BEYOND THE HORIZON

BEYOND THE HORIZON

The National Library of Poetry

Laura Fiorini, Editor

Beyond the Horizon

Copyright © 1998 by The National Library of Poetry
as a compilation.

Rights to individual poems reside with the artists themselves.
This collection of poetry contains works submitted to the Publisher by individual authors who confirm that the work is their original creation. Based upon the authors' confirmations and to the Publisher's actual knowledge, these poems were written by the listed poets. The National Library of Poetry does not guarantee or assume responsibility for verifying the authorship of each work.

The views expressed within certain poems contained in this anthology do not necessarily reflect the views of the editors or staff of The National Library of Poetry.

All rights reserved under International and Pan-American copyright conventions.
No part of this book may be reproduced, stored in a retrieval system or transmitted in any form, electronic, mechanical, or by other means, without written permission of the publisher. Address all inquiries to Jeffrey Franz, Publisher,
One Poetry Plaza, Owings Mills, MD 21117.

Library of Congress
Cataloging in Publication Data
ISBN 1-57553-425-8

Proudly manufactured in The United States of America by
Watermark Press
One Poetry Plaza
Owings Mills, MD 21117

Foreword

Throughout life, we store information collected from experiences and try in some way to make sense of it. When we are not able to fully understand the things which occur in our lives, we often externalize the information. By doing this, we are afforded a different perspective, thus allowing us to think more clearly about difficult or perplexing events and emotions. Art is one of the ways in which people choose to externalize their thoughts.

Within the arts, modes of expression differ, but poetry is a very powerful tool by which people can share sometimes confusing, sometimes perfectly clear concepts and feelings with others. Intentions can run the gamut as well: the artists may simply want to share something that has touched their lives in some way, or they may want to get help to allay anxiety or uncertainty. The poetry within *Beyond the Horizon* is from every point on the spectrum: every topic, every intention, every event or emotion imaginable. Some poems will speak to certain readers more than others, but it is always important to keep in mind that each verse is the voice of a poet, of a mind which needs to make sense of this world, of a heart which feels the effects of every moment in this life, and perhaps of a memory which is striving to surface. Nonetheless, recalling our yesterdays gives birth to our many forms of expression.

Melisa S. Mitchell
Editor

Editor's Note

Boundaries determine our lives. A boundary can be either physical or psychological—poor beginnings, for example, may limit future choices, much as a psyche burdened with hopelessness may be unable to transcend a self-imposed notion of personal limits. A horizon is therefore a boundary, in both the physical and psychological senses: It is the farthest distance or limit an observer can view when looking toward the juncture of earth and sky, based on the observer's position. However, psychologically, a horizon can be either a possibility or a limit, depending on the narrowing or broadening of an individual's perception. When perspectives widen, hope flourishes; when perspectives constrict, despair dominates. Beyond the horizon lie our hopes, dreams, and dearest wishes, as well as future limits to surmount.

One poet who prevailed over his modest origins and limited horizon was Irish poet Thomas Moore (1779–1852). Despite his family's relative poverty and the stigma of being a Roman Catholic in Protestant-dominated Ireland, Moore achieved entrance to Trinity College in Dublin, later attending law school in London. The English government appointed Moore the Registrar of Admiralty Prize-Court in Bermuda in 1803 after he gained favor in London's social circles while in school there. He later left his deputy in charge so he could travel to Canada and to the U.S. to pursue his poetic career. Although Moore earned some praise for his work, one of his strongest critics, Francis Jeffery, wrote that Moore was "the most licentious of modern versifiers." In a turn of bad fortune, Moore's deputy in Bermuda embezzled upward of 6000 pounds, leaving Moore responsible for repaying the debt. He went into self-imposed exile while the debt was settled, returning to England in 1822, poor once again, with a diminishing following for his poetry.

History has not looked kindly on Thomas Moore's poetic efforts. Although he was lauded in his time, modern literary circles view him as one who did not strongly impact the creative world. Twentieth-century Irish poet Patrick Kavanagh (1905-1967), in his poem "A Wreath for Tom Moore's Statue," echoes the modern critical view of Moore's work:

> *The cowardice of Ireland is in his statue,*
> *No poet's honoured when they wreathe this stone,*
> *An old shopkeeper who has dealt in the marrow-bone*
> *Of his neighbours looks at you.*
> *Dim-eyed, degenerate, he is admiring his god,*
> *The bank-manager who pays his monthly confession,*
> *The tedious narrative of a mediocrity's passion,*
> *The shallow, safe sins that never become a flood*
> *To sweep themselves away.*

To Kavanagh, Moore's poetry is a "tedious narrative" that is mediocre, "shallow," "safe," and passionless. Moore's statue "admir[es] his god" in perpetuity, ignoring the matters of this Earth, much as Moore did in life.

As Kavanagh criticizes Moore's poetry for being devoid of emotion, John Paul McCaffrey emphasizes the tedium of Moore's poetry and his soiled public image in the poem, "Thomas Fudge" (1). Moore wrote *The Fudge Family in Paris (by Thomas Brown the Younger)* (1818) and *The Fudge Family in England* (1835), two light satire collections from which McCaffrey's title emerges. As the poem's title is taken from a satirical work, this suggests that "Thomas Fudge" is also a satire on Thomas Moore's life. McCaffrey highlights Moore's religious bent as well as his inability to keep his personal scandals from the public eye:

> *Piety grew so early for Thomas Fudge.*
> *Blessed with his mother's laundry,*
> *He strung his daily lies from sodden porch to post.* . . .

Moreover, religious imagery permeates this poem: Moore was "blessed," or bestowed, with the boundaries his Catholicism placed on him in Protestant Ireland. He was "witnessed," or affirmed, little by his contemporaries, and was "shrouding" the truth to gain renown through his superficial verse. Fudge also "lies," much as Moore hid his being Catholic when he registered at Trinity as a Protestant in order to gain admission.

McCaffrey uses words like "grew," "sowed," and "fielding" to illustrate a connection with the natural world, intimating that a religious focus was natural for Moore who grew up in a country beleaguered by religious strife for much of its history. Moore plied his trade of poetry through assiduousness, much as a farmer would sow seeds to reap a harvest: "Thomas sowed and sowed again to wrought following, / Shrouding the visceral truths in silence." McCaffrey's suggestion that Moore had to exert such arduous effort to garner regard for his work implies that if Moore had been more inherently talented, he would not have had to virtually wring acclaim from the public and from the critical world.

McCaffrey indicates that when Moore fell into debt because of his deputy's fund embezzlement in Bermuda, he "failed his . . . sons," leaving them virtually penniless. In the same vein, he went to Canada and to the U.S. to publish his "visceral truth"—his poetry—ignoring his duties to his country, as well as to his family. Moore's social rise in England led to his appointment as Registrar, but he later wrote scathing political satire that sent him into "social darkness." Lord Byron, a fellow poet, ridiculed Moore for his failed attempt at a pistol duel, his "menacing arts," against Francis Jeffery. It was later discovered that Jeffery's pistol was not loaded, but Byron's stinging satire of the duel erroneously named Moore as the one with the unloaded pistol. Moore then challenged Byron to a duel, but the misunderstanding was explained, and the two became friends. Eventually, Byron gave Moore his memoirs with instructions to publish them after his death. A dispute over the memoirs' ownership followed Byron's passing, after which Moore burned the manuscript. This action literally may have cast to dust authoritative information on Lord Byron, one of the age's defining characters—Moore, as McCaffrey writes, in effect "field[ed] the summary of his ages."

McCaffrey also amplifies Moore's responsibility for his own hardships. His absence from his post in Bermuda because of his drive to publish his works, his great defensiveness concerning his art that led to two duels, and his failure to gain a strong artistic following all indicate that "He loved his dying god / And lied unto himself." Moore was his own god: He subordinated everything to his art—he "married his muse." Since his favor with the public was waning, his art was dying, and he continued to lie "unto himself" until his life's end concerning his art's importance. By reaching outside the horizons of his own life into literary history for inspiration, John Paul McCaffrey exhibits a refreshing perspective on current literary thought. It is for the eloquent and accurate rendering of such a complex individual as Thomas Moore that John Paul McCaffrey was awarded the Grand Prize in the contest associated with *Beyond the Horizon*.

Tracy Carignan, in "At the Old Fort in Annapolis Royal" (73), also reaches beyond the horizons of everyday life, discovering the uniqueness of personal experience. Wandering with a companion through a landscape filled with vitality, Carignan's persona experiences the inspirational powers of nature:

> *The sunlight tastes of saltspray and summer's last flowers.*
> *By a wrinkle in the river, we sit entwined in the afternoon,*
> *while ancient whispers escape the sweaty stone walls*
> *and slither amongst the verdant blades caressing our limbs.*

Later, the narrator's tone changes, moving from a soothing reminiscence of a journey over peaceful hills to a straight commentary on how a change of environment and of perspective can influence poetic creation:

> *The words of too many poets have been read upon this levee*
> *by too many lachrymose young girls—*
> *the air is full of old love and regret and farewell—*
> *but the warm breath of a southern flow*
> *whisks the ghosts away*
> *and we are the only two who have stopped just here to rest*
> *in this quiet and moldering place.*

The setting allows the "two" to push aside thoughts of the thousands of others who have felt a tenderness for the landscape and a romantic love in the same way as they do. By creating an original poem from this particular, perhaps overly-romanticized, scene, Carignan asserts that every experience is unique, even in the same setting. Although this natural place is an inspiration to numerous others—past, present, and future—the manifestation of these romantic images in each individual's creative process will ultimately end in becoming something entirely novel and full of worth.

Another change in perspective inspired Rishad Patel to write "Distances from a Train" (145). Gazing out a train window at the vast expanses of the land rushing by, the persona's horizon broadens and constricts simultaneously. Ensconced in the train's industrial, man-made disconnection from the land, Patel's persona senses humanity's separation from the natural world. However, the persona also briefly glimpses the world lying beyond the limited horizon of industrialized life. Illustrating the transient moment when the persona's life intersects with the natural world, Patel writes:

> *We bluster on, an ancient lyric. A humid man yawns.*
> *Those that are outside are perpendicular to their earth, to my life.*

The word "perpendicular" indicates a fleeting intersection instead of a lasting oneness, both of the people with the land and of the persona with nature, emphasizing the permanent detachment from nature experienced in modern life.

While a knowledge of separateness exists in the persona, there is still "a beckoning somewhere," a search for a kind of meaning aching to be culled from this encounter. As the train continues its journey and the landscape changes, the rhythmic, choppy bursts of Patel's language—"hushed hollows, hasty leaves"—suggest a mysterious unraveling of nature's secrets in time with the train's movement. At the instant when the search for significance should be rewarded with an answer, the persona concludes that "only a portioned rattling stares at me"—mere noise, devoid of meaning, confronts the persona. Eventually, Patel's persona tires of this fruitless, rhythmic search:

> *So I shall yawn now, like the animals.*
> *I have heard the land, its livid lie;*
> *The sky hangs broken, primal river watching.*
> *Frenetic. I wait for capture; I am a spy.*

The persona "wait[s] for capture," becoming a non-participant in the search for meaning. The world's mysteries remain shrouded in silence, even amidst the clamor of the train on its tracks. Patel's concluding with such a resigned statement reinforces that the industrial world can only hope to intersect in brief flashes of union with the natural world. In this case, an enlarging of perspective led back to a narrowing, a separation closing in on itself.

Perspective not only transforms based on communion with or separation from nature, but also regarding other individuals. Joe Grey's poem, "An Impression" (236), exemplifies the sharpening of perception brought about by finding oneself alone within a group. Grey's persona seems to be at a social gathering in which a feeling of isolation becomes desperately magnified. Grey opens with a concrete statement: "The conversation's lacking." Then the persona's language shifts to abstraction, and still the persona cannot derive the situation's meaning: "Nothing significant in a close space provides the key to understanding." The "key[s]" are perhaps a means of interpreting symbols in life and in poetry—they provide a method for understanding and for perceiving this world in which there is "nothing significant."

Though the persona concentrates on the tangible objects in the room—the clock silently ticking, the smoke "dispersing evenly" (acting as a screen that makes communication nearly impossible), and the laughter in which the persona does not share—the gathering's human elements are surprisingly absent. Omitting details concerning the gathering's participants casts the focus on the space left in their wake; the persona is utterly separate and unable to glean meaning from this disunion:

An impression really,
for which there is no basis.
Lost in the cushions of the couch are the keys.
I lost the keys, and that's really all that matters.

The persona knows where the keys to understanding are: They are "lost in the cushions of the couch." Although aware of the keys' location, the persona does not retrieve them for use, indicating severe resignation to the disturbing idea that, even with the keys to understanding, there may exist nothing to understand. To the persona, there is, in fact, no meaning, and the persona's attempt to use the keys would reinforce life's meaninglessness, a discovery that would be devastatingly paralyzing. Hence, the horizon that should be wide and full of possibility in a social gathering becomes grievously constricted and absent of human connection.

In this volume, several other poets exhibited through poetry their individual interpretations of their personal horizons. I suggest you carefully contemplate the differing perspectives offered by the following poems: Tom Hardy's "In Arcadia Ego" (205), Johannes Beilharz's "At Forty" (165), Lorelei E. Smith's "Everafters" (95), Shawn O'Halloran's "Platte Creek" (212), Samantha

Wright's "(No ducks)" (147), Elana Wolff's "Old Photos" (86), and Sylwia Gustyn's "Tall Dwarfs" (227).

Congratulations to the artists featured in this anthology. I hope you will all persist in challenging your personal perspectives by searching for poetic inspiration beyond your own horizons. In all of your creative endeavors, I wish you success.

The publication of *Beyond the Horizon* is a culmination of the efforts of many individuals. Judges, editors, associate editors, customer service representatives, data entry personnel, office administrators, and administrative services staff have all made invaluable contributions to this effort. The editors are grateful for the assistance of these fine people.

Laura Fiorini
Editor

Cover Art: Steve Kimball

Grand Prize

John Paul McCaffrey / Port Aux Basques, NF

Second Prize

Johannes Beilharz / Voehringen, Germany
Tracy Carignan / Trenton, ON
Joe Grey / Puslinch, ON
Sylwia Gustyn / Windsor, ON
Tom Hardy / London, England

Shawn O'Halloran / Hamilton, ON
Rishad Patel / Bombay, India
Lorelei E. Smith / Woodbridge, ON
Elana Wolff / Thornhill, ON
Samantha Wright / Stouffville, ON

Third Prize

Andrew Agostino / Pointe-Claire, QC
Yue An / Xinjiang, China
Paul Aspland / Victoria Harbour, ON
Anne Marie B. Bacani / Toronto, ON
Stanley Branch / Scarborough, ON
W. L. Dafoe / Toronto, ON
Candace Demone / Chester Basin, NS
Deanna Di Lello / Richmond Hill, ON
Kristy Dossor / Mill Park, VIC, Australia
Natasha D'Souza / Dubai, UAE
Severino Enopena / Manila, Philippines
Jean H. Esannason / St. Thomas, USVI
Damian Glover / Hamilton, ON
Susan Goguen / Moncton, NB
Joan Gordon / Winnipeg, MB
Erin Gray / Mississauga, ON
Melissa Hahn / Port Lambton, ON
Elizabeth Hamulka / Toronto, ON
Natalie Hanak / Sidney, BC
Sheri Harris / Toronto, ON
Brooke Herwig / Calgary, AB
Mary Ioannou / Rome, Italy
Geneva Janzen / Halfmoon Bay, BC
Lisa Kireef / Lethbridge, AB
Martin Linton / Edmonton, AB
Shawna Linyard / Milton, ON
Marc Lishchynski / Ottawa, ON
Ann Lok / Vancouver, BC
Fini Lokke / Froerup, Denmark
Brian H. Luimes / Winchester, ON

James Majoros / Toronto, ON
Cecilia Mavrow / Victoria, BC
G. McAndrews / St. Catherines, ON
Klaus Michelsen / Vancouver, BC
Murungu / Harare, Zimbabwe
Ritika Nandkeolyar / North York, ON
David Norman / Cornwall, England
Iheanyi Okeke / Imo State, Nigeria
Doris Elizabeth Palacios / Toronto, ON
Jane Collins Philippe / Whitby, ON
Charles Pilkington / Pierrefords, QC
Tania Poggione / Hull, QC
Lana Rovere / Vancouver, BC
Mala Rupnarain / Sherwood Park, AB
Bonnie Ryan / Moncton, AB
William J. Sampson / Mississauga, ON
Vivek Saraogi / Ayuthaya, Thailand
Jane Silva / Toronto, ON
Kurt F. Svatek / Breitenau, Austria
Tim Thompson / Kamloops, BC
Ted Traill / South River, ON
Margaret Tribe / Scarborough, ON
Janet Renee Tucker / Edmonton, AB
Melissa Turner-Chambers / Rockford, MI
Alfonso Velis / London, ON
Paula Whittaker / Toronto, ON
Elizabeth Williams / Tyrone, PA, USA
Kent Wilson / Calgary, AB
Ken Zokol / Coquitlam, BC

Grand Prize Winner

Thomas Fudge
Piety grew so early for Thomas Fudge.
Blessed with his mother's laundry,
He strung his daily lies from sodden porch to post,
Witnessed least by kinsmen,
Viewed most with amity and tolerance,
Thomas scuffed his soulless heart to suede
Spending youth in lieu of brass.
His mettle frayed, the strands sopping
Social darkness, he continued to ply
His menacing arts and married his muse
To feather the travelling castle.
Thomas sowed and sowed again to wrought following,
Shrouding the visceral truths in silence.
He cleansed his sorrowed bones,
Fielding the summary of his ages,
He failed his calloused sons
To roam corduroy lanes,
To seek audience to truth.
He loved his dying god
And lied unto himself.
  John Paul McCaffrey

Seasonal

When did the summer flower fade?
Yesterday!
The world became a windmill—
And I hung upon its blade.

When did the winter blossoms blow?
Today!
The world became a glacier—
And I shivered in the snow.

When will the crocus bloom—in Spring?
Tomorrow!
My sad cocoon will rend itself—
And I'll spread my folded wings.

But, oh, will Autumn sere the leaf?
Never!
A constant love will feed itself—
From the bosom of belief.

Eleanor Selby

Wonders of the Moon

The night is garbed in grandeur
as the moon lights up the sky;
It heightens all humility
as it kisses both heart and eye.
Its heavenly splendor shimmers
'midst a spectacle of stars;
Reflections move the senses and
romance soars on past Mars.
Humbled by the beauty of that
moon just hanging there,
We tiny creatures gaze in awe
with silent, honored stare.
Ordinary landscapes are
sculpted lavishly
By Nature's rhythmic prelude
to perpetuity.

Joan Adams Burchell

Mother

A mother is patient and giving
Right from the very start
Someone who will go on living
In the soft strings of your heart

A mother is love and friendship
A love that never ends
No matter where life sends you
You two will still be friends

A mother's love is wonderful
A love matched by no other
One that comes from in the soul
That's why we call her mother

A mother is God's creation
Sent from the heavens above
If all your friends desert you
You can count on mother's love

Shirley Jean Srigley

Till We Meet Again

Please keep my heart, no strings attached,
I ask for nothing in return,
though from my eyes you've surely learned
my dearest dreams and wishes.

Keep all my love, no strings attached,
I ask for nothing in return,
though you must know how much I yearn
for your sweet lips and kisses.

When you come home with all your love
I'll walk with you in paradise,
and sun and moon and stars will rise
to celebrate our wondrous love.

Till then my soul will dream of you
and of the love for which it yearns,
while in my heart this fire will burn
for your sweet lips and kisses.

No strings, not now, not ever,
but say what you desire
like set the stars on fire
I never will say never.

Gordon Enright

Nature's Charms

The beauty of the woods surrounds me here
As I gaze out upon the silent sea.
Contentment. Vales of wonder, far and near.
All nature sings in quiet harmony.

Entranced, I watch, as sunshine's silver rays
Caress the treetops, hills, and valleys green.
A breeze from o'er the distant seas now sways
The ever-changing, scintillating scene.

Ah, that these hours of heav'nly splendour here
Continue evermore. But now appear
The distant, first faint glow of sunset's rays.
Though I must leave, the charm of nature stays
In myriad patterns, ever to amaze,
With all its treasures, those who stop to gaze
In wonder, heartfelt praise.

Clifford W. Ketchum

Beautiful Joe

Dedicated to Victor and Dorothy Sherman, Port Dover, Ontario

Sixty-nine years I had your trust,
Side by side since age of six.
Love unfailing,
Unyielding,
Sometimes undeserved.
Rutherford and Sherman a joyful mix.
Shared laughs, smiles, tears, and sorrow.
Her matron of honor and my dearest friend,
In April at her funeral,
I asked, "Josephine, will I see you tomorrow?"

Evelyn Hunter Clark

Reach Out

My son? my son? Ramir, my son!
To my skirt and fingers, hold on!
Why should those tears not freely flow?
Why should those lips withhold your woe?

Blurt out the pain, lighten your heart,
Shout to the winds the thought that hurt.
Lean your head upon my bosom,
Reach out to God, let His love bloom.

Soak up in God's loving grace,
Hold on to my skirt, walk in peace.
Learn to smile, laugh, and prance again.
God's love and mine will soothe the pain.

Please walk with me where flowers bloom.
Sing the hymns that gladden the gloom.
I'll kiss your tears away, hold on!
My son, pour out your heart, my son.

Don't wrench away the life in me.
Fill my empty arms, set me free
From fears and anxiety of parting.
Whisper to my ears what is hurting.

Pacita Labayen Aliermo

ECHO LAKE: July 1997

Toes dipped in the shadows of a chocolate silence,
   in the voiceless void of Echo Lake;
eyes fixed forward to the hugging forest there,
   to the strange tree-stands surround;
thoughts melding out the memories we once knew
   as children, in fields of yellow flowers;
we tasted the honey and the salt, recalling years
   flowing down our cheeks to mouths-held-open.

So it was, two friends from long ago, alone,
   listening for the heartbeats of the Lake,
     water, wood, and air; aware and longing.

The diver took this moment with a laughing cry;
   a Loon, breaking surface from his fine feed
     beneath the mirrored waters, now in-wave.

We smiled, within, without, and at each other;
   laughing eyes met, thoughts t'ward Gaea—
we felt her warmth surge up between our toes,
   from the distance heard her echoes;
in our stillness, silence blossomed secretly,
   love and friendship bloomed, eternally.

David Bosomworth

Mind Search

Middle age is misunderstood
Its recognition lies in, if only we could
Aspire to endeavors that rekindle our youth,
Like a child receiving their first adult tooth.
We patronize and praise our steadfast ways,
Lost and lurking in a hopeless maze.
Confusion sparks our creative drive,
Often leading to a spiritual dive.
Search, discover our limitless quest,
For that is how we truly can test.
While the boundaries of our existence unfold
With more love, laughter, and joy yet to be told.

Betty Klimitz

Joyeus Noel—Merry Christmas

Frost crackles on the window pane
And sled tracks going down the lane,
Depicting that yuletide is in store
With carols, sugar plums, and more.
Grandpère sits by the fireplace,
The children's snow boots to unlace;
His rosy cheeks and white moustache,
And pockets bulging, not with cash.
His tummy round and toothless smile.
A sight like this you'd go a mile
Before another such you'd see,
And in the corner stands our tree.
The packages are not yet packed.
In yonder cupboard they are stacked;
And in the woodshed there does hang
A wild goose, Pierre,
I shot with a bang.
This land of ours does supply
Food aplenty, we'll not cry.
For want of pies and honey pure
We'll all be fed, of that we're sure.

Evelyn C. Zink

Realia

Neither happy nor unhappy,
the real stands between us.

What can we do then, to explain
that what is palpable is not enough,

that the impression our steps have left
on the green grass means more to us?

What were the streets without them,
and what would things be without hands?

They would be real, but to us
they would be obsolete, and die.

Fini Lokke

Aotearoa

New Zealand has sports
which are with limitless everyone
and we will hope that everyone
shall enjoy themselves with fun.

Although a very small country,
one can travel around and see,
mountains, farms, lakes, and beach:
all of them within easy reach.

A flightless bird, the brown kiwi,
for people is fascinating to see,
and always hunts for its food at night
because it gets blinded by daylight.

There are many caves and sights
and glow-worms with tiny lights.
Land of the now extinct moa
is New Zealand—Aotearoa.

Noline A. V. Johnson

Precious Moments

Take each precious moment,
Treat it with loving care,
Hold it gently in your hands,
Don't let it fly away.

Hear the happy birds that sing
To wake you in the morn,
Feel the earth and smell the rain,
And know when spring is born.

Hold the "little" things to heart,
For one day you will feel
How these things have really counted,
And they'll always help you heal.

Take each precious moment
That makes you love—or laugh.
Throw away the sad or bad.
Never hold the chaff!

Some day you'll know that memories,
Tho' comprised of joy and pain,
Are just mostly precious moments
That come back, and then remain.
Audrey K. Thompson

Winter's Frosts

Misty lights
frost winter's hillsides;
Frost,
snow-white on shaded lawns;
Mountains,
far and smoke-hazed,
grow snow
like frosting on their peaks.
Isabel E. Larsen

Buskerville

If life was just a fairy tale
No busker would oblige
To be an inspiration
In a world without the wise.
The twangin' and the jammin',
"Entertainment from the soul,"
A guitar case, your pocket change,
A wishing well, you know,
When offering artistic pomp,
The vain deserve the fame.
Ignoring the creative code,
They put themselves to shame.
The lofty in a cruising world
Can call themselves adjourned.
The joy and hope in "Buskerville"
Are lessons to be learned,
The buskers keep the flaming heart
In others still alive
More than forgotten tiddly-winks
Of art in pompous eyes.
Diane E. Babcock

The Bridge, II

He lived beside the busy river
where there was much coming and going.
The bosom of the river was full
and there was the hurry of many boats.
Above him was the bridge, which
would take him to the other side.

What would it be like on the other side?
Would it be derelict and destitute
with wide streets and paper blown
by the wind and broken windows,
unpainted stores, and grey people?

Or would it be lush and green
with fine homes, bright colours,
the flash of smiles and gaiety,
and the tune of wonder?

Soon he would gather himself
when he heard the fog horn
in the evening dusk
when there was no one there,
and cross over the bridge.
H. N. McLeod

River Rising

What horrific pictures we all see,
Flashing out from our TVs . . .

The red river is again in flood,
Village streets covered with water and mud.

People struggling to save their homes,
A hopeless task in the danger zones.

Citizens from across the land
Have rallied together to lend a hand.

The aftermath is sad to see,
Victim's faces reflect their misery.

But their dauntless spirit is alive,
Yes, the valley will survive.

The task ahead is a disheartening one,
But the restoration has already begun.
William Ott

Thoughts Versus Fights

A thought of fights
A fight of thoughts
I thought of thinking
I thought of fights I hadn't fought
I fought for thoughts I have never thought
—A thought never fought for—
A fight never fought
A fight never thought
A thought never thought

I never thought I would ever fight
For such thoughts,
But I've fought!
What a fight it was!

I've never thought I would ever fight
For a thought I never had before
Alexandre Clemente

Son of Man

Kidnapped by a unicorn's beauty, an
incredible angel holds the power to
make a rainbow sparkle brightly.

On the ground, next to a castle,
wakes a garden of roses
elegantly enhancing the castle and
next to it stands a princess with tears
sparkling in her eyes, as her prince arrives.

Sometimes as the day begins, the princess
opens her eyes, and standing
nearby is a unicorn, and

Off in the distance, the princess
finds a rainbow sparkling with beauty.

Midnight arrives, and all fall
asleep, the stars sparkle brightly, and
next to the castle, the angel watches over.
   Steve Gillespie

Stop the Wind

Child's face pressed against the pane,
Sill held tightly, fingers imprint the dust,
Trees sway far down the lane,
Eyes scan the fields as weeds sweep the crust.
Child cries, "Stop the wind, stop the wind."

Child's eyes searching dust-filled sky,
Swirling weeds tracing furrow's depth,
Watching as they tumble to places by
Twisters twirling, tearing fields by heath.
Child cries, "Stop the wind, stop the wind."

Child searches toward the browning shed.
Dust swoops and swills on slats so worn.
Where are the cows? Perhaps they've fled
To nestle between the stacks just shorn.
Child cries, "Stop the wind, stop the wind."

Child peering toward the barn-topped cock,
Whirling faster . . . blurring, no detection,
Then slowing, silence creeps to unlock.
The wind subsides and with elation
Child cries, "All is well, all is well."
   Judy Mooney

I'll Never Forget

I'll never forget the way you lied,
That was the night my childhood died.
It's a pain so sharp I know it's real,
It's a scar so deep it will never heal.
The tears I cry are all my own,
I've had to bear this all alone.
I was innocent, but I've had to pay,
Now it's time you hear what I say.
How can you call yourself a father?
What have you done to your only daughter?
You've destroyed my life and my will to live,
Now I have nothing left to give.
They've always said, forgive and forget,
But your time is coming, you'll get yours yet!
   Christa Jones

Moonlighting Memories

A bulged red hanky sits on the floor,
guarding tin soldiers and tanks of war.
Superman peers from comics piled high,
creating fantasies for this little guy.
Over the bed silver wings dangle low,
splashing bold colors of red and gold.
Sneakers embrace the leg of a chair,
spilling gravel from who knows where?
Across the dresser blue jeans sprawl,
brimming pockets with fat gum balls.
Up on shelf, a train glows light,
puffing musical bells in the night.
Under red curls he slumbers a grin,
stretching freckles across the chin.
Butterflies flutter indelible joy,
moonlighting memories
in the room
of my boy.
   Barbara Moyer

Forever Angels

For all the children who are taken away,
Our hearts are broken
Ne'er to be the same after that day,
In solitude we shed a tear;
A silent prayer for Him to be near.

To all those who die young,
Who'll always be remembered,
For the happiness they spun,
Who'll never grow and we'll never know
What they could have done.

Forever angels the children will be,
With Him for guidance
They'll always be free;
Forever angels playing in the clouds
Forever angels, forever proud.
   Terry Gorley

Visions

Treasure few secret glimpses
Through mystical windows of time.
A kaleidoscope of moments
Forever labelled: "Mine"

The stained glass of time's capsule
Reflects silently its glow. . . .
Imagine to revive
Shapes of days, years ago. . . .

Deep within the soul's chapel,
Meditate near a looking-glass,
Try not to feel the hours,
The fleeting minutes as they pass. . . .

Caress silently a dream,
In deserts mirages are free—
Assume how soft morning mists
Will unveil new days to be. . . .
   Hana Gerzanic-Hons

A Christmas Card from Urumqi

From October to the following April
Sometimes even May
This long time white
As snow and lifelike as death
I can't remember
For how many days
I haven't been outdoors
Drinking at home alone
Often I lift the cup over my head
But stare elsewhere
As if examining some disaster
Nothing yet has ever happened
And I fling myself abed
Swimming into a dream like a fish

Yue An

Minute Hand

To step beyond the minute hand
Mere seconds it takes to understand
A single star shining in the sky
Leaves us with questions wondering why
As seasons change from warm to cold
Memories fade from young to old
As the driest eye sheds a single tear
Whispered dreams are what we hear
Words written upon the page
Wisdom coming as we age
Hoping for a single friend
To stand beside until the end
To step beyond the minute hand
Mere seconds it takes to understand
That with focused eyes we can see
That we control our own destiny

Kenneth R. Rath

A Face from the Past

Stood aware
In the morning
A face from the past
A memory that will always last
Your eyes
As were
So long ago
Could it be
Or am I remembering
Something so strong
Too strong
I may never know for sure
Yet it remains
In my heart
Although just a part
It still remains
Your smile
My memory
For me
I still can see

Kenneth Rath

If There's a Path

Before you cried and pled for more
God knew your death and birth,
Your days were counted long before
You set foot on this Earth.

And some, upon arrival wonder
Too fearful too fulfill,
While others stand outside in thunder,
And hope not to be killed.

And in their days some people lead
Or stand firm with defiance,
The rest can't hunt, nor kill a weed,
Their lives based on reliance.

Some in each day, find time to heal
While others are in need.
Some fail to see life's path is real,
While in that path others succeed.

Some see a path, but do not try,
Too scared of unknown fate,
Now, life's seen them, and passed them by,
They'd go, but it's too late!

Gila Ashtor

Glimpses of Worth

I see a life's path, all long, winding, and narrow
A path I have no earthly choice but to follow;
In spheres of bright light and patches of darkness
My journey is fraught with decisions and courses.

Illusions take shape and in radiant light
Identity begins and my future takes flight;
Humanistic qualities metamorphose, evolve;
Values, priorities, and problems to solve.

Concerned with improvement and building foundations
I expand explorations, respond to life's stations;
Commitments are made, I need discover my bearings,
But confrontations can alter responsible empowerings.

I have glimpses of things of inestimable worth,
Gained a sense of fulfillment, a reason for birth;
Truth plucked from the shadows and ideas aligning,
I embrace my inner work, awakening my "shining."

So wanting set free, I build a ladder to steeple,
Stop projecting my shadows onto other people;
And asking myself what inner conflicts must endure
I awaken to spirit, bright, constant, and pure.

Elsie Loke Linholm

We Fall Like Waves upon the Shore

I see the waves leap in the air
Full of triumph and life,
Before falling with a crash
Against the golden shore.
Children are on the beach
And, like the rocks, don't seem to care,
They run and call, they are so free,
I shiver though it is not cold.
While one is born, another dies,
We come, we go, we rise, we fall.

Melanie Hurford

Who Am I?

There comes a time in our lifetime
When we need to sit back and think
About human life, our own life,
About its substance, its essence.

We reflect on the creation,
Its source, its purpose, and its function;
Reflect on ourselves as humans:
What really are we human beings,
And how did we come into being?
What is our link with our creator?

There comes a time in our lifetime
We need complete isolation,
And we need everlasting time
In unbroken silence and calm,

A time of deep relaxation
To lose ourselves in reflection:
By the way, who and what am I?
And why am I where I am now?
What are my real place and function
In this vast, complex creation?

E. N. D. Obinze

All Creatures Great and Small

Sunken islands, vast miles do span,
built by marine creatures, unaided
by man . . . what man cannot venture
little creatures can:

Once their solid foundation was laid,
they built till Australia's great reef
was made . . . a huge honeycomb, a building
adorned with plants and rock, where
fish make their home:

Reefs and Atolls . . . exotic . . . extolled,
are growing monuments
to these creatures alone.

Sylvia Brewster

A Guest in Egypt

Egypt's moon shines drunken cups tonight,
shaking her triple bowl through haze.
The wine's sharp fires have seared my tongue,
and glutted food has sickened my taste.
The eunuch stands beside the jewelled door
that sways its panels over golden plates,
and slave girls bear the silver dish of fruit;
they come in mist, like waving fans,
in double forms of grace.
The hour has childed dreams,
and what my Eros seeks
bends like the reeds to Cleopatra's wish,
where love reflects her thousand mirrored forms
in shapes of beauty from the brazen walls.
White arms like roots lift up their hands
to draw me downward to the fecund marsh.
My mind's pool swirls its vortex of desire;
a brilliant sheen, it twists around her eye,
coiling toward her gently moving bed.

Ian MacLennan

My Heart Is on Fire

You are my burning desire.
My heart burns like a raging volcano.
Oh, my love, I thought you should know,
It burns like the Sahara in July.
This, my beloved, is no lie.

Consumed by the flames of your beauty,
I ask for your love, not your pity.
My heart burns beyond my soul,
Deep within the walls of my psyche.
This news only you I have told,
'Cause you set my heart on fire, fire!
You are my burning desire.

Desmond D. Harris

There Is a Way

There is a way
and it is your way.
You must walk through him.
There can be big stones,
strong storms,
in your heart you can feel:
heat like in a desert,
cold like on the polar ice.
There can be truth and lies,
love and hatred,
war and peace,
sorrow and gladness,
and many things more.
You must accept all,
because you are on the way,
on your way.

Irmina Wrezounik

Awakening

Silent screams echoed
Through the hollow ink-stained night.
Shadows stole through the
Creeping walls.
Memories, a thousand faces,
Drifted away.
The raft raised its head up, through
The gentle ripples of a placid river.
And then he emerged,
Through the forgotten mountain crevices,
His gold-rimmed head shone,
Brilliant and iridescent.
Ghosts faded away,
Fear killed its encroaching tentacles,
Mellifluous music filled
The dew-drenched air,
Then, I opened my eyes. . . .

Rubaiyat Khan

Untitled

Be yourself.
None should or could exploit
Or discriminate, if you're you—
Totally,
Completely,
Unabashedly.

A person is not judged
By the color of the skin,
Or by standards external.

It is the heart, the truth within,
The inner glow, the burning flame
That you must tend.

Be true to your inner self—
Enthusiastically,
Joyfully.

Break down the barriers
Of fear, suspicion, worry,
By the power
Of your liberated heart,
And your own uninhibited spirit.
    Sebastian Mattapally

Mythological Iolaus

My love came from Barnegat,
The sea was in his eyes.
He trod as softly as a cat
And told me terrible lies.
His hair was yellow as new-cut pine
In shavings cold and tethered.
I thought how silver it would shine.
By cruel winters weathered . . .
Will he never come back from Barnegat
With thunder in his eyes,
Treading as soft as a tiger cat,
To tell me terrible lies?
    Donna Bilous

Diana Princess of Wales

In the city of light,
On a dark, starry night,
You left us forever, Diana

You left us alone
For your heavenly home
Where you'll find
No sadness or sorrow

If you only knew
How much we loved you
And we will forever, Diana

Our sadness we know
Won't ever go
For you, beautiful Princess Diana
    Dennis Joseph Kelly

The Gunman and the Armless

One thousand guns, one thousand swards
Are in your hands, son of my eternal lords.
And I, the armless, empty hands have,
With no billy, nor arrows, neither a sword.

In the den of lions you are born,
Have the same claws and canines they have,
In the desert, as a poor, I born.
I have the same humility and servility it has.

Does the God gathers the two Antipodes,
In the paradise, or at least at its threshold?
You are the fire that can burn the world at whole,
And I am the water that will put it out.
I'm the smile and the laugh of the world,
But you are the death when its teeth are bared.

I'm walking in the way down-headed,
Avoid, not to lean from one side.
By you walk in the middle, swerved from it aside.
Be whomsoever you want to be in this stockade.
God for each manner, already a destiny made.
    Dirar A. Aldaim

The Sun

A ball of fire, set in motion
Parading proudly across blue skies,
In its daily trek of orange glory,
The showpiece of a master craftsman,
Created majesty, clothed in morning brilliance

Run! It's coming, the heat of the blazing sun.
Take cover! Go hide from its powerful rays.
They're much too strong for your gaze.

The wilting flowers bend their heads,
A feeble effort to dodge the sweltering heat.
They close their petaled doors
As if to hide their beautiful faces,
While the sun, in hot pursuit,
Moves gracefully across the skies
To close one day and open another
In its circuit of fervor.
    Pearline Ann Donalds

New World Times

And now we, who ought to be in New World Times,
It's time that we ought to present past signs,
Showing as friends we can learn to live in peace,
Believing we were created by "It" in "He."

"It" is the spirit of the spoken word.
"He" is the flesh of a walking man.
This story of man began when word was at his hand.

Perhaps we can live in the best type of freedom
To fulfill the phases of life to come.
With truth in power of the soul in me,
We can change this place to a space of the free.

Oh, yes, our rarest race can return and rise
By finding a path to walk that is wise.
Then soon you'll see that love is me
In this long and testing journey.
    Michael Allan Long

Our Love Remains

Youth's glory goes,
The first dreams fade.
Time hurries on with flying feet,
But we have kept the pledge we made
When our love was new and life was sweet.

Swiftly the changing years go by,
And loving affections deeper grow.
We have been faithful, you and I,
True to our vows of long ago.

We have learned much from love,
It teaches us to share,
To sacrifice, to sympathize,
To give, and to forebear.

Without these we would soon become
A dull and soulless clod.
Let's cherish this most precious thing,
It is the gift of God.
Mary Moore

Musicart

Beautiful music,
One also can see like a picture of art,
A symphony in color.
The air is full of music,
Healing for the soul,
Exiting, warming,
Consoling in sorrow.
A rainy day, the drops are falling as tones.
In the sun the music glitters,
All the sadness is forgotten.
Everyone enjoys the music,
A colorsymphony,
To the picture created by lovely tones.
Solveig Olsson

Mystery of the Words and Some Gestures

With your eyes filled with softness
You bring the cheerfulness every second.
You relieve my sad little heart,
You take away my fear who fertilizes oneself.

Your look is so dazzling.
Your hand is filled with heat.
Your eyes are very mystifying
Even your cheeks are glowing of color.

With your hand of tenderness,
Your smile full of wisdom,
You cover up my heart of kindness.
Your face seems full of valor.

When I hold your hand
All my body warms oneself up.
Our happiness will go far.
My feelings warm oneself.

There, the magic settles oneself.
The confidence brings us nearer to our faith.
Then we share our secrets everywhere.
The presence invades us at every time.
Suzette Charron

A Poem for Jane

I copied out your poetry.
It seemed the thing to do.
You see, you mean a lot to me,
It's like sharing what you do.

I wrote this little poem.
You inspired me to.
It feels like coming home,
And it's my way of thanking you.

I keep thinking all in lines,
And of words to put together,
And I keep thinking in rhymes,
And I hope that It'll get better.

It's opened up my mind
To write it all down.
It makes the world seem kind,
To add my own sound.

It must be a wonderful thing
To express yourself this way,
To make all the words sing.
Do you think this way all day?
Lynn Lee Meaney

Dad

There's an inner strength within me
That comes from loving you,
And if I searched the world and back,
No one could fill your shoes.

You are extremely special,
Your qualities are rare,
Whenever I have needed you,
Like magic . . . you've been there.

You taught me about life and love,
No lesson could compare.
The most precious gift you've given me
Is the depth with which you care.

I'm very rich for having you,
My heart is filled with pride.
I need for you to realize
the way I feel inside.

You've always been my Daddy,
You'll be my hero until the end,
But most importantly of all,
My very special friend.
Tina Cooper

Cold Beauty

Icy pearled icicle.
Sculptured glassy point
Congealed water,
With pellucid splendour.
Studded, spangled ice,
Reflecting radiance.
Ornament of grace
Suspends,
Hard and cool,
To its point.
Dolina Davidson

How Absurd

Poor cousin Fred
Was sitting in bed
Spreading butter on bread,
When he stabbed his head
And so profusely bled
That the bed bugs fled
As the sheets turned red.

So Fred was led to a hospital bed
And that filled him with dread,
For someone had said
That he'd end up dead,
But the gash in his head
Was sewn up instead.

Dear Uncle Ned,
He so loved his son, Fred,
That he took his stead
On the boat to the Med
And nearly ended up wed
To Bull's fiancee, "Red."
Now Ned, and not Fred, is dead!

Alana Coolen

Please Try

I need you to understand me,
I want you to try.
I need you to support me,
Without asking why.
I need you to care for me
With a tender touch.
I need you to believe in me,
Without any doubt.
I need you to trust me
With all of your love.
I need you to guide me,
Whenever I am lost.
I need your honesty,
So I know the truth.
I need your protection,
So I'll never lose.
I need you to be my friend,
I want you to hold my hand,
I need you to love me,
So I won't be afraid.
I need you to be a part of us,
So I can be one with you.

Cathy Henrich

Jubilee 2000

God journeys with us
Roman Catholics
in our Jubilee 2000 celebrations,
unites us on our upward way,
blesses us for the best,
inspires us internationally,
is our Light and our life,
assists us in our evangelization,
on Earth reveals
His epiphanies to us,
in ecumenism aids us to trust
in the work of the Holy Spirit.

Gina D'Agostino

The Old Lamplighter

Remember the old lamplighter of long ago,
Who changed the night with a rosy glow,
His footstep ringing down the street,
A nod, cheery smile, to people he did greet?
Nothing stopped him, hail, rain, or snow,
Always on time with a cheerful hello!
The village, just a few lamps, a few people,
An old Norman Church with a small steeple,
But to him the lamps were his kin,
Like children to him, his everything.
He lit them with care each night
So they would shine out and give light.
The world progresses, gas lamps are no more.
Electricity is here—not such a warm glow.
I remember the old lamplighter of long ago.
So sad the lamps and he had to go.
I think I hear him as twilight falls,
His solitary whistle and cheery calls.
Maybe he has a job on high
Lighting the stars in the sky.

Eva Preston

A Journey to Peace

A single dove swept down to Earth,
Wrapping its wings as if to comfort him,
Surrounding him gently on a journey to peace.
Beckoning all who cherished him not to cry,
Directing eyes to the Heaven above the sky,
Delivering him to a beautiful place.

Both wings are free now to carry on,
Waving with a graceful good-bye.
Memories live on and will never be gone,
Envisioning his gentle, smiling face.
Look up to the sky with a smile, not a cry,
God has the true answer; we should not ask why.

June L. Bowe

Cleopatra

Oh, Cleopatra, Queen of the Nile,
After years of searching they still cannot find
Where time has not touched you,
Your last resting place.
Yet there you still lie, serene in your case.
Scepter and orb rest in your hand,
Somewhere under Egyptian sand.
Envied by women, worshiped by men,
No woman has matched your beauty since then.
Bedecked in jewels, bathed in milk,
Groomed and pampered, dressed in silk,
Your love was Mark Antony, but it wasn't to be.
So, with a bite from an asp, you set yourself free.
Men have pillaged, defiled, and stolen,
And what once held beauty are now empty holes.
Barren now is the Valley of Kings.
Gone are the mummies and all precious things.
Over the years they have found quite a few,
But where, oh, where, Cleopatra, are you?

Maureen Collins

The Catskill Hills

Walking through this maze of trees,
On such a ripe autumnal day,
All green and bronze, these golden seas
Of late October pave the way.
And life's own sweet forever song,
Runs in my veins, and I grow tall.
Then thoughts of other times, now gone,
Cast shadows on this wondrous fall.
God's falling leaves have touched my heart,
Have stirred lost thoughts within my soul,
In life; what really is our part,
And wherein lies our final goal!
Why, just last night, the stars all cried,
The falling tears came raining down,
And somewhere in my dreams I died.
In a pool of stars, I dreamed I drowned,
But like the beauty of each leaf
Falling from God's clear blue sky,
It's somehow helped me to believe,
It must be beautiful to die.
   Ronnie McGinn

Moons of Time

For many moons of time we've been far apart.
I could not express what I feel in my heart.
It just doesn't work in trying to shut you out.
I tried to cast you aside, even tried to shout.

But somewhere along the way you took that part,
You extracted love from my heart.
It may have been from times before,
Or just when you walked through the door.

Another love of my life,
Simple and Free,
Within arm's length,
And I wonder if it will ever be meant to be.

Not just yet to move on this one,
But someday soon it will come.
When the time is right, my heart will lead the way,
Giving life meaning with each new day.

Friends forever, wherever we are,
Whether we are near or far,
Whether it be within the physical reality,
Or whether it just remains a dream and fantasy.
   Jaye Low

Dreaming

Under the sky of dreams we sleep,
Wishing for the love that's sweet.
You and I will all our fantasies,
Sharing this love which could be our destiny.
Giving and understanding the stability we need,
This true love we feel is meant to be.
Sharing our lives, in love forever,
I dream of thee, in memory so sweet.
I dream of thee, and the life that could be.
Will true love find its way someday?
   Linda A. Buck

The Search

I've often wondered
About the things I'd say
If that someone special
Came my way.
I've often wondered
Of the things I'd do
If that someone special
Would feel it too.
I've searched this world
Through thick and thin,
For that something special
That comes from within.
The time has come
As I always knew,
That my search has ended:
The day I met you.
   Sandra Raco

Confession of a Raven

(As I smelled the cemetery breeze):

My son,
Look at the gate outside:
What freedom does it hide?
Do you see your pride
Fade away with the moon and the stars
As you reached the cold clouds?
I felt death.
He blew a whisper
And I felt him
Up against my body,
His breath
Full of stench,
His eyes
Full of hatred,
His pulse
Full of anger.

Death to death and pulse to pulse
He took away my last breath.
   Fajr Al-Ajaji

Once upon a Banana Peel

I slipped and fell
Hard, I think, yes, I did, I know.
I'm here, yet my thought are still
Falling!

How amazing the thought
that thoughts can be in limbo,
yet moving and sliding and slipping,
Whoops!
"Here I go!"

But, you're here too.
Where did "you" come from?
The unknown, the unthought of,
the question!

Who are you?
Why did you walk onto my sidewalk
To place the banana peel of my fall?
It hurts. I'm confused. It hurts!
   Kay Brick

Untitled

Where is it all,
there was an abundance of it,
perhaps too much,
Sometimes not enough?
When there, it's often abused.

It passes by,
it cannot be retrieved.
Once past, it is lost.
Who knows that is left
or how much?
Its value is beyond price.
It cannot be bought
or borrowed.

We watch it, we cannot stop it,
not even for a moment.
Falsely we believe it can be con-
trolled,
but it controls our destiny.
And when it is over,
so are we.
It is time.

Gerald B. Edwards

Canadian Scenery

Sunsets of gold
with clear skies above,
shimmering ice fields
and you, my love.

Turquoise waters,
clear and calm,
towering mountains
love, tender and warm.

Green, dark trees,
tall in the mist,
the beauty of nature,
I love to be kissed!

Anna M. Ward

To Wishaw

A little rabbit running by
Said, "Have you heard the latest,
At Huron Park, there is Someone new,
They say he is the Greatest."

Going by I heard the words,
But thought they were just Funning.
No sir, see, it was not birds,
Wishaws were having a Son-in.

There sits Paw proud as Punch,
Saying, "Oh, there's nothing to it."
Watched the Smothers, had a hunch
As they said, "Do it, do it, do it."

So take this roll, wind it on,
Set shutter gaily clicking
At parents, Brother, Tiny One,
So friends will get a look in.

Marion U. Taylor

ELEGY

When I look at the trees and evergreens we planted
   In front of our house as they grow,
And hear the birds sing on their branches
   And you're not here, alas; all this to enjoy.

Getting longer are the days,
   For I hear bird songs coming near,
The sun straightens out its slanted rays,
   And observing all this, I think of you, my dear.

The trees are getting dressed
   The flowers in colors diversified,
My heart getting more depressed,
   My soul without you, mortified.

You strove in this world so unfair
   At times with my caprices and whims so mutable;
O, Mary, if I only wrongs could repair
   When you invariably were so sensible!

O, Mary, dear departed shade!
   Where is your Elysium of Blissful Rest?
Can you not see me so heavily laden
   Bearing this Grief, that rends my Breast!

Joseph DeMelo

Tremulous Leaves

Why so much tremble
in the most tender leaves
when all lamps must be glowed?
Could be apprenticeship life, in silence,
while all steps see to grow their measure?

Oh, the nervous innocence of fresh lily
amazed for prism which project dawns of days!

Flowing voltage in changeable veins
while, dense in the glass,
is drunk the breath.

Who knows from where is guiding us
the heavenly body?
In which fold of soul
it is reclined the secret
of the last sparkle?

Replying is in silence the flint-stone voice,
and make tremble the leaves,
the signs that ride on breeze
of the everlasting mystery.

Carmen Garbarino

Joy and Beauty

Joy and beauty are everywhere, they are not far away
   Take time to see them, feel them, each and every day
The sound of the birds when they sing
   Autumn, winter, fall, and spring
   The rain and the snow and the sun
   Children laughing and having fun
   All the flowers and the trees
Calm lakes, the mountains, and the ocean breeze
   A kiss, a hug, a squeeze
   A bright moon and the stars above
   And peace, and joy, and love

Laurie Reid

I Dare Not

I dare not stand aside and look,
And say I do not care,
Nor can I give a passing glance
Or even try to look askance
At what's happening in the world today.

The restlessness, the poverty, the greed,
The suffering, and the inequities,
To these thing I must give heed.

I dare not say I cannot change
The lot of those in need,
Or say the hungry, starving millions,
Alone, I cannot feed.

I am committed to do my part,
For even one lonely, hurting heart.
How could I ignore a suffering face,
When I belong to the human race?

I dare not.

Gloria Sutherland

Verse: 2000

Bards play with words
Pushing them into piles.
They forget thought for which words were made,
Smugly they arrange styles.

The world drowns in a blood bath,
Starves for peace.
Which suit a dead child?
Which bring surcease?

Our Father who art in heaven,
Blindly we hear Death rave—
Hallowed by Thy Awesome Name . . .
Abba, Save!

Maureen Ehman

Hubble's Flight

Sleep, sleep, lie down to sleep.
Keep calm, so calm, unable to weep.
Order is cheerful, chaos astounds,
Astronauts tumble, nowhere is found.

Six trillion miles elongate the mind.
Stretch out to nothing, no end to the line.
Where was the beginning? Where is the end?
Knowledge restrained by the limits of men.

Hot, hot, the hottest of stars
Unfasten the Hubble to drift ever far,
In coldest surroundings, endless endeavor,
For answers are somewhere, lest somewhere is never.

Wake, wake, gain nebulae insight,
All order, all chaos in Hubble's great flight.

Come back to Earth, to imaginable aura
Where secrets are closer than northern aurora.
Unfasten the mind to drift ever far.
Dimensions are boundless wherever you are.

Greta M. T. Tratt

'emptiness'

"Welcome to the wonderful world of
imagination!" screams the sign
on the silent door as I walk
by, entering my mind that is
mazes upon mazes of mirrors
reflecting myself
over and over like some
twisted kaleidoscope; blue, red,
green, pink, grey, and sky,
coming in, enfolding me and
setting me in the depths of
my soul, deep down, one-hundred feet
below the surface of my
mind. I scream to be released
from myself only to
my own voice
Echo in return.

Sarah Mayell

Wherever the Road Takes You

Wherever the road takes you,
you ought to remember:
Things are not always as you hope for,
life isn't always fine weather.

The days are not always sunny,
for clouds often times gather;
Just when you expect bountiful harvest,
what you get is much, much leaner.

Oft times the sea is deceptively calm
as a gale brews into a squall;
But if it's not time to hit rock-bottom,
there'll be a sudden lull.

Today you may be on bumpy road,
no reason to despair;
Move on, who knows,
ahead lies a well-paved thoroughfare.

Wherever the road takes you,
there's no cause for alarm;
Just reach out to the Father
who extends His loving arm.

Nicanor P. Tiosen

Untitled

I drink my tea in the morning
And also a cup at night.
I enjoy it with my jam and toast,
For me, it tastes just right.

My tea may come from England,
From France or even Spain.
I add a little spice to it,
And sip it with no pain.

I sometimes drink my
   tea at four,
And add a little rind,
But then of course, my
   delicious tea,
Tastes like no other kind.

Rosaline Clark

Your Son Is Dead

As the sun goes down on another day,
And everyone is sleeping in bed,
The message comes
That your son is dead.

What do you feel?
First confusion and disbelief set in.
Then comes the never ending pain,
And the thought of what could have been.

What can you do?
His life is over.
Could it have been avoided?
Maybe if they'd been sober.

Now what do you have left?
An image in your head,
Some pictures and memories,
And an empty bed.

So now we say good-bye,
For one last time,
To the man we all knew.
The waste of life is such a crime.
  Michelle Hill

Things Remembered

Snowflakes, and dew drops,
Icicles, and rain drops,
Whirlwinds, and stillness,
Wintertime, and chilliness,
Summertime, and ice cream,
Springtime, and open streams,
Butterflies, and annoying gnats,
Elephants, and circus acts,
Teddy bears, and lots of hugs,
Barbie Dolls, and Persian rugs,
Cold night, and fireplaces,
Happiness, and smiling faces:
All things to remember.
  Kimberly J. Brown

Significance of Life

The magnificence that is life
Can get passed by
And still we must pass
And yet we will buy
And buy
And buy
While stripping life down
Until all has been bought

But in the sky it is sought

The seekers will find it
Then make a great speech
"The seekers find life,
but well out of reach"
  Jason Michael Belanger

Lost Forever

You looked at me once
with bright, shining eyes
filled with love, laughter, and happiness,
but then you went away,
far away, and left me behind.
I don't know where you went
although you never left my side.
You spent so many nights in that room
with the door closed and me on the other side.
Your arms showed the traces,
but not of our love,
I never thought,
although I wish I had.
If I did, you would still look at me like before,
but now you are gone,
your soul lost forever.
  Tara L. H. Miller

Never Thought

When I first saw you
I admired from afar
Then on the day I met you
I found out how beautiful you really are

At best, I thought
We would meet from time to time
And it never really struck me
That one day our lives would entwine

Nothing has come easy for you
I can feel it in your hands
It seems that every time you tried to smile
The world had other plans

Yet I've never met a soul
So selfless and caring
It would appear your goal in life
Is simply to promote sharing

For this and more I love you
More than I could say
And the amount of love I feel right now
Is surpassed each and every day
  Glen Kaiser

Wanderer

A traveller was wandering through the Arctic,
Leaving his footprints in the fresh white snow.
Walking to the north, south, east, and west,
He was not quite sure exactly where he should go.
Wearing his tuque and his large, thick coat,
He was still thoroughly chilled to the bone.
And with the pain of lost love still in his heart,
His tears froze quickly, and he was alone.

And as his shed tears froze quickly,
His cold-battered body was freezing as well.
Without any food, he began to starve,
And he was fearing a miserable hell.
Gentle snowflakes fell on his misery,
And came down harder as his misery increased.
Death came to him on a cold, snowy night,
When the beating of his sad heart suddenly ceased.
  Jonathan Summers

The Comet

The seers atop the ziggurats in Babylon exclaimed,
"A miracle! A blessing! A powerful portent!"
Now, in scientific complacency, it is called Hale-Bopp.
The comet cares nothing for names.
It hurtles through space at alarming speed,
trailing its great, long tail.
It passes our planet and showers us with
the dust, the particles, and the energies
from the other end of the universe.
Dreamers sense the altered energy shifts.
Leaving our bodies safely in bed,
we travel in spirit and gather up
the dust, the particles, and the energies
from the other end of the universe.
Our chorus rings as we harvest its gifts.
"Sweeping up the sparkles of the bright night sky!
Hale-Bopp, Hale-Bopp, Hale-Bopp!
A miracle! A blessing! A powerful portent!"
Leila Friend

The Awakening

While the serenaders sing their song,
close your eyes and drift away.
A place far beyond your locked doors,
a land where fears and emotions lie.
Inhale the essence of a sigh,
as you revel in the divine energy.
Fall in love with the awakening,
never assuming it's all you can see.
Reflect within yourself your forgotten past
to achieve the uplifting in the cycle.
One must understand her reason,
for this is the love of an angel.
The guide has come to find your peace,
your decision must be made here.
Thy symbolism has come to give
what language sees not clear.
O, the path I have taken
to see the light to let you in.
She has surely come to me
to let our past finally begin.
Shayne Dawn

UMDLOTI 1997

Quilting clouds burden the sky
Threatening the darkened landscape
Until they drape the sea
In a mantle of desolation
Joining all in grim matrimony.
Fine rain punctuates the breeze
And conjugates its wail
Into a mysterious whisper.
Burdened sky, burdened widow's heart,
Brought here for sun and balm!
The clouds knowingly continued their obsequies
Till 'twas time to go home.
Journeying homeward, upward looking to the Berg
The widow's heart is lifted
Through the now-cleared sky
By the glistening snow-capped peaks,
And is blessed with Nature's balm.
Vera Marie Mecl

At the Crest of the Canyon

I stood at the crest of the canyon,
So deep, so dreary, so vast,
And a solemn thought swept over me:
It is like my stormy past.

The howling of the vicious wind
As it tore through the moaning trees,
Reached out and touched my troubled soul
As if a kindred spirit with me.

What cruel tricks fate played on me
To make me feel so prone,
As memories tumbled through my mind
That chilled me to the bone.

The chasm yawns beneath my feet—
Will the struggle never cease?
In the realm of my twilight years,
I only ask for—peace.
Jean Porter

Life Can Be

We travel down many highways,
Some are smooth and some are rough.
We travel over many mountains,
Some are easy, more are tough.

Which way are we all now walking?
Which way will be for the best?
Which way will be the lesser heartache?
Sometimes we must stop and take a rest.

Take time out to help a brother,
Take time out to help a friend,
Take time out to help an enemy,
Someday you'll profit in the end.

While I'm here, I'll help you smile.
While I'm here, I'll listen too.
While I'm here, you won't be lonely,
For I love each one of you.

Life can be so many heartaches.
Life can be so many dreams.
Life can be so many crossroads.
Can we always work out the schemes?
Jeni Chapman

Bewitching Hour

Bewitching hour came to be,
blacked flower's eerie trees.
Alone she stood in a fog-like cloud,
her chants becoming ever loud.
From a tree came a spirit free,
its branches dancing mystically.
Flames came from this tree within,
and she moved ever close.
Sparks danced upon her skin,
flames circled, then engrossed.
Her laughter grew to a deafening pitch,
then silence echoed the wind.
Richard M. Donnelly

Yuletide

Christmas is nearing,
Children are cheering;
Our hearts are warming
As we go swarming
From store to store,
Then door to door.
For months on end
It's all been a dream,
Then reality becomes
A frantic scene.
But isn't it wonderful
To see smiling faces
When you are traveling
To so many places?
A thought comes to mind
As I ponder this rhyme:
Wouldn't it be thrilling
If all could hear
The throng of Christmas
All through the year
With love—goodwill and cheer . . . ?
Diane J. Gibbs

No Matter Where You Are

No matter where you are,
I will always be there.
I will try to protect
The friendship that we always had.
No matter where you are,
The sun will shine
For both of us.
The clouds will never go dark.
They will always be silver.
The sky will be blue,
And the mountains will never fall.
No matter where you are,
The seas will rise
And the rain will make a rainbow.
No matter where you are,
I will always be thinking,
And loving you, no matter what.
Jennifer Abel

Soup

We are soup,
A bowl of leftovers,
A mix of vegetables.

A dash of spices,
Compliments of our chef,
Organizing our ingredients.

We each have a donation,
From talents to spirit,
And effort too.

In a pot we all go,
With lots to give.

"Together we are one."
Astrid E. Hardjana

The League of Thrashing Tails

I heard the crash, felt the vibration
Of the glass breaking on the linoleum
You think you're safe in the dark
Hiding like a thief in the park
I see your amber eyes glowing with satisfaction
From the top of the refrigerator—your bastion
You think you're safe in your position
You will never see my submission
Against the evils of humankind you rail
You and the League of the Thrashing Tails

Your partner in crime comes to your rescue
As she sends papers on the table flying askew
Eyeing me from either side, you leap
After awakening me from my sleep!
I chase you here—I chase you there—
Hey! Let go of that underwear!!!
Whoever said that pets are calming
Must have needed some embalming
In this one thing I cannot sail
To tame the League of the Thrashing Tails
Krista G. Brown

Token of Affection

My token of affection to the Nation
Is not made with gold nor silver:
It happens to be love, my eternal devotion,
Yesterday, today, tomorrow, and forever!
My thanks! It is never, never enough,
To express my sincere gratitude,
Because you never impose any impasse
To those who came to this Land for good:
Bless this people, oh, Lord, I pray,
This Country of ours with this magnitude;
Make this Place safe by night and day!
Agostinho Sendao

Serenity

At this northern lake, as darkness draws nigh
Evening shadows creep in slow,
Prismatic hues, streak twilight's sky;
Red orb on horizon sinks low.

Two foamy white flecks slide into shore
And glide silently on the ebb
In constant calm, repeated o'er;
Soothing, in its stead.

A quiet stillness settles all about,
Save the gentle ebb and flow,
One star in velvet sky, peeps out;
Moon, beams her silver glow.

And somewhere hidden in darkness' veil,
Crickets and bullfrogs start to croon.
Then is heard the sound, a lonesome wail:
The nightly call of a loon.

Wisps of haze at dawn's first blush
Will wrap the landscape in palest gray,
With the increasing light, another hush
Beckons the coming of day.
Norma J. Suddard

Timeless Hills

To gaze at those gentle rolling hills,
those green hills, of my beloved Wales,
hills that watch silver clouds sail by
like giant galleons, across azure sky.

Hills that lie dreaming, content, in the sun,
caressed by soft breezes, when day is done.
Hills that stare back at the moon's silver glow,
dreamily wondering, when did time go?

Hills that once echoed to the sounds of battle,
where now graze sheep, and gentle cattle.
Hills that watch ghostly armies march by,
silently screaming their battle cry.

Hills as old as the beginning of time,
when strode princess and heroes, all powerful, sublime.
When rides Arthur's Spectre, in coat of mail,
and Lancelot still, seeks the Holy Grail.

Hills that like beloved sentinels stand,
guarding this ancient, mystic land,
eternally listening to the soundless beat,
of time long gone, and time yet to meet.

Elizabeth Rees

Tony

My brother is dead
Yet I still laugh and dance.
My brother is dead
Yet I still have a chance.

We walked together for a while
And worked and were sick together too.

I did not see or call him much,
But had always hoped he'd make it through.

My brother is dead
And his wife is alone.
My brother is dead
Only grace she has shown.

Robert L. Miller

You're My Everything

You're my everything.
You're my sun.
You're my rain.
You're the flower of my soul,
My lost
My gain.

You're my river.
You're my stream.
You're my intimate, romantic dreams.

You're my sadness and sorrow.
You're my sunlight of a brighter tomorrow.

You're the clothes that I wear.
You're the water when I thirst.
You're my yesterdays and tomorrows.
You're everything to me that comes first.
You're my everything.

Nelson James Mackoy

Good-bye

While I stood there that day,
All alone and shaking,
As the Greyhound drove away,
Did he know my heart was breaking?

Did he think of me as weak
Because I couldn't hide my pain?
But as tears rolled down my cheek
I could only call his name.

I stood and stared awhile
As that bus speed him from my life,
But as mile passed after mile,
The pain cut me like a knife.

I knew why he had to leave,
And someday he would be home,
But it was at that moment, I believe
I had never felt so alone!

Karen Falkowski

Reflection on Aging

Once dominate forces
give way
to allow the parade
of decline
to march by in twos,
uncertain and fragile,
forgetful and frail,
vulnerable and self-doubting,
each one casting its shadow
on what once was.

Bruce MacDougall

How Does It Feel?

How does it feel
To be loved by you?
Temptations real,
Stronger than steel,
How does it feel
To hold you tight
And never will
Set you free?

How does it feel
To be someone who's
A friend 'til the end,
Forever will mend?
How does it feel
To bring you down?
It's so hard to think.
It makes me weak.

Joselito H. Sandiego

Sunset

I wish I had the time
To spend it all with you
To see the places,
Or laugh with the faces,
That make memories remain in mind.

I wish I had the words
To tell you how I feel
Every moment that you are near,
Each time that you smile,
And to describe the joy I keep inside.

I wish I had the courage
To have done more than I did,
To say the words that matter,
Or show the feelings I felt,
For every moment that I spent with you.

I wish most you weren't leaving,
Taking with you my dreams,
And though I can't be with you,
No matter how hard things might be,
I'm always much nearer than it may seem.

Michael Mugambi

Untitled

Piercing eyes
and excessive lustre
we move quickly
and attend for hints
and cast for that moment
of short transitory view
having plausible words
we contemplate with evil
satisfaction
towards the fall
of the evening;
obscurity and thick shade
sadness, darkness
of prospect
showy, specious and striking
sorrow's aspect.
could not await
could not await.

De Cesare Alessandro

Untitled

Little kids play marbles
in the rain.
They smile
beyond the pain
they carry inside.

Andrea Druhar

Existence?

Trapped in my own world,
I long for my other existence,
For then and only then, will my
Soul be content, free of people
I detest, meaningless, materialistic
Things that mean nothing to me.
But one must coexist!

My ailments that I, and only
I, can comprehend, restrict me
From living my existence how I please.
For some there's only grief and pain,
Loneliness and hardship, followed by despair
and the madness within.

Only grace, inner peace, humility,
and mercy can mend a broken heart,
cleanse a soul, and clear an absent, cluttered mind.

There is more beyond this
physical being, but where,
when, and how?
If I must I'll patiently wait!

Shirley Jacobson

Always, I Shall Remember

It shall be forever,
A feeling of aspiring endeavor,
To wonder why this land of the Fleur de Lys,
Has filled my heart with endless glee.

With its bubbling human effervescence,
As if some magical equation exists—
Within its presence, that knows no bounds,
And fills me with thoughts that keep stirring around.

And now, embers burn within my mind,
That leaves me with a feeling of a kind,
Pressing for answers of things to come
in the land of the Fleur de Lys.
Have we forgotten how to love as one?

Is it too much to ask,
or can we fill the task?
So that glowing embers can light the way,
Filling my heart with endless glee to say:

It shall be forever and here to stay,
A burning ember of love, we shall not stray,
Always, I shall remember, this compassionate ember.

Thaddeus Rogers Couvrette

Cat's Eyes

A pair of cat's eyes, twin embers burning in the night,
Sometimes emerald, sometimes amber sparks of fire,
But always able to see the very darkest sights,
Loathsome, evil deeds that are most dire.
Black as night, their fur stands on end.
They watch as one friend stabs another friend,
Then scurry into darkness just around the bend.
Who will they tell of this murder, each other,
Their father, mother, sister, or their brother?
I think not, for they are solitary beings,
And keep to themselves these solitary seeings.

Nancy Chatten

A Raven Calling

Once upon a mountain, some twenty odd years ago,
The warm winds of spring had melted the late April snow.
This was grizzly country, there were lots of fresh signs,
A big boar bruin had made his mark high on a pine.

There was a large silver tip in the area, I'd been told.
I was hoping this fine spring weather would take a firm hold.
This was the bear for me—no matter what it took.
From all indications, he'd surely make the record book.

Over the next several days, some nice bears I did see,
But my trophy silver tip, not a glimpse—where could he be?
Then one afternoon, as I crossed a nearby slope,
My heart raced; where there had been doubt—was hope.

For there in my binoculars, was the bear of all bears,
The King of the Rockies—a true bow hunter's prayer.
Swiftly and quietly, I maneuvered into position for a shot,
Coming to full draw—sighting in on the vital spot.

Then out of nowhere, came this loud, chattering sound.
Before releasing my shaft, that bruin was off on a bound.
Every time I recall that day—it just seems more appalling,
The shot of a lifetime, ruined—by a raven calling.

R. H. Cleet

Solitary Journey

Across the floor of this deathless valley I walk,
Words become silent here, only my innermost feelings talk.
Lungs of thought inhale their breath into me,
My outer eyelids close, yet in clearness of solitude's vision I see.

I drink of the fluids but my thirst still leaves me dry,
The void of lost memories empties me, yet my soul continues to cry.
Increase of consumption here somehow leaves more to take,
My spirit's essence yearns for sleep, but I am totally awake.

The eagle of my passion screams, yet takes rest upon the dove,
Footprints on my heart have left their imprint in my love.
An echo reaches back from the canyon walls of aloneness sent,
As I realize this is but a gift of even greater values lent.

Gary Brothers

The Handbag

There's something ladies have to carry, some are big and others small,
handle, straps for handy passage, all are gripped when in the mall.
There's pockets on the outer sides, inner, zippered compartments tease,
key chain latches stick out so that keys can be found with ease.

No matter how the design is, small is never enough,
but when it becomes a satchel, you tend to lose all your stuff.
Have you seen women shaking the bag, playing a game of show and tell,
jangling keys to locate inside, identifying objects by their feel?

I see young mothers carrying babes, juggling youngsters in their quest,
trying to free a hand to venture into a bag and keys to wrest.
Perhaps, like kitchens, it takes us gals to design a functional tool.
If we know what it's used for, you'll soon find we're nobody's fool.

I know we carry too much around, everything but the kitchen sink,
jewelry, makeup, monthly bills, directions to gym and skating rink.
We're forever losing something in them; it's a great, cavernous hole,
and as we tunnel through the maze, we feel like the garden mole.

Not keeping track of what's put in, an inventory we need,
a checklist at the end of day, it could be the way to proceed.
If all the bags in the country could be turned inside out, what a drag,
we'd find the treasures of the world, in some old lady's handbag.

Deidre Simpson

Winter in the Tropics

You miss the gentle breezes that never feared to blow,
Yet survive quite gracefully the ensuing stress.
You crave the frightening animals that in the darkness glow
When winter days make you, oh, so darned depressed.

Soothing sounds of soft rolling Caribbean waves
Barely reaching the moon-bathing shores'
Assorted trees, tall-standing and seeming just to shave
The vilest clouds stretching high to heaven's doors.

You yearn for the quiet walks through dense brush at dusk,
Lust for exposed bodies in one unbounded embrace,
All nature's sane creatures innocently locked in eternal trust,
Sweet scented roses dying to entertain your darling's grace.

Come hither . . . walk fondly back to where you oft recessed,
Sing sweetly, invoke the memories of those early days.
Thus beckons the rugged hillside where you once your soul invested
And reclined voluntarily in so many sobering ways.

Might the winter go away and take with it this annoyance?
Would you then crave the great solitude that offers moments so deep?
Is your mind vainly confusing and your choices wholly left to chance?
Must these tropical episodes fulfill . . . but thenceforth only in your sleep.

Bert Riviere

In Retrospect

If we could travel back in time and be young once again,
Would changes make a difference? Would they be made in vain?
If we were wise beyond our years and could start afresh,
As we look at life in retrospect, would it be without anguish?
Would we change a single thing as we reflect upon our past,
Would we live a different life, or would we stand steadfast,
Believing we were always right, in everything we'd done,
We'd made all the right decisions, each and every one?
We would be rather foolish, if we thought this to be true,
Not everyone is happy with everything we say and do.
We must have offended someone, somewhere along the way.
Why did some things go so wrong, and relationships decay?
Often, we ask ourselves, did we make the right decision?
Only God Himself can choose with absolute precision.

Brenda E. Denomy

Sarah's Secret Garden

Dedicated to Sarah Jean Hunter

Heave ho, hidday—ho, hop, skip, and jump-off we go
where fantasies soar and a child's wonderment is at full play.
A dew-covered spider's web in the hay, or a peacock, what can I say?
Down a country road, around the bend, over the fence, under the thicket,
we are there.

Hyacinths, daisies, larkspur, day lilies, and Canterbury bells
Through the trellis's, down the steps, the smell of roses fills the air.
Dew on the grass that feels sweet to our feet,
Robins chirping, the sound of music, and Sarah's laughter
make my heart swell
A blue jay yells from the gazebo
and squirrels go dashing at the commotion.
Asters, Iris, morning glories, lupines, peonies, and poppies;
the butterfly bush moths and monarchs are buddies by choice,
Wild and free, feeling as happy and fluttery as we.
No castles, no stone walls, but we can dream;
See trumpet vines, moats, and secret locks,
Anemones, her ladies in waiting, bowing for all to see.
Up and down hill 'n dale,
Orange candleflower, allium, and crown imperials,
Nooks and crannies, even the crocus, none forgotten.

Evelyn Hunter Clark

Thrust and Parries

Passion is wonderful, as you know,
With the thrusts and parries as you go.
But the tender touch and compassionate caress,
Make the meeting the absolute best.

The joining of the mind and the spirit
Is something we have done and not feared it.
The merging of our bodies at an upcoming date
Will continue to embody us as total soul mates.

With this thought I speak with glee,
For one day soon we will be free
To run and to play and to see,
A beautiful future for you and me.
Rick Morris

Exit Right: A Play by You

The world glows, glistening with golden plums.
Wafts of burning leaves cross the stage.
The set bubbles, pot-light bright:
seasons, tornadoes, mists, summer nights
until the little hidden cancer
   blurs a colored scan, for
   the lump is not benign.
The light stops dancing on the waves;
the talking walkers are silent.
You look around you,
you've been cut from the cast.
Whoa.
You work the curtains alone in the dark.
The mangled menace dangles in the ropes,
a jolly, jumping clown
mocking your silly art forms,
your auditions   your masks   your love scenes,
piercing your head with sharp, quick, tearing terror.
You set your life down on a packing box.
You will miss the cast party.
Cecilia Mavrow

Call upon the Angels

Call upon the angels,
is what she had said.
As a girl, dreams were worth having.
As a woman, those dreams are all dead.
Call upon the angels
when the colours all turn gray,
when the light is too dim,
and there is nothing left to say.
Call upon the angels
when your life runs out,
when the face in the mirror isn't yours,
when the walls begin to shout.
For, when you feel dirty, she said,
use the Lord as your soap.
Dust off your dreams
and carry your hope.
Remember what she tells you,
for it is all true,
because the angel to which you were calling
is the spirit that lies in you.
Eugenia Medeiros

Just Growing Up

Precious are the moments
Shared by a mother and a babe.
The love that grew from a tiny seed
Should never, ever fade.
One heart did beat just for two.
One body did its part,
And nine months later a little child
Stole everybody's heart.
First he started crawling
And getting into all he should.
And then he started walking
As if he always could.
The first days of school,
They came and went so fast,
And suddenly he was a teenager.
Oh, my, how time flew past.
Then off to college and away from home,
Each moment breaks your heart.
Before you know it he is married,
And his own family he'll soon start.
Patricia Jackman

Untitled

I'm not ugly?
I'm not beautiful.
I don't know about you,
But I'm being truthful.
I don't know much about my looks,
But even ugly people can make good cooks.
Rebecca Nielsen

Stress (Spin-Off)

From ingesting media tripe,
Breathing political hype:
Onslaught of stress will occur!

Bosses—money—and sex . . .
Other things also vex,
Cause metabolic stir!

Brain and body parts wrestle—
Straining each bone—each muscle—
Causing a spin-off from stress.

And when stress does occur,
Victims seeking a cure
Will turn to friends for redress!

Beware of the friend with stress!
Take care of him—none the less.
Stress has a virus—like flu.

Oh! Be sympathetic,
Not too empathetic:
Spin-off will fall out on you!
Reg Dockrill

Unintelligent Thinking

With absolute individuality,
relying on no dependence,
amplified enormously,
confidently carried,

Poised by certainty,
combined beyond question,
resulting in triumph,
become source of envy.

Resentfulness eyed,
judgements passed,
ruled conclusive
from one's opinion.

Assumed impressions,
truth unknown,
hearsay babbled,
friendships off-course,
astray,
jealousy won.
    Donna F. Grimsley

In My Heart Daddy

Not here,
But always here in my heart,
Far away,
But not far away in my heart,
For my heart can hold things
that hands cannot:
Like my love for you.
    Melody Nicholls Allingham

Untitled

I never answered the question
eternal
I only walked to work
each day.
I sat in every barroom
and every cafe
I watched every movie
sometimes by day.
I sat in every classroom
with every professor of faith
I thought I saw the earth
turn on its axis.
I did not know a resurrection
of promise
I did not know a basis
for faith.
I crossed each ocean
and every bay but
I could not walk the water
as on a previous day.
    Steven E. Clark

Forever and More

Look within and what do you see . . .

A heart, a soul
Rent asunder, yearning to be free

Sweet sighs the breath of that soul
Slowly beating . . . slowly waiting . . . slowly crying

Soft fall the tears of the heart of that soul
Slowly crying . . . slowly waiting . . . slowly dying

Sad lies the hope of the heart of that soul
Slowly dying . . . slowly waiting . . . waiting

Forever and more the heart must wait
Forever and more the heart must cry
Forever and more . . .

Until the healing touch can be found
And heart and soul are whole and one
Forever bound
    Jennifer Willow

Being a Friend

Be kind to someone, answer their call.
  Give a helping hand to one and all.
Sometimes you might think it's not worthwhile,
  But friendship always brings a smile.

It brings a warmth into your heart,
  Just knowing that you've had a part
In making someone's day a bit brighter,
  In taking their hand and smiling, a "Hi there."

By letting someone know you care,
  By telling someone you are there,
When someone needs someone to talk to,
  Just say I'll be there.

Extend your feelings by lending an ear.
  Some have troubles that bring real fears,
Things from the past that have gone wrong,
  Worries of a future that are so strong.

They cannot relax, unless they can smile,
  So help them today to go one more mile.
Bring some joy into their heart,
  And maybe then, they'll make a new start.
    L. Beckett

Peace

I rest my eyes—closed, they reflect my exhaustion
I float in a concert of shapelessness
My breathing calms—I begin to drift
My thoughts search for a measure of serenity
I feel a sense of movement—a sense of time
Stress is unlocked—my senses take wing
A tireless bliss calms my being
I breathe deeply from within—I hear, I listen
A concert of shapeless calm cloaks my thoughts
Relaxation spreads through my body
If only—I could hold this moment
    Eilleen Ackerman

Mother-To-Be

My babe, my child, please come to me soon.
My heart has been breaking each year about June.
The children are playing outside in the park.
All my world feels is empty and dark.

For, deep within my womb you sleep.
Only God knows if we shall meet.
My precious angel, one you day will be
At home, at rest, peaceful as me.

I ache for you, the world thus knows.
My days go by, so slow, so slow.
The simple things, the sky so blue,
I have not yet shared with you.

Who keeps us apart? Unjust, unfair!
I wanted you yesterday under my care.
Many women, empty, like me,
Won't be the mothers God said we could be.

I love you! I love you! And yet you're not here.
Please tell me, God, when will you appear?
So sad as the days keep passing us by,
The pain and the tears till the rivers run dry.

My son or my daughter, how special they'll be,
When one day my love will be shared by thee!
Barbara Lynn Young Mackay

I Promise

I've tried,
I've believed,
I've wished upon my wildest dreams.
To have you here, to have you close,
is what I need to have the most.
I know in my heart
you were there from the start.
I knew all along we would be the ones to stay strong.
I'm glad that I have you,
I'm glad that you're mine.
All I want is to hold you for the rest of all time.
I want to be with you,
I want you to know
I'll love you forever,
I promise.
I'll show it to the world, and to just you alone.
I want to be with you,
I want you to know,
I'll love you forever,
I promise.
Jasmyne Cunningham

Spring

The rain is wet.
The rain is cold.
The sun comes out and then a rainbow shows.
Lightning flashes and thunder rolls.
Spring has arrived.
Flowers have bloomed.
Spring has come to last one more season.
Karen Norton

My Hands

My hands flow in grace,
My hands are writing music,
My hands clap to praise!

My hands are caring,
My hands are always helpful,
My hands share with you!

My hands are happy,
My hands applaud to others,
My hands express love!
Kailee Anne Cherry

Time

To win may make a hero
But time itself wins all
It paces itself beside
Until our judgement call

We wile away the hours
No thoughts as seconds pass
Alone upon life's ocean
No eyes upon its mast

Twilight may be setting
Or sun on heavens rise
Past memories lie silent
Behind our befit eyes

Each hour walking hand in hand
With days and weeks and years
Time marches on with everyone
Through happiness and tears
Brandy Lane Rose

Celebrations of Life

Like wining and dining until midnight,
Or making love until daylight;
Like April showers bring May flowers,
Or lying on a beach for hours;

Like the moon glows on a starry night,
Or the sun shines under daylight;
Like walking through a misty fog,
Or watching a shooting star fall;

Like lying under a shady tree,
Or being sprayed by the sea;
Like the smell of homemade apple pie,
Or fresh air in the countryside;

Like being in Paris in the Spring,
Or hearing the sound of birds sing;
Like celebrating the fourth of July,
Or looking in your lover's eyes.
Daniel Earl Devine

Emotions

If unhappiness were a rose,
Then I'd be a thorn,
Its perfume held in tight,
Fragrant petals withdrawn,
The fluffy white clouds,
Turned inky black,
Rain down like teardrops,
Never to go back.
Megan Kerr

His Hand in Yours!

The images,
So neatly filed
In the drawers of my mind
Manage to escape
And play with me today—Father's Day.

The image of his little hand
Held securely in yours—

Walking together
At the park,
The zoo,
The beach.

Discovering—
Trusting—
Loving.

Thank you for being his Dad.
Josianne Rodier-Paris

Approach

Awake me from this demonic slumber,
you, God, I beg you God of thunder.
Cast aside my tears and my pain
by bringing me back the babe I gained.

My heart hath broken,
the eternal fire left unstoked.
I cannot ambit, nor can call.

Lay me in thy casket;
I dare you shall
wake me from this slumber,
end this horrendous thunder,
give me back to thy world
if you shall not . . .

Take thine eyes, for they are blurred

Wake me from this eternal slumber.
I pray thee now, do not me sunder!

Neonate rewards,
come rest my bosom, elate my heart,
and arouse me from this demonic slumber.
Why you do not, I will evermore wonder.
Heather Hiseman

The Religion of Life

A brilliant light
near the end of the tunnel
beckons.

A tranquil serenity
pacifies apprehension surrounding
the unknown.

With infinite clarity, sunlight encompasses
the simplicity and complexity
of life.

Nature challenges our
strength and spirit; adversity tests
our will.

We experience a mesmerizing
breadth of love to share our soul
with another.

Giving birth to the culmination of
such profound devotion is simply
heaven on Earth.
Pat Brimblecombe

Forevermore

A man came into my life recently,
with him I've experienced feelings I've
never known before.
When he walks into the room,
my eyes twinkle like the stars on a
clear summer night.
I feel the warmth and love between us
before we even touch.
My skin tingles as my heart skips a beat.
So safe, secure, and out of harm's reach
when I'm in his arms.
Hoping the time will never come when I must say
good-bye and leave.
Without him and his love, I feel so lost and alone.
My fear of losing him and never being together again
breaks my heart.
This man who holds the key to my heart,
I cry for and long for.
I'll love him now and always,
I will love him today, tomorrow, and forevermore.
Debra Grills

I Enjoy Watching the Sodomites Embrace

Because I enjoy watching
The Sodomites embrace, they want
To sing to me under the peach tree—
Close to the tomb of the Ripper.

While smelling their lovely hands and nails,
Thoughts of a vast blueberry garden
And morning drizzle arouse my laughter
And bring shivers in my mouth.

Meditate with your decisions;
I'll wait and wonder if the tea
Will be cold if I cry in it.
Tania Poggione

Old Age

Silent they sit now, the lost and lonely ones.
Longings, like hunger, unappeased save for the familiarity of daily bread,
And expectation a condition scarce remembered.
The day near ended, eyes and ears are ready to receive the whispers
  that spell life.
The cooling, creaking timbers—a fall of ash in the dusty grate.
The old dog snuffling and snorting, reliving scents and sounds
  again in dreams.
The clock-monotony reassuring, soft raindrops on the window,
Reminder of the world outside.
All listened for, garnered, and held precious against the hours of night.
Credits a grain of living still in hand,
Awarded and unspent to greet them with the dawn.
When sound and sight meet sleep's slow overtaking,
Even memories, like a tree's last leaves:
Strip them one by one and leave them bare.
Their spring stays underground, and winter
Glances back no more at the green leaves of the past.
        Marjorie Copleston

HE IS I

HE HEADS FOR HOME AFTER DAYS OF WALKING AROUND
HE HAS HIS EYES DOWN TOWARD THE GROUND.
TIRED, YES . . . HE DOES SEEM.
CRAWLING BACK INTO A BED MADE FOR TWO,
FEELS BRUTALLY MEAN.
HE FLEES TO A WORLD HE HAS CREATED,
A WORLD THAT AWAITS HIM WITH MEMORIES
THAT YOU HAVE STATED.
YOUR SILENCE BRINGS TEARS TO HIS EYES.
TO CEASE THE PAIN OF A WORLD WITHOUT YOU,
HE WOULD GLADLY DIE.
HIS LAST THOUGHTS ARE ALWAYS OF YOU
AS HE WEEPS INTO DREAM, TO A LIFE, HE ONCE KNEW,
AND HE WILL NEVER GET OVER YOU.
FOR, HE IS I. . . .
        Scott Anthony-Hale

Thoughts on Changing Seasons

I look out my window as Winter draws near
And see the rooftops which once were bare
Covered with a mantle of golden leaves
While others rustle beneath the trees.

The busy black squirrel scampers about
And finds a grey squirrel stuffing himself
On nuts the other had stashed away
So his hunger in winter could be assuaged.

Smoke curls lazily in the frosty air
And children scurry along the way
Watching a chain saw taking its toll
On a Maple tree barren for many a year.

The crisp, tangy air makes me catch my breath
As I pick up the papers that somebody left
On my front porch to blow all around
Unless I collect them at break of dawn.

The Seasons continue, each with its own tasks,
But somehow seem sweeter for the thoughts that have passed.
And the things which I see will constantly change
When I look out my window again.
        Eileen Lockstein

My Dog Is Gone (The Sorrows of an Eight Year Old)
This poem was completely written by my eight-year-old son, Athony
My dog is gone.

My dog is gone, it is so unfair.
My dog is gone, she ate my underwear.

My dog is gone, she is not here.
My dog is gone, she bit my rear.

My dog is gone, oh, what a bore.
My dog is gone, she wrecked the floor.

My dog is gone, she is not there.
My dog is gone, I wonder where.

My dog is gone, it is the end.
My dog is gone, no more best friend.
   Anthony Reynolds

If I Could, I Would
If I could take the colours of the turning leaves of fall
I would join them all together and one race there'd be for all

If I could take the hatred and the hurt from every man
I would join them and dissolve them and then peace would fill the land

If I could take the sweetest songs of all the birds that sing
I would join them all together, peace and harmony it would bring

If I could take the sickness and the pain from those who ail
I would join them, make them disappear and good health would then prevail

If I could take the water's salt and ripened fruit so sweet
I would join it all together, and everyone would eat

If I could take the innocence and good in everyone
I would join them and instill them so the wars would then be done

If I could take the happiness and love and joy we share
I would join them and you'd see that for each other we would care

If I could take the faith and hope and charity from us
I would join them and enhance them, then in God we all would trust
   Annette Chambers

In Loving You
In loving you I had written this in your honour,
Since with every breath I took,
I thought of you and only you.
For me, you were the reason each new day dawned,
Because I loved you so much, and I knew I always would.
For, in loving you, I had learned
What it was to forget my own misfortunes,
To forgive those who had hurt me.
It was you who had opened my eyes
To a brighter, more sensuous life,
And helped me see myself before it was too late.
In loving you, I had tried to restrain
My emotions to the confinement of my own heart,
And often had succeeded in doing so.
I may go on into bigger and better things in life,
But you will always be a part of me:
On every corner I turned, I saw you there,
And every night I faced, I prayed to God to keep you safe and well,
And maybe someday we'll meet again, and I'll have the courage to tell you
That "In loving you," my life was worth living.
   Karen Anne Roy

Above All

There's a man looking down on Earth.
Hidden behind the clouds, he beholds its chaos.
He sees restlessly acting people embedded in smog,
Coping with their fears and dangers.

A global village is the concern of some people.
Isn't this the beginning of all evil?
Result will be total control of human beings,
Of their relationships, and their feelings.

Not only political struggles or drug abuse,
But cloning and copying people for scientific use
Are mankind's obsessions
In order to get power possessions.

But nature will present us the bill.
New diseases will make us ill.
You never know how God will decide
When you want to challenge his indulgence.

How shall we behave in this situation?
No one can prophecy our development in future.
Where are our limits
Not to provoke the rage of God?
Trojer Guenther

Ode to Spin

There's something magical about you
that always makes me smile if I'm blue.
When you cast a glance, you cast a spell,
without you life would be hell.

When people insult you, it makes me want to cry,
because I know that you're a good guy.
It doesn't matter what you do or say,
you rock my world, and I'll love you anyway.

At the end of my dark tunnel, you were my light,
like a star in the distance, sparkling bright.
Everything pales in comparison to you,
if only you could feel the same way too.

Sometimes feelings don't need to be said,
so you let your eyes do all the talking instead.
Sometimes waiting is a hard price to pay,
but if that's what it takes, I'll do it anyway.

I'd given up on romance,
and now because of you, I believe I have a chance.
If I were to lose you, I'd be sad.
Could it really be painful to lose someone you never had?
Amanjote Sidhu

Little Wind

Once as a child I caught some wind in a jar.
I tightened the lid and watched it try to get out.
I looked at it there, that little wind,
That piece of the storm,
That smidgen of omnipotence—
Trapped.
The jar soon fractured, disintegrated;
The little wind looked at me,
Gave a little giggle,
And flew off to join its mother.
Darryl Jones

Thinking of You

I don't need a birthday
Or a Christmas bright and new
Or any anniversary
To make me think of you.

For, you are always in my thoughts
From morning until night
Or until the smallest stars
Have faded out of sight.

I think of you at work and at home
And every place in town,
Or whether I am happy
Or my world is upside down.

You are the music and the words
Of every song I sing
From summer into autumn
And from winter into spring.

And someday, when the sun goes down,
Beyond the silent blue,
I know my parting thoughts will be . . .
Another thought of you!
Sandra Cheong Robb

It's the Thought

When the snow is lightly falling
And a song is in the air;
When hearts are light with laughter,
And a sense of Christmas is near;
When a smile comes from a stranger
You meet upon the street,
A nod, hello, how are you,
With a "Merry Christmas" greet!
A time that is meant for giving,
And sharing things not bought,
And leaving smiles behind you,
Remember, It's the Thought.
Kathleen M. Stoodley

Untitled

Shoot for the moon
your heartache will keep,

your dream will speak pictures
as you lie fast asleep.

Temptations will soar

as fears do resist,
but fate will throw in
an unmentioned twist.

Hold tight to your thoughts
the image remains,

this moment is yours,
the passion explains.
Christine Joshua

A Home

A roof, four walls, a floor, some
furniture and faces of loved ones
plastered to the walls; nick-knacks
and curios placed here and there.

Somebody lives here. No,
more than one lives in
this house, eating foods
of personal choice.

Unity, comfort, security, love
envelop the people
who sleep in these beds
and shower in this bathroom.

All are one, yet separated. They
belong here, to each other to this
house, those clothes lying on the
floor next to a well-read book

This, I want. I want these feelings,
this belonging, this unity. I want
to see my taste reflected in what I see
around me. I want a home.

Andre Bradley

Butterflies

A myriad of butterflies
On gossamer wings
Dazzle the eye
Of all who behold
Their fragile beauty
And kaleidoscope of hues
As they soar upwards
In a freewheeling cloud

Susanne Noordyk

Spring

The melody of creation
is sounding forth again.
We see it in the budding trees
and the gently falling rain.

Bush and flower push their way
up through the stubborn sod,
The birds return from their winter haunt
and render praise to God.

Our spirits rise within us
and our hearts attuned to Him,
The God of all creation
Saviour, Lord, and King.

He leads in paths of righteousness,
and all His ways are truth.
The melody of creation
is living, breathing proof.

When trials and temptations
seem to come our way,
we trust in His unfailing love,
His Word, our strength and stay.

G. Winnie Kierstead

I Wonder

I look at myself and I wonder
What my mother thought I'd become.
Have I done some things she'd be proud of?
Would she be glad that she was my mom?

Are my fingers the same shape that hers were?
Are my eyes quite that big or that brown?
Do I care for others like she did,
Or did I sometimes let other folks down?

She must have been tired and weary,
But I rarely heard her complain.
She'd sit down and pick up her prayer book,
And get herself back on track again.

This great lady received no medals,
No honors were given her name,
But she was gentle and kind and I loved her,
And I so wish we could talk once again.

Mary Anne Castells

Sacrament of the World

The wonders of the world,
They'll never be untold.
Violence, love, and faith,
They can all be a big disgrace.
Perhaps not yet, but let's not forget
We have lots to learn, we'll all get our turn.
For, now we are sure,
The secrets that are kept
Will never be a threat.
Never do forget, we are not sure yet,
Until we unfold, our pasts that are untold.
They will always remain
Inside for us to hold,
Shining in our eyes, to let out that big surprise,
Where we should sacrifice
The telling of our lies.
So let us not forget
That we will be next.
Judgment Day remains there to be foretold,
In the sacrament of the world.

Piera Passaro

Struggle Pattern

In the midst of the universe
Lies a misunderstood image
Formed by the human race.
Opinions, ideas and beliefs vanish,
Broken and fragile wings to fly above from,
Move in relentless echoed motion,
Circles and circular patterns embrace the city's edge.
Darkness encounters fears within.
Sunlight's rays warm the uncertainty.
A faraway whisper is heard through confession.
The guiding light remains filled with hope, tears
and our perseverance.
The flight continues as an open-ended battle
Inviting a struggle pattern to enter the
Streams of paradise.

Melani Sinicropi

Railway Commuting

I met your unsteady gaze
As you hopped in reluctantly
Before the doors closed shut.

Beads of perspiration glistened
And trailed down your glossy forehead.
With trembling hands, you unbuttoned
Your collar and quickly gasped for air.

Your large black pupils flitted,
And so did mine, I found out,
Searching for something, nervously roaming
Our fidgety, overfilled car.

I couldn't figure out my restlessness.
Still, I reached to pat your shoulder.
"You needn't be afraid," I assured you.
And then I saw my hands, pale and shaking too.
I touched my neck and felt
My skin cold and damp.

Suddenly, it dawned on me,
Like the girl before me,
I, too, was claustrophobic.
Rosalia A. Bayan

Playing

Children playing on a lawn,
How calm they are, like light that shone.
Their little minds, so ever turning,
Yet having faith that they are still learning.

They calmly trust in God above,
For they will believe, without a shove.
Enduring faith that they have,
Comes in like a refreshing draft.

Us, though thought old and wise,
Disbelieve in faith, searching for a compromise.
We think we know how to truly trust,
All the while we often hate and lust.

We should try and learn from the young,
So in time we will not be stung.
Have faith in a quiet calm,
For there will always be children,
Playing on a lawn.
Christa K. Egli

Mending Terra Firma

My repentance is inaudible,
as the trucidation of Earth nears.
Worldlings are ingenious and applaudable,
yet we can't stop this prodigious fear.

Squandering aliment while others raven,
ravaging terra firma expeditiously.
We are the decapitators of our own haven,
unascertaining to pandemic delinquency.

How can we halt this marring
that creates an epidemic of stupidity?
Dubiety has rendered me expressing
trepidation, befuddlement, and animosity.
Susan Goguen

For Children

All God's animals are nice
And all Lord God's animals are nice
But some are fierce some of the time
And some are dangerous some of the time
John H. Ursell

The Wind

On the wind I hear the heartache
Of a thousand lonely souls
Screaming out in pain
From the love that someone stole

I taste the salt on the wind
From someone's bitter tears
Shedding them forever
And releasing all their fears

The wind slashes at me
Like a lover done wrong
From waking up on stormy night
To find that he's long gone

An' on the wind I smell the passing
Of a love so vilely wronged
The end of love from broken trust
Has forever been prolonged

The wind, it tells a story
Of a love that's dead and gone
But the memory of that love
Shall live forever on
Kellie Spray

Truth

Who would have guessed
that in my quest,
knowledge profound
drove me to the ground

And then I stood
that rotten wood
had let me down,
drove me to the ground

I thought it was I
that led to the sky,
and wearing the crown
drove me to the ground

My humility,
led me to see
knowledge profound,
and I had found . . .
some truth.
Andrew Campbell Christensen

Floating

Looking out the window today,
I saw a cloud to take me away.

Resting on its peaceful embrace
put a smile on my face.

In a time of pain,
this little cloud keeps me sane.

Sun above me,
troubles below,
on this cloud as white as snow.

This little, white, fluffy cloud
keeps me drifting day by day,
helping take the pain away.
Carrie Streilein

Untitled

I'll bang my drum
till you all just go away.
Then I'll dance myself dizzy
and ask for rain.
I can see you in the distance
and I know you're coming back.
I know you think I'm crazy
and that's not fair.
No one said it was
simple.
No one ever touched
me.
So I'll bang my drum again
hoping it'll scare you
one last time.
Now I can hear your quiet crying
and I can smell your salty tears,
but I'm still dizzy
from the dancing.
So I think I'll lie down.
Clint Gibbons

We Two

We are alike,
You and I

Spirit housed by body
Both imperfect

Struggling our own way
For enlightenment

You take one road
and I take my own

But we are alike,
You and I
Pamela Dawn

My Car

Today I got my blue sports car,
Will take me near, will take me far.
Of all the cars that I did see
This was the car that fancied me,
A smooth, sleek style with speed and grace,
I knew could conquer any race.
The price a bit beyond my goal,
But greed was working on my soul.
By then I opened up the door,
And slipped my feet upon her floor.
The seat, it moulded to my back,
Design and glare it did not lack.
I locked the door, I took the key,
And now I travel far and free,
And I'm so happy I did see
The car I'm sure they made for me.
Noreen Paulsen

Mind Meld

Dressed in paper gowns and garbage bags
Angels roast Barbie dolls and green bananas
On the rusted gold bar-b-que
Dousing the bizarre concoction
With antifreeze and cyanide
Shoving mouthfuls of food and painkillers
Down our closed mouths.
TV dances with radio gods,
Static infiltrating our tangled minds
Poisoning us
With cardboard angels and false idols
Burying us in radiated soil
And contaminated flesh.
We are their little puppets
Broken under their steel whip and tarnished spikes.
Our plots in their graveyard
Empty and barren
Because we forgot to fight back.
Shawna Linyard

Reality Halts

Have you ever listened to the sound of a mountain
It enchants like a winged melody
Believed there is youth in a fountain
But of youth in mankind not to be

Could you fly through the air without falling
Over a Valley where mushrooms were playing
Or hear little Leprechauns calling
If their gold-bearing rainbow has vanished again

Would you ever make out to be something
Like a whale "Moby Dick" avoiding all bait
Or thought of yourself as a melon
Being shipped across sea in a crate

If you've never seen to two trees kissing
Or an Octopus doing a waltz
Then you surely don't know what you're missing
When your mind's in Reality Halts.
Jamie James A. Webber

A Cry For Help

As long as I can remember

I was scared and so alone.
Though I had a mother and father
it was never "Home Sweet Home."

All the torments and the beatings
started early each and every day;
ended with me crying in my room.
Why did I have to live that way?

My teddy bear would sit and watch
as the tears ran down my chin.
I was on the inside looking out
while he was on the outside looking in.

As if I were trapped in a bottle;
that message floating about at sea,

No one knew that I was missing
'cause no one was looking out for me!

Couldn't they see I was shy and withdrawn,
or is it people just don't care?
All the signs should have told them;

They listen; they just don't hear!
Paul A. Doucette

Undying Love

I sat upon your window ledge one night,
only to see you lying peaceful in your bed asleep.
I watched over you, and one lonely tear
streamed down my cheek like melting wax of a candle.
How I wanted to reach out and touch your face,
once more to feel the softness of your skin,
to be able to lie next to you
and hear you whisper sweet words of love,
which you often spoke in my ear.
I remember all too well the times we shared
and thoughts that were spoken.
Yet I love you so much,
it hurts that I cannot take you away to my world
where I can feel the way I used to feel
when we were together.
Such a passion we shared, and now all you have left me
are the memories of our love and life.
All I have left to give in return
are the words of my undying love for you,
which you will never be able to hear.
Rachel Ivy Graves

My Favorite Season

Far away, from a distance,
When you look down from the sky
You can see a boarder
That splits prairies from the pine,
And when you look between summer and fall,
You can see green colors turn to all.
Then when you look between winter and spring,
You can see the snow turn into a hummingbird song.
When everything's all right and everything works out
You can turn into not only liking one season,
But all.
Jill Bradshaw

Powerful Music

Today is a day
which is like no other
Within are joy and peace
the life and splash of water

The Earth is full of joy
and pain, frustration,
in music is the power
to make or break a nation
Jason Uppenborn

Mother's Hands

Mother's hands are lined with
frets of crooked crevices
hoarding her heart.
An 'M' in her palm,
caked sweaty in dust,
spilling loose copper and silver
amongst transit digits
to appease our bellies.
Brittle tips of slender peaks
refined by less flamboyant rainbows
grasp time steadfastly.
After weathered bones had not pained,
when time once held her,
with my head cradled
in the safest bonnet.
The clock of the palm
palpitating since my birth,
except when I first slid
my hand rightly in hers.
Mala Rupnarain

Willow Trees and Angels

Willow trees and Angels
Are connected to you and me
They both have a reason to be here
They are both very beautiful to see

When a willow weeps
The Angel collects its tears
She keeps them close to her heart
To be released throughout the years

The tears she keeps to remind her
How wonderful they can truly be
For as the rain cleanses the earth
Our tears clear our eyes to see

So when you see a willow weeping
Know it's okay to weep too
For its Angel will always be beside it
Just as your Angel will be beside you
Kathy Jefferies

Miss Twist

Miss Twist
Was Kissed
By her Love
From Above
The Thought
Where it Ought
To be at Last
Then it Passed
and
Miss Twist
Hissed
In Agony
Her face Stoney
As he Turned
Anger Burned
Light was Dim
And she killed Him.

Gerry Caulfield

Anticipating Salvation

Alone in a room,
While dark flowers bloom.
Thunders and lightnings,
Hercules' might.
Come, fierce shower,
Bleach shadows to a dye
Whereupon here I lie,
My body sinned.

Su Maung

The Beggar Man

In silent tombs of somber streets
They gather with their shattered dreams
To remember days of glory past
And beg for dignity.

Their garments mend with fragile hands
That once and still a mother's pride,
And mysteries of a fallen sheep
That wanders in our countryside.

Their eyes that pierce the darkest well
That long for more than mortal gain,
To dance and play in summer's rain
Like children . . .

They smell the fear of wolves at prey,
Some too weak to fight the kill,
Nature's rage that lives at will
Or so they say.

And so they will lie in state
Like pawns of chess moved by hand,
As mirrors tell the revealing truth
Of who really is the beggar man!

Jonathan Beers

Keanu

I'm here for you!
Why can't you notice me?
I won't make you cry, but it's hard
to say good-bye to me; you're like a candle,
you sparkle every day, and every night.

You'll probably never see this,
Keanu Reeves,
although I wish you could know
the feelings I have for you,
even though they may never show.
Why can't you notice me?

Seeing the sunset across the sea,
looking at the golden leaves
on the tallest trees,
Keanu, seeing the sadness in your eyes
always makes me wanna cry.

My heart skips for you all the time.
But my love for Keanu Reeves is all just
a wonderful dream; I think of you deeply,
but why can't you ever notice me?

Tanya Brown

Lonesome Woman

As a girl I was lonely.
Again and again it happened.
I knew I was born lonely and alone.
A girl without a family,
A woman with family apart.

My life was filled with envy, jealousy, and hatred.
Each angle I went, I stepped on envy and jealousy.
Each side I turned I stood on hatred.
I was born rich and married rich with good education,
A good home with happy family, two of each.

My head ached, my eyes filled with tears,
My throat sore with blisters,
My body tired to the bones,
A sleepless night with empty stomach.

Each day I shuttled from GRA to IBA.
The car engine roars.
All money gone on repairs.
Each day gone followed by another.
A woman with family apart, just for a while.

Adepeju Ategbole

Kevin's Eyes

As I look at those beautiful blue eyes,
I want to take an adventure.
I want to see what he sees.
He sees the bright blue sky,
And a sun that has already risen.
The rays reflect off his crystallized stare,
And soon that stare envelops the darkness.
He glares at the moonlit night,
As the stars surround him.
My journey ends,
And I am leaving those glorious eyes behind.
A tear and a smile come over me.
I have to leave and say good-bye,
Good-bye to Kevin's eyes.

Esther-Michelle Romeo

To Be with You

Hours drag by and I think, I think endlessly of you,
Of those blissful days with you, that were but so few,
That were so short-lived like bubbles, like the morning dew.

I miss you, you are everywhere, I see your silhouette all around,
I hear your whispers amorous, euphonious in every murmur, every sound,
I see your images in the fleecy clouds, as I stand on the grassy ground.

The rose buds remind me of your lips, violently does my heart beat,
The twitters of the love birds on the leafy branches are like echoes sweet.
I long for you, never to part, with all the adoration, we have to meet.

No more of this distance, nearness to you I desperately need,
Just to think you are so far off, makes my heart bleed.
The blossom of love with tears,
 I nurture you in my heart, have sown the seed.

Beyond the tree tops, from the craggy mountains, you seem to peep,
How long and dreary are the nights when I simply cannot sleep.
My love, no longer can I this veneer of composure keep.

To the Almighty I pray, begging him ceaselessly day and night,
That very soon we unite, and get locked in an embrace long and tight.
To be with you, my love, every odd barrier, I can dauntlessly fight.
Nilofer Sultana

Sir Winston Churchill

Black despair and grave dejection gripped the nations of the world
For the tyrant, now triumphant, marched ahead, his flag unfurled.
Wickedness and hate his hallmark, dread and fearfulness he spread,
While free nations were a'searching for a man who'd be their head.

Previous leaders had been failures, they had known but to appease,
All their energies expended, trying wicked men to please,
But their efforts came to nothing, nothing as indeed they must,
For attempts to please a tyrant, fated are to come to dust.

But when happenings most dreadful shook the Earth, a voice was heard,
"Never must the wicked triumph. We'll prevail. I pledge my word!"
Everyone who cared for truth to Winston Churchill's banner came,
And together they fought bravely to extinguish evil's flame.
Eric Gutwillig

Black Hole

Black Hole, Black Hole, within the atmosphere,
Who knows where you are, so far away or near?
Within the clouds, it must be more!
No one can see you, or I would not ask so.

Scientists with telescopes don't give us hope.
They tell loud and clear, "It's much too near!"
Politicians and all, wake up from your dreams!

Puffing in the air, pollution everywhere,
No matter which way we look,
We are grabbed by the hook.
Black clouds from industrial area,
Where can anyone go to breathe fresh air?

Defiled is the ocean, also within the mountains.
Imagine in a city, or if one goes near a fountain,
It's written everywhere, "Do not drink here!"
Looks even disgusting, when someone gets near!

We must get together, think about our future
Black Hole in the air? That is not fair . . . !
The whole world is affected, some places worse than others.
Let's all hold hands, and help each other!
Maria Carlino Bressi

The Awakening

From the darkness of my soul the light pours in and down it seeps.
I forget the sweet smell of life, the joy each new day can bring.
I begin to awaken from my long, sad sleep.
Away in the distance I hear the church bells begin to ring.

I feel the pain and sadness begin to fade away.
I listen to the trees' soft whisper and the birds' sweet songs.
I turn my face up and feel the sun kiss me today,
So long I felt my heart was dead, how wonderful to awaken and find
I am wrong.

Long ago I forgot who I was and along the way I lost me.
So desperately hard I tried to please and love those whose hearts
were cold and empty.
I wrap my arms about myself and thank the sweet Lord above.

The love I seek and have finally found begins first with me.
I've learned most important to love me, myself, and I.
I drink in each new day with the awe of a fresh, new baby.
So to those who feel as I once did, love first yourself, then thank
the Lord up in the sky.

Julie Burke

The Birds

Birds are very unique and everywhere for us to enjoy their beauty.
They possess the inner strength we lack so often in our daily lives.
They are wonderful creatures and carry so much niceness,
that we fail to notice for being self-absorbed.
The crow is the wisest according to the wise man,
who once said that they lead us to our paths
if only we know how to listen and follow their teachings.
They have much to offer to us, and have been here longer, I'm told,
therefore possessing much wisdom and clarity to clearer paths.
Birds are here for our enjoyment only, until we learn how to converse
with them and share Mother Nature's beauty,
leading us to glory and wonderment, until we reach our true destiny.
Double Amen for the furry little creatures, big and small, and all their
wonderful lessons for us to follow.
Let us grow with them until we both find each other again
and share our wonderful lessons together for once.
May we all live together in total bliss, happiness, and much freedom.
Truly Amen.

Frances Killeen

A Hardened Heart

Turns away from caring,
and denial blocks the sensitivity from sharing!
Perception and motivation to live a full life become hazed,
and silent anger is easily raised,
Oft begrudging the closeness of family and friends willing to draw near,
and love's joys become fettered, when driven away by fear!
Self-induced loneliness obstructs life's grounding unto a healthy love
song. Fear sallows a friendly charisma, and the spirit lies low,
While stresses continue to build, and communication stands still.
An obsessed urgency to belong enthrals a dogmatic routine construed
with the excessive, "I love you's," and flowers with hopes to renew
the faded, once wholesome love, now wasting within,
never to ponder whence the sadness begins?
Attempting to calm the silent rage,
working physically and mentally to remove a lengthy submissive core
that grooved the wounds without the tears of yesterday!
A hardened heart slowly pumps life away,
no longer to feel its song and sing, only the guilt and blame remain,
bring forth a bitter note that rings, leaking with impatience that led
a hardened heart to cling, without love!

Patricia Palmer

Ode to Sam

Today I saw a doctor
A decision he left in my mind
He told me my best friend is sick
He told me he's going blind

He says the decision is left to me
With me he can stay
The other decision he left with us
Is he can be put away

For me there's no decision
Because he is my best friend
I loved him since he was little
I'll love him to the end

They say a dog is man's best friend
I know that this is true
For he's always watched out for us
Now we'll watch out for you

They told me it won't be easy
Constant care he will need
Well, hey there, buddy, I'll be there for you
The way you have been there for me
    Terrance Keith Nichol

Nostalgia for Unity

'Twas no long time since homeland behind
Road of life so distant pursued weary days and nights,
Dream of adventure almost has been tired.
Stranger's land well known of theirs and mine,
May it be home living among those dear ones,
Ancestral soul cherished, fraternal love at one.
Life's what? No other than a cloud drifting
Morn' till sundown wild wandering,
Then mounts and vales brood at twilight.
Adored are those eves tinted in golden light,
Gabled roofs with blue smoke o'er hovering.
Birds feather alike the earth over winged scattering!
Weary, tired wings of miles long been flapped!
Home sweet home, eternal nests of fate,
Beauty: how beauty is the unanimous swarm . . .
Lofty, it's lofty, the love for homewards.
Place where all life's memories printed.
Place where all the past shadows rested.
Place where nourished the strong belief,
That him among men and men among him indeed.
    Quy N. Vu

Magical Form

The sonnet's author is not wholly honest:
Conjuring with this magical form, he would,
By illusion, suggest Petrarch's brotherhood
To exalt himself as sublimely blest.
He'd charm from thought the lovers in your past
And render your heart an immaculate womb
With his love first-conceived. Then he'd presume
Eloquent delivery would make him your last.
Disbelief is suspended—yet, I fear,
If the spell of words fails to hold, you will
Find me to be what I do not appear:
A clown or fool performing sleight of hand.
In order to keep my enchanted jewel,
Love, I do the desperate tricks I can.
    Ken Zokol

Hourglass

As I look through the hourglass of time
I hear whispers
Of past lives
Calling out to anyone who will listen

In a way like the wind
Blows and dies
The whispers follow

But who will listen
When I am gone
Joining the whispers
Forever

As I walk away I wonder
Will the whispers follow
In a way I hope so
As I walk away
Into the silent night
    Jennifer Elizabeth Sych

Do What You Can

Today did arrive
But now is passed
Yesterday is gone
But mustn't be forgotten
Do what you can with tomorrow
Through tomorrow's living
Are born yesterday's memories to cherish
    Maureen Hanson

What Is a Friend?

A friend is Someone who cares,
Someone who understands,
Someone who's willing to listen,
and willing to have good times,
Someone who will not judge you
for however you might look,
Someone who will forgive you
if you haven't been so good,
Someone who will be with you
in the good times and the bad,
Someone who will talk
if you happened to be mad,
Someone who you can lean on
if the things don't go too well,
Someone who you can trust
and you know that they won't fail.

This is a friend according to me.
This is the friend I want to be.
    Zut-ying Soto

Untitled

Don't give up
The world I know
'Cause if you do . . .
Till death do us part
And love do we hate
Forever we shall live
In death.
    Kamerine Adams

Nighttime

Oh, what a beautiful night
With stars that blind the eye,
Jewels of Heaven, up above
Encrusted in the midnight sky.

Gentle music of the evening
So far away, yet so near,
A tranquil calm spreads like fire:
Air so fresh, so clean and clear.

Trickles of water echoing
Through the meadows, over the hills;
There's plenty of life all around,
But it's sleeping so very still.

The love for peace and quiet,
A passion so very strong,
To think we have to sleep and miss
This wonderful sanctuary, all night long.

Jennifer Gautreau

The Night We Met

The night we met,
I knew it was right.
When your eyes met mine,
my heart took flight.
Just before Christmas,
nineteen eighty-three,
we were together,
it was meant to be.
We're still married
after eleven good years.
Let's keep on going,
even when there's tears.
Through good times and bad,
you were never away,
always with me,
each and every day.
When you asked me to
marry you, I couldn't say no.
I loved you back then and
now more than you know.

Susan Taylor

Summer Love

The Thrill of first glances,
a brief touching of hands,
that sudden attraction
a heart understands.
Long walks on the beaches,
long walks without an end,
a first Kiss in the moonlight,
as your heart takes her in.
The passion of summer
in the heat of the sun,
the pleasures of nightfall,
when two becomes one.
Promises whispered
in the cool of the grass
of a love that will linger
when summer has passed

Nakules Somasundram

Did You Ever

Did you ever love someone
and know they did not care?
Did you ever feel like crying
and think you were nowhere?

Did you ever look into her eyes
and say a hopeless prayer?
Did you ever look into her heart
and wish you were standing there?

And when it starts, you don't why;
you will wonder day and night.
You see, my friend, you're loving her
no matter how you fight.

Love is fine but hurts so much;
the price you pay is high.
If I could choose between love and death,
I know I would rather die.

And so I say to you, do not fall in love.
For, one day you are happy, the next day you are blue.
You see, my friend, I ought to know:
I fell in love with you.

S. S. Basra

The Name'd Days

There is a size to some proud days,
The days that rise and blind with memory,
That shout and rail against
The laying of all hard things to rest,
The name'd days are they.
If we should ever gifts be given
And choice be ours to name the prize,
The weary ones would bless the giver
Who drowned the days that would come in size.
For then that day is just as others,
Whispering gently of other tymes; but
No face clearly and no heart dearly
And no hopes nearly
To end upon.

Paul Aspland

The Hurting Pain

When life seemed confused, what do you do,
All that was good turned into sadness, it's
not that life isn't worth living, it's that
life just keeps on dreaming. Sometimes
I think and sit and say, I wish I could just go
away. Why do I feel like this, why is life
such a given death? Then you know why
you want to go away. When life seemed
confused and the rain turned into tears,
you start singing the blues of your most
frightening fears. Life is a gift given above.
Life is death without love. Your heart is
your last token. Feeling free, free above, that's
where your heart is, that's where you'll
feel loved. A hurting pain is a crying
shame, but it isn't anybody's blame. But
when you do feel loved inside your heart,
that's when life really starts!

Tami Renz

Open Your Eyes

I can't let go
Of what we almost had.
As I sit here alone,
I can't help but feel sad.
We always talked,
And were the best of friends.
I prayed to myself
That it would never end.
But it was I that wanted more,
And I told you so.
I asked you if you felt the same.
All you could say was that you didn't know.
You now know how I feel,
And that for you I'll always care,
But why won't you open your eyes
To the one who's always there?

Cynthia Brault

Uncertain

It was a day like any other day.
Or was it?

It felt like the whole Assyrian fold
descended and pounded me to dust.
Was it so?

Did the Hand of God reach out to me,
like a Phoenix rising from the ashes?
Could it be so?

The windows of the mind give a
glimpse of a sure, confident, and somewhat
arrogant self.
Or was I?

Each day now faced, uncertain, angry, and sad,
for what was stripped away.
Was it really there?

One thing, certain that I am,
that God's love and presence are always there,
Of that I am very sure!

Margaret Ayre

Give Yourself

Who can give himself, will never die;
others will continue his ideals.
What the life deals,
puts out before us on the table.
If we are able,
we play the cards the best we can,
hoping we won't be the big losers.
Sometimes we win, sometimes we lose,
and we take it all with dignity.
The main thing is sincerity.
Good example we have to show;
for what we sow
today, will be tomorrow's harvest.
So, do your best,
and others continue your ideals,
as the life deals.
Trusting: Who can give himself, will never die.

Ilona Kiraly

Now That You're Here

The light,
once subdued,
is bright again.
The air,
once stifling,
is crisp once more.
My heart, once forgotten,
beats strong in my breast.
Its beat is only for you.
The colors, the music,
the soul of the rain,
have a different feeling in your arms.
Where once there was nothing,
there now is so much.
more than I ever could have dreamed.
Happiness has meaning,
peace has a name,
forever looks wonderful,
now that you're here.

Michelle Thornton

Forgiven

Shattered.
Spirits fragmented beneath
the Dragon's breath. It calls
but I cannot respond.

Broken.
It cracks the bow of tides;
wanting, wishing, waiting.
I have no answer.

Rain.
Sins of reckless ends shower
upon my callous soul.
"Father, what must I do?"

Absolution.
I want.
I wish.
I wait.

Ronnie Lum

Reflections

I used to be young
Curled up warm with my blankets
My dreams
Content in my innocence
Ignorance
Naivete
But all this was
Ripped from my grasp
Torn away
Shred
By
Shred
Till there was nothing left
Nothing
Save this deranged
Distorted
Image
Of former confidence

Carrie-ann Brumwell

A Single Rose

Standing all alone,
for she has no friends,
not a soul to speak to,
but the little buds,
who could not yet speak.
All of her friends have been taken away,
for they had more beauty and radiance,
than she.
She stood there weeping and
every day she lost a new
part of her past and her present,
every day falling a little more behind.
She had to hold on to what she had
until the very end of her time.
When she would soon turn old
and die.

Robyn Cowper

Heart Broken

As I sit in the hospital,
I remember that smile.
Always warm and caring,
I never thought it was only
for a little while.
I remember the times we shared,
Happy and sad.
I thought it would be you and me
Forever.
Then, like it was no big deal,
You walked out of my life,
Taking away my happiness
for life.
You didn't care about the
memories we shared,
Good or bad, happy and sad.
You thought of you,
And only you.
So you ran away and left me
to die.

Prabhjot Lotey

Sailing

I have a boat,
but do not have a goat.
I love to sailboat race
and paint my face.
Jim flies the jib
and also tells a lot of fibs.
I race against my brothers
and have fun with my mother.
When we cross the finish line
we all go out and dine.
I love to sail,
but do not like to bail.
Oh, Sailing,
Bailing,
Oh, is my boat ever failing!

Lyndsey Boston

Mon Chou

Outside the rain falls.
Inside my heart calls
Andrei....
Where are the days we dashed together
through the rainstorms,
catching a bus,
lining up for a movie,
trekking through the woods on a hike?
The rain splashing so fast off the cars
reminds me how fleeting your life was.
Bubbles floating in the puddles are like my teardrops,
drifting off and disappearing,
yet resurfacing again after the cars go by.
These bubbles are not coloured though, like most,
they're grey and misty like my soul.
They only float for such a short time
with rings around them,
rings that grow bigger and disappear from view,
like you, Mon Chou.

Teadora Szalanski

The Window of the Soul

My eyes are but windows unto the world.
They never get tired of absorbing
The beauty that surrounds them.

My heart is but a window unto the world,
Never afraid of being hurt;
For, this window in my heart
Is open to everyone.

My soul is but a window
That only God and I can see through.
No one can ever take it
Away; it exists forever.

My love is but a door without
To be opened by anyone.
Fortunate, those who open that door.
Few are those who see beyond
Their own reflection in my window.

Norma Palumbo

Almost Sunshine

Whirlwinds of faces become a blur
as they are engulfed by the madness of normality.
Tornadoes form in the darkest of undiscovered corners,
waiting for the winds to become as one.
Screams echo off the images in my head,
while familiar voices twist into unrecognizable sounds.
Sanity dances in me, like a leaf caught in a rainstorm,
while hidden rainbows fight to shine.

Captivated by familiarity,
observing through stained glass windows,
encompassed by confusion.

Eternally handcuffed,
where sanity and insanity are disguised as one,
and I am almost sunshine.

Kelly Ward

Forever Bliss

Trapped in the illusions I dream of,
My own secret world.
Nothing is tarnished, lasting love,
I wake up tightly curled.

Sinking deeper in the core of my throat,
Reality stinging, pain is what I truly know.
I wish I could hide under a coat,
My coat of dreams, dreams my escape from sorrow.

Walking day by day,
things being black and white,
Melting in pools of grey,
walking each year closer to light.

I feel sore and bruised all through my soul,
lasting happiness, only in the sleeping state.
Eternal sleep, has no toll.
Forever bliss, I shall not be late.
Jessica Pyringer

The Epitome of Life

For, it is not the cold, heartless world,
But the cold, heartless people that She contains.
In the still of the night,
There is always some light shed.
But you have to find it, you have to see it.
The glorious happiness is always there,
But if you cannot see it, then you are blind.
You are dead.
Maybe, if people are unbearably used to the darkness,
They cannot adjust to the splendid light.
They may see it,
But refuse to believe,
Not only in the light,
But in themselves.
I see that light.
I yearn for the light.
Life is a precious gift,
That I can see,
And not that I accept,
But I treasure.
Jennifer Rinaldi

Fear of Myself

Dark eyes in the dark night,
Dark shadows in the dark light;
There is no light but there's nothing I fear.
What is that noise, what do I hear?
It's only the laughter inside of my head.
I can no longer sleep in the warmth of my bed.
I'm trapped in a nightmare but it is so real.
The wounds seem so deep, but I can't even feel.
I am not frightened, but I am so scared.
I wanted to scream, but I wouldn't have dared.
I might have awoken the evil that lies ...
Lies in the depths of my swollen-shut eyes.
The voices grow loud, the spirals don't fade.
I'm caught in the middle of the horror I've made.
I created the evil but it's after me now.
I will never escape. I will never know how.
Alaina Mellon

Aurora

Colours roll across the sky,
Banners ripple, miles high.
In the dark immensity
Light comes streaking suddenly.

Blazing rainbows captivate,
Arc above, then hesitate,
Glowing moments only then,
Colours melt and soar again.

Stretch your mind to grasp the size
Of this glory in the skies.
Blending, flowing colours pour
Where the darkness was before.

Glowing light has dimmed the stars,
Aurora hangs in radiant bars.
Unforgettable this sight;
Brilliant splendor fills the night.
Lola Alsmo

Setting Free

I sit and think of all I have
And see my life has not been bad.
I have had times that have been hard,
But always you had a soft, kind word.
The good, the bad, it all must be
To help you grow, to set you free.
We've started a life of tenderness,
The love we have could not be less.
If I had to do it all again
So much that I would leave the same,
So thank you for the life we have:
The caring, friendship, and the love.
Edward Cochran

The Pain Won't Be Spoken

The pain won't be spoken,
The hurt goes untold.
Beautiful or not,
I could never be so bold.
I wish upon a star,
Yet it is still much too far
To be heard,
To be listened to.
I want to laugh happily,
I want to dance the divine.
I want to hold you close,
I wish you to be mine.
I dream of being in your arms.
Hopes of being near,
Prayers of loving you,
Are much too far,
Yet, oh, so dear.
Elizabeth Wilson

What You Are . . .

You are a friend to me,
And so much more.
You are a reason to be,
And the one I adore.
As the day passes by,
And life's lessons occur,
I think of one person
And sharing my lessons with her.
When the day is at end,
I turn to my friend.
It is you that I think of.
It is you that I love.
In times of great joy,
In times of sad pain,
I want you to know
I love you the same.
You are a woman of beauty,
Of warmth, and of care.
You are the one I want always
And forever to be there!
   Kevin Duval

On the Edge

I'm lying on my stomach in the gutter.
I can't seem to find my mind.
Do you mind if I join you?
I need to waste some time.

Buzzards are circling overhead.
Are they here for you or me?
Death is on the doorstep,
But he isn't real to me . . . not yet.

Wandering blind through the desert,
Looking for a good mirage,
Offer me a safe future.
I'll choose a Start in my garage.

Hope is a golden ladder.
I'll climb it in futility.
It's better than getting mired
In the quicksand of reality.
   Kenneth Paulson

Wishing To Be Me

I might never save the world,
I may never own an isle,
I might never name a star,
I may never sail the Nile.

I will never sculpt a David,
I will never walk the moon,
I won't swim the English Channel,
Or ever write a tune.

Mona's smile I won't be painting,
Just one thing I wish to be,
It's not the Queen of England,
I wish only to be me!
   Naomi Taylor

Untitled

Well, Stephen, the time has come, to make your move,
To settle down—for twelve weeks, get in the groove.
You are going to enjoy it, your dad and I know—
For we did the same—as that in WWII show.

You are going to meet a great bunch of guys,
Around your age—and around your size.
And they will stick with you through thick and thin,
As you carry on, that's what it takes to win.

Oh, you will meet the odd flake, from day to day.
Best thing—is just keep out of their way.
Soon, you will get new adventures, see the world.
As you march along—proudly—flags unfurled.

We will all be proud of you—you surely know—
As we stick out our chests, for it will show.
Take it seriously and the remarks will be great.
Do your best, at all times—leaves nothing to fate.

In two years' time, you will have to make a choice,
But you will be in a position to raise your voice
And you will be listened to by your peers—
As you decide on the next four years.
   A. G. Moore

Changes

Living on the West Coast was supposed to be cheery,
But the winters, tho' warm, were incredibly dreary.
Tragedy brought us to the prairies, come fall
Where the cold, and soon snow, made their winter call—
Heralding the hardest winter in years.
Tho' mourning our brother with sorrow and tears,
We kept thinking—The brightness! The sunshine!
Not much rain in the summertime.
So we packed our bags, had a garage sale,
Sent our address change so we'd get our mail,
Left the mountains, valleys, and pollution,
Then headed east seeking a life-style solution.
Less traffic, less pressure, and wide open space,
Less stress, friendly people, a much slower pace:
This we agreed was how we wanted to live,
Enjoying the sunsets with the time to give
To projects and hobbies, to finding our way
In our bright, new future with bright, sunny days.
Although not quite settled, the spring warmth of May
Assures us our life change is good, so we'll stay.
   Janice Caulien

A Proposal

It's time to address the matter at hand.
To me, there's no other in this fair land
Who I would cherish and love, and want as my wife,
So I hope you will consider sharing my life.
My dear, it's only you, I hope you can see,
Who is special enough to warrant this plea.
With heart in my hands, and baring my soul
(Evidently, it seems, Love has taken its toll),
I come before you, as sincere as can be,
And put forth this question: Will you marry me?
   Frank Beghin

Sunday Bells

When the Sunday church bells rang, there were those who made
their way to their favorite place of worship.
There were those who played a musical instrument or sang gospel
songs with joyous hearts.
There were those who watched the preachers on television,
or listened to their voices on radio.
There were those who visited the sick and less fortunate
in hospitals and institutions.
There were those who volunteered their services in the shelters
for the needy and the homeless.
There were those who strolled through God's Earth to enjoy
and to attend His Creations.
There were those who found solace in reading the Bible
and sought the meaning of each verse.
There those who made a meal for family and friends.
There were those who remembered that warmth from photos,
letters, and souvenirs.
There were those who rested, or read, or studied for their
long journey ahead.
And the Sunday bells rang for those who heard them.
Kay Fairman

Reflections

She wandered lonely by the stream, the lilies at the fore,
Golden skies and lush green hills shone like never before.
The silent water kissed her feet and washed away her agony.
Entranced, she left her life, its inquietude and monotony.

The reflections she saw beneath shook her unto the core,
A caged bird in this solitary world, who now sang no more.
The love that she had yearned for all through her years,
Its elusiveness and transience had even dried her tears.

As the twilight faded by and the moonbeam lit her shore,
The heavens showered upon her, the love that only dreams assure.
The smile got back to her lips, the one that was lost for years,
Even today in the same dreary world, its sweetness still lingers.
Kalpana G. Samant

A Silent Prayer

The dark side of life we take for granted; from the day
we are born, we live our lives through dark and light.

Open eyes for the light of day, darkness comes with the closing
of our eyes, a sleeping peace, dreams of living,
sleeping thoughts: love, happiness, hate, God,
which takes us through the darkness of night.

Dawn awakes a lifting of the sun, just as Christ rose,
gives us a presence for the new day, God's belief not to punish,
the mind filled with fear, but also laughter and love.

Blow the devil away, the truth of religion a heaven,
miracles as the finger of God points at us; we are built
in a prison of life, a sentence which the Bible can't change.

The one great curse we have in life is the end, we all say
a silent prayer, an act of worship attracted by God,
is this greatest cruelty, life is a marriage with death.

We come from the dark, we don't know why our bodies fail us,
as heaven calls the time, the light following us through
our lives, God is with us to the darkness of the grave.
Malcolm Garrett

Encounter of a Curious Kind

Pulsing, droning, lurching, it descends slowly, ominously.
Hovering, it follows my fearful flight with great, flashing eyes.
Panic and strength ebbing, I succumb to a strange serenity.
Sleep, oh, yes, sleep, yet dread lurks within as if in disguise.

Strange, the odor permeating the senses, not of my world.
Sounds, intermittent, faint, as from afar, yet dangerously near.
Lifted, suspended, then descending to lie defenseless, inert,
Bereft of strength to resist, somewhere within, traces of fear.

Probing, tugging, poking, violations sensed without feeling.
Sharp sounds like snapping teeth or cracking bones of white,
Silence, a silence that ushers me from inertia to wakefulness.
With lifted head, weak, I strive to rise, to once more take flight.

I see them now, there, by the sinister object with eyes that glint,
Slight of body, upright, staring with large, dark, gleaming eyes.
Into the gaping belly of that thing, they disappear, one by one.
Roaring into life it drones, pulses, and slowly begins to rise.

I marvel at my deliverance, unscathed, from that eerie encounter,
Save one ear, something there, yet no pain, how strange it feels.
Driven by gnawing hunger, my unsteady gait cautiously quickens
Across the cold, clear, vast expanse of white to water, fish, seals.

Jean Weymes

An Ode to Saint David

In Hallowed Llanon, was blessed David Born
Showing humility and grace, from that first morn'
Growing in stature and bearing, like the field corn
Nurtured by the waters, light and lively
Of the Towy, the Taff and the Teifi.

David took his priestly vows, and taught the Gospel freely,
Founding churches in the villages he loved so dearly.
His many Christian virtues, the people saw clearly,
As did the whirling waters, light and lively,
Of the Towy, the Taff and the Teifi,

And good David grew old in the service of the Lord.
Guide, protector, friend, ministered with the same accord
Becoming all to all, and so gaining all to the Lord.
He rests now, near the waters light and lively
Of the Towy, the Taff and the Teifi.

Royston Loveluck

My Compliments

After you get through the age-old question,
"To be or not to be?" those of you who decide on the former
Choice have a great many more questions to answer:
To be corrupt or true to self?
To hate or to understand?
To judge or to accept?
To be selfish or to stand united?
To take advantage or to nurture?
To see as an object or to respect?
To use and abuse or to love?
To turn my head or to look over the flock?
To be evil or to forgive?
To control or to share?
To capture or to set free?
To push aside or to listen?
To deceive or to be honest?
To neglect or to do my best?
To attack or to be at ease?
To let die or to be sensitive?
To be alone or to believe in God and His time be near?

Peter Warnock

The Old Country Store

Supermarkets are the rage,
Bigger and better in this modern age.
But give me the old-fashioned country store,
A family-run business with charm galore,
An air of nostalgia within its walls,
A community connection you don't find in malls.
The country store promotes local wares:
Prize-winning foods from county fairs,
Cattle feed, fertilizer, and treatment for weeds,
Meats are cut to suit individual needs.
Remember the old-fashioned wheel of cheese,
Hand-scooped ice cream, any flavor you please;
The best sodas and milk shakes you've ever had,
Timeless treasures, gifts from mom and dad,
Books and magazines, mail orders from Sears,
Monogrammed hankies for a loved one's tears.
Old men gather to keep up with the news
And interact with locals of differing views.
So next time you pass an old country store
Stop and take time its charms to explore.
Linda Hawkins

Thank You

It's not good when you cannot breathe
You wait and wonder for a donor to be
Giving a lung of a loved one he knew
And now it is your turn, your transplant comes through
You wonder if your life will change
Will you look at the world and your life the same
I know in my heart I will not be a loner
'Cause the courage it took to be an organ donor
Was something the donor had already planned
To save someone's life would be just so grand
To save someone's life and his spirit live on
To guide someone else down the path that was drawn
By the Lord up above when he put us on land
To help someone else to lead by his hand
So thank you, to the one who has given to those
Their organs to people they don't even know
God bless you, and I want you to know
You'll not be forgotten or passed down the row
You made a decision to help those in need
By giving your organs and to sow a new seed
Robert B.

Eternal Damnation

Day after day, those hollow, lifeless eyes
burn deep into my soul
and glare at me in disbelief,
confounded by my audacity
to embrace the fires of Hell
and fall victim to the manacles of
Art!

Heaven forbid I should reject the wonders of Science;
Lord help me if I crave Byron and Scott;
God have mercy on my creative soul;
Lord, forgive me, for I have sinned.
The road to eternal damnation
is a labyrinth of poetry and,
God help me,

I love it!
Andrea Leblanc

Little Ones Take Care

Little children everywhere,
Running here, playing there.
Children have such a flare,
For simply saying, "I don't care."
Happy children mostly are,
But don't you wander off too far!
Watch out for the stranger's car,
That might have stopped on the tar!
Run away ever so quick,
For all you know it's just a trick!
Don't stand around like a stick,
It might be you who they'll pick.
Off you go now, run to Mummy.
Eat your dinner and fill your tummy,
Veggies are ever so great,
All your dinner, you ate.
Before you go off to bed,
Tell your Mummy what's in your head,
And just what that stranger said.
Always remember this poem you've read!
Vicki Grech

White Man's Wailing

I am the weather,
The sun and the rain.

I am the feeling,
The joy and the pain.

I am the beast,
Wild, unkept.

I am the human,
So easy to tempt.

I am the truth,
So hard to tell.

I am the dead,
I lie where I fell.

I am life,
The perfect gift.

I am love,
The heartbeat's rift.

I am not blind,
But I cannot see

That I am the Earth,
And the Earth is me.
E. Jones

Homeless

Nowhere to sleep,
All I need is a place to eat.

It's beginning to snow,
And I have no place to go.

I'm lonely, frightened, and cold.
My face is turning frail and old.

If only someone could help me,
And yet again, set me free.
Joanne Maillet

Crushed Dreams

Darkness falls over the sky,
The stars shine out so bright,
The moon hangs so high,
You look up at it with delight.
Through the shadow of the moon,
You start to dream
That one day soon
With happiness you'll scream.
When the stars start to fade,
The darkness is covered by light,
The dreams that you have made
Clearly come to sight.
You start to wonder
How you can make them come true.
The dreams are crushed by thunder,
Back to reality you come to.
Rachel C. Pottebaum

The Power to Compete

The power to compete
Is a natural force,
Like a flower unfolding,
With a desire to bloom.

And where does this energy
Flow from?
It flows from your
Inner being
Where it has been nurtured
Since your birth.

Consciously you release that
Power into your mind,
Body, and heart
Until it connects
To your soul.

So fear not your limitations,
For like a flower
The spirit chooses
When you shall bloom.
Suzanne Y. Cuell

The White Dove

It was morning
As I lay down
under the sun.
I saw a dove up above,
flying in circles,
caressing the sky.
I was pleased
to wear a wreath
of olive leaves,
when the afternoon
came—and the walls
were torn down.
They started slowly
when they began to speak.
At last, we can breathe
From detente to rapprochement:
We now have peace.
Anastasia Papageorgiou

Imagination

There is a land away from here,
Away from horror and without fear,

A place where the hate will depart,
All will be well deep in your heart.

This land exists, trust what I say.
It is inside you, you'll find a way.

A land of dreams, a land of faith,
A peaceful land, where all is safe.

There are mountains high, the sun shines true,
And gentle streams, crystal blue,

Animals running to and fro,
And lush green plants boldly show.

Enchanting colours brilliantly shine,
Nature's true soul is all in mine.
Erin Kelly

Infinite Horizons

Darkness shifts to light where
Early morning eyes once again
Greet the star of day.

Luminous rays wash over the city's plight,
Summoning a newness from previous haste and flurry.
Time progresses, never ceasing.

Hope's destination draws from
Peripheral quarters to the heart's power,
Home to modern superstructures
Silently watching the beings of their origin.

Rampant motion scheduled for the future
Leaves behind the unacknowledged present.

Tomorrow is today for yesterday
Creates tomorrow in
Linear stride.

Predictable life cycles generate
Unpredictable chaos in the
Infinite achievements held by
New Age hands.
Sarah Jane Graves

Fearless

Under the eye of the eagle i wonder
Wondering when it will attack
I find myself endlessly looking over my shoulder
Trying to be perfect for everyone but myself
So i go through life as a follower
But i can't any longer
So i step up and spread my wings
Without a worry in the world
I venge through all the steps
Of my new life
Still confused by myself
I start to believe in myself
For now i am myself
And no one can stop me
For now i am fearless
Melissa Neumann

The Heritage of an Adopted Child
(Love from Aunt Grace)

Once upon a time, there lived two women,
Who did not know each other.
The first one you could not remember,
The second is the one you first called Mother.

One is the Star that guided you,
The other, the Sun that gave you warmth.
The first one gave you Life,
The second taught you how to live.

The first one gave you the taste of love,
The second was there to love you.

The first one had to give you in adoption,
Because she had no other choice.
The other prayed God to have a child,
And God led her to you.

Which of the two, Heredity or a good home
has influenced your destiny?
Neither one nor the other.
It is simply two loved ones who gave
The best they had
To form the great gentleman you are today.

Grace Martin

Pathemata Mathemata
(In Suffering, There Are Lessons)

High on bloodstained cliffs,
Sacrificed by Deceit's onslaught,
My Self lying gently on Hades' door.
Like a modern Prometheus,
I am pinned
By scenes of you and him.
My soul shrinks,
Consumed by Opprobrium's ravens,
In the wake of the day's moon.
In my dreams, I wish I denied man fire,
Till I awaken, singing my pain-embedded song
Far, far into the night.

Martin Linton

Our Mystery

How is it that we came to be,
On this planet that we call Earth?
What created both you and me,
And where was our initial birth?

Did we quickly pass through a beam of light,
Or enter under the cover of night?
Were we bits of dust blown from beyond
That drifted into this embracing pond?

We have yet to discover our origin,
But religion has taught us we came from sin.
Through all of these teachings have we been conned,
These questions should be our common bond.

The answer to this, we will someday find,
By reaching deep into our minds.
However it is that we came to be,
Will forever remain our mystery.

Susan Mackney

Untitled

As I sit here pondering,
my thinking becomes chaotic.
Where is my life heading?
Why is it going this way?
I want to go my direction,
not where others have traveled.
Leave me alone!
I am silently screaming.
Find me peace . . . somewhere.
When will I find my real identity?
I want to cry out,
but people will stare in pity.
I don't want your empathy.
I just want my life.

Katherine Ratcliff

Untitled

In early morning,
I am death.
A few more moments,
I take a breath.

And then it comes,
My time to grow.
A few more moments,
And then I'll know.

I am alive,
And straight from hell.
My soul is not
For me to sell.

A few more moments,
I'll start to nod,
And then I'll know
That I am God.

Michael D. Cartwright

Little Buggie

Little buggie on the wall,
Little buggie do not fall.
Little buggie up so high,
Little buggie cannot fly.

Little buggie got so big,
Little buggie ate a fig.
Little buggie is so cute,
Little buggie plays the flute.

Little buggie on the wall,
Little buggie he did fall.
Little buggie on the floor,
Little buggie here no more.
Poor little buggie.

Jonathan Clubine

THIEF

As the sun breaks through
The morning mist onto our faces;
And the waves roll over
The smooth rocks below,

I steal a glance.

You are lost in your world.
The ocean breeze
Blows your hair back from your eyes
That sparkle full of this
Beautiful morning's light.
The sea birds cry for a share
Of the fisherman's catch.

I am warmed.
I am in love
All over
Again.

Lloyd E. Graham

Remembrance

You are so beautiful:
A bounty of beauty,
An ounce of gold,
So fragile to hold.
I long to hold your hand,
and be together in one band,
As my life drains so gently like sand.
And just to see,
To feel a breeze,
And be thankful that you can sneeze,
To remember me.

Mohsin Saeed

Reflection

The window fades
outwards and inwards,
mirrored,
a faint face
reflects
back,
staring beyond
without seeing.
This morning behind,
in front of, the window
a cold world
lies frosted by the night,
divided by glass.
Now upon the world
sunshine falls,
illuminates,
melts the ice,
yet still part
remains
sheltered, frozen.

Rene Magnus Jarosch

Hero

Amidst the shadows, the darkness of fear,
His blazing image holds me near, To save me.
When trapped in lust and heartless desire,
Like a gallant bird he'll lift me higher, To save me.
Depression like a pit, a chasm like a throat
That swallows your joy like a storm does a boat,
Then his long, mighty grasp will be like a rope
That turns desolate sadness into great redeeming hope,
To save me.
Candy-coated filth and available trash,
Coat our world with an unclean rash,
When suddenly the sun which is he lights a path
To guide all my judgements, and rescue me from wrath.
The paradox becomes clear, a hero need not have might
To intimidate enemies, or fill you with fright,
But with gentleness and guidance to show me the way,
He'll keep my thoughts pure so I'm not led astray.
The gratification of others is not needed here,
For I know when he's close and holds me near,
He came to save me.

Zachary Peters

Baby Girl

Deep, dark, screaming out,
Hiding, hidden, dancing about.
Missing, gone without a trace,
Cold, alone, tears roll down her face.

With problems like these she thinks she must run.
Before they knew it, her life was done.
Forty-six pills were gone the next day.
She knew she had to get out, she chose the easy way.

Her mother feels like doing the same.
She decides not to, inside she holds the shame.
She'll never forget this tragic day,
The day when her baby's life faded away.

Ten years from that day, she still looks back,
She thinks of the happiness that her child had lacked.
A lot more emotion is felt than is seen,
For her Baby Girl was only fourteen.

Rebecca Tottenham

A Man's Mistake

Ready for war, ready to fight,
He marches on out of sight.
He hears the fire, he hears the yells,
But not the sound of his own death bells.

He sees the faces, he sees the tears,
He feels his family's worries and fears.
The smell of blood covers the air,
But standing proud, he doesn't care.

He's ready to go, ready to attack,
He walks away without looking back.
He smells the danger, he hears the shouts,
He looks around, but there's no way out.

Ready for war, not ready to die,
Under the grave, that's where he lies.
He heard the fire, he heard the yells,
But not the sound of his own death bells.

Michelle Ang

April Thoughts

I'm out in the yard, raking leaves, with Homer running wild.
I see the same leaves, a generation ago, when you were only a child.

The sky's the same, the day's the same, and through these eyes I see
A boy, a dog, in the April haze romping through the leaves.

A beautiful dog, that couldn't stay tied, always wanting to be free,
And at the boy's command, away they ran into the "land of make believe."

One small, lonely boy and his faithful pal, went through childhood, side by side.
The problems and joys that they shared together,
from each other they could not hide.

The years have passed, some good, some not, the boy is now a man
His life touched greatly by a childhood friend few people could understand.

I close my eyes, as my thoughts wander back, and I see again
A little boy with his black dog coming home in the snow or rain.

Then one sad day, all things must end, the dog went to sleep, so they say.
But the dog lived on in the boy all his life, and was never far away.

The leaves are all raked in piles, Homer is still running wild,
And I know what a wonderful life I've had,
just being touched by a dog a child.

Mom
Ethel Robins

Things to Do Today—Friday

I'll triumph over those who've fallen, and lie in wait for you
I'll sacrifice my unwanted forgetfulness, for everything I do
I'll hide from all your malice, and then I'll gratefully forgive
I'll carry on old, forgotten dreams for everyone that ever lived
I'll remember hopes that never were, and carry them all until
I'll heal all the injured and then mend the human soul and will
I'll exist just to serve your every whim, give you everything
I'll sympathize with your sadness and accept what it will bring
I'll happily remark on your beauty, and weep when you shake your head
I'll forever cry inside myself for the things that remain unsaid

Jayson Cardinal

Cry to Silence

One of life's greatest treasures is a newborn baby.
I was born on a Wednesday in nineteen ninety-three.
I arrived in this world, a cry healthy and strong,
But what started so right, turned out so wrong.

I arrived a little too early, too weak to be able to eat,
So dependent on others, for my newborn needs to meet.
I grew stronger day by day and finally gained some weight.
Mom and dad wanted to take me home, they could hardly wait.

Not prepared for all the time I needed, soon caring turned to rage.
Alone, crying for hours, while I starved behind the bars of my cage.
A burn on my leg, broken bones, a skeleton covered with skin,
Did no one care enough to question or realize the danger I was in? . . .

Why must healthy, innocent children endure such agonizing pain?
The system seems to fail us and it happens again and again.
How long before someone listens and justice prevails to stop the strife
For children who suffer at the hands of those entrusted with a life? . . .

I never celebrated holidays or had my first birthday.
Life's greatest moments awaiting me as my life was taken away,
But at last I am at peace now, no more pain and no more violence.
My soul soars in freedom as my body lies in silence.

Heather Sylvester Giroux

Unknown

I once thought of you as a friend who was true.
But is a true friend supposed to make you feel so blue?
When I see you, it's like you don't know me.
I know you care for me, so why can't you show me?
Sometimes I wonder why I even bothered to be your friend.
You obviously wanted to see how far I would bend.
I would tell you I'll always love you in my heart,
But you would throw it back at me just like a dart.
There's only so much that a person can take,
Before the pain and anger cause the heart to break.
I know in my heart I must move on with my life,
Even though it feels like someone is ripping out my heart with a knife.
For, now I must forget about the past,
And find a relationship that I know is going to last.
I must close this part of my life just like I would a book.
Maybe someday when I am ready I can open it back up to take a look.
But for now I must say good-bye as I watch our friendship
Just like a flower DIE.
Before I go I must say one thing,
I'll always love you and you'll always be in my heart within.
Good-bye my friend, good-bye.

Glenda Andres

Dying Cries

Innocent children run up and down the streets,
Used ammunition falling at their feet.
Screams are so loud, they can no longer be heard,
Death is crying out as the repeating word.

Soon, one child is left,
Alone and frightened.
He has seen all of his playmates murdered,
The thought sank in as he shuddered.

Thoughts of his toys and games seemed to be so comforting,
As he was aware he may never again see any of those things.
He then wished that he had never played with toy guns
and that he could fly away with some wings.

Somewhere, far-off that child is crying.
Somewhere, far-off that child is praying,
Wondering why he was chosen no witness this Hell,
When all of a sudden he was shot dead, and to the ground he fell.

Kathleen Culshaw

Love at First Sight

Love! Where have you been all these years?
Snooping around for a precious soul, I hope.
Have you got any time for a desert island?
Can you spare a dime, now a dollar for a phone call?
How long should I wait again for an answer?
Oh! Times have really changed for the past years.
No way we can cope with such a pope.
No place on Earth for a lonely man.
The world has gone that crazy for a ball.
Nobody seems interested to put love on paper.
We still say, "Where there's life, there's hope."
But we don't say, "I love you without soap."
"Where have all the flowers gone?"
There's no love anymore at first sight.
Everybody knows the rule, the money on rocks has grown.
And if love builds up its nest, ahoy we bite
At each other to see who's better.
What a pity, poor thing, it looks bitter.
So if love at first sight has disappeared,
Maybe, I say maybe, the cross of Jesus bright and shining will appear.

Bernard Beland

The Last Good-bye

It's such a hard word to say, good-bye,
Especially for those who have reason to fly.
Usually this work is as safe as can be,
But like most of life, there's just no guarantee.

Leaving for weeks at a time can be hard,
Hoping that fate won't deal you the wrong card.
Promising kids you'll be home before long,
Praying each time that you'll never be wrong.

This business we're in has so many good men,
But Destiny takes one now and again.
We can't change a thing, you or I, it is done,
That cruel hand of Fate, once again it has won.

All we can do is the best that we can,
For living in fear is no life for a man.
We must carry on with our spirits held high,
But we'll always remember the last good-bye.

Mark Drew

These Seething Eyes

The air beyond is midnight black.
These seething eyes burn in your back.
These eyes of green are yellow too.
The darkness around sets fear in you.

The sun is shining, the stars are bright,
The soul is there between the light.
The spirit escapes from the dark.
Its burn has left its only mark.

The wolf is around and all is still.
Its instinct is raw and its prey to kill.
The dark is frightening and in it fear.
The days seem cold and the night is here.

A chill runs deep inside the bone.
Fear has left you all alone.
Look in the dark and you will see
The frightening death that faces thee.

Kim Bonnar

No Longer Yours

I love you,
But love isn't being possessed.
I'm still yours, but no longer yours;
You must understand
I have to do this,
For I love someone more.
I have to do something . . . not for you.
Please don't be upset;
I know what you wanted,
But that's not what I need.
I need to do something by myself,
Make my own decisions;
I'm young in age but I know what I'm doing.
I'm sorry if this hurts you,
I'm sorry if this scares you;
It scares me too,
But it's something I must do,
Something I want to do.
I love you,
But I'm no longer yours.

Michelle Mathewson

Home Is

Home, I want a new home
Far and away from the city,
A home that is peaceful and quiet,
One that is soft and pretty.

It would be nice to be in the mountains
Where the air is fresh and pure.
The pine trees blow with the wind
And the birds glide quick and sure.

I'll have two dogs and a horse,
Two cats to kill the mice,
A big room to look out:
Wouldn't that be nice?

Amanda-Beret Shaw

What I Have Yet Not Seen

Many days have passed,
and I have yet not seen
the sweet flowers bloom, the warm,
golden sun rise, and the clouds shading
the grounds.

I have not recognized the silent wind
as it tumbled through the trees,
flowers, and grass.
The rivers have not swayed to the wind,
and they lie with silence
between the moss and trees.

Many days have passed,
and yet the moon has not shone
in the summer's night,
and I have yet not seen
the sweet flowers bloom.

Patryk Polec

My Bronze God

My bronze God cries
For His lost people,
The lands lost in years of war.
The white have won again.
My bronze God cries.

We have to move to a new land.
We must find the Great Spirit again.
The men die in war, the women
In the village.
We have to move.

Our way is gone, lost in the view.
The white men have killed the animals
Too.
We must go out and find it again,
But our hope is gone.

My bronze God cries,
For His soul is dead.
It dies with the land, it dies with me.
My bronze God cries,
For I have died.

April Esson

For You, My Dear Mother

You, my dear mother,
are one of a kind
your courage, your strength,
your beauty, your mind.

You mean more to me, mother,
much more than it seems.
You're in my thoughts every day,
and every night in my dreams.

Between a mother and a daughter
is a relationship so rare,
full of faith and of pride
that will always be there.

Remember the good times,
the memories we've made
as mother and daughter
unable to fade.

You are truly an angel
on whom I depend.
For, you, my dear mother,
are my very best friend.

Cindy Menchenton

After Effects

I woke up this morning,
With a heavy feeling of dread.
If you keep up this lifestyle,
You're going to end up dead.

Some days I feel I've lost my mind,
I feel I'm losing touch.
With all the love I have inside,
That's giving up too much.

I watch everything around me slide,
And wonder when I'm next.
I see so many lights go out,
I know, I'm doing what's best.

I've thought about all the good times,
Mixed in with all the bad.
I wish I could remember
Which time I really had.

This day, for me, I know I must,
If I don't, whom can I trust?
I feel a life inside, you see.
It's me, inside, I see.

Tim Pederson

Wish

Our wish for you:
Laughter to cheer you on,
Faithful friends need you,
And whenever you pray,
Heaven can hear you.

Lucinda Coker

Expression of Love

How I must give thee all my love
Expressed always through my voice, my eyes, my smile
Almost as if it derived from above
It has been in my heart for a long while

In a touch of my hand, my fingers burn
Of passion that I feel inside of me
In my mind, so much runs through and does turn
Of the love inside that will always be

Will you ever decide to come my way
And share the bright light that shines in my eyes
I will wait with the patience till that day
Long as before, the world I say good-bye

Till then, come take with me a walk in hand
I'll dream, being with you in distant land

Michelle Argier

VI

Rising from the lost generations,
Calling my Heritage in mournful wails,
It harkens me listen.
Intrinsic to the wafting tones,
The cries of Joy and Pain recalled.
Inside this shell, a Mind.
Inside this mind, a melange.
I am Poet and Warrior.
I embrace in Passion, Life,
And most Horrific Death.
They are one among rocky crag,
Barren slopes spotted with glacial witness.
Left to stoic testimonial of Clans and Heroes,
Of Dead Vanquished,
Of Dead Victorious.
Among such Brethren Souls,
Lochs lie silent with bated breath,
Awaiting the Ritual Purification
Wrought from the cacophonous Love Dance
Of Broadsword and Flesh.

Stephen Cliffe

Beyond the Heart

Who would have thought we'd meet like this,
Thousands of miles I'd send you a kiss,
Over land, across the sea.
I touched you, you touched me.
Beyond the heart, that's where we've gone,
Lived our dreams. Sang our song.
Beyond the heart, that's where we'll be.
Close your eyes, sail with me.
Who would have known there'd come a time
When we'd talk to one another on-line?
Future changes pave the way
For strangers to make new friends every day.
So many words to be said,
Some not on paper that should be read.
A voice within crying out,
A Struggle for freedom; we know what it's about.
Beyond the heart, that's where we'll be
Read my thoughts. You can see
Beyond my heart.

Dale Barfoot

Untitled

Ere the warrior on the knoll,
commissioned to protect my soul;
Against the Enemy, he stands firm,
willing not to pass his term.

In Darkness, I approached his post
and begged, "Dear Sir, please let me pass;
my thirsty soul cries out for more
and you'd complete your term at last."

"Milady," he reminded me,
"Weakness becomes neither you nor me.
'Tis better I should slay us both
than let you pass and lose your soul."
Angela Brandt

Toy Soldiers

In two separate worlds
The wars are fought.
Young, brave men are sold.
Cold metal, ammunition, are bought.
The earth saps up the red blood of men,
Their graves are moistened by the frost.
Their wise old mothers pray to God for sanity,
To these boys the true meaning is lost.
The price of freedom
Is blood and tears.
One wonders what will become
Of our neighbours over the years.
Will they trade money for food
As they have their souls for land?
Will they forever envision the tragedy
As they march forward, their eyes covered by the hand?
Love for them we all feel, pity as well
For the end result may in no way,
Compensate for this hell
Which we, humanity, created. Hell on Earth.
Diana Vrdoljak

Bedtimes

Stillness in motion, stretching emotion,
Magic potion, cheap miracle lotion,
Need something that is unattainable.
Disillusioned as to what it is.
Flow of energy ebbing to nothing
Like a moving paralytic,
Semi-blind reader and a deaf singer.
Twirling through the night,
Closing lids to the world,
Straps falling, smells drifting, music floating;
Too tired to concentrate.
Beauty is not unnatural,
But is ugliness?
Decide die to the side.
Will you dance with me tonight?
Will you come and hold me tight?
Shield with words.
Protect with touch.
Contaminate my mind?
Please? Tonight and forever.
Eimear Quigley

A Better Me

I think of you often.
It hurts me inside.
Want to grasp you in my hand,
The desire is hard to hide.
I mask myself with a smile
And try to carry on
While in my mind—there you are,
The burning that I long.
You don't just go straight to my head,
You take my longing to be,
My self-esteem, my inner peace,
My sense of morality.
I will fight you and I will win
While I still have some sanity.
I won't give in to temptation,
A bumpy road it will be.
So, when the craving is just too much,
I'll be strong, I won't be sick,
I want to be a better me,
Not an alcoholic.
Tanya Goddard

Celestial Bliss

As I lay myself to sleep beside
your heartbeat,
I long to feel your breath upon my soul.
I reach to touch your shell of
tenderness and hear the murmurs
that silently recite the words of
sweet sins upon my ears.
I caress the warmth of your every limb
and become paralyzed by the way you
seduce my fragile body
into a flight of angelic love
and cosmic clarity that retire in a
praise of enchantment and become
reciprocals of ecstasy,
as we ignite the sparks of unity
refraining from the world and
becoming one into our dream of
celestial bliss for all eternity.
Mariela Izquierdo

Untitled

I try to see the world
through the eyes of an angel.
I try to see the world
through the eyes of a sinner.
I try to see the world
through the eyes of a child.
I try to see the world
through the eyes of an adult.
I try to see the world
through the eyes of nature.
I try to see the world
through the eyes of animals.
I try to see the world
through these eyes of mine,
and through my eyes
I see the world, differently.
P. Porto

Drowning

Its mighty hands reach out and grab me
With a force I have never felt before.
It pulls me under its shroud
In an attempt to smother me.

I will not surrender so easily.
I thrash at its smooth, pure skin,
But it will not let go.

Soon the dark blue
In front of my open eyes
Turns to darkness,

An eternal darkness.
Andrew James Spicer

The Wolf

The black silky sheen
Of the mantle he wears,
The cold, deadly light
Of his eyes when he stares.

The lithe, quick grace
He exudes when he stalks,
The soft, cautious padding
Of his paws when he walks.

The quickness of mind
He uses when trapped,
Just in the nick of time
Before those steel jaws have snapped.

The questions he asks
Of the moon in the night
Speak of great loneliness,
Power, and might.

Understood by so few,
And hunted by many,
He stays in the shadows,
Not see by any.
Kristine Nichols

Silent Symphony

The ribbon of road winds in between
The banks of frozen snow,
While farther back the evergreens
Stand in silent row.
Here and there, the aspens
Dressed all in lacy white
Of hoar frost lend their beauty
In the dusk of early night.

The silence wraps its mantle
Like a peaceful, misty shroud.
A moon, like some shy maiden
Peeps from behind a cloud.
A fairy land of beauty
All around in splendor lies,
And the music of its silence
Lifts to the vaulted skies.

Agnes Hamm

Prayer

Oh, father, the creator,
What are you waiting on to cast the unjust asunder?
Oh, Jah, do you see how your people are suffering
under the hands of the wicked king?
Can you convert this world
into another garden of Eden
and cast Satan away from your children?
The payday, I feel justified about,
But do not let it be long and drawn-out.
Get away, Satan, while we work,
please do not let him lurk.
Sorry if I am grumbling,
but you know I want to commit no sin.
Sometimes the Evil elements are so confusing.
Despite everything, life is a blessing.
Oh, Jah, I fear nothing.
In your hands I put my life.
Oh, thou righteous king,
Creator of mankind and everything,
Thank you, father, to be living.
Denise Palomino

Wisdom

If you go out of the noise and haste,
you'll see how much time you've wasted.
See how much peace there is in silence,
so much heartache and pain in violence.

See how wonderful a world it could be,
a paradise for you and me.
Be on good terms with others.
Think of your fellow men as your sisters and brothers.

Don't let loneliness fill you with fear.
Think of everything you hold dear.
Don't compare yourself with others;
you are different from your sisters and brothers.
Don't be what others want you to be;
be yourself for everyone to see . . .
Jasmine Uys

The Sea of Life

Life is like the sea
Waves of wishes disposed on the shore
Some go answered
Some without plea
Some people in life always want more
Always wanting, but never wanted
Trying to break free
The sunset on the towering waves
The reflection of the fire-some sky
Sometimes reminding myself of me
People never wanting to be slaves
Always afraid to die
Yet always afraid to be
Feelings drowning in the current
Being conscious nor unconscious
Feeling the force of glee
Always but never feeling embarrassment
Hiding under the water's surface like a fish
Floating in self sympathy
The tide comes in, the tide goes out, and so does this
Mallory Hinrichs

Blue Spruce

Once upon our lawn, there was a Spruce tree blue and small.
And if you look you'll see it still, though now it is straight and tall.
Around that tree my two sons played and grew as did our tree.
First it was tag, croquette, or football that I'd see,
But as it grew, so they did too, and soon grew into "teens."
Then there were lots of girls and boys—all dressed up in "blue jeans."
One Christmas time I had a great and wonderful surprise:
My boys had trimmed our "outside tree," a real sight for my eyes.
Then they needed only the old stepladder and the lights
'Cause then the tree was not so tall—and they were still just "mites."
The oldest was the first to go—as so much all young men.
I'll miss him, but at least I still had one to go on then.
But now the time has come, the youngest one will go,
I'll miss him as I missed the other brother,
But want them both to know—
If they can keep on growing,
Straight and tall as did our tree,
There's not much more this Mom can ask
For they'll be men—and free!

Dorothy I. Hitchins

Untitled

She was standing alone by the river
As she does not have any kind of fear
But she has a fear of being poor and bare.
Suddenly a huge wave started getting her near,
Though she tried not to get near,
But her mind persuaded her she should not care,
Because how could a small wave make her life full of fear?
As in her eyes this fear was nothing to bear.
This girl's life has become so miserable
That she could not even think to live further.
But there comes a voice from some small portion of her mind
That life can be both harsh and kind.
I ask you, my fellow, not to worry about anything,
'Cause your worries will not change your fate.
If you want to do something,
Just do it and do not hesitate.

Worry is a kind of a disease; it often comes, but nobody sees.
Then it starts killing people,
Making them feeble. You can fight back against this disease.
It can be done only if you have faith and strong belief.

Tayyaba Jabbar Khan

I Saw an Angel Cry

Yesterday I saw an angel cry,
She said, I just saw you die.
Right there just a minute ago,
No time to even let the good Lord know.

She cried again, as my soul started to move on.
When asked, she answered, your directions are all wrong.
The Angel said she had a number, I was to be heaven bound,
But somehow the devil, a deep hole had found.

That angel, to my soul she held on very tight.
For a few minutes, it was one awful fight.
Then the Almighty Lord seemed to enter the scene,
For right before my eyes appeared a sky blue beam.

That Angel cried again, with my soul clutched in her hands,
When suddenly I heard the sweetest melody band.
My destiny had truly been for St. Peter's gate,
But then the Lord stepped forth and proclaimed I'd have to wait.

Again that wee Angel cried, as she hurried my on my way.
To your body, the Lord says, a while longer you must stay.
The doctors and nurses were just about to give up,
When that little angel, my soul, to my body shot.

James Souter

As I Am

To the Emperor
You are the moon
As I am the star.

You are the wolf that wanders from the shadows
into the full bloom of night,
to raise your head and voice; your sensual, eerie call.

As I am the maiden sent from tear's shed,
healing all hearts wounded in the battle of love.

You are my odyssey to be discovered
As I am your future sent back to you from unfinished past.

You are the oracle which reveals our revelations,
As I am the prophesy of divine guidance, in bringing forth our union.

We are mortal as our destiny is mystic.
To understand is not yet understood, only flashbacks flash
to some other time. We are connected of the spirit and soul
And friends is what we are to be, to be now the present
For the lives that have passed.
I was to you as you were to me: your deepest of all love.

You are, as I am.
    Jazz

Night Whispers

My heart whispers to my soul, I hear them late at night.
They talk about the fire they feel, the power and the might.
Sometimes I understand them, this is true but very rare.
They seem to speak a language they seldom wish to share.
If only I could decipher the code they hide within,
Then I would know what I should do—
With confusion wrestle, just to win.
The hidden inner meanings, they work so hard to hide
Would really help the battle with this fear I feel inside.
Ever am I searching, the endless waves of time,
The strings that tie together this complicated rhyme.
And if one day I see it, the truth for now that's lost
Perhaps I will obtain it, despite the bitter cost.
For now I'm trapped in limbo,
It has seeped into my mind,
But one truth I am sure of—
I could not leave it behind. . . .
    Julie Seguin

Edith Goes Home

The time is now for my journey.
It waits no more.
Its power is greater than mine.
I hasten to ready be, for I must go as one.
Watch for the guiding hands of loved ones gone before me shall I,
And listen for little footsteps.
Might there be a nudge of a soft, wet nose, a wagging tail of my
   beloved pets
To help me should I stall along the way?
My anger I shed as a soldier sheds his tattered coat,
And wonder of its worth.
My hands I empty of all borrowed treasures.
My heart and soul rejoice as they're freed from all bondage.
I feel no wind, sun, or rain,
For I am now all of those.
The darkness hides its head in shame
As the light does so me bathe.

I feel His loving hand touch my brow.
I weep for joy . . . I am home.
    Hope McNabb

Each Day

The changing of shifts, the chirping of insects,
Dusk approaches, broods return from endless searches.
The glowing moonlight brings another twilight.

All is torn from toil and worn.
The mortar sounds afar, tongues engrossed in palaver
As they wait to dine in twain,
A prelude to the final rest
That welcomes the beings of the night.

The night is at peace, the spirits at pace.
Children in a cluster as close as they could muster,
Eyes widely shining, lashes keep fluttering,
Waiting for the gradual deliverer
To be devoid of that morbid fear.

A gradual changing of shifts, the crowing of the cocks
Brings forth the sunrise twilight.
Activities clatter, faces broadly lit
Of children released from their cluster,
Just like the sun, aware it's now their turn
To inherit the dawn.

Iheanyi Okeke

Memories

Dedicated to my Grandfather, Captain Lawrence R. Peel
When the lightning cracked and the thunder roared,
A little girl looked seaward in fear
Watching the ships, their riding lights on
Tossing and pitching in the might of the storm.
How safe she felt, standing firm on the land
Looking outward to sea.

Her grandfather laughed as he held her hand
When the sea is angry, her power unleashed,
White waves crashing, high winds shrieking,
Gulls all wheeling, and spume flying high,
I feel safer at sea," he said, "than here on the land,"
Looking outward to sea.

After the storm is past and the night is clear,
The moon makes a wide silver path on the sea
The path of souls, so my grandfather said,
Leading to Heaven perhaps, or maybe to Hell?
Now I stand here alone and I wish he was here
Looking outward to sea.

Jane A. Patterson

lightjoy

my love for you
not confined in words
emanates from my skin in light waves
beams from my eyes like an eclipse reversed
skips like sunlight across water
illuminates every corner of this room
dances over your skin
 come play with me
love not committed to words is free
only as heavy as a garland
scented of sun and earth
soft and potent
as summer sun
on skin.

Laurie Aldred

Ode to the Sun—That Huge Ball of Gold in the Sky

At sunrise, we see the sun
Like a golden ball in the east
But before we start the fun
At breakfast we start the feast.

After winter comes the sun,
When we all go for our run
As we enjoy the sunshine days
And warmth from the sun's rays.

In the city we look above
Where we all welcome the sun
And all the crowd is having fun
As the sun sends heat from above.

We row in the heat of the day
To catch moments of sun's rays,
And from a bird's eye view of the bay,
We see the mighty "blue jays."

Alas! the sun sets in the west
Like a ball of gold at rest,
As we lay our weary souls
To soothe our blistering soles.

Edwin Ivan Weekes

I Am

I am young, I am old.
I am meek, I am bold.
I am strong, I am weak.
I am cool, I'm a freak.
I can hate, I can love.
I can hug, I can shove.
I can smile, I can frown.
I am up, I am down.
I am here, I am there.
I'm a truth, I'm a dare.
I am no one, I am someone.
I am boring, I am fun.
I am happy, I am sad.
I am good, I am bad.
I'm a lie, I am true.
I am me, I am you.

Katrina Dusterhoft

Autumn and Age

Though music's scattered round my path
From nature's boundless store,
Yet all the fairy charms of life
Entrance my eyes no more.
The falling leaf, the withered flower
on every hand I see;
The bounding pulse, the fevered brow,
Now come no more to me.
I court no more the joys of time
Fast fading to the view;
But, onward look to fairer scenes
than Eden ever knew.

Lynda Williams

Funny Dog

Funny dog, funny dog,
Where have you been?
I've been bugging people
Because I am mean!

Funny dog, funny dog,
What did you play?
I played Monopoly
And checkers in May.

Funny dog, funny dog,
What did you drink?
I drank a club soda,
And that made me think.

Funny dog, funny dog,
What did you see?
I saw a cow
That looked like me!

Tyson Browatzke

Time

The hands of time we cannot stop.
Those measured hours upon a clock,
With every stroke they fly away.
Their revolutions mark the days.

Seasons dance in timeless skies.
Lives are born to later die.
Shadows lengthen in the sun.
The fate of man has just begun.

Light years flash but in a wink.
No time to stop, no time to think.
Spectrum colours turn to rust.
Eternity lies in the dust.

We dream of future days to come.
Who knows the total of the sun,
The wrinkled face upon the clock,
The hands of time we cannot stop.

Dieter Ender

I Do Love You

Let me hold you by the hand,
Together, caring as we stand
To take our vow,
To share our love . . .
Forevermore.

From here on we will be as one,
A promise made by Father, Son,
Through smiles and tears
For all our years . . .
To come.

I promise to love you, come what may,
Now and forever and a day,
To share our dreams
Both old and new . . .
I do love you.

Charles E. Baker

Fireflies

Last night I saw a pretty sight.
It made the darkness seem so bright.
Little sparkles here and there,
In fact they seemed to be everywhere.
These were not stars from way up high,
But close to Earth and nearby.
They were the fireflies flitting by
With tails so bright they matched the sky.

I stood in wonder at this sight
Of dancing flies in dark of night.
What a shame they'll soon be gone.
They never stay for very long.
I just hope that come next year
They will return to sparkle here,
And I will stand and watch in awe
As I have done many times before.

Kaye Sheldon

Failing in Flight

Caught behind the bars of a gilded cage,
the unhappy Hawk views the distant world.
Her wish was to be free, her wing unfurled,
wishing to prey but restrained 'til old age.

Caught behind the bars of a gilded cage,
a place where no light comes in or escapes,
no light, no meat, all attempts become rapes,
wishing to prey but restrained 'til old age.

Caught behind the bars of a gilded cage,
the Hawk strives to answer her desires.
Her attempts are ashes beneath fires,
wishing to prey but restrained 'til old age.

Caught behind the bars of a gilded cage,
not a hope of escape save that of death;
until then she will be, with every breath,
wishing to prey but restrained 'til old age:

Caught behind the bars of a gilded cage,
wishing to prey but restrained 'til old age.

Lisa Jury

Pets!

One day, I decided to get
The sweetest, cutest little pet.
I headed off to the store.
When I got inside, I did explore.
"I have a problem," I said with a sigh,
"I don't know what animal to buy."
I decided to go to the turtle cage first.
When I got there, I thought I would burst.
"Wow, a turtle! Look at him go.
That wasn't fast. That was too slow.
I want a lizard. They look neat.
Gross, bugs! Is that what they eat?
Maybe a dog, they're always nice.
Holy cow! Look at the price!"
Looked at the time. It was already eight.
"I better get going or I'll be late."
Then I left the animal store,
With nothing more than I had before.

Tamara McIlhinney

Tear
To Helen
In a single tear, you tell me of when
Your life was so full of laughter and song.

In a single tear, you tell me of
Your love for one man, so happy, so strong.

In a single tear, you tell me of when
You believed in forever, 'til forever was gone.

In a single tear, you tell me of when
Your joy turned to anger, heartache grows near.

In a single tear, you tell me of when
Life was so hard to begin again.

In a single tear, you call his name.
You see his face, warm and dear.
You reach to touch,
Breathe soft, and whisper, "Tibor, my love,"
In a single tear, "I need you near."

You miss him so, this I know, 'cause
In a single tear, you told me so. . . .
   Arlene Hoey

Living
I sit here alone and start to smile
Realizing I don't need to live in the past anymore
The good times I will cherish
The bad times I will forget
Only living for the moment
And for what is to come
The burden slowly lifts
No more pain, no more anger
Just silence
Eternal peace
I've been so many places and seen so many things
An overwhelming feeling of closure takes over my body
As the pieces of the puzzle finally come together
I can't promise that I'll never look back
But I know now that forward is the only way to go
   Michelle Hundert

In the Swing to Mania
She is tired and cannot stop its propensity;
She is undaunted by insidious incoherency.
And not effective was the Ativan;
Useless still is Diazepam.
She cannot stop her persistent touching,
Always punished for continual hitting.
Now in restraints she feels the strain;
Her body and mind becoming lame.
Yet she knows she cannot fail;
On and on agitations prevail.
Over there is Kraepelin painted black;
She finished him while she was on Prozac.
Always searching for some middle ground,
Criticizing herself when she is down.
These days and nights in close observations,
She recounts her trials and tribulations.
With the restrictions set at her evaluation,
She scorns the increase in her medication.
   Maxwell Lloyd

My Child
He is snuggled in his nest
of blankets,
impossibly tender,
dark lashes frame translucent lids,
blue veined, baby bird skin,
silky cheeks, soft sighs;
I smell his warm milk breath
and gaze at his perfection.

His rosebud mouth
dew wet, suckles at an imagined breast
in his dark dreams of urgent need
of sustenance and protection.

Light shines through a persimmon ear
and my eyes trespass
onto the silent march
of his body's mechanisms
ticking like a clock,
changing and evolving
before my eyes.
   Joan Sylvain

Inside the Mind
At first I was strong,
but weakness overcame.
Listening to lectures so long,
repeating my new name.
Nights are mine to see,
living like this all day.
Moments of doubt fill me,
as reality leads the way.

Is it worth the fight?
Do I let them enter?
If an end was in sight,
would I bite the lure?

Alone fills within.
I am here to lie;
once only a sin,
now makes me die.
As they push me down,
as I step aside,
I hear a guiding sound,
my lonely friend inside.
   Jodi Avery

Leaving Mount Hermon
In a wilderness of winter snow,
So akin to barren desert,
Swirls of wind imprint
The ice-encrusted earth.

Envision a cactus in this world
Where no cactus ever grew.

A few hundred meters below,
That cactus grows.
Does it dream
Of snow?
   Deborah E. Shapiro

A Whisper of the Spirit

Ragged lips and yellowed fingers,
perching unobtrusively in a cafe.
Walking everywhere, drinking coffee,
smoking, reading, writing.
A brain like wet mud,
the silt and sludge of the gutter.
Dark, dank, putrid thoughts;
unspeakable, about unmentionable things.

A bag of blood and bones and muscles
sitting here, puking it out on paper.
Positively, purifying,
painstakingly, perfectly nothing,
but smoke in your eye,
and a whisper of the spirit am I.

Margaret K. Schroeder

Voices in Time

When I was a boy
I loved to listen
to the voices of my friends,
the frogs chanting love and
signalling desire, in the
gentle night suddenly un-stilled,
as the symphony rose hauntingly
through the tingling gurgles
of the trilling stream below
the echoing bridge, against
the resonance of crickets
drumming in random cadence,
and the almost silent whirring
of bat wings silhouetted against
the blue of silent sky and moon
made naked by cloudlessness.
O, tranquility! O, peace!
But now, only silence
and the sounds of dying.

Stanley Branch

Untitled

Without you
my days count slowly,
second by everlasting second:
They drag themselves
like a sled over gravel
to where I don't want to be.

I do not fear time;
only time without you:
Time, stuck like a pendulum
without a time piece
in perpetual futility.

No time or slow time,
makes no difference
to nowhere.

I need you
to make my seconds count
and accelerate my time.

Horst Ulrich Sikora

Dawning

Is it night disguised in primal glows
which hide the dark's disgrace?
Or could it be mere wonders illuminated
in corners found and freed
of shadows?

And so this circle curls like snakes;
becoming once again
where once it wasn't,
clothed in roughened skins to shed the fear
of terrible forevers.

Thus arises one more beginning
leading to an end
of all and nothing;
filled with spaces where we sow and reap
the lives on which to feed.

This day shall bring us to another;
sun burning us into light,
afresh and saddened on vast horizons,
replenished by the death
we're doomed to breed.

Jane Collins Philippe

Cyber Love

Between you and me in an alternate world
Our thoughts and feelings exist,
Although transformed and demodulated,
Received by you through space
Like a black hole absorbing goodness and light.
I walk on the edge of your event horizon,
Never daring to get closer for fear
Of losing my soul in your darkness.
A claim of immortality compels
Like a magnet to cold, hard steel.

We created this world we live in
Without touch or any sense at all.
Only our minds can see one another.
Only our hearts can feel the distance.
No light shines around us.
No glimmer of hope escapes.
Caught in a web of our own devices,
Chances that love dare be real,
Diminished when I open my eyes.

Debbie Deegan

Sounds

i remember the silence in between
when a glistening bead fell from my brow
and entered your eye
you
smiled
as
you
winked
and just then i wanted to tell you how much
but the words got stuck in my throat and
the
silence
remained

Andrew Agostino

Like Some Forever Song

I tried to trace river's flow, which ran through my brick city.
I strained to hear a river's words, which sang against stone banks,
and tore against stone ears,
which sounded deep below stone roads,
and sprang again from where they had buried it, singing.
Mislead through subdivisions,
hemmed in by rigid grids,
its patient valleys turned the roads,
and ran in steady pitch and speech,
like some forever song, forgotten into silence.

This is the song I heard:

You are so hard you would not break,
So still you would not shift.
I am so broken that I run
in changing, rolling drift.
You are so proud you stay to rise,
for I am will-less low.
I am so humbled that I flow.

It sang until the skyscrapers melted in the rain,
and until I remembered again how to cry.
Steven Lorimer

Untitled

Crowded yet alone in the night
Thoughts race in turmoil, poised in constant flight
My singularity of purpose isolates me
My dreams and desires are a beacon to be set free
As I wander and stroll about
I am filled with many feelings, least of all doubt
For as I walk this narrow road
I realize my aloofness is self-imposed
I choose my life for better or worse
Despite my ideals it is not a curse
For as I proceed along this course
My vagueness and doubt have become less of a force
Truly alone, my thoughts no longer a goad
For now I near the end of the road
Only to realize that once you start
The possibilities are endless, because you follow your heart
Joseph Ivancic

Totem Pole

Standing so tall and so strong, rigid and unyielding,
Your many faces so firmly set with eyes unblinking,
Stoically guarding your secrets,
   your knowledge held firmly to your breast,
Who are the ghosts of your past?
With the wind whispering and the ocean sighing,
   they share your secrets.
Who has carved their thoughts on your faces,
   so finely sculpted your body?
Your creators, so human, their souls crying out
Who are the ghosts of my past.
Dear grandparents, you left with no chance to share your secrets.
Your knowledge lies quiet in your breast,
   a brief life etched on your faces.
Your bodies broken from living, so human, your blood is my blood.
My soul cries out with unfulfilled knowledge of you.
Stand proud and strong, great totem pole, guarding your secrets.
You represent a great nation.
As the wind whispers around you and the ocean sighs,
They know, as I will know.
Peggy Fraser

Back in the Hands of God

My heart sunk down into my feet when I heard my friend reply,
"The doctor said we'll be leaving soon,"
My lungs emptied with a sigh.

My eyes welled-up, I turned back on, I thought this was absurd,
I looked at her, she looked back at me, we hugged, without saying a word.

I tried hard not to think the worst,
As my thoughts raced quickly by,
Are they giving Jean the "death sentence"
Just sending her home to die?

My hopes, my dreams felt shattered,
My heart raced, but not with joy.
I felt like a little youngster
Who had broken his favorite toy.

"It's no surprise," she said to me,
Without expression on her face,
"They'll have their conference Friday,
The Doctors of "this place"."

He said some things that eased her mind, now soon onto home we'll trod.
The time's not right, it's not meant to be,
Now it's Back in the Hands of God.

Kathleen M. Stoodley

The First Snowfall of May

I walk outside into the bright sunshine and guess what I see?
I spy with my little eye a deer, a rabbit, and a bee.
Sunflowers, a robin, two chipmunks, and a snake,
some ants are building a hill.
A tree toad, some tulips, a spider's web,
some blue and yellow daffodils.
I pause to look at this wonderful scene as I turn on the garden hose.
Then, all of a sudden, things don't seem so perfect
when a snowflake lands on my nose.

Adrienne Tilson

Ocean of Love

With unfailing regularity rushes the water,
Building into waves and breaking along the shore.
Likewise, you are always there for me:
With such security, I could never ask for anything more.

With mighty power the water crashes,
Wearing the rough edges of the rocks away.
With your strength of spirit you soothe my soul,
And turn every tempest night into sun-kissed day.

From off the ever-tossing ocean
Blows the wind with its salty force;
Just as your smile sends my troubles away
And keeps me guided on my life course.

The mist from the dissipating waves
Falls as a refreshing, gentle rain.
Your hopes and aspirations are cleansing,
Your purity and dreams washing away all my pain.

The ocean is a vast expanse of water,
Stretching beyond the horizon for countless miles.
When I am away from you, for your love my heart yearns,
But no distance is too great to feel the warmth of your smiles.

Rachel Lea Heide

Sacrifices

I want more
more excitement
more affection
more appreciation
I'm tired
tired of making all the sacrifices
tired of waiting for my life to begin
tired of sitting here watching the world move ahead
without me.
But I will stand it, and be strong;
I will not let this break me.
I know this is what I have to do;
it is important to my family.
So I will continue to make these sacrifices and wait.
My time will come . . .
But for now, this is where I have to be.

God, keep me strong
and help me to be good.
I don't want to lose myself.
     Karen Vander Zee

Come November

The daylight shrinks and senses narrow,
the plowshare challenges the fog
to come and go among the furrows
and hide, and hide, from sunlight's glow.

The raw and frigid silence screams
so loud, so loud that hardy birds
have left their summer perches:
their singing gone, a season passed.

A single leaf on birch or ash
resistant to its fate,
clings stubbornly to mother tree,
so proud, so strong, so weak.

It numbs all life, this frost, this cold.
It numbs what warmth once gave.
Once gave, then took, then gave again,
all life, all life, all feeling.

To take one step, OH, MY, the noise,
the noise of grass blades breaking,
and words that steam on fogged breath
beg gently, "Come November."
     Rudi Stiege

Ripples

I still feel the wind's fingers
Tousling my hair, brushing my face.
This haven tempts me, lures my return.
And as the whitecaps retreat,
A fresh smoothness overtakes the waters, in harmony
With the loon, beckoning my ear to follow
Through the shallow waters, underneath the dark cliff,
The tempting danger looms over the water
Disrupted only by occasional ripples,
As the loon's intermittent cry ripples out
Across the lake, to the dock, up the cliffs,
As far as the wilderness reaches.
     Elaine Strohm

Torn between Two Worlds

Torn between two worlds,
One in Canada, the other in Japan.
Right or wrong,
Neither the same.

Born in Japan,
Existing in Canada.
Torn between two worlds.
Whirlwind of feelings
Enter my mind,
Echoing through my body,
Never ending.

Torn between two worlds.
Wondering,
Observing,

Wishing to
Obtain unity.
Reaching the path by
Learning to communicate.
Defeating
Solitude.
     Yoko Chijiiwa

A Good-bye Is Not Forever

Your soft hand brushes my cheek,
and out the tears leak.
You whisper softly, I'll be back.
Good-bye's aren't forever, it's a fact.

You walk through the door,
I long for you once more.
I dream that you are here
To feel your strong arms near.

But now you are gone,
To hear your voice for which I long.
Everyone cries, but I remember,
When you found out that December.

We'll meet again,
We all go down that lane.
Someday I will join you,
Together we grew.

I think of the times that we shared,
I wanted not to believe that I dared.
We will reunite,
With the dawning of the light.
     Rachelle Jackson

Hopeful Despair

A petal may fall,
Does one hear it weep?
A far away sigh,
Or cries from a forest asleep.

The stock will stand,
Shall God's will be the seed?
A wise man's throne,
Or a blind man's greed.

The roots must decay,
Is not Earth just a grave?
Where ancient prophets still whisper,
"Tomorrow we can save."

The seasons will continue,
Can yesterday be returned?
Endings before beginnings,
One man has learned.

The air brings a chill,
Is time able to breathe?
The petal has fallen,
May it never, ever freeze.

Ray David Stasiulis

An Ode to My Brother

On sober days, your talk is small,
You tip a few, and tell me all,
Yet every few that enter you,
I know, not slow, will help you fall.

Your door is seldom open wide,
Still oft I try to look inside,
But I must pry for lock and key,
And pray, from me you will not hide.

If I could be all that you see,
Perhaps then, I would find that key,
Perhaps each day to come this way,
You'd say that you believed in me.

My brother's share has none to spare,
Yet, he pretends he does not care,
And he pretends what makes amends,
Is what he fends without a prayer.

I wish I could confess somehow,
The love I'm feeling for you now.
Despite the struggles we've been through,
Throughout my life, I've cared for you.

. . . I would confess without a sigh,
But you would only ask me, "How?"
And I could never tell you why.

Michelle Michaloski

Strength of Love

With your heart I fly so high
Sweet kisses of velvet trace my lips
My heart beats faster as time goes by
Your sweet scent shall grow the tulips
I smell the love so soft and free
You should know the way I feel
But you must open those eyes so you can see
They shine so bright with much appeal
Strength of passion, our love grows strong
I promise you we will not be wrong
Love is strong and so are you
Fate and love, just you and I,
You must realize that I love you
Will keep us together until we die
That noise you hear is only me
Through our mind, body, and soul
Walking my road with a love destiny
Will make you and I together as whole
Sweet adoration lasts ever so long
I promise you, nothing will go wrong

Brian Nelson

Cathedrals of Time and Space

Atop the Canyons
Woven in Time
Through the fabrics of its first peoples,
Striations of our lives
Reaching out to the skies
In celebration of life's cycle.
It is a part of me
In another time; I, a part of it.
Dancing together to time's beat,
It feels my presence
Like an age-old friend,
Touching my soul,
Exchanging a rhythm,
Transcending space.
The form that binds us answers not to eternity.
Mutual beauty
Whispering to its lover,
Inhaling Divine breath,
Exhaling silent worship;
Masterful temples of unity.

Susan Teed

I'm Only Human

I'm sorry I can't do everything you want;
I'm only one person.
I'm sorry if I make mistakes now and then;
I'm only trying to learn.
I'm sorry if I hurt you sometimes;
I'm only trying to help.
I'm sorry if I say or do the wrong things;
I'm only trying to please you.
I'm sorry if I don't always mind my own business;
I'm only trying to protect you.
I'm sorry if I don't live up to your standards;
I'm only being myself.
And most of all—
I'm sorry if I can't always make you happy;
I'm only human.

Johanne Charbonneau

Image

I look in the mirror and what I see
Is a fragile face staring back at me.
Full of hurt, I see the pain,
Like a dark cloud looming, before the rain.

As I watch my image on the other side,
I can't hold back . . . I start to cry.
Everyone thinks I am so strong,
I whisper to me, "They are so wrong."

What would be their thoughts at this time,
If they looked into this mirror of mine?
Would they understand, if they tried?
I must keep it hidden, covered by pride.

Perhaps one day I will show them all,
But for now it belongs to my mirror
On my wall.
   Teresa Oliver

In Heaven Above

From the Garden of Eden, to the falling of man
God's love will be with us, we need just take His hand.
To show God's love, He sent His only begotten Son
who died for our sins, every last one.
Our Lord Jesus Christ, we should worship each day
and ask for forgiveness of our sins while we pray.
God is calling us now, His children He will lift
up to the Kingdom of Heaven, a most precious gift.
For all life has reason, that the Lord will reveal
on our Judgement Day, which is now close at heel.
So praise be to God, Lord Jesus, the Son, and
The Holy Spirit in all, for all three are one.
I now give to Thee, my heart with all love
to the Lord Jesus Christ , in Heaven above.

With inspiration from my Lord and Saviour, Jesus Christ.
   Paul Green

Undying Love

When I am alone, my thoughts just drift,
To a time when I had a precious gift:
A gift of love that came to me,
A love I know that will always be.
I close my eyes, hold back the sigh,
To let it go I just know I'd cry.
I was yours and you were mine,
We made a vow 'til the end of time.
A choice was made and now I see,
The choice I made was wrong for me.
Where are you now? I wonder yet.
I loved you then and can't forget.
You made the stars dance in my eyes,
You held me close and heard my sighs.
Deep in my heart I know there's a flame
That dances and flickers when I hear your name.
To feel your touch, when things go wrong,
I know that now, it's where I belong.
I pray each night to God above,
To send you back—I need your love. . . .
   Vera Dickens

The Victim

The wind whispers sadness
And cries outside my door,
For I fear the chill of rain
As I lie wilted on the floor.

The night brings haunted images
That dance before my eyes,
They plead with me for strength
To take a final stand.

They are the faces of my victims,
So bruised and full of hate,
Angry visions of the future,
Which I helped create.

Suddenly they fade from me
And the whispers die away,
The door which once was closed
Now lies open to a sunny day.

How can I teach with silence?
For, beneath my fears I hide.
How can I help others,
For what my heart cries most inside?
   Mark Grant

The Tides

The tide recedes,
exposing
sand,
Grains
unique
in shade
and size,
piled
one
on
one,
left to
chance
for what
may be
a lifetime.
The tide returns
To start anew.
   Rick Gianfelice

Imprisoned Within

The silent self,
Entombed in an eerie interior,
Is constantly communing
With an audience of one.

Messages stealthily moving
By nothing at all,
The mystery of speech
Carried on the wind.

Who can know
The content of a soul?
Total communication
Is imprisoned within.
   June Anne Malloy Prebble

A Reader's Dream

I want a private library
A place my books to spare
A room of high shelves
A tall lamp and deep chair

And a window's view
Should I drift from the pages
Of fiction and fact
All down through the ages

A thick carpet below
To squeeze 'tween my toes
As I disappear
In the writer's prose

I'll lock out all care
Behind the French door
To search many shelves
Of literary store

Then, a steamy pot of tea
With a pretty cup and cream
Will settle me to slip
Into an author's dream

Patsy Payne

Like a Dove

The dove, she sits upon her nest,
Upon the nest of her happiness.
She's just like you who gave to me
Precious life and eternity.

She sits there perched, she does
not rest, she protects her eggs
from unpleasantness.
She's just like you who gave to
me freedom from my enemies.

The rain comes down, still she
chirps, she thinks of spring
and her baby birds.
She's just like you who gave
to me forgiving love
and care for me.

The rain had stopped, the
dove had died, a predator found
to stay alive.
She's just like you who gave to me,
crucified love and eternity.

Tracy L. Glaster

The Birthday

One final push.
Relief devours me,
A tiny one is born:
Daughter number three.

Not only her day,
But 30 years past my day.

Alicia M. Surette

Missing You

Dear Dad, we miss you so,
We hated to see you go.
We know your last months here were
Sad, lonely, and filled with pain;
No sun allowed to brighten your days,
No family allowed to ease your pain,
No friends allowed to pass the time.
Dear dad, we miss you so,
We hated to see you go.
We know you are in a better place,
No more pain, no locked doors, no more loneliness.
We loved you, Dad,
We miss you so.
Take care until we meet again in that better place.

Michelle Gilbert

Shattered Hearts Sinking

My heart shatters one more time,
I promise, once again, it will be the last.
Nothing will ever go right
While we fake our love of vast.

I'll sit down against the wall
To prove to myself that I am still here.
I watch the world spin around me,
With vision blurred, I wish it clear.

My heart sinks deep into my chest,
Those constant tears living in my eyes,
The headaches, the stomach pains!
When will I return to being me?
Will I ever re-become alive?

Lauren Elysia Harrison

I Wonder Why

I wonder why I am so poor,
I wonder why?

I wonder why I am not rich,
I wonder why?

I wonder why chance is selfish to me,
I wonder why?

I wonder why Luck is not close to me,
I wonder why?

I wonder why I can't get out from poverty,
I wonder why?

I wonder why I don't succeed,
I wonder why?

I wonder why my life is not comfortable and at ease,
I wonder why?

I wonder why I cannot figure out the path to victory,
I wonder why?

I wonder why I am not happy,
I wonder why?

It is because I am trapped with the question,
"I wonder why?" . . . THAT'S WHY.

Louella Marie E. Andrada

The Tango

Pelted the rugged Indian bark with the leaves of my kiss,
A bored, sensuous bother.
The ground is a marvel of liquid literature.
During sun-splashed seasons,
one is dazzled by the shadows of flocking birds,
obese, heartless trees,
streams of moss-filled caves,
webs, and calms.
The forest is an advocator of growth . . . you know:
bugs and bees,
twigs,
prone to fall cones of pines,
dreams, clarity, shrubs,
dogs and joggers,
a wooded brothel,
       a forest's theater.
Now, fancy seed,
that ancient, wishful, old, gauged medicine:
. . . . creation. . . . .
Someone calls the poets day tailors.
This path needs a gig.
   James Majoros

A Story

A story told by my mother's father about, oh, so long ago.
Before the soundless talk, before the ever-falling snow,
Of a perfect world with music and flowers they all had,
And something called trees and honey bees before his world went mad.
There were bombs and firestorms and a star war that failed,
A ghost of a smile used to cross his face as he spoke of that perfect race,
And told us of the last hope of man on the last shuttle ship that sailed.
Of how they'd searched for people near and far and couldn't ask for more,
One hundred men and women of Earth and home
   and not one who thought of war.
A story of how the good news came before the radios died,
A story of a perfect new planet found and how for Earth they'd cried.
   Rick Barnett

Memories of Yesterday

When I'm with you my heart soars
To heights I've never known.

The moment we first met strange feelings came.
I even said, "I love you," the first time we met.

But I was failed for so many reasons,
Yet this was a challenge for me.

I believed that my sorrows and failures
Will be enlightened for sure,
Because of my faith and hope.

What matters today, I have to face it,
And tomorrow expect the best at last.

Everything is just a fantasy, time heals body's wound,
But cannot touch the heartache

Because parting is not so easy.
Those sweet moments we were together were great memories for me.

You'll always be in my thoughts.
I'll look back to those days being with you
To be reminded of the memories as I wanted to be,

Because the supreme happiness of my life
Is the conviction that we are loved. . . .
   Jocelyn Marybeth C. Salazar

To Be a Grandma

To know just how a grandma feels, you'd have to know for sure,
It matters not how old you are, or if you're rich or poor!
For, grandmas come in lots of sizes 'n every creed and race,
And most are beautiful to see, with lines upon their face.

I've just become a grandma and it's so very pleasin'
To think that I could be a generation beyond teasin'!
The thrill of that great birth event—you feel it, but no pain;
No feeling sick the last nine months, and not one ounce of gain!

My grandson is so lovely to look at and to hold.
I know he will be wonderful for me as I grow old!
For, now he coos and gurgles, whene're I talk to him.
I just could sit and watch him sleep within his bedroom dim.

And I can hardly wait to hear him when he starts to talk,
And soon when grandma holds his hands, he will begin to walk!
For, I will be his buddy and friend with which to play,
And I will read him stories—every single day!

For, now I rock and sing to him and kiss his dimpled cheek.
He looks around and smiles at me, every time I speak!
I feel a warmth and love for him—I see him as such fun.
A grandchild is the greatest gift since God sent his own son!
   Wanda Cross

Neko's Song

Chesai Neko, how I love you, and no words can ever say,
how much I need and want you, every minute, every day.
When the sun wanes after twilight, I look up and I see,
the eyes of my Neko, in the night, a'twinklin' down at me.

The gentle beams of moonlight dancing fiery in the air,
make me pine for all the beauty of my Neko's auburn hair.
The velvet red of sunrise kisses soft the sailing ships,
and the color thus reminds me of My Neko's sweet, soft lips.

Tho' there's miles and miles between us, many days and worlds apart,
my soul keeps right on dancing to the beating of my heart.
Chesai Neko, how I love you more and more in every way,
my love will burn much brighter every passing, lonely day.
   Daniel Newton

Darkness and Light

A buzzer sounds, a gate opens, a man emerges,
20 years, his name, a number stitched on his clothing,
Etched on his soul forever, yet on this day
A man reborn takes his first steps into the unknown.

He dons a white shirt, no number, and a suit
Reminiscent of an era long forgotten.
A buzzer sounds, a gate closes, and the man,
He walks on without even a glance back at his youth.

A tepid August breeze, hints of wildflowers on its breath,
Whispers by as the sun breaks through the clouds.
The yellow globe shines upon him more radiant than any God.
The sounds of life assaulting his solitude become a symphony of nature.

Some take for granted freedom's beauty.
This man, he stands in awe and reverence
Looking to the heavens for answers,
This man, on his day meets his fate.

A horn sounds, a truck delivers a man to his faith,
A gentle breeze whispering by finds a spirit absolved of sin.
Then pushes it lovingly, smile and all,
Straight to the light from the walls of hell.
   Michael Sabourin

Until Tomorrow

Let it Pass
For it Shall
And the Darkness that seems to
Flood the Night
Will mitigate and fade given time
For sorrow brings not peace
Despair pleases only itself
There is no rush
The questions can wait for tomorrow
When the tears will be forgotten
For this living breath
Is like the tide
That brings both dead and living
To its shore
The next minute both have been washed away
And it is from this ocean I will rise
And in these seas I will drown
These waters have no end
And their secrets are only hidden
By the flimsiest of dreams
Brett Raycroft

strawberry blue

twisting the tangles of strawberry blue
wasting the moonlight of day
living a death on top of the moon
i stand in the field where i lay
the twists of good sense cloud up my head
and the language of silence rings true
the symbols of birth lead me to my death
in a tangle of strawberry blue
stone cold in the heat of the fiery night
surrounded by no one but me
i run to get back to the place where i was
and i step in the cage to be free
in a bundle of nothing, the driest of waves
courses the air and i wish
that the shadows of light and the pieces i save
could fly through the air like a fish
all of these twists run through my mind
in a tangle of strawberry blue
and i look for the thing that i know i can't find,
but i'll know when i find it, it's you
Kristy Dossor

Within

I closed and turned my outward seeing eyes
and looked within, where no sunrise
enlightens, and no falling rains refresh
my brain-directed factory of flesh.
I saw no living machinery, no heart,
no instrument that might have been a part
of some unique assembly gathered there
to keep a body functioning in air;
only a garden, pale in mystic light,
where two white butterflies in futile flight
above the long-stemmed, twilight-purple flowers
frittered away the endless inner hours
in empty places where a soul might be;
pointless, in prison clouds of ecstasy.
Bernie Bedford

Sprawled Across

To feel like a page
In an unwritten book;
To utter simply wasted wind,
Blowing in the vast treetops;
To be heard,
And rather not.
Words unspoken,
But dramatically thought;
A distortion of prosperity
Sprawled across
This ever-changing realm
Of the mighty lost.
James Gallinger

Stars

They look down on us
From the deep blue sky.
I wonder why?
God put stars in the sky,
But now I know why.

God put stars since the very first day.
Stars lead us on our way.
They forever guide
Through the dark.
Some say they mark the
Way to freedom.
Others say they're stars
From Bethlehem,
But I say, "I know why stars are there."
They are God's angels,
Looking down on us
From up there.
Lorianna De Giorgio

True Friends

In my life I've never had
A friend as good as you,
A friend who will always be there,
A friend considered true.

You've always been there for me,
Through the good times and the bad.
You always set a good example,
And make me happy when I am sad.

I've never, ever trusted
Someone as much as you.
I can tell you anything.
You're my friend through and through.

I'm so glad I have you
In my life and as my friend.
I know you'll always be there,
From now until the end.

Friends Forever!
Stacy Little

Nearly an Angel

He stood there
His hair so fair
Impish smile upon his face
How could one so young
Have this grace

He smiled
With eyes alight
Showed me love and delight
How could one so young
Have this sight

He laughed
Soft, rolling notes rang
When he spoke, he sang
How could one so young
Know where love began

He did not whine
As the needle entered his spine
He did not cringe or rave
How could one so young
Be so brave

Tanis LaCharite

The Road of Black and Gold

Marriage is like a road
Trod before by many feet
With little trials along the way
For each of you to meet.

The trials you meet without true love,
When you allow it to go slack,
Will be the ones most trying.
The way will seem most black.

The tests that you are given
And face with a love so bold,
Will become all your treasures,
Rays of shining gold.

So on the road of marriage,
When things go right or wrong,
Only when you share your love
Will your marriage be so strong.

So as you begin your marriage,
Announced with love so bold,
Only together can you travel
The Road of Black and Gold.

Judy McIvor

Forever

Press your sweet lips to mine, dearly beloved,
and forever itself shall come within my reach,
and flowers shall bloom and spread their soft
perfume while I upon a silver cloud shall feel to be.

Hold me within the circle of your arms
and life shall be forever full of bliss,
and I shall close my eyes and feel again
the wonder and the sweetness of your kiss.

Providencia Martinez Martinez

If I Were to Die Today

If I were to die today,
would tears be shed, and flowers thrown,
hearts broken and families torn?
If I were to die today.

If I were to die today,
who would notice and who would care,
who would feel all the pain that I bear?
If I were to die today.

If I were to die today,
would friendships pass and memories fade,
letters be lost and photographs laid?
If I were to die today.

If I were to die today,
what would I be saying? Will anyone hear
of the problems I face when no one's there?
If I were to die today.

If I were to die today,
how would you feel and what would you say?
Is there a hole in your heart, tears in your eyes?
If I were to die today.

Katherine Reid

The Odd Couple

Have you ever seen an unusual couple
Who look so strange in the eyes of people?
Facing the society with head up high,
Cares no one, but them,
The affectionate odd couple.

Here are the routine day by day:
Walk in the park, strolling at the seashore,
Watching the late movies,
And holding hands along the avenue,
To drop by the shop to buy the chops.

What if she is tiny, and he is heavy,
Does it really matter?
If the Lady is blue, he is blooming,
Trying to be funny and clown
Like a comedian playing his role.

Though they are an odd couple,
Picturing their faces contented,
Existing in the world,
Where odds are enormous,
Happily satisfied and don't bother at all.

Ester S. Cayanan

The Soft, Fluffy Clouds

Have you ever looked way up high
And studied the clouds in the sky?

Soft, fluffy clouds floating slowly by,
Some down low and some way up high.

Like giant, comfy pillows, they are
On a gentle journey—going so far.

With various shapes of every kind,
Animals, trees, and angels you'll find.

Sunbeams streaming through white fluff,
Awesome beauty—just can't get enough.

But the large, dark clouds—so menacing,
Can send down rain—like never seen.

Anxious to see angry clouds move on,
Replaced by white ones and the sun.

Clouds are a divine creation in our land,
Free to float the sky by the creator's hand.
Marlene Simons

My True Friend

It forms from billions of pieces
Crystal shards
It forms a broken picture
My black heart
It is a monster in my head
Almost a feeling
It is the abyss
A waking dream
It flows up underneath
Enclosing darkness
The light then cast upon me
Cold and lonely
Like the kiss and empty promise
Of false love from one to another.
A reminder of the nothing that I have so much of
Fills my eyes with crimson rain
Thoughts of you drift lightly crying from above
Desolation, my friend, my pleasure, my pain
Karen Lipinski

The Graduation

She sought wisdom and knowledge for lofty flight.
She spread her wings and set her sights.
The gruelling hours, the sweat, and the toil,
She fought the winds that battered her soul.
Look deep, now deeper, and deeper still.
She struggled within, she challenged her will.
But, oh, the sense of sweet victory.
Now, look, she's won, she's finally free!
Where to now? What's wisdom gained mean?
The thirst for more, her journey's not done,
She knows that she knows less than when she'd begun.
This knowledge, however, is fragile and pure,
Its tendrils entwine, possess her, and lure.
Oh, she'll party at first and revel in it,
She's earned it, she needs it, her soul demands it!
Then once again she'll set her sights,
Spread her wings, fly lofty flights.
Linda Doyle

To My Love

I've been taken from you
In a harsh, evil way.
I'm dying inside.
I feel I have been betrayed.

My tears fall like rain
Every second of every day.
I long to be with you.
I have to get away.

I miss you so much,
"Like the desert misses the rain."
My heart is breaking.
I am in so much pain.

When I am away
I feel I am losing you.
I will never leave.
My heart will always be true.

I hope you miss me
And love me, as I love you.
It was finally going good,
But somehow I always lose.
Lindsay J. Davies

A Year to Remember

The August moon shone down
On my dear friend and I,
Standing on the deck of the ferry boat,
Watching Bermuda skies.

We were returning home,
Leaving that island of fun,
But we would never forget
The sea, the sand, the smiling sun.

Walking among the Oleanders,
The Lilies, the Passion flowers,
The delicately tinted Hibiscus,
Gave us many happy hours.

Boys in their white jackets,
Girls in coloured gowns,
Riding double on motor bikes,
Riding into Hamilton town.

We boarded the plane.
It took off into the blue.
We strained our eyes for a last look
At the island's colour hue.
Dorothy Hoffmann

Bird in the Sky

I wish I could fly
Like a bird in the sky,
Over the trees
So wild and so free.

Birds know no worry
And are never in a hurry.
They shed no tears
And they know no fears.

If only I could be
Like that bird in the tree,
So happy and gay,
Singing all the way.

I won't wait another day,
But fly far, far away.
Little bird, think of me
When you fly over the sea,

'Cause I'm all alone
Just like a child without a home.

Jasmine Uys

Untitled

It was windy.
The trees looked like dancing
that has many leaves.
Our life is just like this, what I guess.

Tetsuya Shiraishi

Life Is a Gift

Every day life goes by fluttering
Like a butterfly, strong and high.
It takes away the badness,
Leaving only the good and brings
Me happiness whenever I am with you.

Life is a gift of joy blowing through
The wind whispering your name
That only I can hear. It's a world
Full with magic, a journey you
And I will take and touch the
Highest star and make our wish someday.

Life is a gift, that will apart
We will be together someday and
Fulfill our magic moment with
A gift of yesterday.

Raquel R. Perez

Nighttime Tranquility

The soft scent of orchids pass by my face
As a gentle breeze dances through my hair,
Matting it in its attempt to escape.
The tickling sensation soothes me.

I look to the stars,
But all I see is their burnt carcasses
As the black sea washes over them
Until they are no more.
The crimson liquid erupts and bubbles over,
Filling the bumpy craters of gold,
Dimming the world.
The moon is red tonight.
I can smell it in the air,
The blood lust of a thousand wolves
Circling around me
Until piece by piece
I slowly drift away.

Teena Beckett

The Dog Team

Ahead dogs pull, harnessed in a
double line.
Soft
fresh
snow fell the night before,
cushioning the trail so that
the only sounds were of the
dogs' feet and their breath.
Looking past the double line of
bushy, curly
tails, I see miles and miles of emptiness.
But I don't feel lonely at all,
because after months of dog sledding
a bond of trust as well as
Love
formed
between me and the dogs.

Linda Grace Brooks

What If

What if the animals could speak,
And share the wisdom that we seek?
Would the creatures of the sea below
Relate the wonders that they know?
Would the feathered guardians of our sky
Show us what it's like to fly?
The wild forest creatures, all,
From very large, to very small,
Could teach us much we need to know,
To nurture life and let it grow,
If "man's best friend" could make us see
The worth of love and loyalty.
But what if the answer truly lies
Beyond our human, selfish eyes?
What if Nature has spoken through all the years,
But her voice has fallen on deaf ears?
Perhaps our hearts should strive to care,
Our minds, a new beginning christen;
Then, may we be allowed to hear,
When quiet, our souls are prepared to listen.

Daniel T. O'Brien

Loyally

Every second you breathe, every minute you take
Every laugh you laugh, every day you cry
But time waits for no one . . .

Every morning you wake, every day you survive
Every night you recall those moments—those times
But time waits for no one . . .

Time can be but a moment, it can be a day, a month or a year
Time can be now or past, it can never be replaced
and loyalty, it will only give you what you take
But time waits for no one . . .

Time, it can be said, is a friend, a good friend in a sort of way.
It teaches and matures. Develops, creates and strengthens.
But time waits for no one . . .

Time is the most precious thing we have
our existence depends on it
our soul thirsts for it, our future relies on it
But in the end what is there that makes us want,
makes us need, makes us realize we all only have one. Time.

But, time waits for no one . . .
   Sean E. McElligott

Best Friend

My best friend is a friend indeed.
She is there when she is needed and when she's not.
Always comforting, loving, faithful, honest, and true:
makes her the friend you trust in.
She always seems to have the answers to your toughest problems
and never wants anything in return.
She is there for your moods, crying moments, thick and thin,
and crazy, trouble filled ideas—
and still manages to see the best in you.
They are gifts from God.
When you can't seem to rely an anybody else, they are there,
for making a friend only takes a moment,
but being a friend takes a lifetime.
   Tracie Ford

"Angel Dust"

God proclaimed to all the world—"The tiny, wee souls I dub Angel Dust";
Everyone in His realm agreed, but shouted back vehemently—
"loaned out—only in trust!"

God whispers to the wind—His stories to unfold;
And you, my darling little boy, a story yet untold!
So it was your life got started—small footprints in the sand;
Remember, God is always there to lend a helping hand!

A very special place a firstborn takes;
Like the joy of Christmas, Easter bunnies, and birthday cakes!
The easy laughter bubbling from your heart
Was yours and mine right from the start!

The first halting steps you took filled my heart and memory book!
And the first time you placed a little hand in mine,
I knew a love transcending time!

Your feathery kisses, soft, gentle hugs, and other wondrous things
Brought to mind the tender caress of a butterfly's wings!
So with these thoughts, dear heart—I bid you a happy life;
One without struggle and one without strife!

As for me—my life has changed forever, blessed for eternity
   by this one small treasure—my very own piece of "Angel Dust!"
   Marilyn Haffner

Dream Alive (A View from Space)

Stunning peacocks of land, massive mountains,
All that is important in this tiny blue and white swirl
Earth like a rocket, flying through unknown black
Expanses of the universe and one little ball,
Skin of an onion, atmosphere, protecting the history of mankind.
Dreams alive, wild, and colourful,
Spectacles of fury and bursts of fire,
Tones of light illuminating the electric sky,
Then blackness, vast silence.
Rugged contours vie with the magnificent shade
Of ocean depths, swallowing masses of land,
Our life on this place of blue beauty.
Bursting flames and white tropical fury
Bring it all together,
No race, no religion, oneness.
Creeds dissolve into nothingness,
One with itself and each other.
Terra firma rises from coral and deep green sea,
A map come to life in all reality,
Incomparable, unconquerable, unimaginable.
   Danny Auron

At the Old Fort in Annapolis Royal

The breeze pushes fingers of air across my face
as we wander the grassy embankments under a poignant sky.
The sunlight tastes of saltspray and summer's last flowers.
By a wrinkle in the river, we sit entwined in the afternoon,
while ancient whispers escape the sweaty stone walls
and slither amongst the verdant blades caressing our limbs.
Down through Covert Way, the path is narrow and firm,
annealed by centuries of icy winters and fervent summers,
but here, the hillside pillows our languishing bodies
as we, little heliotropes, follow the sun
wheeling relentlessly across the sky.
The words of too many poets have been read upon this levee
by too many lachrymose young girls—
the air is full of old love and regret and farewell—
but the warm breath of a southern flow
whisks the ghosts away
and we are the only two who have stopped just here to rest
in this quiet and moldering place.
   Tracy Carignan

The Attack of My Love

The attack of my love,
I'll not forget,
I will live and outlive each chapter,
Whether in embrace,
Or in war,
I will have, has felt the same.
Like a wall built up,
Like a bird in a cage,
Either way it's all the same,
The perils of the life I know to grow,
On different sides of a line.
It's all printed in black and white,
For all to behold.
Attackers of love they are here, there, and everywhere,
They are the shadows of eternal rest and yet the shadows of the living,
They've won, and I've lost.
I will be theirs for all life time till I'm set free, to live.
Turn a new leaf
And you will see
The story of my attack of love, clearly.
   Anita Luo Selvaraj

Hope

One look at love
And you will see
It weaves a web of mystery.

All ravelled threads
Can rend apart,
For hope has a place in the lover's heart.

Whispering world,
A sigh of sighs,
The ebb and flow
Of the ocean tides,
One breath, one word
May end or may start.
Hope has a place in the lover's heart.

Look to love,
You may dream
And if it should leave
Then give it wings,
But if such a love is meant to be,
Hope is home,
And the heart is free.

Amy Sanderson

The Trash Man

Suctioned to the icy iron bed,
With my naked mind open
And body immobile,
Their work is less difficult.

The latex hands crossed
Through my thoughts, searching
Me for me.
One rubber worker falls from the fold
And steps into sponge.
My face jerks a smile.
He curses.

The machine hums as
It pulls me out.
The reels roll ahead, from childhood to now,
Only an instant to remember
Before it is gone.

Then, my mind folds back.
The humming expires.
"See you next week."

He left before I could answer.

Tim Thompson

Anchovies

I waited all day for my anchovies,
For they are my favorite food.
When my brother said they would climb up my nose,
I said he was rather rude.
I finally got to try.
Those succulent little fish,
Although I wish I listened to my brother,
Because they jumped right off my dish.
Now stuck here up my nose
Are those deadly little fish.
Help!

Anne Bossio

The Mystery

How can it be, You think of me?
That all my thoughts You see?
In spite of all, You love me so.
It cost You Calvary.

The wonder of Your love for me
Has won my wayward heart,
And by Your grace and pow'r divine
I'll never more depart.

My soul now sings, my eyes behold
The beauty of Your ways,
The glory of Your purity,
The souls You died to save.

Lord, help me do Your work today.
Help me the needs to see,
That I may show some sin-sick heart
The Lamb of Calvary.

Shirley Campbell

of some complaint

i thought of ALL children
living in a world of theatre-frame
      lost
calling to the walls
of earth and care
      lost
diminished by the arrogant blame
of where thought ways dwell

and the reasons embroil again

we bleed
we seed too much
as children fallen
to a heartless drain
      cast
low or high
never ending
by those who would a power gain
then loose on us
their selfish plain

Margaret K. Smith

Little Love Song

Blue sky, white sand,
Warm lips, cool hand,
Pink toes, hair shine,
Love ya lots, girl of mine.

Have to go, see you when
I get back again,
Don't leave, don't grieve,
Sit tight, just believe.

Believe in me, believe in you,
One and one make two,
But two together makes one
New life just begun.

Pearl Swain

A Bar of Soap

I want to be all over you
Just like a bar of soap,
To feel you close and get to know
Every inch of you up close.

But don't you get the wrong idea
And think I'm being bad:
I want to be all over you
And see what you're about.

I see you're different in every way,
But that could be an act,
To please or fool or play with me
To get what you really want.

So I want to be a bar of soap
And feel the real you;
Only then you'd be your real self,
Only then would I know too!
Joanne Scourakis

Awesome

I paused in my walk,
by the dawn's early light,
admiring the dew
that had fallen last night.

Each blade of new grass
held its own special gem.
The beauty enthralled me.
Awe embraced me and them.

The slope of the hill
was gentle and clear.
The rising sun's rays
brought Heaven quite near.

Many years have vanished
since that morning's delight.
My memory holds fondly
the awe-inspiring sight.
Sis. Patricia Kelley

Untitled

The world is falling apart.
The trees are falling around me,
The ground is shaking under me,
The clouds are rolling in above me,
And the rain is falling down on me.

My world is changing.
Can anybody save my world,
Restore the trees,
Steady the ground,
Remove the clouds, and
Stop the rain?
Will my world ever be the same?
Melanie Brownlow

What Do You See?

What do you see?
I see the colors of a new day.
I see fire burning bright as the robe of night passes over the sky.

I see an uncurling leaf,
I see a new world, a labyrinth for the mind.
I see life begin to grow.

I see a river of wisdom,
I see fool's wisdom and wisdom well-earned.
I see sorrow in the water.

I see an old face.
It has seen pain and remorse.
It has seen pure joy.
It has seen fool's wisdom.
It has seen the day depart.
What do you see?
Christina Vasilevski

Our Boys

Our boys are resting in foreign soil
Where they fought so hard the foe to foil.
They fought for freedom in mud and mire,
Where they laid aside their own desire.

They fought through valleys and hills and roads,
On they pushed amid bombs and foes.
Tired and weary from no sleep,
Our Armistice for them we keep!

God bless each one of you
Who went to war and fought so true.
Us young ones cannot understand
Why wars must be through the lands!

Why can't love and friendship reign supreme,
In countries blessed with nature's dreams?
Men full of greed and power and glory;
It has always been the same old story!

Let us try to strive each day
To make this world more happy and gay,
And teach our children to be friendly and kind,
Then peace throughout the world we'll find.
Ashley Vickerson

Devotion

My mother,
who is miles away by land, by sea
is really not that far away from me.
I keep her close inside my heart and mind.
In fact, I have tea with her all the time!

Our phone calls are many, our letters are few,
but what are a mother and daughter to do?
Our time is precious, our adventures are great,
when I know you are coming,
I just can't wait!

So, let's hurry the time between now and then,
so it won't be that long 'til I see you again!
Sandra Joanne Stewart

Not-So-Terrible Two's

Congratulations and best wishes,
you are now a perfect two.
You've learned to laugh and walk and talk,
and flash those baby blues.

You'll learn of many wondrous things
throughout this coming year,
and with God to love and guide you
your heart will know no fear.

Keep your eyes on mom and listen well,
she'll help your heart stay true,
and keep your eyes on dear ol' dad,
he'll help to guide you through.

Take heed of all you see and hear
and keep your spirit free,
and soon, before you know it,
you'll be a perfect three!

Delores S. Sellers

Down Skid Row

For Dr. Diane Wozny
Like-mind
Parallel theatre:
The dips of lips,
the swaggering of sips.

I eye flat coffee in oil-spill crusts,
the hands defy my mind-Virtues,
Habitue the faces in movement,
Hand down on Holy, it stings the palm.

Wet flesh from flight,
sweat feeds The Hunger.
For now, sleep, be still, be awake.
Later, standing on streets, walk.

No hydrant leaks like shower curtain's veil,
just golden ponds that drip down stares.
Like the forest, Man that is,
clear-cut patches, unsigned trails for masses.

My mother put these genes on me.
I have not taken them off.
My father makes spill of the pool,
Never taught me to swim, just floated. . . .

Ann Lok

Turquoise Truck

So your hair was wrecked by a turquoise truck
While you gazed at your gasoline-enhanced
Reflection in the noncommittal puddle.
And now, the traffic moves on unaware as always
And you stand there dilapidated
With your famous hair dripping
Into the autumn morning gutter
With the red and yellow leaves
And the liquid gurgle
Of the swirling,
Swirling
Whirlpools.

William J. Sampson

No Need to Argue

With tribute to "The Cranberries"
There's no need to argue anymore.
Just look at others' feelings,
And look at yourself,
And see how selfish you've been.
There's no need to argue.
We all have feelings
And reasons for those feelings,
But always one of us
Is being selfish.
So open up your eyes.
Is it you being selfish?
There's no need to argue.

Alexandra Coumont

Between You and Me

The memories of our friendship
Are strong as can be.
They are flowing so freely
Like leaves on a tree.

The trunk is our lifeline,
So solid with age.
It grows with prosperity,
Unlike a bird in a cage.

The branches reach out
For the whole world to see.
They are the providers
Of love and eternity.

The earth gives us strength
To stand on our own.
If you follow the horizon,
You will never be alone.

The formation of the roots
Will bind us together,
As distance has brought
Two friends close, Forever!

Janis Tripp

Princess Bride

A gown of pearls and shimmering lace,
A crown of pearls surround her face.
Skin like ivory and hair of gold,
A wedding march as in days of old.

Pearl buttons and satin bows,
Satin white slippers upon her toes.
Golden hair and ruby lips,
A train prevailing from her hips.

Standing tall and full of grace,
A smile she wore upon her face.
A veil she wore and deep inside,
She became the princess bride.

Rosemary Armstrong Chatten

A Nature Poem

Saw a fawn,
Ran away, now it's gone.
Heard a trout,
Splashed up the stream and out.
Touched a frog,
Hopped away in the log.
Smelled a skunk,
Sprayed my sister, then she stunk.
Heard the leaves rustle,
That's when I noticed I liked nature.

Constance Cammack

I Remember

I remember when life was simple,
Easy to understand.
Not a hand was raised to me,
No degrading words spoken.

I remember meeting him,
Everyone telling me he was bad news,
But I wouldn't listen.
I gave him a chance anyway.

I remember
The first time he hit me.
The pain and confusion I felt from it.
How lost I felt without him.

I remember
Thinking it was my fault;
Maybe I still do.
I went back to him,
Because I thought I deserved the abuse.

Cathy Robinson

Forgotten

The laughing
And singing
Are gone.
I am forgotten.
No more phone calls.
No more sleep-overs.
No more parties.
And no more
Birthday parties.
I tell myself
It's them
Not me.

Angela Cruickshank

Follow Me

Will you follow me wherever I go?
Will you follow me even when I go slow?
I shall look behind me,
hoping to see your beautiful face there.
I will fly with you.
I will swim with you.
It will be you and me,
just two, not three.
It's all I ask, follow me.

I follow you, you follow me,
and to see you there
it will set me free. So follow me.
You are my love, you're in my soul.
Deep in my heart there is a hole no more.
Your personality is sharp,
as sharp as a knife,
and without you, there goes my life.
You are an angel to me, you set me free,
So please with all your heart,
Follow me.

Kyle MacKenzie

A Dancing Tree

Leaves rustle at a glance
And a tree begins his dance.
Then slowly the little fingers wave gently.
Other fingers join soon, shaking rhythmically.
Now the strong arms and the crown
Sway to swelling, symphonic,
Sibilant sound of music.
The arms flap, the fingers shiver,
And the hips now writhe and quiver.
The movements gather speed,
And more restless becomes the deed:
There's fluttering, whistling, and bustling!
Suddenly an arm, a small one, wriggles itself free,
But unmoved, the unflagging and indomitable tree
Continues his convoluted dance
In a vigorous, supernal trance,
This way and that way, and that way and this way,
Swinging and juggling in joggling the best way,
Faster and faster and faster
Under the direction of his dance-master!

Vina Kandavanam

Weeping Rose Red

Weeping rose red, why do you weep?
For, the colour of you is sweeter than sweet,
And your fragrance is as light as air
As it drifts with the wind into a beautiful somewhere,
And when you awake with the morning light new,
You are glittered and sparkled with sweet drops of dew,
And the softest skin that holds within
the secret of its bright, wild beauty,
And birds that could see this wild rose free
and growing in a meadow along
would not make a fuss if they could just
sing a soft wind song,
And your colour a red blaze
As people stop to gaze
At the sight of a weeping rose red.

Chantel Lussier

The Short Life

The shortness of life, me thinks about the presence,
The past to erase, to be drawn ahead.
Wherever the sweet melody of mystic music plays
With a romantic song of love,
Through the strife and toil and all the pleasure of dance.

Momentarily time allows the music to tune,
Not to weep, nor mourn, but to be content,
Of the rainy showers of spring season,
Of the affection of the morning dove and red-breasted robin.
The blackbird flipped their wings of feather.
They light full strength on each blanket sheet of pine tree.
Foretell it a beauty nature mine.

A serene day to rake the mown lawn and sweep the sidewalk clean,
To amuse most of the neighbor of our existence.
The cool breeze of humid air blows tenderly on me.
Treading along strolls a dull-grey slim squirrel over the rumpled leaves.

A short life.
A dream for happiness and everlasting love.
Enveloped and sealed for a keepsake, carries onward beyond measure.
To be embrace in the beauty of love and creation.

Shirley Walinga

"A Silent Cry"

As the stars drift silently across the darkened sky,
The sleeping babe awakens with a sharp and yearning cry.

As the drops of rain beat slowly against the damp terrain,
She feels her soul grow hollow under her body's burning pain.

As the wind slowly whispers through the dark and tiny cave,
She dreams of her love's reflection within an open grave.

As the rain plays its final notes and covers the Earth in mist,
She looks a last time at her hungry babe, then to her bleeding wrist.

As time fades into morning, and night's dark face drops,
The crying of her newborn son slowly,
Quietly,
Stops.

Paula Francis-Browning

Take Time

Are there times when you wish you were far, far away,
That you simply can't take anymore,
Your world's closing in, you feel all alone,
When you seem to succeed, someone closes the door?
Then take time out—build up your strength—listen to your inner voice,
Cut your losses, move on with your life.
Find something uplifting—you DO have a choice.
Take a moment, take a step back, get a picture of what's going on.
When you find the cause you'll find the cure—it's time to get tough,
Do what needs to be done.
When you're down, pull yourself up—always think positive thoughts.
Focus on how to right the wrong—you'll find a way out.
You'll become wise and strong.
Take time for yourself, begin making amends,
It's never too late to start—stop feeling sorry—
Put the past behind—don't bury it deep in your heart.
Take time to enjoy what life's all about;
You'll never know when it may end—
If you let others control the way that you feel,
You'll find that you'll never be FREE.

Maureen Clarke

Song to the Youth

Life is a kaleidoscope with varying colors and shapes.
Everything is always changing.
Nothing stays the same.
It is filled with choices and responsibilities,
Which each of us must fulfill . . . for a better world.

Life is a stage.
We all have roles in it, but which is mine?
How must I know and fulfill the role that has been cast?

My life . . . is my journey
And I must journey alone, like the young eagle
Who leaves its nest . . . and flies against winds and storms.

Will I have the strength to fly?
I can find the answers . . . by knowing the song in my heart,
by listening to my conscience, and responding to the One Voice
who speaks through the rivers, the One possessing all good.
Then will I know the answers.
Then will I brave the storms of life.
Then will I find my path.
Bianca Von Muhlfeld

The Silence

Quiet, quiet, it's all too quiet,
an unnerving silence between the group.
Not a word's been spoken since four hours ago.

People thinking inside their heads,
but never speaking. Too quiet, too quiet,
too quiet for me.

I'm going to take the plunge.
I'll speak out the first word, breaking the silence,
that's too quiet, too quiet for me.

The people are speaking loudly, laughing, and smiling.
We are all friends again,
now that I have broken the silence that was too quiet for me.
Stacey Kilvert

The Forgotten Child

Alone in this dark, callous world,
Under a diaphanous cloth he is curled.
Each hand in hand,
Feeling as worthless as any barren land.
A forgotten child

Quietly standing on the side of the road, pubescent and delinquent,
He knows no work-load.
Forced to steal and exist on his own,
This is the reason his conscience would moan.
A forgotten child

As time went on, the offenses grew.
The worst came when he murdered a few.
The judge, jury, and trial came,
And it was found that he was to blame.
A forgotten child

He was led to the noose, there in the gallows hanging loose.
Flying motionlessly in the cold, wintry wind,
This appeared to be the end.
A forgotten child

Here lies his grave now; for his actions, he deserves no bow.
No man nor woman would pay their respect,
For he made no mistake except:
He was a forgotten child.
Dilraj Singh Ghumman

Caira

Insatiable chelonian crawling on obtusely
pointed dreams forever seeking
to satisfy your staunch desires
beyond reward and punishment
yet blemished by fissures of affection
your origin has made you bitter
and threatens your fight and argument

In the trench of your domain
your theme song simmers and shimmers
silhouetted against the pell-mell ridge
the bleak bell begirded with crimson silence
infested with chagrin
piquant with grief drops
insidious secretions on your flame
the acme of arpeggio your release
calloused hands and prodding words
embraced in subliminal ecstasy your peace

Frank Nagler

Words from a Teacher

Sometimes my class is like a volcano—
Serious, intent, but ready to explode;
At times my class is like a quiet street—
Empty, but echoing the day's reading mode;
Often the class is like a short field trip—
Full of animals and children who can learn;
Sometimes my class is like a fiesta—
Partying and games, with joy you can discern;
Our class at times is like a healthy meal—
Satisfying, tasty, pleasing to the eyes;
At other times it's like old history—
Violent and happy, filled with long good byes;
Often our class is like an encounter—
Filled with words and wit and wisdom you can see;
But on all days it's like an earnest friend—
Flawed but perfect, and always precious to me.

Patricia Lewis

A Day at the Beach

Nice, hot days and chilly nights,
Lots of children, petty fights,
Cold blue water, sandy towels,
Children with their pails and trowels
Burying Father in the sand,
Mother gives the kids a hand.
Bathing beauties, bikini clad,
Turn male heads, even Dad's!
The smell of wood smoke and briquettes:
This is something a beacher never forgets!
Hamburgers, hot dogs, pop sickles too!
Repellant, horseflies, and pine-goo,
Sand-caked bathing suits and saggy trunks,
Sand castles, beach balls, and toy trucks,
Sun burns, mosquito bites, and goose bumps too;
"Gee . . . I'm having fun; aren't you?"
Rugby, volleyball, and horse shoe play,
Speed our day along the way.
The sun is setting in the west.
Home is where we make our nest.

Rae E. Bracke

Judged

I can't take this any longer.
Speak and I get stronger.
Who are you to judge me?
Your mind is filled with jealousy,
You're not God and you're not my mother.
We don't have to hate each other.
You haven't been where I've been.
You think I'm evil, that I'm a sin.
You haven't seen what I've seen,
But you don't have to be so mean.
You say that I can't think.
My self-esteem starts to sink,
But I hold my head up high.
With my mind I touch the sky.
Judge me, that's all you do.
I still don't hate you.
I know you're the ignorant one.
I'm the one with wisdom.
My mind is on fire,
Wanting to call you a liar.

Sarah Boyd

Mirage

My heart beating
I reach out for you
I hear your voice, I take a breath
In bewilderment, I picture you
Your features unclear
I close my eyes
Lost in a dream of you, I sail away
You say something, I laugh anyway
You bid me farewell, I wake up
Where are you—just a mirage

Murtada F.M. Fadl

Nighttime

In the wake of darkness lies
a mysterious force uncovered by
the moon, that lurks inside every
shadow that creeps along like an
invisible force waiting to prey upon
the souls who wander off into
the night. Beware of the places
where the light refuses to shine,
because no one knows what
lurks inside the wound of barren
darkness where nothing can be
seen! A sudden noise can start
to make the image notion run
complete, until the source of
it is discovered.

Melanie Richer

Sincerity

Of late why don't I notice thee?
I searched all over, even in me.
In India, you surely are extinct,
Your total scarcity is distinct.

I see you at the end of every letter
For reasons known to all, better
Satisfied are we with this ritual,
Doing no more to save thy actual.

You have fully dissociated all,
Whatever the status, tiny or tall;
Departed from our teachers,
Tracelessly left our preachers.

In all professionals you're scarce,
Putting up show, so farce.
Matters not what's their vocation,
For them, you are in forever, vacation.

Vanishing from children so tender
As they raise to show their gender.
Corrupting their minds like a curse,
Replacing with greed to fill the purse.

D. Vijayaraghavan

Chiang

She spread her wings
Slowly fluttered into flight
She soared a moment up above
Then was lost to sight

Lena Winter

Reach Within

To find your soul you have
To reach within yourself not
Others. Yes, you're lonely, but
Not alone; you have friends
And family who care, not because
You're sick, but because they care.
So reach within, because
Nobody can do it but you.

Theresa D. Scott

Deep, Dark Back of My Mind

In the deep, dark back of my mind,
I can heal my sight.
I cannot find anything lost.
Someday it will turn out right.

In the deep, dark back of my mind,
I can feel my touch.
Everything lost is found,
And has all turned out right.

In the deep, dark back of my mind,
I can touch my taste.
Now I see what life brings,
And what I am to do.

Carly Ann Brundritt

Spring

Spring is gently walking around the land.
Smells of earth below me, rise like music in a band.
Abundance of sun pours down, like liquid gold
Steadily working now to take away the cold.

Scattering around the yard, traces of yesterday,
Leaving the pavement looking dirty and grey.
With sudden bursts of energy, then it stops to rest;
Letting winter snap back in a laughing jest.

The two they play, until a season change,
When summer enters to dry and rearrange.

Doreen Perry

A Homing Maiden

A homing maiden hastens in vain
To escape from the fury of rain.
She struggles through stormy weather
With all the courage she could gather.

Voluptuous volleys kiss her face,
Unkindly blasts of wind embrace
Her tremulous form; her restless eyes
Watch fleeting clouds bow in the skies.

As darkness deepens threateningly,
Lightning flashes unwittingly
A halo of enchanting grace
Over nature and beauty matched in race.
Through creaking trees and foliage bright
At last she sights the flickering light.
Her anxious mother, through wink-less night,
Had kept alive lest she have fright.

Thy loving lap, oh, Mother, is
As Heaven on Earth can be,
For, God's wisdom and His
Grace are embedded in Thee.

Chatar Ahluwalia

In Memory of Paula's Father (Raymond Sutton)

I drove down to the lake last night
where I often go to think,
To be alone and collect my thoughts
and get my life in synch.

Last night my thoughts were very sad
and tears streamed down my face.
As I looked across the water,
I put myself in your place.

They say not to take life so seriously
as you'll never get out alive,
but they never prepare the rest of us
for what it's like to survive.

For, life is a vicious circle
with ups and downs as you know,
but it's the love from your friends and family,
that's needed to make you grow.

Use the strength that he's given to you now,
to keep your chin up high,
and though I know you will really miss him,
his memories will never die.

Allison Laing

Memories of an Angel

Loving sister and loving friend,
seemed like her days would never end.
Her words so gentle, her face so fair,
did everything with so much care.

Fallen from grace is what they'd say,
a loving angel every day.
The songs she sang would warm your heart,
and never failed to do her part.

She lived each day with so much joy,
and cared for each and every toy.
When she was there the sun would shine
warm and bright and ever so kind.

Lived for others without regret,
each and every promise she met.
She never failed to keep her word,
no matter how strange or absurd.

She wished for others' happiness,
and what she felt, you had to guess.
She did not live very long,
but her joy will carry on.
Elizabeth McLaren Wickens

When

When all the light's gone
and your road grows longer,
it's then, they say, you must be stronger.

When your love is lost
and you cannot find hope,
it's then, they say, that you must cope.

When your heart's been broken
and you've no more strength,
it's then, they say, go to any length.

When your tears have fallen
and your world becomes cold,
it's then, they say, find courage to hold.

But when you've lost
what once you had,
They cannot say you must not be sad.
Angie Waldo

Amnesia

The yard is cluttered and uncut,
Ruins of buildings that once were spotting the uneven ground.
The driveway is rough and unpaved,
Yet, somehow, it feels like home.

The floors squeak,
The hot water tank is small,
And the tile is worn.
Yet, somehow, it is familiar.

I don't know when I've been here before,
Or even if I have,
But the people are kind,
And the faces are welcoming.

I like it here.
Sara Damgaard

Two Brothers

In the center of the world,
Where God's word was told to us,
Two brothers fight,
Two brothers kill,
Two brothers die.
They must be insane,
As brothers they are.
They praise the same God,
And live in the same house.
But unlike Cain and Abel,
They have begun to forgive,
To pray, and to be brothers again.
May God forgive and bless
Both brothers the same,
For it's easier to fight
Than to surrender and forgive.
May your holy house
Be prosperous again.
May both brothers at once
Hold the sacred olive branch!
Pablo Aguirrezabal

Deadly Shadows

As I'm trapped away,
The voices quiver and haunt.
As my life splatters to the floor,
My silence is being heard,
Only after death has begun.
Sandi Peacock

The Magnet

There was this magnet
right down below,
the bottom of the sea
being its place by rights.

I dove sixty feet
and gazed fixedly,
dared not touch it with my hand—
so sweet—a white line in the blue.

I gasped for air,
such was its drawing power—
a hand, then a leg, then a fin.
How could one escape from this?

I rolled over twice,
feeling the soft sand moving;
it went up in spirals,
the current catching us adrift,

so we all moved—a ballet
around the rocks, the corals, the algae;
but my magnet kept me tightly knit
to the wonderland down below.
M. Vaz

The Secluded Heart

To thy gentle love I surrender not
For no man has shown yet
What cannot be destroyed
The lips that tell to all of joy
Are still to reach the heart in me
The separation of soul and soul
Are equally in the past
As the separation of body and mind
Love not for what the fingers touch
But for what you see beyond sweet flesh
A pure love will sure prevail
Should the entity be found
But faith condemned for acquaintance of
The deep address of impudence
The secluded heart is with just cause
and so
To thy gentle love I surrender not

Angi Smith

Because You're My Friend

Chuckle me not, guy,
'cause laugh never can I.
Let not you cry,
though sorrow narrow your eye.

Don't ever you try,
hide low tie.
While no jolly can you buy,
nor he, does she know you lie?

But I find it high
through your silent sigh.
Always I close by
and never say good-bye.

Riyun Chai

My Mother's Face

As I look into the mirror,
It's my mother's face I see:
All her faith and wisdom,
All the love she wrapped in me.
Although my hair is shiny brown
And hers a silvery gray,
It's my mother in younger years
In the mirror I see today.

Lisa M. Gagnier

I

I am many things,
To too many people,
But I am me
To myself.
The inherent logic of insanity.

Garry Roberts

Tears

they slide gracefully down your cheek
as they gently tickle your skin
they may appear at any time
no matter which mood you're in

they're the drops of the ocean
inside your heart
they're the emotions that you keep
bottled up
they're the feelings that you hide
inside your soul
they're the thoughts that you have
when you're alone

they're clear as crystal with nothing inside
yet they carry all the feelings you hide
they symbolize all hopes and fears
they're the hidden pearls we call tears

Sara Noble

Wine Goblets

A black and white photograph.
Early 1930s, a village in northern Italy.
An osteria-bar.
Three youthful women,
each holds a wine goblet,
replenished with a dark liquid.
Red wine?
The aura defines simplicity.
Yet perplexed.
The pose: A nonchalant display.
Yet sensing rigidity.
No passion.
Characterization obscure.
Secrets.
A salute,
to a mysterious destiny,
or,
to a friendship,
or,
just a photograph.

Maria Zanella

Bingo Beef No. 1

Heavens to Betsy! The language is gross
When a voice yells "Bingo!"
And someone's that close
To winning.

The macho-est of men would blush bright red
At the words that some young chicks have said.
O, horrors!

But whether young chicks or older men,
Please—don't pollute our ears again,
Have pity!

M****! Take this advice:
Using foul language just isn't nice—
So don't swear—
It sounds like hell!

Wanda Wlodarski

Spirit Walk

I'm bewildered by the shapes and shadows in this murky atmosphere
Altercating with the light as it broaches near.

I'm bemused by transformations of this languid, liquid air
As its tendrils curl around me and pretend it isn't there.

I'm seduced by distant memory as it leads me to the edge
And it whispers softly to me, assuring solemn pledge.

It beckons, this strange calling, as it strokes a smooth caress,
So inviting, seeming pleasure and it promises deep rest.

I merge with unnamed presence and seek its inner quest
And hunger for the knowledge it withholds 'til final test.

We motion now together in the shadows of this place
As we weave and now behold us; I cannot see its face.

I feel its subtle, warm embrace and know the choice is really mine,
As it shows me peaceful pastures and endless, deep blue skies.

I'm lulled by gently swaying trees and sense sweet, fragrant puffs;
Benign, as though a friend may blow a dandy's little tuft.

I'm immersed in this serenity and captured by its lure,
I do not wish a harsh return to the land where pain endures.

I release this moment with a longing in my heart
And try to quell this desperate yearning for the gentle spirits who depart.
    Lola Feusse

The Honest Room

Alone, in her desolate room, so restricting and so cruel,
a tortured spirit silently murders her tormented soul.

With no distraction, no distortion, she reveals her dying bravery.
There is no tragic depth to disguise, no heroic image to defend.

The room glows with ruthless honesty.
Unrelenting fear emerges from a daily disguise.
A shattered spirit lures her away from the abandoned truth.

The room preys on this truth and unites a fearful future.
The room grows with a darker honesty, hidden amongst the silent ghost of a mortal soul.
    Andrea Aceti

Untitled

I always thought that blood was red.
The purple juices that curdled on the snow, were no less life than red.
The thick black hair, fanned out upon the sidewalk,
Face cuddled into soiled footprints,
Thin, denimed shoulders, hunched against the cold,
Adolescent wrists, poked out of sleeves,
Palms up, and still fingers curled as if to catch the flakes . . .
When he was born, did his mother
Stroke that olive face and breathe, "Oh, precious one!"
Or did she shriek, "Not mine!"?
When brown fingers brought her a dandelion,
Did she show him who likes butter, or did she push away?
Was he one or one of many? Did he live in hut or teepee?
Was he often very hungry? Oh, what brought him to the city?
Ah, those thin puppet pant legs lying there,
Shoes so cruelly worn!
"Yes, lady?" the sure young man standing, hands on hips.
"Move on, please. We're waiting for the cops.
Yeah, dead, I think.
It's just an Indian, you know."
    Phyllis Noble

A Life in Solitude

Confused whether or not to return from the shadows,
She feels a certain degree of need to.
Her time is over, but her life had just started.
The chair in which she sits is older than her,
Yet as it rocks without feeling,
She knows that she will go before it.

The wind from outside her window rustles her white locks,
Swirling them speedily into seclusion.
A clock above the mantle snaps time greedily,
But she does not desire its custody.
For, she has heard the clacking for eighty-three years.

To her, the life she once had is not forgotten,
But merely not remembered.
To her, the life she once had never ended
Until just the other day.

Alone in her room on this warm sunny day,
The cry of a baby outside her door makes her smile.
She knows that her life has accomplished
More than what she sees in front of her.
Whatever it is, it is done. Whatever it was, it is done.
William D. Jackson

Each Day with You

Each day with you, I feel the warmth of love between us,
The joy and happiness deep within us.
I feel the beat of your heart saying, "I love you,"
And that I will always be the only one for you.
Sweet dreams and promises we made for each other,
Is a very special thing for us to remember
That nothing and nobody can ever come between us,
No matter what people may think or say about us.
Our love for each other is growing much stronger
Each and every day that we spend together.
I knew it from the start that we are made for each other,
Because of the love that we feel for one another.
Isabel A. Plata

Just So You Know How I Feel

Two months have gone; a third is on its way,
I think of you every moment, ever since that tragic day,
when you slipped so far away.

I wasn't there to see it, and I couldn't say good-bye,
Instead of all this pain I feel, I think I'd much rather die.

I wasn't there to comfort you in your time of need and pain too,
But I want you to know that the loss of your presence,
just tears my heart right through.

I know that ending your pain and suffering was the right thing to do,
And sometimes I feel, that deep down inside, my heart knows it too,
But lying on that silver table, so lifeless and sound asleep,
I still can't picture you.

It could have bitten me right in the face,
and I can't believe I was so blind,
and every time I close my eyes, I see you in my mind.

They told me that forgetting it would mend all of my pain,
But I think I'd like to tell those people,
I think, that they are quite vain.

They say they know it's hard, and they say they know how it feels,
But they can never know, until they see someone they love drop dead,
head over heels.
Patricia Anne Mastromatteo

She's Always There

There's a place I can go in my dreams, far away,
And as she sits and watches me,
Far beyond the clouds—all I know
Is that she'll never leave me.

She knows I'm lost, and falling apart,
Reaches out her hand, hoping I'll take it,
And a single tear streams down my face,
As she comforts me with her warmth and grace.

I look up at her, with a twinkle in her eye.
I realize that things will get better,
With the help of her, she'll lead me which way to go,
And she'll be telling me, there's always tomorrow.

I just hope and pray that she'll be by my side.
Loving as she's been, it'll only get stronger.
Until the end, life travels on by,
With the help of each other, our love will never die.

I love you, Mom!
Erin Blackstock

Old Photos

There you are, back-to-a-tree
with me in your arms,
the sea splashing blue,
out of its element.

And there you are, blown dry on a rock,
by my side in the wind
in the sun,
sleeping rapt and unafraid,
no outrage to connive.

When we fell into the arms of love,
the whole world was a lamp:
Light, the scent of roses,
constant as a soul.

We were so well-meaning then,
just look at how we reach.

How could our arms have shrunken so much
to limbs the size of whirl-a-gigs,
dwarfed and disproportionate,
and torpid even in the wind?

Come. Let's stretch.
Elana Wolff

The Special Person in My Life

A mother is a person on which you can depend.
Any problem you bring forth, she will surely mend.
A mother always believes in you,
That everything you wish for will come true.

She's the one who comforts you
When everything's wrong and you feel blue.
Whenever you begin to cry,
She is right beside you, near your side.

She teaches you right from wrong.
She makes memories last long.
She loves you with her heart and mind.
She is the one who is always kind.
Inês Ribeiro

Dying to Live

I wish to bond with nature,
To fall face front
Into growing grass.

I need to grasp fresh mud
And feel Ms. Nature's
Delicate pulse.

I yearn to meet water's waves
And float upon
Her soothing skin.

I wait to speak to trees
And hear the gentle whispering
Between wind and leaves.

I hope to see some of this life,
To enjoy the loving company
Of a dying branch.
Andrea Venantius

Innocent Heroes

Cries of sadness hit your eyes
People mourn the loss
The children of the world
Get buried in the toss

It happened in Oklahoma City
On that day nothing was very pretty

It happened in Scotland and Australia
Innocent heroes pay the price
Of some evil mania
They never get to roll the dice
Skies of spirits tell the truth
Of innocent heroes in their youth

May we learn and stop the Earth
From turning backwards in its time
Through the complications of life
And the convicted of their crimes

Users of compassion
Aim the lasers of emotions
While we struggle through morality,
The laws, and our devotions
Francisco D. Reis

Friends

F un to be with all of the time,
R emembering to share also the cry,
I in being selfish sometimes,
E specially there in moments of
N eed, indeed
D ear to my heart,
S o special are thee.
Ingrid Maria T. Sestito

He Sang

My head was lying on his lap
He was driving
The song he was singing
Was something about a saddle
And an empty stall

I was ten
We were together
It was somewhere in Alberta
He drove
And I listened to him sing

When he sang
And when I slept
With my head on his knee
I had not a worry in the world
And I was ten years old

Time is such a scary thing
It's been such a long, long time
Since I rode with him
My head on his lap
And he sang me his favorite songs
Jim Warren

Immortality

The poppies spoke to me today,
As I walked o'er the plain.
They spoke about the battles here,
And of the many slain.

Yes, the poppies spoke to me today,
About the cannons' roar,
And how the bombs fell from the sky,
To kill and maim below.

They murmured softly in the breeze,
Of valor glory-bound,
And asked me but to softly tread
Upon this hallowed ground.

And as they spoke throughout my stay,
These gallants who have died,
I wanted to kneel down and pray,
But only cried and cried.

Yes, the poppies spoke to me today,
Of those who perished for you and me,
To never forget the price they paid,
For our peace and liberty.
Norm F. Stevens

Subway 1

The train gasps and slowly the
gray-tiled station disappears,
replaced by the charcoal darkness of the tunnel
snow boots leave gray slush footprints
on the faded blue floor

The stop, the whistle, the doors open and close
a couple, sitting together, switch newspapers
the ritual of the long, familiar ride
electric lights,
cracks in the tunnel through which the sun seeps,
slip by infinitely
the stop, the whistle, the doors open and close

As the aisles crowd
the coughing and swaying of the train
crushes the cold isolation of strangers
in a clumsy, voiceless intimacy

We're clanking,
clanking into the charcoal darkness of the tunnel
Konstantine Stavrakos

The Mountains of Vancouver

They rise so high 'twixt sea and sky,
Mountains of mighty mold.
They catch each ray of dawning day
And wrap themselves in gold.

Or they look down with angry frown
In austere, threatening might,
And lightly swirl soft mists of pearl
About their rugged height.

Towering, broody, wild, and moody,
They watch the years go by.
Ever changing, colours ranging
To match the mood of sky.

When chill winds blow and bring the snow
To drape the peaks in the white,
In awe folks gaze, their souls give praise
For this celestial sight.
Sybil Byrne

Elizabeth Robinson

The angels were circling one night in flight
And saw a soul who'd been in pain.
They gathered her in their arms and wings,
And took her home again.

Betty was like an angel to us,
And we all loved her so.
Now we know she's well in Heaven's grasp.
We'll see her again, I know.

How wonderful to have spent time with her,
As her earthly sojourn grew near.
I know she felt blessed by your presence and care,
To be surrounded with those she held dear.

And now celebrate her beauty, her strength, her life,
As from heaven her spirit draws near.
She's with the angels.
Maureen Tays

Stepping Up

I visit a friend, a clipping, poetry contest
Ye, I'm glad to see.
Why don't you enter?
Disclaimer: me don't write poetry.
Your journal: eloquent, beautiful, write so well.
Block to you from my heart.
Write me from your heart.
Gut-wrenching disclaimer: write, no encouragement.
Do others decide for you??? . . .
Quiet, deep inside, a rumble, stewing stillness,
My friend so powerful, discerning time passes.
Evening, four hours sleep, restless
My friend phones, the voice stirs memories, a rumble.
Dreamtime: it comes once twice, write or no peace.
Comfort songs come this way, it is the process.
I write, tears flowing, my offering, my angst.
I will send it to wait with trembling.

My friend, you touch me deeply.
Shirley Nichols

Mind Power

As we lie there thinking
Of what's to become,
Our heads go ablaze like a fiery sun.

The thoughts about life and how it's arranged;
But one little slipup and then it's all changed.

Thinking of yesterday and what tomorrow will bring;
But then knowing about one important thing.

Something that's strange, true but yet kind;
The power we all have in one little mind.
Ken McIsaac

A Dream

It begins as a seed
in a heart
that's ready to receive a vision
of what might and can be
if only it is embraced, treasured, and believed.

And the truth of it is spoken
and known
only unto its author and its receiver,
the promise of things to come.

An appointment with destiny
rings true
and a path is set,
a goal is set,
and the road to victory has begun.

Dare to dream,
Dare to embrace, and
Dare to be
all that you were made to be,
And discover who you really are.
Maria Noël

Black

It is quiet and dark,
The shadows are
taking over
And your mind is hazed
by the black fire.
Your soul yearns for
companionship
In the deepest sea
of envy and hate.
And grey eyes stare back
at you from the endless mirror,
A corridor of shadows
that won't let your thoughts
flow,
breathe,
cry.
All is black.
and then you open your
eyes.
Leah Jan Chutko

Winter Night

Gold orb rises 'pon indigo sky
Bold black spruce
Throws long, dark shadows
On twinkling night-grey snow.

The world is still, so quiet.
A lone wolf howls afar;
His echoes carry such loneliness,
As the hush again envelops.

Timidly, a nearby coyote yips.
A hesitant moment, then
Answering chorus of jubilant
Yodels serenade the moon.

Northern lights begin their dance
As stars crowd the sky.
A "silent" winter's night unfolds
'Neath the brilliant glow.
Shirley A. English

My Wall

Why do I cry these tears
Why do I have these fears
Built up through all these years
That built a wall
It's getting so tall
I'm walled away from happiness
I'm walled-up in loneliness
Behind my wall
There is nothing at all
Except me and my hate
I'll have to wait
I cry so much
I'm losing touch
I'm going to drown
Without a sound
I sink down and down
In pools of tears
And walls of fears
Dana Baiton

Nature's Path

When man doth look around and see
What nature has accomplished,
He can't but struggle inwardly
And feel himself admonished.

The gentle breeze, the starlit sky,
The beauty of the seasons,
Make all his efforts somewhat vain,
No matter what the reasons.

For falling rain and sun's warm rays
There is no substitution.
Our Earth's determined to go on
In spite of man's pollution.

The lords of science exert powers
That challenge God's creation,
But now and then catastrophe
Wakes up each sleepy nation.

'Tis then we stop and reassess
Our success and our failure.
We never have and never will
Outdo old mother nature.

Mary T. Bunting

The Land Speaks

The land speaks
Its voice can be heard
It flies high
Higher than a bird

The land calls
All plants and animals
Each one shows
They are special

The land meets
Waves from the ocean
Feeling its
Soothing lotion

The land greets
Winds of change
Types of weather
On its range

The land speaks
Listen and hear
Words that are
Actively dear

Vernon B. Dziedzic

An Angel's Harp

The melody of an Angel's harp
In harmony with the beat of the heart
Where goodness abounds
Sin is repelled
And the love of God within e'er Dwells

Lorraine L. Wysynski

The Mark on the Wall

I put a loving mark on the wall,
As my little children were growing tall.
They would stand on their toes,
Not for me to see,
And keep hoping taller they would be.
Then back to back we would go,
They on their toes just like before.
I would smile at them and say,
Haven't you gotten taller since yesterday?

But yesterday has gone too fast,
And I am looking up at last,
For they are big and I am small,
It is their turn to put my mark on the wall.
I was blessed with eight of them,
Seven children, one angel among them,
For this little one cannot stand at all,
But I will still put her loving mark on the wall.

Phil Coughlan

From Dark Below

You want to steal away,
furtively, softly;
that is: to warmer regions,
heart-southwards.

Off from the tables of the regulars,
to be no longer cut
by sharpened words
spoken imprudently.

And more: you don't want to
give up your fantasy
fragment by fragment
at your strength's expense

to get astray neither in chimney's forests
nor, as you reckon,
in others' egoistic feelings.
And yet, you won't be able to detect an exit.

Kurt F. Svatek

Wind Song

Oh, wind, you are so bold
You make me restless, you stir my soul
You touch my cheek, you tease my hair
You dance around me everywhere

I feel you bite my ears and nose
My cheeks you colour like a rose
You move my body, you push my feet
You hurry me along the street

I see you hiding in the trees
I feel you dashing past my knees
You dash, you dance, and turn the dirt
Like maids a-dance in frilly skirts

At times you're quiet, then you're strong
You bellow out your dancing song
The highs and lows though eerie be
Your song—a wind sung melody

Kath Jacquier

Precious Imagery

My granddad was the captain of a ship that sailed the seas,
And when I was just a tiny tot he'd sit me on his knee
In the rocking chair that rested on a scary black bear rug.
I'd snuggle in, get comfortable, and give him a big hug.
Then by music from the gramophone we'd venture off to sea,
In those wondrous recollections I would hear so eagerly.
Soon the main-sail would be set, and the winds were blowing sure,
And it wasn't long until we were a long way from the shore.
The sky was darkening today. It soon became like night.
A storm soon raged. All hands on deck—oh, wasn't that a fright!
As they tried to lower sails, the waves were lashing at the men.
The great ship lurched and pitched as waves washed over her again.
How amazing that the sailors didn't get washed out to sea.
Somehow fastened to the riggings, they worked on most gallantly.
Now the lightning flashed and there was soon an awful crash of thunder,
And on granddad's knee a little child, whose eyes were filled with wonder,
Soon realized the sea was calm—the rocking chair had ceased,
And the gramophone had run right down, her small world was at peace.

As he wound the gramophone again, he scanned the stormy west,
Then gathering up the little one, he'd rock her off to rest.

Charlotte Baraniuk

Sunrise

It touched the still waters of the pond,
and was reflected in its clear, glistening surface.

It shone on the snow-covered hill,
Making its cool white top shine like silver.

Its gentle rays penetrated through
the tangled web of grass on the lawn and soaked up the dew.

It stole through the windowpane,
and gently warmed the face of the child sleeping there.

Its wonder filled the old man with gratitude,
as he woke to another day.

It had an indescribable beauty,
the artist knew he could never capture it.

Its significance was never forgotten;
since Rome, man had symbolized the dawn with a promise.

Kathleen Loo Craig

Exposed

It little profits an idle man to know no King.
Upon a churning time I sit, under a purple sky,
Gone gray with man—and I stray, without a conscience,
Without a mindful thought or thing my own.
The sky? The sky above (gray yet) the sky, it's not so high anymore.
It little profits to struggle, to fight, to stand, to cry and strain,
And lose and lose—again and again.
It's no use anymore . . . what will?
The true, the fine, the poor, the honest, and pure, chaste few are few and
Less and less. But profitable still.
And what, will this hand never be clean?
And what part of my avarice, my greed, my mind needs it thus?
It doesn't, I think—
So on cruel spot! On!
'Tis too late to seek out new worlds; we'd ruin them too.
So run and run and run away.
The sky is gray and falling down—We'll cower beneath our gold,
Survive ourselves to mete and dole, corrupt the young, betray the old
And it matters little to me.
I am exposed.
I am exposed.

Kent Wilson

From a Bedroom Window

In an hour You plastered the torment of a fallen battalion to Your heart
and sucked that torment dry,
and robbed the crash from westering lightning above war fields,
booming into a galaxy that barely survived;
in an hour You better than battered the threads of time,
those threads agonized and torn in line;
in an hour, oh, the castle of cards You carefully erected,
so that for eternity You could muse and play,
threaten to blow it down and away,
and snap Your monstrous finger and thumb over our heads
to have our hearts buckle up dead.

Great, great beast, roaring, raw thunder,
of what stuff You are made I wonder,
and long for, so that I may be You, and You me,
and I may shatter Your dreams as raucous as can be,
and You will awaken from distempered sleep to see just how we see,
from a bedroom window rocked atrociously,
frantic and frightened,
but through and through in awe of westering lightning,
and in an hour You will crumble to nothing, that which is me.
   Damian Glover

God's Gift

A tiny seed is graced by God to grow inside of me,
Its very being left in the care of only you and me:
A little one to share our lives and to be a part of
Every hope and every dream and fill our wanting hearts.

To feel its tiny movement is a joy I can't express,
To hold it close, inside me to my heart impress.
There has to be a power more divine than you and me,
With his love did shower so we two can now be three.
To have within his mighty grasp, and now with life I flow.
To plant within this woman and watch this little one grow.
Each day is like a glowing smile because I feel sublime,
For in a wondrous place in me, is a wonder, a beautiful child.
A feeling only a mother can know, whose heart is filled with joy,
To very soon bring to the world a little girl or boy.
We are to be parents, my love, to watch, to teach, and to guide,
For God above has blessed our love with a wonderful, beautiful child.
   Judy Bearns

Hope Never Fails

In the midst of oppression all dreary and dark,
hope turns on a light, and clearly lights a spark.
When moments seem final, and no one can ease your pain,
hope embraces all emptiness, and fills your heart again.
After you've cried all the tears your eyes could flow,
hope comes to rescue floods of the heart, and soon the calm will show.
When today has lost all its meaning, and sadness makes time stand still,
hope strikes a hand that only fate can fulfill.
If love has its purpose, and it hasn't yet taken its place,
hope conquers all reason, and peace fills the space.
Some days you will feel beaten, and all out of ammunition;
hope then puts on your armor, and clothes you with ambition.
In days when you feel you've breathed your last breath,
hope kisses your heart and breaks the hand of death.
In the morning when you awake,
hope will offer a life today that you must take.
For, now is the day hope will show you new trails;
So grab the hand of hope—for, hope never fails.
   Michelle Kutney

Reflections

When you look into the mirror, are you satisfied
With the image that is looking back at you?
Do you like your face and hair,
And the style of clothes you wear?
Is there any need for changes you can do?

Do you like your own reflection?
Do you like all that you see?
Does it all pass your inspection?
Well, that's the way it all should be.

When you see yourself as other people see you,
Does your opinion of yourself go up or down?
But no matter what you wear,
Just put it on with care
With a smile on your face, not a frown.

    Beryl Pauls

A Request for Cremation

Take me west to the mountain peaks
Where the snow falls on the mountain creeks,
Where the coyotes howl and the wind blows free,
And scatter my ashes on the lone prairie.

Take me high where the eagles soar
And the roses bloom on the valley floor.
This is the place I wish to be,
So scatter my ashes on the lone prairie.

This world has been good,
But it has come and gone,
For I know I'll never see another dawn,
So God bless you all and do not cry,
For there is nothing left but a sad good-bye.

Take me up on the great divide
And scatter my ashes far and wide,
Either in the air or on the ground
Just so I can keep moving around.

    Jim Burnett

Is This the Right Place to End

In this dead end,
Yes, it's true,
Where bad and wrong
Mix up,
And truth
Doesn't show up.

Where souls and people
Aren't the same,
But with our eyes closed
Who's gonna guess?

Yes, this is the place
Where anyone can say a lie,
And nobody dares to tell the truth.

Maybe this is where we're supposed to end,
Or maybe not.
But again, is this the right place to end?
Well, I guess we'll never know.

    Elba Yesi Gerena

Our God

When we are weak,
He makes us strong.
He tells us what is right,
As well as what is wrong.

When we are doubting
And filled with despair,
Feeling, oh, so lonely,
Seems no one to share.

His promises He will keep,
And stay close by our side.
Give to Him your troubles
And in His love abide.

    Willa E. Vansickle

Perfection

When caress crop out
before the subtle word,
When we would learn to give
without losing time,
complaining on pains of others,
When we would search quick solutions
to satiate hunger
approaching bread at proper time,
When we would give drink to thirsty
without being asked,
Then
We would have advanced something more!

    Mary Rosa Calvino Citro

Jason Mason

He started young, as most kids do,
Maturing slow, his faults were few,
Thick blonde hair and big brown eyes,
Was no one sweeter, amid the sighs.

Energy, yes, he had it all,
A handsome boy, and growing tall,
Always curious, always sweet,
Polite to others, and fun to meet.

The years go by, a child grows,
There is no stopping the way life goes,
Leaving home, a man must do,
Working hard, that's all he knew.

Ethics, yes, he found his way,
The future bright, he earned his pay,
Liked by all, his spirits high,
It's sad to say our last good-bye.

You see, we loved him, then we heard,
He'd lost his life, our lives were blurred,
We had but one, our only son,
He'd left to young, age twenty-one.

    Paul Mason

To Be Happy

I wasn't happy the way I was before,
So I wanted to start over again.
I changed the way I looked and even acted
And those who I considered my friends.

Then people started talking,
Because they wanted to know.
One hears this, the other hears that,
And soon your life is one big show.

Then I asked myself and wondered,
"How did it come to this?
It's when I wanted to be happy again,
And it was my smile that I missed.

I thought that if I changed
Everything would be all right;
But the only thing that I noticed,
Was more problems in my sight.

At times, I look back at it all
And those are the moments when
I ask myself this question,
"Will I ever be happy again?"
   Raissa Bernabe

Frozen Forever

They stand motionless, dismal.
Effect of still moon, observing,
Scattered; no pattern,
Like a board of chess
frozen forever at the climax of the game.
Kings and Queens stand tall,
masters of the court.
Pawns go unnoticed,
tiny stones, marked.
For chess:
fairy tale knights, wise bishops.
Each piece polished fine
portrays its importance in the game.
Each tomb,
each graveyard's woe, depressed;
remains eroded, stained,
decorated, or bare
to reflect the death of life . . .
marked prominent.
   Cara Pentney

Safe Inside

I'm somebody's baby
Whose—I don't know.
I go to all kinds of places,
But never see faces.
I hear things that are nasty
And things that are sweet.
I've felt the cold, and now
I'm feeling the heat.

My world is a dirty one.
To others it is clean.
My thoughts are my secrets;
My feelings—known only by me.

I'm living in the dark.
Don't show me the light of day.
Don't kill me that way,
Keep me safe inside you.

I know so many people but no one knows me.
I'm so alone in my dark, lonely world.
How will I survive all this confusion
At nine months old?
   Pasqualina Scala

Runaway

I sit and stare at the sky
as a single tear falls from my eye.
I am left to face the unknown,
afraid to walk this world alone.

I have only me to carry this load,
heading down a dead-end road.
I am consumed by the dark and can't see the light,
there seems to be no end in sight.
   Gina Clark

On a Spring Day

The sun shines in the cloudless sky,
On this beautiful spring day,
But no matter how beautiful the day may be,
It can't wipe my tears away.

Thoughts of you always linger in my mind,
Not letting me forget
The laughter, the smiles, the tears we've shared
Since the day we met.

One day we may be together again,
And in my heart I know,
That you still love me very much
Even though you don't let it show.

Until the day we meet again,
I'll always be waiting for you,
Hoping that all my wishes and dreams
You'll finally make come true.

Hoping for the day when you come back
In my life to stay,
When you replace my tears with laughter,
On a beautiful spring day.
   Katherine Vavaroutsos

Earth's Greatest Treasure

Of all the wonders of the worlds,
The treasures great and small,
The many miracles of Earth,
Which one surpasses all?

Is it the frost-drawn pictures,
And soft snow on bush and tree
That herald winter's presence
For all the world to see?

Or is it the emerald beauty
Of summer and of spring,
Bringing forth the joyous songs
Of birds upon the wing?

Maybe the warmth of autumn,
Its colors bright and bold,
Is the greatest of all treasures
That Earth's bounty can unfold.

No! The greatest of all treasures
That comes from heaven above,
That lights our eyes and brightens our smiles,
Is the precious gift of love!
   Betty Domolewski

Love Eternal Will Not Be Denied

Somewhere in Time
We turn, we churn, in an evolutionary thrust and spasm
To kiss the Abyss, and walk the chasm
Between the Sacred and the Profane, Pleasure and Pain,
Bliss and Insane, Voice and Refrain,
Telling everybody that it's his name.

Inhale, exhale, savour the pleasure
Beyond all our dreams, buried treasure.
No scope, no probe, can begin to measure
The Passion, the Sorrow,
Only the joy of yesterday's Tomorrow.

Eyes touch, sublime transduction
of Lovers entwined,
Immaculate Seduction.
   Douglas C. Headdon

Time Is Near

Are we ready or are we not?
For, we know not the time we've got.

He's given us a choice for thousands of years,
but the time has come, for he is near.

The gift he has given cannot be bought,
so put away your money, insult him not.

Open your eyes, he's made it quite clear;
your minds, your hearts, and your ears.

He'll be here to collect; he hasn't forgot;
and reward us for our battles we've fought.

So, praise the Lord and give a loud Cheer!
He gave us Salvation; you and me, Dear.

So use your time wisely, the time you've got,
for he is coming, Ready or Not.
   Peggy Audrey Minchan

Cats Sleep Anywhere

Cats sleep anywhere:
On top of a table, any chair,
On the rug, or a bed,
Up in a tree, or a shed,
An open drawer, on a shoe,
Anybody's lap will do!
Cats sleep anywhere:
Close to fire,
Even on top of the refrigerator!
They just don't care!
   Addana Lewis

Solitude

A solitary life
In peace and tranquility,
Drowned in loneliness
Yet so safe and secure . . .

What does it wonder . . .
Watching the tiny ripples
Or the changing colours
On a silent, dusky eve.

Is it lost in a huge world
Or did it choose to be that way
To avoid life's illusions
That fills its heart with pain?
   Lakmini Baumgart

Cocoa Loco

A crocodile
Living by the Nile,
Fancied a cup of cocoa.
He left his lair,
And soon was there,
Cruising up the Orinoco.

It came to an end
Around a bend,
When he turned tail to go.
To all he'd seen,
He'd yelled, "Where's yuh bean?"
But the natives didn't seem to know.

It appears to me
If moral there be,
Then we should really mark it.
If one gets such a yen,
One should think once again,
And first try one's supermarket.
   Brian B. Kelly

Fate

To be caught within the boundaries
of belief and disbelief,
Distrust so great that
nothing is really real,
even within grasp.
All reason escapes logic,
only that one lost feeling,
as if an instinct to assume
all is simply a dream,
that can never be awakened from.
Endless sleep is a pattern
within the cycle of being.
Must break free.
Kandice Doucette

Dreams

As I sit with light of fire,
In my thoughts I dream awhile.

The thought of light,
The dream of fire,

Make my life seem worthwhile.

As love will fade, so shall I,
In my dream I shall die.

The light will dim,
The heat seems cold.

Darkness grows upon my forehead,
For love and life must be taken.

Death is always awaiting!
Sheila A. Durack

Everafters

Cinderella does not always
find her Prince.
The magic slipper often
doesn't fit,
or, if it does, it pinches
when you walk.
But somehow, we believers
always wait,
watching the darkening skies
for a daring white stallion
and gallant redeeming Prince.
While, in the sodden fields,
the waiting pumpkins rot,
and apathetic mice infest
the house.
Lorelei E. Smith

Untitled

The things I wish not to remember, I do.
The things I wish to forget I don't.
I tire at what excites me,
And live when there's nothing to live for.
I know what is wrong,
I dismiss what is right.
I love you with all my heart,
But I choose no to indulge you.
When I need company,
I sit alone.
When I need privacy,
You don't leave me.
I cry when I'm happy,
And smile when I'm sad.
You make me laugh
When I don't feel like laughing.
You burden me with your frowns
When I want to sing.
Is the world upside down,
Or am I its reciprocal?
Katherine Warzecha

Forsaken

My mind has been denied, and my heart forbidden.
Eyes that see, and hands that feel,
That leave a sting too numb to feel.
Only pictures, that are lifeless, with two-dimension
innovated—neediness.

That rages through the mind of insanity, of madness.
Thoughts twisted and eroded,
The mind decayed and unfolded.
Obsession?
No! Deception.

The serpent lies within the mind,
Search for it and you will find
Evil rage, plunder, and raze,
Bewildered—confused in the incense haze.

The sweet smell of the aphrodisiac,
Combined with hands that touch,
to some it really doesn't amount to much.

Have I been forsaken
and my life lost and taken?
Peter Paulozza

Untitled

The gray skies of life envelop the world in a
shroud of gloom.
Only mankind can help to light up the universe
with love and trust.
Gray can turn to golden warmth . . .

Suffering—tragedy, will eternally be upon us,
only to be eased by sharing our hearts with
our fellow man.

The spirit must constantly be nourished
or it will die,
the most tragic and saddest
death of them all.
Suzanne Kallman

To Mother with Thanks

You have given me a very special gift,
to capture more than what the eyes are meant to see.
When I walk into nature's wonderland, not only do I notice,
but touch and experience her beauty. I thank you.
Oh, a significant role you play. You are a link to the chain
of life and survival.
For when the last dew drop falls,
and mother nature tucks in her last group of children
with a comforter of snow,
everything grows quiet,
the lonely whispers of the wind, calling out to the endless
patterns printed upon nature's formations,
while the special bonds of silence assemble themselves
to the bottom of her forest floor.
The harmonious effect that it preys upon all who see it,
remain in awe, while her story of existence is taken
prisoner. I will be gone, but you won't.
Those footprints that you made for me, I will walk upon
forever. And that one semester of time, will educate me
for a lifetime.

Lisa A. Davenport

My Anxious Plea

Give me peace, put a hold on the anxiety and tears.
Release the tension from constant stabbing fears.
Relax my nerves by running a warm, comforting bath
Of understanding, and don't expose my tender loin to wrath.
I am just a frail human, prone to misery and weak.
It's only a humble life, of reasonable comfort I seek.
You can't imagine the depth of humility I feel;
It overwhelms my desperate vogue of ardor and zeal.
If I were a cloud I could dissipate and reemerge,
In a new mental capacity of confidence I'd surge
To spread my new-found courage into a sound mental frame,
Without malice or bitterness, no scapegoat to blame.
A courageous spirit may become void if ever daunted:
Losing faith sends vibes, leaving a mind quite haunted,
Searching for peace in a world of intolerance and greed,
Leaving a trail of lost souls homeless and in need.
If a refocused mental network can only take command
Like the hot sun rays drying the rain-soaked sand,
This new circuit of energy in dormancy is pent
'Til the air waves are opened and a message is sent.

Jack Brock

Royal Memories

The tasty Sunday lunches when all were summoned
Sitting in the gallery, trade winds blowing, palms swaying,
Listening, your mother talk of days long gone

Laughter, chores, family sharing without regret
Everyone aware of rewards to get, Memories, History,
Feelings of belonging, these treasures, not monetary

Vivid memories of overnight sleeps when there were many
Securely, five girls, aunts and nieces, horizontally share one bed
All welcomed to partake, though not plenty, what was there

Your thirteen, and their many claimed you as Royal
We called you Queen or Mom, not granny, grandma
You wove in the blood, strength, grace, dignity

Spreading your priceless seeds across the seas
Now radiant blossoms bloom among thorns
The Spirit of your legacy continues

D. Patricia Makeiff

Ode to the Atom

Four very scientific guys had had their say
To what we all know and learn today.
Have you ever wondered what things are made of?
Dalton had a thought that everybody loved.
Atoms, as he realized,
Are how things materialized.
From Dalton's earlier mistakes,
We now know Thomson's model, similar to little cakes,
But scientists always have to prove or compare,
So it didn't just end there.
There was Thompson and Crooks in the 1890s,
Britain's James Chadwick in the 1930s.
And the Gold Foil experiment conducted by Ernest Rutherford,
Indicated to others he was not just a nerd.
From the Periodic Table much is to be learned,
Isotopes aren't listed, but don't be too concerned.
Now it is much easier for students in classes,
When the Periodic Table provides atomic numbers and masses.
As you can see from previous mistakes,
Discovering the structure of the atom was no piece of cake.

Victoria Fung

Mother Earth

The shadows, like ugly trolls, dance naked in the evening
worshipping their God—the moon.
And the wind, the voice of their evil chant,
whips the leaves about their feet.
Death is in the air tonight;
The smell of it—like fear,
It is suffocating.
The taste of it—like vomit,
It is choking.
The sound of it: silence.
Silence but for mother's words;
Softly now, quietly. Whispering out of the darkness.
Confused and tormented,
yet relishing the prospect of final retribution.
For, the scars on her body shall never heal.
The evidence of her rape, her degradation for all to see.
Tonight she sleeps,
Tomorrow . . .

Denise Somerville

Migration

Am I sight-seeing for my synapses?
Experiencing new context for familiar stories,
Searching for faces to give features to old expression,
Hoping that new form will finally expose meaning,

Lassitude.
An electrical impulse
Driving an insane need
That responds to:
Tangier, Rangoon, Yaounde, Tamiahua, Qiryat Shemona, Guantanamo.

A litany of memories
Yet to happen to me, at least.

Loneliness,
The hidden cost of a bargain made in the basement of airline consolidators.
A life in the skin—the surface of human interaction.
A guest in a stranger's economy,
A scrapbook of farewells that never create lasting sorrow.
No one to take presents home to.

Why wander?
Why wonder?
Understand. So I can rest without apathy.

Ritika Nandkeolyar

St. Catherine's Street: A Sorry Pair

I heard two songs fight for sway, on that distant day.
Two musicians did erstwhile play,
One in the light, one in the shade.
One in garish cloak and purple pants,
The other barren of romance,
In earth attired under brimful hat,
Mourning his song and the words that they spat.
The one danced in step and kicked partout,
The other looked as if the day he did rue.
One set of fingers sang a merry tune,
The other cried a melancholy note.
And so while one craved of you a boon,
The other was silenced too soon.
The song of the one drove out the other,
Not knowing he was his sister's brother.
Yet were the hands that played awry;
The sax merrier than the trumpet shy.
  Brendan Gluckman

A Toast to the Future

Why it's so hard I don't know,
Why so many changes affect us so.
The future is exciting and new,
The challenges there are not few.
We should use the past only as a guide,
Not a place where we can hide.
If the past is where you choose to dwell,
It could make your future a living hell.
Every day we test ourselves.
It's who we are that brings us wealth,
Not the money we can make,
Not the people we can break.
Success is measured in who we become,
Because we are the only one
That needs to be happy with the decisions we make,
Along life's path that occasionally breaks.
These challenges make us change and grow,
Successful people will tell you so.
To the future—raise your glass!
The future starts now and past is past.
  Marie Mushing

Sonnet

It's hard the life, poor man, that we do lead,
In tempest locked, and swayed and lost out right.
Sometimes the heavens shine, and upright then
Our portly keels do skim our danger's fleet;
And we, like birds of ocean, sometimes meet
And sometime miss, all wind-tossed without maps;
Sometimes the waters spraying, buffeting surge
Must make us flap, or bound over waves,
Or tired stand on feet when we would fall.
Yet preference keeping mirth, her will to go
Through roaring tempests, dashing waves or sun,
Makes us go encased in thought, not willed to die
By our necessities. Our clime this Earth is
Storm and sometimes sun we must not shun,
But whether storm or whether sun, kneel high or fly.
  Julio Gianni Toro San Martin

Game

There are two ways to hunt.
The first, by sport,
Requires strategy, stamina,
Determination, and skill.

The prey becomes alert to pursuit.
Fear drives it to flee, wounded perhaps.
Time and suffering and knowing slow it
To exhaustion and inescapable death.

The second way
Is by stealth;
The prey, suddenly
          come upon.

There are two ways to kill.
The first is by torment:
Terror—glistening in the victim's eyes;
Slow, labouring pain as life leaves.

The second
Is instant,
Painless,
Over.
  Donna Morhart

Heaven

As I lie in a field,
I listen to the breeze.
It whispers your name,
As it blows through the trees.

The bright yellow sun,
shines through like her smile.
I think to myself,
she'll be here in a while.

Together we lie,
like a ball in a glove.
We walk in the flowers,
and then we make love.

We walk on the beach,
holding hands in the night.
It seems like forever,
until morning sheds light.

She says that she loves me,
and I say the same.
We were once really happy,
we can do it again.
  Scott Tragvair

Innocence

The world looked so much better
when you viewed it
hanging upside down
from the monkey bars,
letting all the blood
rush to your head.
Clouds made different shapes
for your entertainment,
never letting on
that it was the wind
who created them
and not the power
of your mind.
Back then you never doubted
that your dreams
wouldn't come true
because you knew
in your heart
that anyone could make it
if they tried.
Deanna Di Lello

Remember

Remember our walks
In the parks so far.
Remember our games
We used to play in the car.

Remember our love
That we have to this day.
Remember our hugs
That help me in every way.

I guess I'm saying
I love your sweet touch,
And I love our love, oh, so much.

Happy Mother's Day, mom.
Erin Duffy

The Old Ones

The moon and sea akin to me
they speak to me in ancient tongues
of deeds undone and things to come
they speak to me of times long past
when I was young, but not so they
of times when man was yet to be
of times when all there was to see
was the moon and the sea, the endless sea
Karen Burns

Oh, Canada

The day is quiet, the weather tranquil.
Two old men on a park bench sit side by side.
The pigeons are cooing, the talk is wistful.
One man says, "Now begins the Change of Tide.
We must change the Outrage that's hard to kill.
The strength of man's hate for man
That continues to resist man's deepest will,
No matter how the word denies, it ran
To murder, maim, hate, and kill.
A religion, tradition, nationality, and race,
Because of color, style, and a prayer to belong
To true honor, loyalty, and a hope to live
In peace, tranquility, a place to be safe.
Things a new country to give,
Not a place where real beliefs are a disgrace,
A place where promises of safety were assured:
A place called Canada!"
Jackie Nikolic

One Old Man

Gray hairs, knowledge to spare
Must keep yourself sane
Shaking hands, year-old muffins
Your cat's dead in the lane

Dust, grime, and a filthy bed
All alone, wife is dead
Weeds overgrown, locking you in
A whole year passed, not one word said

Tea cup, dead mouse curled up inside
Forty-year-old dentures, dirty and misused
House alone in the neighborhood
Simple things that you confused

One group of family visits
Those kids make me feel young
They drive five hours and still feel guilty
Now you're happy and unstrung

While they're here, life is great
Then they have to leave
Once again you're on your own
Another year to grieve
Nicole Robertson

Requiem for My Father

Quiet and humble, with the strength of ten,
Grace and charm unequalled among men.
Did for his family each day his best,
The travails of life put to the test.
His faith in God and simple commands
Met squarely all rigours and demands.
Gentle and kind, old country ways,
Slow to anger in all his days,
Took no advantage, nothing done fast,
Put others before, himself the last.
Character deep as his love was true
Solid, reliable, through and through.
True to his word be ever sure
Memories of him to last and endure.
Husband, father, friend, all had—
That quiet man who is my Dad.
Gordon Drybrough

Flowers in the Field

Poppies wave from left to right,
Crying, shouting, and yelling for help,
For the war goes beyond the bright light.
Tanks and guns are going off while the dogs yelp.

Receiving the award and respect of those who won,
But now we cry for those who are gone.
Beyond the golden bar ahead for one,
Share the tears that we have shed upon.

No fighting here, for we need a day of peace.
Quietly the ground shakes upon life,
A second of your time, for all is released,
To sing out loud, to share what's left of life.

To gladly say the war is over for all,
For those we thank who fought for us in our big ball.
   Sherri Ann Horne

Beyond

May we go beyond our Earth
Beyond the stars, skies, and seas,
Farther away than any mortal eye dare sees?
To disappear into the gleam of darkness
Beyond trees, branches, and boughs,
Beyond the distance that time allows
To venture to the unknown,
Beyond any human confrontation,
Beyond the boundaries of mortal imagination,
To seek new worlds
Beyond hour, day, and night,
Beyond the speed of Apollo's light,
To seek new life
Beyond the human civilization,
Beyond the hope of returning from oblivion:
These I seek for
Beyond the pain that cuts like a knife,
Beyond the chambers of mortal life.
   Stephanie Fohring

Dream of Love

I dreamed I was standing by the ocean,
Soft sands beneath my feet.
A gentle breeze was blowing,
Cooling the summer heat.

I dreamed you were standing alone nearby,
And as the moon lit up the starry sky,
We were drawn together by the power of love,
Speaking silently with our eyes.

You gave me a rose and took my hand,
Led me along the shore lovingly.
We stopped, but the hours passed us by
As the young night faded quickly.

Then, as magically as you had come,
Something took you away from me.
You left me with a salty-sweet kiss,
And soon I again stood in solitude.

I dreamed you were dreaming of me,
Dreaming of you dreaming of me.
I dreamed we were both in love,
Always were, and forever will be.
   Connie Fan

Think

Thoughts that I have never had
Are faces in my mind:
I think I see expressions of
How old I am in time.
I walk away from who I was,
And ahead of me I know
Are those that tell me who I was
Before they have to go.
I followed them until I saw
They were not friends of mine,
Just old-time thoughts
That I'd forgot I'd had
In the expressions of my mind.
   Gary L. Gordon

Sixty Below

Hard on the heels
Of the wild north wind
Comes the bitter cold.

Locking the land
In a frigid vise,
Converting the lake
To a plain of ice,
Cracking the hearts
Of the helpless trees,
Driving the animal world
To its knees.

And all the land
Is still as death—
Even the air
Holds its breath.
   Gordon L. Perry

A Friend

I go and visit
In a Chronic Care Wing,
My Senior lady friend
And a man named Jim.

He has no family here
That I do know of,
So when I have the time
I pop in to say, "Hello, luv."

I do most of the talking
As he has difficulty,
But when he starts to laugh
It's very heartily!

Yes, it is good for him,
And I like to see this too.
I feel that I help a little bit
To make his day go through.

Sometimes I hold his hand,
To show that I'm his friend.
Though I'm a little Nutty,
I'll drive him around the bend!
   Morag Slicer

Awakening

The winter snows have melted,
And its cruel winds cease.
The gentle lamb emerges from hiding,
Bringing peace to the Earth.
It has vanquished the lion,
And has gathered the clouds.
The first sound of thunder is heard,
Signalling the birth of the new season.
Rain begins to fall softly to the earth,
And like the waves of the ocean,
Life spreads across the land
And death itself fades away.
The sleepy awaken,
And a world of wonder dawns,
As does the morning sun.
David Cameron

Sunflower

You are as beautiful as
the summer's sunshine
with cerebral orgasmic
beauty and I find
myself caught in rapture.
I long to hold your hand,
walk with you through the glory
of your rainbowland.
Pretty little flower
with your lovely way,
let your color shine out
with every passing day.
You're glorious in essence,
a character, my sin,
and as we exchange letters
I wonder how this did begin;
A shout through the night
from a stoned mouth hurled,
those two christened words
loudly called, "Hello world!"
Jodi Pallagi

Suicide

When the sun goes slowly down,
I am sitting in my room,
crying about my dumb room,
and wetting my purple gown.

I look at my hated face,
don't want to see it anymore.
My eyes are so sore,
of this piece of fat without grace.

What is the worth of life,
when nobody loves you,
which is my fate, too?
So I take the knife.

There's blood all over, it's done.
Finally, I am gone.
Arlette Huguenin

Sailor's Wind

The wind that makes the wide ship sail
It's sunny out, no clouds, no hail
The waves that ripple through the sea
A far-off sound that haunts me

The wind that gives me one good chance
The breeze that makes my blond hair dance
The wind that whistles way up high
Overpowers some horn you buy

Countless shells upon the shore
Your heart tells you to sail no more
The gulls that soar away up high
Saying to your sea career good-bye
Heather Agnew

Lullaby for Liam

Go to sleep, my baby.
Wait for me in your land of dreams.
It's early yet for you to sleep,
But your wee body was so easily tired.

Go to sleep, my baby,
Safe and well in your land of dreams.
Time there is, but not for you.
Please wait for me in your land of dreams.

Stay asleep, my baby.
Walk in mem'ries of your short life.
Cry no more for life slipped by,
I'll see you when it's time for me to sleep.
L. Monica Stevens

A Baby's Face

God took the blue from the sky,
And dropped it into every eye.
Angels wove golden threads,
Then placed it on their tiny heads.
Form delicate birds God plucked the down,
To make their face's soft and round.
From in the sea, down beneath,
Came the pearls to make their teeth.
With careful hands, soft and strong,
While angels gathered with a song,
Full of light, love, and grace,
God made what is a baby's face.
K. Hotson

Redemption

Leaving the womb of the car
Outside a coffee shop in Brantford
On the first Saturday in November
A wind mean as January, came knifing at me.
Fumbling, I tried to zip and Velcro my jacket shut.
Too late, the damage was done.
The mind shuddered in unison with the body
As a pastiche of winters recalled
Frosted the window of my soul,
Until ambient warmth and the aroma of coffee
Embraced me as I entered the shop.
John B. Traynor

A Pretty Neat Little Love Poem

On the first day that I saw her
presence clutched my heart and held it tightly
(rendering the rest of my body paralyzed, unable of speech and control).
I was helpless, nervous, and totally in love.
Her touch: soft and warm.
Her skin: smooth as silk.
It numbed my hands to caress her beautifully curved body.
I was under her spell,
a spell which I couldn't break
(a spell I didn't want to break).
Year after year, my love never faltered,
it only grew deeper with every passing moment.
She never complained, only listened with everlasting patience.
She was always there when I needed her,
she never abandoned nor deserted me.
She was faithful and honest.
She was the one.
She was my first love.
She was my first car.

Cory Stevens

Elusive Sleep

Sweet sleep come, woo me down the long grey lanes of mist,
Swirling and haunted by the memory of a gold time.
The soothing breath of Morpheus, let me not resist,
But on gossamer wings bear me away,
Till, as the brittle rime does melt and fade from off
the chastened flower,
So woo distress from me, that I may rest with happy mind,
and for a while forget my care, in thy secluded bower.

Oh, sleep! Elusive sleep, that mocks at wealth,
Yet steals upon the poor with tender stealth,
Touching the work-worn heart with peace,
That brings it near to God,
Have I offended Thee, that thou my weary eyes have scorned to kiss,
Locking my turbulent heart from out the vale of bliss?

Come, let me rest, down deep within thine arms.
I would unruffled be as mountain lake, that nature's
furies only leave more calm.
Soothe from me maddening thoughts, with all thy charms,
That I may wake with spirit bold
To meet with fortitude whate'er the dawning day may hold.

Mary B. Lemon

Please Stop the Blame

Rich against poor, "majority" against "minority,"
Black against white, brother against brother,
Parents against children, please stop the blame!

Nation against nation, blood against blood,
Why does this happen, why does this go on,
Teaching our children these shameful deeds?
Please stop the blame!

Politics, religion, race, culture, status,
Each blaming the other, not accepting their own responsibilities.
Please, please stop the blame!

Bloodshed and tears, heartache and pain,
Why must this go on? Who are we to judge
Those we stand beside, those who share our space?
Please, please stop the blame!

Why must innocence die to have hatred take its place?
War over love, hatred over unity?
Death over life?
Someone please, please, stop the blame,
Before it's too late to turn back!

Cory Whitecap

My Tears Can't Change the World

They know! They know! A man yells as I cross the street.
A tear falls from my eye, it's the middle of the winter,
And the poor, old vagabond has nothing on his feet.
His eyes are bloodshot from the lack of sleep,
And the cuts on his feet are mighty deep.

Help me! Help me! He begs and he pleads,
Help me! Help me! I'm down on my hands and knees.
The man he's talking to turns and walks away,
Do I have to see you bums each and every day?
It scares me to see the coldness in his eyes.
That man couldn't care less if the vagabond lives or dies.
It hurts me to see the blood pumping through his veins.
For, the blood that pumps in me is pretty much the same.

And a tear falls from my eye and drops down on my heart,
And that sweet and helpless tear rips my heart apart.

Retard, retard! You're nothing but a retard!
The little kids sing and cheer.
And the little boy turns and walks away helplessly
And sets forth a little tear.
A little girl screams out, "Look at that stupid walk!"
    Cedric Jean Marie

Carry Me

Carry me toward a never ending path.
Carry me out of the darkness and into the light.
Carry my thoughts, my dreams, my heart.
Carry the love you feel, but carry your mind, not your heart.
Carry your mind into a cloud of dust.
Carry your love away from mine.
Release your madness.
Release your pain.
Release me forever and walk into the rain.
Release your mind, your thoughts, your dreams,
Darkness forever.
Leave your soul and carry your mind.
Darkness I shall live in;
Darkness, for I can see
Darkness make me blind.
Darkness I shall live in.
Leave me behind, for I am blind.
Soft wind creates the whisper.
Carry me out of the darkness and into the light.
    Diane Fiorini

Bow to the Ring

A roar erupts
as the Matador strides confidently into the ring.
He salutes to the cheering crowd,
and turns to face the undefeated Black Bull.
Silence envelops the once-frenzied crowd.
The Black Bull excitedly tears at the ground.
A tear glistens on a woman's cheek.
The cage flies open
and the eyes of the combatants become fused.
The Matador stands rigid with a crimson cape at his side.
With the grace of a dancer,
he glides away from the charging Beast.
Frantically, the Beast turns and faces his challenger.
With the torment of a thousand years etched on its face,
it charges with unbridled fury.
Sweat falls from the weary Matador.
He knows the Black Bull cannot be defeated.
Lovingly, he looks at the weeping woman,
and bows to the Beast.
A tear drops, as the soiled cape falls lifeless into the open ground.
    Brian Long

Inside My Head

You'd see the sun, the driving rain.
You'd see the hurt, the blinding pain.

You'd see the memories of a troubled past,
When you're always picked to finish last.

You'd see the strength, no room for wimps.
You may see weakness, but just a glimpse.

You'd see the shame, you'd see the guilt,
And all of the walls that I have built.

You'd see the truth and the times I lied.
You'd see the blue of the tears I cried.

You'd see the love that I wish to share.
I look around but no one's there.
You'd see the rage and explosive flame
And all the demons inside my brain.

You'd see the dark that brings the dread.
It's really not nice inside my head.

You'd see me standing, the only one,
A flash of light and all is done.
Now all is quiet, all is dead.
There is nothing left inside my head.
  Shawn Scott

Vengeance of Ease

In the silence of the night
Lies a soul who has betrayed,
Taken away by a crazed insanity.
All thoughts and feelings are strayed,
Beckoned by the whispers
Of the sinful, dying wind.
Perched upon a ledge,
Remembering back to all the times he sinned,
Rising from the darkened stillness,
Above the cries of the wild
Is a man who thinks nothing of himself.
His anger and unspoken words seem mild.
His life shall never be regained.
Because of one moment of vengeful anger.
Mistakes are often left, overtaking ourselves,
Thinking of only pain and not the danger.
  Shawna Croy

The Lucky Team

Four to four, tie game it was.
The score board was soon to ring a buzz.
The crowd was cheering, players sweat,
For the air was warm, sticky, and wet.
The ball went up, up, and down,
Then into the net and on the ground.
The buzzer had now given a loud ringing.
Then players danced and began singing.
As players began to take a bow,
The crowd was screaming out loud, "Wow."
At the end of the game, players sat in the shade,
For that's the way soccer is played.
  Marissa Mangano

Strung-Out

When I'm a walkin'
Don't come a knockin'
'Cause no one's gonna be in.
I'm floating high
And when you come by
You might bum me out.
I'll be up,
Like a twister in the sky.
I'll be up,
And then I'll be all right.
  Neeraj Jain

The Answer

To be or not to be,
That is the question, which
Through the elect arises,
But everyone is said
To the election rises.

To be and not to be,
That is the answer,
Which
Mankind in him awaits,
Whenever quest is inward
And inward strike its waves.
  Popescu Elena Liliana

Everlasting

Change and rearrange,
behaviour of a free man.
No persona non grata,
out of fata morgana.

They don't need to speak,
they don't need to seek
when they know the reason why,
and only they can try.

Like the names of seasons are to give,
to say, to pray for a free way to live.
Into circumstances, making chances;
no more questions, taking advances.

Romancing time to run free,
although reality makes you see.
'Cause what we see is everlasting.
It means almost everything.
  Benjamin Marijanan

Friends

We depend on our friends
Our friends depend on us
If it weren't for our friends
It would be a hard life
Friends give us advice
They help us along the way
Everyone has friends
We have a best friend
We tell friends our secrets
And know they won't tell anyone
Friends are the best gift in the world
  Sophie Bastarache

Let the Wind Blow

Let the wind blow,
Whatever way it wishes to go.
Let the wind blow,
Let it fly with the crow.
At last, may it stop gently,
And let it past just the same.
Let it breathe in, let it see,
The wind is never tame.
When the crow takes the soul,
It will sometime
Let the wind fill in the hole.
Then allow it to climb
Back into the sky
Where it will meet its past.
Let the wind blow.
It could happen so fast,
Let the wind blow,
To leave the human eye.
Let the wind blow. . . .

Cynthia Byrnes

Brighter Days

Sad, confused, and alone,
she cries herself to sleep;
for, deep within her broken heart
are secrets that she keeps.
For, so very long ago,
she lost her heart to love,
and lost her faith in everything,
and cursed the gods above.
There was no turning back,
nor excuses that would do;
for, when it came right down to it,
there was no question who.
But over time the wounds would heal,
her—sure of her way.
Longing to feel loved again,
she dreamed of brighter days.
There were no guarantees in life,
she knew, and expected none;
and when she fell upon true love,
her brighter days would come!

Kerrie Dart

Sunflowers

Sunflowers smiling
Happily toward the sun
Shifting into brown.

Angelica Kilander

Truth?

Truth knows you.
Do you know truth?
Do you speak, creep, or cry?
If you tell wrong, you prove my point.
So do you speak, creep, or cry?

Bonnie James

Thanks Be to You

Thanks for the sunshine warm and bright,
Blue skies up above—
Thanks for the laughter in my life,
Many blessings of love.

The gift of bird song, free and sweet—
Tiny animals at my feet!
Thanks for this life, and trees so strong,
You made nothing that was wrong.

Help my heart to soar with you,
To dance with joy at life's rainbow hue.
Guide me kindly day by day—
So that I may grow and follow your way.

Thank you, Lord, for being there,
With you I have no fear!
You guide my steps, you hold my hand,
I see you in this perfect land.

So help me daily, to say thank you, Lord,
And may all men with one accord
Know that life without God's care,
Would mean that no one would be here.

Shirley Maypother

My Friend

Please accept me as I am,
For I am me, there is no other.
I am a friend God chose to walk with thee
Even for a time, along life's way.
God caused me to pause and stop awhile,
And talk and share sweet memories
Of the past, precious dreams of the present,
And desires of the heart's tomorrows.
We have walked betimes, hands clasped
In love's friendship, each heart beating in rhythm,
Each mind's thoughts tuned to the other's.
Yes, we have been close, two spirits entwined,
Each in the other, God between
Makes friendship gleam, it can but grow,
Though time and distance may part us.
For, I am me, and you are you,
And God hath joined two hearts as friends
Just like no other.

Hilda Vaughan

The Silent Room

In the vacant silence of the gloomy bed chamber,
I stand weeping,
weeping for one passed away,
in the very room in which I stand.
Then upon my shoulder I feel a hand,
and a presence,
which lifts me from my misery,
and a voice sounds in the hollow stillness,
and a footstep behind me
on the stair,
and I turn,
to find no one there.

Ian Mallov

Please Remember

Remember all the times you and I have shared.
Remember the times we showed each other we cared.
Remember our laughs, our tears, and our feelings.
Remember our fun, our games, and our healings.
We were friends, best friends in fact,
But I know I've lost you and couldn't get you back.

For years we were together
And hope it'll last forever.
But we lost each other during a fight
And I hoped things would turn out all right.
But it didn't as I know so far,
And I still keep on wishing up upon a star.

I know I was wrong and you were right,
And I'm sorry 'cause it led the fight.
I'm really sorry deep in my heart,
'Cause I know that's why we're apart.
Now you're gone, gone to a deep sleep,
In a coma you stayed still from head to feet.

Forgive me, please, and please do remember
It's me, your friend, your friend forever.
I'm here for you like I used to be.
Forget the fight, but please do REMEMBER ME!
Michelle G. Daculan

Bahama Bay

Walk within sight and sound of the water,
And look with awe at this side of nature,
One moment calm and self-contained, it moves
With sudden fury to foam-flecked anger.

Alone at dawning on an ocean strand,
Oft times in the stillness a voice can be heard,
A mermaid singing her soft siren's croon,
Beguiling words drifting over the sand.

Tenderly teasing, she waves her finger,
Across delicate script upon the shore,
Where sand crabs scrawl subtle lines and angles,
And above fading stars seem to linger.

And it's there in a soft shawl of misty blue,
I am sitting proud, regal, Neptune's daughter,
Barefoot with sun-kissed shoulders, still and straight,
Uplifted and crowned in the sun's golden hue.
Molly S. Taylor

The Rebirth

From a dark womb have I sprung forth untamed,
The beast, unclothèd and coolly suckling,
In wailing lament eternally shamed;
The wicked babe thrust unto the living.
Mine love's humour doth wrest the savage bane
From the stone where flows a steely river;
Unto its veins her tears pour crimson rain,
And beguile nature's parchèd wither.
Clad no longer in matted fur am I,
O, noble hound of happy countenance!
But should love leave the filthy brute to lie
In mockery of manly radiance,
Then content am I with mine beastly state,
For, the beast hath conquered animal's fate!
Christian Szabo

Not Ever

I have sailed upon the high seas,
and I've sat in the shade
of the world's tallest trees.

I have seen a silver rainbow
dancing in the Kalahari
midnight sands,
and I've stood beneath the floor
of an ocean,
resting high on a mountain top.

I have walked in the morning
mists of south east Asia,
and I've bathed in the heat
of Costa del Sol afternoons.

But never have I known a splendor
to equal the light
that shines in the loving eyes
of my one and only Miriana.

Not ever.
Robert Downing

Mirrors

Everywhere around,
Just take a look:
Walking, siting, talking,
Mirrors of the life.

Many, many mirrors,
Each can only show
Small part of the game,
Big game of the life.

Many books are written,
Many movies seen,
Parents shown children
What is good and bad.

Mirrors showed a lot.
Still always one can learn,
If eyes clearly see,
And ears want to listen.

Walking among them
Trying just the best,
Sometimes seems so hard,
Giving a right reflection.
Vedran Dilberovic

The Elements of Love

Only the sky knows
How much my love for you is true
Only on the wind flows
All the love that I have for you

Only fire's desires
Our love inspires
Only the heat of the day
My sadness takes away

Only water shares
If destiny will happen
Only the ocean
Can contain our cares

Only the Earth knows
Without you I can't sleep
Only nature shows
How our love is deep

All these elements
Prove that you and me
Will reach beyond eternity
And forever our love haunts
Sebastien Roy

I'm the One

I'm the sword,
the one that kills everyone.

I'm the eagle,
the one that flies to the sun.

I'm the fire,
The one that burns.

I'm the blood,
the one that flows through my veins.

I'm the heart,
the one that keeps you alive.

I'm the evil,
the one who controls the hell.

I'm the power,
the one that gives you the light.

But I'm not GOD,
Because I don't feel love!
Leonardo Bertschinger

Blood

At the moment He took His last breath,
the Earth died.
The floodgates of heaven opened
And down fell the tears of His Father.
The sky became like night, black,
full of hate and revenge.

Vengeance is mine, sayeth the Lord,
but this was not vengeance.
It was an eternal outpouring of love.
It was a gift,
It was life
To live abundantly,

From the moment He took His last breath,
To the minute you take yours.
Jenni Reich

Feelings

I love you, I swear,
Because to me, you're so dear
That whenever you're not near
I shed a tear.

Your sweetness
Is my weakness,
And your tenderness
Is endless.

Every single day,
Every night I lie,
Though you're far away
It's you I dream of, always.

You're the light
In my night
That shines so bright,
And I can't let you go, but hold you right.

My feelings for you will never
Change whatsoever,
So let's be together
And have something to cherish in or lives forever.
John Odede

Lustre

Somewhere in a place . . .
Two hearts crossed in space
Enveloped by the power of grace
Beating in rhythm at the same pace

Fulfilling two lives with a profound love
Glowing bright like the stars above
Embodied souls becoming one
Embraced in a life that has just begun

You arouse in me your warmth and splendour
And entice me with your passion so tender
In my mind I see your smiles
Filled with beauty between the miles . . .

Of my feelings you made me aware
Giving my eyes a sensuous glare
Though the distance keeps us apart
You are always in my heart
Carla Marisa da Fonseca

Untitled

As I look down on this world I see,
the lack of love intimidates me.
My tears become rain and pour down on what's beneath.
They do now make a difference, but without any grief.
The birds look different when you are up here:
Freedom beyond with no limits, no fear.
A flower now blows in the heavenly winds,
Take notice how unlimited one flower is.
Everything I imagined simply became real.
The sun brings the warmth I always can feel.
The crickets in the night are composers unseen,
In this cathedral of life, or is it only a dream?
The night summons the stars like a king on a throne.
The moon commands the waters, but everything's un-shown.
But I am up here, alone like before,
Taking for granted my life in this game once more.
When I look down this time in fearless pain,
Something happens, unreal, I feel my rain.
There is nothing left up here to see
Except for the loneliness that is there for me.
   Angela Barkhouse

Someone to Watch over Me

Many days have now passed since I last saw her face,
and she knows that I regret not giving chase
to the many open miles that have kept us apart
since the last day we spoke and she knew to depart.
Her departure was quick and she did not feel pain,
but not saying good-bye left me something to gain.

The feeling that I carry when I know she is near,
and she kisses my cheek and says, "Good night my dear."
I often wonder how she lives her life now
between the world I am in, and it seems that somehow
we are not far apart and when I feel sad or sublime
she always seems to have enough time.

For, the ones who still love her and call her by name,
they will always be close and their admiration still the same.
Since they do not need to be afraid when their time will come,
She will protect them from harm lost in the sea.
Their simple reminders are still lost in the sea,
for that's where she is, a wave's kisses away from me. . . .
   Lisa Cyr

Musings on an Airline Flight

Like a bird, our plane is poised
To climb to the high reaches of the sky.
Testing the thin air, soaring, reaching,
Carrying us to our destination to arrive by and by.
From our eyrie in the high blue air,
We look down like eagles upon the fastened Earth
As we soar above serrated rows of clouds
That depend upon the very air for birth.
Passing high o'er snowy farms, woods, and silenced waters,
The route north over frozen wastes with tortured rivers,
We pass unknowingly in the air
Perhaps only a misty, white band that quivers
To mark our passing.
Seeing frozen circles—perhaps a meteor, who knows?
The glaciers that scoured the land,
Leaving their marks down the millenniums, across the snows,
Sunlight reflecting as if off bits of glass.
Sky now misty with high cirrus,
And so we fly on as the hours slowly pass.
   Lyn Collis

Clearwater, My Home Town

Memory of a little town that nestled on the hill
The valley down below it lay very, very still
With cattle wandering here and there and a river running by
A swimming hole where we would go has now almost gone dry
The long train bridge that spans across stands out against the sky
The large school bell whose toll was heard
Sits silently as you drive by
The old school house has been replaced
New schools, new times, and new ways
The churches still welcome all who come
A welcome with music, hymns, and praise
The park where baseball games were played
Continues there in bigger ways
The rink my father loved so dear
The call of the skips so loud and clear
I wandered back after many years
To see what changes had been made
That warm welcome has always stayed
I thank you kindly for the welcome you gave
The day I went to my home town, Clearwater

Beth Parkinson

To Whom It May Concern

I'm writing this just to say good-bye.
It would be rude not to, then go off and die.
So, please don't forget to cover my bird at night.
When people come in the room he gets an awful fright.
Also tell the lady down two doors, that I won't be able to clean her floors.
Oh, come on now, please don't cry, if you hold on a minute
I'll tell you why.
You see, life's really getting me down, and people don't listen when I make a sound.
Me and the folks aren't getting along, everything I do seems to be wrong.
When you think you really know someone, they turn on you,
And it's really hard to be happy when you feel so blue.
So please don't worry, it's not anyone's fault.
All good things in life must come to a halt.
I'm not addressing this to anyone in turn.
So I'll guess I'll just put down,
To Whom It May Concern.

Andrea O'Connell

My Twin

The meaning of twin to me
Is much more than the name implies:
It is sharing a lifetime together
From the moment of conception.

A bond forms with every heartbeat,
With the nourishment of one mother at one time,
With the soothing motion of the amniotic fluid,
With the warmth and closeness of another human being forming.

We were as one. That moment of birth that most experience alone,
You shared with me. We landed in a soft bed,
Were hurriedly wrapped in warm blankets,
And placed side by side to face the world.

We absorbed the love encircling us,
Each nourishing gift shared between us,
A little for you and a little for me,
Shared equally so that we would both survive.

The bond we share is still strong.
Life's experiences cannot severe it.
It has wound through our being since birth,
Growing stronger as we did.

Lois McGuire

Passing By

Springing up
Fresh and new
Like flowers on a spring day
So colorful and life like
Our friendship is
Devoted,
Full of trust,
And filled with laughter
I see the moments
Pass by too soon
Caring,
And full of help
You are there when I need you
But we are getting older now
And our lives are becoming filled with others
I see you are hurting
Wishing for the past
To regenerate
But life must move on
And now I am gone. . . .

Tia Kennedy

The Seed

God gave you a child to love and raise
With kindness, beauty, and a lot of praise.
You'll teach them to walk and talk, and then
You'll let them go their own way in the end.
The words you plant at an early age
Will grow like the oak with beauty and grace,
Or rage like a bull let out of the gate,
To destroy and create a great deal of hate.
Each child must learn the right from the wrong,
So teach them beauty, give them strength to be strong,
Create for them a life of which they can be proud,
Don't let them walk within a permanent cloud.
Teach them the meaning of sunshine and rain.
Show them the meaning of life and its gain.
Give them now what they really need.
Give them yourself, you've planted the seed.
Nurture that seed and watch it grow.
Bless their young lives and don't let them go.
Show how forgiveness, understanding, and love,
Were given to all from God up above.

Brenda J. Ollson

Those Dreadful Memories

The time has come,
When all I ever had has come undone.
But memories still linger to haunt me forever,
to ruin the remnants of my life,
to kill the joys,
to enhance the sorrows.
Memories which were once cherished,
now cloud the mind
and heave the heart.
I sit in hopeless wonder
and ask if they will ever vanish.
I receive no reply, and all is dead . . .
except for those dreadful memories,
which are here to stay forever.

Farah Shariff

Flowers

On the coldest night
When the moon shines bright,
And the stars twinkle above,
Flowers grow
Beneath the snow
And fill the ground with love.
When the snow goes away
And the cold's held at bay,
The flowers begin to sprout.
Out of the trees come the deer,
Then their fawns appear,
And we know what love's about.
The flowers stand by
As the bumble bees fly
And spread the nectar around,
So when the cold comes again,
We can all depend
On the flowers beneath the ground.

Andrea Van Tine

A Summer Scene

The busy bee, a bumbling buzz,
A blessed life of pollen and fuzz,
A shallow frog of swamp and mire
Watching the sky for a simple flier.
A row of mums, of colour, and care,
A bumbling bee found his way there.
A one track mind, a focused chore,
A slimy frog, sloth and bore,
A flower happy sharing its seed,
Bumbling yellow, and then the deed!
Sharp snap of power, a lightning crack,
Bewildered bee and lips that smacked,
A gross ribbit, a lonely mum,
A restless stinger in a tummy tum tum!

Jon ImBeau

How Soon?

How soon is too soon
when you're waiting to be?
How soon will the heavens
stretch out to the sea?
How soon will an angel
reach its precious birth?
How soon will the flower
reach the precious earth?
How soon will it take
for her wounded heart to heal?
How soon is too soon
for our lives to become real?
How soon is too soon
for our tears to run dry?
How long will it take
for us to ask why?

Lisa Disanto

A Friend Like You!

A friend like you,
Is hard to find.

You're always true,
  You're always kind.

Where could I find,
  A friend like you?

A friend so kind,
So good, so true!

Bobbi-jo Schell

Endless War

Light there is,
Shadow there will be,
Kindred as brothers,
Foe to each other,

Silent war,
Raging peace,
There is no ending,
Nor any beginning,

Dragon twins,
Of endless strength,
Mighty wings,
Of boundless length,

Spreading life,
Spanning death,
Time itself
Cannot hold their breath,

Burning night,
Glooming day,
Fight by sight,
And vantage nay,

First of all,
End of nothing,
There is no ending,
Nor any beginning . . .

Sevendalino Khay

Good-bye, My Love

Good-bye, my love.

As we lie together again,
You on my left as usual,
Everything seemed so right.

Our emotions took us over.
The passion soon followed.

Everything seemed to stop.
We travelled back to the past.
The bed had become our
magic carpet through time

To another bed, to another you,
Another you, and another me.

Luigino Centritto

Gram

I sit here thinking of times less sad:
My visits with you, how many we had.
Your smile could brighten any room.
Your wisdom, love, and caring bloomed.
As we prepare to say good-bye,
I have to ask, I have to know why.
God answers my questions, as I look to the sky.
Your time has come for heaven above.
I love you, Gram, soar like a dove.

Carrie Billings

White

White is the colour of peace and purity.
Thinking of white reminds me
Of snow and winter, soft and cold,
My grandma's hair, so kind and old.
White is the happy bride of black
And the colour of a white dove's back.
It is a silk wedding veil.
White is a Beluga, a sleek white whale,
A mysterious ghost, visitor from the past.
A guardian angel to watch you to the last.

Samara Leibner

Unfailing Love

Imagine a love wider than the ocean.
Imagine a love higher than the sky.
Imagine a father who will give his son.
For our forgiveness on the cross he must die.

When you're lost and have no one to rely on,
When your heart is bleeding from pain,
If you'll have faith and trust always,
Relief and comfort are yours to gain.

As humans we expect too much,
We demand and depend on each other.
We lie and cheat and murder
Instead of loving our sister and brother.

When your lonely heart aches with hunger,
And your soul is dry with thirst,
Your life will become richly blessed,
If you'll just accept Jesus first.

He's a friend who is always patient and forgiving.
By your side he will faithfully stay.
His ears are always listening,
All you ever have to do is pray.

Laura Diane Grona Morin

Pain

Raindrops sliding down the windowsill.
Tears streaming down my face.
Everything goes wrong for me, nothing ever goes my way.
Thunder.
The pain in my heart that never seems to cease.
Lightning,
A flash of my past,
Grey clouds roll overhead.
The days are passing by,
As I drown in my despair.

Hinna Memon

Yesterday's Tear

A tear every night for eternity straight
Whispered in silence during hours so late,
No one can hear them, no, they'll never know
Of the pain overwhelming me, this undertow.

It's dragging me under, drowning my soul.
As long as we're apart, I'll never be whole.
So with each tear, I say a small prayer
for an end to the torment, does anyone care?

I cry every night, I wish to die every night.
I wake in the morning in terror and fright,
Knowing only that you are not here,
Then calmly I wipe away yesterday's tear.

Now eternity is ending, a blessing has come.
My prayers have been answered like a love song.
God only knows of the pain I still feel
Whenever you're gone, the ache is so real.

I cry without you, I die without you.
Yes, I need your love to
soothingly dispel my fears and
calmly wipe away yesterday's tear.

Dale Sarver

Society Masked

False faces engaging in trivial talk,
Carefully concealing forbidden thought.

Heartaches frozen deep within
Revealed emotions, an unwritten sin.

Society dictates the way to be;
Young rebels, revolt, this is me!

Dare reveal with an open heart,
Dare abandon a dictated part.

Consequences seen freely, ill health abounds,
Spirits stifled on others grounds.

Time to break the crackling mold,
Let not your soul be sold.

Cory D. Staal

The Life of a Trucker and His Wife

From city to city and town to town,
And down the open road,
"White line fever" makes our blood pound,
As we drive on to deliver our load.

Our "home away from home" is our '93 Mack
And we're as comfortable as can be.
We don't work; as a matter of fact
We're "Professional Tourists," you see.

Continuing to travel through this great land,
Free from worry, stress, and strife,
God covers us with His great hand
And carries us safely through this life.

So, the life of a trucker and his wife
Is very blessed, you see.
We have God, a good job, and each other,
And that's everything we need!

Eva E. Brewster

Hidden Feelings

No matter how much I hate it,
It hurts that you don't care.
The time without you by my side,
Has been extremely hard to bear.
I am trying to forget you.
What else is there to do?
You've found a new girl already; now,
Did I mean that little to you?
So, now the days go by so slow,
It's like I'm in a daze.
Why does my life now seem to be
An endless, hurtful maze?
I wish I had the answers,
I wish I knew what to do,
I wish I had you by my side,
To tell me . . .
"I LOVE YOU."

Sabrina Mondello

An Escape

THE WINDOW IS CLEAR,
THE VISION IS NOT,
THE SURF IS CLEAN,
THE SUN IS HOT,
THE SURFER IS A DREAMER,
HE LIKES DREAMING A LOT,
LIFE IS HARD,
BUT OUT IN THE OCEAN,
THE SURFER FORGOT.

Sally Macneill

Unquenched Desires

if only i could dive
to the ocean of your soul
i would surely sacrifice
my life on the shore

wash if i could
your feet with roses and my soul
and then dry them good
with kisses "oh, my goal"

if only your happiness
i could make divine
if only your sadness
i could make mine

oh, my dear love,
my life's all grief and sorrow
if only you could come
and change my tomorrow

they fake my attire
my heart is on fire
i'm burning entire
with unquenched desires

Farzana Yaqoob

Green Grass Grows

green grass grows
without saying,
though
no hard feelings

adjust the beauty,
the beauty
of it all,
to ART

and the grass
grows
green
with saying

Arno Neele

Untitled

What a world we live in,
where fear and horror
play an intricate role:
A world that thrives on
despair and chaos
and degradation of the soul;
where couples fear to bear children
due to social breakdown
and a rise in crime.
A place where even small towns
are no longer safe, and
we are running out of time.
Although this all seems so
very bleak, know that there
is hope, there is a light.
The one Way to true happiness
and ultimate salvation, is
through the One, Jesus Christ!

Thomas Geier Jr.

Confessions

Another fruit has fallen
and landed at my feet.
I picked it up and looked at it
and knew that I could eat.

I knew that I must have a bite,
if only to confirm,
that this particular apple
most likely had a worm.

It came from neighbor's property,
so I really had no right.
But if I pass the opportunity,
I could starve before tonight.

I think up all the excuses
my little brain can find.
I finally decide to compromise.
I'll leave the core behind.

Melissa Turner-Chambers

Untitled

Why can't I just say: I love you, you're the only one,
I've never loved anyone this way before?

Why is it that I can't even call you?
I'm even shy on the phone.
If I could kiss you once then I'd leave you alone.

But I really couldn't,
'Cause I'm hooked,
I'm obsessed,
Your face is all I see, 24 hours a day.

What is it in me that keeps you away?
I only want us to be together,
Forever.

Is that too much to ask?
I know it is,
'Cause a kiss is too much.
Even in front of your friends you can't talk to me.

So I'll just keep dreaming
Until I die.
I'll die thinking of you,
Saying the words: I love you.

Dominique Dube

A Stranger's Good-bye

A woman steps out from the corner's shade.
The daylight is slipping and starting to fade.
The blood drips from her once-beautiful face.
She is wondering how she got to this place.

Taking a step the wrong way,
So many walk by, but they have nothing to say.
She turns in circles, as if in a daze.
She asks for help in so many ways.

The woman realizes she's not going home,
So she turns again and starts to roam.
Each step makes the tears run twice as fast.
How long is this woman gonna last?

Three more steps; she's almost there.
No, wait. She hasn't gone anywhere.

A woman lies in the dark alley street,
Black and blue from head to feet.
When that woman dies who will see,
That the woman was a friend to me?

Josie Kelly

Freedom

Freedom is the most wonderful thing.
It sounds like a bell with a sweet sounding ring.
It's a peaceful way to live and die.
It's the thing that lets you say hello and bye.
It's a bird in the sky, when you let him soar.
It's at dawn when you watch the waves lap the shore.
It's the gargoyles that sit on buildings at night,
Watching the street lamps give off their golden light.
It's climbing a mountain with the ground far below,
With the sun over top of you, golden-yellow.
It's why you don't have to do all with a reason,
The freedom to let creatures change with the seasons.

Lori Groening

Death

A lonely cornfield lies with a lonely path is what I see,
But leading to where?
To death or to a world of new life?
As the black bird flies north facing away from me,
Why do they face away from me? Why is death so crucial?
Why can't we live a long and a happy life?
Oh, but we must go on to a new world, I would hear often.
Oh, but why?
Oh, no, I don't want that to happen to somebody I love.
But what can death do for you except leave you to weep?
Is it a darkness that covers our hearts?
A death of somebody you loved can be cruel to you.
Somebody that did nothing, will hurt you with incredible pain!
My loved chicken died. Oh, how crucial, oh, how terrible!
Oh how I want to be with my small warm yellow, soft chicken.
The death of Fe Fee, oh, how will I ever forget that death?
Oh help me, God, oh, please. Please bring my beloved Fe Fee to me.
The death of Fe Fee blackened my heart!
Now I will never . . .
You'll soon understand why I wrote this sad poem.

Lois Y. Lee

Mania

The waterfall of my consciousness rolling, churning part of me, hating
me, hating part of me, wars waged inside of me, wrist-slitting,
pill-popping nightmare, dream, blessing.
Keep your crack-crank-hash-herb, reality is already warped, mirror to
my mind, bulged, stretched, cracked, distorted view, is this me
and where do I end and you begin when you are over and over and under?
Where are the angels to restore my faith? No slick-dressing, smooth-
talking, ice-dancing angels here, no sloe-eyed Mohammedans
rising before me ascending, descending that endless ladder
running straight, not like my mind twists and turns back on
itself, a Celtic knot of endless intricacy and mind-shattering complexity.
No Alexander to solve my Gordian brain, only a riot squad of Aryan
cherubim blasting me to my knees with fire hoses of censure,
damnation, drowning me with jets of theocracy.

Brooke Herwig

Unconditional Love

There are many lonely people in our world today.
Visit someone in a Nursing home,
It helps them pass the time away.

Some are lonely and forgotten,
You just smile at them and say:
Let's go out for a little walk,
It will brighten up the day.

Sit and talk or read the news
They so want to hear,
Or hold their hand a little while
As they keep rocking while you're near.

Make a cup of tea for two,
Goodies on the side.
Pour the tea in a china cup,
To them it will mean so much.

There is joy of caring for others,
As we will be old one day, we may sit in our rocking chair,
Wondering why no one has come our way.

Love is a gift God gave us, unconditional in every way.
To those who are lonely and broken, these words our Lord has spoken.

Carmen Gass

Imagination

Honey colored sunbeams wash teasingly at my senses, taunting me.
I struggle but cannot ignore their power.
My mind wanders outside to that large expanse of freedom.
The minister's words diffuse quickly like a soap bubble.

I give in to the power, carried away on the wings of fantasy.

I step into the deepest recess of my soul and close the door behind me.
My heart beats slowly to the rhythm of my imagination.
I climb to lofty heights.

I am suspended above the cloistered surrounding of my ordered life.
For a moment I am ruler of this world,
Commander of events,
Adjudicator of my feelings,

Singing.

The door opens and I am thrust back into my abyss of order:
a world of laws,
of four corners.

Will I someday get caught in one of those corners
and never again be able to escape?

Bonnie Ahearn

Tattered and Torn

It's a constant struggle to keep the tears from falling.
The frustration is unbearable. On the outside peace is
Battling to hold on. While inside a raging storm, twists
And torments the soul. Strength and courage are running out.
I feel so alone inside and out; yet, it is the summer and
The air is warm upon my face, all I feel is cold air
Turning me inside out, making my heart hurt with the cold.
My heart aches so badly at times—I fear the pieces will
Never cease falling into shattering piles. The raging storm
Is wreaking havoc and is taking all prisoners against their will.
When one does not know how to swim or does not have that hand
Reaching out to grasp—the life line is so thin, so fragile.
Is it worth the struggle to reach for the fraying line only
To have it break once again?
I beg for peace, for the pain and hurt to dissolve.
Maybe it is sinful to want to vanish; but anything must be
Better than the hell I endure in this heart of mine.
I beg to be released form this loneliness, from this worthless
Body that has no will to go on any longer.

Joanne M. Camerson

My Mother

She stands tall, proud of her being,
Aware of her responsibilities, announcing her title to the world.
She's my Mother.
She's worth more than anyone can afford;
She puts all strengths forward.
She's a leaning post that will never fall; she's my Mother.
She's a rainbow in the sky with her inner beauty shining through;
She's my Mother.
Her courageous character and jovial laughter, her bright smile
And her uplifting spirit encourage everyone; she's my Mother.
She's faithful and honest, trustworthy and easily admired;
She's my Mother.
Our time with her is always cherished, whether we reflect it or not.
It will always be there and so will she; she's my Mother.
That one little word is used so often we tend to forget its true meaning,
Taking her for granted; she's my Mother.
She fulfills the word so greatly; hopefully, I will do the same,
Being a leader just as she is; she's my Mother.
These reasons and more explain mother's love.
Although it's time I let you know why I love you so much,
Because you are my Mother.

Angie Clearly

Remembering

How shall we honor them this day?
We, who remember longingly our glorious dead,
Who in the morning hours of life
Left home, to loved ones bade "farewell,"
And went to fight a war
For country, God, and King.

If only they could speak!
They'd tell us where we have been weak,
And show us where we've failed them so.
They'd give us strength to right the wrongs
That still exist in this old world of ours.
Then, with God's help, we would more nobly live
And, thus, to them a greater tribute bring,
When we in silence stand, remembering!

Carl Currie

Undecided Seasons: The Lovers That Never Were

Sordid yet alluring seems the winter's snow,
Blanketed in stillness is the life we know.

Winter's wrath undaunted, silent, freezing vale,
Melting, glowing, warming, gentle breezes sail.

Patient, thoughtful, guiding, springtime silhouette,
Sympathetic, smiling, ready to forget.

Delicate persuasion, trustworthy and fair,
Courteous, kindhearted, filled with utmost care.

Confronted by darkness, somber, unrefined,
Suddenly uncertain, outcome undefined.

Sneering, so untrusting, as she backs away,
Confident and forceful, winter's here to stay.

Tenderly persistent, comfort in her heart,
Free of hesitation, knowing he must part.

Obligingly docile, melancholy frown,
Abiding her wishes, slowly stepping down.

Heavenly spring returns, after winter parts,
Loving life and nature, opening our hearts.

Magda Mizgalewicz

The Miracle of Life

A bird flew today,
And so did the breeze.
It whispered in my hair,
it became teased.
A child walked today,
with his granddad.
This made him happy,
yes, it had.
A rabbit hopped today,
so did a kangaroo.
Guess what a child did:
a child did too.
A husband kissed today,
he kissed his wife.
Are you wondering how this happens in one day?
Well it's the miracle of life.

Angela Shantz

Tribute (Tribute to Kurt Cobain)

My soul is filled with fears,
And with shouts and lots of sorrows.
My eyes hide the uncried tears—
Am I gonna die tomorrow?

My wild love is now no more—
I hope his soul was somehow saved—
Between us there's a locked door.
If only I could see his grave!

My wild love is now a dream,
Buried deep down there,
Worms and de-carnation are a team
And that isn't damn fair!

Will I end the same way?
Will my youth revolt and moan
That I should stop it now, today?
Can't everybody leave me alone! . . .

Ioana Jurcovan

My Love for You

I'll love you when your hair turns grey,
I'll love you when you're old.
My love for you, it burns so hot,
It never will grow cold.

I'll love you when you're happy,
I'll love you when you're sad.
My love for you, it is so great,
That I'll even love you when you're bad.

When we are together,
The world's a happy place.
Whenever you want to see it,
Just gaze upon my face.

So don't you ever worry
That my love for you will die,
Because I'll love you forever,
Even when you make me cry.

Patricia Read

Trapped Inside

I met a different girl today,
Although she wasn't really new.
She got deeper inside my head
Than I thought could be true.
She showed me she was strong.
She showed me she was tough.
She taught me in anything
Good is not good enough.
She didn't let anyone hurt her.
She never showed her pain.
She made a promise to herself:
She would never cry again.
This girl I met today is loose,
And I learned something instead.
This girl I met today was me,
Just trapped inside my head.

Jackie Joudrey

Vanity of the Beauty Queen

So soon, my sweet, without a trace
The dreary look of ageless time
Will come to claim your pretty face,
Put powerful wrinkles in your prime.
Elwin Neu

Words to Live By

Life is so precious.
Living each day as the last,
Look towards the future
As you reflect on the past.
One minute you're fine and well,
The next could be lived in
Agonizing hell.
Don't take anything for granted.
Don't waste what could be kept,
Because you never know the
Next thing you could get.
Keep peace between your loved ones.
Be true to all your friends,
And remember to have faith
Right up until the end.
As I end these words to live by,
Remember what they say,
Be true to yourself and others,
Each and every day.
Nyomie Ray

I Am Not Stone

With rush of blood, my heart beats,
Sends warmth to my flesh and bone.
In glory, my spirit leaps.
I have life, I am not stone.

But, in the darkness I fear,
My spirit scorns the unknown,
The dread my heart cannot bear.
I wish I were made of stone.

In the midst of pain I weep.
Silence echoes my heart's moan.
All grief my spirit can reap,
Why am I not made of stone?

And yet, after the darkness
Is light, a promise of hope.
My heart feels its warm caress
Upon my vain spirit's grope.

The soothing laugh of a child
Numbs the pain my heart had borne.
In my bleak spirit, life smiled:
Yea, I'm precious, but not stone.
Ofelia Francisco Pabalan

A Woman's Wish

As a little girl with a doll I did play
Knowing that I'll be a parent someday

Then I grew up and soon I got married
Hoping that soon a baby would be carried

With one doctor's visit nothing mattered
All of our dreams were simply shattered

A newborn baby I would not hear cry
This realization just made me die

No one can know how this can feel
That a child to me can never be real.

What really hurts is to hear in the news
Of parents who their children abuse

A precious gift they take for granted
Something I have always wanted

Why can't they treat these children like gold
Hold them precious until they are old

For now we just have to go on
With just myself and my husband John

Even though we may never have children together
We'll have each other forever and ever
Susan Muller

There's No Way Back

Snow falls gently from the blue sky,
Swirling, twirling, it seems like they are
Laughing and giggling and playing tag
In the drifts of the wind.
Some land on branches and lose
Their friends, others fall to the
Ground and make a cotton-like blanket
On the ground.
New footprints haven't been made yet.
The wind picks up again and the
Blanket is ruined. The little flakes
End up where they started.
Falling . . . falling . . . gone. . . .
Sandra Miller

Untitled

I sing of peace like a sweet candy.
It feels like a cool breeze touching
My face and sounds like birds chirping
In the distance. It looks like a paradise
With green trees and a babbling brook.
The smell of wild, exotic flowers is in the air,
As I sit in peace.
Ryan Winn

Life

The sun is leaving, the moon is coming.
The leaves are falling, the trees are balding.
A baby is born, an old man dies,
then life continues.
Sheena R. M. Belisle

The Doctor

Daily he goes upon his rounds of mercy,
This doctor with the charming smile,
Probing the mystery of disease,
To relieve the suffering of his fellow men,
A special kind of man is he.

When I was sick, struck by an illness,
Terrifyingly rare,
I sought him, and placing my life
Within his care, I found compassion, goodness,
Gentleness, humility,
And hope, when hope had ceased to be.

Under the skill of the surgeon's hands,
With the great physician's healing touch,
A miracle was wrought in me,
For I was given life a new, I was made whole.

Can I repay these dedicated men? Nay,
But I can pray for them each day
And humbly give my thanks
For the gift bestowed on me,
That priceless gift of health.

Margaret Giles

Mobius Strip

There is no line between love and hate
Just like winding roads are in some ways straight
Two things opposite are always the same
The ones you forgive are the ones that you blame
There is always a beauty to the things
that disgust you
The ones who tell you everything are the ones
who don't trust you
The light your soul feels is the
darkness you see
The sky for which you reach is the ground
beneath your feet
Life is death and death is birth
Just as value has absolutely no worth
The things you know now you must learn
Whatever you extinguish somewhere still burns
The only thing real for me is but a ghost
I hate the one I love the most

Victor Joseph Lorentz

Peace

Peace is the still waters of the shadow-filled lake.
Peace is the beautiful sounds that the loons make.
Peace is staring, looking at the night sky,
Peace is everything: the world passing by.

Peace is beauty, pure and sweet.
Peace is the spring breeze blowing at your feet.
Peace is a wide-open field filled with dreams.
Peace is a wonderful garden, jumping with light beams.

Peace is hope, peace is a dream,
Peace is a child, peace is a team.
Peace is the flowers, the sun, and the sea.
Peace is our world—can you not see?

Meghan Bruni

Him

Don't let him take over your feelings.
Don't give your heart away.
It will hurt so much less
When he lets you go someday.

Don't be so quick to believe
Something could happen so fast.
It will hurt so much less
When he is haunted by his past.

Don't believe he could be different
When they are so much the same.
Don't blame yourself if it goes wrong.
He too, could be the one to blame.

Don't take him for granted;
It is the worst thing you can do.
For, if it is meant to be, it will be.
If not, the only one hurt will be you.

Amanda Recsetar

Forever

Dedicated to my sister, Dia

I went to a better place, Dia,
A place where all is well.
A place where all is white, Dia:
It's opposite from hell.

Tell mama and papa not to cry, Dia.
Tell Ebeca to be strong.
I will see you sometime again, Dia,
Soon or maybe long.

I know you're praying for me, Dia,
Every single day,
But please understand, Dia,
That I had to go away.

In the other life we'll meet, Dia,
And I'll see your beautiful face,
But first I'll see you in heaven, Dia,
Heaven, a happy place.

You'll always be in my heart, Dia,
As much as I can give.
We'll always be together, Dia,
Forever we shall live.

Amy Lamothe

In Hiding

Burn the candle deep inside,
that's the place where I must hide.
Rays of light that pierce my eyes,
screams of terror that reek the skies.
Heal my wounds without a trace,
Love like Death, without a face.
Time is never time at all,
throwing stones that ne'er will fall.
Broken fragments of the past,
incompleteness that will last.
Death alone will soon arrive,
Joy and Sorrow can't stay alive.

Cynthia Buitenwerf

When There Is Hope

It leads the mind to sober thoughts,
composes the heart to beat with time,
and not retard with despair;
Hope alters the disconsolate soul
to evoke ineffable joy;
In the depths of every heart,
it lies in a tomb;
From the shadows of the past
it emerges, even from ashes,
clear and new, like a beautiful
pearl from the oyster.

Albeit a flickering flame,
it sees us through vicissitudes
one can only imperfectly control;
It revives the glint in the once-
agonized gaze, and even the
quivering lips curve to form a smile.
Transient man has the blessing of
Eternal Hope.

Geeta Pani

Hope

The pain, the hole, how wide, how deep?
Only God can know.
God can fill it with His love.
His comfort—it will show.

Lean not on yourself through this.
God will see you through.
Trust and lean on Him alone.
He will carry you.

He knows the plans He has for you.
He sees the start—the end.
He knows exactly where you are.
Ministering Angels He will send.

As He raised Christ from the dead,
His resurrection power.
God, our Rock, our Refuge;
God our Strength, our Tower.

God did not start this work in you
To leave you on your own.
He'll carry you to completion.
You will never be alone.

Maxine Grimes

Remember 1939–1945

In solitude they lie today
In distant, foreign lands
Their souls have passed the heavenly way
Like winds across the sands
But in our thoughts they still remain
Remembered with love and pride
Their sacrifice was not in vain
In our hearts they still abide
They died for us and won acclaim
A deed remembered by God
So now in Heaven's hall of fame
They rest on clouded sod

H. Ross Hill

Imagine

You're standing on a long, dark road,
no moon or stars in sight.
The only thing that you can see
is the far away flickering light.

You start to walk, you do not run,
your heart is pounding fast.
When suddenly it's standing there
and you have to stop and gasp.

It's big! It's huge! It has 10,000 arms!
Oh, what can it surely be?
Will it keep you here or let you go?
Will you be present or past history?

You stand so still, you do not move,
you dare not even breathe,
and now foolishly you realize
at last, 'tis only a tree!

Melissa Clarke

Is It Love?

Is it love, or just a fantasy?
When you can say I love you
With every part of your heart,
When you can look them in the face
And smile with wide eyes,
When you're willing to let them go
To see if they'll return,
When everything you do or think
Is about or for them.
When every tear you cry
Is for their well being and safety,
When you're willing to do anything,
Even just be their friend,
When you can listen to all their
Thoughts, feelings, and ideas with open ears:
When you can respond in such a manner,
There's feeling and caring behind.
Is it love, or just a fantasy?

Amy Parkinson

Memory

The rain pours down and it feels like tears.
This feeling will stay until the sky clears.
I think back on life, what has been gained?
Nothing but pain that grew when it rained.
I think back on last love,
Never once feeling the dove.
I've gave love and never did receive;
After all this time, I wish I could relieve.
Pain will come and pain will go,
But I am left in forever sorrow.
The smile is make up, it can wash away,
Only it is reapplied each and every day.
The loneliness dawns on me from time to time,
Revealing my emotions I feel like a mime.
Try and try but never understood;
To be understood, if only I could.
Empty, alone, one and oneself;
I can only pull through if I believe in myself.
Independent I stand, alone I am,
One man standing, then the sky clears.

Jeff Philip

Suicide . . . Second Chance

Fragile as a spider's web . . . swinging in a gale force wind,
A twig flies by . . . a corner tears . . . hanging on . . . when will it end?

One day merges with the next, hardly leaving time to breathe;
Escape preoccupies the mind . . . looking for a way to leave.

Problems, once your challenge, now magnify in size,
As any hope and faith you had diminishes and dies.

For a while the bottle helped you cope; you thought it was your friend,
The freedom that it offered you, trapped and tangled, in the end.

And now it seems too hard to bear, each day longer than the last;
One clean cut to end it all . . . a second cut . . . you're slipping fast!

Pain and anger well within; blackness fills your very core;
A white light beacons up a path . . . on the threshold . . . through the door.

As if through mist and swirling fog, you strain to hear a muffled voice.
Your wife is standing by the bed . . . tears are streaming down her face.

Suddenly the world seems small; you and her, guilt and pain;
All those things you never said; the untold times you tried in vain.

Support you thought you never had, arrives from far and near;
And in your deepest knowing, one thing is crystal clear:

Your time to go is not quite yet, you cannot leave the dance;
You still have lots of work to do . . . you've got a second chance!

Ronald J. Boeur

Peaceful

The rays of the morning sun beam down upon my face;
The cool breeze brings a swaying movement to my hair;
The tall oak tree rustles its branches as a robin lands and sings a
Rhythmic tune to relax me;
The rushing water of a nearby stream may be heard as it bathes the
Rocks in the way of its never-ending course;
The moisture of the dewy grass cleanses my skin as it touches my
Pores with tingling impulses;
The quietness of this silence inspires my mind with its presence and
Makes the atmosphere ever so peaceful.

Gloria Zasonski

Past and Present

As different as we all are, we may find things the same as others.
Memories fade like dreams you can't remember.
Friends fade as though you have just met.
Leaving your family, leaving your friends,
Wishing never to return like stars in the sky.

Leaving home, like the moon on the horizon leaving for the day,
Breaking away from fighting with brothers and sisters,
And bond that is soon to be broken although you keep in touch.
Only to remember the good times that were had
Can only make you want to stay.

Growing up on Flintstones makes people see they're all the same.
Hearing things go pop and bang, makes you see it was not all me.
Catching the first butterfly, baseball, are all memories to keep.
Hearing brothers and sisters in trouble, happy it was not you,
Smelling the smell of campfire, freshness after the rain,
makes you want to stay reaching for your parents on that special day,
showing them you have done what you have dreamed of,
wanting them to know you have tried your best.
While you taste your last home-cooked meal before leaving the nest
that they have provided on your way to your new way of living,
only to come home to visit.

Robyn Sieger

Infinity

Infinity is timeless, as the ever-rolling sea.
The sands of time drift aimlessly to find where they should be;
They stand as silent sentinels, protecting you and me.

And as they stand, so silent in their never-ending task,
They beckon through the ages
And call us from the stages of the world where we may pass.

The call: it is a song of life, a melody sublime,
Enriched by many harmonies
With ever-changing cadences of haunting, restless rhyme.

At times, the harmonies are harsh and jarring to the soul,
Their rhythms racing helter-skelter, trying to find the goal.

But then . . . through all the noise, the stark cacophony, the maze . . .
There winds a tiny melody . . . a small, intrusive courier
That speaks of better days.

This melody remembers when the Earth was just begun,
The mystery, the moodiness, the rising of the sun.
It hears an infant's feeble cry . . . the ecstasy of love.
It strokes the soul with healing balm; it celebrates the poet's song;
It rights our worst-imagined wrong,
And sets our path, directs, displays the time that's yet to come.

Barbara Andrus

Untitled

Missing you,
It feels like my heart is being ripped from my chest.
Real love is vulnerable when you let someone see who you really are,
and they love you anyway.
I have done that, and stand before you exposed,
A child in love.
Love grows expectations.
It is a dependency,
Mutually fed,
Mutually enjoyed,
And I am so afraid to depend on this! (Lest it all disappear)
And perhaps, though mostly aware,
I have opened myself up to so much disappointment.

Pamela C. Quait

Why Must We Die?

Because nature says we must?
Once we have had our years on Earth—the winters hard, the summers fair,
But what of little babes and sucklings who go oft before their time
With hardly a deep breath of Earthly air?

No! That cannot be the reason that we die,
say I who lost a precious mate of nearly fifty years
and have been searching for a key to unlock
the pain that festers in my heart.
It is a puzzle that tormented my endless
waking hours whilst I shed blinding
tears and wept for one last embrace.

But now there is a cry that struggles within me to be heard, a cry that grows,
for at last I know why the dead have died.
In the ordinary passage of time—days, months, years,
were all lost in the turmoil of living,
but when man dies, he dies to be remembered
every day from that day forth by loved ones, friends, and even foes.

There is no escaping memory until we in turn become a haunting daily
diary of time gone by, to be remembered with tears, pain,
guilt, immeasurable loss, and love and
love and love eternal.

Harriet R. Wagner

Time Well Spent

When I was but a child of three,
I used to climb on Nana's knee,
Where I would curl into a ball
And feel quite safe, away from it all.

She taught me rhymes and the ABC's.
At four o'clock we'd have our teas,
Sandwiches, cream cakes, a currant bun:
Nana knew how to make it fun.

We'd often go to Whitley Bay
Where in the sand we'd tirelessly play,
Or walk the causeway to St. Mary's lighthouse
And listen to the herring gulls grouse.

Sometimes we'd go to Leazes Park
And sit in the grass where we would talk,
Stringing together daisy chains,
Sauntering home through drizzling rains.

Sitting in front of the warm, coal fire,
Toasting bread on a fork, as we'd try to get drier,
Comfy and cozy in her peaceful home
Where still today, my thoughts often roam.

J. Wallace

The Drop-Out

Hey, man, listen up for a minute,
There's a story you should know,
About someone who made a mistake
And to education said "No!"

I was going to make big money
And I'd be real cool,
With fancy duds and a fancy car.
Who needed to stay in school?

They're having a class reunion next year,
But I know that I ain't gonna go.
The past ten years of my kind of life,
What have I got to show?

Whiz-kid Bill will be there,
He's now a big shot CEO,
With an expensive car and an expensive house.
I hear he's really raking in the dough.

And sweet Joanne, she owns a company,
Publishing magazines and stuff,
How did she ever make it through?
She always found schoolwork tough.

David Armstrong

A Lonely Road

As I walked one day on a lonely road,
all alone and far from home,
I hoped to meet a magical fairy,
for I was young and believed in fantasy.
Perhaps I was smarter then,
for now no mother or father
to guide me through this stone cold world;
now when I walk on this lonely road,
I do not think of fairies,
but think of luck and God itself,
to ensure me of my lucky days.

Ravi Chander

The Planet

What in tarnation is it all about,
The world and people on it?
The planet is such a wondrous place,
And yet, we can't help but destroy it.
The lakes and streams and oceans:
Such beauty you can't believe,
But what do we do, we contaminate
and kill the fish too, if you please.
The forests, God, it's hard to believe
That people higher up,
Who should do better but
apparently do not.
Poor Mother Nature must be crying
To see such damage done,
And our pure, fresh air that
That once was there
Has flown with the midday sun.

Doris Mae Donald

So Do We All

So do we do in coming to
The life that will be lying,
And bearing on the life to do.
Our doing will be dying.

So do we go in going to
Together time unbearing,
As we will know the life we through
No longer will be caring.

Then so we do each day upon
The time that has us sharing,
To have the pain that has us on
To other lives comparing.

But so we wait on time too late,
Tomorrow we'll be crying,
For we've too little done to date
Will move undo to sighing.

So do we all our life undo
To bear we've come to lying,
To life once had to going through
And we so do in dying.

Paul Anthony Lee

Chosen

Isolation extends her welcoming hand
to share in cutting the silver cord,
Hurling the jagged mark of terror
downward by the shrieking sword.

Flailing arms of motherhood,
Injustice to this world she bore,
Seventeenth day of April Fool,
severed, silenced evermore.

Fatal heartbeat, midnight air,
Secrets of the sister dawn,
Chosen fool of Easter prayer
dances with death's dark song.

Brenda N. Quick

Precious Gems

No one having silver and gold
Will treat them carelessly
Even though they are old
They want it to shine properly
To stay in good condition
Locked in proper place
For the next generation
That no one should displace
Those who have them feel great
But thieves will hunt their gate
More precious than these gems
Are the kids God gave to you
How are you helping them
In life to make it through
Leaders for the future
Teach them great things to do
As you learn their nature
They are God's heritage
For him they should engage
He will ask you for them

Gerald Butcher

Mother's Life

The most sacred name in the world.
In times of joy and pain
We could always count on her.

From your first cold
To your first day of school,
Marvelling at your first communion,
For the big piano recital,
To your first pee-wee league goal.

Your graduation from high school,
From your first date with love,
When your love leads to marriage
And she marvels
At her first newborn grandson.

From first presents during Christmas
To your first Thanksgiving dinner.
Mother in all times and occasions,
Most trusted friend and confidant,
You are cherished and loved.

Peter Nikolantonakis

Perish

Horror thought.
He thinks wild.
He drops under no reality of
weakness.
Resisting his inside friends,
defeated he wasn't.
The silence was.
He befriended peace until the hour,
the hour of reasoning.
Now he thought without a smile,
what a senseless reason to perish.
All eternity lonely.
Peacefulness replaced with emptiness,
bravery with fright.
Insanity was by far the best.

Corey Scobie

A Cry in the Night

Walking in an alley in the heat of the night,
running from the danger that will rape me in a fight,
I try to stay calm, I try not to cry.
I pray to God, "Don't let me die."
A fear of panic creeps down my back
as I cross the road of Major Mack.
I'm almost home, I'm almost there,
I won't look back, should I dare?
But as I walk, I can almost hear
the sound of footsteps coming near.
When on my neck I feel a hand,
I turn around to see him stand.
I try to scream but no one is around,
all I can hear is my heart pound.
He pulls me close, I pull away,
the harder I struggle, the more I pay.
It's almost over, "Please! No more!"
I begin to cry as I'm thrown to the floor.
Suddenly, I wake up, my mind filled with steam,
only to realize it had been a dream.

Stephanie Daniele

About Him

He writes
but it isn't just words
the inspiration flows through him
(as it does through me)
escaping through his fingertips
and even if he wanted to make it stop
he couldn't
because he doesn't know where it comes from
just a growing idea like a disease
inside his brain
an ache that won't fade
until everything is out on paper
and then he can rest
and then he can wait
for another voice that needs to speak
its sorrow
and uses him as a way
to be heard

Jessica Wallace

Spring

The buds starting to bloom on the trees,
The grass and plants begin to sprout,
It's spring, the season for growth.
Warmer and warmer each day,
There's green everywhere
And it makes the world look so peaceful.

The birds are chirping their prettiest songs,
Making nests for the young.

The rain falls,
Feeding those beautiful flowers and plants
The water they need to survive.

The sweetest time of the year has begun.

Cheryl Muir

Love Is the Answer

Love is an attitude, love is a prayer.
Reach out to someone and show that you care.

Encourage the heart
That is aching and blue.
It will comfort them,
And uplift you too.

Burdens change shoulders
When prayer is in place.
It will be so plain
On that loved one's face.

Do it now without delay.
Someone is waiting just for you.
Don't put if off another day.
The master is counting on you too.

Love while you can with cheery word or smile.
What's done with a loving heart
Is treasured and worthwhile.
Even if you have nothing else to give,
You can always give encouragement.

Encouragement is the oxygen of the soul.
Florence Thurston

Tears

The tears of joy that glisten on my cheek:
Words, happiness I cannot speak:
Of them what could be said,
From my sure heart they are fed.

Only to see things from a different scope!

As they slowly drift down my face,
From a soul of satin and lace,
My poor head must deal
With the deep-found love that I feel.
Like a heart of knotted rope.

From my brain to my lips,
Like some internal eclipse.
From front to back,
In pure emotion I do not lack.

Of this I can cope!

Only from them I can see
The beauty that exists inside of me.
Like sweet water to right the wrong,
The taste of salt that makes me strong.

In this song of hope!
Philip Edward Porter

A Gift of Love

Happy are the moments I am greeted with each morn.
Love is the essence with which I'm adorned,
I feel life in its fullest as it bursts from my heart
Allowing me to see light where there used to be dark.
To share this with another is a desire unbound.
This power of love is ours to be found,
Allow me to give this gift to you,
Then you will be giving it back to me too.
Judy Swallow

Toronto the Good

The endless trains of time
Prey upon my mind.
Let not the noise,
Confusion of the city
Block out the good.
Sing in my heart
The roasting chestnuts,
The art work for sale.
The excitement surrounds me
And enriches my heart.
Sherry Normandeau

Big Bro

Green, shiny eyes,
Goldish-brown hair,
Has a cheeky grin,
And swings on his chair!

When he is puzzled,
He'll scratch his chin.
He has very white skin,
And is very thin.

Thinks I'm made of glass,
And though I'm very tall,
He still thinks I'm a baby,
All delicate and small.

When I'm bored,
He'll tease me,
Or help me build a sand castle,
When we're by the sea.

I love my big brother,
For when he is near,
As if by magic,
My troubles disappear.
Donia Sawwan

In the End

Thunder roars,
Rain comes down.
Her cries are heard
Throughout the town.
Another loved one gone
For her to cry tears.
So as she leaves too,
The whole town will hear
A very sad tale
About a very sad girl
Whose heart could be shattered
Like a glass-plated pearl.
She'd lived a sad life,
That's what the papers had said.
Two shots to her heart,
And the sad girl was dead.
Virginia Matthias

Kin Dread

Wrapped in a layer of warmth,
Not even taking a breath,
Quietly lying very still,
Using my strength of will
To hope and to pray
That it will go away,
That twisted face of hate.
Or is it to be my fate
To look into those eyes
And wish that I could die?

Years have the memory faded.
My mind through mire has waded,
Awaiting the hoped-for day
When all the horror goes away,
To claim that time as mine
And never will I pine,
To be back in a home
Where I always felt alone
Amongst souls pulled apart
By a vile, evil heart.

Debbie Duffy-Bone

Transitions

The dark is coming.
Now land grows silent and still.
Morning changes all.

Michael Fleming

St. Valentine's Day

Hearts and flowers and candy
Are appearing everywhere.
With fancy cards, with bows and lace,
That day is drawing near.

St. Valentine's, the day of love,
And Cupid with his bow,
And little arrows filled with love
Will soon be letting go.

He shoots them here and everywhere
With hardly any thought,
And you can't hear or feel them
Until they hit your heart.

So on the fourteenth of the month
Be careful no to tarry,
Or you'll be next to fall in love
On the fourteenth of February.

Adam Lewis

Untitled

Fear employs me—the work need not be explained;
Hand extended, fate uncertain . . .
Legend tells no other exists above
Your trust, your word,
My religion.

Memory allows me to presume all will be conquered.
Weight, pain, struggle, exchanged in binary system:
Stars, two, compatible evolution,
Burden, flash; magnetism strong,
Death inevitable.

It is about me—although you believe you;
Standing in my way—the legend I believe
Laced with forever and eternity for always,
My decision to abide killing me.
It competes with you—you hate to lose.

Mass, a measure of what is within.
Do I speak of mine or yours?
This binary system, orbiting around a common mass,
It is mine.
All within you absorbs into me.

Nicole Neverson

Lovely Feelings

What are my feelings?
Are they anger? A furious burning
Inside that can control itself but still
Is ready to burst?
Is it sadness? A great depression that
Sucks the scorned life out of me?
Or is it love? A desire to feel love,
Yet express love at the same time, and
A desire to feel the power of love so they
Can overcome the anger, burning,
Sadness, depression, and just pure
Hate that a thing can feel?
All numb, dead feelings lurking and
Searching for their next victim.
"Love will redeem," they say, some believe,
But some fear love; they fear that their
Hearts may be broken and dreams shattered.
Yet, if they open their hearts and shed
A little light on love, then slowly, slowly,
Life should come together.

Dani Jackson

Unforeseen Singular

Upon this lifeless world alone I stand,
Looking onto those who've tread this way.
Searching for a stable, open hand,
And one to tell me of the coming day.
But one advice has helped me live thus far,
It is to know that life is but a game;
On which to act and wish upon a star,
In hopes to someday win fortune and fame.
But till the day my pawn becomes a queen,
I'll think of all the places that I've gone.
No longer with the dice between my rings,
I shall throw away all chance, and spread my wings.

Melissa Ramballie

Silent Despair

Lonely is the word today.
I feel pain. I feel dismay.

All depressed and nowhere to turn.
No one understands this joy for which I yearn.

This powerful pain so deep in my soul,
is dragging my heart inside the big black hole.

No one understands this pain that I feel,
'cause Cupid has captured my friends, my peers.

I stand by watching with these single eyes seeing
a parade of lovers walk right by.

This pain in my heart, so deep in my soul,
hurt by Cupid, but not by his bow.
These wondering eyes have nowhere to turn,
instead of the dreamy haze, I see the emptiness of my heart, of my soul.

No one knows of this path that I feel,
'cause it's locked up tighter than a vacuum seal.
But I'm ready to burst, to free my soul,
to open my heart to some happiness, not sorrow.

Crying in the rain, with water down my face,
so my friends won't see this empty space.

Kimberley A. Hoch

Not Weeping

Dedicated to the goddess Diana

Symmetry drawn and settled into place.
Gentle ridged valley-sides reflect in Nemi's waters
their double-image
one surfaced as the real,
the other submerged into the cool
separations of memory.

Set below the village is Diana's moon-shaped lake,
glass-fired and concentrated in the explosive
desire to release her waters into adjacent valleys.

Droplets find their way into uplifted crevices even when
a sag in the surface suggests a momentary
decline, inmost and obscure.

We know that the lymph seeps out from
carved-in tunnels; it rushes through spaces
to fill the body's cavities.

We watch the outpouring,
continuous and unreserved: steady rivulets of spring
waters to be collected with care into green-stained
bottles set aside for the after-moments
when the thirst of your nearness awakens.

Mary Ioannou

The Satisfied

We scorn the drug addict,
despise the alcoholic,
for both cloak what's real,
what's conscious, and what's logic.

We applaud the business man,
cheer the powerful, the wealthy.
We salute the honest,
the gentleman, and the lady.

I fare just like all people.
I honour the mighty, the good, and lovely.
But still . . . there is something amiss.
Why are they and I still unhappy?

Why is the millionaire so lonely, the business man lost?
Why is sometimes the addict more alert than most?

Is the drug and alcohol addict the only one spaced-out?
Ain't I cloaking my life, building my wealth, my honor, my love?

I look around and see a mesmerized world
not knowing where it's going.
I see a very sad world pretending to be gay.

Then who is living?   The satisfied, the contented.

Anthony Zammit

Childhood Memories

As I walk in the halls, people stare and whisper.
Why do they do that? Just because I'm deaf? Shy?
"Look!" they say, "She's short and ugly, she's too shy
and never talks, she's deaf and dumb!"
Go away. Keep away. We don't want you to be our friend.
You're too shy and stupid!
I feel so lonely, I can't stand it anymore. I want to hide so they
can stop hurting my feelings.
I can't stand the whispers and stares anymore.
No friends, oh, how I wish I had friends.
Why are they doing this to me?

They do not know the real me, since I'm shy and deaf,
then why do they hate me so much?
What did I do? Why won't they give me a chance?
I try to make friends, yet, only a few
will be my friends.
I wish, oh, how I wish they would give me a chance to be their friend.
Tasha S. Wigley

Dinonychus

Dinonychus was quite fierce. Its dagger claws could slash and pierce.
Its teeth and foot claws swung about, and made its victim's guts fall out.
It ate all stomachs, fat, and veins. Its belly bulged to show its gains.
The goopy gizzards, blood, and gup were consequently gobbled up.
You see, this creature bit on sight. It went on like this day and night.
It was so greedy, it was said it ate not only meat, but head
And foot and tail and mouth and claw of almost everything it saw.
So finally, it grew so round, its stomach huge and vast and sound,
So massive, fat, I now can prove that when it woke, it couldn't move.
Of course, it bellowed loud for aid. It screamed and yelled, but firmly stayed
Rooted steadfast to the ground, and quite a crowd soon gathered round.
These other dinos watched until the fearsome predator was still.
Then, once full certain it had died,
They cheered and whooped and roared and cried.
They threw a party, saved the whale; they opened up the bottled ale.
Then, as the party gained some throttle,
They even played some spin-the-bottle.
(Just for fish, you understand. You don't find much of those on land.)
And once they'd made and ate some stew, they ate up Dinonychus, too.
Mike McGovern

The Mind's Eyes
Dedicated to my son, Jessie James

As I ride down the bicycle path, legs strong, arms strong,
The sun shines bright and the wind blows strong.
I pedal faster, faster; my heart beats in a racing rhythm.
My mind wanders to the time when Jessie was fine.
He is always on my mind, although he's no
longer with me at this time, only in the eyes of my mind.
I pedal faster, harder; I feel angry inside.
Why me?
I arrive at the end of the bike path.
I sit near the lake shore, enjoying the bright sunshine.
The wind blows the waves onto the shore bank;
Though the day is bright my heart feels
no delight, and my eyes cry for Jessie who is no longer in my life.
As the wind blows on my face and through
my hair, Jessie will always be with me
in the gentle breeze of the wind, the waves
in the water, the brightness of the sunshine,
the hummingbirds in the sky, and the tears in my eyes.
Gloria Battersby

The Lake

In a land where I've never been
There is a lake that I've never seen
Yet this lake it is so real
It lives within me, this I feel

Only a picture have I seen
This lake that is so very green
Reflections from it shimmer through
The effect it has, almost untrue

Yet this lake lives in my mind
It's in my heart and soul in kind
It haunts me with its shimmering colour
This wondrous sight I now discover

As I see it my thoughts unwind
A loving picture springs to mind
A moment of joy and happiness
Shared with a loved one, with sweet caress

The emerald lake, that's how it's known
Beneath a mountain that God honed
That moment I'd have loved to share
Oh, how I wished that I'd been there
B. K. Williams

Be with Her on the Other Side

When Shadows surround you, disguising your fate,
And you sense the presence, the one who awaits,
You run and you hide but know it's too late,
You can't escape the embrace of the one you don't hate.

Its chilling sensation brings you to your knees,
And before your eyes the serpent dangles the keys.
Its glare horrifies with the greatest of ease,
And the demons, they linger in the whispering breeze.

You turn just to see how you got to this place,
This crossing, this channel, the empty embrace,
And there through the darkened mist is her face,
Her beauty shines through the mist with its grace.

Her body inhabits a place you can't see,
But her soul is released and now becomes free.
You know she is where you want to be,
As the tulip beside you falls dead at your knee.

Your love is too strong; you know you must go,
You having nothing left so let it be so.
The reaper, the river, the serpent, they know,
You enter the boat as you let the blood flow.
Daniel Reiff

Snowflake

You were like a single snowflake
So unique, independent, and fragile
Without him
Floating from the sky so softly and unaware
That once you hit the ground
You would become just like all of the others
No longer unique or independent
But still fragile
Melissa Marshall

Friendship

Friendship is farther than a star.
It plays a song by guitar.
Friendship lasts longer than time,
Is a beautiful design,
Makes the coldest night warm,
Is an invisible form
Of something deeper than love,
And more crucial than blood.
Cristin Alsop

The Power of the Rose

A rose can be given
At any time or day.
It can be used as a thoughtful welcome,
Or farewell when going away.

A yellow rose is saved
For the very best of friends,
A sign you hope your friendship
Never, ever ends.

A wilting rose can be a sign of death,
But you should remember life.
This flower has a mystic beauty
That cuts sadness like a knife.

A red rose is a love,
A love that you must share,
Given to another,
Signifies you care.
Lisa Manuel

The Key

Show me the way
And my heart will follow.
Find me the night
That leads to tomorrow.
Bring me the sun
That lights up the sky.
Find me a place
Where nobody cries.
Give me your love,
For that is the key.
Be by my side
As lovers should be.
Adolf Curtis Jr.

The Snowman

He stands there in the snow
With a giant carrot nose.
He loves to play with children,
But soon comes March.
The snowman saw the temperature rise.
Don't you worry.
Don't you cry,
Just build me some other time,
Good-bye!
Jeremy Zorzi

Meet Me at Midnight

Meet me at midnight
out by the dock,
under the brilliance of the stars.
There we will be together,
till the lark sings its sweet song.
Then our parting must take place,
and I, never to see your face again.
Winnie Hui

flight path

one day a body awakens
and knows itself to be
part of the flight
path of its soul.

free-falling becomes
first nature then.

eagle intends its downward rush
held by its own reflection
in a salmon's eye.

salmon hurtling skyward knows
itself to have wings
in another dimension.

where water meets air,
the self-horizon
shifts into rapture,

and breaking upon
the abandon of form
the silence finds the poem.
kim mallett

The Elevator

Sixteenth floor, going down . . .
Life is like a cop's duty,
If done wrong,
You'll get the booty:
Booted right down to square one,
Where there is no possible fun.
During this time you'll want to quit,
Dig yourself down into a six foot pit,
Covering yourself with lots of dirt,
Making the ones around you hurt,
Going straight down to hell,
Where the Devil knows you well,
Ending your life, before it's been lived,
Giving back what hasn't yet been given.
You think you've thought everything through,
But you've got to know what's true to you.
You've got to listen to your heart,
To find out why these things do start.
You could've stopped this in mid-stride.
All you had to do was get rid of your pride.
Shalynn Pauls

The Game of Love

Tears and heartache and pain and all;
Are just part of this treacherous game.
Insecurities, jealousy, and control;
Are just weapons with a name.
This game is a serious one,
Where wonderful dreams of sweet romance
Give power to schemes of deceit.

By now you should know the name
Of this exciting, yet dangerous game;
Whose joy-filled moments of sweet romance
Entice us to gamble, again and again.
Yet, no matter which move a player makes,
Though the pieces may still separate,
The board is in continuous play.
Lillian Brummet

The Swallow

He soars on high and dips and weaves,
gliding deftly between the trees.
Then his purpose realized,
the saga unfolds before my eyes.

He alights on the box, but alas it is taken
by a pair of small sparrows, who appear to be shaken
by the gall of the swallow. Thus setting in motion
the instinctual need to defend. Prove devotion.

For all of their nestlings lay huddled inside,
awaiting the food that their parents provide.
In complete unawareness of what is ensuing,
their eyes not yet open, no chance for a viewing.

And so with gesture the swallow is chastened,
a peck to his head decides flight should be hastened.
He soars, gives his call, and is joined by his mate.
Together they fly, for the eve is now late.
Joyce Laura Bailey

Time Alone

My time alone is precious to me,
It's time to sit and look and see
All the things I did that day
And how I helped in my special way.

I do this where I see it fit,
Where I won't miss one single bit,
Where my thoughts flow wild and free,
Where no one else can bother me.

I ask myself, "Did I live for the Lord?
Did I follow by his accord?"
And most often I'm proud to answer, "Yes,"
Because I know I tried my best.

I pray each and every night
That I might shine with His Holy Light,
To be an example to all I know
That they too will see His awesome glow.

So now I leave you with this thought
That you might learn and be taught
That Jesus is the one and only way,
And see our Saviour Lord someday.

Corinna Fetter

In Memory of Sandra

A friend of ours died suddenly the other day.
When we found out, we didn't know what to say.
We were simply shocked, to say the least.
It's hard to believed she's gone . . . deceased.

So young and beautiful, yes she was.
We all did love her, but why? Because.
We'll never know except for her,
If we could only go back to the way we were.

We sit here and wonder and ask ourselves why,
Why did she leave us, why did she die?
We all did think of her as our friend.
Too soon did her life come to an end.

We will remember her bright blue eyes,
Hear her laugh, see her smile,
Her beautiful, long blonde hair,
All the good times that we shared.

We didn't think her life was so bad.
Now that she's gone, we're all feeling sad.
We keep on asking ourselves why,
Why did she have to go and die?

Marion Thompson

Untitled

Stepping inside to take your place in the bank lineup,
Warm, dry air envelopes you.
Taking off the colorful scarf
And fashionable winter hat,
A spasm of electricity encircles you.
And through thousands of extensions of your scalp,
You are unknowingly connected
To the face, arms, and chest
Of the particularly handsome man behind you.

Nanette Beaulieu

Homework

Homework, oh, homework,
Some do you quick as a wink,
But every time I think of you,
My brain begins to shrink.
Just how can they remember,
If 6x12 is 72?
I never, ever, get it right,
It's way too hard to do!

Ratika Srivastava

The Bridge of Time

I looked into a baby's eyes
And saw the bridge of time,
Within those pools of innocence
In liquid blue sublime.

I saw reflected in those eyes,
The face of one whose form
Was shaped and moulded by the ties
Of those he saw perform.

And realized the weight we bear
In caring for a child,
Whose life is shaped by those who share
Her time, her love, her smiles.

For, someday, when these eyes will gaze
Into the innocence
Of yet another infant's face,
Our presence will be sensed.

Wilfred J. Martin

In the Spring

Little lambs, so soft and fleecy,
Daisies white and leaves so lacy,
Bless nature in the Spring,
Clouds that float and birds that sing.

Thank we now our Heavenly Father
For the springtime joys we gather,
With the birds that soar in flocks,
From sparrows to the gliding hawks.

Joy to all beneath the sun,
As the Lord's love-work is done,
And we each partake the blessings.
Free to all are nature's lessons.

Alda Ogilvie

Champagne Lover

Dedicated to Jens Meyer: 'Twas a dream that should be remembered

Drown thyself with me
In a pool of champagne.
Pure, fiery, cool;
'Twill satisfy pain.

Tingling icicles,
Sparkling passion,
Together we swim
In kinky sensation.

Confess to me thy evil,
Share with me thy bliss,
Reveal thy fantasy,
Give me thy kiss.

'Tis a reverie we breathe;
Erotic, exotic,
Heat calmed by the breaths of the winds,
Their whispers hypnotic.

Full moon cases bewitching luster,
Diamonds above inspiringly glow,
We are together as one when
In champagne we flow.

June Chu

Summer's Youth

In the endless fields
Where lost love rolls
Taken off our shoes
We run on naked soles

Under the daisies under the sky
Rolling in the sunlight breeze
Crouching in the sway of green
Hidden in grassy seas

The waves of the sun break
By clouds few and far between
Lifted hearts of lifted dreams
What may be next and what has been

I couldn't see you for the sunshine
The rays of paradise everywhere
Could it be an angel
Thought I, seeing your glistening hair

In these endless fields
Time's passing in denial
I found heaven in your eyes
When I saw you smile

C. Graham

Friendship

Friendship: It's really
a wondrous thing to have,
because it gets you through tough times
and it makes you feel good.
Yet, some people think
you don't need it.
Friends: People really good at heart.
Life is full of confusion, misery, and death,
but friends get you through it.
Without friendship,
there's no point in living.
Friends are also people
that are not racist.
All over the world in different
places, people suffer with the
cruelty of racism.
Peace and tranquility will one day
return again.
Friends: you can't live with them,
and you can't live without them.

Davina Mendoza

Till the Fat Lady Sings

There are times in every life
when we feel hurt or alone,
but I believe these times
are bridges yet full grown.

We struggle to recapture
the security of what was
and the thing that happens next
happens just because.

And almost in spite of ourselves
we emerge on the other side
with a new understanding, awareness, and strength
that time has chosen to hide.

It's almost as though we must go through the pain
and find the strength to rise above one's slights,
for this struggle is a path that we're destined to take
to grow and reach new heights.

Steven Mckegney

Salvation

She stood at the edge of the hill,
seeing things,
so clear, so still.

Her white dress flittering in the glossy air,
should she fly?
Would she dare?

Life gets clarified, life is clear,
simple things
were so near.

She felt a plunge of enduring strength,
then dropped
a lingering length.

A smile was seen across her face;
the clumsy girl
has left her trace.

Laura Partyka

Untitled

When the world amazes me, could there be endless possibility?

When there is nothing left to show
And the night puts an end to its undying glow,
Is there more, somewhere out there, is there anyone who will care?
We can make love to share, across all the oceans or here at my motions,
Could there ever be someone, without any potions?
With a mind to be thinking, if he'll ever have someone to be,
It's all a little weary, but I wonder if you can hear me?

From all this I am going to make a wish,
Through heaven's delights, the devil we will fight,
To live in a world without the fall, with everyone in a harmonious peace,
To have money without greed, no disease that can't be cured.

The essence of life comes through a seed,
Fertilized through phallic rhymes, sex would be so pure,
That it would cause no one pain, we would all stop playing this game.

So dark it makes us pure, it hides our sins,
Now we can feel in ourselves secure.
Everything works in such a rhythm, that to disturb one thing
Would leave a wound that needed to heal,
Like in Scotland the field full of cattle, for then the world is real,
Back the next day ready for battle.
Robyn Brandt

Sign of Life

Stuck to a lamppost on a crowded street,
Lost among the million papers
Telling people what to do, where they are, or where to go,
The sign flutters in the breeze;
This lone paper quietly asking for attention,
Asking for help it so desperately needs

People walk by without even a glance,
Staring straight ahead, not wanting to see, not wanting to care.
The cloudy sky looks down and laughs.
Suddenly a drop of death falls on its face.
The ink, like its life, starts to run down into nothingness.
The wetness seeps through and the sign is destroyed;
The little sign that simply read, "Help Wanted. . . ."
Brigitte Curé

My Love for You

Sometimes like a storm, violent and proud,
Raging ever more ferociously by the hour,
Sometimes springing forth softly and shyly,
Like the littlest petal on a delicate flower;
This is how it comes, with faces of two, my love for you.

It can be the deepest, darkest inferno,
Sinister, amber flames, craving, consuming,
Quenched finally by its own pearly perfume,
Enrapturing all with the heavenly scent of the blooming;
Of that which comes, in colours white and blue, my love for you.

It wears the mask of a foamingly mad beast gone wild,
Whose growl is meant but as the whimper of a newborn child;
It is dauntingly vast, wide, and infinite,
Yet fragile as each and every passing minute;
It is all of these and much more too, my love for you.

One final note, this love with me does not die,
For certain things, throughout the ages, remain immortal and high;
In every generation or few, love, a true messenger does retrieve;
Always remember, no matter how well the surface may lie and deceive,
Believe it or not! For, honest and true will always be my love for you.
Ryan Beaton

The Pain

Like burning needles slamming through my mind
Nowhere could I find, to get away, a place to hide,
A place to find, and so I hid the pain in my mind.
The belt rose and buckles shone and swiftly on the back
And legs and arms and head the sound did crack,
The screams and cries, and so I hid the child I was
Within my mind and shouted, I will never cry for you again,
Then froze within my mind the child within in diamond case.
The pain did stop and thereafter no pain would come.
From any person, near or far or breaks of bone nor cry,
For, I was hidden in my mind alone without pain, to die.
I did not know my child would die or whither up and never cry,
So adult life just struggled by and the belt fell and buckles shone,
On and on. Taking pain to others with blame unforgiving,
Looking for release from diamond case, and in my mind
A hidden place someone did see and cry, let him free, and I heard the screams
of torment and anguish and heard a voice say, take a deep breath, you'll
be okay, and on my shoulder I felt the hand, and it was I that gave that
horrid cry and shattered the diamond. My child was free and I was looking
into to me and understood at 53 . . . it's over.

Stan Jarvis

Inside the Blink of an Eye

Inside the blink of an eye:
In the midst of the vicious circles of life,
In the disturbingly sonorous thunders,
And in a state of mind in utter helpless imbalance,

My voices of sincere distress echo in the skies;

Where the rage crashes onto the Massive Mountains,
Its free-running shouts collide against the inclement waters
And its vulnerable wounds bleed into the vibrant winds.

I attack the waves—waves of recycled pains.
I relive within each loud outcry—cries that reverberate in my mind.
I know no peace for the while—
I have since been a captive of the hands
 of time.
I sway in passive rhymes, in silent—loud yearnings entwined inside my
 galaxy sublime.

Anoush Demirdjian

The Tree

I knew that human beings and trees were friends a long time ago,
But almost people had already forgotten about it.

I stretched arms as far as possible,
And I brought the shade for children from my heart.

I brought the lullaby and peace of mind for children
From my soft voice.

I was the spiritual community.
children, birds, and animals made one world!

Sometimes I led children to the dreamland
As if I were the west wind which swifts and never stops moving.

Every morning I was looking forward to seeing children
From the bottom of my heart.
Why?

My mind was opened by children,
And children only have the key which used to open my mind.

Teruo Abe

Thomas Fudge

Piety grew so early for Thomas Fudge.
Blessed with his mother's laundry,
He strung his daily lies from sodden porch to post,
Witnessed least by kinsmen,
Viewed most with amity and tolerance,
Thomas scuffed his soulless heart to suede
Spending youth in lieu of brass.
His mettle frayed, the strands sopping
Social darkness, he continued to ply
His menacing arts and married his muse
To feather the travelling castle.
Thomas sowed and sowed again to wrought following,
Shrouding the visceral truths in silence.
He cleansed his sorrowed bones,
Fielding the summary of his ages,
He failed his calloused sons
To roam corduroy lanes,
To seek audience to truth.
He loved his dying god
And lied unto himself.

John Paul McCaffrey

Wall of Darkness

As I wait day and night for someone to come,
I realize that thought was somewhat dumb.
No one has come for many long years,
And stretches throughout my many fears.
I feel I'm alone in a gigantic Earth,
I know it's been like this since my birth.
I have nowhere to go.
And no one to know.
So I lie at night and think in my head:
With this going around, I wish I were dead.
I guess this won't end,
And will not fully mend.
I simply can't beat it by using my smarts,
I will be guided along with my hurting heart.
I feel all alone, and if alone it must be,
At least let me keep my dignity.

Deanne Richardson

Dreams

From faraway places
To faraway times
From the wide open spaces
To the small and confined

A place to escape
To where peace can be found
Where sadness is taken
And happiness found

Where the heart is free
And where love is always round
To where tears leave
And where we can fall and not hit the ground

Where we lie in the clover
That's where we want to be
But when the dream's over
We're sent back to reality

H. Rolufs

Diaspora

Where do the exiles go?
Upon which paths?
Where is their refuge?

Will they ever return?

Oh, people of hunger and cold!
Guests of the cliffs
or huddled in the breezeways,
my heart, too, follows that path
and sighs, shouts, and cries,
and still, none comes to ask us . . .

In what gourd does our hope rot?
Where are our lawyers?
What horror!

The honey of our lives
spilled along the floor.

Huge is the heart of the earth
where our refuge lies.

And alone the roads,

they are full of watchtowers,
barricades, and checkpoints.

Doris Elizabeth Palacios

Fantasy Dream

As I arose from my beauty sleep
I placed afoot on the grounds.
I was in a princess' chamber,
So I took a look around.

Oh, the palace made of gold
As I rushed down the stairs,
I ran outside,
glaring at flying horses in the air.

Leprechauns were gardening
With their little green crew.
I ran near an ocean,
So shiny and sky blue.

I dove into the clear water,
turning into a mermaid of mer.
I saw the God of water
Who turned me into a mortal warrior.

I fought with my sword of silver
Until my enemy killed with a sword.
I lost the battle of justice
and my soul went up to the Lord.

Priya Sen

And Yet I Dare

I dare not think,
but it weighs my soul
and pleads my senses,
begs me to.
I dare not think,
of withered dispositions
and weathered faces,
of spent childhoods and jaded youths,
of precious, young dreams ebbing way,
hopes woven in the knots of a carpet,
the clatter of a loom,
of backs bent from unending labour.
I dare not think,
but I can hear the laboured breathing
and sense the cold hand of despair
grip the young hearts.
I dare not think,
and yet I dare,
for to think is my forte,
and to incite thought another.
   Bushra Aimal

My Life

I've lived a rather full life,
My ups and downs I've had—
Blessed with a loving family
And friends, both good and bad.

I fought a war, helped win the peace—
I've traveled far and wide;
To some I lived a model role,
To others—well, I tried.

Good health was mine, but sometimes
The going has been rough;
I found that childhood dreams come true
If one tries hard enough.

I chose my mate—no—she chose me,
I've often wondered why.
We raised a child—beloved son—
And the years kept slipping by.

Now I find no valid reason
My final days to dread—
Just think! I'll have a head start
On the life that lies ahead.
   Robert M. Fish

The Resting Place

The warrior lies still and alone.
For him, the battle has sung its final song:
The blood soaked clothes,
His face that is wrecked,
The bullet that pierced his heart
When it entered his chest.

Photographs lie by his side
Of a day he took a bride,
When he said his vows
Like death do us part.
Did he realize he would take a bullet in his heart?

What was the last thought
When the bullet struck home?
Was it for his country
Or his loved ones at home?
   Paul Pears

Blind Ambition

My friends I used,
Their trust I abused,
My family my mind forgot,
For things more important,
Or so I thought.

All I wanted was everything,
Not for a moment knowing what that would bring.
Now as I sit and listen to the wind,
I stretch my arms as though to find a friend,
But I always find there's no one there,
No one there to care,
Whether I breathe, live, die,
Or whether I rise to reach the sky.

I did what I had to to reach the top.
Nothing or no one could make me stop,
But now that I've reached my mighty throne,
I find I stand alone.
   Starla Esak

Iniduoh

Touch my body.
Sink your hands
Into the folds
Of my belly.

Reach up inside of me
And grip my heart.
Try to crush it underfoot
With the heel of your boot
And crack open the old wounds—soft white scars
Like the jagged lines
Running from one end of my wrist to the other.

I ran all the way to India
To find God and my soul.
But I lived a lie
Because all I wanted
Was to fly and plunge down
To escape my demons.

It was only my faith that pulled me back.
   Anne Marie B. Bacani

Untitled

I'm losing all my powers of concentration,
Forgetful of my smile and repartee,
In a crowd I can get lost in isolation.
In my mirror I am losing sight of me.

You brought me to this place of introspection,
Led me here and left me on my knees,
Where I'm shuttered and confined by my confusion,
And stripped of my delusion that I'm free.

Your eyes spoke short good byes in consolation,
Like a sullen sunset fading out a sea.
Now your darkness draws me on to destitution,
And a darker dawn is calling out to me.

As my reflection wanes in resolution,
My waking hours grow shorter by degrees.
I'll stand in shadow 'til time brings solution,
And wait in wasteland for someone who sees.

In other arms I'll find my absolution,
And other eyes may drown all urgency,
As morning light will shatter night's illusion,
So other lips will loose your hold on me.
David Norman

The Red Horizon

Dark grey monstrous clouds
That flare with fire and slats of ice
Death of the raging red sun of life
And azure cerulean skies
Deep violent shrieks and cries
Of horror and wrath arise each hour
Devilish screams of malignancy and murder
Haunt the foul-stenched, mucky air
Day shall vanish and night shall be ruled
By wicked spirits and satanic followers of Lucifer
Disease and poverty will engulf all
The creatures of Earth and turn them insane
Doomed are the deviations of this world
For they are the hideous demons of the mortal soul
Deception and scandal shall devour and enslave humanity
And pollute the thoughts of innocence
Damned are the mortals that provoked such
Evil explosions of lust and desire for they will
Die in perfect terror and sin
Qing Huang

A Fierce Battle

Kitty, kitty, I see you there,
Sitting on that velvet chair,
Licking your paws after your lovely feast,
Watching out for that creeping beast.
Sitting crouched, very still, taking aim,
You pounce and get your game.
He tries to run, but he will find
That he is caught, and you don't mind.
You bite him, he bites you;
He screams to get the last of you,
But you are lucky, like a four-leaf clover,
To rest again, for the battle is over.
Kitty, kitty, I see you there,
Sitting on that velvet chair.
Angela Parks

As I Drink My Drink

As I start to drink my drink, I don't
make a single peep.

I can hear the mice squeak.
The mice are beneath the floor,
Under one of my wooden floor boards.
Now I hear them no more!
As I'm in the middle of my drink,
I suddenly think of the colour pink.
I think of the roses that sit in rows.
Now I see those pesky crows.

As I drink down the rest of my drink,
With a little slurp,

I suddenly hear birds chirp.
I can tell it is spring.
Birds fly with a flap from a wing,
As I watch the birds fly by
In the blue cloud-streaked sky.

I wonder where those beautiful blue
birds are.

I figure they can't be far!
Tara J. White

A Golden Beach

Alone I walk on an ocean beach,
dimpled footprints behind me reach.
'Tis quiet, no sound to be heard,
except the cry of an ocean bird.
Gentle waves caress the shore,
erasing footprints forevermore.
The log upon which I chose to rest,
tells me of its lifetime quest.
Its lines and scars tell me tales
of mighty seas, sun, and whales.
A sand bug jumps and when it lands,
it disappears among the sands.
A tiny crab scurries seeking shade,
to find a new home that nature made.
Gentle waves once lapping the shore,
now vent fury with an awesome roar.
I must retreat and head for home,
dimpled footsteps, now covered by foam.
Boiling waves toward me reach,
A story on every Golden Beach.
James R. Coxon

Awakened

When the green weaving leaves
reach for the sunlit sky,
the loon whispers its lonely cry
echoing through the water's edge;
all awakes when a sudden
splashing ripple,
bounds across the disturbed,
glossy mirror;
all is awakening.
When the darkness becomes white,
this is the morning light
awakened by the gentle chill
of an endless blow of air
flowing across my lazy eyes,
all as I can see;
I, my life finally free,
awakened by the morning light.

Calvin Flanagan

His Hand

His hand created the beauty around.
His hand made man from the ground.
His hand gave us the wind and rain.
His hand created man's pain.

His hand gave us the birds and bees.
His hand created all the trees.
His hand gave us his only son.
His hand gave us the Love of this "One."

His hand took away this gift.
His hand gave the world a lift.
His hand did this so we would be
With him, in all eternity.

Gloria McLeod

A Blink of Light

Darkness takes me over
like a nightfall in my mind.
I'd like to run away from here
but there's no door I can find.
My will to live just fades away,
but then there's a blink of light.
The blink means you, my saviour;
only you can end the night.
I was about to lose my hope,
but now I just have to fight.
I have a dream of holding you;
I keep it living and hold it tight.
The love I feel is real and strong;
when I'm lost, it is my guide.
You are the only one I have
when even friends just step aside.

Oskari Ratinen

Everything

Got away from town,
lonely, feeling down,
problems, thoughts, my mind spinning round.

Drop my shoes away,
nothing left to say,
naked feet on ground,
walked away, far away, from town.

Sat under a tree,
I was feeling free . . .
nothing to be found
just a simple sound . . .
birds were singing
and my brain kept on thinking.

Nobody told me . . . I will cry . . .
nobody teach me . . . the way we die . . .
nobody said . . . that I will lie . . .
why-why-why-why?

I am good and bad
and fool and mad . . .
I smile and cry
and live and die . . . why-why-why?

Agis Lambrakis

When You Need a Friend

Whenever you're feeling down and blue,
remember that I'm here for you.

I'm going to stay right by your side now
until the day I die.

Even if you feel alone, sick, or need
someone to hold, I'll be there, I
promise I'll never, ever disappear.

You can trust in me, my friend.
I'll be there to lend a helping hand.

If for some reason we have a fight,
we'll talk it out and make everything all right,

Because friends are forever.

Gillian McMaster

Thoughts of You

When I think of you,
I know Heaven must be real;
It must be the reason true,
For the way you make me feel.

Whenever we are apart,
Only you so much could I miss.
With every beat of my heart,
I think of your smile and its warm tenderness.

Every morning you are my first thought.
You are my last thought every night.
No doubt by Cupid's arrow I have been shot.
How I dream of holding you in my arms so tight.

No thought or dream of you is ever as dear
That it could ever truly replace
Actually having you near,
And seeing your smiling face.

Stephen George Dugan

For Dad

To my father, Bruce Arkilander, who died suddenly on October 24, 1996
I wonder if you are the wind now, whispering through the trees,
or the bright sun in the early morning, shining to say hello.
I wonder if you are an angel, if you have wings, and if you can fly.
I wonder if you'd let me stay a while, with you, up in the clouds.

I wonder how you fill your days, your evenings,
or if you even know the difference.
I am blind; I can't see anything but this world,
an empty world, without you. . . .
Is it empty there, too, Dad?

I wonder if we'll meet again, if I'll have a second chance . . .
Will you still know my name, my face, my voice?
Sometimes, I feel your voice slipping away,
a fading sound, a distant dream, a ray of sunshine I can't grasp.

I wonder if you can see me smiling.
And, I wonder if, when I smile, it makes you happy,
because if it does, I will smile.
I will smile for you, for Dad.

Adrianna Arkilander

Eternal Rapture

Do we betray our hearts, our souls, our very being?
What is this feeling of love? Why does this emotion
control the air we breathe, the life force that pulls us,
the ever aching beat of our heart?
A love so strong, with no barriers to separate one being from another,
two souls forging as one, living, loving, existing
for every waking moment created together.
To look upon with longing and excitement, to long for
and cherish what is, and what can be!
To feel for and want for the highest of dreams, redeemable in the stars.
To accept, not expect, to give, not take, to appreciate, not idolize,
to place above all others, material or otherwise, to grow within
that heated essence, vibrating from their eternal soul.
How do we begin to understand the chaos, bewitching as it may be,
lying endlessly in wait for our souls to be united in eternal rapture.
To awake to a glorious morn', sunshine filtering through your vision,
arousing the sensations of heaven above, to feel and see the vibrant
life force driving you forward, through the eyes of someone so dear,
to look upon that face, to memorize every contour, for precious it is.
This being, this essence of life, this person you love and adore,
gives you life, unconditional love, endlessly and forever eternal.

Christine Henderson

Man and Maiden

Behold her now, the maiden, so devilish and divine.
Her heart enclosed by venom, yet overflowing with kind.
Berry lips, doe eyes, and raven tresses,
ravish the inferno within his breast.

She is freed from the manacles of the demon's abyss.
He intoxicates each fibre, and allows her to know bliss.
He conquers every dragon, that stalks her nightly dreams.
She enchants the beast that torments his soul, his deviation she redeems.

She heals his bleeding wounds and scars, from hearts' battles deep inflicted.
She is the bond that sets him free, when of a crime he is convicted.
He lilts to her the serenade that dances in her soul.
He beckons her to stay with him, to cherish, have, and hold.

They rise and fall with ecstasy, in a sensual embrace.
They have discovered Eden, beneath Heaven's beauteous face.
Their two souls now weave to one, beyond the burning flesh.
Transcending through eternity, this love shall never perish.

Vivi J. Dabee

Timeless

As I sit and reflect about the years gone by,
Each day, each night,
I watch the clock slowly tick off
Another second, another minute, another hour,
And I realize how, when you're watching the clock,
Time goes slow. However, when you are thinking of other things,
Time rushes by you.
Time is like life, when you stand by and watch it,
It goes by slowly,
But when you take chances and dare to live your life,
Taking advantage of every opportunity,
Then life is lived.

When things in life twist and turn,
It's challenging you to live it.

When we're together, time goes unnoticed.
It seems like we've never spent enough time together;
Like we've been having fun, falling in love . . . while time rushes by us.

Life challenged me.
Time wouldn't wait for me.
And I fell in love.
Tammy Hall

The Mistake

You stare as if I am the fire to light your soul.
Eyes so piercing, they see right through me.
Consume my last breath, and make me feel I am without life.
I breathe in, afraid to let it go, as if it is my last one.
My heart beats thunderously.
I know I am still alive, hypnotized by your gaze.
You raise my head with your hand and kiss me.
I see you thrive on every touch, each one more
intense, you want more.
I do not feel in control, my feelings take over;
They roll like the waves in the sea.
All that I see is blurred by my guilt-filled tears.
They burn my eyes, all the pain and confusion
seem too real for this dream; I can't do this.
I want you, but the door cannot open.
It will not open, it is locked, and you
don't hold the key, not for long anyway.
My true soul mate waits for me elsewhere.
Jennifer Williams

To You We Throw the Torch

To you we throw the torch, oh, children of the now generation,
Be yours to hold it high and lead us to a new dispensation.
To you we throw the torch, oh, children of the now generation,
Be yours to hold it high and lead us to a new civilization.

Show us what we could only preach,
And scale the heights we could not reach,
Destroy the shackles—every kind—
That have enslaved the human mind.

Replace true love where hate abounds,
En-tune your hearts to cosmic sounds
Transcending race and creed and clan,
Promote the dignity of man.

Redefine nationality's worth,
Make man a citizen of Earth;
Untie the knots of "cult and "place,"
Answer the challenges of space.

Banish the tyrant and his might,
Thunder again, "Let there be light!"
And when all anxious strivings cease,
Bequeath to mankind Eden's peace.
Harry S. Haughton

The Ghost of Annie

I remember Annie—she wore flowers in her hair
when she danced in fields of daisies.

Now whispers in the wind remind me of her song
that chants the story of a young girl's dream.

Her eyes were callow when I made her cry
through broken promises and countless lies.

With these memories now that haunt me
remains the ghost that follows.

Prancing round these empty halls,
like a lingering curse, a spell long since cast,

An endless, aging torment—a price to pay
for debts long since made,

And how these days tick by
with silent movements of a clock,

Ticking time with fleeting pace
upon the pawn who fell from grace.

The ghost of Annie shall make her peace,
I'm sure, one day when I'm asleep.
   George Porro

Psalms of My Tears

O, love, O, love,
My joyous love,
As the tears sing of this weathered place,
And dance with glee in untamed grace,
When bits of teardrops fill up high
To glorify your love
And so do I,
This brook of teardrops
Muted in thy sight.
When valved tears streamed
This very night
With lanes coating my eyes,
They will show there are no lies.
As like children leaping over the hills
In wandering of tenacity's will,
All is gathered when teardrops sing
Of the last elated flame
When feathered wings of haste do spring
From my eyes,
For which my whole being bears the blame.
   Leroy Burgess

Words to Describe You

I wonder if there are words to describe you.
I wonder if there's a poem I could write
About your charms and desires,
About your beauty and might.
You are a most wonderful person.
Your features are so divine.
There are not enough words to tell you
How much I wish you were mine,
But please don't take this seriously,
True as it might be,
For I could love but one person
And that one person is me.
   Lloyd H. Metzger

Change

You said
she soon will change
you hoped
in time he will alter
yet heard lies
and saw her falter
and him doped

So now make a u-turn
let the tire burn
and the fire retire

Lessen the range
review the facts
limit the scope
go on and adjust
yardstick your acts

Modify your plan
for she will not alter
and he will not change
but my friend then
you can
   Paul Hartal

Abandoned Memory

Lonely soldier standing there,
many people stop and stare.

Few, they know the reason why,
the day had come for you to die.

For most, they come and only look,
recalling writing from a book.

They know not why, and less they care,
of battles won in ice-cold air.

But as for me, I wonder how you feel,
underneath that look of steel.

Then as I watched the crowds go by,
a single tear fell from your eye.

The hours passed, the sky turned grey,
their reverent thoughts are stored away.

But, as for me, I'll persevere.
Good-bye, my friend, until next year.
   R. A. Bob Schneider

A Matter of Principle

Dare not to test me,
For you will be sorry,
And disappointed,
We may just fight and argue.

A brother, a sister, a friend,
An enemy, tough or frail,
I'll send you to jail
Rather than lie for you.

But if you are right,
I'll give up my life
To sacrifice for you;
I'll die to protect you.

So, you live and I die,
To you, this I sigh,
Life is worth living,
When there's a reason for dying.

For what good am I to you,
If to stick to principle, I fail?
Honestly, I love you,
And I'll visit you in jail.
   Alejo Galahad Parucha Jr.

The Crow

Black crow, dark as night
Show me the way
To eternal light.

Black crow, upon my shoulder,
Show me the path
To the love I desire.

Black crow, angel in disguise,
Compel me to become
Very forceful and wise.

Black crow, whom I've come to tame,
Keep bearing gratifying messages
As you've accomplished in my name.

Black crow, whom I know,
Return to me
As you did today . . .
Hope for tomorrow.
   Louise Brunet

One Dark Night

In the dark I lost my path,
And all I could see were the words upon my epitaph.

The branches are thick and cover the light,
I am falling—deep into the night.
A mist enshrouds this maze of trees;
It makes me feel weak, and I stumble to my knees.

The mist recedes,
But the trees remain there
And I find myself fighting
Against odds unfair.

There seems no end, it eludes my sight,
But my hopes and dreams are burning bright,
Even in the darkness on this one night.
   Michaela Knot

Nor Death Do Us Part

When the moon shines o'er the bay
I shall not be far away
You'll hear my whisper in the wind's embrace
You'll feel my lips caress your face

My song of love will circle 'round
A gentle, warm, and soothing sound
My smile you'll see in the water's glow
Then, my Darling, then you'll know

That I am part of everything
The moon, the wind, the birds that sing
My life still echoes in nature's breath
My spirit surrounds you despite ev'n death

When you look at the sky, I'll come down as rain
Together we'll cry tears of bittersweet pain
But the sun'll come out and still I'll be there
Warming your soul, kissing your hair

So don't let sorrow fill your heart
I'll not let anything keep us apart
A true love like ours ne'er will die
Nor, my Darling, nor did I
   Tracy Lynn MacDonell

Life and Beyond

The flower of beauty lasts but a day.
The flame of sky-lamp shines not long.
The colourful rainbow soon fades away.
The life of man too lasts not long.
The sound of music melts soon off.
The string of joy too breaks tune off.
Life is not like shadow, still
Fades away blooming charm and dill.
The flying clouds go out of sight,
Shining stars in sunny light,
Singing birds in silent night,
Life is not always too bright.
The soul with splendour likens right a bloom,
The flower of beauty lasts but for doom.
The soul, like flower, though does it fade
Blooms in heaven brighter in grade.
   Dr. Cherian Kunianthodath

Breaking Point

Listen to their eloquence
As they sink deeper into decadence.
It's not hard to tell the difference
Between the truth and the lies.
Have we reached the breaking point?
See the skies melting—
What is the breaking point?
See our hearts searching.

Everywhere lives suffocate,
Great lies for millennia circulate.
How blindly we discriminate,
Yearning for the private Eden.
Have we reached the breaking point?
See our children fainting—
When is the breaking point?
See our women lamenting.

Open your eyes, one day mankind will live as one.
Open your mind, one day all evils will be undone.
One day after the breaking point.

Tom Klosowski

Spring Time

Spring is on the way,
The signs are all around.
The winter's snow has disappeared,
I see and smell the ground.

The pussy willows all in bud,
I heard a frog today.
A fly went buzzing past my head;
Yes, spring is on its way.

The school yards filled with jump ropes,
The boys are playing Pogs,
And I see people everywhere
Out walking with their dogs.
Yes, spring is surely on its way,
For the sun gets warmer every day.

Florida Gordon

First Swim

She leads you, blindfolded, into the ocean
To show you how to swim.
Her love's a current that swirls around you
And pulls you under at her whim.
She speaks white lies like her native tongue—
You can taste them on her lips.
She wears her pain like a tattoo on her back,
But it's a tidal wave you just can't miss.
She takes you to the top of the highest cliff
To drink from the fountain of life;
Then she pushes you off when your back is turned
And cries out your name as you dive.
And you die inside each time her love's not there—
It leaves you shaking, sweating in despair.
You ache to have it—to taste it, to breathe it—
Your wants, desires, and cravings need it.
Then you wash up on the shore, surprised to be alive.
The waves crash over you and roll you in the mire.
You watch the water go and leave you high and dry—
She takes her love away, but doesn't tell you why.

Jason Laxdal

Untitled

You sit there quietly,
Afraid to say a word.
I try to break through to you,
But it's like you haven't heard.
What secret
Makes you guard your heart?
What pain
Lets friendship play no part?
Maybe letting me in
Would make things easier.
Maybe telling me your hurt
Would bring healing you deserve.
Keep on being silent,
You'll find your friends have left.
'Cause talking to a brick wall
Makes you think leaving is best.
Then who will be there for you?
You'll be here all alone.
Who will hold your hand?
You'll be on your own.

Hanni Oppel

Reflections

God,
I pray because I know you care.
I pray because I know you
will make my dreams come true.
I pray because I love You.

But, God,
one dream was a mistake.
It was just childish retaliation.

And, I was asleep, you see.

God,
in future
grant not all my wishes
unless they be
what you want
for me.

God,
Why did it really happen?
Why, God?
God, why?

Jennifer M. Garnatz

Silence

The finish of all doubts
where life is like heavenly clouds
and laughter will instantly grow
when peace of mind's coming slow.
Things in life will be far
as more as important they are.
But, sometimes much better it is
to see not the things that we miss,
but more of the things that we get,
'cause this makes us lucky guys yet.

Karsten Kutowski

Taking Space

That's not me
In last year's photograph:
Thin,
Huge eyes,
Like a doe on a country road
Staring at the headlights.

This—I am.
This year the photographer
Had to step back
To fit me in his frame:
Fat,
Full of strength,
With an abundant lust for life,
Smiling, and
Taking space.

Tatjana Kruse

Covert Love

No words of Love are spoken
No signs are made overt
A farewell kiss is all that's shown
Then alone to feel the hurt

With arms around each other
We walk the dog at night
Then talk about the weather
When we greet the morning light

The veil that is the dance floor
Hides the secret touch
And blurs the meaning in the eyes
Of the look that says so much

The distance in between us
Bridged by knowing smiles
Is to the others in the room
Measured now in miles

A secret known by everyone
That no one can reveal
For in the heart of all who know
A covért love can feel.

Brian Bignell

Serenity

In the night
Is a great place to be:
All alone,
Quiet,
Stars,
The trees,
And me,
Alone,
By myself.
The night is a great place
To be me.

Carolyn Sapach

Dying in Silence
(About the Dropping of the Atomic Bomb in Hiroshima)

I, looking at these creatures,
think to myself: they're humans just like me,
although their skins are falling apart,
their bodies in pieces,
their children in silence,
throwing up all the time.

I should go to heaven for what I am doing,
trying to help half-dead and lost people,
and for what I am facing alive: hell.

I rescued a lost girl,
her family dead,
her life tragically affected forever.

As I help these people in the sand spit,
other people don't have anybody to help them.
They cry out for help,
but no one listens.

Hiroshima is gone,
its people dying without a thing anybody can do.
At least we are dying for our country,
dying in silence and great agony.

Felipe Fuchs

God's Plan/Self Will

In this world of ours there's so much trouble.
In this world of ours we're sorrow bound.
If we do not heed the plan God gives us,
We may never hear his trumpets sound.

But, from God's plan, the purity's been forgotten
And self-will takes over when it can.
Leading our souls through to destruction,
Self-will is the ruin of a man.

Some men try to rule the world with their bodies.
Some men try to rule the world with charms.
Some men try to rule the world with their own laws,
And some men, they don't think it any harm.

But look at what man's self-will got us into:
Pollution and destruction to His land,
Now we gnash our teeth and blame each other,
And wish that we had followed God's own plan.

We read so many books we think we're learned.
We put ourselves above His master plan,
Create ourselves a world of self indulgence,
Creating final ruin of a man.

Linda L. Macumber Hirschfeld

Beauty's Truth

I hold my breath for fear of change,
this wondrous beauty known not by name.
Yet the flow of water signifies strife,
flowing forever, water is life.
Protected and sheltered from the cruelest rains,
it is as the child who knows not of pain.
Young and innocent, yet as old as time,
surrounded by beauty and untouched by crime,
born from virtue never to die,
unlike cold hearts will never lie.

Andrea Rector

The Curve Ball

I stand at bat, hoping the pitcher will not throw the dreaded curve ball.
The pitcher tries to stare me down.
He tries to make me crack, but I glare right back.

Will he throw a fast ball, a slider, or a curve?
The pitcher winds up, and here comes the pitch.
I swing and I miss as the ball flies by, faster than lightning.

Again the pitcher throws and the ball blows by like the wind.
I can feel the breeze and hear the whistle as the ball goes by.
Two strikes and one more to go.

Will he throw another fast ball?
No. That is too obvious.
He is going to throw it, the dreaded curve.
I can feel it.

The pitcher releases the ball.
I watch the ball as it comes toward me and it feels like eternity.
Will the ball break at the last second, or not?

Only a coward would move and only a fool would hold his position.
The ball comes closer and I pray; "Will it break?"
THUD
No, it did not. Boy, does that hurt.

Robert Greb

Tears

The tears fall as I prepare to say farewell to you
I wish you not to see them, but I can't hide them from you
These tears bear a special message: They're saying I'll miss you
These tears say I'm sad to be leaving you
The great time we had together
The tears will fall and then we will part
Every tear bearing its own special message for you
Message of missing you and of the love
When you see the tears don't be sad, because I love you
They will come for a while, then it will be better
I may still cry and miss you, don't be blue
I love you

Chantale Trahan

Remembering Ludwig: The Poet I Once Knew

I clearly remember him submerged in his Art,
the pencil in his left hand passionately trying to capture
the pulse of a nation North unfolding,
observing men and women, hating and competing,
as if gladiators.
"Oh, this unbearable nightmare"—the poet would write,
and two continents of sadness,
in each eye on each shoulder he would carry.

I also remember him proudly thinking:
vampires and dead souls, of many wearing shoes,
shinning with Hollywood glitter and customer service.
"Oh, this zero landscape"—the poet would write,
as if a giant,
who is unable to breathe any rhythm, any grace, around him.

So, you claimed it was your untameable passion which guided you,
your passion like a river violently flowing between the size of two
volcanoes turbulent,
but, oh, poet—who was he who reading upside down
he worried?
Oh, river—the gift of love, the gift—did you ever know?

Klaus Michelsen

Girl behind the Eyes

Those eyes of blue I actually had never seen before,
Except those like I had seen on TV,
But the image within them was as crystal as their colour,
And they were more real than I could imagine.

They were fired my way and I openly admit
That it is true, for I had already been looking.
The way they have lasted is so incredibly crazy,
Considering the glance only took mere seconds.

I do believe I shall remember them always,
Maybe because they were so fresh and new.
The shame is that she actually gave me the second chance,
But now I may never know the girl behind the eyes.

My mind was so blistered with so many thoughts,
And her actions hit me nothing short of a shock.
My absentmindedness dimmed my senses.
The brightness of those seas could not reach me.

Then again, I could say they did, a lasting impression
I'd say they left. Those eyes have certainly embossed their mark.
A deep regret goes out to the girl behind the eyes,
I may never see again.
Anthony Paletta

The Old Piano

It stood alone and silent, within the antique store,
A very old piano, from days long gone before;
It seemed to beckon to me, as though to say, "Come, play!"
And such was the attraction, I could not turn away.

. . . Seated at piano, my fingers touched the keys,
And like one who is welcome, I felt at once at ease.
Its tone was warm and mellow, and as I improvised,
I knew this old piano had once been loved and prized.

Then, conqu'ring some misgivings, which long had been acquired,
Quite unrehearsed, impromptu, I played as though inspired.
And unaware the music was heard throughout the store,
Surprised, I heard the people applauding for some more.

To be an entertainer was something rather new,
And with uplifted spirit, I felt creative too.
I played the old piano in sentimental mood,
And fondly I'll remember this cherished interlude.
Joan McEwan

Distances from a Train

This land is meadowy, lush, and lenient;
The train I'm on slashes by its pyrrhic
Edges; its earth climbs the walls of houses.
We bluster on, an ancient lyric. A humid man yawns.
Those that are outside are perpendicular to their earth, to my life.
The land is mellow, accidental, outside.
It lends its men jobs, a theory, a wife.
The tufted tracks are the unused ones.
Life through iron, and they stray (as I must) without
Importance through hushed hollows, hasty leaves;
And I watch the evening drip and brood.
There must be, I think, a beckoning somewhere:
"How must I participate, pay rent, enroll?
Which side may I take?"
But only a portioned rattling stares at me.
The grass is bluer now, for evening takes her toll.
So I shall yawn now, like the animals.
I have heard the land, its livid lie;
The sky hangs broken, primal river watching.
Frenetic. I wait for capture; I am a spy.
Rishad Patel

Poem of Love

Dedicated to Marie Rutka

I am writing you this poem of love
That's a lifetime overdue,
About the pain and joy that somehow stemmed from you.
With the knowledge and expression
From deep within my heart,
I have to stay, I want to say:

The reflection of my childhood years,
Not clear in many ways,
Time has healed the wounds that bound me many days.
Your true guidance and affection
Became a part of me.
Your strength so near, I do not fear.

All the moments when I felt so sad,
You're the best friend that I've ever had,
Our bond will never die.
How the love you gave has made me whole,
Penetrating to my inner soul.
I have to let you know, I need to let you know.
For, what would I do if I didn't have you?
I would not wake with a smile on my face.

Karen Rutka

Courage

Look inside yourself,
What do you see?
A dream, determination, or maybe you see me.

I am courage,
The courage that you always need,
The audacity to do anything,
The will to succeed.

Your wishes will come true,
If only you believe
That you are who you are,
Not what others judge you to be.

Look inside yourself
And just believe,
I'll always be me
In spite of what you see.
I'm your courage,
And I will always be.

Gilese Turner

Wish

WISH
One person, what can she do?
She's totally falling, falling for you.
She leaves in tears,
Her words unspoken,
She knows her heart will only get broken.
But what can she say? It's not the time,
Not today, not tomorrow, probably never,
As her heart fills with sorrow.
But what can she say?
What can she do?
For now she knows,
that her wish will never come true.

Jessi Mccartney

The Summer Dream

Soft, pale wisps
Stream and bulge
In the deep blue sky

Blowing the cares and worries
Of the human kind away
To dreams

Bright yellow faces
Dot the green carpet
On the cool, heavy ground

They kiss the ankles of every human
Who wishes to pad through
The Summer Dream

Allison Brown

July

Swimming,
Splashing,
Smiling,

Steam off the sidewalk,
Shouts from the playground,

Singing birds,
Sandy beaches,

Scoops of ice cream,
Sticky faces,

Sailing,
Sun,
Sweat.

Melissa Romlewski

A Walk on the Beach

Sunlight has never
Caressed features so fair,
Nor wind been so blessed
Such form to assail.
Untethered sea background
Sending waves to your feet,
In reverence like subjects
Thee hoping to greet.

We walked that cool day,
We talked and we laughed.
Enjoyed we the moment,
Yet foolish felt I.
For speech came not easily,
Not focused on words.
Unfairly distracted,
By naught but my eye.

Brian H. Luimes

Untitled

Long days,
Even longer nights,

Hopes and dreams
Lost in time and space,

All reason and logic
Scattered with the wind.

Someone's cries
Are lost in the emptiness.
    Garry Mason

(No ducks)

a man
sits
on a park bench
  a paper bag
between
his knees

s u r r o u n d e d by
marigold triangles
    caught
behind crosshatched
construction fencing
and   caution tape

the man
consumes
his picnic Big Mac
        staring
at a cement
duck pond

cheeks swollen
mouth full
drowning
    Samantha Wright

Visions

The frantic scream hits the forest;
drunk tongues recall the sweet passion
to soar above his bitter shadow;
their ugly void repulsive to most.
Then drive into the storm of death—
Stop! and worship the moment.
For, beneath winter moon white light,
lies a delirious, missed vision.
    Erin Browne

Dedicated to my mom who passed away in November at the young age of 48

I Sang a Song

I often sang when I was happy,
Even when I felt lonely and blue.
I sang to entertain me, myself,
On some occasions other people too.

I sang to overcome the drudgery
Of all those odd jobs which I had to do.
I sang to overcome monotony
When there was nothing else for me to do.

I sang while plowing the fields,
While mowing hay in the meadows.
I sang while hiking through the woods
Among the poplar, birch, and willows.

I sang while driving to town on a wagon,
Keeping in time with the clip-clops and rumbling.
I sang while walking five miles from a dance,
Walking the farmers at two in the morning.

I sang while working on construction jobs,
Keeping in time with the sawing and hammering.
I sang to practice all of those songs
Our chorus would sing that same evening.
    William Dale

The Family

He was a tall, lean cowboy,
'Been married three times before.
The child, a precocious teenager,
Some other woman bore.
She was a mid-life spinster
Who had lost her good looks and charm,
But somehow they all came together,
Shared a home on her cattle farm,
He had a cat and a horse and a dog.
She had several of each.
The child, when she came, had nothing,
Only dreams beyond her reach.
At first they were friendly strangers,
But through winter their friendship grew.
The spoke of their past, their hopes, and their dreams.
They shared what each had been through.
She was already "Mom," by spring he was "Dad."
They did not question the why or the how.
These three complete strangers, unlikely to meet,
Had become a family now.
    Tamaara A. Baldwyn

Beautiful Beast

Beautiful model, horrible beast,
Both if you look real hard.
Binge and purge, I don't see why.
You try so hard, yet you know you'll die.
Beautiful beast, horrible model,
Both if you look real hard.
How can you say you're not as thin,
When your clothes hang from you like your skin
from your chin?
Shh! Be quiet, or else they'll know.
Don't stop know, how far can you go?
Beautiful model, horrible beast,
Both if you look real hard.
    Nir Lipsman

Vision

Along the sea wall, a balmy fall day,
Sea gulls land and fly,
Waves gallop, splash,
Tempestuously beat the unyielding rocks.
Eyes focused over and beyond the angry sea,
Majestic mountains confront my thoughts, my vision.

You smile floating gently, extended arm.
You offer to me an open hand,
While the words "I love you" you mimic.
I sit idle. Not once allowing my thoughts to wonder,
To question those feelings that continue to dwell
Endlessly somewhere among the depths of my emotions.

I feel the warmth of your breath,
Impeccable thoughts flood my mind,
And to the sound of crashing waves.
with you I dance, once more.
Cleonice Biondi Covelli

Dreams

Down the slippery slope we're sliding
With never a worry and never a care
What fate is there for us in hiding
What dreams are there that we do not share

Hear the soothing songs we're singing
Share life's fate with all who dare
Hear the bells so loudly ringing
Love God's world that is so fair

Live your thoughts so truly trusting
Keep your friends so tried and true
Eat your cake with the pure white frosting
See the heaven so deeply blue

Search the seven seas so stormy
Find the ship of life so short
See the white clouds float by softly
Steer your ship of fate to port
Rudy Succhorab

Northern Spring

The sun is warming up the sleeping land;
  The snow is settling now
    Beneath the dormant bough.
The icy spears from roof edge downward stand
And liquid diamonds gleam—a wonderland.

The soft winds gently blow
Across the melting snow;
Like ancient tales, the winter trails
Have faded long ago.
The grasses soon appear
To tell that spring is here,
And in the dell, the blossoms swell—
A sign that summer's near.

New life is surging in the strengthening sun;
  The birds sing mating calls
    Through stately forest halls.
Through woodland vales the sparkling waters hum,
And myriad creatures cry, "The spring has come!"
Helge Hongisto

Alexandra, South Africa's Child

tear gas cannot make me cry
you cannot squeeze
water from eyes already
burnt by white rage
plunge me into dirty water
but I will not swallow
your hate
no wires you tape to
my back can shock me
I know all the names
you have for me
fill my arms with trays
to serve you
I will never hand
you my heart
hide me in your shadow
my black skin will
blend in well with your
fears of the dark
Lisa Kireef

Untitled

As I sit in a daze
Thinking of what could have been,
A transcendent haze
Of all that has happened .

How could I be so blind?
How could I not see?
How could I let it happen?
Bittersweet destiny.

How can love go so wrong?
When you know it's all right,
When the truth starts to fade,
and you pray for the light.

Getting caught up
In a whirlwind outside,
Nothing to blame now,
Just human pride.

Looking out, happens all the time.
Everyone learns to carry on.
The sacred beauty of love
Is all lost in a song.
Samantha Milner

Backward Is Life!

If night were day,
and day were night,
it would be justified,
for us to fight;
to run away,
or feel the pain,
one man's death,
is one man's gain.
I lie awake in the night,
and ponder how to stop my fright.
Now I leave,
hope it is for good,
with blood on my sleeve
and rips in my hood.
All I want,
is to believe,
that the world we live in,
can be deceived.

Christopher Shickluna

The Bells

Some people are afraid to die.
Some people are afraid to live.
Some others even know for what
All is this about.

For some people, love is all.
For some others, it's a sin,
But without it we can't live
Even we suffer for to give.

Who cares the way you feel?
Who says that you must try?
'Cause behind every one of us
There's a great bit of proud.

So, why don't you listen
To the bells of your heart?
Why don't you see
The beauty of the stars?

At the end, everything must go
To the exact same place,
And sharing life with someone
Makes the trip at least worthwhile.

Leda Suzana Klassmann

Mombasa

Brown dugs flapping on dry, wrinkled skin,
A woman fights double bent with overripe sacks.
Old Jesus in ruins,
New Bobbing wool plaits,
And smells:
Arab,
Swahili,
Died fat, and decay.
While spittle-stained pavements hold smiling half-men,
Paws out for a coin, or a lure to believe
That the Coppertoned legs can wrap them in love.
My room tastes of the city: stale, damp,
But a home
Like the women on streets
Who wail for the flute
And drown out the crisp BBC.

Murungu

On a Clear Day

Windswept images of lilies framed with gold,
My heart encased in wrought iron of old,
A whisper in the moonlight,
On the trail of a woodland sprite,
A lost soul out in the cold.

Solitary drops of whiskey float to the floor,
A single stream of blood seeping through the door,
The sun blinds a weary man,
Ensnaring him in the Faeries' plan,
To keep him he knows not what for.

The seal hunters speed up their pace.
A tear slides down an infant's face.
The storm rages violently,
My fear grows silently,
She dances, a ballerina without grace.

Voices from within the silent dark
Flying through the heavens on the wings of a lark;
There is strength in the pain,
To look up once again,
The scar on my heart a fading mark.

Sonja Pecnik

Miss You

I remember
how you used to stare at me all day,
how blue your eyes were,
how soft your hair,
how you were always content just to sit with me,
we didn't have to talk.
I remember
how you made me feel,
free and confident,
how happy I was with you by my side.
I remember
how I died inside when I had heard
you left me,
how my heart sank and
my eyes filled with tears.
Stupid dog.

Katelyn Harker

My Heaven, Your Hell

Look through my window and tell me what you can see.
A haze of weeds, ah no, 'tis herbs of borage and rosemary.
There's lemon grass and sage, but you're not interested, I can tell.
All this to me is pure heaven, but your life seems one big hell.

Look through my window and tell me what do you see out there?
Dratted animals, ah no, 'tis my pets; with them my life I do share.
Cats, dogs, budgie, and my dear old parrot as well,
To me, they are shear heaven; to you, they are one shear hell.

I'm looking through my window, now I'll tell you what I can see.
My garden out there, everywhere shrouded in magnificent mystery
"What's that you say?" Money, more money to buy then sell.
My luxury is here in my heaven, your money is damned in hell.

We are looking through my window, the spirits are saying to us:
Take what nature provides, use wisely, be happy and don't make a fuss.
Life is short, eternity's forever. "Does this to you now ring a bell?"
You can choose to live in my heaven
or you can choose to live in your hell.

Mona Tattam

I Am a Girl Who

I am girl who is afraid.
I wonder if I've made him angry again.

I hear his shouts, like thunder screaming down from the sky.
I see his fists beating down like lightning.
I want to stop drowning in the pouring rain of my tears.
I am a girl who feels like she is inside a hurricane.

I pretend the winds will come and carry me away.
I feel like I am being imprisoned here.
I touch the cold face of my jailer.
I wish that he would finally change.
I cry because, deep inside, I know this torture will never cease.
I am a girl who feels trapped.

I accept that this is my fate.
I say that it's none of their business.
I dream that they all understand.
I try to make everything right.
I am a girl who is already dead.

Lindsay Fern Shessel

Don't Expect Blind Faith

If you're so smart and have all the answers,
Why the hell hasn't anything changed?
Are we supposed to believe your predictions,
Or are we being led astray?
The world if full of cynics who cry
The end is near, we're all going to die.
All this talk of doom and gloom,
"I don't subscribe to that point of view."
The world is full of people who live in hope and die in despair.
You prey upon their weakness, steal their dreams, pretending you care.
Perpetual believers lining up to hear it all,
Waiting for their future as you gaze into your crystal ball:
Tell them anything you want, maybe they will take the bait.
If Euthanasia is our destined fate
Have me committed before it's too late.
All my life I've heard your lies, all my life the truth's been disguised.
Too many times I've been deceived, so don't expect me to believe.
There's just too many Barstool Prophets and Microphone Apostles,
Soothsaying doomsday watchers, Psychic Charlatans, and fakes.
Don't you dare preach to me—don't expect blind faith!

Curits Doherty

Thoughts from a Greeting Card Writer

I make up my own greeting cards, both pictures and design,
Because the words are more sincere and the thoughts are mine.
Oh, I suppose they'd be content with some commercial card,
But I've always found a line or two wish I could discard.
So, on the day of birthdays, babies, or anniversaries,
And, yes, even get-well cards, the lines flow out with ease.
Now sympathy cards need little work because in times of grief,
A sincere line of comfort's best—that is my belief.
A dozen roses and a card are ideal for Valentines,
And a lot of cards are quite romantic, oh, such pretty lines,
But they're not the words I'd say and so I leave them be.
I'd rather that my lover read the words that came from me.
They may not be as flowery or filled with metaphors,
But they are from the heart of one who cares a whole lot more.
Some of my friends have told me, "Man, you could do this for money,"
But then the words would not be right. I mean, how can you be funny
Or say congrats or get well soon to someone you can't see?
No thanks. I'd rather write the words for those closest to me.
    Paul Palace

Friendship Lost

We promised ourselves we wouldn't change and be best friends till we die,
But now I'm not too sure if we should even try.
We used to be inseparable, it was always me and you.
Things have changed and now I ask, could our friendship really be through?
I see you with your "new friends" and at times it's painful to see.
It's hard for me to understand that your best friend is someone other than me.
I really hate to think about it, it's a subject I always dread.
I may not want to believe it, but our friendship is hanging by a thread.
I know that you are trying not to let what we had go through the door.
You do make conversation, but we both know it will never be like before.
At nights I lie in bed and wonder how a friendship like this could end so fast.
And yet it was just like yesterday we vowed that it would always last.

I wish on a star and pray to God that what's left of our relationship
will never be erased,
But even though it may be fading, our friendship will always have its
special place . . .
in my heart.
    Bernadette Cabotaje

Prince Edward Island

I was born and raised on P.E.I.,
Where I shall live until I die.
No place on Earth with it can compete:
A Heritage washed by the waves in A Heavenly Retreat.

One time this land was known as "The Million Acre Farm,"
Which endeared many hearts with a special charm.
Acres and acres of fields with potatoes abound,
With huge potential for markets when leaving the ground.

There are no big mountains or great lakes,
So preferably the fertile red soil is all it takes.
The beautiful scenery attracts artists galore,
And visitors keep coming from away, by the score.

The Island people are so kind and so good,
Always ready to lend a hand whene'er they could.
The air is so clean and the water so pure,
This is my way of life, you can be sure!
    Mary C. Barry

The Child in Me

Happily, I run through the forest.
It's all my own adventure.
I feel the wind blow through my hair,
But am stopped by a creature

Of faith and loyalty,
And sadness, fear, and pride.
It lives all alone
In a cave on the inside.

The creature is not human,
But it is in its heart
It has seen the hurt
Of not getting another start.

It captures and hold my eyes.
It beckons me to stay,
To come inside its world
And see its forgiving way

Of help and letting go of what it really wants,
Of what it ever had.
Even though it's a great creature,
Its life is really sad.

Paige Leffler

Unless We Stop It

The air is dry and dirty with soot.
The water is thick with toxins and oil.
So many houses and apartments,
Too many people
With too many things;
Cars by the thousands, buses, and trains.
Too much violence,
With too many crimes and no justice;
Broken dreams, and hopes shattered upon the streets;
Nobody's there when they are needed.
No time left for love or harmony here.
This is what I see,
Unless we stop it.

Alycia Wiffen

The Changing Forest

Tall, big trees connected by vines.
Wet, soggy soil making my shoes sink.
Dark, shady, humid place in which I walk.
Hot, fresh air, good and pleasant to breathe.
Rushing, hurrying animal, up in the trees.
Peaceful.
The calm before the storm.

Whining, clanging machinery, crashing through all.
Falling, stricken trees, collapsing with a thud.
Screeching, disturbed creatures, losing their homes.
Stench, foul smell, smoke, fire.
Dry, scorching air, painful to breathe.

Nothing left.
Emptiness.
Then rain.
All heaven is weeping.

Aya Kiriliuk

Rain

Rain.
It falls silently, quickly
To the green Earth.
The night falls,
It rains
And rains.
The sun shines again,
And dries the Earth.
All is dry once more.

The bad times pass,
Only to followed
Once more by good times.
With this knowledge
You can fulfill your life, in new ways.
For, when the good times pass you by,
They are only closer to you.
And when the bad (or wet) times come,
They are only farther away.
So go out and live and fulfill and enjoy
Life.

Andrew White

The Sun

As the sun crept over the
peaks of the jagged mountain tops,
pushing its way toward
the dark, everlasting sky, sparks
of effort falling until it gave
one last struggle to touch the sky.
Once again it had saved the
world from eternal darkness.

Christina Davis

Dieppe

Under skies and beaches bled
one thousand Canadian soldiers lie
forever eighteen
the guns of yesterday
silent on this grey day and drizzling
as vets on parade
like sticks against the sky
limp through the rain and muck
sucking at their boots

Gathering in disarray
before the graves
furtive fingers swipe at eyes
turned downward
on tormented memory;
unforgiven all these years
where love lies bleeding

D. A. McRae

The Winter Days

Spring comes unexpectedly,
daffodils peeking through the snow.
A life begins and then you see
a time to learn, a time to grow.

Summer follows much too fast,
a joyous time to chase the sun,
a time to love, a time to laugh,
a time to live, a time for fun.

Like autumn leaves the soul matures,
a rich, dark beauty, stronger still,
a warmth, a harvest that endures,
a molding of the human will.

Then winter days—skies overcast—
with vicious storms or gentle snows,
the stronger will survive the blast,
the weaker crumble like a rose.

Let not your winter days be lost,
in fear and trembling, idle pain.
You can no longer bear the cost,
of squandered time, of wasted gain.
Judy Fiala

A Lost Love

I tried to follow the colours
Of which, the rainbows show
Also walk in the paths
Wherever your footsteps go.

I'd like to shine like the noonday sun
Through white clouds, under an azure sky
Which will set in the western horizon.
Perhaps I'll hear the peacock cry.

I'd like to be the evening star
Twinkling in the sky so blue
Near a big, full harvest moon
Lighting a path in life for you.

I'd like to be in your dreams
Which you dream in the night.
I'd like to help you make life's journey
Smooth, truthful, and right.

I'll keep you in my memories
Although we are apart for miles.
I'll think of you always—as
With bright eyes and sweet smiles.
William J. Lambert

Pretend

Take me down to all places dark and bad.
Take me with you.
I'll pretend to know you, I'll show the way
through the end of the beginning.
I can't face the dreams that were lost at sea,
so take me underneath where all is cold
and bitter.
I'll pretend to be your love, I'll pretend
to be what you need.
Take me there, where you belong.
I can wait there for you, but I can't lie.
Nothing there ever lasts,
so let's go there; we'll live and die a forever.
We'll take broken promises and make them believe,
make them believe they're real,
We can try a truth and make it glow,
I can light a candle, and we can drown in
our sorrows,
so take me with you and we can pretend
to be all we're not.
Natalie Hanak

I Wish I Had a Pony

I wish I had a pony of black,
And yet a hackney at that.
It would be very gentle and tame.
I would have "Midnight" for its name.
It would have a pen of its own
And a pasture where it could roam.

In spring, over the puddles we would jump,
And quickly over a fallen tree stump.
Summer days in the river we would splash,
And bound into the forest, quick as a flash.
Just my pony, Midnight, and me
Go sailing by an old oak tree.

In fall days we would take a hike
In the woods which we would like.
We would get our sleds out in winter days,
Flying across the snow, so happy and gay.
I wish I had a pony of black,
And yet a hackney at that.
Christena Albrecht

My Feelings

The way I feel makes me confused.
I have so many decisions that I have to choose.
My mind says no, but my heart says yes:
I don't know which answer would do me best.
I close my eyes and you appear,
Hoping that the answer is near.
Night and day I think about you,
Wondering what I am going to do.
Why is choosing the right so hard?
I wish it were as easy as opening a card.
Choosing the wrong answer is what I will regret,
And it is something I will never forget.
I guess for now I have to look deep in my heart
To see if you take that special part.
Cristina Nigro

Summer Poem

The poet drinks (a woman kisses his lips)
he gets drunk
(temptations, blood, pain, anguish, death,
hunger, and human misery).
To the health!—
of those who die in order to live,
of those who live in order to die.
The night wears, inconsolable,
and as the moon is being drunk, the poet also drinks
his dreams and songs.
His room and its windows are inebriated too,
but the future belongs to us
(it is a hope),
and then the rose appears, opening up its gowns,
and a robin sings cheerfully on the patio,
and the wind was lost in the nakedness of that woman
until the dawn arrived
with its bare feet.
Alfonso Velis

Innocent Murderers and the Insane

The innocent roam the streets
With the insane and the murderers.
They're all common,
Uncommon.

The murderers kill the insane,
While the insane scare the innocent.
They all want what they have,
Yet they don't have what they want.

The insane claim they're the innocent,
While the murders claim they're the insane.
They can't have what they want,
Yet they claim it's what they need.

The innocent try to protect the innocent
And they end up becoming murderers.
Now they have what they don't want,
Yet they claim they're the innocent.

The world is full of imposters
That claim they know who they are.
All they really know is that they need something,
Yet they don't want what they need.
Jason Hamilton

Carnage on the Road

Pathetic, abandoned, small bundle of fur
Matted into a bloodstained blur
Against the unyielding blackness . . .
Were you recently warm, lithe, and free?
Banished forever from burrow or tree?
Were you loved, fed, and caressed,
Snuggled safely at a yielding breast?

Irreversible mould of death I find,
Man's merciless chariots ceaselessly grind,
Devouring the blackness . . .
In the sanctuary only of my soul.
Illogical desire to make you whole,
A futile wish to recreate.
The carnage—
Some can only obliterate.
Maureen V. Schuil

The Meaning of Life

"A panorama of thoughts
Race around in my mind,
While searching for an answer
I'm sure not to find."

"Sought by the sages
Down through the years—
An enigma of mankind
Fraught with its fears."

"The 'Meaning of Life',
Shrouded in mystery—
A riddle for the prophets
Throughout our history."

"We wonder and ponder
The where and the why.
'Man lives—Man dies—
At the command of the One up on High'."

"He alone knows the answer—
The secret is His.
We're just peas in a pod
Seeking to solve the quiz."
Eva Parifsky

My Mother and Me

You give me an eye sore!
Said my mother to me.
I won't budge an inch,
Not even for thee.

I displease her
Out of house and home,
And so on and so forth,
Lest it be known.

Just yesterday
I was the apple of her eye.
We have seen better days,
My mother and I.

But what's done is done,
What's to be will be,
Remembrance of things past:
My mother and me.
Alexis H.D. Tupper

Diamonds in the Sand

Sand on the beach under the blazing sun,
settled in chaos with order all around,
not just heat but pressure too
will turn transparency precious too.
Life is like this if you look.
Do not read it like a book.
Brad Good

Hate Me No More

Who'd ever thought you and me
Who'd ever know this could actually be
Imagine us together at last
No one would think of it
if they looked at our past
I've touched your hand before
but only to stop your swinging fist
It seems so clear now
look how much we have missed
So pronounce your love to me
and hate me no more
As blind man could even see
Our love ending war

Mariana Oliveira

Universal Mother

My soul is empty,
My spirit has flown.
Deep darkness surrounds me,
I suffer alone.

'Tis the fate of mothers,
To bear such great loss,
To feel wrenched, torn, and worn
Like being nailed to the cross.

For there's no place to go
When the soul is not full,
And the spirit just dies,
An eternal lull.

Oh, Mother! Oh, spirit!
Pray, show me the light.
While the darkness endeavours
To swallow my life.

Josephine Taylor

The Love of Husband and Wife

Love is being together,
Enjoying everything in life,
Overcoming all the bad times,
Never dwelling on the strife.

Our road has not been easy:
Rocky shores, then soft sand.
Rough as it has been,
It's kept us hand in hand.

So many times we have fallen
Kind hands have helped us rise.
In everything we strove for
True love has been the prize.

Now as our time grows shorter
Each burden seems to lift.
We know our love is forever,
Our God's most precious gift.

Eva Kitney

In an Evening's Dream

Secrets shared upon an evening's dream;
Love those eyes that I've seen.
To the girl I spy under my sheets;
To the gentle breath she breathes as she sleeps,
The one I love is the only one I know.
To her my love will gently flow.
Hold and embrace;
Tightly kiss upon angelic face,
I love the girl I see in my dreams.
I believe she is real,
And I know she is mine.
Truly, the hardest task was to find her.

Robert J. Richmond Jr.

The Tree of Life

Mythical worlds we live. Mythical minds we have.
Mythical teachings we're taught. Mythical times
we're in. High and low feelings seem to go
bad together, no matter what the weather.
Just hear mother, you'll discover a whole new
cover, like magic potion, that damages
emotion, mixed up in rhyme, damaging time,
a new leaf, an old role-modeled seniority
into control, analyzed facts, stick like tacks,
building the past-tense emotion, pricks your
senses, into that potion of mythical worlds,
minds, teachings, and times.

James Stanley Chisholm

Sea of Flames

Blue eyes bright as the sky,
I will always love you.

Immortalize our love and cherish it forever.
You are the one I will always remember.
I'm gonna take you beyond the limits of my love,
Flying high on the wings of a dove.

Sharing desire and burning like fire,
Feeling your heart beat with mine,
Lying beside you, fire inside you,
Till the end of time.

I am the lightning that strikes you.
Hear the rolling thunder around you.
Sea of flames won't stop me,
Nor mountain high will hold me.
Heaven or hell I'll follow.
You are the one I hollow.

I hear your sight—you hear me breathe.
Yours is the head for my laurel wreath.

Oded Schechter

I Am Only You

Look for me in the morning mists of the mash,
Find me in the sunset fading across the bay,
Hear me in the running rocky river,
Think of me in the memories of your life,
For I am only you . . .

Robert J. Whitty M.D.

Answered Prayer

One day I tried to call you when I was feeling blue,
"Where are you?" I was saying, when I really needed you!

So I called again on Tuesday, hoping surely you'd be there.
But that ole' phone kept ringing, there was nothing I could share.

I thought that I had missed you in between each call I'd made,
So I tried again on Wednesday, hoping you'd be home that day.

Wednesday came and went, and on went Thursday too.
Here it was now Friday, I was feeling very blue.

On Saturday I did some things to keep me occupied.
And before I knew it the day was gone and another had arrived.

On Sunday I just knew right where you would be found.
I went down there and saw you with your head bowed to the ground.

Where have you been I asked you? I've been blue and feeling bad.
And you looked up at me, with a smile so warm and glad.

I've been praying for you, friend, knowing you were feeling blue.
And now prayers are answered 'cause I'm standing here with you.

I prayed for you on Monday and all the days since then,
That you would find the only one who truly is your friend.

He helped you through another week, you never were alone.
He was standing right beside you every time you dialed the phone.

D. Deforest

Amusement Park!

When we went to the amusement park,
We had a whole lot of fun.
We stayed there until it was dark.
There was a great ride called the "Thriller Run."
We went on many different rides,
Including roller coasters, Ferris wheels, and merry-go-rounds.
You must not forget the amazing water slides.
The park was filled with joyous laughter and happy sounds.
The rides that go up and down really made me sick.
After that I had to rest a little bit.
To help my stomach calm itself, I got a Popsicle to lick.
Some of the rides I did not like, I must admit.
We had lots and lots of fun that day.
I can hardly wait until it reopens in May.

Sharon E. Rose

Freedom

Through stained glass windows
I saw the clearing
Through multicolored leaves
I saw the sun flooding through the trees
And I rushed out to meet it

At the clearing

At the edge, I watched dancing leaves twirl in the sunrise
So did my heart

In the stillness of dawn I knelt down, eyes upturned
Tiny residue of tears mingled with dewdrops from the trees
Caressed my face
Moving me
Despair vanished to whence it came

I rejoice
I embraced Mother Earth

I rejoice not for yesterday
I rejoice not for today
But I rejoice for the morn'
For I have reached the clearing

Lolita Johnson

Mourning

This mourning is invisible, I keep searching on my face,
searching for some kind of change that must have taken place.
Sometimes I may be quiet, not saying anything,
but a breaking heart is silent, no sound, no crack, no ring.
Everything is different now, although it looks the same.
I know that nothing ever will be the same again.
My mourning is worse in morning, I can't really say why,
perhaps because it was this time that she was picked to die.
She will never again be hungry, thirsty, or feel cold.
She will never have gray hair, neither wrinkle nor grow old.
It's hard to hear this silence, which is screaming in my head,
I want to scream aloud: She is dead! She is dead!
Because she loved so many things, I see her everywhere,
in plants, in trees, a gentle breeze, in a strangers' thick black hair.
I'm searching for her in strangers, I look right at their faces,
I'm searching for her, searching for her, looking every place.
It's worse for me in the morning, when morning nudges me,
the truth comes back and covers me with cold reality.
Everything has changed now, it left a gaping hole,
she touched my life profoundly, my beautiful Nicole.

Stacey Smail

Love

In a world full of darkness that never stays the same,
The joys that were once felt always end up in pain.
Like a ship on a stormy night never to reach land,
Bound to the pit of the ocean, to sink within the sand.
It should never have set sail on such a treacherous night.
In a world full of darkness, never again to see the light.
The captain thought his strength could endure through the past,
But what he does not know is that even strength cannot last.
The ship anchors away to its unforeseen fate,
The pleasures of the members not to know until it's too late.
The land behind them disappears, the ocean is now theirs,
For now they are in control, but soon will come their despair.
The waves become fierce as they invade a territory unknown.
Out of control, out of reach, to and fro the members are thrown,
But up ahead lies a river, a sparkling brook with trees.
Quick, turn that way, glad to not pay their fees,
But as the ship approaches, the true figure appears,
And much to their dismay, once again set in their fears.
It is a battle that is forever fought, in the end no one gains fame.
Unfortunately, far too many people treat it only as a game.

Patricia Cusack

My Soul Mate

What is this wonder to have . . . if not an instrument that I may use
To find tranquility
Be still and be quiet and listen to the rhythm . . .
The wonder of it all . . . my emotions cascade over me like the tide
To a place so ravaged and secret none have been there before
Reaching out for understanding but afraid that it may come
If not today, perchance tomorrow
There is a place that I have been touched
That I never thought I would
A place so dark and secret I could not venture there alone
Now a lantern is burning brightly
Lighting the way to my heart
It shines through the darkness with a luminescence so wondrous
It takes my breath away
For this journey I need you to help me find my way
For together the path is less lonely
And because of you I will fear the darkness
No longer . . .

Debra Lynn LeRoy

Victim of My Shadow

My shadow follows me under the midnight glare.
My shadow follows me, people Beware!
For all you can see is not me,
It is my shadow that follows that, you see.

My shadow cannot change although I can.
It cannot laugh or cry like every other man.
My body has changed, my face full of sorrow,
But my shadow remains the same today and tomorrow.

For, I did once sin and I can say I am sorry,
But those who only see my shadow do not worry.
I am a victim of my shadow because I cry.
I am a victim of my shadow because I cannot reply.
Joseph Cullia

Peace of Mind

I've just closed my eyes again
Remembered the hurt and all the pain
Life can be cruel and shatter your dreams
To you I cry out with confusion it seems
For, you are my peace of mind
Which I fear I lost somewhere behind
The path becomes clear with dissolution
The wound seeps in with tears and confusion
As I sit down to write these words
Up in the sky I gaze at the birds
So wild and free with sweet inspiring sounds
To help me reach the outward bounds
As I reach up and touch the sky
I feel so peaceful on this natural high
Now as I contemplate this thought
I begin to realize how hard I fought
To secure my peace of mind
The door opens as the emptiness falls behind.
Anna Teixeira

Brummagem Street

The Beautiful Women of Brummagem Street
Live in Doll Houses
Picket fenced in.

They drink strong Coffee and weak Tea
Artificially sweet—two packets per Mug.

The Beautiful Women of Brummagem Street
Staple their Lashes and Pluck out their Brows.

They Tighten their Skins and Paint on their Faces,
Sculpt their Expressions and Varnish their Toes.

The Beautiful Women of Brummagem Street
Have Poppy red lips, Peroxide smiles.

They Glue on their nails and Implant their Breasts.
They Suck in their tummies and Suck Out their Thighs.

The Beautiful Women of Brummagem Street
Have Silicon wishes and Bourbon desires.

They eat dry leaves with vinegar,
and Styrofoam cakes without.

They dream in Seasonal Plastic Pallets.

They dream in Black and White.
Sheri Harris

Slacker

Boredom
Slicing through my brain
Losing sanity
Feeling a numb sort of pain

Boredom
Knots in my hair
Doodles in my book
Life seems so unfair

Boredom
Pondering my thoughts
Doubting existence
Reality lost

Never should have sat here
Never should have come
Now I'm dead and lonely
No courage, only shame
Jennifer Perez

Destiny

I can't believe you left me,
I was scared and all alone,
Wandering the streets,
No way to get home.

Think of memories we shared,
The endless talking at night,
The jokes we exchanged,
Not one single fight.

Remember the promise made,
That forever you'd be true.
This meant forever,
Not one year or two.

Recall the heartfelt promise,
When you said those words, "I do."
I thought you loved me,
And never be through.

I guess it's "destiny."
Tabitha Marie Hughes

Untitled

I was sitting there
For a long time and
Watching it, the candle.
Then I suddenly
Realized how it was
Clinging to the centre
Of the candle to
Burn.
Ingeborg Dalby

All Alone

I don't know why I'm standing,
standing here alone.
I do not want to be here a
million miles from home.
My home is across the ocean,
the land across the sea
where the heather hills are
whispering, "Please come home to me."

So why am I standing here,
what am I waiting for?
I have a million miles to travel
before I can journey home.
The days seem long, my heart
is heavy, why can't it be today
when I can set my sails forever
round the banks of Kiloran Bay?

Christine A. Campbell

If Only . . .

If only I could hear,
I would listen to people talking.
If only I could touch,
I would hug you.
If only I could speak,
I would tell you how much I love you.
If only I could explain,
I would show you my feelings.
If only I could read,
I would read your thoughts!

Tatiana Georgitsis

I Wish

I wish I were an ocean.
I wish I were a sea.
Everything around,
Is such a part of me.

I wish I were an eagle.
I wish I were a dove.
I could have no enemies,
Or I could mean love.

I wish I were a nightmare.
I wish I were a dream.
I could make you shiver.
I could make you scream.

I wish I were a lot of things,
As I'm sure that you can see.
But I think that right now,
I am quite content with me.

Livia Peyton

How to Fly for a Few Seconds

Climb up the steps
The box, the ledge.
Plant your feet firmly
And balance yourself so as not to fall.
Don't look down.
Line up your toes to the edge
And bend your knees
Keeping your back straight
And your arms outstretched.
Jump high and far,
Pushing off from the ledge into the open air.
Feel the weightlessness as you fall toward Earth.
Make sure someone is there to catch you
Before you reach the ground.

Veronica Ferraiuoli

Two Roads to Take

There are two roads
Which one will you carry your load
Will you go where the life is wild
Or to the one with tests and trials
How about a life of fun and games
Or a life with God which just seems plain
How about a life where something doesn't feel right
Or a life where God makes your burdens light
I pick the second one, how about you
You better pick one, you can't have two

Shinika S. Holdipp

WORDS

I have all these words in my mind
trotting incessantly, searching,
hoping to find finally my lips
to end this race.
All my hopes, all my laughs, and
my nights are frozen in these words . . .
along the corners of my mind they
laugh at my intentions,
daring me to draw them with my voice.
A scream runs along my throat,
hoping to break the silence
only to draw them beneath my skin.
This is not a battle against blood and flesh,
this is a passion against the darkness
of distance and time . . .
time that runs away with all these words,
following this transparent phantom.

Martha C. Inturralde

Waiting for the Time to Go

I'm sitting here, trying not to think about it.
The time was running so fast, too fast.

I'm sitting here, trying to find a solution.
The time is running so fast, too fast.

I'm sitting here, trying to forget you.
The time with you was so wonderful, too wonderful.

I'm sitting here and there is nothing to do for me
except for waiting for the time to go.

Cornelia Berndl

Sisters

We've spent so much time remembering the past,
reliving the good times and bad,
Whenever I sit and my thoughts drift to you,
I'm alone and it makes me feel sad.
Whenever my holiday time comes around,
my plan is to always go home.
My family means so much more to me,
than the lure of the tourist-to roam.

Some days I'll sit and remember the times,
when I've made you laugh till you cried;
Although I'm alone, I'll chuckle out loud,
but, it's more fun with you by my side.
Through childhood we grew, as we both spread our wings,
and we went down our own separate track.
Commitments and jobs now claim most of our time,
but we still love to smile and look back.

Sometimes when I read the letters you send,
a few tears will moisten my eyes.
That you care so deeply-after all of this time,
still catches me so much by surprise.
Rose Marie Pichota

Continuum

When the Deluge came, all the world
Was wet.
Then built an ark, a patriarch,
To save from sodden end the creatures paired
That yet
Would populate a land to be unfurled
Where waters cede to desert parch,
And let
The 'twixt and 'tween land nurture Nature's herd.

Thus all who are, for Noah's sake inspire;
Expire
In given course of time. All dwell
To give genetic leave to those who succeed
To sire:
Begetting constantly does not inquire
To know how or why they propagate so well.
Entire—
In whole because of Noah's knowing deed.
G. A. Hoyland

Teddy (My Hamster)

I would do anything to bring you back, but I
Know I can't, so I have to face that fact.
Life without you is like being in a world without
Light; no matter how hard you try, nothing is quite
Right.
You probably know why I cried and cried. It's
Like winning a prize, and not feeling any pride.
You were my first thought in the morning, my
Last before bed, and it's still the same, even though
You are dead.
I hope you know how much you meant to me,
The world, and to everyone you met.
I will love you always and forever, because
You should know that my love lasts forever.
Laura Dean

Sitting in the Dark!

Looking into the sunset,
Over the deep blue sea,
The colors and the scenery
Keep distracting me.

The soft white waves
Bow gently at my feet,
As the sea gull sweeps
Softly past my feet.

As the sun disappears
And the moon comes to sight,
I can't help but wonder,
'How sad is my life
Without my love
Sitting by my side?"
The dark black shadows
Are the holes in my heart,
As I wait patiently
For my love to find me,
Sitting in the dark.
Claire Fletcher

My Echoes Decoded

By the stage I sitting weary,
The scene echoed in the screen,
Reminding me the living in expire,
I cheered simply I say, Amen.

By the flag I standing preen,
The anthem echoed through the pole,
Warning me the mob dying skin,
I laughed simply I lost hope.

By the grave I staying futile,
The sigh echoed from the corpse,
Telling me the folk buried bundle,
I sneered simply, I born car case.

By the church I attending Sermon,
The toll echoed into my soul,
Suggesting me why not you scorn?
I mocked simply I do console.

By the bed I going asleep,
The dream echoed underneath,
Threatening me I live in pop,
I wondered simply, I trend after death.
Ato Seyoum Dagne Birru

18 January, 1923
In memory of Wallace Reid

I heard a call,
an echo toward the sun,
come forth my heart,
thy wounds lie restless, narrow seeds
upright among distorted rainbows
into darkened storms do shroud
the forsaken road
alone and far away.
A dream in death despair,
the value of true love,
the wisdom of its feel,
has lost its touch.
Time's eager hands did block. . . .

I'll never know
the kiss of fever pitch
thy cheeks best stole,
the song no lyric
ever wore. . . .
Eulogia Rojas Corpus

Spring

The cool winds warn the tiny plants
to snuggle down real low . . .
For, Mother Nature soon will come
And cover them with snow.

The mighty trees all shed their leaves
And hold their bare arms high.
The winds and gales all strip them bare
And winter fills the sky.

As months go by, all stark and cold,
Nothing alive it seems . . .
But slowly, friendly winds and sun
Start pushing through their beams.

Warmer and still warmer comes
the feeling in the snow . . .
For it's now time for sleeping things
To shake their heads and grow.

So, slowly, changes do occur,
No movement . . . not a thing,
But tiny plants push up the snow
To user in our Spring!
Dorothy Mazurik

Working Boy

Every morning up at five,
At the plant by six thirty,
Straight to my station,
Where I will spend my day . . . life
With sweat pouring off my body,
And my head pounding like a drum.
I wonder . . . will I ever break free
From this hell I have to call my job?
I should have went to school.
I should have went to school.
Why, why did I drop out?
I punch the time clock on my way out,
And at five o'clock as I put my key into my door
I hear the cries of my son.
This is why I dropped out.
This is why I will never break free
I go to bed and wake up every day
Hoping my son will learn from my experience,
But will he? I never did!
Jennifer Regier

Love Hurts

Right now my life is a living hell.
How could an angel break my heart?
It hurt so deeply I thought I would die.
Thoughts capture me, prisoner of my breath.
It's hard to go on when my lover is leaving me behind.
The story of my past is so sad,.
Even I have pity for myself
Everything I do makes me feel bad,
And shame makes my days so miserable.
Somehow I got messed up about faith,
Like if I would not have any human feeling at all,
Or like if I am being used like a piece of rag,
And thrown into the garbage.
Despair erases everything I have achieved.
I feel like nothing matters anymore in this world.
Hate makes me think of the ugliest things,
Because I lost my pride and self-esteem for love.
Nobody knows I wish for the end of it.
Every time I seek help,
Death always appears the easy way out.
Bandasack Thilavanh

Pain and Deliverance

"Father," I cried, "the way is dark,
The rocks are sharp, and the mountains steep!"
"Fear not, dear one," returned His voice,
"I will not forsake my sheep!"
"Forgive me, Lord," I called to Him,
As I clutched the hem of His gown.
"You lead the way, I will follow you,"
And my precious Lord led on.
Less piercing now became each thorn,
For He had tread before.
Half my burden He carried,
All of that and more!
Onward together we travelled
'Til we came to a smoother land,
And the piercing thorns
became shimmering jewels
At His feet, in the warm, smooth sand.
Myra G. McCulloch Moorman

I Wonder What They See?

We never stop to take the time and ask them what they see.
We are only concerned with now, not then, and of our industry.
We pass right by a gentle smile without a slight hesitation,
Not knowing that their fate will be our final destination.

But what is wrong with their fate, I ask? Is it such a terrible plight?
For, if being old is so very wrong, what makes being young so right?
We, the young, are fast indeed; but the old have their insight,
And no matter how we hide it, growing old is our deepest fright.

But why, I ask, is that our fear? For, what is wrong with old age?
Growing old and growing wise is the next level the next stage,
But despite this all, we close our eyes and do not see the truth.
We do not think that the elderly were once like us, the youth.

Yet the old still are, deep down inside, right down into their core,
And though they have given lots of love, they have a whole lot more.
We do not see their outstretched hands, but only their wrinkled skin.
Our eyes are open to their outside, but not the beauty within.

Yes! At times I have done this, but I try to live respectfully.
So, now I know what's in their hearts, but I wonder what they see?

Michael Grandsoult

O, Soldier, Soldier

O, soldier, soldier, why do you create so much pain and agony,
When men never return and sons are never loved again,
And still another dog tag fell in the mud,
And still soldiers march,
And only God knows why?

O, soldier, do you remember those far and few in between years?
What greatness we could achieve if only we dare!
And now war birds fly, machines of men clash, whirr, and melt
The world in cinders,
And still soldiers fight.
And only God knows why.

So, soldier, if you must march and fight for us,
Roman, Hun, Spartan, Marine, and Israelite,
You know you always will,
And if you do not see tomorrow, then you shall see eternity,
Because soldiers die
And only God knows why.

Wesley Wiecek

Horizontal Sol

Platonically meshed collapsed receivers
conceptors damaged beyond repair,
I am one of the hundreds. I am without sense, without reality,
without doubt, smite, smote the sky and eye indulged the paired matching,
images and vicariously arranged flocks herded,
entranced and attracted, swaying, warring,
loving wood idols, loved the sweet green grass
forgotten once again, drowned in the sea
of corporate affiliates and florescence.
They ate roots now digesting dogmatic,
cryptic glances, prances about spreading.
The Fake Muse lifts gifts me with vision
so yearned for; I cry at the ecstasy of it all; the
tunnel vision cracked, deposited, grown inside me
and it has a new home; it likes it here, and someday the sun will aid it to
become another hour passed by my processors, my wiring, my nerves repaired
and listening to the baying of a passing crowd, transfixed, loved, and lived.
The other side of the wall, a continuation of past gods so illustrious, so
real, so in front of us. She whispered, go to sleep, little ones, and that is
what I do—I sleep, I dream, and I pray.

Michael O'Toole

Ode to Poetry

Poetry, the loosener of relief, shakes me: a timely utterance,
It gives my thoughts release. And I again feel strong.
But like a laurel tree, and every laurel tree, of many one or none,
Single which I have looked upon,
Doth speak of something that held glamour but now gone.

But thus: the same tale repeat.
And as I age along, so did others but now diseased.
Soon I too shall fade,
But in my heart will be the ones I loved,
And others are whom I had wronged,
Thus to release the wretched will be a pride,
Whilst their failings will be leaned to virtue's side.

Since I live, see, and feel nothing:
Thus only the sad, empty, blessed dust.
Where is my splendour that is so hard to find?
It has disappeared as if it belonged to a myth,
What courage, what pleasure was left for me when old age came?
What joy was given to you when you appeared in this world, my child?
How would joy just turn to sorrow?
And how did all its blessing vanish in the thin air?

Ali Ibrahim

Together

You and I share a love that bloomed just like a flower,
from something so small, that grew so fast, our hearts really
do have the power.
I want to be with you and share my life in every possible way,
so that we can have a family and grow old together, without
you I will not stay.
This day brings joy for all to see as we unite our love together.
We exchange our rings and say, "I do": These are our vows
to keep forever.
This is a day we will never forget as long as the flower lives.
It won't wilt or die until we leave each other,
because our love to one another we'll give.

Maria A. Pirroncello

Love's First Dream

In the middle of a prairie field, I stand on my own,
an unpleasant feeling to be all alone.

As I look in the distance I sense the golden grasslands
waving in the nighttime breeze.
The beauty of the midnight stars helps subdue the loneliness
I feel inside. I close my eyes and pray,
promising to make bad things good, and good things better.
All I ask for is the loneliness be gone.

I sense the twilight as night turns into day,
and open my eyes to the beauty of the sunrise.

I find myself in a place I have never been before,
surrounded by a symphony of beauty, the most beautiful part being you.

We embrace and I begin to sense inside
that my prayers have been answered. The loneliness is gone.

Suddenly the vision begins to fade. In desperation I hold you tighter.
I feel helpless, I'm losing.

My efforts make me shake and quiver, and I awake myself
from a deep sleep. I had been dreaming.

I then realize we were not together,
you had turned over in your restlessness.
I follow you, you turn to me, we embrace,
and slowly drift back to sleep.

Chris Breckon

The Seer

For I am a unicorn,
born of the sun who roams hidden places;
I drink the still waters,
I see the center within.

For I am a unicorn,
seen as a flicker of silver in moonlight,
I ride the wind, I tame the beast.

I am the lawless one
whose name means submission.
I, the wand'ring spirit
capture thy dreams eternal;
I am the spear point of truth,
the carrier of vengeance divine.

I will fight thee!
And ye shall feel my golden hooves
cleave thy evil into nothingness!

I, warrior of unseen forces,
am the master of thy darkness,
the amber sword of eternity . . . for I am a unicorn,
and thy battle with me hast begun.

Traci Saunders

Love

Two hearts beat in rhythmic sync,
Pounding, throbbing, what's this feeling called?
Oh, yes, Love.
Tell me you love me, but is it true?
I will believe it and say I love you too.
The world has no problems as long as we're together.
Could I be yours forever?
The seasons change from warm to cold,
But you remain my shelter.
In your arms is where I'm held.
My love for you grows deeper, much like the snow.
First love, last love, which love could it be?
Take me by the hand and show me the way,
The way to your heart.
Lead me through the maze,
For I don't know where to start.
Two hearts beat in rhythmic sync,
Pounding, throbbing, what's this feeling called?
Oh, yes, Love.

Courtnie Brown

Friends Forever

Our friendship is cherished with you and me.
Together we've been through a lot:
Rough times, happy times, sad times.
We've always been there for each other.

Nothing can ever come between us.
For, our friendship is too strong,
Too strong to be apart.
Well always be friends.

Friendship is something I'm glad to say.
Friendship is something too strong to fail.
Friends Forever, that's what we'll be.
Friend Forever, that's our motto.

Dharsiga Mohanachandran

The Sea Within

When you sail on the sea,
It's funny what the mind
Can do to thee.
Memories come and go,
The future no one knows.
Reflections of lights
Shimmer and glow
And dance on water's night,
Making the heart sometimes light.

Good friends I have lost,
Also many a lost thought.
If you sit and let it talk,
And take the time to sit and watch,
It will leave you deep in thought.
Days come and go
As I travel the waterway,
Weaving and winding the way
Along the coast I love the most.

Captain D. Suveges

Nothing Lose, Nothing Gain

There e'er abode near the great wall
An old man good at breeding horses.
One day his horse ran stray and missed
To the northeast territories.
People fear his troubling at this.
All came to cheer and console him.
He answered: "Lose one horse it seems,
Or perhaps a good thing will redeem."
Of course several months passed, indeed,
The horse came back with a small steed.

A bad luck under some limit
Would turn out indeed a good deed;
A temporary loss may manage
An unexpected advantage.

Hor Ming Lee

A Wonderful Day

Looking outside my window
The roses were red
The birds were singing
I couldn't stay in bed
Today's my birthday
Today I'm eight!
I'm having a party
And I just can't wait
For all those gifts
And all those goodies
To see my friends
And to see my "Dad!"
It'll be the best birthday party
I ever had!

Mary Doucette

She Heard a Song

The song was in her heart.
When she heard the tune,
She had to take part.
Music is poetry with a tune.
You can never hear or read enough,
too late or too soon.
One thing in life
to get rid of one's strife.
You hear, react:
that's a matter of fact.
The gift of music and poetry is
a wonderful thing.
Participate, enjoy,
let us hear you write, read, and sing!

Lorraine Doyle

My Mother's Eyes

My mother has deep, dark,
and bloodied eyes.
She hides them
beneath a Medicare lens.

My mother spies a crucifix
and attempts to climb aboard.
Her arms encircle my griefs and joy.

At times I can be glimpsed
inside my mother's eyes:
Either mirrored,
reflecting her generations,

Or else as a black and callous boot.
That is why my mother shall forever keep
her deep, dark, and bloodied eyes.

Jim Arkell

Trucking

Trucking
Through the highway,
Voice-links contact control.
The road, long ribbons of it,
Leading your power behind the wheel.

Sun-beaten and alone
Between dusk and dawn roadhouses,
Pep-ups of the dark.

Handfuls of food as welcome as the
Gurgle of refuelling tanks,
Boots-riding superiority
To those unable to conceal escaping envy
In the corners of their eyes.

Door-slam,
Secure in your machine.
Comrades on a twilight lurk,
Bypassing hostility. . . .

Sharon Berry

At Forty

I'm overweight, creaky,
have brownish bags under my eyes,
just read five minutes of Carlos Williams

This is a world I've left
I haven't much good to say about it
(might I perhaps be denying the good times the good
to perversely justify the bad of these times?)

The Carlos Williams I have in my mind
is not really the doctor, it's rather
the good looking guy on one of his
New Directions paperbacks,
almost a guy with a scout hat, it seems,
sort of like a Mountie of poetry

Really, not a poet
There's something to say for a guy who
delivered 2000 babies

And about me they (if they will ever bother)
might say: deliverer of thousands of lines
of infertile industrial prose

Johannes Beilharz

Summer

The cold wind blows,
Blowing insecurities into my mind,
Sending their messages of doubt.
Leaves fall to the ground; their lives gone,
Taken by the wind.
My collar up, I battle for my life,
Against obstacles of worry thrown against me,
Armed with the wind.

Suddenly, I stand tall; collar down, coat open,
To pass life's obstacles.
The battle is over.
Summer begins.

Jennifer Kendrick

The One

Could perfection possibly exist?
I see you, I see what I've always imagined.
You're a priceless picture of perfection.
Mere words could never explain this bliss.
You've unraveled the best in me,
Touched the wounded soul in me.
Could you be a blessing from God above?
You reflect the true essence of love.
Could I be bewildered without you by my side?
Could I be strong enough to carry on?
A myriad of questions flow in my mind.
The answers, I only see in your eyes.
They reveal what I want to be revealed.
It's not what I feel, it's what we feel.
I long to see what you see,
Learn what you learn, touch what you touch,
Grow old with you, see the world with you,
And die only in your arms.
You fulfill my hopes and dreams, because
you . . . you're The One I've always been looking for.

Mornie Amin

To Mother Queen

He sings this song to her queen mother
on this tremendous day
when she was born,

And when she came,
the whole world smiled with joy
and Heaven and Earth received her with much pride.
She was the queen.

The budding rose, she then turned soon the flower
and reigned supreme over Earthly things and life,
over stars, the moon, and the heavens too.
She was the queen—queen mother.

She was abounding with charm and beauty
meant for her,
and loved by all her subjects.
Scores of years and more,
her life was full of gladness and good cheer.

And then one day, as if by fate itself,
he found the queen amidst the heavenly stars.
Upon her throne she sat and looked at him
and whispered in his ear. . . .
Peter S. Faminow

The Realization

It is a rare and fleeting moment,
when in your anger you pause
and gaze up to the expanse of the night sky,
cold but soothing . . .

The moon, stark and white—yet inviting,
and the stars twinkle knowingly,
In that instant, ancient instincts flood your heart
with a knowledge . . .

Sounds of crushing snow beneath your feet,
bitter wind nipping your flesh
awaken the sense that we are not the gods,
only mortals.

If ever fostered such feelings
that your spirit's taken flight
with a greater creator, force, or being,
it's this instance . . .

It is a rare and fleeting moment
when the realization dawns.
For one brilliant, peaceful second you were sure
you understood . . .
Ruth Ann Young

Gone

Your eyes pierce me with a deep pain.
Your smile makes me feel uneasy.
Why? Why? Why?
Why are you treating me like this?
Why all the silence?
Why don't you just open your heart to me once again?
Never before have I felt such a deep ache.
But, every time I see you, I know it's all over.
I know it will never be how it was meant to be.
Kamila Duda

In Gold We Trust

Removal of the scintilla despondency,
webbed toes are luminous vapor.

Where a face should sit
dances a child,
ingrained to the cleavage of stain.

Accuracy condenses itself
with rain slaughter,
misty and arbitrary,
bit, fat, and pungent.

Pregnant blood
is urine
leaping from off the night
into the frigid
abduction of morning song.

Where tissue awaits
to rebuild its covet,
a woven sedative
entangles glory
to the purest form of mutilation.
Amanda Mekhael

Untitled

Come look through my window,
approach and see,
Fall's almost upon us.
Reminiscing will be.
Green leaves turn to silver
that in the wind blow.
Bitter thoughts, yet happy,
soon there'll be snow.
Bring memories of the year,
which have gone by.
Sadness, madness,
pass before my eyes.
Pleasure, grief, unhappiness,
love, loving life, passing days,
I sat and watched,
Sierra, my daughter, play.
How lucky I am,
this mortal soul,
though grief played too,
I've reached my goal.
Marian Heibloem Reeves

How Sad It Must Be

How sad it must be
To live a life of sorrow,
To look in the eyes of me
Who gives no real tomorrow.

To hear one speak
The lying words of love
As your thoughts render
So far, far above.

How sad it must be
To live a life so cruel,
To look up in the eyes of God
As he's used up like a tool?
Why be such a fool?

How sad it must be
To live a life of hate,
But for the poor fool
Love has no opening gate,
Only a cold, lonely heart,
And for love he will always wait.

Vivian Ruddell

SCI-FI Legends

A captain larger than life,
a lady's man with no wife,
but a ship and a star to steer by.

An alien in a strange land,
with "live long and prosper" in hand,
and emotion in his logical eyes.

A doctor with more than one face,
traveling throughout time and space,
is a mystery without his own name.

Four cosmic misfits alone,
on a red dwarf as it is known,
find life in a "better than life" game.

A maverick who believes,
his partner who disagrees,
and the truth out there to be found.

A true superman of steel,
a woman whose love is real,
forever is this dynamic duo bound.

These heroes protect our future,
and make our world go round.

Michael Anthony Basil

My Hero
Dedicated to my hero

My hero is someone who came to be,
Someone who's been a part of me.
Nowhere to run, no place to hide,
It came to be I lived this lie.

Digging down to find within
The manly faces to start over again.
To risk this journey once pushed aside,
Is to face who I once had to hide.

Sharing broken promises and broken dreams,
Forgetting the lies and angry schemes,
Learning the truth and learning to be,
Is how to live and set one free.

My hero came many times over,
Wiser and wiser, and much older.
For, the strength and courage and the "Will" to be,
The hero I'd like you to meet is within "Me."

J. M. Chamberlain

The Refugee

Bumping vehicles battle for space,
They halt, screeching, meandering
Slowly to a jerk, then a sudden bang.
Ragged passengers, eyes—bulging,
Their thumping chests beat in rhythmic unison,
As they scamper to safety.
Heavy-laden trucks their wares discharge
In the madding crowd, bulky, skimpy species
Hop, stepping onto the arena, confused.
Here, a sack atop a pair of boots
With sliced or better, marshed human flesh,
Litter the track of competitors
On a walking-race.
Cyclists pedal creaking wheels,
Dragging disease-infested cattle.
Drooping heads on backs of trudging mothers,
Bearing, like Atlas, their world
Of baskets, with ladles and pots
Typical of the African refugee
En route to no destination.

Nuala Obuekwe

Sun King

You are like the morning sun,
Radiating cheerful light.
Your smile is dazzling, warm, and bright.

Your sun-kissed countenance is a welcoming glow.
From your spirit, good feelings flow.

Bathed in your sun-soaked beams,
You have touched my life,
My heart, my dreams.

Circumscribed by the warmth of your rays,
I will remember you for the rest of my days.

My soul is infused with the peace you bring,
Your happiness is my happiness,
My sun king.

Elizabeth O'Brien

Shadow World

The frame is made of coal and tells a story of a same,
Of a soul lost and forgotten without a name:

A victim of a shadowed world with no light to shed.
Where you can dress to camouflage the spirit chained within.

He only smiled for the camera,
He only laughed for the fans,
He only dressed up so he could be the man.

The man that was admired, though he hated the dream.
The man that his father was, though he never wanted to be.

He did not expect to wear a mask, but I guess he always did.
He never knew the soil in his eyes,
Though they were brown.
He never got to inhale love,
He didn't have time to breathe.

He is a soul lost and forgotten,
And a river in a dam.

He is a soul lost and forgotten,
And a sidewalk that ends.

He is a soul lost and forgotten,
Still searching for himself.

Nevres Kianieff

Red River Run Away

Another great disaster has came upon our land,
In our beautiful red never valley
where the river flows so grand.
Many homes were flooded as it overflowed its banks.
They built dykes of a car, struck buses, and sand.
The strong wind tried to break it, but the dykes
were built to stand.
It made a big lake like you have never seen.
Now we have water that should be nice and green.
Soldiers came from near and far to help us in our fight,
And thanks to everyone, the help, we must have done it right.
And now that it is over, I hope it stays in its banks,
And never again shows us its ugly pranks.

Lena Murray

Lord, Can You Hear Us?

I watch you as you lie in bed,
Wishing there was more I could do.
Your body weakens from day to day,
As I try to comfort you.

Your hand in mine as you slowly slip away.
I place a pillow beneath her head,
As I listen to her cries of pain, "Oh, God, how can I take them away."
I feel her hurt as she calls your name, "So I begin to pray."

Oh, Lord, if you can hear me,
I ask how could you let this be.
She can't understand, we don't even know why.
Can you not hear her cry?

Please give her peace for every tomorrow
If she's not ready to leave us now.
Can you not take away the hurt and sorrow?
It's up to you, for I know not how.

Oh, God, take away her fear,
Let your light shine upon her face.
She knows her time is near,
Please comfort Mom as she leaves this place.

Gloria Gouzopoulos

Rosa Moshata

A complex child trapped in the arms of her makers.
Danger is often the parent of fear, so she's lonely in silence.
Freedom is expressed with love to her, so she accepts it with deliverance.

Eccentric child, socially viable for an unknown purpose.
Living her dream, thriving for perfection.
Intelligent woman, so she's frightened to let go of herself.

Virgin child, a vamp for men that fall into her beauty.
Pretty eyes are often reckless, so she's often tempted.
Offspring of vitality, so she's an object of vigilance.

A lady of passion,
Drowning in her own heaven of tears.
Intriguing woman,
Nailing her final fears.

Overnight she breathes the air of love.
Mien of a tigress,
In captivity of mother nature,
Spellbound lady.
    Slavomir Gola

Freedom

Marriage is my freedom.
Like a star floating free in the galaxy,
I am not dependent.
I am not shackled.

Like a star burning against the infinity of the universe
I have my destiny.

And it is intertwined with yours.

We dance our dance in step
with the universal hymn
of creation and life.

We are partners swaying to the joyful rhythm
freed by our love.
Partners by choice;
one with the Spirit who gives us life and teaches us the steps.
    Patricia Corbett

Untitled

There is so much more to see within colourless eyes.
Life behind the blackness. Hope in the white.
One life captured in a picture.
That same life as fragile as the paper it's printed on.
So, rip it, apart.
Who we are is what we're told,
(There is so much that can't be seen within colourless eyes.)
Two lives captured in a picture.
Most of it's been lies.
So, it's, ripped, apart.
Do colourless eyes cry colourless tears? Do they cry at all?
One life where there was once happiness.
One set of eyes where there was once hope.
A soul that is but a walking shadow,
Lost in the blackness. Scared, of the white.
Now, alone in the picture. Not, in life.
    Sandy Mann

The Flight of Life

A child, Now Woman, for her innocence she's given.
Takes up the reins, upon this dark horse ridden.
Faces towards sunlight, a long road is chosen.
In time hearts striving, warm closeness is woven.
Build foundations of stone, masoned to bend, not to break.
Fill it with passion, sharing, patience, and faith.
Hardest to learn, forgiving mistakes.
Raging storms come, turning streams into flood.
Some might take you under, in the great pools of mud.
Reach out, inner strength uplifts you from this bottomless low.
Taste life . . . touch . . . hold . . . and let go.
    Sharon Passero

The Taming of an Arrogant Guppy

A guppy I am, I say it with pride;
Mean and nasty, you better go hide.
I'll hunt you down and swallow you whole;
Deep down in my stomach it's black as coal.

Was that a fish that just swam by?
I think I saw it from the corner of my eye.
My fins are like swords, my teeth are like knives,
And just like a catfish, I have nine lives.

And now it's time to go make my kill;
I hope he's big, so I'll get my fill.
Over there he's hiding behind that rock,
Because he knows once bit, my jaw will lock.

What's this I see? Two big yellow eyes?
He's huge! I exclaim to my surprise.
Oh, no! Here he comes with jaws open wide!
There's no place to swim, there's no place to hide!

It's dark in here, and what is that smell?
I wonder where I am . . . I cannot tell.
There are many small fish that look just like me.
I might stay here for eternity.

Kim Franklin

When I Was Four I Asked (Sweet Innocence)

Uncle Josh, what are those lights above
Flashing on and off behind the clouds?
He said to me, and I believed it was,
The fireworks display of the gods.

"And what is that rumbling noise
That roars and roars as the lights go off?"
"It's the ruffles of snares and drums," he said.
"The gods are on parade."

"Where come the gusty winds
That snap the leaves and rock the trees?"
He said: "It's the gasping breath of sky horses
Of soldier-gods in chariot race."
Pit! pat! pit-a-pat! came the rain.
Pit! pat! pit-a-pat! on the window pane.

Uncle Josh asked me as he tucked me to bed:
"Guess where raindrops come from, Little Brad."
How he chuckled like tickled when I said,
"That one chariot ran over a water jug."

Melchor M. Costales

Aches

I woke up crying on a bright summer day.
I didn't know I fell asleep.
I was sitting, enjoying the sun,
Red flowers in full bloom,
Children's voices bouncing,
And the room was quiet and peaceful.

Yet when I woke,
Silent tears were sliding down my cheeks.
My heart was tired and my spirit was weary.
Did they come from the abyss of my soul?
When did they get there—these tears?

It was a bright, bright summer afternoon.

Miriam Batts

Hourglass

Images of success;
Neglecting pursuit.

Accumulation of items;
Forgetting creativity.

Visions of happiness;
Denying possibilities.

Presentation of caring;
Refusing involvement.

Waiting for the moment . . .
Inaction.
Waiting for the opportunity . . .
Blindness.
Waiting . . .
Time's up.

Lorraine Doucette

Theirs Is Mine

Pitiful roars from
A bewildered, broken self
Sound and resound
As streams rise from
Her hill for flood flow.
And tearing her
Dark pine needles she says:
"They were good after all."

Another smiles in sorrow,
Perhaps for their negatives:
But, both regret the missing.

Gnashing her teeth
Like a cow watching others slaughtered
And rolling herself on the
Brown grained-carpeted floor,
Her reverberations
Again double and redouble.
Now! Not for missing's sake,
But anticipate her day and misses in:
"Tomorrow shall be my day."

Takwi Mathew

Eric in Memory

Your life so quietly ended now,
Rest, by the cypress shadow deep.
The rain falls on our brows,
Our tears console your sleep.

Though laughter ceases to be,
Voice without sound,
And mute is your melody,
You live still, below the ground.

In our care your spirit dwells.
Dear good friend, farewell!

Lola Dunston

Angel of Light

Streams of stars in heaven's night,
Falling echoes, souls in flight.
Heart of darkness, foreign mind,
Go, and let me sleep and find
Peaceful beauty in the sight
Of timeless rolling seas of light.
Trembling shadows, silence singing,
Heart and soul go onward winging,
Beauty that I cannot clasp
Abounds somewhere beyond my grasp.
Clive Rea

War Is, Peace Is

War is death.
Peace is happiness.
War is the battlefield.
Peace is families.

War is a living hell.
Peace is togetherness.
War is torture.
Peace is freedom.

War is suffering.
Peace is Remembrance Day.
War is men and women at battle.
Peace is coming home.
Aaron Feere

The Last

Storm is brewing in my mind
Peace and Love so hard to find
Why is this yearning inside of me?
Blackened hole of loneliness must recede

Away from me
For love of God
Angel's Heart
Must find some peace in my lover's arms

Seasons come and friends go
The pace of life
Like undertow
Lover stands on Holy ground
My goals and dreams no longer found

For love of hate
Angel's Heart
Must find my mind before I depart

To you my life must be hell
To bathe in hate
To grapple with self
That's O.K., I know who I am
Last angel yet to go to heaven
Jason Seeley

Demon Lover

Woe is me.
My demon lover, in her beauty, has taken my heart.
How could this be, am I not intelligent?
Demon lover, taken my soul, forsaken my mortality.
Blood of mine, my captured soul.
Am I not frozen, ice runs her veins, chosen?
Chills through my spine, as she dines.
Spells this wicked love has cast.
Blinded by greed, need more.
My demon lover has borne, child
This cannot be; God, what have I done?
To give this demon flesh and blood.
Demon lover has wished well
Internal light, she will fell,
Break the spell.
Darkness shadows me,
This cannot be.
My demon lover, how I do love thee.
Rick J. Riley

Longing

My lonely self aches every day
To behold you with your ample charms.
If only you could hold me in your arms,
It would feel like heaven, and there would I stay.
I fear, through, that sight is the only way
I could ever take you in, for I disarm
You in my plainness, and there does farm
My problem; beauty from me was always astray.
If only you could see me from deep within
And not be so blind.
For, even though beauty lies not in my skin,
My attractiveness is found throughout in my mind.
The chance, however, that you would see
Would only transpire in a fantasy.
Stacy Grondin

Love's Utmost Treacheries

Love's tornado visits my heart
With storms and shattered dreams.
The rain in my eyes foretells my pain,
And brings winds of my anguished screams.

Caught in the whirlwind of despair,
And carried to depths unknown,
Lightning flashes of love destroyed
By the clouds of shame poured down.

Up from the muddied earth below,
Up past the raging sea,
I ride on the thunder of life's retort
To rescue myself form me.
Glynn Wikstrom

A River's Song

When a river sings a song, it is music.
When the murmur rises low but clear, it is freedom.
All that troubles you today is a problem.
It will, like my waters, pass away. It is a stream.
Charlene Buzzell

Fate

Fate plays her part with thoroughness
not giving more, not giving less.
She is impartial to us all;
through her, we either rise or fall.

Fate gives us all our parts to play;
we have to play them come what may,
but one thing there's to say of fate:
She comes not early or to late.

Fate brings both poverty and wealth;
fate brings both illness and good health.
What's due to us she brings on time,
regardless of whatever the clime.

Sometimes for us life's so complex,
we think on us there is a hex,
but what we sow, 'tis what we reap,
is reason why we sometimes weep.

Let's curb our thoughts, our words, our deeds
before they be prolific seeds
from which could sprout a cruel fate,
a fate we would be sure to hate.
Ansel McLaren

Recollection of Our Reunion

The blissful get-together with you ended only too soon,
When my dear ones had to bid me adieu.
How songs of the good old days we sang,
Immersed us into memory of our golden youth.
I wish I could hold Time from elapsing,
While we lost ourselves in melodies we once knew.
The remaining sound of music lingered in the air,
As if praying for another Reunion soon with you.
Wen Peilin

Honey Bee's Sting

I see you honey bee struggling
to take flight away from me;
seen your final flower,
reached your darkest hour.
No more colour in your sight.
No more wrong. No more right.
In final, desperate passion,
You have lost your sting.
Only noise left: frenzied buzzing.
Poisoned beauty leaving its mark,
thousands of brothers
left alone in the park.
Now reflecting your story in my own life,
I can know your pain.
Remembering our masculine embrace,
nature repeats again.
My lover lies lonely on his bed
leaving his sting of love in me;
he leaves me alone, with my own love at home,
as his Spirit flies away free.
Dai Mason

Love at First Sight

I gaze in your eyes
And see blue skies.

I look at your face
And see that it is you I chase.

I take your hands
And put them in mine,
Then I look in your face
And find it shining with grace.

I look up and I see you;
Out of the corner of my eye,
I see you steeling glances of me
Like you're a private spy.

We catch each other's eyes,
And see there's no lies.

Then it is us we see;
That he is he and she is me.

Then we see a lover
And find that it's each other.
Jody Neil

The Transient Ones

We are the transient ones
Who pass through time.
We choose no place to stay.
We choose no time to go.

When the time is right
And this only we know;
We begin again.
One transition is complete.

We are born of the Earth,
And are lead by our senses,
We seek friendship with others,
But watch as they become memories.

We are intrigued by the future,
And haunted by our past.

We are here, then we are gone,
And we never look back.
Our eyes are dark and sad,
For we cannot say good-bye.

We disappear into the future.
Sometimes we just fade away.
K. Jill McMurray

The Entertainer's Request

I think it's time for a song tonight,
But should it be sad or sweet?

Happy songs are nice to hear,
But they never seem complete.

Sad songs we remember,
We sing them over beer.

Sad songs are repeated
Throughout each passing year.

I'd like to sing a happy song
for everyone to hear.

But somehow it's the sad ones
That keep the customers here!
K. Jill McMurray

Perpetuity

We speak of sticks and stones,
And bones that break,
And say that words "Just don't,"
For goodness sake.
'Cause what's a word
Sent through the air,
Dropped from the lips,
With little care?
But like an Arrow
Sent on high,
It falls to Earth,
We hear not its cry.
As it pierces deep
The gentle soil,
And quivers there,
And does recoil,
So do the Words
Released to taunt,
Forevermore
Remain—to haunt.
Barbara Ruth Neish

Waves

Wandering,
restless waves
rush to the shores
with gleeful frenzy;
expecting to end—
the perpetual search
for an abode of repose.

But, confronting a delusion,
recede
with indignant frustration,
only to be submerged
by cheering on-rushers;
their jubilant roar
overwhelming
the feeble warning
from the freshly deceived.
D. Veeru Reddy

Irreplaceable You

When two hearts unfold their wings of love
No one understands except the one up above
It's the sweetest puzzle to you and me
And Praise God!! Only true hearts can see

Your arms so warm,
So strong, so long,
Relax me as a melodious song
Your lips, so smooth as silk they felt
And suddenly, slowly I'll begin to melt

Your eyes, they speak to me as voices
I know I'm secure, I need no choices
The peace, the joy, the love we share
Leaves me no questions, I just know you care

Your heart, so big, so true, so pure
Weathers all storm and more love implore
With all my heart I love you true
God sure thought me special when he made "You"
Sharon Moodie

Conjecture

Twisting, turning, forever adrift.
Lost in times once lived voraciously
yet never enough, it seems; as I sift
endlessly, memories change.

Tints that were once rosy-hued
become grayer,
as though a bulb that once shone brightly
has begun to finally fade, slowly,
darkening what was once red and golden lights.
Experience shows better
that which youth hides, yet with older eyes,
I retrospect furtively,
piecing together aspects of what never was.

Like layers on layers,
forever covering the truth behind these memories,
now never to be trusted
as innocently as before.

Time fades and, once again,
leaves me waxing eloquence.
Sarah Cooling

A Creature

In a dark chamber, silently I lay
While men worry, in chaos they sway.
Eyes attached yet closed, and knew nothing of.
To life I breathe that nobody could scoff

From outside worries I may be so free,
Aid me, your mercy, nurture me safely.
Sturdy I may survive with mind healthy.
Give me a chance, please let me linger.
For, I crave the light like you forever.

Although pain is inflicted in your womb,
In time, I'm due your life in danger looms.
In spasmodic burst I cry in this land,
Waiting to be touched by your two soft hands!
Ma. Bonita P. Valdez

Poignant Being

With maddening rage, your passion dances from delightful to macabre,
and your grip on reality surrenders to delusion.
Like an alchemist drunk with deranged laughter and greed,
you search for the elixir of life.
Your soul, once ablaze with allegrettos and a sense of peace,
cowers under melancholy's inevitable control.
Because nothing lasts forever, your castle has crumbled,
leaving only a torrent of illusions.
Knowing your morals, you clung to them fiercely,
and refused to let anyone rape you of them.
Bruised from fate's shrieking and moaning,
you tried in vain to choke the past and present.
With faint hope, you waited for the day of resurrection,
but it could never arrive, your nostalgic ways were too intense.
Thus, because of your ceaseless medieval views and naiveness,
your song of triumph was incessantly muted,
and I was forced to watch in silence your pathetic attempt to be.

Candace Demone

My Hopes of Tomorrow with You

Every time I close my eyes, I see you here with me.
I wrap my arms around you, hold you close to me.
I can feel your warm and tender touch,
Your heartbeat close to mine,
When our burning lips unite I feel electrified,
And want to love you till the end of time.

There is something about you I just can't define.
I never met anyone so divine.
You live for love, understand, care,
And are so kind to all men and creatures alike
Your smile brings rainbows of sunshine and lifts up everyone's spirit high.
Knowing you and loving you is a wonderful experience to last a lifetime—
You truly are an Angel from above.

I let you down and caused you pain so many times,
Yet you always stood by my side and never let me down in spite of all that.

I'm afraid to open my eyes as I fear of what I might find.
I now realize I will never find another love quite like that.
If I could only have another chance to show you how I feel,
I'd put my arms around you and make you mine till eternity.

Angelique Fleming

A Dream

One man had a theory that our lives were someone's dreams,
A thought in his subconscious where nothing's as it seems.
The man said there's a world just like the one we know,
But this world is a perfect one without villains on the go.
And one psychotic being with thoughts of hate and rage
Has dreamed a world of violence and put us in his cage.
There is no higher power and when asked what death does mean
The man said rather simply, "We were wished out of his dream."
To know what makes this madman work, to know what's in his mind
Would be intriguing, yet most frightening, for fear of what we'd find.
The open raw emotions of society as one,
Our sick and twisted secrets, are used for this man's fun.
Every move a picture as the camera falls apart,
Only negatives are left in every beat of every heart.
No one has significance, nothing done or said has cause.
Our race would not be bitter if it weren't for one man's flaws.
Though these thoughts are naught but theory,
One question can't be shaken:
What will happen to our world
When this man does awaken?

Amanda Green

The Point of Life

So much stuff is going on around us all the time.
It's easy to get caught up racing for the finish line,
And yet once we arrive there, it never feels quite right.
The road we thought would end we find continues out of sight.

It's not that we've not made it, it's just that we forgot
That life is one long journey, so finishing is not
Something that will ever be; new goals will soon replace
The ones we have been working toward that got us in this race.

For, surely behind every goal lies the search for peace,
And in every achievement we do hope the urge will cease,
Yet only when we recognize that peace can only be
Found when we attend to every moment gratefully.

Will we then experience fulfillment of desire,
The only kind that truly stokes the hearth of inner fire?

So when you start to hurry,
Running past today, my friend,
Remember that the point of life
is not to reach the end.
   Debra McGee

My Wildest Dream

Dancing with the clouds on a cool summer's night,
Gliding through the sky feeling so light,
The wind blowing by, breezy and crisp,
Throwing my hair up with a calm, gentle twist.
A delicate hand whisked by on my face, silky and soft like elegant lace.
Upon my grasp, a faint open hand strives toward a beautiful land,
Escorting me toward a superior castle,
Pondering on without a hassle.
Glancing back and forth with a gleam in our eyes,
Reaching far out, under the skies,
Holding on tight under the stars,
Knowing the moment is definitely ours:
Still in the sky will the night stay forever,
'Cause that's what we'll be forever, together!
   Andrea Vander Loo

Untitled

As I cry myself to sleep at night, thoughts run through my mind:
A vision of paradise exists, a place I may never find.

Far away in a heavenly land, sanity a norm in society,
impossible would be for sadness to expand,
where peace is our root for sobriety.

A world of authenticity, so genuine and so very true,
recognized by its simplicity, ideal for me and you.

Whomever is feeling so troublesome as I, must keep a similar fantasy.
For, with all of these painful tears I cry,
I may drown in this horrible reality.

As I lose myself in this spectacular illusion,
the clock ticks throughout the night.
Just when I feel I've escaped my confusion, reality collides with my sight.

My heart becomes filled with endless rage,
my soul feeling hollow and deceased.
Once again my feelings imprisoned by a cage
until night when they shall be released.

So impatiently waiting for darkness to arrive,
the anxiety builds up within myself hours before my whole being turns
alive, when the reality is placed upon a shelf.
   Jennifer Maharaj

Love Worshippers

It's with us since the day we are born,
And lives with us till the day we die.
It is the one feeling that we cherish, yet mourn,
And all its abundance we defy.

It's our feelings that get confused
As we are involved in this passionate ambition.
In return we heed and abuse,
As it slowly fades away without recognition.

We treasure it, then lose it.
It slips away when we try to grasp it,
And plunges into our hearts
Leaving scars. Our only comforts are the memories.
Emilia Dominguez

Silver Path

When nights bathe the sky in black,
We wonder if there is light.
When drifting clouds shade the silent moon.
They hide our view, then suddenly drift away.
We see the perfect moon, the scattering bright stars
Held in harmony with silver threads.

With night and its soothing calm,
Our thoughts turn to drowsiness.
We think of black hue.
Then our faith renews.

In the vast stillness of night,
When we glimpse a shooting star,
We're held spellbound
Trying to measure distance
And its destination.
Time is limitless
In this divine universe.

On a path bewitched by stars.
Night shadows dance upon our
Tireless, patient moon.
Eleanor Staats

Brides of Snow

The falling snow adorned the trees like brides.
They're all aglow in veils of virgin white;
A slowed car on the highway dips and slides,
While fields and lawns reflect a wintry night.

See how they stand, all dressed and beautiful,
The maple and the pine and all the rest.
A gentle couturier calm and dutiful,
Spreads ermine at the feet of those he dressed.

So there is winter world of moonlit dreams,
We see their flowing, soft magnificence.
"The hunter of the East" with golden streams
Will bathe their hearts in his beneficence.

The morning sun will kiss their veils away,
While nature's jewels on their branches dance,
And bridegroom fills their hearts with his embrace
As they awaken from their bridal trance,
And we in gazing thus recall our goal,
To greet the loving Bridegroom of our soul.
Marion R. McManamy

The White

Peace shouldn't only be
Hoisting of the white flag,
Signing on the dotted lines,
But, "acceptance of it,
In one's soul,
In one's mind,
In one's heart
In one's deeds."
Bad blood between nations, cease.
Pure blood between nations, rule.
Emergence of marginalized love,
To be cuddled by living
Spirit of peace.
And white flag in pivotal,
Majestic role of dominance.
What else is there to say?
Martin P. Monareng

Love

What is love? Is it a rose?
Is it woman's pose?
Some say it is a knife
That cuts you and you bleed,
Like a seed becomes a flower
When you water it.
Is love a river that flows?
Do not know what love is.
I look up and see a white dove,
And it comes and sits on my
shoulder.
Just then I stop crying,
Because now I know what is love.
It's a white dove.
Mae Tzimoulis

Happiness

As I sit and watch her play,
Her smile and laughter, oh, so near,
I feel slight immortality
When I see myself in her.

She is the sunshine in my life,
The laughter in my voice,
The one that makes me feel complete,
And makes my heart rejoice.

In her small face I find more love
Than I could ever dream,
And all my prayers are answered
In this tiny human being.

If I could have just one wish
Come true for all to see,
I'd wish to return the happiness
That my daughter gives to me.
Trudi M. Roth

A Hero Lasts Forever

A hero is looked upon,
Sought out to be a prize;
Found to be a person,
As human as you or I;
Someone to give you a boost,
Someone to help you on your way.
A hero lasts forever.

Someone you know,
Or someone you have never seen,
My hero is someone
Who is very dear to me.
A hero lasts forever,

As long as you need them
And as long as they need you . . .

Michelle D. Pompana

Upsurge

A frightened, lonely little girl
sat crying on the floor.
Four walls closed in around her,
she could not find a door.
This was not the first time,
she had wounds that were so sore.
She had to end the sadness,
she could not cry much more.

So finding all the strength she had,
she boxed free from that room.
She was determined to be happy,
there would be no more doom and gloom.

A courageous and strong woman
smiles at her reflection in the floor,
at the walls secure around her,
as the light shines in the door.
Joyous to be living with a hope
of things in store.
Grateful for the freedom to be
herself forevermore.

Kay Jones

Fossil's Reprise

This is
A tossed salad
Consisting of
A rare libido
Which has been
Marinating within
The uncertainties
Of her lustful life
She has made several
Toasts in regards to
Fulfilling escapades
And yet this rare sauterne
Still tastes of nothing more
Than just aged vinegar

Paula Whittaker

Prayer for My Children

Into my keeping a treasure so rare,
These are the children God placed in my care.
People beginning the journey of life,
Or a road that will often be riddled with strife.
Persons that need a faith that is true,
God give me help in my guidance of you.
I pray you will seek the path less trod,
For this is the one that leads to God.

God, give me wisdom to love but not jail.
Give to me guidance that will not fail.
Let me mould but not break these lives of Yours,
As I seek Your voice to open the doors.
Help me to steer but not lead as I pray
For guidance to start these lives on their way.
As they tackle the road and the road bends,
God, allow us all Earth's time to be friends.

Elizabeth Von Keitz

Princess of the People

Married in a story book romance,
A princess, who was of and for all people.
A loving mother, of two teenaged sons,
who she loved, oh, so very dear.
A true angel of hope and love, for those in despair,
for she loved all, both far and near.

But life is so full of irony and uncertainty.
One never knows what may come,
For on this tragic day
The princess of the people could not be saved.

For a speeding car, the driver drunk,
Behind the wheel, crashed into a
reclining wall, ending the life of princess,
who gave her all.

Oh, Diana, the world shall miss
that smile, your beauty, grace, courage, and faith.
You'll be in our hearts always,
and forever in our prayers.

Stephen D. Pommer

Fantasy

Where were you when I could have loved you?
Where were you when I longed to be in your arms
each and every night?

Where were you when I needed you, to love you
In the fantasy of another's arms?
Was it worth the loss of true love, the
Love that would have loved you forever?

Now you are alone to dream of your many loves.
A true love you will never find,
For the clouds of fantasy,
And betrayed by fall dreams.

When the clouds have rolled away, and you can see
That I was the one true love in your life,
By then I will be no more.

Olga Taylor

Love-Forsaken Soul

Is that a boat I see there on the lake?
Is there a ferry man to take me to yonder shore?
Why won't you answer me?
Can't you say yes or no?
The wind, the waves, the blue sky above,
How silent are thou.
Oh, life's elements,
Yet silent judges of time,
Could you not comfort a love-forsaken soul?
Alone I stand here,
Alone in grief.
Who can I turn to?
There's no one to see.
Please, Mr. Ferry Man, take me across in your boat,
Let me sail on the seas of forgetfulness,
Never, never to anchor again on the shores of memory.
Patsy R. Mohammed

October

I missed October this year
Not because I was basking on some tropical isle,
I was here—alone.
Love seems so close now—
Maybe, it's the maple tree
in mom's back garden
"In Flames. . . ."
Muskoka is alive this time of year.
I miss you so!
October is vibrant—not unlike you.
Being alone, feeling so much from
within—alive with feeling,
Now that feeling is real—stay . . .
I love you—you are the beginning of "October."
Doris I. Karman

Fate

Devilish potters who, with spinning madness,
mold the shape that our lives will bear . . .

Little goblins who, playing mischievously,
blend the essences that will pervade our souls . . .

Diabolic gamblers who, with skillful tricks,
cast the dice that will decree our fate . . .

Sinister puppeteers who, sneering proudly,
handle the strings that will control our hearts . . .

Aliens from beyond the Earth . . .
Eerie beings, distant stars, mythical Gods . . .

I summon you to bear witness to your deeds!

Expose your distorted faces.
Let us hear your discordant voices.

Do not sink into the gloomy night.
Spring forward onto the radiant day.

Stop jeering at our vain efforts,
mocking our pointless pains,
deriding our futile wishes
. . . to attain the bliss of heavenly existence
in this earthly reality of human life.
Beatriz Lilia Solina

Looking Back

John told Mary, Mary told Sam
That I said, Jim was seeing Pam.
I didn't say it, but John did.
I overheard him talking to Ned.

Now Pam is mad at me.
Jim, he's mad too.
With everyone up in arms
What do I do?

I tried to tell them that it was John
Jealous because Pam was gone.
He asked me out, I wouldn't go;
I won't be second and I told him so.

The list goes on of teenage woes
That are very real, yours and mine,
But looking back many years ago
They were only big at the time.

'Cause Ned joined the Army,
I married John,
Mary ran away with Sam,
And Jim married Pam.
Betti Ann States

Conclusion

The clatter of your heels
Upon a charcoaled plain
Above in all you feel
This beautiful, curtained dance.

The neighbor's wisdom does cajole
The words, how nice they seem.
Not all that shines is really gold.
Not all wisdom is itself.

When all the clouds are cold and mean,
And no more corners to turn,
When only one can mediate
This channel of dishonor.

Upon this journey of sinuous roads,
Engaged in laughter immense,
But in the rancor of the next
Continues this morbid dance.

And now concludes this voyage
In sorrow, reprisal done,
Creates another time
When all is really one.
Jane Silva

Diana—Princess of Wales

Sweet Ambassador,
Full of ardour,
Brought love and comfort
To the sick and the poor.

She walked with dignity,
She showed every grace.
Though her heart was broken,
She kept a smile on her face.

She curtsied and bowed,
She traveled everywhere.
The throngs lined the streets,
For she proved that she cared.

Lepers and AIDS victims
She caressed with a touch.
Her devotion was dauntless,
To each one, meant so much.

Her compassion, so genuine,
She was loved far and near.
A true Royal in spirit,
Diana, we all hold you dear.

Nancy Thomas

Bourgeois Burlesque

the aching void of empty sky
wails of torment and despair
as endless oil-slicked gulls are stilled
in deadly ooze and toxic waste

microscopic plant-life strangled
by formaldehyde surprise
dumped into a wordless ocean
by cost-effective, balding chiefs

landfill sites exuding plastics
pools of PCB's flow free
intermingled with ground water
spawning glowing mutant rats

thinning ozone layer threatens
birth defects, a heartsick clue
global warming melts the ice caps
flooded farmland means no food

terror rages through the forest
as animals adapt or die
mothers shelter young with fury
all in vain from rain that burns

Bonnie Ryan

Eventide Tranquility

We walked over hills to our favorite retreat
far from the clatter of traffic and feet
where down in the meadow, air was still
and eventide quietness presented a thrill:
As glowing sunset changed colours of flowers,
we saw through a break in the trees
a yonder green valley and ultramarine lake
where, in the twilight danced a whispering breeze.
Stopping to soliloquize, enchanted by view,
I set up my easel, as painters do,
for, there in the centre of tranquil scene
a black swan appeared as in mesmerized dream.
He majestically moved with noble stability,
proudly surveying evening serenity;
unmoved by our presence, he passed us by,
enjoying sweet fragrance and sun-setting sky.
I painted my picture of an evening enrapture
as only a study in nature can capture!

Sylvia Brewster

Being at a War

The guns firing, the bombs exploding
this is what it is like to be at a war;
children crying, people dying,
this is what it is like to be at a war.
Every soldier,
every single soldier,
keeping a teddy bear, a doll, or a picture
to remember a loved one.
This is what it is like to be at a war.
What causes war?
Hatred, pride, and jealousy.
Why does everybody want power?
Why do people fight to get what they want?
Why must millions of people die because of wars?
Why can't we all live in peace?
Why?
So many questions,
So few answers:
This is what it is like to be in a war.

Tariq Mohammed

Untitled

Statics reside in my fingertips.
Circulating through my thoughts,
Contemplating the present state of disconnection,
i stand in the express line of life
Purchasing artificially coloured cures,
Amused by the toothless grin
Which smiles as it is placed on the grass.
Newly-bought biscuits,
The ungrateful birds, the unforgiving words,
The intestinal clues of compassion
Which compete for my attention:
You have misused my attempts
And now your handsome architecture
Cannot withstand my sand sanity,
For it has hardened
From days and years of solace fears,
Stoned, electric outlet tears.

Janet Renee Tucker

Next Christmas Will Be Different

My Christmas tree fell over when I put the star on top,
The heavy decorations caused the half-dead bows to flop.
The dog ate all the gingerbread and candy canes there were.
Next Christmas will be different, I'm telling you. I'm sure!

The shopping malls were crowded, it was chaos wall to wall,
I felt like decking cashier clerks instead of decking halls.
I had to kiss my grandma underneath the mistletoe.
Next Christmas will be different, I just wanted you to know.

The wreath that hangs about our door fell down onto the stairs,
I tripped on it in my good clothes. My pants now have a tear.
The Santa in the mall took off when I was next in line.
Next Christmas will be different. Next Christmas will be fine.

That reindeer slipped and broke his nose when landing on my roof,
Our colored lights burned out that night and caught its clumsy hoof.
My brother caught the chicken pox and had to stay in bed.
Next Christmas will be different, that's exactly what I said.

I got the same book seven times, and shorts that are too small,
My favorite Uncle Brad hung up on me this Christmas call.
If all Christmases are bad like this, I don't know how I'll cope.
Next Christmas will be different, at least that's what I hope.

Jonathan Love

Dad

After all these years what is one to say
To one she has known all her life but seemed so far away

At first I thought I knew him, in his eyes I did not see
How one small thing could change him from the man he used to be

For as long as I remember he has had a "Lemon Heart"
That was made of golden laughter, but tore his life apart

I despised that endless bottle that stole that man from me
I was jealous of the attention that I did not receive

When suddenly it hit him, his body had enough
Abuse from his addiction, he got rid of that awful stuff

I have never been so happy in all my living days
To see him look so handsome without that gloomy haze

We have had our good times and Lord knows we've had our bad
But I will always be his girl and he will be my Dad

Candace Clark

Racing

As I sink deeply into this kitten's cushion,
It welcomes me. One arm slings over my shoulder,
One arm curls around my waist; embraced
While breath and blood begin to race.
Nine vital men and women circle the engine and me,
Tuning the instrument with catlike calculation.
I keep the pace. Radio? Check. Fuel? Check. Helmet? Check.
Did I mention there are spares in case
My rubber tires? Just me now, waiting.

Another time (or not) as this cat purrs
In the warmth of my mother's quilted furs.
I would be soft in REM,
My feline friend in RPM,
And quickly sleeping I would dream
Of milky places never seen
Where hills are high and fields are . . . Green!
I know how it feels
To be a pebble in a slingshot.

Ryan Keith

My Lady Love

Unbelieving when I said, "Been waiting for you all my life."
"How could you be, when you did not even know I existed?" you asked,
"How could you have been waiting for me?"
You did not even know my name,
You did not even know my face,
You did not even know I existed.

I went to the store to buy a shirt,
Knew there was a shirt out there for me;
Did not know what style, did not know what colour,
Searched from store to store, no haste,
Do not find it today, will find it tomorrow,
Next week, next month, next year.

Driving past a mall, glanced at a store,
What's that, stopped; walked over, that's my shirt;
Somewhere out there; knew my shirt was waiting for me,
Did not know your name, did not know your face,
But knew you existed.

Then I saw you, "Dear God! Here she is,
The other half to complete our perfect whole."
I love you, my lady love,
Now believing when I say, "Been waiting for you all my life."

Leslie W. Gordon

A Rainstorm

I sat by my window watching the sunset,
when it started to rain.
I ran outside in my bathing suit,
and watched the rain running down the window pane.

I ran around, jumping and dancing in the puddles,
getting wet head to toe.
I was having so much fun
that I forgot about going to visit Moe.

I was enjoying watching the rain running down the gutter,
when I heard the thunder.
Then I saw a bolt of lightning,
I looked up at the sky with a face filled with fear.

I ran up to my room,
and wrapped my towel around me.
I sat and watched the rest of the storm
from my room where it was warm and cozy.

Nisha Jeyaseelan

Laura

My heart as stone,
Thoughts of melancholy only mine,
Until you whispered, your Spell covering me,
And I knew again I was happy.

Our walks, talks, our laughs,
No dolor did I sense.
You made me feel good about me, about us.
Laura, beautiful, your enchantment over me complete.

Now, heart of mine is barren,
Chained to Spectres of you.
A wilderness where a garden had been,
I look for Sun's radiance, and only Rain's shadows I see.

I miss, I long for our moments,
Your smile, your laugh,
Your beautiful Emerald Eyes.
A wisp of an elegant vision I will keep eternally.

Our time together tho' too brief,
Know I that we each found someone who understood us.
We bonded, but too short, then we shattered.
You still begin my thoughts, and Dreams of you end my day.

Lawrence Myers

Princess Diana

Although she once was very shy,
She expressed her feelings and would even cry—
She was a story book princess of her time,
With love for others that made her fine.
Always there to lend a hand,
To many AIDS victims, then took a stand.
For any worthy cause today,
There she'd be and there she'd stay.
There is only one question left to ask,
About a fairy princess that's in our past.
Mirror, mirror, on the wall,
Princess Diana is the one to be,
The fairest lady, can't you see?
With her beauty and her smarts,
Forever she'll remain the Queen of Hearts.

Gone but never forgotten.
   Mary Lou Anderson

Ghetto Life

Battered roofs, broken glass
Dilapidated houses, lower class

Children playing in the hood
Mother's praying, God will do them good

Struggling hard to make ends meet
To make it possible for the ghetto youth to eat

Nowhere to play, ghetto youth turn to the street
Get caught up with drugs; wasted, dead meat

As we continue the quest for our cry to be heard
No help from the governor, not even a word

Life in the ghetto, full of struggle and strife
Dreams of turning it around to live a new life
   Kia Burchall

True Meaning of Life

I used to be a potter,
When clay used to get squeezed under my bare feet,
That was the real pride for me,
When the earthen pot used to get different shapes.
That was the real pride for me,
When I used to punch, I baked that pot in oven.
That was the real pride for me,
When I used to paint and glaze that pot.
That was the real pride for me,
But now I have become a pot of earth,
Now I feel really close to God.
   Vivek P. Kalekar

Soldiers

Blood sheds
Babies cry
Women scream for the lives of their husbands
The soldiers
Fighting for their country
Fighting for Freedom
Sacrificing themselves for others
In the midst of explosions
   William Barnes

What the Lake Knew

Cozy, time-weary cottage,
ants and squirrels sensing your death
attack your aged bones.
I struggle to tend your many wounds,
but age is my enemy too.
Peaceful, restorative water,
your tranquil mirror calms my soul,
but cruelly tells the future.
Now caught in time we sit reflected,
seeing truth in your shimmering depths.
Our image fades with gathering dusk,
foretelling the passing of friends.
   J. Lindsay Morrison

Untitled

He gets so emotional.
I end up feeling sorry
For him,
Or else actually just wanting
To be held
Or kissed.
My mind sways
Back and forth;
And before I know it
His face is too close to mine.
And then I whisper
"No."
And it is even harder not to.
   Amanda Lewis

Lost

I see you again
after so long
and my breath comes
gasping down
that still
you do this to me
after so long
and I am happy
that my spirit feels its youth
and I am sad
that my heart lost its truth
so long ago . . .
so long ago . . .
yet
not forgotten
as I see you again
my soul knows
back then
when I was faithful
I cheated myself.
   Joanne Allong Haynes

Desire

I take you down in my desire,
Burning, burning,
Supernova proportions.
You take me down,
I take you higher.
Caught up,
Entangled,
The lovers embrace.
I never saw the warning,
The angel's face
Moving above me
In silent glory,
Reflecting the horror
Of my shining moment.
Innocence
I lost forever,
Dancing the dance
Of moonlight desire.

Amanda J. Hare

I BELIEVE IN ANGELS

I believe that angels fly
That souls gone by
Wear halos gold and fine
And walk a short few steps behind
The people left to survive
This world without their smile

I hear a whisper, smell a scent
I believe it's heaven sent
Angels singing songs on high
From rooftops, mountains, and the sky
They fly to the highest of the highs
And sit beside us to laugh and cry

I believe that angels fly
That souls gone by
Wear halos gold and fine

Debra Harrigan

Dark Rain under a Dead Tree

I sat by that old, dead tree and remember
all the fun we had by that tree.
Then I remembered the fight we had by
that old tree,
and as it grew colder and the rain fell
I remember what you said to me ("I love
you"). That day that the tree died and you left.
The rain fell hard and my tears fell over my
face as I thought of you, where you were,
How you are and what you are doing.
The rain stopped, but my tears didn't. I thought
I could live without you, but I guess I was wrong.
So I'm writing you this letter, so I can say
good-bye without crying, and don't try to see
me unless you want to go to the old, dead tree.
You will find me under one of the branches,
or at least my remains.

Janine Miller

Algonquin Skies

Once upon a time, I saw a long house
In the sky, curiously formed
By the smoke
Coming from an outdoor fire
Improvised by a camping crowd
Visiting the old farmhouse.
The smoke blew across the country road,
Stretching up and over like a bridge.
Chimney smoke from the neighbor's wood stove
Blew up and over to the other side,
Greeting and meeting the smoke
In a bracing effect.
It was May.
The maple trees had blossomed,
And some leaves were in a state of shock.
A sudden frost had occasioned the wood fires.

Francine Bergeron

Do You

Do you cringe when a lion takes a deer
While it was innocently eating grass?
Do you have your reasons for allowing this?
Do you close your eyes when a snake suffocates a frog
While sleeping on a rock?
Do you intend letting me know?
Do you turn your head away
When a farmer shoots a native animal
That he's caught eating on his property?
Do your reasons have a purpose?
Do you cover your face
When a fisherman goes to slaughter a dolphin
He feels is a nuisance?
Do you wish to let me know?
Do you block your cars when a dog cries
After being belted with an iron bar
But can't run for shelter because it's tied up?
Do I have the power to stop this?
Do you?
You do.

Dominique Clapp

The Wind

From seas and rivers, from oceans and land,
you'll find it there in the palm of your hand.
Don't try to see it, just know that it's there,
by the warmth, the rain, and the chill in the air.
It sings in the chimes and blows through the trees.
It waves over grass and plays with the leaves.
It climbs over mountains and runs over ground,
but sometimes it's still and doesn't make a sound.
If you listen really hard you can hear it exclaim
the word you know well as it whispers your name.
It weeps with the willows and wrestles the corn
from dusk until dawn: A new wind will be born.

Andrina Matthie

My Mother

To Mary Ann Sahagon
My mother, the best of all,
Who was always there to never let me fall.
She gave me life and humanity,
And always had pride and dignity.

She was always there to care and love me,
Also gave birth and showed me the world to see.
I really love her with all my heart
And I pray every night for us to not part.

When I am sick she would make me soup,
And we would always stick together like a troop.
She would also cheer me up when I am down,
So she would not see a lonely frown.

If I were happy, but would not smile,
She would make me, and would even take a while.
I was telling the truth when I said I pray,
It's just because I don't want her to go away.

Gina Sahagon

Maternal Love

I lie here in the womb of my mother.
I am not born but I already have a home.
I hear the voices of two happy people
As they thank God for making me.

I already know my mother's voice.
She speaks such loving words to me
Even though I'm not full term,
And I kick my legs as a response.

She listens often to my little heart,
And cries her tears of joy.
I used to think it was sadness,
But then she'd rub her stomach and say, "I love you."

For nine months I stayed that way,
Growing a little each time,
My little thumb jammed in my mouth,
Listening to her beautiful words.

The last thing I remember is her cry of pain
As I anxiously pushed my way out.
The love she showed me when I was inside,
Is nothing compared to now.

Arlene Versteeg

Wash Me Free

Your eyes reflect
the fear
I hold like a well
You know more than I
why I can't let it go
It holds me closer
than your arms
Controls me
when I feel
I'm beyond control
Pulling away
it only stays with me
a blown-glass aura
counterfeit safety
Gather them up
the four corners of my heart
In a cradle of your tears
wash me free

Beverly Bouma

At My First Glance

I thought you were a weed
But upon I closer look I noticed
You were a rare, exotic flower
Beautiful in your simplicity
Yet complex in your many colours
Each petal taking on its own
Shape and individual identity
Absorbing the warmth of the sun
Exploding with a sweet scent
As I look around
I see many footsteps around me
And I begin to wonder
Did they think you a weed
And just pass you by
Or did they, like me
Stare in amazement
At a rare, exotic flower

Lana Simpson

Life Is Pain

Forever in the death
of my heart
I feel such a pain,
like a knife wound
that won't go away.
But I can deal with it,
I have before.
It's nothing different now,
it's not something I have to find
or have found.
And if it went away,
it'd be too late.
And if it left me now,
it wouldn't matter,
for I've died before.

Veronica Lynn Ann

A Tribute to Diana, Princess of Wales

Diana was a shinning star
on Earth,
but now,
she is a shooting star
in the heavens above.
Even though she is
no longer here,
her light is brighter
than any candle,
or even the sun.
Her kindness broke any wall,
but now,
will the walls build again?
Only a shooting star will know....

Natalie Hughes

John

Eyes of the clearest blue
Framed by lashes of velvet
Clash with the strawberry stubble
And thrust to his chin.

His smile is captivating;
The grin of a mischievous boy
Shines on the face
Of an undoubtedly grown man.

Cockily he struts his self-confidence;
His air of righteous independence
Is tangible—
No harness could subdue this spirit.

He is intoxicatingly sexy,
Yet a glimpse within
Reveals the tenderness, the vulnerability
He so struggles to masquerade.

Eyes of the clearest blue
Framed by lashes of velvet
Complement the rugged beauty
Of the man's soul.

Angèle Messer

My Friend Is Gone

I was all alone the day you left me,
I didn't say good-bye to you.
Now all I have are your memories,
the days we hung out.
I sometimes speak your name
to people who ask about you.
I often think about you, with God in heaven.
I dream about you running through
the beautiful flowers, with the breeze in your face.
So I will say good-bye one last time,
and cry for you one last time.
Our friendship will never end.

Cassandra Strub

Distance and Time

You are like the sun to me,
Always shining, always lighting my life.

You are always there,
And although sometimes I cannot see you,
I know you are shining somewhere.

My young son, lost far too soon.
To my son, a gentle prayer.

I endure the night,
Because I will see you soon.

Clouds of time may interfere,
But I feel your warm breath.

When it rains, I know you are trying
To rid us of the tears that fall.

I see you smiling in my thoughts ... so beautiful.
So I'll see you soon, and you me.

Someday the sun will shine forever,
And we shall be eternally together.

K. Jill McMurray

Diana

A fairy tale dream that didn't come through,
A life shortened that was sometimes blue;
Diana came to us on a summer's day,
Warmed our hearts, and took our breath away.

A princess young and innocent,
Charm and beauty you did transcend.
Into a storm, Diana, you were thrown.
When it was over you held your own.

To the world, Diana, you were a friend.
A gentle touch, a heart you'd mend.
Pain and suffering you shared with all.
The people's princess you were called.

You left the world a part of you.
In William and Harry your precious two
For whom you loved and deeply cared,
Diana, the world will forever endear.

Diana, princess of style and grace,
With love and compassion the world you embraced.
From this world you were suddenly called,
But will forever be loved by all.

Mary Mahadeo

Sensation

Luxuriate in the silken darkness,
Reveling in the aches,
Stretching and curling with leonine grace.

The scent lingers,
Like the smoke of incense,
Hidden pleasure insinuated in its presence.

Desire-whetted bodies
Heat the turgid air,
Still expectant and unfulfilled.

The silence rings,
With half-forgotten,
Passionate murmurs, delightful sobs.

Salted essence clings
To swollen, moist lips,
Hungry mouths descending on forbidden secrets.
   Rachelle Redford

My Sleeping Love

You lay your head atop my chest.
You gently touch my breast.
A smile drawn across your lips
as you fall asleep.
Ever so softly I caress your face.
with my finger I trace
your sensual features; your eyes and ears
and you fall asleep.
I close my eyes and see the dream.
Reality is not always what it may seem,
though you are real, as is our love,
and the life we hold in each other's arms
shall continue together.
Forever.
   Julie Desilets

Apathy

As I look across the mountain,
what did I see?
The smoke-filled sky and polluted streams,
The anger of the people through their selfish greed.

As I sit in my mountain retreat,
what did I do?
I thought about the s**** below, their gloating faces,
their posh places.

As I look from my mountain,
what did I see?
People starving,
people fighting,
mothers crying, and fathers dying.
My mountain is safe, from that hell of a place
where people don't care,
they just sit and stare like me.
   Brian Pearson

Lust, Passion, Sexuality

Lust, passion, sexuality,
it is in our society,
it is everything describing me,
the physical side of me.

Lust, passion, sexuality,
it's a form of personality,
it's many people's reality,
it affects our morality.

Lust, passion, sexuality,
it is my identity,
it is what I show,
and what you see.

Lust, passion, sexuality,
it can be wonderful,
it can deceive,
it can relieve,
it can intensify,
it can magnify,
but ultimately can destroy
our spirit and our soul.
   Nancy Murray

Nicotine: You Filthy Queen

In the morn' I love thee
With my cup of coffee.
Prime time for consumption
Is after sex, no gumption,
Which brings the exclamation,
Ahhh! The realization
That you, dear Queen,
Are best not seen.
I shun you now, you filthy cow.
I am so pure but even now,
One scent, one whiff, one puff
Would be enough and, oh, so tough.
Avert my eyes, hold my breath,
Dull my senses, you'll be my death.
All my life you'll be my wife!
In my dreams, you filthy queen.
The b****, I cannot ditch.
Queen, you evil witch,
Ah, it's all manure 'cause I'm so pure!
It isn't s***; I've really quit!
   Thomas Meredith

I Just Want a Dad

A young girl lies, her
Innocence whole, till
She came to the age, when
She had more. What
Was it, dear Mary, that
Your daddy stole? could
It have been the
Heart of your soul? What
Would you do if
You could punish him now? Would
You bind him in chains? Would
You kill him somehow? Would
You just ask him why, how
Does his soul smell, and
Is he afraid of
Burning in hell? But
All that you want is
Just what you had, the
Love that you knew before
You lost your dad.

Russell Dobson

Howling to the Moon

How could I have loved you yesterday
without restraint, and not forget
that love is just a trifle left behind,
forgotten, atop a chair?

Or maybe draped over a velvet sofa,
or next to a hydrant in some street corner;
an intense, sonorous interplay,
at times just sighs, moans, and silences.

Had you understood it somewhat sooner,
that same day you left so hurriedly,
wearily along the winding road,

You could have left me, as a memento,
hanging from the moon in its last quarter,
your bra and your panties dipped in syrup.

Jose R. Vales

Love Infinite

The moonlight splits the night,
Like a sabre through black velvet;

A rose petal falls on my breast
Like a bead of blood on white satin;

Candlelight shadows your warm body
Beside me, touching my soul;

You kisses teasing, pleasing;
Your hands caressing, undressing;

Your tongue and lips searching for forever,
And forever is this moment of our oneness.

Elizabeth Radmore

Women

What more do you want from me?
You have degraded me to this.

You have told me that I am this.
I am a sexual object, not a person.

I am your toy, not your co-worker.
I am your b****, not your wife.

I must stand in front of you, legs spread and naked.
I perform on command.

But I am not that.
I am a person with talent.

My gender has worked too hard for me to lie down.
Treat me as an equal, no better or worse.

Respect my values and myself: There is no weaker sex.
I am a woman who could have been your mother.

Janice Moser

Our Innocence Is Gone

I see it with my own eyes,
babies having babies, babies taking lives.
There seems to be no more talking it out,
the talk is gone; now it's all clout.
The future looks dim if we continue with this trend.
The killing has to stop, the violence has to end.

I watch the news every night at six:
people getting hurt, junkies searching for a fix.
This unfortunate truth that is so clear,
the criminals are younger, the violence is near.
It's gotten to the point, going to the store is not safe.
What used to be the playground, is now a killing place.

When does it all end, when will it stop?
It's not safe nowadays to even be a cop.
There's no fear or respect for the police,
the attitude is "sc*** you," they do as they please.
We have to find the answers to what's gone wrong.
The criminals are younger, our innocence is gone.

Kenneth Edwin Garland

Headache

He ripped out his hair by the roots.
He pounded on his skull with closed fists.
He knocked his forehead against a concrete
Wall until he bled a wash of red.
He drilled a hole in his temple with a hand driller.
He gave himself a lobotomy with a rusty spoon.
He pushed a rail tie spike through the soft spot
On the back of his head.
He deep fried his face in boiling oil.
He did everything he could, but he just could
Not get her out of his head.

Brian Webb

Humanity?

Once again, I find I'm shedding tears,
not tears of joy, love, or grief.
These tears fall when I look at our society.

A baby is crying, while a single mother tries to feed!
Homeless children wander aimlessly, with no place to sleep!
No medication for a war veteran's pain!
No shelter for a young family thrown out in the rain!

Humanitarianism has fallen from its state of grace.
I can't say I'm proud to live in this place
where laws protect the guilty or insane.
I think we need to re-evaluate,
correct our laws, and bring them up to date.
Forget about you, forget about me,
human rights are for our longevity!

Young punks beat up a grandmother, just to take her purse;
they will get nothing of what they deserve.
Why do we let a convicted child molester sleep
So at night he can dream of loving somebody else's baby?
Sweet sixteen, she won't be coming home late,
tonight she will be dinner, on a homicidal rapist's supper plate!

Ritchie Greves

Collect

I just spoke to someone who showed me the way
To beat all the traffic, to get through the day.

A ride on a cushion so soft and so light,
A beautiful, bright, shimmering flight,
This feeling of rapture, so sweet and so fine,
Can be yours, you good people, for the price of a dime,
Just call your pusher collect.

Stan Cameron

Restoration

A stupid mistake I made long ago, hurt you so much, that I know!
Yet after that all I can say, is forgive me, dear, in any way.
I never wanted to hurt you so much,
So, my love, I show you through my touch,
My heart hurts with every step I take,
Just thinking of how much I made you ache.
Your love is all I have, it's true, but don't forget I love you too.
I never wanted to make you cry, I still ask myself, "****, why?"
You probably say it's nothing to you,
Yet through your eyes I see it's not true!
Darling, you know that I love you so true,
And a stupid mistake, again, I won't do!
I never intended to break your heart.
Boy! I was so close to having us apart!
I know that inside you still ache, and that smile I see, I know it's fake!
You can always lean on me and cry out your tears,
Count that I'll be there to chase your fears
I know I hurt you so badly, it's true, but I am trying to make it up to you!
So if you can find it deep in your heart,
Then forgive me, dear, and let us restart. . . .

Bedoor Khalaf

Longing for Adultery

My face grows numb with alcohol . . .
The butterflies in my stomach are calling for you.
You left in a hurry. You seemed too anxious to leave.
Was is something I said? Or something I didn't say?
I want to f*** you. There, I said it. But you already knew that.
I dare not initiate anything—my conscience forbids me.
When you make advances, I cast them aside heartlessly.
I'm sorry. I can't help it . . . yes I can, I'm sorry.
My face grows numb with alcohol.

When you brought me to your place, I felt I was home.
You've captured my heart.
You're living a life I wish to lead. You inspire me.
When I look into your eyes, I am saddened.
Your eyes reveal solitude, freedom, wisdom, and truth.
All that I wish to behold. All that I lack.
I want to come home to you.

You have given me more than I realize. You are beyond words.
You speak to my soul, whether you are present or not.
If it were in my power, I would crown you the God of intensity.
But these are mere words, and you deserve so much more.

Noelle Murphy

Reflections of the Heart

The love once awakened, brings joy in every simple thing.
You see the world with renewed joy.
In simple pleasures there is such depth.
It is eternal summer in your heart.

True love shimmers your heart with laughter.
There are no rules or principles that you would not bend.
You make any sacrifice for the warmth of the look,
To simply drown in the loving depths of those eyes.

True love is felt in just remembering that loving smile,
The smile that lights up my heart and the world around me.
Like the summer sun, the warmth lingers . . .

True love opens your heart to love profound.
Your heart overflows with, oh, such joy!!
Thank you, my love, for I never knew
Such love as you have made me feel.

Bharti Patel

Tonight

Tonight I kissed the man I began an affair with 18 months ago.
His eyes sparkled as I entered the room and he held me in his gaze.
They beckoned me to share the secret thought of intimacy to come.
As he spoke my name, my heart tightened with desire
and I was instantly jealous of those standing close to him.
His hand brushed my side as he walked past
and I burned with aching as the sensation of his touch remained.
Tonight I kissed that man.
After hours of talking about the reasons we could never be,
the moment arose and we were.
He held me close and then cupped a gentle hand to my face
as he inhaled my neck and paid homage with lingering kisses.
Desire tore from my heart and shot through my body.
Passion danced through me like a flame searching for his touch.
I whispered his name, barely breathed it in a sigh of passion laced with
tenderness and the reply was a touch of tenderness laced with passion.
His restraint evident in the trembling of his fingers on my face
and the dusting of touch on my lips,
I gave in to our fever and melted against him.
Tonight I kissed that man, and I won't ever be the same.

M.C. Francisca Sinn

When I Think of You, My Love

I live in the faith, I practice charity.
I wait for a favor, the heart of my lover.

Under the sky of Trenton, there is one heart that I love and cherish.
This heart is yours, Kathy.

Oh! Say Yes . . . Say No, tell me that you love me, "yes."
Love is like a candy bar, everyone would like to take a bit of it.

Under the starry night, I love to pass the night.
Close to your heart, receive from you your soft kiss.

I'm so joyful . . . to be loved by the one I love so much.
Demonstrate your love for me, tell me, do you love me?
Try only for one day to be together,
To be united forever.

It is not too hard to answer to your request.
I'm prepared to realize all your requirements.

Give a Kiss, it is a holy gesture.
To grant faith to the one who is receiving,
without discouraging the one who's giving it.

From my heart, listen to my voice
That is telling you with energy, I only love you . . .

The letter is a letter of gold.

Serge Lalonde

Survival of the Young

I know the redundant, chaotic era of youth
Like a hypnotic picture show for your bored entertainment.
On material, glossy paper you are pasted,
Shooting aimless energy and
Crying at your tentative nature, discontent,
Sighing at nothing and laughter that is the same,
And the energy is your happiness.
Absorbed into blank walls you cover with a
Talent, and we are all stars,
But each an enigmatic universe;
You are lost and empty and afraid
And you make your motivations so you'll
Never have to fake it:
Alone in company and awed at the blank spot.

Youth are lost souls seeking definition
Until they've been conformed, innocence promenaded,
Youth detained and aged: and I feel so old, but beautiful.
So glamorous are the stars.

You were a generational era,
But I am the epic denied.

Geneva Janzen

Birthdays

Every year you have a birthday to remind you of your first day here.
Every birthday also reminds you that you get older
  after each and every year.
I've had many birthdays, and can't go back, but only ahead.
I have so many memories to share, all stored in my head.
Each birthday is a new beginning, a chance to start anew,
To look into the future with high hopes,
  and to do what you always wanted to.
The garden of knowledge and wisdom you've planted
  will neither wither nor die,
But will blossom in much more beauty,
  as the next birthday passes you by.
So don't wish to live your life over again, don't worry about the past,
Because another birthday is coming, and they all go by so fast!

Stephanie Fiorini

Sister Moon (To My Bride on Our Wedding Day)

The clouded sky makes dark tonight
The land that lies below.
For years of months and weeks, no light
To make its river glow.
A few small twinkles, a few small brights,
Yet nothing made this current show
Its water's impassioned toil, or its torrent's playful flight.

But, stop! Tonight, do clouds recoil?
A shaft of Light spills through
To touch the waves and raise the iridescent dance.
What Luminary? From where this dazzling Hue?

It's YOU, my Sister Moon.
The Light streams from your face,
A borrowed Brilliance, not your own.
Of every good and perfect gift, the Source,
Your heavenly Light, from the eternal Sun.

Could there be a dance tonight
Of Moonlight with the magic water?
Will the moonlit sky make bright
The land that lies below?

Andreas Tabert

Lost Soul: A Sonnet

Sometimes I wonder what I've ever done wrong.
I know I've sinned, but can hell be this long?

I'm lost in frustration, blinded by my tears,
held down by my uncertainty, hindering my fears.

I've lost my faith in people, it's hard to look them in the eye.
They've stolen all my willpower, making me wonder why.

I've locked up my heart and thrown away the key.
My emotions and my soul fastened deep inside of me.

Will things get better or will I be stuck inside
This pit of despair that I've been trying to hide?

It's been a year, every night a tear,
Never once a real smile, never once no fear.

I'm searching for that key, I'm trying to get off my knees.
Help me find myself. Someone help me, please.

Tamara Ann Eidsness

Free Us

On the verge of insanity we kneel to our God,
Praying to kill our weaknesses one by one.
A simultaneous metamorphosis from leper to leopard?
We are all wild animals waiting to be freed.
Isolation clouds our minds,
Hallucinations play their games.
We are all followers in this twisted world of semantics.
Take us to your predecessor; we are all as one.
Change is for what we thirst.
Peace is for what we hunger.
We brainwash the wretched.
We defeated the purpose of humanity,
Focusing our concentration on a crevice in our brains.
Reality has shifted; still we think we're all sane.
We hum the tune that only we can hear,
So serene, so pure,
Yet sour and disturbed.
Our flight has arrived, though only in our minds.
We will ingest change and devour peace,
Only to reawaken in an entangled web of nonexistence.

Vicki Metcalfe

You Can't Stop a Heart from Loving

No matter how much you try
To build a wall around the pain,
No matter how much you don't want to cry,
You'll always feel the rain of tears in your heart.

You meet someone and then get hurt,
You rebuild your wall of stone
Hoping it won't be blown to pieces by someone else.
This time no one will make me feel like dirt.

Time goes by, you meet someone
Who turns your world upside-down.
You don't know how or when,
But you fell in love again.

You can't stop thinking about
Why you let another in,
When you know about the pain in the end.

You can't stop a heart from loving . . .
No matter how much you try . . .
No matter how much you cry . . .
No matter how much you don't want to love again . . .
You can't stop a heart from loving!

Christine Rivest

Queen of Hearts (In Memory of Diana, Princess of Wales 1961–1997)

Hers, from childhood, the bitter pain of tears,
Dreamed of a peep-shy wedding to a Prince,
Her one longing, to be cherished through the years,
By a lover, husband, brother: not since.

The beginning of time a perfect love be found
To ease the pain of separation and of grief;
She gave to others her complete round
Of love, compassion, yet was taken by a thief.

To steal her image, peddle it to crowds,
Make the true love of children mawkish;
In death, we realize her vision through the clouds,
Her smile, radiant, joyful, a little rakish.

For hers is the queen-dom, the love, and the glory,
Alone at the Taj Mahal, rapt in the story.

Rosemarie Rowley

On Reaching the Grand Age of 13: A Wish

I long to have a friend who's just my age,
A friend who thinks and feels just as I do,
A friend who never tells me in a rage:
"I'm older, should I not know more than you?"

I want a friend who knows not how to sigh,
A friend who thinks not always of her charm,
A friend who uses not the ugly cry:
"I'm so unwell, can't even move an arm!"

I long to have a friend who's frank and true,
A friend to whom my dreams I could impart,
A friend who'd never cease to love me true,
A friend I'd always love with all my heart.

Oh, friend, I'll never cease to search for thee;
Oh, friend, wilt thou one day belong to me?

Mary Massoud

How Do You Say Good-bye?

How do you say good-bye?
Do you say it in a burst of tears,
Or in utter silence?
Do you say, "Thanks for everything,"
And take a last look at your lover
Only to discover
How much you really care?
Do you say, "Good luck,"
And smile a sad smile
When your heart is breaking all the while?
Do you kiss farewell,
And pat his hand?
Do you say, "I'm hurt, but I understand?"
How do you say good-bye?
In a burst of tears,
Or in utter silence?
I think I did both,
When we did part.
I left in silence,
But tears burst in my heart.

Joyce Kowalchuk

Woe to America

America with lands of vast,
From sea to shining sea.
Why is it now, that your God's Wrath
Is raining down on thee?

With floods and fire and winds so strong,
What is it telling you?
Could it be that you've done wrong,
And death will follow through?

America, you've taken grace,
You've turned it into evil.
Gangs and guns are now your face.
You're playing with the devil.

But deep within the heart of you
A truth will soon begin.
With people who are sure and true,
America, you'll win.

America, our hearts and souls
Will always be with you.
Please stand on guard, America,
Our faith and trust are with you.

Florence Connolly Hood

Mother and Child

Those eyes first blink.
This body no longer sinks
From a nurturing womb of yours.

Colors of the new world to dwell,
Curly lashes of yours coy,
Shed with tears of joy.

I first fell in . . .
Your warm embrace,
My life was so enlivened with God's grace.

Sweet kiss that is undying
On whose presence I'm relying,
Oh, a face so simple.

Bonded in one cord,
Nourishing my every artery,
Lying myself in you without query.

It's only you I've got.
You're the best.
In your arm do I rest.

Yes, God's unrelenting love
Sent me this creature, my mother,
Who cares like no other.

Irene Grace Wong

Loneliness Kills More People Every Year Than . . .

I look around at others, especially the old,
I see their dismal four walls
and how they grow so cold,
how they grow hungry and wither away
with loneliness a constant diet,
day, after day, after day.

Loneliness is a killing thing,
it strips your heart and soul.
The desperate need lies there
aching, hopeless, but not told.
Is this what they live with
the rest of their lives,
growing old, growing old, growing old?

See them sitting in the parks
or wandering aimlessly about,
day in, day in, day out.
Look into their eyes sometime
and tell me what you see.
Will it be you that you see there
or will it—God forbid—be me?

Joan D. Draper

Golden Maple

The majestic gold of the maple
Will soon now fade away
As the rain and winds blow
On this mid autumn's day

Soon your limbs will be barren
Exposed to the cold days ahead
Thinking only to spring once again
A revitalization from looking so dead

Your beauty is still appreciated
Through days of frost, ice, and snow
But unfortunately you cannot understand
These thoughts and feelings that only we know

Take your short rest for winter
For you've earned it, and take in pride
Because you change with all four seasons
But you never lose your beauty far or wide

If only we could express our feelings
To let you know what beauty we see in you
Then your leaves of green, yellow and gold
Would never need to leave, or need to be renewed

Diana Gwen Garrison

The Old Steel Water Tower

Do you remember that old steel water tower
Where we spent many and many an enjoyable hour?
That big black tank suspended high in the sky,
The rivets, the beams, the crisscrossing cable ties,
That tall, mysterious, silent aqua tank
Was the object of much pleasure and many a prank.
That lonely, scary ladder to the uppermost part
Accommodated only the daring and the stout of heart.
We'd climb part way, half way, all the way up,
As if we'd win the bronze, the silver, or the gold cup.
The ball at the apex was the most valued prize;
We'd sit on the lofty tip observing miniature size.
As often as we'd climb our high steel friend,
Not one of us ever met with a dreadful end.
It was exciting, stimulating, like being totally free;
I wonder, was it as much fun for you as for me?
God, I loved those venturous times from our past;
Time and youth fly by, but memory of good times last.
Do you remember that old steel water tower
Where we spent many and many an enjoyable hour.

Edward John Page

Resolution

What else, in truth, could I have done?
I hardly know what else I could have said.
Better to release the hand I cannot hold,
Better to disregard the life I could have led.

Always it was the jeering of the crowd,
The fear of it, that stole my peace away.
But I know now that what I said and did
Were at the crucial moment all I knew
To do, all I knew to say.

Shall I make my every word and deed
Soft pillows for my foe to lay his head?
The feathers on my bed are mine and mine alone.
I will myself to sleep when all is done and said.

Joan Gordon

The Enemy

You are my enemy, mine:
Enemy mine for all time.
I will never let you rest;
I will hunt you with great zest.
Even now I approach.
Soon will I encroach.
You are walking the line.
You, my enemy, mine.
    But as I draw near
    I begin to fear.
    Is it really you I seek?
    I fear I am growing weak.
    Could there possibly be,
    A foe we fail to see?
    A foe so very great,
    He could cause this hate?
        He is the author of all things bad.
        He is the one at whom we should be mad.
        Not at our brother;
        Not at each other.

Brian Lange

Native Ecology

We stopped by the roadside in the sun
where the peasant was selling melons,
golden and green and rose-color flamed,
cantaloupes, Persians, and some unnamed
we had never seen before, since we'd come
so far from our native land, abroad
as conquerors, carpet baggers, felons
in uniforms of lust and greed, war's frauds.
And then at a bend in the country road
there were the melons, all green and gold,
silent and innocent in the sun,
and we wondered what it was we'd won,
when the peasant who'd never drawn his sword
laughed—and gave us—his land's reward.

Betty Bagart

Wishes in the Breeze

If I could touch yesterday once more,
I would be happy and heartened to the core.
If the joyous voice of youth rang out once more,
Resounding over shimmering sea and sunny shore,
Knocking, full of innocence at life's door,
Oh! If only I could relive yesterday once more!

If I dressed myself in yesterday's hue,
I would look a million dollars, a woman new!
Full of the joy and sparkle of spring,
With not a thought of what tomorrow may bring,
I would dance away the night in yesterday's garb,
Away from critical malice and cruel barb.

The harsh light of today blinds my eye,
As winds of change around me sigh.
Gone is the simple way of life,
Facing me is uncertainty and strife.
Yet, in a lazy moment I live again,
Yesterday's joy amidst today's pain.

Dr. Anjana Rai Chaudhuri

I Love in Silence

"Under all speech that is good for anything
    there lies a silence that is better.
Silence is deep as eternity; speech is
    shallow as time."
—Thomas Carlyle

I love in silence
    like the moon that watches
    over me in my deep
    slumber
Unheard of,
Unspoken of

Gazing far from a distance
    to a wide plain of sadness
Contented with the mirage
    of white-colored sprinkles
    of happiness

Allan T. Masuda

Obliterated Inspirations

Wanting nothing and receiving such
my heart had turned to stone
Seeing light through the darkness
my angels had left home
Beacons of hope to shield my desires
your touch has seared my soul
Laughter's light within my reach
insecurities begin to unfold
Melting facades emerge unyielding
before your amorous eyes
Depths of emotion overwhelming
my spirit can no longer hide
Heights of heaven seem so near
when within your arms I lay
Love's greatest treasure retreats so swiftly
when faced by the light of day
Dreams of forever challenge me
strike the falsehood of my existence
Now true love whispers so clearly
You leave me no resistance

Catherine Kelly

Love

My love is strong like the north wind,
As sweet as the flowers in spring,
Deeper than the reddest rose,
To whom can I it bring?

It blossoms more and more each day,
Like daisies in a field.
It spreads its wings like birds in flight.
So what now does it yield?

It yields just the one I need,
Who's lying next to me.
His body warm and tender,
Oh, is it meant to be?

I need him, for he's strong of mind,
His will is greater still,
But tender is his warm embrace,
My arms I know he'll fill.

Deanna Bird

Passionate Poem Pirate

I am a Pirate in search of a poem,
for a poem is a very special treasure.

Using my Imagination,
I wear an invisible Pirate Hat,
my eyes become my Treasure Map.

My mind becomes my Pirate ship;
I will sail through books and magazines
that turn into oceans and seas.
Each page in a book or magazine
represents an island, state, or country.

I will explore each island, state,
or country for poems.
When I find a poem, I can share the
poem with a teacher or friend
at school or at home.

For safe keeping, I will bury each
poem in my very special treasure chest:
My heart; and lock it with my soul:
A very special key that will never get lost
or from me depart.
Joleen S. Quintanilla

A Simple Wish

She often stares out her window
Admiring her favorite star,
Wondering what life will bring her.
This journey seems so dark.

Taking each day one at a time,
She feels she gets nowhere,
Goes back and thinks of the little girl
Who had so many dreams to share.

As the path she follows gets longer
And as narrow as it may seem,
One thing she knows for certain:
She'll hang on to all those dreams.

A silent tear, she makes a wish,
Her star begins to fall;
A simple wish on life's challenges easier
For the baby down the hall.

Closing he window, she crawls into bed
And turns off her night-light.
Tomorrow she'll admire a new star,
Keeping a simple wish as tonight.
Christine Bojarski

Summer '89

One hot day in '89, a family was on tour.
Who was to know they would visit me?
As they started to explore,
They were anxious to find some lodgings,
And ice to cool them down.

This family of Americans
Descended on Retford Town,
A small corner of Nottinghamshire,
A market town of old,
Where local folk are friendly,
And numerous goods are sold.

I allocated ice at once,
Explained just where they were.
I fixed them with a guest house
Where facilities they could share.

They were a smashing family,
And now we keep in touch.
I am so glad we met that day,
And value their friendship much.
Valerie Morgan

The Present, the Future, and the Past

A trace of what was
an inspiration from the past,
but now? The present!

The present, the future, and the past.
The future, the present, and the past.
The past, the present, and the future.

Events in our lives
have to do with time or the wind?
Knowing, waiting, walking.

Waiting for it to happen in the future,
Living it in the present
Until it becomes past again.

Becoming, everything becomes
Experience,
Life itself.
Ednilson Turozi de Oliveira Sx.

Autumn

Rainbow-coloured trees
Swinging and whispering in the breeze.

My heart, enraptured and enchanted,
Feasted on these and was delighted.

Surely, these are but dreams
Of a soul that yearns
Of a flight beyond grip.

Yet I, sensing all these,
With a sigh dying in the breeze,
Caught hold of its fleeting flesh,
Stood still . . . in its caress.

Then sadly, my heart remembered,
These too shall cease
With winter's embrace.
Esther Rivera Limsiaco Stansfield

Justice

A loud, vestige roars over the darkness,
Very ill, weak, and hopeless.
The lamentation is too loud,
Yet nobody could hear it among the crowd.
(It breaks the silence of night, and bears a tear each in every road.)

Nobody verifies the truth of morn',
They all spin a yarn.
There's no change brought about,
. . . Year in, year out.

Everybody seems a coward,
Not even a short testify toward.
Justice really has a blindfold,
Imperfect balance, and a chain made by gold.

Is there a source of light
That will guide justice right?
How I hope there's a bright tomorrow, beyond this sorrow.

My dear friends, "don't point fingers to justice,
To let the verdict be wise."
If you will hide beyond those yesterday tears,
Justice will never prevail, not in a hundred years!
    Rochelle G. Lopez

The Gardener

The leafless tree releases
its final fruitless effort at life.
Each hope stolen
by the cockroaches whose tracks journey from the past.
NAIVE
could be read backwards through the cracked plastic bottle
discarded in the shadeless grove.
The gardener hasn't tilled his soil in years,
yet the clay-baked earth sprouts no weeds.
His unused tools lie among the emaciated roots,
their blood tarnishing everything near.
Man's final attempt,
He himself lies buried beneath his spiritless garden.
Only the question remains:
Did he reap what he did sow?
    Lana Rovere

Upon Awakening

A cricket's last sound of night,
The birds' first song of day,
The morning sun's
First light creeping through my window shade,
Rainbows dancing from prismatic fragrances now gone.
Those pink fingers are crawling over the mountains of purple hues;
I only have a moment to watch,
a moment to see . . .

Silence still owns the time,
I'll capture it while I can;
Before the smell of coffee lingers in the house—
All the quiet will be gone.

Blades of grass will be swept away by silver teeth,
Leaving behind a sweet green smell that brings back "good old times,"
Did you run your feet through the cool emerald blades?
Curl your toes to feel the dew left from the night before?

Did you see?
Can you now?
If even one more can see as I . . .
Then my day is complete before it ever begins.
    Betty Loise Gjesdal

The Melancholy Creatures

We are the melancholy creatures
Born from her womb and tasted her milk,
The murderers who killed her.

We are the listless, dejected, and mournful,
Trodding across her invisible limbs
And condoling our guilt with a respectable tear.
As if that's all it took, as if it covered mistaken steps . . .
As if it made us innocent.

But where are the clean, clear air of her breath
And the silvery streams of her life-giving tears?
Where are the selfless gifts of her very own children,
Her insurmountable beauty, and the splendor of her simplicity?

She is gone, stamped out of existence, taken advantage of, and ignored.
For, who cared for her screams of horror
Amidst the bombs of war? Who saw the look in her eyes as
We coughed darkness into her skies?

She deteriorated without acknowledgment,
Our mother, our protector, our safe haven.
Today the sun sets on bitter horizons, for we are
the melancholy creatures . . . eyes open and seeing nothing.

Elena Anciro

Image of a Twister

Bold and beautiful, she came dancing across the valley
with magnetic force. She pulled you closer till you could almost feel
the vibration. She danced a haunting, spiral movement,
leaving a path of devastation in her wake.
As you got closer, you could feel her emotions.
Pain yet no shame. Extreme grace but very out of place.
A burning rage but a search for peace,
kind but ruthless like a green-eyed monster.

If you were lucky and made it to her centre,
you would find a good but confused soul mate.
But, as of all twisters, she must keep moving and conquering new
territories as boredom would be her death. You can't capture
a twister, only go along for the ride and only hope the spiral dance
will come to an end when the winds calm and the core strength
increases to conquer the turmoil of emotions.

Susan Scholes

Faces

Not only fathers die, but mothers too.
Systems shut down, it seems so cruel:
The erosion of the spirit and the flesh.

"Am I going to get better?"
How can you tell an intelligent person that black is white?
I settle for shades of gray, dark gray.

Roles reverse whether you're ready or not.
Better be ready!

Messy business and a major inconvenience for the coldhearted,
Harrowing and overwhelming for the warm.
Somewhere in between is where I try to tread.

Selfishly, I pray for the inevitable spring.
Devotedly, I endure the interminable winter.
Incredibly, I prepare a face for all the faces that I meet.

It's my father's face.
It's my mother's face.
It's my face.

Charles Pilkington

I Walked in the Garden with Jesus

I walked in the garden with Jesus.
Bright flowers were blooming there,
But little I saw of their beauty
For my heart was laden with care.

I talked in the garden with Jesus,
And unburdened to Him my woes,
Nor could I conceal my impatience
As He stooped to pick up a rose.

Then he said in accents so tender,
As He placed the rose in my hand,
"This well-loved flower has thorns,
my friend, do you understand?"

As I left the garden and Jesus,
Bright flowers were blooming there,
And I wondered at their marvelous beauty
And the absence of all my care.

Edythe Manning

New World

It's here, it's there, it's everywhere
The new world of hope and peace
New thoughts beget new attitudes
Replacing old, barren platitudes
Of rulers now, of rulers then
Who saw themselves as prudent men

The cry of the pitiful, hungry infant
Is no longer far, no longer distant
Realities of global interdependence
Enforce a calm, cautious coexistence
The scourge of wartime tragedies
Still brings forth fatal maladies

The new dawn succeeds the long, dark night
A new world basks in greener light
The pride of some in far-off lands
As scads of wealth are changing hands
The old ways doomed to lie at rest
Humanity struggles to stand the test

Len Moore

Glen Garry Dirge

Cry no' for me, MacAllister lass.
Cry no' for the blood, spilt on this grass.
Cry no' for MacDonnell nor Stewart brood.
Cry instead for the lies, against us spewed.

For on this bonny, Garry Glen,
against us evils, were set in pen.
On Friday eve, before Beltane,
all was lost for folly's gain.

Upon yon hill, sin siriche du
looked out and smiled, he liked the view;
and in his blackest, elven way
he taunted the elders and made them sway.

Sin siriche du, he wrote in sin.
Fears he fed, 'tween kith and kin,
and upon this bonny, Garry Glen,
blood, deceived, flowed from his pen.

G. McAndrews

To Our Son

Life is not always easy
To decide which road to take,
But wherever the path may lead you
We're behind you all the way.

There will be many curves and bends,
And some may go straight through,
But remember when things get rough
We'll still be there for you.

It's always a parent's wish and sorrow
When our child leaves the home.
We feel we're losing a part of you,
But we're also proud how you have grown.

You have always been a wise little bird
Who has flown our little nest,
But as you soar away on your own
We wish you all the best.

Every parent wants to give their kids
The things they never had,
But there's nothing more important
Than life, family, and friends.

Karen E. McDonald

Angel Voices

Trim the wick of your lamp,
Replenish the oil.
Shine forth upon the cities and fields.
Like moths, pulled against their will,
Souls in the darkness will see your light,
Flutter closer, closer—ever closer.
What will you do?
Will you turn down the lamp,
Leave only darkness and misery—or,
Offer more light
To souls lost in confusion?
Now is the time!
A good time—to
Break the bars of selfishness,
To offer your hand—
To put it in ours.
For, together we can do all things.
We can live with love!

Doreen E. Andrews

Pain of Aging

There she sits, small and frail, in her chair,
Sometimes falling to one side,
Unable to control the deterioration
That time chooses to vent on her body,
But she's so bright and alert,
Dispensing wisdom and humour,
Aware of the latest on the news,
Putting visitors at ease with her wit.
How can it be so hard to watch?
Why can't the ravaging stop?
She hopes there's a purpose in living.
Selfishly, we can't let her go.
We want her laughing and loving,
So forgetful of her pain and suffering.

Tish Robertson

Hectic

Rolling along on the bus line,
Going back home for a rest,
Just spent a week in the city
And it's cruel, cold, and hectic at best.

I thought to go down for a visit,
Get away from frustration and such.
I think I must now have rocks in my head,
Or at best, with reality lost touch.

Just kidding myself as usual,
Thought I'd get comfort at home.
I'm so tired and weary of living
And it cuts to the quick of the bone.

If you're thinking of rest and contentment,
Never go to the city to dwell.
It will drain you of life's vim and vigor,
And make your life one living hell.

The city is just a gannet,
It sucks out your strength like a leech.
It's so good to go off on vacation,
But for me, I'll go down to the beach.

Gordon D. Buchanan

Fall

I'm sitting in the tree house with my dolls
to watch the squirrels after all
they put some food in a safe place
where they can get it later on
when old man winter comes along.
And who is coming round the corner there?
It is mister rabbit, to steal some carrots yet.
The birds are singing in the tree
as if they never did it see.
O, boy, if mom finds out
she will tell dad about.
You think he can smart him out?
I hope he will not catch him,
because I like him round the house.
There are so many things that I can see
when I'm sitting over here.
The sun goes down and dark it gets,
so better I will go now in the house
where mom and dad are waiting for me now.
Good night, I see you all tomorrow back.

Margot Frick

Little Boy, Quiet

It was to be the last poem, said he.
All yes, on him, and this solemnly.
Poor child, no tools to express his desires.
Poor child, like singly battling great fires.

As days passed by, he felt so muted,
Words and speech, his mind convoluted.
In great despair, he sobbed: "These curses!"
"How can I stop these many verses?"

He knew from within, that out they must go.
He knew deep inside, a flame not to blow.
With renewed respect, he cherished his choice,
And hence reclaimed his own little voice.

Stéfan Lévesque

Retrospective

I was born of the dawn
from the merger of an unexpected verb,
from the enigma of a touch,
the opening of another unawaited enigma,
yet warm.

I bloomed barefoot,
shaking with no duty other than crying,
with no goal other than the daily routine.

I have come from afar,
pronounced defenseless, wet,
carrying centuries of sadness,
bearing the pain of mankind,
bearing the hope of mankind.
This is not what I want . . .
I will go back today.

I must reverse my birth,
reverse my blooming
to position myself in entrails
in a caress,
in a word.

Patricia Laborde

Stay

Crying out of thin air
And somehow it doesn't seem fair,
A cool breeze enters the room
Full of sadness, empty promises, and gloom.
I'm throwing punches in the air.
You said you would always be there;
Another promise, gone away.
You have no idea how much I miss you today,
What I would do to have you here.
I'd hug you tight, I'd hold you near
I'd make you see how wrong it was
For you to leave just because.
I still can't see what went wrong,
That you were unhappy all along.
I always dreamed of being your wife,
Now I feel I've ruined your life.
If only I could turn back the hands of time
I'd make you now and forever mine,
But nothing I can do or say
Will ever make you want to stay.

Melissa Karen Rivera

Untitled

I cannot sleep, nor can I die
God put me on this world just to cry
I have no hate for you, but I lost all care
In trying to make a love where all is fair
I tried to be what you wanted to see
I tried to be who you wanted me to be
It's too late to turn back now
But I still love you, somehow
Through the love, I knew all along
That it was a joke, and I was wrong
To fall so deep into your heart
Only to be left with us falling apart

Natalie Wowk

Nature High

I love the sun, it's so bright.
When I wake up, day's full of life.
The sun is what cheers me up
When I'm sad in the corner, curled like a lump.

With the sun I see the sky,
So blue and bright it catches my eye.
In the sky there's cotton clouds;
It's so beautiful, so quiet, not a sound.

I see birds fly by,
So cute and adorable I could cry
The cry of joy and of a wonderful day,
Not of sadness that would ruin my way.

I love the flowers and the trees.
I'm nature high as you see.
I love the wind and its cool breeze.
I love how it blows on me.

I wish I could see more in life,
Travel around the world to the height,
See what I can reach,
For I could be as nature high is to the peak!

Roanna T. Cruz

The Forgotten One

Sitting alone wondering.
Doing nothing but staring
Into the open sky ahead.
Tilting till he can his head.
Waiting for something to happen.
Waiting for his dull life to brighten.
"What would I be doing if I were there
And not just sitting idle here?"
Where that "there" is, he alone knows.
Now sitting with his eyes closed,
"Life's not fair," says he.
"Why shouldn't I have the key
Of happiness and prosperity
Instead of this boring stupidity?"

Now he's lying down straight,
Thinking about his happiness-deprived fate.
"Why do I always sink
While others get saved by the brink?
I don't even want to live anymore.
I'm fed up with this life 'cause it's a bore."

Sikander Iqbal

Mother

Her hands are withered and calloused
From the years of hard work and caring
But look closer and you can see
The love and the sharing
But when she holds you
These hands are soft and loving
They never ask for anything in return
But a loving touch would be payment enough
All too often we forget to
Show her we care
Till one day she's no longer there
"Loriflynn"

Geraldine Chittick

Him

Ouch, I'd say,
And he would immediately come running
Down the narrow hallway of our apartment
To ask if I was all right,
And of course I was.

Five minutes after he had gone
I'd do it again.
I'd lie on the edge of my bed
Making myself purposely fall off.

I thrilled at the thought
That he would come running
At the merest thought
That I might be hurt.

No matter how uneventful
My pranks might be,
He'd come running.
I think he enjoyed it
As much as I did.

Melanie Aubin

Memories

In loving memory of my dog, Patches
An old grave, much grown over,
A brick cross for my love.
She is gone, but her love lives on
Even though she's up above.

Every day I brought her flowers,
Whole nights I spent weeping.
I realize how much I love her,
Now that she is gone.

A flowerless rose bush at her head,
A cold, bleak winter with her dead;
No flowers every day for her,
No pretty roses red.

The days have gone by and drifted into years.
Years since I have last shed my tears.
But I'll never forget her, no.
Or why would I cry today?

Noelle Palmer

A Friend

How is a friend made?
Is it a strange chemistry,
A chance meeting we get to meet
Basically strangers off the street?

Who is a friend?
Someone like me to you,
A person to share those special times,
Sharing laughter and tears together,
Someone to share those innermost secrets.

What does a friend mean to me?
Someone to share my thoughts,
A shoulder to cry on,
Someone to fill those empty times.
A friend is someone like you to me.

Robert Bickerton

From a Mother to Her Child

It's a very special love
between a mother and her child.
And I wanna say to you,
I'll love you till the day I die.

I'm proud of you, my baby,
that, I wanna say to you.
You are the light of my life,
and I'm counting on you.

Be strong and be brave,
don't you ever give up.
If it's something you want,
you'll work your way to the top.

At the end of this poem,
it's just one thing left to say:
My baby, you're so strong and fine,
I love you, and I'm proud to say you're mine.
From a mother to her child.
Toni Nordrik

Sun and Moon

The sun kisses the moon to the night
Sweet, gentle, lingering kiss:
Breath and ecstasy withheld until
The final moment
When the sins of the world,
Of the father,
And of the soul
Evaporate, leaving behind only gentle coolness.

What seems to the world without,
Seems not to the world within:
Only the liar will not reveal,
Concealed so well.
Deep and many layered is the skin,
Deep and many layered are the thoughts,
Scented with sweet perfume
That even devils be fooled.

Breathless, yet deathless colour of the night.
One half is not half without the other:
Deep, dark, stingy deathlessness.
Death without death,
Salvation minus the hope,
And fear unchecked.
Derek Fung

Dreams

Never lose hope of your dreams,
For one day they may come true.
No matter how big or small,
Hold on to your dreams

Whether a rainbow with a pot of gold
Or an adventurous quest,
Never dwell on the sadness life brings.
Hold on to your dreams.

Growing up dreams change
From lollipops to millionaires.
If you believe enough
You can never tell what's going to happen.
Hold on to your dreams.
Virginia Kernel

Memories

They say memories lie within,
Not a person's mind, but his heart:
Those special times cherished most,
Which shall never be forgotten.

An important part of my life
Has been shared with you, my friend.
The experiences you have taught me,
Can never be erased.

For the times when I thought
Life was too much to bear,
I only had to turn around
And you were always there.

Your company, support, laughter, and respect
Have helped me to understand and grow,
And for this I sincerely thank you;
How much, you'll never know.

Our friendship is like a story,
That never has to end,
But while this chapter in my life closes,
I'll never forget you, my friend.
Petra Herrenkind

Peace

The call of the eagle reaches my soul,
causing me to stand in awe
at the glory that surrounds me.
The spring thaw shows its power
as the great mass of ice
breaks up along the shore.

A tiny squirrel scampers to the end of a limb
and stops to stare at me.
He chatters ceaselessly,
and I wonder what his message is.

Robins, a sure sign of spring,
flitter to and fro around my feet;
as the bank swallows, chickadee, and crows
all seem to call for my attention.

Sprigs of new life
peak up through the moist earth,
and fresh dear tracks
line the path before me.

We pass this way but once; shadows,
casting light or darkness upon the whole.
Viola Doncaster

Mistaken Identity

Dragging weight of confusion's fatigue
Spurns an exhausted flop of inevitability,
An urban cot of unforgiving,
The only home in wayward spinning.
Eyes of scorn pass him and judgement
At a battered shell.
A concrete ornament
But raise the horizon to see the truth
A blinding spark skyrockets aloof.
Although they look down to spew
His mind still soars, bird's eye view.
Christopher Danby

Untitled

She ascended the stairs.
The dust rose around her like a cape, encompassing her every movement.
The webs hung declaring the existence of the past and yet shrouding it,
 veils concealing breath.
The air was thick, her palms sweaty.

Why was she here?

The answer remained in the shadows of her mind, refusing to come forward.
Suddenly she remembered a child of years past.
Long blonde hair, big, wondering blue eyes and a wide open smile.
The picture faded, replaced by a scream . . . her scream.
Her mind refused, her eyes closed.

In a dimly lit room, the sun trying to break through thin, wispy rags
 hanging over a shattered window, the child reappeared.
The smile gone, the mouth a thin, straight line, the eyes no longer
 wondering.
The picture did not fade, her mind accepted, her eyes remained open.
The image, reflected in the dresser mirror, was her,
 time had passed.

Anne Scott

Final Plea

Unaccepted and excluded. Where did I go wrong?
Unwanted and unhappy. Nowhere to belong.
Hanging on without support. Painfully turning me away.
Now, encountering loneliness, I'm left empty and astray.
Solitude infests my soul. Bitter life I must face.
I want to escape this agony. My value is a disgrace.
Worthless and abortive. Kick me, I am down.
My self-esteem is slaughtered. Leave me here to drown.
Turbulent and instable. The shallow spirits flee.
Drained of all my confidence, there is nothing left of me.
Withdraw me from it all. I no longer want to abide.
Sorrow is quickly creeping in. Banished from my pride.
Inattentive of my error. Respect impaired by stress.
I cannot bear this spite and live with this distress.
I need to be released. I want to become free.
End all of my torment and grant my final plea.

Beverly Bilusack

A Reflection on Evolution

The dawning of man was a most momentous thing,
but nothing could prepare for the terrors it would bring.

Humans alone brought pestilence and disease,
which kill thousands with relative ease.

Yet worse than that was an inquisitive mind,
to research, to learn, and also to find.
Fire and electricity are but a few of many.
Curiosity brings little hope, if any.
But with each thing created,
almost all affect the Earth in some minute way.
Species extinction, soil degradation,
and deforestation still happen to this very day.
Yet, there is also medicine and alternatives
to pollution which are good, if I may say.
Humans are dooming their own existence,
By creating without caring about the consequence.

Weapons of war, created to kill,
Inflict death and also fit the bill.

The destruction of Earth and the creation of hell is almost complete,
With humans accomplishing almost all of this feat.

Chris MacDougall

Stand Together

Sleep, my child, for today can wait as the wind blows softly,
don't sleep too late.
Morning softly kisses your face, arise, my sweet, and shake off the
nightmares that lie down deep.
Fires of rage in the early morning sunlight,
the men on horses take to their flight.
Your grave, I can feel your soft hair through the wind (memories).
On the sixth moon, they danced with whores and witches,
for the seventh day the harvesters could rest.
The land we share is of sweat and blood;
together, my brothers, we tear it apart!
She, the one with long, sun hair, dances in circles.
Why should we care?
She offers Ravens of sleep.
Lie down, my brothers, our hearts we must keep.
Protect our keys for the moon is green; rise and be strong mountains,
pour oceans through torn hearts.
Noah, my deep, fine feathered friend, Ravens of morning you must send!
Owls of evening seem to crave the flesh we leave in our grave.
   Robert J. Valiquette

My Train

The flowers turned dull in pity,
The old willow drooped for me,
For I sat there staring,
Eyes blurred in tears;
Everything was nothing and I was nothing carrying everything.
I had been waiting for my train for some time,
But seconds seemed like minutes and I was a second.
There was no one else in the station,
But everyone was looking at me,
And everyone was talking about me,
But it did not matter anymore.
I could not correct my wrongs,
They were not there to be made right;
I was alone with nothing to hope for.
Life had nothing for me and I had nothing for it.
I had no purpose and no smiles left;
My train was arriving, ready to kill;
It had only to have a victim,
I stood up and took a breath;
It was my last.
   Paul Heideman

I Can't Tell

I can't tell how I feel, I'm not sure what is real.
It has to stay in my head, circling silent and unsaid.

I'm not mentally unstable, rudderless, adrift, or unable
To steer with true resolve, the bind is if to involve.

A parallel soul in life's business, to see the very is-ness,
The species wield power by fear, who see not the mirror.

To look life in the eye, yet decree how we live or to die,
Armies on a grisly game board, add more to their hoard.

The money changers of old, now they trade paper for gold.
Nations entwined in their grip, of coiled snakes in a pit.

Let's lift our torch and light the way, to the dawning day,
To know thoughts unspoken, the curse of silence is broken.

Again their tables are turned, driven out, paper burned.
Eons of repeating the past, ah, but this time is the last!
   Glen Nichol

Rock My Babies

One little baby, with one on the way,
I ask myself should I leave or stay?
With a blackened eye and a swollen cheek,
I rock my baby fast asleep.

Two little babies and another one soon,
I hide myself inside a room.
With a broken arm and missing teeth,
I rock my babies fast asleep.

Three little babies and another one coming,
I quiet their cries with gentle humming.
With a broken nose and my lip cut deep,
I rock my babies fast asleep.

Four little babies and another on the way,
my life's filled with violence more each day.
With a broken leg thrown down stairs so steep,
I rock my babies fast asleep.

Five little babies alone on the floor,
Because I am not there to rock anymore,
but down from heaven I will peep,
and I'll rock my babies fast asleep.

Shelley Craig

Oh! The Tree in Autumn

Oh! I know thy sorrow,
To loose the dress you borrow.

When the wind swiftly blew around and kind
Thou gave a hand and danced with the wind.
The wind gave thee the lovely dress,
And I slept the nights without stress.

Now, the howling wind roars in the night
Saying, it's not fair or right
To keep the dress you borrow,
though it's hard to loose without sorrow.

Oh! Tree, give it back without a fight
And tell the wind it is right.
Show thy grief, wear the silver dress,
Mourn and cry and see the mess.

When the nights get cool and calm,
Let the wind come back with its gentle charm.
Get the dress back and let it grow in the rain.
Never forget to give it back again.

But, I know thy sorrow
To loose the dress you borrow.

Delcia Abey Wardene

Reincarnation

The ship sails the sea of dissipation
Toward a crimson waterfall
Where a thousand fireflies
Pirouette in a pulsating rhythm,
And man rides the sea of reincarnation.
Destiny beckons like an orange mushroom;
Bursting in flames of brilliant agony.
The thirsty traveler touches the rainbow skies,
And man is born again.

Hrilina Tagore Mederacke

Untitled

I met a boy, his name is Jeff.
He brought us joy, but then he left.
Whatever did become of him?
His future not bright, but certainly not dim.
As memories of him come flooding back,
I'll remember forever his certain knack.
He'd be beside me and help me through
With all those things I couldn't do.
Without him life is not complete,
A play that I am watching repeat.
What a mistake to let him go,
But at the time I did not know.
If my boy Jeff could see me today,
I wonder what he'd think with dismay.
Am I the person that I should be,
Or is there something I just don't see?
Have I done my best throughout my life
Or go about angry, causing strife?
Think about it, are you today
The kind of person you'd like to stay?

Lindsay Schmautz

From Inspiration

You were born out of inspiration,
My mind, the mould,
My spirit, the fire.
You were born from within,
From enthusiasm, from interest,
From the deepest thought, from the shadows,
From the far distance, you came.

You are phrase, you are sentence.
From my lips I roll you out,
To touch, to feel, and to form.
I mould you into what you soon become,
I mould you from within,
I mould you, from inspiration.

Like water, you run.
Like stones, you fall.
Like the waves, you roll.
I build you to heal,
I build you to soothe,
I build you to be used,
I build you, from inspiration.

Justina V. John

Summer Memories

The sun, the rains, the flowers, the sea,
memories of the childhood dreams.
Happiness, smiling faces, holding hands,
memories of the gone summers,
part of the endless friendship.

The summer,
the full moon, the dark summer sky,
an old man playing a saxophone,
the deserted, dead houses,
a lonely dreamer on Broadway,
the calming streets of the city, New York.
The summer is over.

Hanna Valtonen

Communication

Communication is a skill,
Which takes true efforts and a will;
It takes much practice day by day,
To talk to others in right ways.

Communication must be clear,
Be understood by those who hear;
One's actions go with what they say—
Will help or hinder in some way.

Assertive we must learn to be,
Our thoughts and feelings speak more freely;
To others, bring our thoughts across—
Provoke no anger, cause no loss.

And if we don't communicate,
A mixed-up life can be our fate:
For our emotions get suppressed.
Rage on the inside—won't let one rest.

Let's strive to speak direct and calm,
To speak our feelings, lessen qualms,
Communicate with confidence,
With firmness, kindness, and making sense.

Keturah Hiebert

Living with Love

That someone special
Has come into your life
Full of promise, fulfilling
His plans to make you his wife.
Does he love you the way
A husband is to love his future
Or does he love you for his convenience?
Love is serious and
Dangerous as well,
So keep your eyes open.
Don't end up in hell.
Communication lines must always
Be open, and if they are not,
Then no words can be spoken.
Aggravation well set in as if
It were invited,
But let living with love
Keep your love life excited.
Motivate your lover as if it were yourself.
Keep all emotions flowing
And you shall stay in good health.

Kim Saulnier

Puzzle Pieces

Life is a puzzle, we are the pieces.
Either you fit, or you don't.
The people that fit, flaunt it.
The people that don't . . . want it.
Myself, I am from a different puzzle.
I can fit, if I make myself.
I may be there but no one wants me to be.
Will I ever fit?
Maybe.
Eventually.
I hope.

Jackie Dougall

In Arcadia Ego

I feel part of the city tonight,
Greeting Ellsworth like a long-lost friend,
Driving open-topped and wired,
Fired like a rocket with a Tarmac trace.
Eyes like cut crystal,
I course through this city
In a state of grace.

I sound my yawp to the engine's hum as
Neon shards rain silent on alabaster.
There are those of us who drive
To a different drum.

Essence of rose in a sweet petroleum pall,
In this Tarmac Arcadia
I have it all.

Tom Hardy

Gone Away

I'm leaving you,
I don't want to look at you,
to listen to you,
to love you anymore.
You mean nothing to me.
No, it's not your fault,
or mine,
I blame time and the world around us.
Maybe everything would be different
if we lived in another world,
time, space . . . But . . .
Don't be afraid of life,
Live for yourself . . . 'cause . . .
Another's eyes will look at you—maybe
even prettier than mine.
Another girl will love you—maybe
more than I have.
I know that it's hard for you now,
but it will pass soon, I know.
And soon, believe me, you'll be happy again.

Milica Janosevic

Stranded in the Dark

Stranded in the dark,
I don't know where and how to start;
Living life again without you . . .
You sentenced me for life,
Condemning me of a sin I'm innocent of . . .

You didn't have a heart,
You just burned bridges down,
Never forgiving . . . never considering . . .
Never caring to look back!

All I thought that love was fair,
that you would always stay . . .
I thought you would always be here,
Ready to listen . . . willing to understand!

Now . . . for what seems eternity,
Trying to get over you . . . trying to survive,
But only time will tell,
How long will I be Stranded in the Dark!

Rubella B. Baria

Untitled

United by an air of trust,
we are divided by centuries.
Timeless, we are together.
Immortal.

Artifacts of life and love,
death, pain, and power,
transcending time.

Our words, our words are a will to power,
bitter nights wedded with
supreme sadness.

My mind, my mind is a grace of being
and nothing less.
Stop the ceremony!
Resurrection of madness.

Individuals quest for power.
Will they get it?
Possibly.

Mountains of light show the way.
I know you can follow me, but you won't.
On my desperate quest for . . .

S. W. McAdam

A Heart in Flame

Do you really love me
Or is it just a game?
Am I just your summer lover
Whose heart is afire with your flame?

Your mixed signals, they confuse me.
You hide so much behind your eyes.
Are you ever going to let me in?
If you do you will be surprised.

The feelings that I have for you,
In a lifetime they only come once.
When I met you I found my destiny,
And, darling, you know that I'm no dunce.

The love and compassion that I have for you,
There is not anything that could compare.
I found in you my perfect mate,
And what we share together is very rare.

Please tell me you really love me,
And, my dear, this is not a game.
You are not just my summer lover,
And it's my love putting your heart in flame.

Brian Joyce

Dying

Why do you stand there, watching me dying,
barely breathing. I can't stand, I'm lying.
I try to speak out, asking you in plea,
but I am dying. It's not me you see.
As I lie there, my eyes fill with tears.
I try to speak out telling you my fears.
Why you ignore me I'll never seem to know,
for I am dying and soon I will go.
But before I am gone I want you to see
that there is a real person inside of me.

Amber Burke

Quidnunc

"Is there anything I should know
before I leave?"
Yes, be strong and have great courage,
for, life is not for the weak.

"Is the path I must take
straight and true?"
Not to the naked eye. For, you will
set out looking West and arrive
in the East.

"Will the people I meet along the way
be gentle and kind?"
Only if you show them your heart first,
leave your Ego here with me.

"When I do all these things, do you promise
I will find riches?"
Yes. It may take a thousand lifetimes,
but in the end, you will find the
greatest treasure of all:

You.

Megan Bishop-Scott

Devil in Disguise

On a cool fall day
I thought and angel came through my door
I thought he was here to stay
I thought I had to search no more

He would whisper so softly
His touch felt so right
He would talk so sweetly
He seemed to have an angelic light

With every wind that blows
All of the given and taken lies
Out the door my love goes
With another devil in disguise

They don't care if they hurt you
They don't care if they tear you apart
When finally they are finished and through
They walk away with your heart

All of my regrets
Of what I let my heart say
I can't believe I ever let
A devil take my heart away

Tabitha Grozik

Piece of Heaven

A Piece of Heaven, in the middle of Hell,
So much promise, yet no one could tell.
Looked over by ignorance, forgotten by all,
So it would sit there, and its tears would fall.
When it stopped crying, it then did discover,
The tears it had lost had become a great river.
So down the river and into the lake,
It swam and swam, until it was late.
It crawled upon shore and across soft sand,
Looked up to see another's strong hand.
Two pieces of Heaven together in Hell,
So much promise, yet no one could tell.

Jc Pope

Pen Pals

Calm. Thoughtful. Lonely.
The struggle of the gloomy days is over,
Faded in the foggy sunsets
Of the quiet hills.
Memories of the good old days
Draw a smile on the idle mouth . . .
The sun feels warm on the eyes
Closed to the pink shades
And to a blurred reality.
Images of funny faces,
Laughs with no noise,
Music, color, places,
And a silent voice
Meet me somewhere, draw me to you.
Dear friend, so far apart,
Yet so close, so missed . . .
The breeze blows a smell of sweetened air . . .
For a while, you were here
Or . . . was I there?

Mirta R.B. de Fiaño

I Spoke

I spoke of memories as my heart
pounded against my chest.
I spoke of the innocent child that
lies quietly within me; the one that
laughed and cried;
the one that wrote his feelings as
my eyes cried, knowing this would
be the last, the farewell to yesterday.
I stood brave and glorious to their eyes
as I trembled and came undone within
these walls.
I spoke freely as my words bared my
heart, leaving me with nothing but
the memory.

I spoke and I told the story of a child who
reached for his dream, the dream that began
this journey that I have begun.

Le Sand Duane Taylor-Arenas

I Sat Beneath the Desert Sun

I sat beneath the dessert sun,
My body bathed in golden sand.
The air was hot across my face,
My steps I could not retrace.

The lizard green with eyes of glass,
Sauntered by with just a glance.
His shadow or mine, I could not tell,
A blanket to cover my mind and soul.

The desert is brazen, harsh, and hot,
I must go before I see
Mountain streams, cold and white,
Or Island solitaire, forever me.

Would he lead straight way
To velvet lawns and crystal seas?
Beyond the endless dunes, it lay,
A splendid land of purple, spice, and teas.

Penny Boyes

My Sisters and I Together

My sisters and I are going to be together,
I hope forever and ever.
Kristine, Karrie, and I laughed day by day,
We were there for each other all of the way.
Crying, someone dying, happy times, sad times,
and even bad times.
Time goes by too quickly—
Kristine already has a family and I like
remembering the good memories.
Karrie is engaged and I feel happy for her.
Every day I will be there for her all of the way.
I just remember the good times.
Even though I wish they were here today,
they will watch me graduate.

Kelly Symington

Our Savior

What a day of rejoicing it will be
When the tears of Blessing fall on thee.
Sweet words of wisdom you shall hear
As the Blessed Savior draws you near.

Hand in hand, come to me,
For all the beauty you will see.
All the mysteries shall unfold
Of all the things we have been told.

Remember when darkness begins to fall:
Only my name you need call.
I'll come rushing to your side,
And in me you shall abide.

Laughing and talking, singing your song,
For you are home where you belong.
Nothing more to dread or fear,
For you, Blessed Savior is always near!

Lisa Scott

A Star

What is in a star?
Is it a glowing light that shows us
our dreams or is it just a shape
Made by millions of little glowing crystals?

Does a star bring a wish that gives
us hope in the world or in our hearts,
or is it just a magical myth created
to bring joy to everyone's life?

Is a star a guiding light to our
future that helps us with our thoughts,
or is it just a plain old light created
by the sky up above?

What do you with a star?
Do you carry it in your pocket for good luck?
Do you look at the silver shaped crystal
and wish for happy thoughts to make
your dreams come true?

A star is not a plain old light,
for a silver little star is within
us all.

Shelly Breen

At the Beach

As the tide advances, the waves crash
against the shore in a steady, rhythmic tempo.
Later, as the tide wanes, the water laps at the shore's edge.
Again, the steady beat yet fainter . . . so much fainter.
The ocean reveals itself slowly, over time, to the watchful eye.
Like a curtain being pulled back, the tide unveils
hundreds of metres of wet, sandy, tide-marked beach
to be enjoyed by all who frolic at its shore.
Beach balls, Frisbees, and sand castles suddenly appear
and fill that sandy bar, newly taken back from the sea.
For a few hours those inhabiting the beach are given free reign
to spread out and explore this new terrain.
A game of catch casually unfolds with young and old alike at play.
Children explore aquatic life in the pools
left behind by the retreating tide.
They dig in the wet sand to create towns,
cities, and castles from their inner eye.

What is it that I've seen at the beach today?

What I've witnessed is the Earth
Lifting the hem of her skirt to give us a glimpse of her beauty.

Catherine Lynch

The Sense of Life

This world is filled with many wonderful things:

The beauty of a sunrise,
when the world begins to wake;

The smell of a summer rain,
that reminds us of a world just found;

The sound of silence,
that lets us hear the little things the world has to say;

The light touch of a flower's petal,
to offset the harsh pain of life's thorns;

And the taste of life itself,
that makes you yearn to experience these things all over again.

Gordon Courtney

Untitled

Why can't we enjoy life for the moment?
The future holds uncertainty, this we know,
but if we only search for what may be,
we lose sight of what currently is.
How does one smile with the day and close that chapter for the night,
only to start a new page with the rising sun?
I really do not know. I wish I did, for life would be different:
Many lost treasures of the past could actually
be fond memories in my heart.
I struggle to hold on to a life sign,
while nothing seems to entice the spark of happiness.
Contentment with what one has—how does one learn to value
and appreciate it?
Laugh. Smile. Have a sense of humour.
Envelop the beauty and strength of others:
Use that to fuel your own fire.
But the trick is not to ride their wave;
you must find your own path and travel it on your own. Initially, at least.
Then, you can choose who else you want
to see the beauty you have found:
the beauty of the Self, the Inner Soul.

Jagjit Kanda

Shadows

Long and in front are the shadows in the morn',
Short and below the feet are they in the noon.
Long but behind they stretch late after the noon
They vanish at night—those shadows of the morn' . . .

Run after the shadows to catch them on the run,
Those two dimensional shadows—they also run!
Through lowlands, highlands, valleys, or mounts
Those flimsy shadows—they spoil all the fun . . .

Desires are long in the morning of life,
They narrow to a circle during the noon of life,
They are senile and inactive in late years of life,
They no longer stretch during the night of life . . .

Desire is a shadow—a storm it could be.
Greed is a whirlpool—a monster it could be,
Pride is a precipice—a trouble it could be.
Egoism is a volcano—disastrous it could be . . .

Ignore those shadows, they are ephemeral ones,
Greed, pride, and egotism are the undesirable ones,
Righteousness is the one—the most desirable one,
For it can be the torch pointing to the Ultimate One. . . .

Siva Wimaleswaran

Hoping for Success but Achieving Failure

I tried to love, but all I had was hate!
I tried to mingle, but I was ridiculed!
I tried to give, but I was abused!
I was sincere, kind, and generous before,
but now I'm a selfish, arrogant witch!
I was tame, silent, humble like a saint,
but now I'm wild, weird, horrible like hell!
I was slim, beautiful, and attractive before,
but now I'm a bloated, ugly, disgusting pig!
Once I had seen light, hoping it might renew my sense
of regrets, but all I saw was darkness!
Once I had felt a soft hand, patting and comforting me,
but it turned out to be dusk of sands covering me with sorrow!
And once I had smelled freedom, being free to wonder
and explore, being free to be yourself, but
I had found myself trapped, a victim of fantasy
and illusions, and all of these are the causes
of lack of love and confidence!

Maria Gerardee Rubio

Rockies after Rain

Walking through the meadow—fir trees all around.
Clouds are clinging to the mountain wall,
Blades of grass are swaying, while the trees move in the breeze,
And I listen to the crows and ravens call.
There's nothing quite so pretty as the Rockies after rain,
And I hope that I can pass this way again.

Waking in the morning to watch the sun come up
When all the world is waken'd by its light,
Each day a new beginning that will soon be put to rest
As the same sun falls and darkness fills the night.
But there's nothing quite so pretty as the Rockies after rain,
And I hope that I will pass this way again.

Mother Nature glistens with pride for what she has,
A baby fawn just learning how to stand,
The prairie dog that whistles to a friend across the way,
And the streams begin their journey through the land.
And there's nothing quite so pretty as the Rockies after rain,
And I know that I will pass this way again.

Delphine Riehl

My Heart

Dedicated in memory of Edith Joan Mcnamara
I will never hold your hand again
Or even touch your face,
But with all the love you've given me
In my heart you'll have a place.

It may sometimes feel so empty
And I may feel so blue,
But because I know your love's inside,
My heart belongs to you.

You mend it with a memory
Of the life that we once shared.
You bind it with the love you gave
And the thoughts of how you cared.

My heart is heavy and full of hope
That one day we shall meet
Along your path to happiness,
a road that's bittersweet.

Janette Mcnamara-Comeau

To Start Again

I'm starting over, over again.
How I decided, I don't know when.

My slate is clear, wiped free of chalk.
My mouth is free of evil talk.

But the road is, oh, so very long,
And the wind's my friend, my only song,

Because no one would talk to me,
For fear of what they might see.

But that's the past and now it's done,
And in the east I see the sun.

It's rising to a brand new day,
And all I do is look and say:

The grass is green, the birds are singing,
And today, my friend, is a new beginning.

Danielle Suchet

Rainbow's End

The hazy sun of the afternoon
Is changing places with the moon.
The sounds of summer round my head,
While others tuck their child in bed.
What greater gift have we been given,
The flowers, the trees, the changing seasons.
No greater quilt could be designed
With all the colours of nature in mind.
The roar of ocean, wind, and rain,
Snow, sleet, and hail and hurricanes,
Flowers, insects, birds, and bees,
All have their place and have their needs.
The greatest gift we have been given:
To see, or touch, or smell the heavens.
So, take a moment of your day,
See just one miracle along the way.
These wonders given all to fend,
On the walk to rainbow's end.

Mary Reyno

After the Rainfall

I saw the sun today
and almost felt its brilliance,
its beckoning embrace.
I almost called my friends today, to say,
but not—I could not bear.
They only would have told me, look, we know,
the sun's been shining every day.

How could I see,
when all I think about is he
and feel the pain, the clouds, the rain.
Why cannot they see?

Maybe next week,
I'll see the sunshine almost every day
and feel the hopeful rays that touch your soul
and give you happiness.

Irja Ketola

Peace

Our soul toward caress incline
As thirsty lips towards a brawling spring.

Heliotropes tilt to face the wheel of Sun
And the condemned head
the headman's blade averts,
Craving for the leniency of the Judge.

Our body tends toward the calm
As tired hands toward the sky of blue.
Loins lean toward the stalk of
Spring and desire's crest
detests the hammer of Time,
longing for the readiness of the Lover.

Our soul t'ward Peace incline
As eels toward fresh water.

Konstantinos Bouras

Nature and Poetry

Nature as I look upon, I can see its uniqueness...
Like the trees, the flowers, the birds,
the butterflies, the sun, the rain,
the bow across the sky, and the open
countryside, in these I find my joy...
in time of grief, walking beneath
the moon, listening to the sound of
waves soothe my bitterness.
In response to this idyllic rural charm,
my experience is a form of escapism...
a retreat to nature.
Near the heart of Romanticism lies
a kind of subjectivism, merely an art
of expression or imagination.
Thus, Romanticism is a return to
nature; nature is one of the great
themes of Poetry.

Simon Leong

Dreams . . .

A curly lock of jet black hair
Entwined around little fingers,
An empty look, a blank stare,
A shiver as she tingles,
The world around is busy with life.
The world she's in is free from strife,
As she cuts through the clouds like a knife.

The tree and clouds
transform without
her having to think much about.

In winds they drift
and are soon caught,
as the strands shift,
in a poem, they are sought.
Po Li Loo

One Mirror, Two Faces

When I pass by the mirror,
When I see it,
I see your faces.
You're an angel, you're a demon.
I know the heaven with you,
But also I know the hell.
Like a hurricane that breaks the branches
Of a strong tree,
You broke my heart and my soul.
I see the mirror again
And what I see is a beautiful world behind you,
And I think that like a masquerade I take it off;
I take the best things and reject the others.
I take the world
And replant my spirit.
Zeny Hernandez

The Saint

Kiss the saint, let his lips purify your soul,
hold his tender hand,
feel the embrace you giveth to him.
Look into the porcelain eyes and believe
you are of a clear conscience,
push the door open from the gospel,
pound your feet to the pavement,
light your cigarette, and begin anew.
Hold your child in your inner self,
buy the book and flick a dime
to the man sitting on the corner,
pick the weed from the garden,
chew the end bitter as you were,
a new start begins.
It will also be done in another
time . . . clock out.
Elizabeth Williams

One Nation

We have gathered together as one Nation
And ask you to join our celebration.
We miss our Homeland, that is true,
But came here to start life anew.
As we roam this vast, wide Earth,
Our lives receive a second birth.
As we live from age to age,
We share with you our heritage.
Natives, English, Scottish, Germans, just names a few.
Be it in harmony that we live with you.
This is a land where freedom rings from shore to shore.
This is our Homeland forevermore.
"Good Bless North America"
Anne Nethercott

Him

One night as I lie awake in my bed,
I look up and I wonder,
Where is he? What is he doing?
Is he in the clouds? Sleeping?
For, it is a man I love and believe in,
But I cannot see him. When?
I think to myself,
Will I ever get to see him?
All I can do is dream and wonder about him.
My heavenly Father, Oh! I love him!
If only I could touch his soft face.
I must be patient. Then someday,
I will. I will.
Danielle Little

Memories

Did I tell you, my love,
How your memory lies upon my mind
Fresh as the morning?
Were it not true,
Would I not a long time ago
Have folded the memories I have of you
And hidden them
In the secret spaces of my mind
Like some half-forgotten poem I once wrote?
Yet, is your memory so dear to me,
Fostered and cherished, the thought of you,
Oh, the thought of you
Rings like a cheerful chime
Of crystal, rare and fine.
Elizabeth Seddon Webster

Sunset

Down, down through trials of smoky mist,
The weary wanderer slowly slips
To bathe in lakes of lemon clouds
And scorch the hems of velvet shrouds
That loom above the mountain tops,
So still and silent as they watch him
Ease into a purple robe,
End his journey 'round the globe.
Wink farewell to the dying day,
And dawn a new one far away.
Gordon W. Power Jr.

Shattered Hopes and Broken Dreams

As she looks into the mirror, what does she see?
Hopes and dreams tormentingly fading away like a breeze
Pushing clouds torturously slow, seemingly never ending into nowhere.
Images through her mind, pain surging through her heart.
An ache, an emptiness, a part of her soul goes missing.
A never ending yearning that is not in control.
An expectation, a for-granted, a planning-on,
A wanting, a hope, a yearning, a desire.
All has been cruelly ripped away.
She feels raped, intense rage, hatred, anger.
She feels a part of her missing that she'll never know.
She feels a dull, throbbing ache intensely surging throughout her being
until she feels absolutely nothing but worthless.
Again she looks into the mirror, now what does she see?
Shattered hopes and broken dreams.
With no more thoughts to hear but dead silence,
She bows her head in shame and turns away, this childless woman.

Jo Ann Nuttall

The Sun

When the morning sun rises above the calm and clear water
and the pure, angelic clouds gallantly give way for its glitter,
our humble souls and trembling sights elated to their highest wonder—
with its piercing glow and warmth announcing a precious new day,
our grateful praises to the Creator for gifting us to such display,
our hearts, our entire beings blessed with such deep intensity.

When the midday sun shines with its bright and forceful light,
its warmth, its power, its brilliancy refurbishing our daily lives,
amidst our awes, amidst our praises to such heavenly sights,
we carry on our daily marches with great vigor and enthusiasm
for the mysteries of this ethereal and boundless sacrarium,
remain spiritually engraved and appreciative for our equilibrium.

When the sun reaches its hazy ways to the peaceful blues crepuscule
its gleaming rays, its flashing display comfortably fading over the hill
once again, we remain speechless at such constant phenomenon.
Giving its daily glory for the heaven to be adorned in such distinct array
with zillions of bright stars as mysteriously captivating, in
countless ways we close our eyes, and with submissive dignity, we
cherished that day that the Good Lord, in his infinite kindness, has
bestowed to us so freely so we can witness that miracle, of the sun
rising, again, in its grandeur and sanctity.

Blondine Vortmann

Platte Creek

In the morning of my days, the silence broke early in bird song
And my first hours carried me wild and free over the open fields,
Riding high above the little house, where generations of my blood
Had lived and died beneath the turning wheel of the heavens,
And solitude reigned under the soaring cathedral of the trees
Where we splashed wet and were baptized in the shining, rushing water.

And as the noon burned bright and the meadows lulled,
Half-dazed in the sullen callings of the cicada we sprawled,
Refreshed in the thick, cool shade of ancient stones,
And like our first awakenings a new note struck
Sounding depths of our wells, our backs felt a new weight
On the turning of the handle and the rising of the water.

And when evening came arcing on the wings of swallows,
And the whippoorwill sang in the dark just beyond the window light,
We closed our eyes and watched the self-made stars
Until we sank beneath the silence,
Broken only by the echoing laughter of the moonstruck silver river,
And we slept with the peace of the innocent.

Shawn O'Halloran

Despair=Existence

No lonely night such as this when time's velocity
is speeding so fast and suddenly stops at the center
of my melancholic life; my soul is poignantly brimming
with so much angst and despair
and I cannot see any glimpse of way out,
except to immerse myself from this absurd ordeal.
I wanted to tear my flesh away
to feel the uncanny beatings of my heart,
and listen to the precarious murmurs of my blood
pulsating through my arteries and veins,
or maybe break my skull open to explore whether existence
occurs only in my brain or whether my mind took over
all my senses to trap all the pains of this lonely world.
I do not know and I do not care anymore
who I was, who I am, who I will be,
and for whom I was existing.
Only one thing of which I am certain
at this particular lonely moment:
that I am living in dark despair
and my despair is my existence!
   Danny C. Sillada

Reflections of the Heart

The love once awakened, brings joy in every simple thing.
You see the world with renewed joy.
In simple pleasures there is such depth.
It is eternal summer in your heart.

True love shimmers your heart with laughter.
There are no rules or principles that you would not bend.
You make any sacrifice for the warmth of the look,
To simply drown in the loving depths of those eyes.

True love is felt in just remembering that loving smile,
The smile that lights up my heart and the world around me.
Like the summer sun, the warmth lingers . . .

True love opens your heart to love profound.
Your heart overflows with, oh, such joy!!
Thank you, my love, for I never knew
Such love as you have made me feel.
   Bharti Patel

Visions of a Dreamer

Artist at the easel, facing canvas bare.
Dreamer deep within himself with stories none can share.
Echoes of a mem'ry drowned beneath a flood of tears:
Answers come so easy, it's the question that he fears.

Artist dabs his pallet, but no hue can ever tell
Of secrets in the dreamer's souls where nightmares' dragons dwell.
Hope, the bride, in myst'ry veiled, cries loud her virgin's song:
Truth, her valiant lover, for whom she's waited for so long.

Artists sees the vision pictured in the dreamer's mind:
Truth is sailing homeward, but deep darkness lurks behind.
Hope, the captive princess, from a castle tower stares
Out across the sea of life horizoned by despair.

Cloudy skies are weeping and the thunder roars in grief.
Inward longings failing, falling like the autumn leaf.
Artist paints the picture: wistful dreamer lain to rest.
Hope now waits in silence, ever loved but not caressed.

Winter world is dying, silent darkness is its grave.
Spring's new hope brings promise that life can yet be saved.
With each storm, a rainbow: see the Artist paint the sky.
Dreamer, seek eternity, for there your treasures lie.
   Bruce Mitchell

The Song of the Spirit

I hear the Spirit singing in the wind, blowing through a tree,
A tree planted by the river, its branches raised to thee.
The song is one of praises, of hope, and of eternity,
Forever giving glory to your name.

I hear the Spirit singing in the river running free,
Flowing down the mountain side, it's rushing joyously.
The song is one of praises, of joy, and of blessing thee,
Forever giving glory to your name.

I hear the Spirit singing in the mountains above the sea,
As He leaps upon the high places, they join in harmony.
The song is one of praises, of strength, and of majesty,
Forever giving glory to your name.

I hear the Spirit singing of a hill called Calvary,
Where, for the love of all world, the Son died on a tree.
The song is one of praises, of forgiveness, and of victory,
Forever giving glory to your name.

Kathleen McQuade

Back Then, Oh, I Remember

Back then, oh, I remember,
Those cold, chilly days of December.
The light turns to dark, the days are shorter,
The whistle of the wind from the crack in the mortar.

We lit up the coal stove, that we now call a furnace,
To heat the house, cook the coffee, but hope it doesn't burn us.
Coal and wood are burned, we now call combustion,
Trying to start a fire from the fierce wind often causes frustration.

The warm wind whispers, "Snow, you're going to melt."
This is the spring weather that mother nature dealt.
The melting of the snow leaves the brown hills bare,
Magpies and black birds that you can scare.

Brown land, filled dam, expected calving cow,
Put on the boots, harness the horse, and hook up the plow.
The team of black belgians working all day long,
Pulling behind the man who plows and sings his song.

The song he likes on the radio that's just come on the air,
The song is sung by Elvis Presley, "Let Me Be Your Teddy Bear."
Field got worked and got seeded, my plow has got a dent.
Being my own boss, working manual labour, doesn't cost a cent.

Darryl Brown

My Mother

A tender touch,
a warm breath,
a silent nudge when I needed to be pushed in the right direction.
With a persistence you stood by me,
never allowing me to fall too far.
I have learned to be strong, yet soft in your arms.
With you as my teacher I learned to be human.
When I shed each tear you were there to catch it.
You, the amazing sculpture, molding me into
what I have become.
Throughout each hardship I endured, I have found a
solidity and peace in your eyes.
A friend, a parent, and a wonderful soul:
With the truest of all loves, I love you.
My world, my universe, my sanity, and my mother:
One in a million times can someone seek out a friend as
true as you.

Christa Hayward

Tiptoe with Arms Spread

Fragile Mercy, unto thee I come; with my arms forever gaping to be
forgiven of the inflamed injustice that is ripe within my wounded soul.
Risen out of the ashes of earthly darkness,
like a moth to the flame of light,
I come.
I come to embrace the friction of unending glee,
but it seems just an illusion;
An illusion to satisfy sinners and make holy men beg forgiveness.
Silent ember voices rain down upon my salted wound
and like hail they clear my mortal thought.
With fortune's luck, the ivory gates open.
They beckon from beyond,
and now my unworthy flesh feels forbidden lights.
Soon the naked envy is liberated from faithless thoughts,
and all that is forever takes hold upon my every being.
Soothing emptiness fills my heart and I dive breathless into eternity;
I breathe the essence of heaven and realize finally what true love is.

Chad Loker

Cat Tales

Tiny kitten paws batting at my hair,
Helpless little creature, dependant on my care.
The outside world awaits till she's grown a little more,
A garden full of wonder for Chloë to explore.

We chose the name of Holly three Christmases ago . . .
A kitten seeking shelter from the bitter wind and snow:
Affectionate and playful, a real beauty, too;
Calico in colour, with eyes of greenish blue.

Big brother Bow was another Christmas cat.
Loves to cuddle on your lap, tho' he's very big and fat.
He's Chloë's lumbering playmate, like a giant teddy bear,
When he isn't busy snacking or napping in his chair.

Arthur, stately lion king, with mane of reddish gold,
Orphaned from his mother, only ten days old:
Nine years later . . . still a baby, very shy;
Demands his morning grooming with a plaintive little cry.

With his boxing glove paws, Duke's the grandpa of the five.
Seriously injured by a bike, we're lucky he's alive.
With his silver tipped grey fur and emerald green eyes,
He's everybody's friend and loves to socialize.

Joan M. Chapman

At the Shore

Here, at the shore, where warmed water laps stone,
burning sun on bright water, the flinty scent of hot sand,
responding to relentless tug, the quieted lake
stretches long, unbroken, but pliable—ruffled here,
now there—the gently questing wind.
A boy, maybe nine, hair wet and plastered, shivering
under towel, chest panting to stepping rhythm,
splashing ashore, to watch younger brother.
Small boy clutches red shovel, contented by
scrunch of sand, enchanted castles, imagined dragons.
A moment passes and another. Distant splashes, voices,
laughter, rise and fall. A cannonball splash leaps high.
But now, smaller boy is not in sight. Frantic
scan for wondering toddler. Annoyed. Look again.
Now fear twisting stomach. Brother gone. O, God!
A panic search, a pounding heart, eyes bore near-shore
murky water. He must be found. He must be here. And
then—near surface, thin wisps of small boy's hair.
Reaching urgent. Spluttering child pulled to shallow shore.
And now, a small boy clinging tightly in his brother's arms.

Bryan Karney

The Journey

We all start life as a baby with an unknown journey,
And love with an unknown strength.

The journey has many roads of life:
Fast roads,
Bumpy roads,
Roads without control,
But whatever road you are on you will find some happiness on it.

Some journeys will keep you close with family and loved ones.
Some journeys will take you far and away from the ones that care.

But when the journey is coming toward the end,
You will always find the way back,
To get to the place where you are happiest
With family that loves you and cares for you.

When you get to this place, you can say that the journey is then complete,
And those who traced your journey here
Will have enjoyed the end of your journey with you.

We thank you and say our love for you will continue on.

David LaPlante

Everything's Gonna Be Okay

To expose your heart to danger when you know that it might break,
To take a risk of pain that you know you shouldn't take,
To fall in love with someone thousands of miles away,
And to know he sees his first love every single day,
To hear him say he loves you and wonder what else he'll say,
You don't wanna be that selfish so you can't ask him to stay.
He's asking you to stop worrying, for he's always there for you.
You wish you could believe him, but it's the hardest thing to do.
So scared that he'll forget you when he stays back there for a while,
So scared to lose your biggest love and live without his smile,
You sit and remember the fun and joy you had together one day,
You sit and wish from all your heart that everything's gonna be okay.

Dina Mamdouh Zahran

The Jewel of Your Life

I bestow My most precious jewel unto you.
This jewel, although it merits wealth is not of the material order.
For, this jewel is not a trinket that can dangle at the center of your chest.
Know this jewel and its wealth can be seen even though it is veiled.
For, this jewel I bestow unto you is the heart that beats the drums of life.

This gem I offer to you is the host of My life force.
It is the carrier of My radiant Divinity and will remain forever aglow.
Know it is with purpose that you are so endowed.
Experience the significance of your uniqueness, for you are life.
Understand that it is by design that I have chosen you.

Know that it is through the heart that I speak to you.
Experience intuition's insight and wisdom, for they guide you in being you.
Understand that there are other life forces that will try to influence you.
Do not sway to influence's way, for I am here to stay.
Behold the yearning for divinity's truth, for it is strength.

Know that in the spirit of inner strength you can become all that I am.
For your soul is stronger and more brilliant than the world's strongest gem.
Experience that it is in and through you that you and I are one.
Hail the bounty of our oneness, for liberation and deliverance await.
Understand I love your soul, unconditionally, for within your jewel I am!

Paula Fleming

Ode to a Grandchild

Did I see an angel flying down to me,
Or a ray of sunshine sparkling through a tree?
A lovely little girl, with silky, flowing hair,
Come running through the garden, her rosy face so fair.
Her name is Rachel Jane, and she's five years old today,
A precious ray of sunshine to warm us on our way!
Alas, time rushes by too fast!
Only sweet memories will last.
No longer does she run to me
To wipe a tear away, maybe.
She kneels beside me, holds my hands
And gently says she understands.
Gold tresses pressed against my white
Eyes growing dim, but not her sight.
Glowing cheeks, her smile impresses,
Twinkling eyes, my hand she presses.
Soon our Ray will fly away;
She was never meant to stay.
Childhood dreams too soon have passed.
Only love for her will last.
  Winifred Jean Hodge

Prisoner of Monday Night

This precious sunset is fading,
sweet denial shall soon set in.
I wish to be free of such concrete dreams
and their florescent simplicity which can't be destroyed.
This pathetic regret decorates me with hate.
Indecent, silent destruction.
Pain plagues the mind as the stench of fear is absorbed,
the world is in its grave of space.
I reach out and the darkness conceals my hands.
It pulls me into the maze of truth
where heaven and hell collide.
Where dreams are reality and
reality is a dream,
we are all puppets whose strings are tied to the clouds.
Flirt with fate and fate will flirt with you.
Dare to make a difference.
  Tara Cadrain

No Soul Can Contend

The greatest thing about having a friend
Is having someone to talk to,
Someone who will listen, respond, and care,
Someone just like you.

To have a friend like you would create in the world
The luckiest people alive,
People who would be happy, blissful, and free,
And would have motivation, incentive, and drive.

Although these friends improve people's lives,
There's nothing like the real thing.
You have absolutely no idea
Of the happiness to me that you bring.

Your wondrously caring nature
And overwhelming enthusiasm for life
Have inspired me to be a better person,
And develop this poem in my strife.

You're a very caring, generous, and lovable person,
Characteristics with which not a soul on this Earth can contend.
You're one of the best friends I've ever had.
I hope that fact never ends.
  Robert DeAbreu

A Wounded Soul

I'm angry now, angrier than I've ever been.
I no longer think of you
even as a friend,
For you ripped out my heart and danced upon my soul
without even a glance or a nod.
You're not the knight in shining armour I
thought you to be.
You're a devilish, foul sod.
I no longer think of you with fondness or bliss,
for you robbed my heart with tainted endearments
that flowed from sour lips.
You kissed and lied as you looked me in the eye,
but when you see thine own reflection, how can you not shame?
For, you are a con-man playing the Puritan's game,
but all comes back to those who perform
wicked deeds—and I'm certain you'll get yours.
It's the only repercussion to your selfish plan.
You see, my friend, God chases and catches those
Who stole treasures and hearts as they ran.

Paula Burlock

Sonnet: War and Peace

War.
Silence! The guns. Grey monolith knoll tanks.
Extol not ranks of sons marched in starched suits
To decimation. Limb loss. Sightless boots
For foals no more to climb sun knolls, snowbanks.

Silence! Infants cry. Children treading planks
Of hate. Want gaunt fingers dreading stones. Roots
Of earth hurled. Youth unfurled. Silent, dead lutes,
Poisoned juices in silver fluted tanks.

War! Feral Stealth. Stealing wealth, gun glory,
Despots bereft of bank deposit soul,
Conscience!

Peace. Foliage park strolls, Shakespeare scrolls, story
Libraries, prairies, skating, "Skoal!"
Music, art, a body part, in twin towns.

Shirley Anne Counsell

Imagination

I called to my friends, one fine winter's day.
I asked them to come over, I asked them to stay.

We pinned a sheet to the end of my bed.
We got a paintbrush and painted it red.

When in a flash we were sailing the ocean.
We were planning to find a magic potion.

At a big island we met three ugly men,
They were trying to find the ink to a pen.

They ordered us to sail the seven seas,
Then 'cross the ocean to the island of Shmeezz.

We did what they said and sailed the seas,
Across the ocean to the island of Shmeezz.

But when we got there no ink was found.
It was then when we heard a horrible sound.

'Twas my mother saying it was time for dinner,
For if we didn't have our veggies we'd get thinner and thinner.

So bye-bye for now, see you again.
Next time we'll tell you the beginning to end.

Kristi Higgins

The Burning

One day this man I loved told me
that my poetry was too "sickening, too emotionally laden."
So I burnt them, all twenty-seven years of my life.
I burnt my dead mother and my still living father,
my sisters and my brothers.
I burnt friends and acquaintances.
I burnt people on the metro and trees on the street.
I burnt happiness, sadness-anxiety, and all my fears.
I burnt the rain, the sun, my daughter, and son.
I burnt cities and mountains, and love and hate, and I burnt the moon.
Had to keep opening and stirring these in the stove,
as they took time to burn. Finally I succeeded in burning . . .
you and me, and birds and butterflies.
I burnt newborn babes and dying millions.
I burnt war and hatred. I burnt the anxieties of love.
I burnt snowfalls on a winter day. I burnt everything beautiful.
I burnt everything ugly. I burnt everything that I ever knew,
or had encountered . . . all of it . . . too emotionally laden.
So I burnt it! I burnt this life right up!
Except I did save some because I really couldn't burn it all . . . my life.
Eleanor Jones

Bleak Horizons

Lingering memories whisper among the screaming voices,
My heart crying reluctantly, thinking of feelings before,
Concocting the chemistry between us,
But you don't know, you'll never know.
Why should I sit and fret when reason dictates that I rise,
Ascend to the realm of the sensible, the prosaic, the heartless?
But emotion rips through the dividing wall,
The denizen of dreams where he and I ruled alone,
When his every delectable feature lay magnified in my memory.
Trying to sew together patches picked hastily with sense
Into my heart's intricate blanket,
Gently using the fragile string of passion and the needle of reason,
Fingers too often pricked,
My bloody dreams dying with every falling drop.
Your last sight plays before my mind,
The flame dying out on this candle of young love,
Fading into smoke from your absence.
Yet I search blindly for your lost presence,
You who never belonged to me
Anyway.
Natasha D'Souza

Ode to a King

When I lie back a ponderin'
about this world we're wanderin',
that the world's moving so fast,
that it's passing you by,
that it's getting you down,
that it's taking its time.
Fewer answers than questions.
It slips through your fingers without the slightest detection.

Memories are what get me by—
that glitter in your eye,
the time you told us all that lie
about the rat that bit you in the thigh,
and all the while couldn't bring yourself to cry.

I never got the chance to say good-bye,
and I won't bother asking myself why.
I know I'm going to find out the day I die.
These are just a few words I wrote for you, Dan.
Good-bye for now, my brother.

You were a king!
Michael G. Webb

Offering of a Yellow Dog

This lovely mole, this star-nosed Talpa,
Stalked among the lilac roots, buried for seasoning,
And now exhumed to tempt your appetite
Is but the smallest testament of my affection.
Or if it please you more—this eloquence in bone,
This skeleton emptied out by some departing bird.
Perhaps this wing that once assaulted heaven?
Or then this breast? This chalice for a heart,
This ribb'd cathedral sweetened by the earth,
This harp that holds the rigid echo of an elegy.

Or should your hunger stem from needs no temporal treasures fill,
If your distemper springs from moments fled through time
To haunt some outer space, returning only in the sweeter sweetness
Of remembering—then touch my head, and touching it recall my love.
For, all this ecstasy that marks your presence, this joy
Resurgent only with your footsteps, I would return, retaining nothing.
All I am, or would be, all I own of mind, of energy, or of bone,
(These only now exhumed or these my own still sinewed)
Would cross the world to lay my heart in tribute at your feet.

W. L. Dafoe

Did You Ever?

Did you ever hear the cry of a wounded fawn,
Or see its mama with pain, long after dawn?
Did you ever see a baby seal plead for his life,
Or his mother consoling him after the plight?

Did you ever see a mama bird pick her fallen one,
And see her gather the fallen eggs one by one?
Did you ever see a mama turtle trying to shield her eggs,
Or guard her newborns with tears, fearing the dread?

Did you ever see a baby separated from its mother,
Just after the umbilical cord was severed forever?
Neither mother nor child knows of this bondage.
To both it's a big world—to whom do they pay homage?

So is an anguished soul that utters: "Hear me" —it dares,
Knowing well no one listens or cares.
His fate he debates, doesn't know if it's too late,
Those silent morns, not too many can or will to relate!

This is the heart that yearns to be understood,
Finally settles down to solace and solitude,
Empty and aching, finds peace in meditating,
Surrenders to the world—there's no debating.

Marguerite E. Rolley

The Night Before Easter

'Twas the night before Easter and all
through the house, there wasn't a sound except for a bunny.
The baskets were laid on the stair with care, from which
they tumbled and landed on the hare.
Suddenly the bunny heard a little crack.
He regarded his eggs, then a chick popped out and bit his leg!
"Ow!" the bunny shouted. "What was that for?"
"Look up," said the chick, going out the door.
What the bunny saw was a broken shelf
mounted pot of honey. The honey dripped all over
the poor little bunny.
They honey stuck to his body-so-hairy, as he wondered,
"How come these things never happen to the tooth fairy?"

Matthew Scribner

"Too Wonderful To Be . . ."

A war, of musical high and low colours, e-x-e-r-c-I-s-e . . .
LARGER than smaller, growing stronger with each pulse . . .
Yellows, every shade,
Oranges that ooze . . .
and, red, right up to fury!
THEY
spark . . . then ignite . . .
flame . . . into dynamic rapture.
It,
cannot be controlled, curbed, or confined,
this happening, has come to life. . . .
There is smoking . . .
scorching,
. . . then the paper is consumed!
Everything is snuffed . . . doesn't exist,
gone free . . . !
— . . . Alas . . .
a masterpiece,
"Too wonderful to be. . . ."
Diana L. Ludlow

Never Forget Remembrance Day

As I lay in bed feeling sick one day,
A scene from war came to my mind as I lay:
Dead bodies lying on the dirt,
With mud streaked across their shirts;
Soldiers hiding here and there,
Shooting bullets and bombs everywhere;
Explosions shooting flames across the land,
And soldiers marching with rifles in their hands.
I get sad thinking of those who died,
Those who no longer get to see the bright blue sky.
I also feel happy for those who survived,
Those who were thankful to be alive.
Today is the day I should pray,
Because I'm just sick and not dead where the soldiers now lay,
For being warm and safe from blood and war,
For our freedom given to us after the war.
And on this day
We should give thanks,
Because it is Remembrance Day.
Stephanie Siu

Depression

I lie here in bed,
Wishing I were dead.
I have so much to do,
Yet no energy comes through.

I wish I were well,
But there in the depths of depression I dwell.
I know I'll be myself again,
But how can I live through all this pain?

The doctor tells me my illness will go;
But what if he's wrong?—Oh, I just don't know!
I try to be happy and cheerful,
But instead remain sad and tearful.

I try and I try,
Yet all I can do is cry and cry.
Oh, God, please help me to fight,
For, I feel like ending it right here tonight.
I know that I'll be all right.

Day by day and night by night,
Hoping the next day I'll feel all right.
I wish I were well, but here in the depths of depression I dwell.
Patrick Sikka

I'll Always Remember

My childhood years were carefree and timeless
Each day a new beginning—long-lasting and forever
So much wonder to behold, exciting and captivating
Like a butterfly dancing in a dream

The trees standing high bearing strength
With leaves spreading beyond into the night
Stars twinkling and the moon shining on the water
Still-like and mesmerizing

Feeling the warm and gentle wind against my being
Languishing and relishing and held in its caress
Taking me to a world of yesterday
How I longed for that feeling time and again

I never chose to grow older, with age innocence is lost
Though I cannot regain the stolen years
I can go back in time . . . with my mind
I can touch the wind, I can feel the sun

I can see my being a child again . . . a child again
The laughter, the innocence, the joy
Yes, I can recall the years and never bid them farewell
For as long as God gives me breath . . . I'll always remember

Rose Nicholas

Little Lil's Nature Lesson

I would if I could, but I can't so I shan't,
said little Lil, to her dad.
You see, I want to stay around, to see the snow
coming down just for once, and not be sad!
My dear little Lil, you will soon see
that mother nature's the one, who will put you to bed.
Just like all lily pads, including your dad,
we're only to sleep, so don't be sad.
So let us remember, as days go by
We would if we could, but we can't so we shan't.
But, we'll return next spring, said little Lil and dad pad.

John D. Veitch

Heroine's Journey

Assaulted by familiar faces,
They leer like jackals and sniff at the fresh tear
Left by the lash of their barbed, bitter tongues.

Their eerie laugher hides in shadows and mist,
Lingering in cracks and crevices,
Hushing the voice of the soul desire.

Messages veiled in an assassin's script,
The saboteur's identity is cleverly masked within a loving grin.
Sinister warnings like mines are carefully placed along the path.

Ashes to ashes,
The woman's spirit turns to molten embers.
The winds of adversity strike a blaze across the heart,
Illuminating her infinite and indomitable will.

The foundation's burdened by the weight of intrigue,
Defiantly gives up the ghost.
The sorceress's genius transforms the waste and ruin left in its wake.
With her sweet breath against the dust, she imbues it with the divine.
It awakens to become
The musician's song
And potter's wheel.

Kathy Lynn Treybig

The Absence of Father

Father, I do not hear your words.
As in quiet space and black night . . . I am.
Where is your discipline?
Gone . . . nonexistent.

Father, I do not see your love.
A vagabond heartless, lacking warmth . . . I am.
Your creation, broken . . . shattered.

Father, I do not feel your tenderness.
As in whiteness of coarse rock, rejected . . . I am.
The rain falls, limestone . . . crumbled.

Father, I do not smell your maleness.
The "Old Spice" of a substitute, a product of such . . . I am.
A surrogate on trial, imposter . . . unreal.

Father, where is your strength?
It was used up for I am.
You gave it away.
The spawn of your existence,
The seed of your lineage.
Who are you?
To me . . . nothing.

Daphne J. McIntosh

One Night

The warriors have been at battle all night,
breakers crashing against the rocks, thunder
crackling the air—the sky is alight;
winds charging, demanding to enter.

Through the window, a glimmer of awe in the eye,
but stare on, to see what lies in store.
Lightning exploding—let out a feeble cry.
Deafening gust rapping at the door.

Slowly, beams of the sun dispel the clouds with light.
Fireworks have subsided as has the commotion.
Where is that chaos, that dreadfully wonderful night?
Now hear not a sound, calm are we, devoid of any vibration.

Sana R. Kapadia

The Lonely Teen

She was left all alone
to face the problems he helped bring on.
It takes two to tango, so she was told.
Now all alone, since the seed has been sown.

What is she going to do now?
Where can she run to get out from under this cloud?
Who can she talk to? Where can she turn?
How is she ever going to explain this to mom?

She didn't mean for it to go this far,
but his talk was smooth in the back seat of his car.
He had all the answers to whatever she asked,
his answers were self-serving, truth wore a thin mask.

Now she faces pregnancy all alone,
fifteen years old, and now a runaway from home.
She cries all the time, no one to talk to,
and in her confused mind, there's only one thing left to do.

"What a tragic scene," the newspapers read.
Why on Earth didn't she seek the help she needed?
The irony of this sad story is, she reached out and tried,
but there was no one there till the day she died.

Kenneth Edwin Garland

The Crystal Energy Den

So special a being you have sent to me
To assist me with my books of poetry,
To share the time and space just being,
And April will be the keeper of the Crystal Energy Den that is to be.

The fairies surround April with love.
The spirits give April Crystal Energy from above.

She'll serve you sweets as treasures:
Coffee, tea, or whatever at your leisure.
She'll share with you love, peace, and harmony,
And the Crystal Energy Den will be her artistry.

When I pass by I'll stop in for a while.
Spend some time giving the Crystal Energy Den my energy,
So April can create what she wants it to be,
And when I walk away I'll wear a smile.

And then it will be time to continue on my journey,
Covering many miles before I return again,
Never being in any great hurry,
And always sending April energy in the wind.

The Great Spirit will guide you along,
Keep you wise, healthy, and strong.
Jaye Low

Anna

Inspired by a girl I saw playing the part of Anna
Though half an hour late was I, the result was still the same.
I would not let the night go by till I found out her name.
Her voice was sweet and pure, strong yet petite.
It unlocked my heart's door as I fell at her feet.

"Anna" they called her as she danced across the stage,
A smart English wonder who never seemed to age.
Though a cumbersome loop lived in her dress,
Of the maidens of the group, she danced better than the rest.

I tried to pay attention to the rest of the play,
Intentionally turning my head the other way,
But success did not come, much to my chagrin,
And once more I was pensive in sin.

"What could I have done?" I ask myself now.
There was nothing I could do but exclaim, "Wow!"
For, her face was perfect, her expressions real,
With the voice of an angel . . . at least that is what I feel.
Matthew Espaldon Wolff

A Doe at Evening

As I went through the marshes
a doe sprang out of the corn
and flashed up the hillside
leaving her fawn.

On the skyline
she moved round to watch,
she pricked a fine black blotch
on the sky.

I looked at her
and felt her watching;
I became a strange being.
Still, I had my right to be there with her.

Her nimble shadow trotting
along the skyline,
she put back her fine, level-balanced head.
And I knew her.

Ah, yes, being male, is not my heard hard-balance, antlered?
Are not my haunches light?
Has she not fled on the same wind with me?
Does not my fear cover her fear?
Giovani T. Aligaen

Loss of a Father

"Cancer . . . Multiple Myeloma, " the doctor said,
And we're off! Dad at the wheel, mostly in control for seven years,
At times veering and careening.
Then the viper, poised to ambush, strikes,
Merciless, devastating, swift.
The black widow scuttles across her web, injecting deadly poison,
Cinching her victim in sticky threads.
Where now is the shepherd boy with five smooth stones?
The major organs fail one by one.
Fever rages.
Consciousness comes and goes . . . and goes.
A once-massive frame is now merely skeletal.
And then . . .
"Peace I leave with you. My peace I give unto you.
Not as the world giveth, give I unto you.
Let not your heart be troubled."
And now, no more pain, not for Dad anyway.
And now, peace, for Dad anyway.
I pray, for the rest of us, it will come soon.
Margaret Tribe

Dusk at Seashore

Dusk makes its long-awaited appearance.
Its faint light glitters on the ebbing waves.
Sea gulls hover gaily in the crimson sky.
The setting sun beams wearingly halfway above the horizon.
Crickets sing merrily, welcoming the impending night.

I've always liked the magnificence of sea.
It can be calm as still water on a fine day,
But ferocious as burning fire on a stormy day.

As my moods rise and fall unstably
I ask myself,
Why I come here every day,
Especially right at this time of the day?

From the bottom of my heart
A faint voice seems to tell me
It's this spectacular sight—the ephemeral dusk at seashore
That I'm after,
To search for evidence of God's existence.
And I know I've found the answer!
This is part of nature—God's wonderful creation
That manifests His greatness.
Sun Tze Yun

The Stranger

The stranger approaches her calmly
on a deserted street corner.
He introduces himself to her;
they are no longer strangers.

He takes her hand,
leads her through his heart,
down the street,
and across his soul—she never looks back.

This instant connection
filling her body,
she yearns for him.
His lips land softly on her ear.

A shared night,
shared hearts,
shared souls,
and shared hands.

He leaves her standing miles from where she started
and disappears into the shadows.
Trembling, she runs his scenes through her head,
touches his soft familiarity once more—he never looks back.
Andrea Wardrop

Poem Transcending

Forever . . . we live through eternity. . . .
Each passing lifetime . . .
  forms and flows into the next. . . .
Do we realize the significance of it all?
  Spiritually and emotionally connected . . . forever . . .
A destiny . . . few experience . . .
  seldom wish to . . .
or perhaps fail to recognize its call. . . .
  Beyond our dreams . . . our physical beings . . .
souls reach out in the void . . .
Hoping to endure the pain . . . or explore the pleasure . . .
Connected through time . . .
  Is it love we remember? or a strangeness that binds . . .
so strong nothing can free . . . or disillusion . . .
Transcending everything we understand . . .
Spinning a tale . . . a poem . . . a rhyme . . .
  Reaching out to hold the truth . . . in such tiny palms . . .
Feeling only the limits . . . the boundaries of life . . .
Miracles appear. . . .
For sometimes . . . we feel the connection . . . the greatness . . .
and the beauty of it all. . . .
    Stephanie Ho

Home

The little cottage father built was nestled under trees
And inside by the crackling hearth boiled gently ham and peas.

The walls were chinked with plaster, with floors of rough hewn plank,
And children sat on barrels, watching butter churned by crank.

The wind grew loud and vicious, cold air came seeping through,
And snowflakes drifted under doors while smoke pushed up the flue.

The baby lay in cradled warmth and cooed his pure delight;
Oh, Lord above, my mother said, let him survive this night.

The storm, it shrieked and hissed with rage; our home began to quiver,
And in spite of blazing logs, we couldn't help but shiver.

Then just as we were bedded down with blankets filled with feathers,
The wind and snow just ceased to blow. And God released our tethers.
    Shirley Paquette

Rick

Nine years ago today our lips last touched.
Nine years ago today our hearts last touched.
Nine years ago today our hands last touched.
Nine years ago today and I still miss you so much.

It seems like yesterday that we laughed and carried on.
It seems like yesterday that I listened to your song.
It seems like yesterday we were having lots of fun.
It seems like yesterday there were two of us, not one.

Just the other night we held each other tight.
Just the other night everything seemed all right.
Just the other night we sat and watched the rain.
Just the other night you left me with this pain.

Nine years ago today you teased me like you did.
Nine years ago today you laid upon our bed.
Nine years ago today it was you I was seen with.
Nine years ago today my heart broke when you were touched by Death.
    Annie Thurgood

Tall Dwarfs

Breaking through the patterns allows us to laugh.
And so we laughed . . . all the way from the coffee shop,
all the way down the street, up until the bend.
And then you stopped and asked me why I've been laughing all the way
from the coffee shop.
And I wondered if you could judge laughter by distance.

But I have the cure for giggles:
one life,
one wall,
and a drop of fear.

In the coffee shop where we go . . . on a picture . . . it says:

Recognize your insanity.
And I wish that I were free from myself,
and I laugh while walking from the coffee shop
all the way down the street
up until the bend.
Sylwia Gustyn

Treasuring a well-spent life

Years long ago, I laid my head on cold, dry sand,
Close to where the seashore gave way to the ocean,
Stretching out my frail form facing the star-filled skies;
The sound of waves gently breaking on pebbled shore,
The pale moonlight glistening over the restive sea,
And the balmy breeze caressing softly my face:
At age nine, I thought then, life must be so precious
To possess jewels like these.

Now, I, past forty, staring at my weathered hands,
Tasks that they've done etched the marks of demanding dues
And wearied strength, sapped by promises left undone,
Still prodding the heart to desire for one more blow;
And rising to heave this aging body, I dreamed
Of that moment, when in my youth, thought of this hour;
Far from the gently breaking waves on pebbled shores,
Treasuring a well-spent life.
Severino Enopena

Of Vibrational Soul

What of the self—the Soul—
remaining long after easing off its fleshy coil?
It soars!

Leaving indelible marks on those it touched—embraced—uplifted—called out to.

Once more like—the wind—a raw mass of boundless energy flowing.
It moves through TIME—silently knowing.

Alongside rushing gale force winds where hawks dare fly—
likening itself to wildly charged, colorful displays of
flashing currents—bolting through the Heavens!
It rides each crest—forever showing.

Breathing in fresh, palpable gulps of Eternity—
picking up flitted currents passing.
Somehow aware of its purpose—it lands.

Other time frames await!
But now—its plotted course resonates—of gentle motion rocking.

Swaddled in rapturous folds of Mother's arms—Soul again meets its fate!
To stay the while—to ignite the day.
To move in TIME—until home again—it must fly.
Pamela Wollinger

Whales

The winds blow out across the bay,
The water high along about May,
There are black-eyed Susans back on shore,
But you won't find whales out here anymore.

The capt's cursin' out some song,
He's been away from home too long,
And all the rum now he's glad that he stored,
'Cause he can't find whales out here any more.

And still he sails across the ocean dreaming through his tears,
He'd taken almost 20 thousand back across the years.

The shadows roll out across the sea,
There's nothing there and there'll never be.
The old man lies dreaming behind his door,
But he can't find whales out there anymore.

And he really knows how it used to be,
How you'd hear them pushin' down through the sea.

Let's both have drink now, but I'd better pour,
'Cause you won't find whales out here anymore.

And still he sails across the ocean dreaming through his tears,
He'd taken almost 20 thousand back across the years.

John Christopher

Remembrance Day

The thunderous shots are heard all around.
It frightens, it kills, it tremors the ground.

The terrified people flee far away,
But the scared-to-death soldiers all know they must stay.

Wars are caused by anger and greed.
People write down the fight for others to read.

Shots are fired and bombs explode,
But those brave, young soldiers are still fighting bold.

When the war is won and survivors go to their homes,
They can still feel the fear within their bones.

We here stand on this day;
We stand here in silence, we remember and pray.

Respect that time when the horns strongly play.
Stand up and remember, it's Remembrance Day!

Amanda Bryan

Hallowe'en Poem

Hallowe'en is here! Hallowe'en is here!
As orange pumpkins glow in the night,
Ghosts scream and dead leaves fly,
As Frankenstein thunders by.
The top of the casket creaks open and bats shiver, petrified.
A witch's and warlock's poisonous brew boils over the cauldron,
And the full moon stays in the sky.
Costumes flare and children cry,
"Trick or treat!"
As the skeletons dance throughout the night.
But then the spooks melt to soft ice,
"Hallowe'en is gone!" wailed the ghosts.
Then they leave,
For next year they will come back again,
To give a scary fright!

Clarisse Sly

Where Are They!

Skies of blue ribbons and white hairy wisps,
Deep in the valleys of my mind,
Looking up on mountains high
Beyond the farthest sight of mankind.
Seeing places not yet beheld:
Jupiter, Mars, Saturn, Neptune, Mercury, Venus, Uranus, Pluto.
Releasing energy, imagining a response,
Trespassing through holes in the sky,
No fear of what might have become.
Officials concerned, but denied, not told.
Humans are everywhere, even not known.
Yet in minds deep it's felt there is
A perfect world not yet known,
Purest and holy one in the hearts.
No boundary of hatred already seen.
Behold, you must admit time is now.
Yesterday is gone and yet to come
Moments lost reconcile later.
Never let go, you mustn't,
There are Aliens here: Find them!
   Verona Henry

Then She Came

There was a time when pain was king, submission was his game . . .
then she came with her structure strong, head held high;
walked to them from the sky.
She was radiant with hair of golden silk,
scent of sweet perfume, and eyes of sparkling diamonds.
She took the discomfort, held it in her hands,
rolled it into a ball, and threw it.
Her rosy lips smiled an enchanted smile,
the people filled with laughter, and everyone cheered.
She is a role model; so peaceful, innocent, and strong.
They trust her to help them when things go wrong.
She attends the searches the people create
to bring them together and those that wait.
She is a great friend, can stand up to hate.
Her confidence allows for her advice to mend.
She brings joy, she brings great life for all those that live with strife.
Her strong respect and love for all show her intelligence
when put to the test.

She is Faith, the one and true, she is there always for you.
   Angie Marie Christensen

Papa's Pipe

You went with him most everywhere from rise to setting sun.
Some people need a dog or friend, with him you were the one.
I wish you could relay to me his thoughts. If you could have read
His mind, I'm sure there was love so pure, and fear, yes fear, and dread,
Days ahead with little hope, naught from the past to care,
Empty heart, no work to start, plenty of time to spare.
The days grew better, a job, a letter, this to us all was new.
He wrote the letter with hope in his heart,
his nearest companion you.
Then illness came upon him, he suffered much as before.
He was used to pain of a different vein, 'twas ever at his door.
If you could just tell, I'd know so well, what this man did think.
Now you are wrapped in a tissue, kept in a drawer.
All dusty, smelly, and forgotten, to be used no more.
You had your day, when peace you gave.
You stayed by his side, till he went to his grave.
   Teresa C. Davis

The Magnificence of God

The pearly white sands
The immenseness of the blue-green water—
The continuity of the waves,
The happiness and innocence of children's laughter—
The blue sky—white and grey clouds,
Tall, stately pines—craggy rocks—
Majestic green palms waving in the breeze—
The "meeting" of the sky and sea,
The sound of waves crashing upon the rocks and shore—
The fresh ocean breeze—
The chill in the air—the warmth of the sun—
The salty sea air,
The beautiful sunset of crimson gray and orange,
The gathering dusk—are all signs of the magnificence of God.
Amongst all of this there is peace . . . a deep inner peace—
And my God spoke and said: "It is wonderful—my handiwork.
Enjoy it—it is yours just for the asking."
These wonderful signs that proclaim the magnificence of God
Remind me of man—because they reach their final destination
The shore—recede and come again. . . .
   Donald M. McCartney

THE MUSIC OF SILENCE

I listen to her singing in the valley of silence.
So sweet is the sound when her tongue utters no word.
The harmony of that timeless moment echoes around.
Those speechless thoughts fly over like the wingless bird.

Our eyes talk to each other without any gesture.
Her lips stitched still convey all the emotions.
The cool breeze brings the warmth of her on my face.
Far still close, her heartbeats speak for her notions.

The murmur of her wavy hairs cry out in my ears.
Flowers sigh when her crystal brows look in coy.
That serene face embodies the cool of nature.
Feeling her soft complexion, wind dances in joy.

The soft music of her breath prowls down to my heart.
Those slender, snowy hands chant with my mind.
Words may not accompany, still I hear her so clear.
The gentle thoughts and calm desires are only of her kind.
   VIVEK SARAOGI

Forever

Don't cry, for I am not gone.
Don't forget I will always be
There for you in life or death.
Forever.
Don't be sad, because I am there to laugh with,
Don't let a shadow come when you think of me,
Think of me as I was,
Happy and emotional forever.
Don't mourn my death, for my heart still beats, listen.
Can't you hear my voice, my laughter?
Look . . . can't you see my smile, my worried face? Forever.
Don't stand under the stars wishing I was there,
My spirit surrounds you, I'm always around.
Hear my words, listen to my advice,
I always care, I will always be there.
Forever.
Don't look down, keep your head up and feel for me,
I am always around you, never forget who I was and am.
Don't cry, for I am not gone.
Forever.
   Dayna Lynne Barrett

Freedom Is a Word

They told me I was lucky when I was young,
You live in a free country unlike some.
I wondered for many a year just what these words did mean,
Not drinking water from a stream, or having skies clean,
Not gathering foods from forest, for those doors are closed,
Not walking alone at night, or to march for opinions opposed.
Don't step on the toes for the violence did silence those
Who strapped themselves to trees
When the delays they caused were increasing the fees.
The contested view winds up being the arrested
To appease the few who own the world,
Making freedom just a word. Sad to believe the lies you're told
That politics should be about economics
So that it provides lush lining of pockets.
Wealth before health is the call of the day,
So another sick dollar we spend for this way.
Know better than I the rulers say I speak for us another day
One where people look at the sky and cry,
Where the need for clean air leads many to despair.
Leaders are trusted in employ with our lives, 'tis not yours to toy.

Anita Carter

Untitled

He weeps and crosses his arms to protect his soul.
   Crouch down beside him,
and you will hear his heart pound miserably behind his flesh.
Crimson fear boils to invoke—
the treason and neglect and blank greeting cards.
Do you really care?
   Sing lullabies—he loves to croon
   And mock.
He rises slightly at the sound of someone entering,
but settles suddenly when no sight is granted.
Alone in black demise,
stopping only to allow someone to gently penetrate through his life.
A smile released, never anything more beautiful.
Eyes of deprived emotion and delicate jurisdiction,
he looks right through me
and touches the crevasse of neglect I've been building for so long.
I interpret this in my wild imagination
as his voice spills over my body and prickles every nerve.

Joelle Mozak

Untitled

As the dying road appears before me, there is
No more search of truth as the mirages go by.
There is no turning back now, my life is over.
There will be tears of sadness—my life went by fast.
Yet people talk, I listen, what am I missing?
The joy of my childhood will not be forgotten.
The funeral was terribly sad, though in our ears we
Can still hear her sweet voice that we won't forget.
Days go by very slowly; it is not the same,
Yet those days at play with friends are but memories
Of random, skittery thoughts. Now the autumn dusk is here.
Thoughts come, there is loneliness, though I still wait for
My baby girl to come home.

Meaghan Pluss

Sensational Tragedy

Princess Di is dead, without a bullet in her head,
and now, somehow, prince Charles seems like the "Juice."
With paparazzi chasing, a car flips, now they're tracing
the outlines of bodies for the news.

Nicole passed away in an most unnatural way,
and Goldman bit the big one too.
Their deaths were a sensation on TV's across the nations;
The ratings did not go into the glue.

DeNiro found his fury when his vision became blurry
from the flashbulb of some money-hungry jerk.
And the Fresh Prince went so wiggy, got arrested by a piggy—
in an airport where the paparazzi lurked.

But Jr. J.F.K., one time he got away,
To a tropic, secret spot to take a bride.
So the flockings took their cameras, packed up all their pajamas;
but couldn't find Jr. no matter how they tried.

This wave has long been mounting, the moments we've been counting,
the day has reared its ugly head. How can the media live with themselves,
how can we agree to such sensational tragedy?
Especially now that Lady Di is dead.
   Jeffrey D. Palmer

A Beautiful Day

A miscellany of grasses, perfumed and gay
With wild lotus and musk flower
Where crested wavelets play
Boats with white sails moving swiftly by
Where the gallant commander forever watches on high
Seeing ghostly blue figures surging, advancing
And now in the distance, majestic and strange
Gallons of white water crash and roar
Perhaps Indian maidens peer through the mist
Forever keeping their eerie, mystic tryst
While sturdy little motor boats are bob, bob, a'bobbing
Bearing cheery blue rain-coated figures
Looking around with awe and longing
Cameras at the ready to record forevermore
The pageant of sun and water and Niagara's beauteous shore
   Eileen Mitchell

Will Love Prevail

Dedicated to Judith Czar

I love you, though you might not believe it to be true.
It hurts me to know that you doubt my love for you.

Since we went our separate ways, I can't help but think
And feel, that losing you may once become my deepest regret.

You taught me that the most important thing in life is love.
I have come to agree with you from the bottom of my heart.

I know of faith, hope, and love, but the greatest one of these is love.
I pray the love I have for you will one day mend the pain
And broken heart I caused you.

Please forgive me for all the harm I brought upon you, for
It was not I, but my weaknesses and sinful nature that
Played out their maliciousness around you.

I have faith, hope, and love that one day you will
Forgive me without fail.

Although I wonder as time goes by, "Will love prevail?"
   Gabriel Morgan

Dad

In memory of my Dad

Although he is but a memory now, I often feel him near,
Still a vital part of who I am and all that I hold dear.
I believe he is watching over me as I live from day to day,
Guiding me with his gentle hands when I have lost my way.

He's with me every waking hour and even in my dreams,
In fact he never leaves my side; at least that's how it seems.
I see his smile that was just for me, the twinkle in his eye,
And I can hear his tender voice, fainter now as time goes by.

He touched my life so long ago with his love and his affection,
He taught me tolerance for others and gave my life direction.
He was my rock, my anchor, always there for me to lean on,
Even after all these years it still hurts to think he's gone.

"He is the wind blowing free, a leaf falling to the ground,
The rain against my window pane, a snowflake swirling round.
The silver sand beneath my feet, a wave breaking on the shore,
He is a part of all these things, for now and evermore."

The pain has lessened now, time heals all wounds they say,
But that hollow space within my heart will never go away.
It's still there when I think about him, but I try not to be sad,
For I know someday I will see again that man I called my dad.

Sharon Lynn Fehr Revels

Sadness

You do not have to speak, my dear,
For, sadness is written on your lips,
And your eyes seem to reflect a look of sorrow.
Your hair, once so smooth,
Now seems limp and weak
As does your heart,
Beating with a sound of sadness.
So, now, my dear,
You know how I know of your pain,
For, even though your words speak not of this tragic emotion,
I know what you feel,
For, words are not needed to show
That sadness is what you are going through.

Sonja Dale

No Music?

Have pity for the man who has no music in his soul,
No classic note of Mozart, no beat of rock and roll,
No famous Broadway melody, no sweet song of romance,
No tune that he can whistle to, no tune to make him dance.

Have pity for the man who has no music in his heart,
No lyrics to elate him if his world should fall apart;
No toe-tapping inspiration, or nostalgic refrain,
No song to hum in sunshine, or sing into the rain.

Have pity for the man who has no music in his mind,
No Country Western sad songs, no forgotten words to find,
No rhapsody of spirit, no jive, no jazz, no blues,
No rhythm to propel him, no "special song" to choose.

Have pity for this man, he is missing all the best,
A pillow of soft symphonies on which his head can rest;
The sing-along of friendship, the harp, the violin,
Have pity for this empty shell, try not to be like him.

Rusti Stauss

Did You Ever

Did you ever gaze into a mirror wondering who you are?
Did you ever peer inside yourself not getting very far?
Did you ever feel an angel's tear fall down as hard as rain?
Did you ever dream a thousand dreams you'll never dream again?
Did you ever feel your insides dying, lacking a desire?
Did you ever feel your heart tingling, flaming with a fire?
Did you ever wish for something even though it had no chance?
Did you ever want to look at something, but couldn't bear a glance?
Did you ever want to change the past, but knew you never could?
Did you ever want to be something, but knew you never would?
Did you ever trust a person who just threw your trust away?
Did you ever have to leave a place even though you longed to stay?
Did you ever feel the heartache of leaving someone dear?
Did you ever you make a chapter close without your conscience clear?
Did you ever try to love someone with hatred in your heart?
Did you ever try to just walk away, but couldn't tear yourself apart?
Did you ever see one's suffering, but couldn't heal his pain?
Did you ever wish you could start all over and try this life again?
Did you ever want to shrivel up into a little hole?
Did you ever want to leave your body, just to be all soul?

Natalya Grod

Sonnet

Search for me among the trees, for there I weep.
Like rivers do my tears flow from mine eyes.
Gushing floods of sorrow do wet the thirsty earth,
for I have truly lost the one for which I have striven.
Moans are flung above the treetops; sobs assault
my tortured soul. My beloved's farewell resounds
inside me; her good-bye breaks my tender heart.
Her hasty parting leaves a gaping void.
My heart rent in twain by the sudden, violent act.
Together, our quivering hearts beat doubly as one,
but split apart, one surely quits; the steady beating slows.
It slows, it stops, coming eternally to its rest.
I watch as my beloved one sleeps eternally in death;
oh, hasten the bloody hour that I follow her to rest!

Robert R. Gibson

The Raven

Far up in the northern sky
I heard the Raven Call
For his mate to watch him dance.
He is the greatest bird of the north.
How many hard, cold winters did he survive
Already? Never goes south, north is his home.
Warm March winds, he starts his mating dance.
He goes far up into the deep blue sky
Until you can't see him disappear.
Then all of a sudden you hear his cry
As he comes tumbling down.
All of a sudden he stops. On the
Highest pine tree sits his mate.
Then together they fly, soaring round
And round, catching the wind currents.
They mate in flight.
Through rain and hail, blizzards, snow storms,
He survives them all; he is the strongest bird of the north.

Rita M. Owl

Break Down

Break down social barriers, let Christ and conscience be our guide.
End violence, pride, war, drug abuse, corruption, and ungodliness.
This world would be a better place if we persevere with love,
If we we'd be to our fellowmen kind and give a helping hand.

True to his call, God creates us all,
To be more like him, to be pure within.
Through disobedience sin came forth,
Thus alienating man from God.

To have no chance we had no choice,
To get a chance we have a choice.
So the saviour bridges the gap,
And through his grace we all are one.

What greater love could one bestow
Than that of dying on the cross?
Why segregate and separate, living the present as the past?
Be wise, think twice, pride bears a price—disguise: It's the
sword of the anti-Christ.

Be not like Cain who murdered his own or living by standards
As in days of old.
Cease now all war.
Too much blood by far shed by mankind on each other.
Gloria Fraser

A Canadian Autumn

As we walk through the woods, the trees with their vibrant colors bow over us making a beautiful arch.
Suddenly, among all this beauty, an evil chill creeps up my spine.
He with his arm around me feels me shiver and pulls me close to his warm body.
The chill leaves as we follow the path over a high bridge that crosses over a beautiful shimmering pond.
When we come to the top of the bridge, he drapes his coat over my shoulders while we watch a flock of Canada geese rest on the pond as the fallen leaves weave around their bodies.
As it starts to get dark and we finish our walk, with a kiss
I now understand why I love a Canadian autumn!
Jennifer Thomas

Untitled

I saw you on the subway, Jesus.
You were so dignified, but why didn't you wear socks?
(Your feet were trapped in deerskin moccasins.)

I wore a black wool coat with a cleverly cut collar,
You a modestly fashioned jacket.

My hair was neatly slicked back,
Yours fell to your shoulders in perfect disarray.

I chased my thoughts,
You seemed to catch them with velvet smoothness, amicably.

You emanated serenity and warmth,
I sat immersed in my vanity.
You made me think,
I . . .

But why didn't you wear socks, Jesus?
Elizabeth Hamulka

A Conversation with God

"Can I help you?" God asked of me.
I said I want to fly over the ocean,
I want to be free.
"Free from what?" came his reply.
Free from everything that holds me back,
I said with a sigh.

"Can you elaborate?" he exclaimed with a smile.
I sure can, but it might take awhile.
"I have eternity," he stated with great patience.
As I tried to explain there was so much ambivalence,
I found it hard to know where to begin.
I said, Lord, it's that I feel I have sinned.

"Child, we all go through times of trouble.
You can't live your life wrapped in a bubble.
There are times when you will fall and all you have to do
Is pick yourself up, dust yourself off, and continue on through.
You see, my child, you will learn from your mistakes,
And I will not give you problems that I know you can't take.
I am a loving God and all I want of you
Is that you send out love in everything you do."

Dawn A. Douma

An Impression

The conversation's lacking.
Nothing significant in a close space provides the key to understanding.
An arbitrary symbol? The digital clock silently ticks out time,
without having momentum—no distance to measure.
Smoke and laughter.
Smoke comes from the mouth and nose, acrid and heavy,
dispersing evenly in the place, making it difficult to see,
and the happy sound that follows it is like that sound
that comes after something forced.
An impression really,
for which there is no basis.
Lost in the cushions of the couch are the keys.
I lost the keys, and that's really all that matters.

Joe Grey

My Heart's Quest

Trapped and impaired, my heart grows weary,
from the turmoil of endless pain.
My heart is trapped by demons,
as my mind plays host to their wicked games.

Though battle-torn and bleeding still,
my heart limps forward, the steepest hill;
To end the eternal conflict for love,
the tiresome fight for the devil's kill.

In its quest for love, my heart's desire,
lie ashes of dreams charred and marred.
Blinded by smoke, my heart pushes on,
in a futile hope all demons are gone.
From my heart to your heart is the quest to find comfort,
happiness, and rest.
My heart's turmoil to give all,
stumbles wearily from each painful fall.

The lonely battle rages over tear-stained fields;
my onward heart to razor scepters yields.
Battered roses wilt in the fields of myrrh;
the quest goes on through hell's eternal fire.

Demons tricks cut deep and quick.

K. Jill McMurray

Why?

How many times do I say sorry?
How many times do I say sorry for my hate?
How many times do I ask forgiveness for what I've become?
Our society: We abort and kill and murder.
How long does it take for me to see that I'm wrong?
Our society: Corrupt to the center, for what? Love?
And why? Why do I say sorry for who you are?
And why? Why do I care what you've become?
As the questions swirl through my head, we need to help,
Change, what we've made? The questions again swirl through
my head as I ask the question: "Why?"

D. Porritt

Leaving

As I sit here quietly watching this woman die with grace
I stare around at pictures of her family in a wonderfully kept place

I noticed all the sweetness and glow about her face
She knows what lies within her future, and she thinks of that other place

I ask myself how I would feel if I should know my faith
And then I quickly ask, "Oh, Lord," please do let me wait

She moves her hairless head aside and I smile deep inside
As I feel the life which she had known with honor and with pride

She sleeps peacefully, now unaware that I am writing her this poem
With pen in hand and many thoughts that flow

I sit and ponder alone, I shall miss this dear, sweet lady
When it is time for her to go

Margaret Roote

Beginnings

As the seed is introduced into the earth,
Two people meet.
As its roots burrow deep into the soil,
A friendship is built.
As the stem pushes its way through to the sun,
A relationship grows.
As the red petals stretch gracefully in the morning's dew,
Love is exposed... but, unlike the rose, love never wilts away.

Aimee Lewis

Taking a Walk inside the Zoo

Taking a walk inside the zoo,
I glance up and paralyze at a gaze,
Where eyes of the richest amber stare back at me.

They radiate a fake fierceness,
And hypnotize me to look deeper
Past that facade and into their hidden soul.

I probe, peeling back a mask,
And plummet into a tiger's mind
Whose emotions fill me, overflow, and spiral around.

An innocent helplessness
Lies within, a sadness so never ending
Into which I melt, becoming a part of its infinite depth.

Me and this sadness,
This complete sadness, threatening, forcing,
Bullying its way into my mind, my spirit, my very nature.

Crack! A whip sounds and I fall,
Emotions bang a shield and I stare now at a retreating tiger's back.

I do not move, I cannot move.
My vision blurs at the memory of what I had just seen and felt and left,
Taking a walk, in the zoo.

Aisha Magsad Hussain

Seasons of Mother Nature and Mankind

It is Spring, we are new, Earth Mother and Mankind.
Shades of cherry blossoms, apple blossoms in our hair,
Skin soft as rose petals, hair like thistle down,
Shades of daisies, tulips, daffodils at our feet:
We are bedecked with the pastels of this season.

In the Summer of our youth, Earth Mother and Mankind,
Darker shades we wear as is befitting to this stage.
Our greens are rich, our pinks are red, our blues are royal,
We revel in our youth, and learn of love and life,
And the responsibilities of our pending adulthood.

In the autumn of our days, Earth Mother and Mankind,
We seem to deck ourselves in even darker hues.
The blacks of the night, the navies of the evening skies,
The orange, purple, red, and brown of falling leaves:
These are the badges for the good we have achieved.

Winter, the final season, Earth Mother and Mankind,
A mantle of white we both now wear upon our heads,
As with dignity we greet the era of our passing near,
Symbolic of our purity, our perfect state of being,
Until again we rise with joy to greet the dawn of Spring.
   Hazel Rice Harper

Life without Love

Love is not something I have had the pleasure to know.
I have not nurtured it, enjoyed it, or helped it to grow.
I haven't had the chance to grow close to those nearby.
I simply haven't been loved and I often wonder why.
Is it me? Is it them? Is it something I might have done?
Is it that when love confronts me, I just turn and run,
Or is that there is simply just no one that will care?
When it comes to the crunch, no one is ever there,
No one to comfort me when life gets me down.
When I just need a little love, there's no one around,
No one to tell me, everything will work out O.K.,
No one to hold me or comfort me in any way,
So I go through life alone, with no comfort, no love,
And maybe when I die, I'll find comfort up above.
   Joanne Hendriksen

Good-bye

I have no time for you today,
Said a man to his best friend.
I must run, I'll see you soon.
The price I'll have to pay.
I know just where I'm going
And how long I'll be.
Then if things don't go just right,
It's you and me, you'll see.
I know I really do love you,
But things do have to change.
I cannot go on this way
Hearing the things they say.
The real life facts I'll face
Of comings and goings each day.
So I'll say good-bye for now;
To hope our love keeps its vows,
That when I return home again
I haven't put you through too much suffering and pain,
Hoping things have gone better for you,
No more struggles, or crying, the blues of our last "Good-bye."
   Fran Halladay

My Dog

You were brought to me one cold, dark night
Your heart full of fear, your eyes full of fright.
I knew it was love, with one little look,
One glimpse of that puppy was all that it took.

Strayed from your mother—days later I'd learn.
The bond grew between us, so strong and so firm.
A sweeter little puppy I never did see.
No one could ever dare take him from me.

Weeks turned to months, and months into years.
You grew into adulthood, so big as a bear.
I could tell what your thoughts were, as I looked in your eyes,
Two big, shiny brown ones looked back into mine.

The sound of your tags as they jingled on your chain,
The clippings of grass on your paws when it rained,
The tip of your tail as through bushes you went,
When wonderful days at the cottage we spent.

The years have gone by, day by day they have passed
Since the vet said so sadly, "It's over for Chance."
Each night at my bedside when I talk to God
I'm so thankful for owning that wonderful dog.

Elizabeth Sheppard

Snow Scapes

Twilight lies o'er a patch of snow that dusts the foliage below,
And from my perch at window sill I, watch the striking scene so still.
Then through the frosty pane I search for signs of feather upon the birch,
I listen for the silent sound of wintry birds that can't be found.
The moon is chilling for October, the twinkle in the stars is sober,
A lonely night, it takes its toll, a dreary mood stirs 'round my soul.
The silk robe draped around my shoulder provides no heat and I grow colder,
So from the hearth I would engender a roaring fire of great splendor,
But as there's not a stick to burn, back to the window I return.
I gaze at numerous branches bare and until April I sit and stare,
And long for days of sweet spring rain, streaming down my window pane,
When once again I'll come alive and warmth within my soul will drive
A passion and a strength of will to lead me from my window sill.

Beth Ann Ward

Is the Natural, Natural?

A nature lover, an herb eater, a flower picker, that's my friend Rick.
He tells me interesting Hasidic tales, writes fantastic stories,
Does a mean massage. That's Rick.
I think he's intelligent, but what the heck!
Does it really matter?
What I think, what you think, what anybody thinks?
Suffice it to say, Rick is a simple person:
A naturalist, a great thinker, a farmer, a barefoot walker.
But underneath the naturalistic layers, the deep-set eyes,
and faded, soiled clothes,
I see a cunning, shrewd man.
Now I ask myself,
Is his natural really natural?
In the final analysis, does it really matter?
Because you see, I like Rick.

Jean H. Esannason

The Unloved

My clothes are torn and ragged.
I have no shoes to wear.
I look sadly at people in their cars,
But they do not care.

The street-side is my playground,
And abandoned buildings my home.
And from where do I get my food, you ask?
It comes from the gullies that I roam.

Look at me! Look at me!
Am I not the future too?
Does it matter if I don't have appropriate clothes to wear,
Or a good pair of shoes like you?

I am human! I'm an orphan.
I'm one of the outcasts of the world.
I need someone to wipe away my tears,
To support my dreams, and to control my fears.

To myself I am a person.
Like you, I have memories and dreams.
But in the eyes of the better off,
I am no one, it seems.
    Marisa Harris

Reflecting

The many seasonal faces are a wonder to admire,
But autumn is a special time, to sit beside a fire,
To marvel at a harvest, ripening in the sun,
A joyous, sweet reminder of a season just begun.

In solitude we ponder, then possibly reflect
On the distinct greatness that sometimes we may neglect.
Leaves carefully tinted in orange, crimson, and gold,
A gift from above before the season grows cold.

Alas, the north wind that always rolls around
Permits the leaves to dance, someday paint the ground.
Blending in the breeze, we can revel at the sight
Of nature's infinite wisdom created in God's light.
    Cheryl Ann Stead

To Me, You Are

Layer upon layer, layered so smoothly,
Long, lustrous, enthralling locks,
My sense of touch yearns for their silky sensation.

Like two celestial spheres drifting in deep space,
Eyes so incredibly dark and bold,
I can't seem to resist their gravitational magnetism.

A nose that knows it has its own beautiful place
Resting among its surroundings.
My nose knows too, its sensuous softness well.

Lustfully glowing lips
Shine like the sun sinking into the sea.
Oh, to set sail on their soft waves.

And when you smile,
The stars light up in the sky and the moon shines,
And I find myself forming my own symbolic constellation.

And all of this makes up a face
So poetic in both beauty and grace
I read between its rich lines
To uncover all of its literary gold.
Ah . . . beauty, what a wonderful thing to behold.
    David Grosfield

Raindrops

The sun is deciding to leave or remain.
Blue sky is fading, it's going to rain.
Wind calls to the clouds, meet one and all,
Join hands together, get ready to fall.
Fluffy white clouds, turn on a frown,
Make your face dark, cast your eyes down.
Wind whistles around, trees answer back,
Sky moves closer, the earth gets black.
Birds scurry away, some shelter to find,
Ducks on the pond, they don't seem to mind.
Flowers bow their heads, ready for rain,
To smile on the world, when sun shines again.
Rain starts to fall, the clouds they are crying.
Earth gathers their tears, none are left lying.
A small patch of blue appears in the sky.
Clouds start to drift and float on high.
Sun shows her face, waves good-bye to the rain,
Flowers open their petals, say hello once again.
Clouds lined with silver as they slip away
Leaving a rainbow of colours to brighten our day.
The sunshower has gone and all that remained
Are tears on the flowers to show that it rained.
   Doris Crain

Travailing Spectre

Travailing spectre, what holds you bound between
Shadow and light? Did your life force rise without
your knowing, or was something left undone
preventing you from finding the light that leads
to peace? Do you linger in silence, was your entry
barred by violence, or perhaps you are lost, seeking
yet finding not that which would ease that lonely
pain that haunts you? Are you a reflection left from
mortal breath, or simply unhurried in your journey? You
are a mystery to my senses and to many others
that exist is not consensus. Yet I think upon such
a lonely fate and can only pray that God will
intervene and lift you from that place. Perhaps you
gaze above my shoulder and read this poem once,
twice over and as you read, perhaps you see that
you are not alone, for people pray as I do
today that God will take you home. You are both
spectre and spirit. Use your spirit. He's bound
to hear it and lift your soul on high. Amen.
   Mike Wydenes

I Know This Love

I feel like singing a song of joy from within my heart.
The way that I feel has been strong from the very start.
Now that I know how to word how I feel,
I know my love for you is real.

It isn't every day that people feel this way;
Like sharing every thought and everything they say,
Making happy times and moments for each other.
It will continue on, I need not wonder.

Love brings many splendorous situations,
Love takes a very special combination.
We're that special pair, I know we can make it.
We have what it takes, I know I'm not mistaken.

If it's fifty years or more,
Be it rich or be it poor,
Be it sunshine, rain, or whate'er the weather,
I know that you and I can last forever.
   Vivian L. Thompson

Tears Are Falling

The tears fall freely down your empty face,
They're caused by pain and suffering time can't erase.
So when you find yourself standing lost and alone,
Remember all the heartless cruelty you to have shown.
And when no one stops to wipe the tears away,
Remember it was you who laughed only yesterday.
You walked pass a dying man and never gave a smile,
Was it too hard to stop and help him travel life's final mile.
He asked you for your help and you kept walking on,
You claimed you were right and he was wrong.
You cry not for no one will lend a helping hand,
As you find yourself in the shoes of that old man.
You say if you could travel back through the years,
You would help him to his feet and dry his tears.
But it's too late for the wrong is done,
You've played your games and had your fun.
So when the tears fall slowly down your face.
Remember you to helped others lose the race.
   Shannon Michaud

The Teacher

True greatness pushes the limit and height of aspiration
To an ever-expanding plane of achievement.
The gift of enlightenment so eagerly received is its legacy.
It is pure, generous, and freely given,
Yet so rarely glimpsed through the passage of time.
We felt its kind power, we felt it enshroud us and lead us
And tuck our minds safely in under a blanket of wisdom.
At that unnoticed moment it will let us go,
But still held by its enthusiasm, we chase our own dreams.
Who is it? It is he, this communicator of the ages,
This gentle pervader of so many revelations.
Sharing ideas with us was the heart of his science.
We came to understand them in the light of clarity.
We shall not let his passions and hopes fade,
Nor ever will he become just a name from the past.
Rather his spirit will lift us time and time again,
A teacher of the world, of the cosmos, Carl Sagan.
   William Campbell

Thoughtful Thoughts

For people who speak slowly I can wait,
Perhaps they are thinking thoughtfully while they hesitate.
Thoughtful thoughts seem to take a little longer,
While thoughtless ones don't take any time to ponder.

Thoughtful thoughts expressed in such a way,
Could lift up the spirits in someone's day.
For, the thoughtless many times must say,
I am sorry; I didn't mean it that way.

If only thoughtful thoughts were allowed in our heads,
One would not become one that others dread.
If only thoughtful thoughts were allowed to be said,
Would all that thoughtfulness like gossip spread?

Imagine a thoughtful thought being worth a million,
Would we be quickly cashing in the billion?
The thoughtless thought only worth a penny,
Would we be so quick to have so many?

Think the thought, but think it through,
Try not to let the thoughtless one come from you.
Thoughtful thoughts cannot be measured,
For the one receiving one, it will always be treasured!
   Yvonne A. Macdonald

The Problem with Our Marriage

Drove him to the mall: He had some shopping to do.

I had opened my mouth, asking questions,
hoping a little truth would show between the answers.
He doesn't like questions.

Then, in the parking lot, I said,

"The problem with our marriage
is you expect me to be your wife
but you refuse to be my husband."

I turned my back.
I should have moved out of the way.

He kicked: end of argument, beginning of monologue.

I didn't say anything more: I stayed out of reach.

I was guilty of deliberately embarrassing him in public.
People in the parking lot had seen the kick.

We went into the mall to do his shopping.

The footprint on my leg turned purple,
size twelve, extra wide.
    Vivien Broughton

Do You See What I Say?

To my autistic son
Please watch, and learn to listen to me,
for I'm unable to talk. I'm locked inside me.
I get frustrated and angry. I don't speak the same way.
Please try and hear me. Please see what I say.

I speak with my hands, nod my head to reply.
I throw things in anger and wipe tears when I cry.
I speak with expressions and actions, you see.
Please see what I say. Please do this for me.

I clench my fists in frustration, bang my head in despair.
You won't listen to me, it just is not fair.
My hurt will release all the tears that I cry.
Don't you see what I say? I ask you to try.

I need understanding and patience, not pity or fear.
My language is different than any you hear.
We'll learn together, both me and you.
Please grasp what I say. I pray that you do.

As you open your eyes and begin to see,
a new day will dawn as you listen to me.
You start to understand what I'm saying to you.
Do you see what I say? I think some of you do.
    Cheryl Schofield

Catherine

The little smiles you send our way,
And the endless hours of wanting to play,
Great big tears from a girl so small,
And teasing the dog with her polka-dot ball.

Quiet moments with kisses and hugs so tight,
And stubborn stands with all of your might,
Laughter contagious, we burst at the seams,
And the peek-a-boo times filled with laughter and screams.

Sad times of misery you insist we all share,
And the sly, innocent eyes melt all with their stare.
Although there are moments of anger and shout,
My littlest angel you are without doubt.
    Claudia Herr

Letter to a Stranger

I'm writing to you, though I don't know your name,
But I know your heart well; it's ready to tame.
If I reach out to you, I know you'll appear.
If I cry out to you, I'm sure you will hear.

I'm writing to you, though I don't know your face,
But I'd recognize you in a vast, crowded space.
Your eyes would be warm, and your smile would be too;
Welcoming me, beckoning me toward you.

I'm writing to you, though I don't know your voice.
But with your soft, songlike tone, I would have no choice
But to listen to you, and answer your pleas.
I know you hurt too; that's why I'm at ease.

I'm writing to you, a pure stranger to me,
But God gave me eyes, eyes destined to see.
He gave me a heart, to get love and to send,
And God gave me you, my stranger, my friend.

Sonia Myre

Extinction

A flower, as immortal as the day it lives on, withers.
It begged for a hint of hospitality and care. We ignore it.
"Survival of the fittest," we would say.
"It's not our fault," we say. "Is it?"
Why are we dying?
I ask myself as I lie surrounded by blood and tears,
I ask, "Why are we dying?
Who did this to us?"
And I listen for a response.

Now as my body lies dead and I stare blankly into the
sky . . . I hear a voice among the guns and crashing explosions.
I hear Him whisper . . .

"You did."

Jennifer Desmarais

Your Loving Ways

Vision always comes and goes . . .
Your image and the wonderful things you do.
Moment of happiness is there to recall,
How wonderful to know someone like you . . .

When I am in distress and in low down profile,
I think of you always; loneliness subsides at once. . . .
The way you do care for me, the sweet face to show,
Makes me feel renewed, the good side of the point of view. . . .

Day by day is not easy to overcome . . .
Specially when you have a troubled mind . . .
Feelings of insecurity from someone you care,
Afraid of loosing you as day pass by. . . .

The time we are together, my life seems so nice.
My heart is full of good thoughts in your loving arms. . . .
Whisper of your loving ways, I appreciate it so much . . .
Love that is precious in my heart and mind. . . .

There are times as if I can not let it go. . . .
The heartbeat I felt, the wonder it gives . . .
Joy of your words, expressions, excites me so much,
Sign of love that comes deep inside our hearts. . . .

Julie Mahal Amor

Drawing the End

The end is drawing near, my life is full of fear.
Wondering when death is coming.
Thinking to myself why I'm here.
My life is empty or is it?
I sit here drawing the end.

People take empty glances as they walk by like zombies,
Wondering were to go and how to get there.
Fathers away for weeks sitting in empty hotel lobbies,
Picture of their family in one hand, hooker in the other,
Sitting there drawing his end.

Violence causing the news headlines as the days go by,
Wondering what big news report will be there tomorrow.
Wives getting slapped around and just want to die,
Thinking they can change their man,
Sitting there drawing her end.

People living their destiny in pain,
Wondering where their next meal is coming from,
As they lie there looking lame,
Collecting cans trying to make money,
Sitting there drawing their ends.
    James R. Mitchell

The Red Maple Tree

Its leaves, crimson like the blood of a passionate lover,
Flirt with the sun with such intimacy
For all the world to see.
Soon they will be gathered in the arms of the fickle wind,
Carried on the wings of its song
To heights and places unbeknownst,
Then let fall to tremble on the ground.
The tree, now naked, has no regrets,
As that of a betrayed woman,
Like a great performer
Stands in wait—
To play her role once again.
    Hope McNabb

Untitled

I wish I could be the one you need,
A modern embodiment of Ophelia
Who could suffer and die for you
And bask in the pleasures of unfulfilled desire.

I wish I could hide myself from the truth
So that I could pursue your love with hope,
Unperturbed by your withered esteem for me,
Ignoring the unalterable past.

I wish I did not have the misfortune of understanding you
So that I might die fighting for what can never be,
Chasing your heart as you take it elsewhere,
Reinventing myself to alter what cannot change.

I wish life were less real;
My sense of reality threatens my sense of love.
If life were an illusion
My life would not need gratification.

I wish you could acknowledge my pain
To undo this plight you created
So that you could be my order
And I could be your life.
    Marc Lishchynski

A Light in the Darkness

The light is fading.
Shadows of you
Dance along the walls,
In silent stillness.
My heart is as an empty void,
No longer filled with laughter.
It is consumed by the darkness of your death.
But when I feel alone,
I see your smiling face,
And hear your soothing voice.
Your warmth removes the cold anger that burns inside me.
With the brilliant radiance of the sun,
"You light up my life."
I can see more clearly now.
The walls are torn down,
And the shadows melt into smiles
On the faces of young children.
And morning comes.
It is another day that I'll never forget
How much I love you, Papa.
    Sarah Stapley

Distanced Shadow

As I walk through my distanced shadow
I see the pain and laughter that I put on people's faces:
All the tears, all the joy,
All the good and the bad.
As I walk through my distanced shadow
I see all my obstacles I must overcome.
I see my distanced grandpas lying in their beds fast asleep.
As I walk through my distanced shadow
I see all the offset colours that brighten the world.
I see the hunger that destroy many lives.
As I walk through my distanced shadow
I see people killing people for more control.
I see the lack of trust in everyone's eyes.
As I walk through my distanced shadow
I see battered women hurt by their loved ones.
I see young children beaten every day.
As I walk through my distanced shadow
I begin to wonder what kind of world is this
and why am I here?
    Toni Clark

Falling Rainy Stars

Quietly, softly—like in dream—
on that rainy day
the tiny golden leaves,
autumnal but still dreaming about the spring,
were falling down with rain. . . .
I listened to the rhythm of heaven,
music of flying stars on the roof of my car.
I watched the gold from the sky in various sparks.
How they are flying down to choose their own place
on wet and colorful natural space. . . .

Oh, yes!
Even the forest feels sad and crying after summer's gone;
it pours the rainy tears for summers of many years,
my feelings and dreams were also within
in all their beauty and richness.
The sky and forest were in tears,
like me with many unfulfilled dreams,
with many from heaven falling stars. . . .
    Marinko Grk Croata

God Is Love

Dear Heavenly Father up above,
We thank Thee for Thy great love,
for health, wealth, and loving care,
to know that Thou art always there.
You gave us a mind, clear and bright,
knowledge to know what is wrong or right.
There are those that live in doubt and fear,
do not know God is always near,
nor do they realize that every good—perfect gift
comes from the Lord above.
We must help our neighbours and love them too,
pray for guidance to see it through.
We know if we ask, believing, we will receive
the strength to carry on, to help those in need.
Each one can do his part to help in the heart of healing
what a blessed life to us will be given,
the art of really living.
God is love.
  Sarah Simnett

Ode to Landmark

The months have passed since September the sixth
When we left for landmark, from the land of the sticks.
Down the valley we did go—
With great expectations and faces aglow.

After years of frustration with the school work here,
We were expecting a super year!
It meant my third baby was leaving the nest,
Oh, but it was all right if he could just pass those tests.

The days, weeks, and months rolled by.
You were happy and doing well and I said, "Oh, my!"
Your weekly summation book had great things to say,
I said, "Thank you, God, this is a great day!"

The work got harder but you didn't mind.
The harder it got the more you climbed.
You pleased your mother and many folk,
But yourself was proud, we can't revoke.

I wish some M.P.'s could be here tonight.
No, we wouldn't pick a fight.
Just for them to see those proud, happy faces,
Who through their short lines had many disgraces.
  Judy Lepper

The Attic

Behind the attic door
lies imagination.
An ancient doll lies dust covered
on the worn, time-forgotten floorboards.
A neglected rocking chair, stuffed in a corner
without an arm and a leg, holds a moth-chewed
photo album of the happy years.

Silver light from the moon shines on a
cedar chest covered by a musty, paint-stained sheet;
Inside holds another new world of joy.
Costumes of the years, forgotten by the elderly,
books, letters, and emblems hidden away
for any inquisitive mind.

The attic is getting chilly and there is a storm brewing.
I am frightened.
I must leave this new world.
Behind the attic door lies imagination
and curious temptation in a child's mind.
  Kirsty Meldrum

Diana, A People's Princess

They strew flowers in her way,
Who goes in triumph even unto death,
A solitary figure of astral luminescence,
A light to shine in the hearts of the bereaved.

We knew her not, and yet we missed her so.
She lived her life for others where royalty dare not go . . .
The sick, the maimed, the despised, the voiceless.
They were hers and we will never forget.

We feel the power of genuine love and truth
In the death of beauty and of youth,
A magic so strange and overwhelming,
A people's Princess endowed with Divine blessing.

We so often learn from other's fate,
And hasten to correct before it's too late.
To do good for others in worsened state,
Diana, our model, she couldn't wait.

Let not her death be in vain,
For she showed us the path again and again,
The sick with AIDS, the homeless, land mine victims:
This to a person we admire . . . rest in peace—Diana.
    Robert Madhosingh

Perfect Angel Jobel

Nights to nights, dreams to dreams,
Light from light, as it always seems.
By hand, by kiss, by love and trust,
To keep a promise from dust to dust.
To give, to make, to love, to take,
When two souls meet for love and sake.
For joy to love that's in your heart,
The bond between us shall never part.
To hold, to cry, to never let you go,
Our bond together is sweet as the mountain's dew.
Fresh and clean and has been seen,
When two hearts beat as one.
For, this is now the time to tell,
As I stand before the most perfect Angel who I call Jobel.
    Mary Jane Zapanta

Mother Africa

Give me a reason—a purpose where there's no doubt.
Tell me the truth, something that I can shout out.
I paused with a cause, so people hear me now,
Mother Africa is in turmoil.

But who's to blame? Who, me? I ain't callin' no name,
Seeing that it's so easy to explain.
And it's with regret and shame—having to suffer
The agony and pain, being a true son of the soil.
But look, even now, I remember . . . Mother Africa.

Now listen to me, my friends . . . someday it will end . . .
When? That will depend on who's on our side.
Yet in a twinkling of an eye, as the years roll by
There will be no more sparks left to ignite.

And who from among the old should leave behind
The stories that are to be told about
Mother Africa, than I.
    Irwin Da Costa Yarde

Beyond the Rock at Sunset

Evening thickens the lake. Shorelines disappear.
Darkness swallows the beach.
The water dims,
And the Great Pine leans deeply into its own reflection.

My craft glides at my lonely will, moving as I wish it.
I know the paddler's art:
I watched his shoulders that no longer bend over the bow.
I learned to read the ripples by the muscles of his back.

His sureness overcame my fears.
Now I am safe in all weathers and all waters.
I long to share his strength and skill,
But it is night. I forge on alone. I am a solitary expert.

Stephen Day

Above and Below

A technicolor bird soars gracefully through the air.
The clouds move silently out of its way.
The fluffy white clouds turn a deep grey as the bird flies past them.
The sky that is blue rains from strips of white pounding
continuously on its surface.
The drops from God's eyes moisten the Earth and comfort the children.
Everything is peaceful.
Everything except for that technicolor, man-made bird,
causing pain and agony from the clashing of forces together,
causing flashes of light and deep, frightening rumbles.
The Earth is silent, yet the sky is not.

Tacia Lee Kilty

The Color Fields

Shall I paint you a picture of words and of scenes
Of fields to all and fields in between
Some are of wheat, with their wisp-green heads
That roll in the wind like the waves on the seas
Some are yellow, from the potent rape seed
As a honey-gold carpet, in a sun-drenched breeze
Some are of scarlet, with the waif-poppies as fire
Which then smoulder to crimson as the sun reaches higher
Some are of purple, as a bright royal crown
With their velvet-rich texture as a deep eiderdown
And some are as white as an ocean of brightness
With their tone as startling as a brilliant light
This constitutes my canvas, constructed with words,
And as bold a reflection as the fields and their colors

David Whitby

Plentiful Fields of Gold

Oh, Maryland, oh, Maryland—
you are a merry land!
With fields of gold
so plentiful,
no one can say it's dull.
I roamed around
and what I found
surprised me to no end:
That fields of gold
had in their fold
so many weeds—you see.
But what is to one a symphony
is just a discord melody
to someone else's ears—so it appears.
Oh, Canada, oh, Canada—
it seems you had a ball:
To gather in the fields of gold
in Maryland this fall.
America, America—from north to south, from east to west,
You surely did your best: to touch us all!

Edeltraut Scheffler-Plath

And the Roses Bled

Caught in a web of dreams,
Reality's but a far cry away.

Although this thing between you and I
Can't withstand the light of day,
You didn't bother to fight it,
Until the very end.
Hurt beholds a fictitious will.
Pain subsides in the heart of the unjust.
Making sense of it all just seems to confuse.
High hopes neglected for peaceful souls.
Candy-coated sweetheart is the secret to success.
The blind and brokenhearted left to go unnoticed;
Only in the end will the blind see
And fools will reign in error.
For, it is times like these
That princes may be comparable with Earth's floor.
Yet, in seeking truth, may find it all a misunderstanding.

Caught in a web of dreams,
Reality's but a far cry away.

Kristy Lusk

Jeremiad (A Tale of Woe)

The cryptic, nebulous nature of your loss,
Ambiguity spilling over the edges,
The used and neglected carved out of stone,
Always with identity,
Yet somehow unknown.
The ambivalence of your love overshadowing my pain,
The hedonic youth of summer slipping away with the rain,
My codified mind believing your meaningless words to be pure,
Your inexcusability sickening,
And my nescience unbelievably nauseating as it spews out with the love
Fulsome to the pleasantries of time,
Abuse replenishing in the form of tears,
Factitious amazement soon buried by your grave,
And endless, twisted remnants of constricted memories.

Erin Gray

Be

When there must be a word for humanity,
For love, child, shepherd, hope, and vanity,
For words lost upon the fields in period thought
Heard only by the speaker, and that sage
Speaking only profanity.
It is unto itself and for itself
That the draught of Eden is offered
Unto the better half and wiser tree,
Upon which words have grown, around which
We are allowed to simply be.

But pick the fruit and Conscience sees you;
Drums fall like fetishes into the night
Of a memory not yet won from creation,
A conscience again possessed by a power.
Drums, drums, drums, before the music starts.
The human contributes toward the evaporating bliss
To find hedgerows and porcupines in his head, in his bed.
Drums, bidden, like planets to the suns,
It is Adam and Eve,
Eve and Adam.

Ian Basson

A Tear

The silence of our land seeps into my soul.
The rage of our ravished, desecrated world hangs on,
In the stilled and silent winds.
A tear glistens, falls, and a world is dying.

The young, the old, embrace each in their grief.
Wars are fought, the Mother Earth's children
succumb to the realities of the long-fought feud.
A tear glistens, falls, and the people starve.

Souls taking to the wind, the air is hot, lands
are drying and the water that's left is rancid
and reeks of the poisons of man.
A tear glistens, falls, and our ethics disappear
with the northern winds.

The people rage, embittered, enslaved by the
venom of greed and power.
Our souls wither, hallucinations of reality fade.
Illusions walk the land.
A tear glistens and falls, Mother Earth weeps in desperation.

Lane R. Mortimer

My Love for You

As time goes by, our marriage grows stronger.
You, Tracey, are the best thing that ever happened to me.
Your love I don't have to wait any longer.
Soon we will be celebrating our second anniversary.

We have been through good times and bad,
There were times where we almost said good-bye.
This, my darling, made me so sad,
That it made me happy that we are giving it another try.

Sunsets and moonlight walks are hard to do with a child,
But in my heart these are things I would love to share.
I had to grow up and stop being wild.
I do love you, this I declare.

I hope you think of this poem when you're feeling low,
no matter what we say or do.
Cupid hit me in the heart with his arrow,
And forever I want you to know that I love you.

Gary Latendresse

Vs.

The love between you and I dying,
Like the final glimpse of the sun over the horizon.
Our time in Eden was short:
We were blind to obstacles in our path,
And now we stumble over their broken remains.
The sparkle in our eyes is fading,
Rendering us vulnerable to the prison of our broken dreams.
Our impassioned thoughts are dwindling,
Hearts no longer beating in the same rhythmic, reckless abandon.
Our hands meet in a hopeful attempt
To rescue
The love between you and I.

Nicole Pastuch

A River

Oh, little river, what is it like to always move so fast?
To forever stumble down the hills as the seasons pass?
To toss and turn and twist and wind however God may please?
To fly so swiftly over cliffs and land with such great ease?
Maybe one day I will follow you to see just where you go,
But I am young, so I'll stay right here, and for now just take it slow.

Christine Van Walraven

White Dove

The house is quiet
every letter, magazine, book
breathes, whispers, waits.

I take your latest letter to the light.
I hear your voice.
I don't understand.

I take the magazine to the table and look at the pictures.
I take the book to bed and sleep between the pages.

You are the heart of the house;
you are the memory
the house has forgotten.

The postmark on your envelopes is illegible,
the letter undated,
there's no return address.

Why do you send me books and magazines?

There is no shelf for your books,
no place for your magazines.

I toss your letter into the middle
of the mystery.
The pages flutter into silence.
    Barry Morrall

Love Calling

They say, "To love is nothing,"
But to me it is everything.
I may have a faith that moves mountains
And speak the language of angels,
But without that one priceless gift,
I am nothing, I cannot profit.
Love is not fleeting, but eternal,
Given of God.
Let it be known that as "the grass withers
and the flower fades, the Word of our God
stands forever."
So shall be love.
As the pearled gates hewn by angels
Stand tall for everyone to see,
Let me show my love.
Let not pride hide that which I have been called to show
Especially with those who mean the most.
    Holly Marlow

Won't You Please Stay

Robin, oh, robin, don't fly away.
Won't you please, won't you please stay?

I'll miss your presence upon me.
Your beautiful colors I won't see.

Robin, oh, robin, don't fly away.
Won't you please, won't you please stay?

You're welcome in my home when you're left in the rain.
I know how you feel because I too have felt pain.
To be left alone with no one in sight,
Don't leave me alone, it just isn't right.

Robin, oh, robin, don't fly away.
Won't you please, won't you please stay?

We can be friends 'til we are friends no more,
Even when each other is who we bore.

Even when death comes our way,
Friends is what you and I will always stay.

Robin, oh, robin, don't fly away,
Won't you please, won't you please stay?
    Nicole Liscombe

This Scared Little Boy

As he ran to his room, he hung his head in shame.
This scared little boy thought he was to blame.
This scared little boy hid between the bed and the floor,
Knowing he wasn't safe until his daddy slammed the door.

Now that he was gone, he wanted to go to sleep,
But all this poor boy could do was weep.
When he awoke, he clenched his pillow with fright;
Nothing could be done when they started to fight.

Then he knelt down beside his bed,
And as he prayed to God, this is what he said:

"Dear Lord Jesus, as I am on my knees,
I'm asking you to help me, please.
God, show me how to love my daddy,
And show my daddy how to love me."

Rudy Fehr

Thank You

Thank you for everything magically real—
Worlds full of wonder, life's mysterious seal.
Contentedly perfect, unfolding dream,
Enchantment lies watching your richly sewn seam.

Beckoning attention's whispering way,
Yours is the cloak of ordinary days.
Your smiling lake, so calm and serene,
Reflects the stars' shining—eyes see where you've been.

Breathing your spirit, the nectar of friends,
I hear your voice from beyond where time ends.
You lead so gently—inspiration's call—
Or with the choking of pride's desperate fall.

Please help me find that which does hide
Inside the letter, word, glance, and sign.
Attuned to creation, knowing your style,
Let me keep feeling love's warming smile.

Steven Lay

Circle of Memories

I was a seedling that was carried far away
Across unfamiliar land, here to a place
where forever I'd now stay.

I hear a creek by my side, smell wild roses below.
I feel the massage of a buck's tines, and see busy squirrels
in this peaceful meadow.

I could tell you a story, from my rings inside:
lighting storms, droughts, floods, all left the scars, but
rainbows, Chinooks, and falling stars
left my necklaces healthy and wide.

Now I've grown old, my bark is dry, my limbs are frail.
I will wait for the final wind to carry my last seedlings,
a gracious, silent fall is now what I must do to prevail.

Claudette Patry

Winter's End

Nature's permission and farewell departure of small white
crystals of frozen water,
The cold, chilly season of the year.
The strong feeling and affection for the thought of cheer.
Gone the Jack rabbit with its eye following trail.
Gone the long, dark, cold nights with their big, tall tales.
Gone burdensome weight of our hats, mitts, and shoes,
And out of hibernation comes the bear from its long winter's snooze.
Nature's so beautiful for our eyes to behold.
Thank you, God, for leaving it here, so it is not left untold.

Theresa Watters

Your Voice

It's your voice untieing the words
Without being them the transporting
But the fragile reflection of loves
And the sound clear of your soul.

It's your voice that with easy calm
Untangle the threads of my mind
And like to the sea the breeze
Passes gentle and caress me

It's your voice that one day at the wind
Emitted a sound with my name
And tell me since that time
That I'll live of your breathing

It's your voice that seduce me
And from my absent will strength
Only rest to me
For living you eternally

It's your voice conducting the soul
That sails soft to my entrails
It stay placid and invades
Fusing with me forever.

Lucia Puyou

Economic Crisis

Her life is packed in a cart,
and on her back is her child;
eyes wide open even when there is nothing to want,
legs dangling restlessly because there is
 nowhere to land.
Where are they going to?
What are they heading for?

She suffers the
un-quantifiable and indescribable pain
that accompanies the loss of an age,
when life was hard, but bearable,
when people were kind and approachable.

Dust for sandals and
a shroud of grief for clothes,
she drags her life in the scorching heat
and cries bitterly for the child
who has not yet lived,
but is forced to die.

Emilienne Motaze

My Special Rose

There's a special rose in my garden
That takes the cold out of winter
When she smiles, she melts the icebergs at sea
She takes the grace from the swans
A nightingale stops to listen to the melody of her voice
Oh! How she thrills me
Though storms, hurricanes, and earthquakes may rattle my bones,
My beautiful rose keeps me calm
The darkest of clouds may dull my mood
My rose brings back the spring into my heart
When I retire from the day, I cuddle to my rose
Which strengthens me for another day

Carl Mullings

Grandmother

Grandmother is just the right name for her, for she is truly grand
Roaming and pacing in the house on the stormy nights
wondering if we are okay
And when she gets the message that we are fine
only then will she rest
Never rude or nasty to us, she's the one we love
Deep as the seven seas with love
Mother of our mother always cares
Oh, grandma, you're the one we love
Her heart always filled warmth
Early she rises every morning
Ready to start the day with a smile

Megan Emberly

Third Deep

Behold, the world outside . . .
So full of treachery . . . I want no part of it.
Come . . . see my world!
A poet . . . content with scroll . . . and pen . . .
 A fancy jar of ink . . .
Time enough to meditate . . . to pray . . . and to think.
Third deep into this world I own
A small, possessive space.
At peace with memories of old—
And the same familiar place . . .
Sans noise and turbulent fear,
Content, I stay
with God's blessings and
His presence very near!

Norma Sherk Henderson

Repeal the Twenty-Line Law

I've talked to William Shakespeare
About this "twenty-line" law.
"Tomorrow and Tomorrow" stays,
But "All the world's a stage" must go.
"To be or not to be" was fine, in 1642;
But now it will not qualify . . . it's over thirty lines!
Unless the Law is modified,
He'll have to rewrite all those plays—
Romeo and Juliet, Macbeth, and all the rest.

He's started a petition,
And put it on the Net;
(It's "Willy S. dot com").

He's got a lot of email
From Tennyson and Keats,
And from the folks who wrote the Bible.
The list goes on and on.

So can the Law be changed?
They're lined up in the streets
And Mr. Shakespeare's at our door,
Petition in his hand.

Ted Traill

A Closer Look

I thought I saw the metallic glow of the brilliant white moon
shining through misty grey clouds upon me in my car.
But as I took a closer look,
I realized it wasn't the hypnotic scintillate of the silvery orb.
It was the reflection of my own verve,
mirrored back through pools of ocean sapphire,
pacific skies,
crashing tides of blue on blue,
echoing through a sphere of white.
My eyes, they told me a story through that window.
I saw my own self as raw and exposed as any creature.
Naked, helpless, hopeless, breathless.
No more.

Melissa Hahn

Untitled

Madness surrounds you like the dark.
There is no escape. It is everywhere.
Slowly it devours you, like a wolf savouring the bloody
pleasures of its prey.
Like a puppeteer, it pulls all the strings.
You are no longer you, you are what it what it wants you to be.
It carries you farther away from your loved ones with its
turbulent waters
and holds you captive in its dense forest of delirium.
You withdraw into your own world of fake bliss and surrender
to its promises of sweetness and security, unaware that death
himself has lured you nearer to your doom.

Antonesha M. Harris

Dead Leaves Falling

As I see a dead leaf fall to the ground,
I wonder, is that how I'm going to be as I get old,
Flying everywhere the wind me blows,
So fragile that even the gentlest touch would shatter me?
And as I get to the ground, will I just lie there, alone, separated
from the rest of the world?
Will I just lie there in silence, watching as all of my friends
fall to the ground?
Will I die and become one with the earth once again, in peace,
or will someone just trample me?

As I see the leaves falling to the ground, I wonder. . . .

Kristian Niemi

I Know This Is a Music Video

I know this is a music video.
How do I know, you may ask?
I know this is a music video because
I hear the music

I know this is an action movie.
How do I know, you may ask?
I know this is an action movie because
I just saw a man save a damsel in distress.

I know this is a heartfelt love poem.
How do I know, you may ask?
I know this is a heartfelt love poem because
I am serenading you right now.

I know this is a math exam.
How do I know, you may ask?
I know this is a math exam because
I feel stress. How do I solve quadratics?

I know this is a poem.
How do I know, you may ask?
I know this is a poem because
I wrote my words, my thoughts; a mirror of me.
Poet

Then Come with Me

Have you ever . . . run in the woods,
Feeling as fleet and free as a deer
Bursting forth, elegance exposed, for a time?
Then come with me! Hurry.

Have you ever . . . walked in the woods,
Seeing the lush, green growth of the seed
Bursting forth, at spring's first sign?
Then come with me! Explore.

Have you ever . . . stood in the woods,
Smelling the warm and pungent air
Bursting forth, full of cedar, fir, and pine?
Then come with me! Inhale.

Have you ever . . . sat in the woods,
Listening to the chatter of the birds and squirrels
Bursting forth, the air full of excited rhyme?
Then come with me! Enjoy.
Rowena J. Ramsden

Friendship

Did you ever stop to think
Before you took that sip of drink
That everything was on the line?
That someone's life was too great a fine?
I guess that your own fate is in your hands.
Do something. . . . Let's take a stand.
I was a victim of a crash.
The driver was drinking and driving too fast.
He never thought of the damage he could cause.
He got out without a scratch. . . .
I lay there injured and sober.
Next time, will you stop and think
Before you take that drink?
Emilie Browne

Faith

I sit beneath a willow tree,
and hail the pelting rain.
So sad that it is falling,
denoting of its pain.

Do the clouds feel remorse,
of the treasures they let fall?
As I'm bejeweled with wonder,
is there any need at all?

The day begins most perfectly
with the christening of the ground.
My peace of mind and fragile heart
are sheltered in the sound.

Coupled with the moonlight,
the thunder shakes my brain,
but scared am I not
of this torrential rain.

It is here that I find my solace,
in feeling so immensely small.
I need not love, nor peace, nor
praise, nor any priestly gall.
Kristy Button

Fluttering Wings

From the core, beyond,
Fluttering of wings I heard,
The soul is flying,
Flying beyond the mortals.
Beyond and above Heaven,
The soul is fluttering,
Fast to cross the boundary
Of this translucent life.
Wasted for long, long years,
The agony and the sins,
All perished in moments,
And the soul has vanished.
Like the sweet kisses,
He poured on our cheeks,
That tasted saline?
Who'll tell us: He is silent!
P. K. Mohanan

To God with Love

Dear God, my Father above,
Thank you for Your infinite love.
I surrender myself to You,
You refresh my spirit like morning dew.

Dear God, my Father above,
You live in me with the peace of a dove.
To you, my Lord, I give my heart,
And pledge from You I never will part.

From this day forward I belong to you,
Help me always to be true.
Dear God, my Father above,
This to You is my song of love.
Lea Mendes

My Heart Will Say Good Bye

The song, will come to an end.
The letter, will sign sincerely.
The wine, will be all gone,
But my love for you
Will always live on.

The music, will fade away.
The night, will only come closer.
My heart, will say good bye
But my soul, wants to die.

I dream of you.
Memories of what could be, us.
I need to touch you.
To kiss you, but dreaming is not enough.

I will live on,
And watch you from the sky,
And when I see you,
My heart will say, Good bye.
Ari R. Kolman

Appeal to Thee—Eternal

O, wretched thief! O, silent sinner!
Bequeath to me the tranquil night
in all its splendour
that I may transcend my mortal bonds.
Apprentice me, thy willing pupil,
in trav'ling this penumbral road.
Two stray lambs, allied in purgatory,
forsaken by life,
forgotten by time.
For thy blood-drenched kisses
I renounce Apollo's golden rays,
and for thy life-giving death,
thy death-giving life,
I renounce hope and redemption at once.
Give unto me thy aconite blood
that my soul may too be tainted with
the poison of a millennium.
And bear unto me thy immortality
that I may love in death
what life would ne'er permit.
Shannon Simson

Storm on the Mountain

I don't want to climb that mountain;
I don't want to cross o'er that sea.
I just want to go on the pathways I know
Where my soul lives peacefully.
I don't want to soar like an eagle
While storm clouds challenge the sky;
I just want to be where a heart can feel free
To watch every storm cloud roll by.

Don't put that mountain before me
Where I can't see the other side;
Don't wash me away in my ocean of tears
I can neither share nor hide.
I don't want this storm cast upon me;
It shatters the love I knew.
I wish I could hide 'til my heart can abide
By the storm as it passes through.
Velma Crabs

Earthdance

And say to death
you shall not have me;
life is my right and
this Earth, my home—
I am part of all things:
You cannot sever the bonds
which link me to this place and time.

You cannot divide my soul from this body:
it is not your hour—
the song is mine:

A laugh in the face of the fear you bring,
a sword in the morning, sun on the hill,
the celebration of blood and bone,
moonrise over an ancient stone.

Love is the reason,
life is the season,
love is the union of heart and will.
Morgan Searle

Fresh Water Poem

Fresh water poem
laced with ivory, curtained by the glass
shielding the morning dew.
Walking in the downpour of the autumn afternoon,
clouds loom overhead as I walk
between the soil and the heavens.
Trees are vibrant,
shaded in orange, yellow, auburn.
Majestically, leaves fall
and are covered by my footsteps.
The rain pours down harder,
trickling off my face, landing in my mouth and eyes:
A blurred vision of paradise.
I can see the city from the mountaintop.
The cold air rushes through my veins,
it's time to leave.
I take one look and I am fulfilled by the
distilled, passionate glance
from nature and tread gently home.
Shoshana Dayan

Untitled

She's light on her feet
Like birds of a feather
As he steps keep in time with the beat.
In the breeze she sways like a flower.

There on the dim-lit stage
Her body sways to the music.
Here is where she earns her wages.
She is gifted with a special magic.

She's a beautiful sight to see
As she stands lightly on her toes.
Then she begins to dance like the breeze,
While her body flows with emotion.

It claims her soul and all her will.
Her every movement keeps in time.
She's like a dove on wings,
The ballerina dancing girl.

Ballerina dancing girl.
Janet A. M. Corriveau

Net Angels

A breathtaking angel I have seen this night,
I must truly be blessed to have witnessed this sight.
A sweet faced doll winking down at me,
her beauty seducing and trapping me.
With fiery hair of hand-spun gold,
and a green velvet dress of old,
smiling to me, she offers her hand.
I wonder what it is she has planned.
As my lil' net angel sings her lilting song,
I know she could do me no wrong.
Chasing away the Moat Monsters that forever plague me,
forgiving public posts meant only for she.
Giving freely her tender, sweet love,
standing in the forest, a fragile lil' dove.
Her eyes shining bright in the night,
her kisses from Gaia, a wondrous delight.
So as I lie at her side and Stormy comes up
as Luna plays with the ocean tide,
I thank thee, Lady Life, for the gift you have sent,
for my net angel and the night she has spent.
Liza Magill

of the death of love

in the deathly stillness of a lonely night
  i heard a heart cry out.
a desperate plea of mercy
  from a long and weary bout.

as the cruel stab of merciless love
  plunged deeper into the soul,
it fell twisting downward deeper
  into life's most dreaded hole.

fate played its most devilish die
  a misfortune being told.
leaving it to wither and weaken
  in the early morning cold.

as the night grew on more wearily
  it gave its most desperate shout.
in the deathly stillness of a lonely night
  i heard a heart cry out.
S. Elizabeth Rousseau

Crossing Lines

How to decide
what's black and white
is not as easy
as it seems.

It seems distinct.
When lines are drawn
in Indian ink,
there is no gray.

However, where the lines
are crossing, black grows deep,
and white looks whiter too.
A space is shown.

It's artificial, though,
it's an abstraction
like experience in one's life:
you only think you know.
Fini Lokke

Sunrise, Sunset

At first sight, such beauty, a vision,
Time passes, interest fades,
Then as in the beginning, aware,
Something of such splendid wonder
Now, slipping away.
T. K. Cooke

The Reverend

In the reverend's heart
Angels live
In caverns warm and dark,
Where no light
Reaches
To show
They are less than dust.
Erin R. Hillyer

Untitled

Shadows creep
As darkness seeps
And all the world lies quiet.

Flowers flow
From valleys low,
While stars drift silently by.

Dewdrops glisten.
Flowers listen.
The night reaches out its hand.

A silent shiver,
The merest quiver.
Night steals o'er across the land.

Forlorn on its own,
Stopped o'er a headstone,
His hope now fading fast.

The child weeps
And slowly creeps
From present into the past.
Kenna Wilkie

Dice

When the loaded dice thrown unchecked
By some queer circumstance,
Fall to disrupt my life,
A jagged tear appears.
Then, each night is agony,
As my mind seethes
In unchartered seas.
Each day dawns
With a promise of new hope,
But the hours pass by
In mock sympathy.
I sit like a beggar
And wait for them
To take pity
And drop a wish fulfilled,
Into my empty bowl.
But then, fate does not discriminate
Nor judge the good or bad
Accordingly; it simply loads the dice
To throw where it will.

S. Nandini Shinde

To Live a Dream

I walked across the dunes of time,
Heard silver notes of chimes sublime,
Saw wings of angles, tones of cream,
I closed my eyes and lived a dream.

In Harmony's house I sang the hymns
Of sweetly melded seraphim.
This sight of sound cannot be seen,
Except when living in a dream.

Through the window crept a chill,
An evil spirit's treacherous will,
From cauldrons deep
flowed martyr's screams,
They sought to scare me in my dreams.

In other dreams of time and space,
I met a stranger, colder race.
Their complex minds could not perceive,
The rich rewards of living dreams.

Their wisest scholars wondered why,
And yet would not even try.
They lived in cities emerald green,
And never knew the hope of dreams.

I've ridden winds of ecstasy,
Through countless, nameless galaxies,
I've seen stars born and planets die,
I've dreamed of life beyond the sky.

Amanda E.G. Gilmore

The Gates

I knocked twice, then tried again, but no one to those
gates came. So loudly I call out my name, this too was
also in vain. Patiently I sit and wonder why, today is
the day they said to drop by. At last I hear the rattle
of a key, then those gates swing open for me. State your
name slowly and clear, tell me what business you have in
here. Well, I replied to this man in white, a cigar in his
mouth that was not alight. My business is with someone
higher, he said it was time for me to retire. That stogey
hung from lips so grim, it was then that I offered to
smoke it for him. His eyes gleamed in evil delight as he
passed me a cigar that burned bright.
"Are you a magician?"
in surprise I ask, as I puff at that stogey and flick off
the ash. The aroma is heavenly, the best I have known,
better than all the heroin I've grown. Inhaling deeply
I enjoy my smoke, before I know it my body is afloat.
That man in white leads me through the gates, I feel I'm
in heaven, but what a mistake. Then grim reality stares
me in the face. I see for myself I am in the wrong place!

Maurice Graves

Forgotten Child

Why am I here? This child. Does anyone care out there?
My body is already tired of living,
chained to this desk, doing something that is unforgiving.
My soul is crying, how do I stop it from dying in this factory?

Chorus, Oh! Stop the madness.
My heart longs for some gladness in all this misery.
Can you help me, my friends? I need to be free.

My hands are small,
but the promise of heaven on earth was made to us all.
I cannot change the system from within
as I am only a child who doesn't know where to begin.
Oh! Let the nations hold hands.
Together, my friends, I know we can take a stand.

I hear the song of the river calling me.
A message of hope, cry not, little one,
your time to dance in freedom is soon to come.
A quiet prayer is heard by the wings of a dove
who will carry to the heavens above.

Kelly McGuigan

The Ballad

The first pitch of the game was a beauty to see,
It was right down the pipe, clocked at ninety-three.

The umpire yelled "Strike!" and the crowd went insane.
The batter stepped back in. Two strikes remain.

The second pitch of the game was thrown with a curve.
The batter just stood there, 'cause he lost all his nerve.

The third pitch was a ball, it was way, way inside.
The batter dropped back to save his own hide.

The fourth pitch of the game was a real hard throw.
"Strike three!" yelled the ump, and the batter cried, "No!"

Ole Anderson

Oh, Lord, We Need Love, Love, Sweet Love

All we hear people talk about this day is birth control and population,
Demonstration and rioting in some institution,
Hijacking and kidnapping, and things we never heard about before,
But we never hear people talking about loving one another any more.

We hear a radio talk show host talking about a murder case,
And a woman running down the street with teardrops streaming down her face,
And some shocking news report every time we turn on the TV.
Oh, Lord, is that what the nineties will be?

We must take better care of this planet Earth.
If we would just look around, we would see for all it is worth.
As we have searched the depths of the oceans and the skies up above,
We have just ignored the clean up of pollution and the meaning of love.

Oh, Lord, we need love, love, sweet love, like we did never before.
We must help each other and care for one another much, much more.
As we have strived for riches and pleasures, diamonds and gold,
We just took things for granted, including this beautiful world.
    Anton Mirc

A Reconvergence of the Twain

Kobe's little fissures grew, flocks of pterodactyls flew.
Eons passed, dactyls died. The little fissures multiplied.
Over the archipelago, things go to and things go fro.
Land forms, volcanoes burst: little faults at their worst.
Men upon the island chain, manlike marched a fissure vein.
Christ and Confucius great, oh, that fault could hardly wait.
Wait it did, it waited more. Signs were simple to ignore.
Gods guide our affairs, down below they stifle their airs.
Level lay Lisbon and Lima. We down sake at baths in Arima.
Pope saw the hero fall, but Voltaire saw the most of all.
Kobe grew by leaps and bounds, and faults bereft of sounds.
Smiles play round faces of boys. Faults make a little noise.
We're safe, up north they're rife, not us, we bet our life.
Faults for ages ignored; it's while we slept they soared.
Ignored for eons and years, it comes jolting the spheres.
Seismic demons out of bed. The quick left, ponder the dead.
Tricked, betrayed, undressed, all is really for the best.
Heirs come into coins. Beasts get fat on corpses' loins.
Climb from rubble, find a niche. For the best, we get rich.
Voltaire's council's sound: Faults still lurk underground.
    Bruce Wiggins

Who Knows?

Who knows . . . as your heart beats faster.
The whisper of a soft breeze in your ear.
Who knows . . . as a simple touch can send a simple rush.
The softest caress means so much.
Who knows . . . how a fleeting glance can make you shiver.
The mysterious forces which bind us together.
Who knows . . . how there is more truth in a kiss than the sweetest words.
The flower can only bloom if the soil has been seeded
with truth and a tender hand.
Who knows . . . the spirit that makes you soar above all oppression.
The wings start their journey in a single moment forever perfect in flight.
Who knows . . . as a tender smile melts the hardest heart.
A connection is made that stands as two souls united as one forever,
joined together, separate, but never apart.
Who knows . . . the warmth of firelight on your skin.
That warmth flows in all that beautiful and serene.
Who knows . . . how to calm the roaring tempest with a kind word.
The roughest storm must weather the rock before they can allow the water to the sea.
Who knows where love whispers your name.
I only know that when it's real, it sends the soul to the purest elation possible.
Who knows if two people can fly in the undercurrent of a colossal storm.
If that tempest has an eye of the hurricane, there is always hope.
    Amanda Wilson

Heaven Cannot Wait

Life on Earth is but a fleeting moment in eternity;
We are born to the world to know and serve God with charity.

The true meaning of our existence is the quest for the truth;
Purpose of life is often forgotten in our prime and youth.

In our teenage years, we attempt to conquer love and glory;
Our youthful pride renders us never to say we are sorry.

In our adult years, we're busy striving for fame and fortune;
In our golden years, we face many of life's misfortunes.

With the passing of friends and loved ones, and our own waning health;
We soon realize that the most important is not our wealth.

All that glitters is not gold, happiness is yet to be found;
No material things can satisfy our souls that are God-bound.

Deep in our hearts, we each have our own problems and afflictions;
It is in God that we find solace, comfort, and solution;

Take stock of life now, wherever you are in the stage of life;
Let Jesus Christ be your anchor in the stormy sea of life.

Heaven cannot wait for us, our eternity is at stake;
"Follow me," says the Lord, He'll lead us on the path we must take.

Ted Ong

Our Love

Oh, how I do love you?
There are so many reasons.
It would take from now to eternity to tell you.
There aren't enough words to describe how much.

I will love you till the end of time.
Being special is what attracts me to you.
Being you is what caught my eye.
Being you is why I fell in love.

There just doesn't seem to be enough time for you.
Each passing day I fall more in love.
The moments we spend together are beautiful and rewarding.
My life is yours and yours is mine.
Fate brought us together, only fate should take us apart.

Love is very special,
And being with you makes it even more special.
Special is what you're all about, babe,
And I want it to last forever.

Ken Chevalier

Protect My Cabin's Home

Known by the local North American Kootanai Indian Band as the
coiled serpent, lies a vast turquoise body of water, named, "Kootaney Lake."
As dawn's first rays break the mist over the lake, the rays of the sun
form a sapphire blue, red, and purple mirror on her surface . . .
Towering above the lake, the mighty sentinel stands like a fist,
high above the town of Kaslo, B.C. . . .
Her profound shadows, from a height of approximately 2,710 meters
above sea level, shining distant peers; Kookanee Glacier;
Woodberry Glacier and New Denver's distant, ice-covered walls . . .
Framed to an artisan's picture, for a mountaineer's dream,
Mt. La Blanc's Glacier, her jagged, snow-crested peaks apocalypse the artist's canvas . . .
Below the frosted fields of ice, giant enigmatic waterfalls dance and roar.
The mountain's basins contrast a sea of colour. For, in the month of
July, blue-berried queen cups, radiant purple flea planes with bright
yellow arnica, hold fields of windswept crimson-red Indian paint brush,
while fragrant-filled wild roses doze lazily along glacier-filled streams.
Only to be surrounded by fragments of sun-enhanced soapstone and
jade-coloured serpentine everywhere.
Contrast the mountain together with
large, gnarled, mystical larches hugging her tree line.

Carl James Golling

Women: Leaders in Our Own Rights

In today's world, more and more women are getting involved in politics.
We believe that the time has come for us to take over leaderships.
Some of us aspire to become presidents and prime-ministers,
Or hold other prominent positions, ministers of governments.
But the greatest challenges facing us, as modern women,
Are the forces of many conflicting and competing problems,
Such as being professional wives and mothers, or single parents.
These situations make it difficult for us to control our commitments
In our endeavour to take on leadership roles.
However, we should continue to pursue our goals.
Becoming great leaders means conforming ourselves to ethical standards
And being courageous against evil inclinations, to compromise those principles.
Most of all, we must be steadfast in our decision making.
Our desires must be to build a stronger nation, and not for personal gain.
Then and only then we will become not only "leaders in our own rights,"
But the kind of women who will dispel darkness, like radiant lights.
Solomon prayed for wisdom and got riches untold.
Some ask for riches and power, which are seldom used for good.

Vivien C. Patrick

Fading Memories

Love is like the foamy ocean waves, rushing to meet the shore
leaving temporary marks, never striking twice in time,
constant in stride and continuous in pace.

Contrary to love that waits to take hold of its believers,
who never know the power of its consequences,
or the force that dwells inside its embrace.

For, love can be swifter than a leaping gazelle—
or slower than the melting ice in glacier form,
heavier than the arduous burdens of life
or lighter than the warmth of free spirits,
bittersweet as the patterned frost—
or soft and caring as a fingertip's touch.

Taken by the greedy, who seek to posses it—
or given by the contented with grace,
ugly to those who sever hearts with lust and wanting eyes
or beautiful as a spider's web that tempts to capture us
with its fragile beauty and fierce lightning strikes
or tranquil as sun rays peeking through clouds after a storm.

Elegant is love to all who dare to embrace it, yet those
who fear its warmth and tenderness, fear life itself!

Monika F. Kruschwitz

Falling

Wildflowers falling from the sky,
  as I slumber into your embrace with kisses.

I imagined you were plucking wildflowers and giving
them to me, placing them tenderly into my arms 'midst
sun drenched fields of tall, straw grass. Something quite
gentle and unhurried, yet you were running, running with
armfuls of love, I imagined, as the tall grass bowed to
your bounding feet, and the petals fell to my face as I
lay waiting. You entwined the petals into my curls and
watched, smiling, as they danced with the sky upon my
cheek . . . and as the sun lit my hair with gold, your
eyes held our glow. I simply rested, silently, smiling,
staring . . . feeling the love . . . and as we sipped the
juice of mangos from thetree, with their pulp you wrote,
"*The nectar of the gods*," upon my flesh.

Wildflowers falling from the sky,
  as I slumber into your embrace with giggles and kisses . . .
wildflowers falling from the sky.

Jill Campbell

Komi

Stunted fir-trees and birches are trembling with fright of the fury of engine,
one kilometer of the well bore skips the vertical line pre-drawn,
at the depth two thousand hundred geophysicists lost their instrument,
the headquarter's command is to plug up: we've tilted and missed the bed.
Tired crew in soiled, wadded jackets are running the bit in hole,
a Mi-eight hovers over the camp, throwing out oils from the puddle;
logging people from Bangladesh, shaken with cold of the Urals,
parry by working-clothes armor the terror of frosts to come.
O, the poetry of strings and crown blocks! O, timely and false spontaneity
of the speech pouring out for free when struck by a well-aimed tool!
Muscles and rotors and pumping lines—all the petroleum industry—
by whom are they always loaded, who does excite them all?
Tell, for whose sake we go, eyes down, getting employed as laborers?
Whose avidity's driving us, cap in hand, to bow to stingy monopolies,
just to the people whose speech is full of ****s and okay's in English,
to work as interpreters or advisors for Shell and the Occidental?
On the top of the derrick they stand as one, mastering tundra like prairies,
Russian tool-pusher from Ukhta and a thorough-fed Texan boss.
The insanity that has become a life is leading due North—directly,
allowing no deviations, like the compass in Gatteras' brain.
   Alexander Gurevich

Untitled

Nestled in the Owings Mills of Maryland,
Amid the wonders of a literary State,
The National Library of Poetry sits, majestic in suite fifteen thirty-nine,
Inspiring young writers to explore their somnolent thoughts,
Ordering poetic verses to come to the fore, from topics of
Nature to romance, even futuristic, any style or subject will do.
Anthologies are born from this cultural mix,
Largest poetry organization in the world, we laud you!

Libraries everywhere should overflow with your works.
Immense knowledge in them is found, from poems written in iambic
pentameter, to those with
Blank verses, penned with brilliance of the writers,
Rhythms and
Rhymes,
Yuletide themes and

Off-rhymes clothe in
Figurative language, personified like actors on a stage!

Priceless organization, the persona of an
Optimistic man emanates everywhere, and
Affects us into poetic gear, enthusiastic Howard Ely, excellent Try!
   Norma Williams Seymour

The Sense of Life

This world is filled with many wonderful things:

The beauty of a sunrise,
when the world begins to wake;

The smell of a summer rain,
that reminds us of a world just found;

The sound of silence,
that lets us hear the little things the world has to say;

The light touch of a flower's petal,
to offset the harsh pain of life's thorns;

And the taste of life itself,
that makes you yearn to experience these things all over again.
   Gordon Courtney

Biographies of Poets

ABE, TERUO
[b.] March 7, 1972; Tokyo, Japan; [p.] Yukie Abe, Sadao Abe; [ed.] Camosun College; [occ.] Student; [pers.] I strive to reflect the goodness of mankind in my writing. I have been influenced by the romantic poets—Shelley and Keats.; [a.] Victoria, BC

ADAMS, KAMERINE
[b.] January 24, 1981; Ottawa, ON; [p.] Keith Adams, Yolande Adams; [ed.] Bell High School, Nepean, ON; [occ.] Student; [memb.] Competitive fastball, competitive hockey, varsity rugby, sr. band; [a.] Kanata, ON

AGUIRREZABAL, PABLO
[p.] Mosen Bernat; [b.] November 24, 1981; Bilbao, Bizkaia; [p.] Julian Aguirrezabal; Raquel Jauregui; [ed.] American School of Bilbao; International Baccalaureate at Gaztelueta School; student; [oth. writ.] Several articles and poems published in the American School of Bilbao Literary Magazine, articles in the Gaztelueta Newspaper, a letter published in Time Magazine; [pers.] I am inspired by current events around the world, and I try to denounce injustice. I owe much of my roots to my English teacher, Mrs. Dyer. My motto is "Lepoan Hartu Tasegi Aurrera" —Put it behind and push on.; [a.] Getxo, Spain

AHEARN, BONNIE
[b.] March 1, 1952; Saint John, NB; [m.] Peter Ahearn; May 20, 1972; [ch.] Jason, Patrick; [ed.] B.A. English; [occ.] Tutor— English and Math; [memb.] "Beta Sigma Phi Sorority," New Brunswick Consortium of Professional Writers; [hon.] Volunteer award from NB Branch United nations Association of Canada, 1997, English and Humanities Award in English, 1992; [oth. writ.] Currently working on a novel as well as a writing course from The Writing School, Ottawa, ON; [pers.] I have great admiration for such writers as Jane Austen and Margaret Lawrence, and I strive to write with the same honesty they did.; [a.] Saint John, NB

AHLUWALIA, CHATAR
[pen.] Chatar; [b.] June 10, 1916; Rajasthan, India; [p.] Ramchundar Kalawati; [m.] Raj Ahluwalia; November 19, 1945; [ch.] Rasuhim Ahluwalia; [ed.] B.A. (Honours) Diploma in Journalism; [occ.] Retired from diplomatic service with the government of India; [memb.] Ontario Real Estate Board; [hon.] President Gold Award; [oth. writ.] The World at Crossroads. Scattered Pearls (poems); [pers.] Service to humanity, modesty, and love for children. A devoted worshipper of my mother.; [a.] Rajasthan, IN

ALBRECHT, CHRISTENA
[b.] December 22, 1983; Mornington Twsp; [p.] Reuben, Ruth K. Albrecht; [ed.] Grade eight; [pers.] First poem that I have entered to be published. Hope to write more in the future.; [a.] Millbank, ON

ALDAIM, DIRAR A.
[pen.] Milad Ghalib; [b.] February 8, 1941, Assab, Eritrea; [p.] Abdul Daium, Nima Issa; [m.] Fatima Baroudia, September 10, 1986; [ch.] Alexander Aldaim; [ed.] MSc Technology in Building, Moscow Engineering Military Academy, 1972. Several courses in Bio-Gas, Alternative Energy Different Inst. USA, Egypt, China, India.; [occ.] Director and Founder of Nowares Al Mocha for Technol-Advisory and Marketing.; [memb.] Unions of Yemeni Writers and Journalists; [hon.] Social Activity Award, 1982.; [oth. writ.] History (Agha Khan publication), many poems, short stories, and political articles were published in local magazines and newspapers. Translation of Scientific articles (Scientific American Arabic Edition). Political and Geographical Articles (Moscow News-Arabic Edition, Asia, Africa today—Russia version).; [pers.] Do the best for anyone, don't look back to what you have done.; [a.] Mocha (Red Sea), Yemen

ALIERMO, PACITA LABAYEN
[b.] January 25, 1942; Philippines; [p.] Sebastian Diaz Labayen and Angela Cazcarro (deceased); [m.] Eduardo A. Aliermo (deceased); June 20, 1948; [ch.] Rodolfo, Reynaldo, Ma. Cecilia, Rolando, Ramiro (deceased), Rogelio; [ed.] Courses in Secretarial Arts and Sciences, weavers, course in Real Estate Development, Management, Brokerage; [occ.] Visual Artist; [memb.] International Society of Poets, International Poetry Hall of Fame, past member Quezon City Board of Realtors, Philippines, past member—Legion of Mary Auxiliary, Philippines; [hon.] Editor's Choice Awards 1995, 1996 (twice), 1997 (thrice); elected to International Poetry Hall of Fame 1996; [oth. writ.] Inspirational poems for hospitals, senior's homes, veterans' association, poetry exhibit in World Wide Web; poems in anthologies; [pers.] Humility will lead a person to humanitarian endeavors and to capture spiritual happiness.; [a.] Vaugh, ON

ALIGAEN, GIOVANNI T.
[b.] January 3, 1960, Manila; [p.] Mr. Pedro L. Aligaen & Mrs. Veneranda Aligaen; [ed.] Nine (elem.), 1964-1968 Sta. Catalina College, 1969-70 Arellano University (HS), 1971-1974 Far Eastern University, (Drafting Tech), 1979-1980 Technological Institute of the Phils.; [occ.] Draftsman; [a.] Quezon Citym Ilocos Sur, Philippines

AMIN, MORNIE D.
[pen.] Emerald Rose; [b.] May 21, 1975; Jeddah, KSA; [p.] Dr. Abdurahman U. Amin and Dr. Indah Kumalah D. Amin; [ed.] Dental Medicine, University of the East; [occ.] Dentistry Student; [memb.] Societes Dentinum Clinican's Club, Leo Club; [hon.] High school Honor Student, high school poetry contest winner, High School Singer of the Year '90; [oth. writ.] Several poems published in local newspapers and school magazines; [pers.] Life entails an abundance of things: love, happiness, respect, rejection, fear, anxiety, and many more. We, as God's creations, should recognize the value of life. Poetry is a way of revealing life's beauteous little secrets, and so, do your share of giving significance in God's gifts through different ways.; [a.] Taguig, M. Manila, Philippines

ANDERSON, MARY LOUISE
[pen.] Mary Lou; [b.] August 2, 1969; New Glasgow, NS; [p.] Colleen O'Brien and Keith Anderson; [ch.] Aaron James Fraser; [ed.] East Pictou Rural High School 1987, Miss Murphy's Business College 1988 (Secretarial), currently enrolled with The Institute of Children's Literature; [oth. writ.] I write a lot of short stories, for young and old. I hope to someday have some published. I'll continue with poerty too.; [pers.] I strive to do my very best at everything in life and go the extra mile. "Hold onto your dreams" is my motto.; [a.] Trenton, NS

ANDRADA, LOUELLA MARIE E.
[b.] May 9, 1952; Baguio, Philippines; [m.] Teddy Andrada; October 21, 1976; [ch.] One daughter; [ed.] Bachelor of Arts in Communications, Masters in Teaching; Guidance Counsellor, Radio Broadcaster, Teacher, Motivational Public Speaker, Drama Direc-

tor; [occ.] Day Care Worker [memb.] Broadcasters' Club, Public Speakers' Club, Teachers' Association, Filipino-Canadian Saranay; [hon.] Best Counsellor of the Month, Best Pronounced Judge during university debate competitions, Top Are Manager—life insurance; [oth. writ] College publications "Myself, as a Student"; [pers.] Don't let fear steal your dreams.; [a.] Edmonton, AB

ANDRES, GLENDA
[pen.] Glenda Andres; [b.] August 23, 1975; Burns Lake, BC; [p.] Reg and Eva Andres; [ed.] Grade 12; [occ.] Food service industry; [oth. writ.] Lots of untitled poems; [pers.] All of the poems that I write directly reflect what I am feeling in my heart. I only hope that the people who read them appreciate them as I do.; [a.] Houston, BC

ARGIER, MICHELLE
[pen.] Michelle Argier; [b.] October 19, 1968; Toronto, ON; [ed.] Bachelor of Arts, English—The University of Western Ontario; [occ.] Product Support Specialist, Sharp Electronics; [pers.] I believe my writing reflects what I feel within, and what can also be felt by others.; [a.] Mississauga, ON

BABCOCK, DIANE ELAINE
[pen.] Dedan; [b.] September 14, 1955; Comox, BC; [p.] Ken Babcock/Bev Urquhart; [ch.] Tyler Austin Babcock; [ed.] Grade eleven, additional: variety of training; [occ.] Bookkeeper; [memb.] International Society of Poets (Distinguished Member); [hon.] Many Editor's Choice Awards (NLP), Best Waitress Award, nominations for "Best International Poet" (ISP), nominations for Best Lyricist/Poet (EN); [oth. writ.] Published book: "Charges" 1994 (Carlton Press), published on WWW: (personal page— "Overdraft" and "Charges 2"); [pers.] Writing for others to relay their intimate feelings toward another allows them, and myself, to experience the extremes of emotional levels. Writing for myself is from a heightened awareness of my surroundings.; [a.] Nanaimo, BC

BARKHOUSE, ANGELA
[b.] March 19, 1974; Lunenburg, NS; [p.] Linda Barkhouse and James Frotten; [ed.] Secondary education at Park View Education Centre, Bridgewater; [occ.] Clerk; [oth. writ.] I have a collection of poems that I have written throughout the years, but I have yet to have any published.; [pers.] I like to write poems to express my feelings. When I look back and read them, I remember how I coped with those feelings and how writing them really helped. I like things that have a lot of meaning.; [a.] Lunenburg, NS

BASRA, SANDDIP
[b.] July 28, 1966; Coventry, UK; [p.] Surjit and Balbir Basra; [m.] Sarbjit Basra; 1996; [pers.] Always strive to better yourself, never give up on your dreams, they are what keep you alive, and honour thy family.; [a.] Surrey, BC

BASTAROCHE, SOPHIE
[b.] February 3, 1985, Ottawa, ON; [p.] Tammy and Jean; [ed.] Grade seven; [occ.] Student; [memb.] Elaine Hunter Dance School; [pers.] The world never ends, it just goes on.

BAYAN, ROSALIA A.
[b.] October 24, 1948; Sta. Cruz, Manila; [p.] Francisco and Elizabeth Angeles; [m.] Cesar E. Bayan; August 16, 1966; [ch.] Leah, Norman and Piah; [ed.] Teodora Alonzo High School, International Correspondence Schools, The Writing School; [occ.] Housewife; [oth. writ.] Several poems and articles published in local weekly magazine; [pers.] I write to celebrate family values and to scrutinize the differing tempers of human adversity. Experience has been my mentor on the why's and wherefore's of authorship.; [a.] Manila, Philippines

BEARNS, JUDY
[pen.] Judy Bearns; [b.] 22 February 1948; St. John's, NF; [p.] Ruth and William Hillier; [m.] Frank Bearns; 9 September 1968; [ch.] Sherry, Karen, Jamie; [ed.] St. George's School, Bishop Abraham High School; [memb.] Pastoral Care Volunteer Health Science Hospital, St. John's, NF; [hon.] Was director with Mary Kay Cosmetics, won Grand Am '94 diamond rings for court of sales two years in a row, Top in Sales in my own unit in NF, many plaques and banners for sales in Canada; [pers.] I have been greatly influenced by my mom who was a wonderful poet, and by Christ, my inspiration and friend, and pray others see his hand in my writings.; [a.] St. John's, NF

BEATON, RYAN
[b.] October 12, 1978; Montreal, QC; [p.] Douglas Beaton, Patricia Beaton; [ed.] Currently finishing CEGEP in Montreal. Going on to university next fall; [memb.] McGill Olympic Running Club; [hon.] High school awards; Governor General's Medal, Class Valedictorian, Athlete of the Year, public speaking; [oth. writ.] Poems and philosophical writings published in regional school anthology; [pers.] We should instill in one another the confidence for each to find his own meaning in life rather than imposing and drilling rigid beliefs into others. This poem written for Allison.; [a.] Montreal, QC

BEILHARZ, JOHANNES
[b.] January 15, 1956; Oberndorf/FRG; [m.] Susan Chelf Beilharz; June 5, 1982; [ch.] Two; [ed.] MA in English Lit/ Creative Writing, U. of Colorado, Boulder, 1981; [occ.] Translator, Voehringen, Germany; [oth. writ.] Various publications in US and German magazines (poetry and translations of poetry); [pers.] Poetry should be a meaningful, concise rendering of human experience. I am indebted to a great variety of poets—mostly modern: John Ashbery, Frank O'Hara, Federico Garcia Lorca, Gabriel Ferrater, Sylvia Plath, and Alexander Lernet-Holenia.; [a.] Voehringer, Germany

BELAND, BERNARD
[pen.] Petrus Romanus; [b.] April 6, 1948; St. John, QC; [p.] Liliane Beland and John M. Beland; [ed.] B.A. ES—Ottawa University, Chambly Seminary—Philosophy—St. Laurent College—Latin/Greek; [occ.] Economist, Humanitarian; [memb.] Knights of Columbus, 3 Degree Vision Montreal Political Party, Maison Grands Parents, Patro Le Prevost, Order of the Holy Fathers of Nostradamus; [hon.] Commissioneer Census Canada, Porte-Drapeau, Knights of Columbus, Poorest among the Poor in Canada, Apostle of Jesus, First Camper at the Adirondak USA 1980-81, Vacation at Cape Cod 1982 USA; [oth. writ.] "How to Survive with The Bible," "Trust and Obey," "Miracles in Jesus," "No Shame in the Cross of Jesus," "All You Need Is Love." [pers.] Once you're born again Christian, you don't belong to yourself anymore. Life has no time. Money is a waster of energy. Poetry has a meaning.; [a.] Montreal, QC

BERNABE, RAISSA
[b.] December 3, 1981; Toronto, ON; [p.] Leodegario and Jane Bernabe; [occ.] Cashier; [hon.] Environmental Studies Award; [pers.] To truly understand human nature, you first must understand yourself.; [a.] Scarborough, ON

BOURAS, KONSTANTINOS
[b.] March 20, 1962; Kalamata; [p.] Nikoletta Bouras/Vassilios Bouras; [m.] Eleni Maniadaki-Mania; [ed.] Mechanical Engineer/The National Metsouio Institute of Technology of Athens, Theatrical Studies/University of Athens, D.E.A. in Theatre/Paris III (Clanouvelle, Sorbonne); [occ.] Mechanical Engineer, The Atrologue/National Tourism Organization of Greece; [oth. writ.] O porfiros Ilios tou Erotake tou Thanatou, 1987; Agouroe Eros, 1988; I Kiladaton Nekron Eroton, 1990; Eros Iliotrofos, 1993; Agabes Eros 1995, Eros Trimargikos, 1997; Stonasterismo tis Hecatis, 1997; [memb.] International Society of Poets, International Writers and Artists Association, International Theatrical Institute, European Institute of Theatrical Research, Centre of Research and Studies in Modern Greek Theater, Greek Writers Association; [hon.] Award of the University of Athens; [pers.] His poetry is marked by the search of the sublime, by lyricism, and by a sensuality in the Kavafian genre, and true to the classical Greek ideal of beauty.; [a.] Athens, Greece

BOWE, JUNE L.
[b.] June 18, 1952; Liverpool, England; [p.] John Joseph Gleeson (deceased) and Florence Gleeson; [m.] Peter James Bowe; October 14, 1977; [ch.] Devon Lynne Bowe and Michael James Bowe; [ed.] Central Collegiate, Durham College; [occ.] Home support worker part-time; [memb.] Distinguished Member of The International Society of Poets; [oth. writ.] Other poems published in anthologies, Shadows and Night, A Treasured Token and Best Poems of 1997, also a poem published in "The Poet's Corner" Haiku section; [a.] Oshawa, ON

BOYES, PENNY
[b.] May 5, 1949; Katrine; [p.] Albert and Allie Northcote; [m.] Doug Boyes; [ch.] Andrea, Greg, Dallas, Brandon; [ed.] High school graduate; [occ.] Homemaker; [memb.] Church Secretary and Librarian; [oth. writ.] "An Evening Stroll along the Beach," "The Swan," "Yesterday's Sorrow"; [pers.] Poetry is a wonderful avenue of sharing the true self. Poets I admire are Henry Vaughn, Wilfred Owen, and John Milton.; [a.] Burk's Falls, ON

BREEN, SHELLY A.
[b.] November 8, 1983, Antigonish, NS; [p.] Mary and Laurie Breen; [ed.] Grade eight—St. Andrew Junior High School, Ant.; [occ.] Student; [hon.] At the age of 11 and 12, I recited two poems for a contest that I represented for my school and received a certificate for each.; [oth. writ.] Entered for a poem contest for Remembrance Day.; [pers.] I enjoy reading and writing poetry very much.; [a.] St. Joseph's, Antigonish Co., NS

BREWSTER, EVA E.
[pen.] Elaine Burtch; [b.] January 29, 1945; Seeley's, ON; [p.] James and Lois Burtch; [m.] Gerald E. Brewster; June 22, 1963; [ch.] Stuart, Kevin, Eva Joyce, Lee; [ed.] Grade nine and business school; [occ.] Housewife. I travel with my trucker husband.; [memb.] WYCLIFFE Associates of Canada; [hon.] Metzler Business College, computer course; [oth. writ.] Memorial Poems 1969; and 1997 in Christian Standard Magazine; [pers.] I write from my experiences. My late father instilled my love for poetry.; [a.] Havelock, ON

BREWSTER, SYLVIA
[b.] March 19, 1924; Aldershot, Hunts, UK; [p.] John Lawrence Brewster (deceased); [m.] Hilda Brewster (nee Beak—deceased); [ed.] Various county schools: Hampshire, Berkshire, and Surrey (UK), currently extra further 'Vital Biblical Education home studies with Sisters Bible and Tract Soc., PA; [occ.] Composing music for my poetry and compiling new edition poetry book; [memb.] FSC UK Supporter Membership, The National Living Paintings Trust, Membership a voluntary charity library for blind and partially-sighted adults and children, reading, Berkshire (UK); [hon.] ICS UK Graduate Rep. 1993, ICS Diplomas: Short Story Writing, Speedhand, Creative Embroidery, Working with Words. 1996 Elected into International Poetry Hall of Fame, 1997 award Poet of the Year (National Library of Poetry and Distinguished Member of ISP); [oth. writ.] Children's short (family) stories, speech therapy tongue twisters, classical and humorous for children and adults, historical articles; [pers.] Poetry writing enhances my daily food for thought.; [a.] Hampshire, UK

BROCK, JACK S.
[b.] February 13, 1933; Harrogate, BC; [p.] Robert and Sarah; [ed.] Grade 12 with university entrance, Diploma at Lady Grey School, Golden, BC; [occ.] Semi-retired; [memb.] Boy Scouts of Canada; [hon.] My award has been the people's support in this small community who have given me tremendous backing in their complimentary words after seeing my work in local newspapers.; [oth. writ.] My Angels of the Night, Wondrous Lights, The Rainbow Cake, The World Cup Skier, Mothers of Durand, I Love BC (in local news); [pers.] I would like my poems to simply create a clear picture of what I am trying to show in words. My courageous friend with terminal cancer inspired my writing of "My Anxious Plea."; [a.] Golden, BC

BROOKS, LINDA GRACE
[pen.] Lynette Tamar Mark; [b.] October 26, 1945; Canada; [p.] Mr. and Mrs. John Shortt; [m.] Dennis A. Brooks; August 27, 1968; [ed.] Grade ten, currently studying best top publishing, children's writing course, writing for stage sireen and TV journalism; [occ.] Housewife, Writer; [hon.] World Decoration of Excellence; [oth. writ.] A Dog for Keeps (Nelson Charlesbridge), The Lights of Home (self-published), Keto, which is to be made into a movie.; [pers.] It doesn't hurt to have a goal in life.

BROWN, ALLISON
[b.] 18 April 1983; London, ON; [p.] Howard and Marion Brown; [ed.] Grade nine student at Kincardine District High School; [occ.] Student; [hon.] Essay won first place about Remembrance Day. Received English Award in grade eight. Won the Fall Fair Award for two years.; [pers.] Nature inspires my writings. Often certain phrases come to me, and I build a poem around them.; [a.] Kincardine, ON

BROWN, DARRYL
[b.] April 26, 1980; Maple Creek, Saskatchewan; [p.] Jim Brown, Linda Brown; [ed.] Last year of Consol High School, grade 12; [memb.] Student Representative Council, SHA Referee's Division, Consul Rockets Hockey Club; [a.] Consul, SK

BROWN, TANYA
[pen.] Teddy Bear; [b.] September 4, 1980; Ottawa, ON; [p.] Joan DesRosiers (grandmother); [ed.] I am attending the Carleton Place Alternative School and in grade 11.; [hon.] I have awards from the V.I.P. It has to do with drugs, alcohol, and peers.; [oth. writ.] I have written quite a few poems, but never had any published—only this one.; [pers.] I have been greatly influenced by my grandmother to keep writing poems.; [a.] Carleton Place, ON

BROWNLOW, MELANIE
[b.] December 20, 1978; Milton, ON; [p.] Carol and Len Brownlow; [ch.] Breanna, Lynne Brownlow; [pers.] Dedicated to my father, Len Brownlow; [a.] Georgetown, ON

BURCHELL, JOAN
[pen.] Joan Burchell; [b.] July 19, 1932; Toronto, ON; [ch.] Janice Beveridge and Sandra Mulveney; [ed.] C.H.S.C., Toronto; [memb.] Past member Ontario Genealogical Society; past volunteer Can. Cancer Society; [hon.] First prize for Romantic Poetry Contest (1989) in local weekly paper; second prize in Poetry Inst. of Canada contest; certificates for three exams, Royal Conservatory of Music; [oth. writ.] Upwards of 60 poems published in "The Record News, E.M.C." Smiths Falls, published weekly, O.G.S. "Newsleaf"; Poetry Institute of Canada anthology; another local paper "News from the Valley"; and a compilation "Our Lever Family Tree," 1991; [pers.] Writing gives me joy. I look for the good in each day and I express my thoughts and feelings in simple words. Each of my poems printed is another rung on the ladder to a dream.; [a.] Smiths Falls, Canada

BURKE, AMBER
[b.] October 18, 1983; Saskatoon, SK; [p.] Debbie Cleaver (biological mother) and Brad Clearer, James Burke (biological father) and Karen Cornstock; [oth. writ.] This is my first real writing but I am inspired to write more, so I'll see where I go from here.; [pers.] I am only fourteen, and I thought because of my age no one would care for my writing. This just proved to me that you can be good at writing no matter what your age.; [a.] Chestermer, AB

BURNETT, JIM
[b.] April 24, 1913; Carman, MB; [p.] William and Ethel Burnett; [m.] Helen Ball Burnett; September 21, 1940; [ch.] Two; [ed.] Grade 12 (Certificate); [occ.] Retired; [a.] Vernon, BC

BUTCHER, GERALD
[b.] December 3, 1925; St. Lucia; [p.] Luvina Anna Butcher; [m.] November 1955; [ed.] Elementary grade; [occ.] Mason and Carpenter; [memb.] Member of the S.D.A. Church; [hon.] Three certificates for songwriting; [oth. writ.] I have five songs on cassettes. I sent to different studio's in America, they promised they'll publish them. Up to this present day, I've received nothing.; [pers.] I was bright in school. I used to play too much. I lost what I studied in school. When I became an Adventist, I began to study Bible history, which makes me what I am today.; [a.] Castries, Bexon

CAMPBELL, SHIRLEY
[p.] Richard and Melba Howes; [m.] Jack Campbell; May 20, 1990; [ed.] RN: Midwifery; [a.] Melfort, SK

CARTER, ANITA T.
[b.] December 13, 1973; [oth. writ.] I am currently compiling a body of work called "Lyrics without Music" that I am looking to publish.; [pers.] Life is being bought with the dollar; I try to teach people the error in this way through my writing.; [a.] Victoria, Australia

CAULFIELD, GERRY
[pen.] Angela Dust; [b.] September 3, 1979; Edmonton, AB; [ed.] High School Honours; [occ.] Student/Dreamer; [memb.] The International Society of People Bent on Extravagant Silliness. SPCA Mascot; [hon.] High School Honours; [oth. writ.] "The Intricacies of Humanity . . . Simplified," "Time and Time Again," "Greetings and Hallucinations"; [pers.] Sing for me, and I will return your songs, unbroken, untamed. I will set them to flight and in doing so, your trust will always light my heart.; [a.] Stony Plain, AB

CHAMBERLAIN, J. M.
[pen.] B.J.; [b.] October 24, 1957; Saint John; [p.] Delphis J. Chamberlain, Marie Levesque; [m.] Divorced; [ch.] Thomas Joseph Gillespie; [ed.] GED—course and workshops on Psychology—dealing with mental disorders, Sign Language Course Level 1 and 2, Typing Course Level 1 and 2; [occ.] Support Worker—"Paul I. Leger" nine years, little facility group in Renous Institution; [memb.] Parish Council, Board of Directors "Beautification" —made Honorary Member Sisters of Mercy, Christopher Course Cursillo; [hon.] November 1995, The Atlantic Institution in the "Understanding Survival Program" for dedication to the inmates at presented to Paul Leger, myself. I am the founder of this program; [oth. writ.] Several poems published, Wild East Publishing—articles published in local newspaper—New Free Catholic paper; [pers.] I strive to embrace (uncover) the dark secrets to empower the memory that once was "me." Thank God and thank you for your kindness.; [a.] Saint John, NB

CHAMBERS, ANNETTE
[b.] October 20, 1959; Dunville, ON; [p.] Anna and Arthur Goodfallow; [m.] Jeffrey Chambers; November 25, 1978; [ch.] David and Gregory; [ed.] Grade 12 Diploma; [occ.] Emergency Room Clerk; [memb.] Recreational volleyball, aerobics exercise member; [oth. writ.] Poem published in The Glow Within; [a.] Dunville, ON

CHANDER, RAVI
[b.] August 24, 1985; Toronto; [p.] Harmesh and Raj Rani Chander; [ed.] Currently studying at Earl Grey Junior High School at Toronto; [occ.] Student; [hon.] Academic Scholarship at Williamson Elementary School; [pers.] The art of poetry reflects what you have in your heart, not in your head.; [a.] Toronto, ON

CHAPMAN, JOAN
[b.] April 5, 1930; Toronto, ON; [p.] Rene and Russ Salmon; [m.] Ron Chapman; November 26, 1965; [ch.] Rusty and Roni-Lou; [ed.] Elementary and secondary school in Bracebridge, ON. Business College in Orilla, ON; [memb.] Girl Guides, Broom and Stone Curling Club, basketball, softball, hockey teams, Toronto Accolades of Harmony, Inc., Happy Trails Cloggers; dance group Shufflin' Slippers; [hon.] First place for bulletin contest with International Harmony, Inc., third place in Toronto Star Newspaper Mystery Writing Contest; [oth. writ.] I write only for my own enjoyment and at the request of friends and relatives for "special occasion" poems, etc. I have never submitted anything for publication.; [pers.] Being an animal lover, I have found that the nicest people I know are also animal lovers. My contest poem "Cat Tales" describes our own five cats. Since

retiring, I spend 14 hours a week with my dance groups, plus public performances.; [a.] Scarborough, ON

CHATTEN, NANCY HEATHER
[b.] July 26, 1946; Belleville, ON; [p.] Arnold and Etheline Weese; [m.] Harry Neil Chaten; July 5, 1963; [ch.] Robert, Lawrence, James, Melissa; [ed.] Trenton High School, grade 12, Loyalist College, Chemical Engineer Technician, Ontario Business College Law Clerk; [memb.] Trenton Community Players Theatre Group, Tops, Writer's Roundtable; [hon.] Professor's Award (Loyalist College), Editor's Choice Award (The National Library of Poetry); [oth. writ.] Several articles published in local paper, articles electronically published on the World Wide Web; [pers.] I find poetry a cleansing form of therapy to resolve emotional issues. My mother influenced me with her own writings.; [a.] Trenton, ON

CHAUDHURI, DR. ANJANA RAI
[pen.] Anne Hogan; [b.] August 15, 1958; Calcutta, India; [p.] Dilip Rai Chaudhuri, Uma Rai Chaudhuri; [m.] Dr. Royston Hugh Hogan; December 9, 1989; [ed.] Bachelor's (B.Sc.), Masters (M.Sc.) in Chemistry, Calcutta, India, Ph.D. in Chemistry—University of Arizona, Tucson, Arizona, USA; [occ.] Writer and Tutor; [memb.] American Chemical Society; [hon.] Gold medal in Chemistry for Masters, Department of Chemistry, University of Arizona, travel awards; [oth. writ.] Unpublished poetry anthology. Nearly finished writing young adult's fiction book. Poetry published on the Internet under pen name of Anne Hogan.; [pers.] Influenced by Wordsworth and Tennyson. Great love for English and American poetry and fiction. I like to make people aware of the sufferings of mankind through poetry. Like to write poignant poetry.; [a.] Singapore, Republic of Singapore

CHEONG-ROBB, SANDRA
[b.] September 7, 1970, Mozambique, Africa; [p.] Chong Gail Kim Cheong; [m.] Brian R.P. Robb, July 15, 1995; [pers.] Life is very short—make the best of it. This poem is dedicated to my boyfriend, now husband—Love ya. To everyone who is no longer with us, we'll be "Always thinking of you!"; [a.] Toronto, ON

CITRO, MARY ROSA CALVINO
[p.] Rosa Citro, Julio Calvino Prada; [ed.] French Teacher, Music Teacher, Lawyer; [occ.] Lawyer, Music Composer; [hon.] Poems: Prix "Fundacion Givre 1982; Editorial Bs. As. Poems 1985. Prix Internationale Lutece, Paris, France 1985. Story: Prix Fundacion Givre 1987 and Prix International Lutece. Paris, France 1985 "Music"; [oth. writ.] Nine books, and six books to publish. [a.] Republica Argentina

CLAPP, DONMINIQUE
[b.] April 4, 1953; Geelong, Australia; [ch.] Daniel, Natasha, Mark; [occ.] Assistant Nurse in Nursing, pastel paintings of animals, writing!; [pers.] We must try as hard as we can to not harm any living creature.; [a.] Wentworth Falls, Australia

CLARK, EVELYN HUNTER
[pen.] Tea Sherritt; [b.] July 8, 1942; Shelburne, ON; [p.] Verna and Milton McKinley; [m.] John William Clark; October 12, 1996; [ch.] Wendy, Curtis, Robin, Beverly, Susan, and Gregory; [ed.] Tyr's College. English Literature. Diploma—Journalism, D.S.W.; [occ.] Writer—Freelance Photographer, Poet, and Author; [memb.] World Vision, Child, Ana Yeli, Mexico; [hon.] AVA, Society P.C. Animals, Girl Guide Lieutenant, poetry 1996—letter from HRH Queen Mother for poem called "Pup"; [oth. writ.] 1996-97 Pup, Jake, Beautiful Joe, Realization, Twins, Zephyr. "Only Once October Comes" short romance novel, Toronto Star. Author self, typist, Trist Smith and edited Colleen Hughes. Love to 16 grandchildren; [pers.] Thank you to the above whose help and encouragement I appreciate. Thank you to Jeffrey and Diana Kerble whose 500 acre estate I have lived on the past eight years at Duncan Lake.; [a.] Clarksburg, ON

CLARK, TONI
[b.] February 10, 1979; Edmonton; [p.] Garth Clark and Cindy Clark; [ed.] Student at Lacombe Composite High School. I'm in grade 12; [occ.] Student; [memb.] I belong to two music clubs and one video club.; [hon.] I received an award for Most Outstanding Student on my grade average.; [oth. writ.] I have an auntie and uncle named Brenda and Mike. They are the best you could ever ask for. I also have a sister (Michelle) in grade 10. Good friends Karrie and Jamie (no other writing ever published).; [pers.] When you fall down, pick yourself right back up and move on. Don't hang around your past.; [a.] Lacombe, AB

CLEARY, ANGELA
[pen.] Angie, Winnie; [b.] October 29, 1979; Halifax, NS; [p.] Michael and Loretta Cleary; [ed.] Currently attending Auburn Drive High School, grade 12, planning to become a Paramedic; [memb.] Member of my school's rugby and wrestling teams; [pers.] Love you, mom and dad; [a.] Dartmouth, NS

CLEMENTE, ALEXANDRE
[b.] January 26, 1967; Araguari Minas, Gerais; [p.] Orlando L. Clemente and Divina M. Da Silva Clemente; [occ.] Teacher at Cultural Brasil Estados Unidos; [memb.] International Society of Poets; [oth. writ.] Poem "Vase" published in the book "Fields of Gold" by The National Library of Poetry, and the poem "Amused" to be published in the book "Best Poems of 1998"; [pers.] My voice is the voice of the mythical searcher who would rather find the answers for life's questions than live the questions themselves.; [a.] Sao Paulo, Brazil

CLIFFE, STEPHEN
[b.] April 25, 1964; Halifax, NS; [m.] Esther; 1993; [ed.] B.A. Honours, Acadia University; [a.] Mississauga, ON

COCHRAN, EDWARD
[b.] December 10 1964; Penticton, BC; [p.] John, Ann Cochran; [ch.] Jonathan, Matthew, Michael; [ed.] Grade 12; [occ.] Aluminum Casting Operator; [oth. writ.] Several poems, none published; [a.] Kitimat, BC

COKER, LUCINDA
[pen.] Lucy; [b.] November 22, 1981; Del Rio, TX; [p.] Rosemary, John Coker; [ed.] Sophomore at Desert High School; [occ.] Student in Desert High School; [memb.] Jewish Youth Group and Nashim or Women and Young Women of Reform Judaism; [hon.] The Girl Scout Silver Award. To leadership awards. A and B honor roll twice. Student of the Month three times.; [oth. writ.] Three novels and 12 more poems, not published; [pers.] I always loved the arts, and I always wanted to show my work to the world so they can enjoy my writing, and to give hope.; [a.] CA

COOLEN, ALANA
[b.] July 23, 1981; Halifax, NS; [p.] Kornelia and Allan Coolen; [ed.] Forest Heights Community School;

[occ.] Grade 11 student; [memb.] The Canadian Chito-Ryu Assoc., St. Margaret's Karate Club, Chester Curling Club, Chester Brass Band, FHSC Choir, Jazz Band, Concert Band, Newspaper, Yearbook; [hon.] National Council of Teachers of English Award, The National Library of Poetry's Editor's Choice Award, various trophies and medals in music and sports; [oth. writ.] "Always There" published in The Glow Within, The Best Gift and various articles in school newspapers; [pers.] Go for everything, back down from nothing!; [a.] Hubbards, NS

CORBETT, PATRICIA
[b.] February 8, 1954; Mayerthorpe, AB; [p.] Edward and Betty Peters; [m.] Leonard Corbett; May 29, 1976; [ch.] Adam and Nathan; [ed.] BEd (U of A), Early Childhood; [occ.] Program Coordinator (High Prairie Day Care); [memb.] Edmonton Autism Society, Association for Community Living (High Prairie); [a.] High Prairie, AB

CORPUS, EULOGIA ROJAS
[pen.] Jean Rojas; [b.] April 27, 1955; Cavite City; [p.] Virginia Salcedo and Hernardo S. Rojas; [m.] Hernani Corpus; October 20, 1982; [ch.] Dino, Ginny, Patrick, and Paolo; [ed.] Three year co. B.S. Nursing, undergraduate—Mass Communications, Comprehensive Seminar for Real Estate Brokers and passed exam for licensure of Real Estate Brokers in 1994; [occ.] Real Estate Broker, President garment manufacturing company (BSR Ent.); [oth. writ.] (Below are all poetry compilations and unpublished works) 1. Errol Flynn: Sketch in Poetry, 2. The Forest of Fear, 3. On the Shores of Sorrow, 4. Storybook Prince and Other Figurative Royalties, 5. Mourning Star; [pers.] Only true love can save this world from total annihilation.; [a.] Cavite, Cavite

COUGHLAN, PHYLLIS
[pen.] Phil; [b.] January 1, 1932; [p.] Nano Long E. David Coates; [m.] Patrick Coughlan; July 29, 1955; [ch.] Eight; [ed.] Primary C. Secondary; [occ.] Housewife; [pers.] You cannot put a price on wisdom. It is one of our greatest gifts.; [a.] Cork, Eire

COUNSELL, SHIRLEY ANNE
[pen.] Shirley Anne; [b.] January 14, 1929; Toronto, ON; [p.] Sarah and Albert; [oth. writ.] Enc. Letter-Book app. 150 pages—Holocaust poetry, unpublished, two-three other books also unpublished, church papers—these are all high school books. First prize—16 "The Season"; [pers.] Each day is a gift. To live, to hear a rift, to visit the sick, quick! Visualize sunrises, sunsets, as glorious new beginnings. Tomorrow!; [a.] Toronto, ON

COURTNEY, GORDON
[pen.] Ellwynn; [b.] March 19, 1962; Calgary, AB; [p.] Fred Courtney, Barbara Courtney; [ed.] Harry Ainly CHS, Northern Alberta Institute of Technology (NAIT); [occ.] Service Technician; [pers.] Imagination is a terrible thing to waste; use it, develop it.; [a.] Edmonton, AB

CRABS, VELMA
[pen.] Songs written under Velma Crabbe; [b.] May 30, 1916; Sudbury, ON; [p.] John and Elizabeth Gutcher; [m.] Thomas Crabs; September 4, 1949; [ch.] Thomas, Jaqui, Dawn, Kim, and Harold; [ed.] Massey Public and High School, R.C.A.F. Radio Direction Finding and Fighter Training Control, Ontario College of Art (painting); [occ.] Household Engineer while trying to find time to write and put together my "big untitled book."; [memb.] I was a mother of SOCAN for several years, but never seemed to find a way to use it. I dropped the membership. It seemed that one could publish if it was sung and recorded by someone.; [hon.] I live in small town where honors and awards are offered for heroics and I won my lifesaving award when I was 11 years old (described in my book). Awards are not offered for saving animals that find a way into your heart through their mind.; [oth. writ.] Three books of songs and a fourth pending, seventeen short stories, so far. I have over 300 photos of our local roadside flowers, 18 or more illustrated poems, and thirty or more others. None has been published.; [pers.] I wish to touch gently without hurting, to provoke only thought, and reach that inner something that makes us human. My only influence is this life we all must live.; [a.] Massey, ON

CULLIA, JOSEPH
[b.] May 12, 1971; Victoria, Australia; [p.] John and Teresa Cullia; [ed.] 1978-1983 St. John Bosco Primary, 1984-1989 St. Bernards College, 1989-1993 University of Melbourne (Accounting/Law); [occ.] Cafe/Restaurant Proprietor; [pers.] At birth we are equal, at death we are equal; let's treat all as equal.; [a.] Victoria, Australia

CYR, LISA IORRAINE
[pen.] Etcetera; [b.] February 11, 1970, Vancouver, BC; [p.] Walter and Diane Driscoll (one brother Gareth Driscoll); [ch.] Two girls—Chantelle 7yrs. and Ariel 6 months; [ed.] Grade 12 at Port Hardy Secondary with some writing courses taken at home while I raise my girls; [occ.] Retail Sales; [oth. writ.] I have only published two other poems so far: "Misunderstood" in Reflections by Moonlight and "Forgotten Secrets" in Poetic Voices of America.; [pers.] I sometimes need to be inspired for my writings to come alive for others to see it as I do. My works are mainly done for life's unusual aspects and creatures: dragons, unicorns, ghosts, to name a few, that give me great joy to write about.; [a.] Fort St. John, BC

DA FONSECA, CARLA M. GRAND MAISON
[pen.] Isis; [b.] June 22, 1970; Mozambique; [p.] Ernestina and Antonio da Fonseca; [ed.] I am currently doing an Associates Degree in Hospitality Management; [occ.] Civil Servant; [hon.] Essay writing competition first place (with distinction) awarded in high school; [pers.] I feel good about myself whenever I write poems. It's a way of expressing myself and sometimes my innermost thoughts and feelings.; [a.] Macau

DALBY, INGEBORG
[b.] June 24, 1981; Oslo, Norway; [p.] S. Lasse Dalby and Berit Karlsen; [ed.] I am now attending upper secondary school; [occ.] Pupil; [pers.] I'm attending the music, dance, and drama department at my school. Drama is my subject. I also play the flute. I'm writing poems when I'm in the mood for it.; [pers.] Do not prepare a three-course dinner when people have just asked for porridge.; [a.] Moss, Norway

DANIELE, STEPHANIE
[pen.] Cheeks, Psycho Babe, Snot; [b.] April 16, 1982; Canada; [p.] Rita and Damiano Daniele; [ed.] St. Joan of Arc High School, grade ten; [oth. writ.] I would like to dedicate my poem to my grade five teacher, Opyio Oloya, for giving me the inspiration to write, and also for believing in me.; [a.] Maple, ON

DAVENPORT, LISA A.
[b.] December 17, 1966; Toronto, ON; [occ.] Lumber, Purchasing, Acting, Broadcasting; [pers.] I believe we should live out every day to its fullest, for there may not be a tomorrow.; [a.] Barrie, ON

DAVIDSON, DOLINA
[b.] March 2, 1968; Isle of Mull Scotland; [p.] McKenneth, Mac Donald, Hectorina Kay; [m.] Ian Davidson; April 27, 1991; [ch.] Lewis John Davidson and Anna Jayne Davidson; [ed.] Finishing math on grade 12 equivalency exam.; [occ.] Housewife, Farmer; [memb.] Home study program, Popular Piano. Stratford Career Institute: writing stories for children; [hon.] Youth Training Scheme (Certificates) Retail Pharmacy, Loreal Hair Care, Computer Appreciation, The National Library of Poetry Editor's Choice Award 1997; [oth. writ.] Poems published in the Russel Banner and the Roblin Review Papers. "The Shell" published in The Glow Within 1997, with The National Library of Poetry; [pers.] Stand up and be counted. . . . Life is what you make it.; [a.] Birtle; MB

DAVIS, CHRISTINA
[b.] May 15, 1984; Victoria, BC; [p.] Regina Sinclair-Davis and Jack Davis; [ed.] I am currently in the eighth grade at Lansdowne Jr. Secondary School; [pers.] All my poems are dedicated to my nephew Jordan, and nieces Ruby and Rachel.; [a.] Victoria, BC

DE GIORGIO, LORIANNA
[b.] October 27, 1982; Toronto, ON; [p.] Pietro De Giorgio, Susan De Giorgio; [ed.] Grade ten student at St. Joseph's College School. Graduated from Holy Rosary Elementary School; [memb.] Once at the Girl Guides of Canada; [hon.] Merit Award, Excellent French Student; Two Year Award at Conservatory of Music, Toronto (piano), Honor Roll for grade nine and grade ten; [oth. writ.] Several poems and some short stories (never have been published before); [pers.] Believe in yourself and you can go far. I try to write poems that bring out the goodness in people.; [a.] Toronto, ON

DE OLIVEIRA, EDNILSON TUROZI
[b.] June 25, 1965; Cafeara, Parana, South-Brazil; [p.] Wilson Candido de Oliveira and Maria Nilva Turozi de Oliveira; [ed.] Elementary school, high school and university in Brazil. B.A. Major in Philosophy, Minors in Psychology and History at Pontifical University of Curitiba, Parana, South-Brazil. Music study in Brazil at Santa Cecilia Conservatory of Music (Curitiba), and at Milton Nascimento's Music School (Belo Horizonte—Minas Gerais). Certificate of Completion of the National Capital Semester of Seminarians at Wesley Theological Seminary in Washington, DC, issued on December 12, 1991. Music Certificate on Classical Guitar and Composition at Sherwood Conservatory of Music in Chicago, issued on July 28, 1993. M.Div. with Mission Concentration at Catholic Theological Union in Chicago, issued on June 3, 1993. MA in Theology with concentration in Ethics at Catholic Theological Union in Chicago, issued on June 1, 1995. Two-month intensive course on literature focusing on Indonesian literature at Sanata Dharma in Yogyakarta, Island of Jawa in Indonesia, April and May of 1996; [memb.] I am a member of a Catholic missionary congregation called Xaverian Missionaries. I was ordained a priest in Brazil in this congregation three years ago.; [occ.] I live in Jakarta and I am involved with Inter-Faith Dialogue. So, I am a young missionary priest doing inter-faith dialogue in Jakarta.; [oth. writ.] When I studied at Wesley Theological Seminary in Washington, DC (1991), I wrote an article for Center Focus (Jesuit bulletin); [pers.] Let us build this world anew and make it a never-ending poem of love, justice, and peace . . . a poem that humankind has been trying to write for centuries.; [a.] Jakarta

DEEGAN, DEBBIE
[b.] December 28, 1960; Montreal, QC; [m.] Jean Paul Lapointe; March 25, 1995; [ch.] Two; [ed.] McGill University; [occ.] Administrative Assistant; [memb.] Secretary, Pointe Claire Figure Skating Club, Soul Trek; [hon.] Awarded rank of Captain in the Soul Trek organization; [oth. writ.] Science fiction; [pers.] The ability to make our own minds is our truest form of freedom.; [a.] Montreal, QC

DEMELO, JOSEPH
[b.] January 17, 1926, Island of Sao-Miguel, Azores, Port.; [p.] Manuel and Maria DeMelo; [m.] Mary Evangelina DeMelo, May 7, 1952; [ch.] Sonia Sousa and Gregory S. DeMelo; [ed.] Primary school, graduated, good grades, diploma, excellent in history, 1945 studied Portuguese, then started learning English, avidly and assiduously, two semesters at Charles Evans Hughes Evening High School—NYC; [occ.] Retired; [memb.] AAA and now CAA (automobile), library membership card—when I was back in the States, now here in Cambridge.; [oth. writ.] In 1945 I was 19 years old, went to work for the American Air Force Base in the Azores. In 1953 I had to resign (after eight years with the Americans) to come to the States. 1953-1983 worked for Carey Transportation, Inc. in Manhattan—then I resigned. I came to Canada in 1984 with my wife.; [pers.] Face life's pitfalls with equanimity, calmness, and resignation. Think that all humans have benign and altruistic qualities. Be content with your lot, and don't envy or try to usurp what's not yours. Don't load your conscience with inquities, lest you'd live miserably.; [a.] Cambridge, ON

DOHERTY, CURTIS
[pen.] Curtis Doherty; [occ.] Musician, Songwriter, Lyricist; [memb.] American Federation of Musicians (AFM), Local 547 Calgary; [hon.] Editor's Choice Award 1997 re: "Too Much Religion"; [oth. writ.] Several poems and lyrics including "Too Much Religion," Editor's Choice Award from The National Library of Poetry, 1997; [a.] Calgary, AB

DOMINGUEZ, EMILIA GRACE
[b.] November 19, 1980; Zamora, Michoacan, Mexico; [p.] Dario Dominguez and Deborah Dominguez; [ed.] Student at the American School Foundation, Mexico City; [occ.] Student, currently a Junior (11th grade); [memb.] Founding Literary Editor of the high school newspaper: The Bear Facts. Member of school organization: Project Lead; [hon.] Named "ASFS Own Poet Laureate" in the ASF "Focus" magazine (summer 1997). Award for "Best Journalist." Literary Editor of The Bear Facts; [oth. writ.] Poems published in school's literary magazine "Reflections." Several articles published in school newspaper. Poem published by The National Library of Poetry, other poems to be published in the future.; [pers.] Be all you can be. Be kind to yourself, and most of all, love and respect yourself. You are unique, nobody can be you. Just be.; [a.] Mexico

DONNELLY, RICHARD M.
[pen.] Rick; [b.] July 22, 1954; Lloyd Minister, SK; [p.] George E. Donnelly and Irene L. Donnelly; [m.]

Lisa Donnelly (divorced); September 14, 1986; [ch.] Michael, Dannielle, Jason, and Kyle Donnelly; [ed.] Grade 11—finished; [occ.] Truck Driver for 25 years; [pers.] Writing poetry was a form of stress release. Now it's an enjoyable hobby, with a strong desire to someday publish a book of poetry. I enjoy sharing my emotions and thoughts on life.; [a.] Edmonton, AB

DOUCETTE, KANDICE
[b.] 5 February 1976; London, ON; [ed.] Studying at Trent University, Peterborough, ON to be an Anthropologist; [occ.] Student; [oth. writ.] In 1990 an anthology of poetry and prose called Ink of Imagination with Jenni Blackmore (Lunn). Then with Trent University's Women's book of poetry Dangerous Divas 1998-1998.; [pers.] Poetry, to me, is an outerbody experience, a chance to look into the soul of the future, to see the paths and patterns that lie ahead, and the past is the key.; [a.] North York, ON

DOWNING, ROBERT J.
[b.] January 8, 1935; Hamilton, ON; [p.] Albert Downing and Dora Figgins; [m.] Miriana Kaludjerovic; September 27, 1980; [occ.] Fine Artist; [memb.] Royal Canadian Academy of Arts, Sculpture Society of Canada, Ontario Society of Artists; [hon.] Seven Canada Council Awards between 1967 to 1985; [oth. writ.] Confessions of a Canadian Sculptor (early memoirs), published by the artist in edition of 30, 1991; [pers.] 77 Exhibits of fine art in seven countries.; [a.] Toronto, ON

DREW, MARK
[b.] September 9, 1964; Quesnel, BC; [m.] Kelly Drew; June 6, 1992; [ch.] Michael, Ashley; [occ.] Aircraft Maintenance Engineer on Sikorsky 561; [pers.] Write from the heart—you can't go wrong.; [a.] Victoria, BC

DUSTERHOFT, KATRINA
[b.] 3 April 1982; Drayton Valley; [p.] Ken and Connie Dusterhoft; [ed.] Currently finishing high school and continuing on to university; [oth. writ.] Too many to say, but my favorites are: It, I Am, and Roses; [pers.] "Only as high as I reach can I grow. Only as far as I seek can I go. Only as deep as I look can I see. Only as much as I dream can I be," —Author unknown. I saw that on a painting at a local art show; it inspires me and my work.; [a.] Drayton Valley, AB

ESANNASON, JEAN H.
[b.] April 19, 1935; St Thomas, USVI; [p.] Carmen and Harold Esannason, Sr. (deceased); [m.] Irving V. Bauman; April 5, 1961; (divorced 1975); [ch.] Susan Ann, Nedina Jean, Ginger Marie; [ed.] C.A.H.S and Vermont College of Norwich University, (Cosmetologist —Caribbean Beauty Institute); [occ.] Retired Educator; [memb.] Life membership in The Mungo Niles Cultural Dancers; [hon.] May 11, 1997 "Mother's Day Award," by Senate president Lorraine Berry, May 25, 1997— "Retirement Award" by Joseph Gomez School, August 15, 1997, "Excellence in the Arts" award by The Governor of the VI, RL Schneider; [oth. writ.] Poems: "1989 Anthology of American Poetry," "Inner Eye Magazines" local newspaper. Books: "If I Perish, I Perish," "How to Make a Fly Catcher and Other Crafts," "Cyril Emmanuel King: A Man of the People." Articles: "The Voice Magazine"; [pers.] I reflect beauty, love, joy, sadness, and pain in my writings because they are a part of life and a part of me, but in all things, I give God the praise.; [a.] St Thomas, USVI

FAMINOW, PETER S.
[b.] Lundbreck, Pincher Creek District, AB, January 12, 1917; [p.] Sam and Elizabeth (nee Holoboff) Faminow; [ch.] Three children —Sarah, Pauline (Polly), and Megan; [ed.] Graduated from University of Alberta with a credit first year Law Degree, completed grade 12 at high school (Lundreck) Pincher Creek Region, AB, graduated from Willamette University (Salem, Oregon, USA) in 1943 with a B.A. with distinction, and received a B.A. of Laws from University of Saskatchewan in 1952.; [occ.] Lawyer with private practice of Vancouver and North Vancouver since 1953; [memb.] British Columbia and Alberta Bar Associations; Canadian and Vancouver Bar Associations and member the Foundation for Legal Research in Canada; Phi Delta Theta International Fraternity; [hon.] Joseph Albert Prize and Chamber of Commerce Oratorical Contest winner; [pers.] My hobbies are gardening, badminton, golf, choir singing, square dancing, and classical and modern music. Both parents arrived in the Port of Halifax at five years of age in 1898. They were raised in mud huts in Swan River, northern Manitoba, and Yorkton Saskatchewan. They pioneered on the prairies and the Kootenays of BC, settling in Alberta in 1916, where they farmed and ranched until retiring to Calgary in 1951. In his early years, my father, Sam, worked on building railroads, forestry, sawmills, and utility construction works in many cities on the prairies and in BC. My parents found creative expression in carving, spinning, knitting, and cloth and rug making. My father won many awards for his creative works at exhibitions. Many of their works have been donated to, and are preserved in, the Gelnbow Museum in Calgary, AB

FISH, ROBERT M.
[b.] November 11, 1916; Toledo, OH; [p.] Harry L. Fish, Velma Kime Fish; [m.] Denyse Pupier Fish; November 23, 1946; NYC, NY; [ch.] Michel Robert; [ed.] Fostoria High School, Fostoria, OH, La Salle Extension University, Chicago, IL; [memb.] American Legion, Paris Post #1; [oth. writ.] Poems published in World of Poetry anthology "Our World's Most Treasured Poems"; [pers.] If my poetry can create a sense of contentment, a smile to the lips, a lump to the throat, a tear to the eye or, as director Frank Capra said of his films, "a glow of satisfaction," then my work will have achieved that which I seek.; [a.] Sevran, France

FRICK, MARGOT
[b.] April 27, 1924; Trier, Germany; [p.] Jakob and Elisabeth Lichtherz; [ch.] Six; [ed.] Business college; [memb.] Orchid Society of Alberta, International Society of Poets; [oth. writ.] Some stories not published, yet one poem published in Fields of Gold. One will be in the book Beyond the Horizon and on the tape "Sound of Poetry."; [pers.] My life is so colorful, it would make a book with lots of pages, but in short I'm still a life and like to write. It started all I was 14, sitting on a tree in the night looking down on the Rhine River, where fog was rising and it looked as if elves where dancing.

FUCHS, FELIPE
[b.] 11 May 1982; Porto Alegre, Brazil; [p.] Flavio Fuchs and Sandra Costa Fuchs; [ed.] High school; [occ.] Student; [memb.] Brazilian Judo Federation, United States Judo Federation; [hon.] National Judo Champion (in Brazil), National Judo Champion (in the US); [pers.] I would like to thank my English teacher, Mr. Wenker, from Parkville High School (in Baltimore,

MD) for all the teachings and for all the life lessons that he gave me in the year of 1996 that I won't ever forget. Without him, it wouldn't be possible for me to write this poem.; [a.] Porto Alegre, Rio Grande do Sul, Brazil

GALLINGER, JAMES
[pen.] Jake; [b.] July 14, 1970; Owen Sound, ON; [p.] Lyn McVey, Bill Gallinger; [ed.] Guelph Collegiate Vocational Institute, Honours (G.C.V.I for short), Toronto School of Business, Honours; [occ.] Customized Golf Club Fitter, Regency Golf Company (CAN) Ltd.; [pers.] Take away all the walls and boundaries, just let it out, write.; [a.] Guelph, ON

GARLAND, KENNETH EDWIN
[b.] July 13, 1954; Scotland; [p.] Janet and Edwin Garland; [m.] Wendy; [ed.] Grade II; [occ.] Tractor Trailer Driver; [oth. writ.] I have many songs and poems, this is my first attempt of any kind to have my work published.; [pers.] I believe, in reality, there is no fairy tale in real life.; [a.] Scarborough, ON

GARNATZ, JENNIFER M.
[pen.] Jennifer M. Daley; [b.] September 23, 1953; Lucea Jamaica, WI; [p.] Rolando B. Daley (deceased), Loreen Sterling; [ed.] C.A.S.T. (secretarial course) Alpha Academy, Blake's Preparatory School Christian Albrecht University and Goethe Institute; [occ.] Executive Secretary/ Admin. Asst.—bilingual; [memb.] G.E.M.A. (Copywriting Society in Germany for Songwriters/ Musicians / Publishers); [oth. writ.] Song lyrics recorded by artists in Jamaica. Dozens of unpublished poems, lyrics, and melodies presently being compiled. Also working on plays, children's stories, and novels.; [pers.] It is my goal to finance an orphanage and geriatric home. Even a dog is worthy of respect. Be kind to and tolerant of each other and help those in need, especially children and the aged. Although I am a fun-loving person, my writings reflect the suffering in the world.; [a.] Hamburg, Germany

GARRISON, DIANA GWEN
[b.] September 25, 1953; Comox, BC; [p.] Robert and Jean Garrison; [ch.] Vicki Lynn; [ed.] North Island College; [occ.] Office Assistant, Mental Health Services; [memb.] Royal Canadian Legion LA, BC Forestry, BC Chapter CMHA St. Johns Ambulance, Diabetic Association, BC Summer and Winter Games; [oth. writ.] 54 Poems published, mostly written about local community celebrations and events.; [pers.] I find writing poetry very therapeutic and strive to create a masterpiece of art through my words.; [a.] Courtenay, BC

GAUTREAU, ERIN JENNIFER
[b.] September 26, 1982; Saint John, NB; [p.] Roderick and Faye Gautreau; [ed.] Still in school; [hon.] Many school academic awards, drama awards; [pers.] Literature is constantly changing my life, and my life is constantly changing my literature. My poetry reflects the experiences of others, along with my own.; [a.] Saint John, NB

GERENA, ELBA YESI
[b.] September 16, 1982; Santurce, PR; [p.] Elba Maldonado, Luis Gerera; [ed.] I'm in tenth grade right now in Colegio Ponceno.; [occ.] Student; [hon.] Third honor of my eighth grade graduation class and belonging to the National Honor Society; [pers.] I'm a very sensible and realistic person, too much for my age, I think.; [a.] Ponce, PR

GHUMMAN, DILRAJ
[b.] April 11, 1978; Toronto, ON; [p.] Sukhjit Ghumman, Harpreet Ghumman; [ed.] Appleby College (private school) undergraduate, studies in pre-med at University of Toronto; [occ.] Pre-med Student; [hon.] Duke of Edinburgh Award Recipient, Honors Student, Optimates Award Winner for Bronze and Silver Level, Certificate of Academic Proficiencies, HDSEF Bronze Level Award, Dean's List; [pers.] In life's journey, let attitude determine your altitude.; [a.] Mississauga, ON

GIBSON, ROBERT
[b.] June 8, 1978; Barbados; [p.] Robert Gibson Sr., Evette Gibson; [occ.] College student; [hon.] Special mention in a local newspaper poetry contest; [pers.] I want to thank my heavenly father for giving me this talent, and my family and friends for believing in me.

GILMORE, AMANDA E. G.
[b.] January 13, 1978; Fredericton; [p.] John and Judy Gilmore; [ed.] High school: Devon Park Christian School. Currently enrolled at University of New Brunswick, Fredericton campus; [occ.] First year University Student and Freelance Writer; [memb.] Writer's Federation of New Brunswick; [hon.] Editor's Choice Award—The National Library of Poetry 1997; [oth. writ.] Article published in local newspaper, poem published in The Glow Within; [pers.] When you find yourself at the end of your rope and about to fall off, look up and see God reaching out to save you. All you have to do is grasp his hand.; [a.] Mouth of Keswick, NB

GJESDAL, BETTY L.
[pen] Betty L. Myers/Gjesdal; [b.] September 16, 1949, CA; [p.] Betty and Ray Myers; [m.] Rasmus Gjesdal; May 30, 1981; [ch.] Shelly, Ana, and Bjorn; [ed.] Crescenta Valley High, Glendale Jr. College, Pasadena City College; [occ.] Seamstress; [a.] Algaard, Norway

GLUCKMAN, BRENDAN
[b.] December 9, 1978; Edmonton, AB; [ed.] I am currently a student at McGill University.; [pers.] We live as we dream—alone.; [a.] Montrail, QC

GOLLING, CARL JAMES
[pen.] Carl James; [b.] August 6, 1956; Nelson, BC; [p.] Mr. and Mrs. Carl Joseph Golling; [m.] Heather Louise Golling; 1980; [ed.] Primary education government schools in Nelson, BC. Secondary education, Royal Roads Military College, Cariboo College, St. Davids; [occ.] Private English boarding school which I attended grades 8-12 prior to college at the Kootenay School of Fine Arts, Kootenay School of the Arts; Graduate, Commercial Gallery Artist; [memb.] I volunteer my time at the Canadian Physical and Mentally Disabled Health Centre as their Staff Editor for their news magazine in Kelowna, BC; [hon.] Nursing-Medical Officers Certificate, service awards, Honorable Discharge from the Canadian Armed Forces with federal disability, government disability permanent disability cheques. Retired from service federal government; [oth. writ.] None except non-profit literary work for the Sword Literary Magazine in BC. By, non-profit I mean the writers were not paid; however, the magazine sold $1.25 per copy.; [pers.] "Remember chance always favours the prepared mind!" ("Notation") My late Uncle Harry Golling who died of cancer, prior to his demise at age of 29—won the silver medal at the World's Fair for his pottery exhibit in the early 1960s.; [a.] Kelowna, BC

GRANDSOULT, MICHAEL
[b.] February 22, 1983; Scarborough, ON; [p.] Cheryl Grandsoult, David Grandsoult; [ed.] Francis Libermann CHS; [oth. writ.] "The Birth of Pride—Canada" newspaper, The Toronto Sun—published, other poems not published— "What Is War?" and "Wasted Heart"; [pers.] Poetry is a reflection of the reality of feelings. To be real, you have to feel.; [a.[Scarborough, ON

GRAVES, RACHEL IVY
[pen.] Waldo Klein; [b.] January 24, 1975; Peterborough, England; [p.] Reg and Janet Graves; [ed.] High school diploma and two years at college for Office Administration and received diploma; [occ.] Office Administrative Assistant; [oth. writ.] My poem has been published before, in another book (anthology book).; [pers.] Belive in all that you are and everything that you can do, because you are number one. My dad always inspired me to write.; [a.] Calgary, AB

GRAVES, SARAH JANE
[b.] 9 August 1978; Kelowna, BC; [p.] Patricia Graves and Nelson Graves; [ed.] Currently attending first year of college at Okanagan University College, Kelowna, BC; [occ.] Student; [oth. writ.] "Shadow of the Imagination," in the volume "The Sands of Time" by The National Library of Poetry; [pers.] Time has such a great influence upon our lives that it becomes subconscious. This is what inspires my writing (exploring the effects of time).; [a.] Westbank, BC

GREEN, AMANDA
[b.] July 12; Montreal; [p.] Gerry Green, Sabina Green; [ed.] Vanier College (first year), St. Laurent 1997-98, Lindsay Place High School, Pte. Claire 1992-1997; [occ.] Student; [hon.] Citizenship Award 1992-93, Honors in Art 1996-97, publication in school board creative writing compilation 1993-94, 1996-97; [oth. writ.] Pennies for a Beggar (short story), some other poems; Thoughts of a Boy, Cemetery, My Son, Never Again, Grip, The Man Who Never Cried, On My Mind, Tinfoil, Silencing the Baby's Cries, plus others; [pers.] The most accurate method of displaying emotions is writing. Never do I hide the truth on paper.; [a.] Dollard-des-Ormealds, QC

GRIMES, MAXINE
[b.] November 4, 1957; Nelson, BC; [p.] Fred and Carla Leeming; [ch.] Pamela Morgan and Kody Michael Grimes; [occ.] Bookkeeper and Korpack Cement Products, Trail, BC; [pers.] I am inspired to write from my heart in hopes to show others in similar circumstances—there is hope.; [a.] Genelle, BC

GRIMSLEY, DONNA
[b.] June 21, 1966; Winnipeg; [p.] Doug and Margaret Grimsley; [ed.] Red River Community College; [occ.] Calgary Herald Newspaper Sales Assistant; [memb.] Curler; [hon.] Canadian Mixed Championship Bronze Medalist; [oth. writ.] "Pure Inspiration" in The Sands of Time; [pers.] My dream has arrived.; [a.] Calgary, AB

HALE, SCOTT ANTHONY
[b.] September 22, 1966; NJ; [p.] Mary M. Ward; [m.] Bertrand J. Fauroux-Hale; April 17, 1996; [ed.] London School of Journalism (currently); [occ.] Writer, Model, and Businessman; [memb.] Brandon Hale Society of Poets, Janice Chilcoat Singers of Los Angeles, The Michael Viscariello Writers at AOL, The Mark Cruz Foundation for Dance; [hon.] The Brian Windom Literary Award, The Nick and Bree McQueen Poetic Writing Award of Excellence, The Karry Allen Beach Dance Honor; [oth. writ.] "I am Raymond Edward I," "Debbie and Gwen go to Mervyns," "Lady Cheri Antionette's Struggles," "The Fearless Efforts of Robert Douglas," "The Terror of Tallon Trevino"; [pers.] As in life, all things, no matter how big or small, are achievable and even more so if you're a writer.; [a.] Long Beach, CA

HALL, TAMMY
[b.] June 1, 1977; Kitchener, ON; [p.] Jim and Dolores Hall; [ed.] Elmira District Secondary School, Wilfrid Laurier University; [occ.] Student, (full-time); [memb.] Ladies Fastball Association, WLU Intramural Volleyball; [hon.] Highest Achievement in French Award, Regional Volleyball Championships. Award of Merit from the Provincial Sears Drama Festival; [oth. writ.] I have my own personal collection of poems what I write in my spare time.; [pers.] I am grateful to my friends and family—especially my grandpa, for giving me inspiration. Celebrating my ability to feel is a way to be fully free.; [a.] Coestogo, ON

HALLADAY, FRAN
[pen.] Skuttle Bug; [b.] June 13, 1944; Delta, ON; [p.] Addison and Loretta Halladay; [m.] John, Larry, and Bobby; [ed.] Grade eight, 1/2 year high school; [occ.] RNA-DSW—Security Guard, Homemaker; [hon.] Memo, Honorable Mention, Certificate, my poem was greatly honored from another, Honorable Mention in book Somewhere of Another Poem and Company; [oth. writ.] I make up poems all the time. I just do this in my sleep, in my spare time, all well. I love doing this.; [pers.] I crochet, knit, and make crafts. I make up poems of all kinds, day by day.; [a.] Odessa, ON

HAMILTON, JASON
[pen.] Sluze; [b.] 7 August 1982; Etobicoke; [p.] Barb and Rob Hamilton; [ed.] Attending grade ten at Sandwich Secondary School, Lasalle, ON; [occ.] Student, Writer; [hon.] Most Improved Student— grade 8, Goalie Award; [oth. writ.] I'm working on getting my own book published, containing 100 original poems and 41 philosophical statements (Sluze's philosophy), all written by me and titled "Fears of the World."; [pers.] "A wish is something you know will never happen, and a dream is a thought of the future."; [a.] Windsor, ON

HAMM, AGNES
[b.] November 8, 1927; Rosthern, Sask; [p.] Jacob and Helena Fehr; [m.] Martin Hamm; April 23, 1950; [ch.] Rita, Ted, Jim, and Judy; [ed.] Grade 12; [occ.] Retired; [oth. writ.] As a teenager, I had numerous articles published in the Western Producer (Saskatoon, SK), also one in a national church publication.; [pers.] As I feel that my talent is a gift, I try to honor God in my writing.; [a.] Prince George, BC

HANSON, MAUREEN HAAKENSON
[b.] 4 November, 1957; Berwyn, AB; [p.] Ada and Malfred Haakenson; [m.] Norman Hanson; February 1975; [ch.] Sherri and James; [occ.] Teacher's Aide; [a.] Red Deer, AB

HARDJANA, ASTRID
[b.] July 27, 1980; Mississauga, ON; [p.] Teddy Hardjana and Theresa Hardjana; [ed.] St. Augustine's Secondary School, Brampton, ON; [occ.] Student; [memb.] The National Authors Registry; [hon.] Short stories and poetry with the Royal Canadian Legion; [oth. writ.] Poetry contests with the Royal Canadian Legion, poetry published with the Amherst Society and Illiad Press and the school anthology; [pers.] I strongly want

to express the trials and tribulations a teen goes through and inspire others. If I can't always be here to change the world, at least my words will live on.; [a.] Brampton, ON

HARRIGAN, DEBRA
[b.] May 18, 1956; Toronto, ON; [p.] Alexander and Constance Whitton; [m.] Michael Harrigan; October 1, 1977; [ch.] James, Adam, Melissa; [occ.] Educational Assistant and Registered Nursing Assistant; [oth. writ.] Several articles published in local magazine; [pers.] My life is greatly influenced by those around me. When someone touches my heart in a special way I love to express it in my writing. This poem is in memory of my dear father.; [a.] Woodville, ON

HARRIS, ANTONESHA
[b.] December 29, 1981; Kingston, Jamaica; [p.] Icema Smith; [ed.] Suthermere Preparatory School, Immaculate Conception High School; [occ.] Student; [oth. writ.] Several unpublished poems; [pers.] My writings focus on human emotions and experiences. No matter what subject I choose, they tend to reflect my inner conflicts and deepest thoughts. As such, I consider any creative work a window into its artist's soul.; [a.] Kingston, Jamaica

HARRIS, DESMOND D.
[pen.] Desmond D. Harris; [b.] May 2, 1965; Clarenton, Jamaica; [p.] Anncella Russell and Fredrick Harris; [ch.] Troy, Travis, Traymon; [ed.] Trout Hall All Age School, Clarenton, Jamaica, Clausle McKay Secondary, Clarenton, Jamaica, George Harveys SS., Toronto, Seneca College, North York, Toronto; [pers.] My writing is a reflection of everyday life experience. I write about what I experience as well as others around me. I started writing poetry in September of '92 as living it since.; [a.] Scarborough, ON

HARRIS, SHERI
[b.] 21 October 1974; Toronto, ON; [ed.] McGill University, Honors B.A., Cultural Studies; MS Journalism, Medill, Northwestern University; [occ.] Writer/Journalist; [hon.] Shakespeare Gold Medal in English, McGill, 1997; Lionel Shapiro Award, McGill, 1997; [pers.] A single word has so many meanings, brings so many traces and images to mind, but to paint a story or write a painting, that brings words to life. And that is not just power, that is simple beauty.

HAUGHTON, HARRY S.
[pen.] Harry Sweeting; [b.] May 24, 1938; Jamaica; [p.] Zachariah and Mable Haughton; [m.] Veronica; September 23, 1967; [ch.] Lisa and Sean; [ed.] Dr. of Education (Univ. of Toronto), Master of Education (1984, 1977), Bachelor of Arts (York University, 1974); [occ.] Professor of Education, Teacher of E.S.L. (Misssauga); [hon.] Win Davies Memorial Scholarship (Ontario Public School Teachers Federation), Toronto, 1981; [oth. writ.] Two books of songs for schools: Leaves on the Maple Tree and Canadian Experience; [pers.] I believe mankind has an obligation to discard many of the theories we've inherited from our parents and teachers and go in search of our personal beginnings.; [a.] Mississauga, ON

HAYNES, JOANNE ALLONG
[pen.] Joanne Allong Haynes; [b.] February 23, 1966; Mon Repos, Trinidad; [p.] Julius and Zita Allong; [m.] Louis Haynes; April 26, 1992; [ch.] Ka'en Christian; [ed.] University of the W.I. (BSC Government.), Holy Faith Convent A Levels, St. Joseph's Convent (O Levels), St. Gabriel's Girl's R.C. (C.E.); [occ.] Teacher (U.W.I. Extramural), Designer—Batik and Tie Dye (Sunstrokes); [memb.] Writers' Union of Trinidad and Tobago; [oth. writ.] Several poems in a collection ent. "Conscious"; short stories, children's stories, and commercial writing; [pers.] I want people to read my work and be inspired to think, change, and do. I want people to be conscious (aware) of the world, life, death, and oneself.; [a.] San-Fernando, Trinidad

HEIDE, RACHEL LEA
[b.] 15 February 1975; Kingston, ON; [p.] Mervin and Pauline Heide; [ed.] Royal Conservatory of Music, Grade Eight Piano, North Dundas District High School (Chesterville, ON), B.A. Honours in History at Carleton University (Ottawa, ON); [occ.] University student, Piano Teacher, Student-Secretary at a law firm; [memb.] Saskatchewan History and Folklore Society; [hon.] Numerous Royal Canadian Legion awards for Remembrance Day essays and poems, Valedictorian at high school graduation 1994, $12,000 Faculty Scholarship from Carleton University for having highest average of all undergraduate students entering Faculty of Arts, $1000 research grant from Saskatchewan History and Folklore Society; [oth. writ.] Numerous poems published in local newspapers, working on two historical fiction novels, working on undergraduate thesis on British Commonwealth Air Training Plan, poem published in "A Season of Flowers"; [pers.] In a world that is often cruel and harsh, I wish my writing (whether prose or poetry) to be a voice of eloquence that creates images of beauty, peace, serenity, and strength in my readers' minds.; [a.] Embrun, ON

HENRY, VERONA
[p.] Maizie Campbell; [ch.] Jermayne Colphon; [occ.] Company President (vice); [oth. writ.] Currently writing a novel that will be ready for publishing very soon.; [pers.] Never underestimate the powers of the mind.; [a.] Pickering, ON

HERR, CLAUDIA
[b.] November 20, 1958; Toronto; [p.] Paolo and Bruna Vanzella; [m.] Hardy Herr; August 28, 1982; [ch.] Catherine and Alexander; [ed.] B.A. Psychology; [occ.] Information Technology Clerk

HIGGINS, KRISTI
[b.] September 6, 1985; Ottawa, ON; [p.] Lynda and Steve Short and Steve Higgins; [ed.] Gr. 7 H.W. Knight PS, Cannington, ON; [memb.] 4-H Program Youth Group; [hon.] Literary Guild, honored to be a semifinalist; [pers.] I write because it inspires me to go out and do more, fulfill my dreams. It doesn't matter what friends think, you just write!; [a.] Cannington, ON

HIRSCHFELD, LINDA MACUMBER
[b.] February 2, 1948; NS; [p.] John and Geraldine Macumber; [m.] Paul G. Hirshfeld; July 15, 1972; [ch.] Virgil and Jason; [ed.] Grade XII Gen. and Business; [occ.] General Cleaning Lady, industrial and private homes; [memb.] Fenwick United Church, Fenwick Boy Scout Group, Committed Nappan Home and School Association, Amherst Mobility Service Award; [oth. writ.] 18 Un-submitted songs, six un-submitted poems; [pers.] God willing, I'll be one half a century old come ground hag's day 1998. I'm a mother of two young men, Virgil age 12 and Jason age 18, they are my reason for existing.; [a.] Nappan, NS

HOLDIPP, SHINIKA S.
[b.] January 15, 1980; [p.] William Holdipp; [ed.] Primary school—Prospect Primary, high school—

Whitney Institute, college—Bermuda College; [occ.] Student at the Bermuda College; [memb.] I'm a member of New Testament Church of God, Heritage Hall, and Amnesty International; [hon.] I have received awards from two of my high school prizes. I graduated from high school in 1997 with a Certificate of Merit with Honours. I have received certificates from Amnesty International Bermuda for appreciation and from New Testament.; [oth. writ.] I have helped my country by doing community service. I assisted at Government Nursery. I thank God for allowing this chance to happen for me.; [a.] Pembroke, Bermuda

HUANG, QING
[b.] January 28, 1981; Shanghai, China; [p.] M. Huang, Hanli Liu; [ed.] Grill at North Toronto CI, Royal Conservatory of Music in grade 9 piano; [occ.] Student; [hon.] Gold Cup Award for highest average in grade 7 out of the whole grade level; [pers.] Water is the blood of life, but a healthy psyche is the key to living.; [a.] Toronto, ON

HUGHES, TABITHA MARIE T.
[b.] August 27, 1982; Calgary, AB; [p.] Elizabeth V. Lister, Robert C. Hughes; [ed.] Cawthra Park Secondary School; [occ.] Visual Arts Major at Cawthra Park S.S.; [memb.] Brownies of Canada, Girl Guides of Canada, Pathfinders of Canada; [hon.] Honor Roll student three years in a row; [pers.] Always strive to be the best you can be, and your possibilities are endless.; [a.] Mississauga; ON

HUI, WINNIE
[b.] December 15, 1985; Hong Kong; [p.] May Hui and Samson Hui; [ed.] Grade seven at Tomken Road Senior Public School; [occ.] Student; [pers.] Always try different styles and kinds of writing.; [a.] Mississauga, ON

IOANNOU, MARY
[pen.] Mary Ioannou; [b.] March 21, 1951; Rhodes, Greece; [p.] Evangelia and John Ioannou; [m.] Dr. Riccardo Duranti; August 1972; [ch.] Irene and Giacomo; [ed.] Public schools in Bedford, Ohio; B.A. in American Studies at Wittenberg University, Springfield, Ohio; [occ.] Middle School Social Studies Teacher and Curriculum Coordinator for Ambrit International School, Rome, Italy; [memb.] E.C.I.S. (European Council of International Schools), M.A.I.S. (Mediterranean Association of International Schools); [hon.] Workshops on interdisciplinary teaching and inquiry method in Rome, Italy; Munich, Germany; Tunis, Tunisia; workshop on poetry and science bridges in Vienna, Austria; workshop for British Council in national conference on E.F.L., Milan, Italy, on using "Multisensory Teaching"; [oth. writ.] A year's program in 17 issues of the educational journal "La Vita Scholastica" in '93-94 on teaching English through the creative arts. My Indian ink prints will be illustrating a poetry book, "Affetnosa Fantasia," pub. Arachne, coming out in December, Rome, Italy.; [pers.] What has influenced my creative works are: my personal/professional mulitcultural experiences, my passion for forming, saving abandoned animals (here on my farm), and the beauty of the diversified Italian countryside, Tess Gallagher's and Ray Calver's poetry/short stories.; [a.] Rome, Italy

IZQUIERDO, MARIELA K.
[pen.] Maii; [b.] Chile; [p.] Mario Izquierdo and Maria Izquierdo; [ed.] Northern Alberta Institute of Technology (NAIT); [occ.] Student; [hon.] Certificate of Exemplary Marks; [pers.] May the inspiration of wisdom, love, and positive thinking shower our hearts to share and write the beauty we were, are, and will become, because we are the creators. Thank you, Pablo Neruda!; [a.] Edmonton, AB

JACKSON, DANIELA
[pen.] Dani Jackson; [b.] January 30, 1985; Hollywood, CA; [p.] Joni Pitters; [ed.] Grade seven Cedarview Middle School; [occ.] Student; [hon.] Two local writing awards; [pers.] I use writing as a way to express my feelings.; [a.] Nepean

JACKSON, WILLIAM D.
[ed.] Guelph University in Ontario—I am studying my second year of English.; [pers.] I hope to further my education and seek a career relating to social issues in which I can work with others. Although I would like to pursue a future in writing, I feel that the primary benefits of writing are ones of personal satisfaction. My philosophy is: One's sun has no light, unless the self believer can see a sunbeam.; [a.] Weston, ON

JACOBSON, SHIRLEY
[b.] May 20, 1968; El Paso, TX; [p.] John, Virginia DiBella; [m.] Ken Jacobson; November 8, 1992; [ch.] Audrey Katherine Jacobson; [ed.] St. Francis C.H.S., ICS, business school; [hon.] Editor's Choice Award for poetry published in 1997; [oth. writ.] Poem published in The Glow Within anthology, several personal writings; [pers.] Poetry is not only the freedom to express: It gives you the freedom to escape.; [a.] Richmond Hill, ON

JAMES, BONNIE
[b.] December 15, 1984; Burnaby, BC; [p.] Carol James and Brad James; [ed.] Marlborough Elementary School, Harold Bishop Elementary, Frost Road Elementary, Fleetwood Park Secondary School; [occ.] Student; [memb.] JOLT, Counter Attack Club, Student Council, Leadership Program, Days of Our Lives Fan Club, IPF; [hon.] Grade four Roll of Honor for Most Improved Student, SAI EHV Contest, Education in Human Values first place, 1997; [oth. writ.] Articles for school newsletters and newspapers, letter published in TV Guide, winning letter published in local newspaper contest; [pers.] I may only be 12 years old, but I believe that everyone has the right to state their thoughts and be heard and respected by others. I write poems as responses to what I see in life.; [a.] Surrey, BC

JANOSEVIC, MILICA
[b.] April 4, 1980; Belgrade; [p.] Bozidar Janosevic, Rada Janosevic; [ed.] Elementary school and I am attending the third grade of XIII Belgrade Grammar School; [occ.] Student; [hon.] First prize for the most creative short-story; [oth. writ.] I wrote over 200 poems, and I'm working on my novel. I also wrote over 150 stories.; [pers.] "They say that hope is happiness," Byron wrote, and how truthful his words are, because hope is happiness, and when I write, I hope, and writing is the only thing that can make me happy.; [a.] Belgrade, Yugoslavia

JARVIS, STANLEY NORMAN
[b.] 24 April 1939; Alberta; [p.] Louis and Mary Jarvis; [m.] Susan Miller; 16 April 1966; [ch.] Two; [ed.] Second year Malaspina College/University Nanamo, BC; [occ.] Self-employed as "World-Win Enterprises"; [memb.] Loyal Order of Moose; [hon.] Past Deputy Supreme Governor, Loyal Order of Moose for BC; [oth. writ.] Numerous poems for friends and organizations; [pers.] The memory and pain are real and

acceptably exist, yet can be overcome with help, and so I've learned to help people, both health- and income-wise, to enjoy life.; [a.] Ladysmith, BC

JURCOVAN, IOANA
[b.] January 5, 1980; Timisoara; [p.] Dorel Jurcovan and Lia Jurcovan; [ed.] W. Shakespeare High School; [occ.] High school student; [memb.] I was a founding member of the "Help the Orphans" club in Timisoara but gave up due to studies, founding member of the "Shake the Spear News," the high school's newspaper; [oth. writ.] Articles published in school's newspaper (I am one of the founders of this newspaper.); [pers.] "Life is what you make of it" (S. Smilles). That is why I try to live every moment of life by choosing a challenging future job: Journalism. I hope to join an US college and after graduating, volunteer to help people in Asia and Africa.; [a.] Timisoara, Romania

KALEKAR, VIVEK PRABHAKAR
[b.] July 7, 1960; Pune, India; [p.] Prabhakar, Vatsala; [ed.] II Class Mot Exam for Engineers by MMD Mumbai; [occ.] Merchant Navy Engineer; [a.] Pune Maharashtra, India

KANDAVANAM, VINAYAGAR
[pen.] N. Veka; [b.] October 29, 1993; Nunavil, Sri Lanka; [p.] Vinayagar- Sinnammah; [m.] Thavamany; August 20, 1964; [ch.] Varanan Varny; [ed.] B.A. Madras, dip. Ed.; T.C.C.; dip. Teaching of Drama, Sri Lanka; [occ.] Mail Manager/Asst. Receptionist, Upper Canada College, Toronto; [memb.] President, Tamil Writers' Association of Canada, patron of several cultural associations in Canada; [hon.] Many awards for Tamil Literature and Drama; [oth. writ.] Author of eight Tamil poetry books and seven books on literary and social topics; [pers.] Highlights moral values in writing and speeches. Likes Shakespeare in English and Kambar in Tamil.; [a.] Don Mills, Toronto, ON

KELLY, DENNIS
[b.] January 11, 1931; Aruba; [m.] November 16, 1957; [ch.] Three; [ed.] High school; [occ.] Retired; [oth. writ.] An Immigrant's Fond Dream, Claneys Wales, Diana Princess of Wales, Princess Diana, Shillelagh; [a.] ON

KENDRICK, JENNIFER
[b.] September 12, 1982; Wolverhampton, England; [p.] Frank Kendrick and Barbara Kendrick; [ed.] Queen Mary's High School, Walsall, England; [oth. writ.] Several poems, short stories, and various articles published; [pers.] I don't know where it comes from. Anyone can find it if she just opens up her mind.; [a.] Wolverhampton, West Midlands, England

KHAY, SEVENDALINO
[pen.] Shawn Fate; [b.] November 10, 1977; Cambodia; [p.] Khay Khun Heng and Khun Srey Mom; [ed.] Royal George H.S., College Edward, Montpetit, Ecde Polytechnique de Montreal; [occ.] College student, Ecole Polytechnique de Montreal; [hon.] HS Mathematic Award, Pascal Contest, Birles Prize; [oth. writ.] Several poems published in personal web site; [pers.] Fate is an addicted gambler. Mankind will just have to play along and best him.; [a.] St. Hubert, QC

KILANDER, ANGELICA
[b.] March 2, 1982; Solna, Sweden; [p.] Svante Kilander and Lotta Kilander; [ed.] United Nations International School (UNIS) of Hanoi, Sigtunaskolan Humaniska Larovekret (SSHL) in Sweden; [occ.] Student at SSHL, a boarding school in Sweden, tenth grade; [oth. writ.] Several poems published in my former school's literary magazine; [pers.] I love flowers! To me, flowers represent friendship, which is why I write a lot about flowers. Every flower is unique, and so is every friendship. This poem is dedicated to my best friend, Dzung, and my family.; [a.] Sigtuna, Sweden

KILTY, TACIA
[b.] September 14, 1983; St. Vincent; [p.] Heather Kilty; [ed.] I am in grade nine, attending Lakeport Secondary School; [hon.] I've received a lot of sports awards, as well as "Student of the Month" awards.; [pers.] Be nice and have fun. Set goals for yourself, no matter how far-fetched they might be, because you can do everything and anything you put your mind to.; [a.] St. Davids, ON

KITNEY, EVA
[b.] September 14, 1928; Niagara Falls, ON; [p.] Adam and Eve Yost; [m.] Leo Kitney; June 10, 1950; [ch.] Four girls, one boy, "Jamie"; [ed.] High school; [occ.] Deceased August 3, 1997; [memb.] Daughters of Isabella Catholic Women's League; [oth. writ.] During her lifetime, Eva wrote 38 poems to commemorate special occasions for family and friends.; [a.] Niagara Falls, ON

KLASSMANN, LEDA SUZANA
[b.] August 4, 1948; Caxias do Sul, RS; [p.] Lothario I. Klassmann, Olinda C. Klassmann; [m.] Mauro V. Centeno; June 19; 1993; [ch.] Daniel Backes; [ed.] Faculdade de Filosofia, Cienceias E Letras Porto Alegre, RS, Brasil; [occ.] Secretary of Literary; [memb.] Literary Center of S. Leopoldo; [oth. writ.] Articles, chronicles about quotidian life published in local magazines; [pers.] I like to catch the feelings of the people through the way of life and somehow "paint" with words these feelings. Poetry gives us the way of saying things with beauty, love, and emotion. In some ways, poetry has the power to change the world for the better.; [a.] Sao Leopoldo, RS

KNOT, MICHAELA
[pen.] M. Knot; [b.] April 24, 1979; Czech Republic; [p.] Richard and Dagmar Knot; [ed.] First year university; [occ.] Student, future undecided; [pers.] I wish to show the strength or response of the human spirit in its environment.; [a.] Edmonton, AB

KRUSCHWITZ, MONIKA
[pen.] Monika Kruschwitz; [b.] September, 1957; Halifax; [p.] Rolf Meier, Waltrant Meier; [ch.] Elise Duellet; [ed.] Maritime Business College; [occ.] Secretary—Dalhousie University; [pers.] Enjoying the awesome wonders of nature inspires and spellbinds my spirit; this gives me la raison d'etre.; [a.] Dartmouth, NS

LABORDE, PATRICIA GARCIA
[b.] August 25, 1954; Monterey, N.L. Mexico; [p.] Jorge Laborde and Maria Luisa Garcia; [m.] Joaquin Pocurull; October 12, 1985; [ch.] Lerida Sofia and Jaqueline; [occ.] Writer and Corrector (Proofreader); [hon.] Winner in several poetry contests, (local). Third place in Second Marie Claire Literary International Contest (1995) (short stories); [oth. writ.] Several poems, articles, and short stories published in local, national, and international magazines and newspapers. Books: "Angulo Sol", (1982, poetry) published "Ecos de Otra Voz" (1995, poetry) unpublished "Historias para el cafe' y otros milagros" (1996), unpublished short stories.; [a.] Nuevo Leon, Mexico

LACHARITE, TANIS
[pen.] TLC; [b.] February 5, 1929; Pas, MB; [p.] Lawrence and Florence Williamson; [m.] Raymond William; September 22, 1951; [ch.] Jay Patrick, Kimberly Rae, Reid Buchcannon, and Hollis Marion; [ed.] Senior Matriculation Commercial College; [occ.] Retired; [memb.] Royal Oak Golf Club, Capitol City Yacht Club, St. Paul United Church, Post Polio Assoc.; [pers.] For every bit of love one gives—it returns ten fold; not necessary to you but someone you love will receive needed blessings. I have great faith in and honor the human race.; [a.] Sidney, BC

LAING, ALLISON
[pen.] Ally; [b.] 26 December 1963; England; [p.] Murray and Rita Slote, Brian Osborne; [m.] Scott Laing; July 1990; [ch.] Jesse and Jordan; [ed.] Grade twelve and a college grad through night school for Early Childhood Education; [occ.] Own home day care center; [pers.] I have a file folder that I don't go to often, but it's full of "my thoughts in writing" as I like to call them. It helps me release my feelings when I can find the time.; [a.] Pickering, ON

LAMBERT, WILLIAM J.
[b.] William J. Lambert; [b.] December 24, 1919; Camden East, ON; [p.] Winnifred (deceased) and John Lambert; [m.] Evelyn; September 21, 1977; [ch.] Three; [ed.] Very little, eighth grade, Soldier, Farmer, Construction Foreman, Gardener, Propane Operator, and Poet. I have been successful in all walks of this life.; [memb.] War Amps of Canada, Distinguished Member of The National Library of Poetry, Poetry Elite 1985, Public Recognition 1939/45 Canadian Forces, 18 Editor's Choice Awards 1993/97, The National Library of Poetry 20 anthologies USA, one anthology Canada, The International Poetry Hall of Fame Museum on the Internet's World Wide Web; [oth. writ.] The Poet's Corner in a local paper for two years. I have four books of poetry on the market, "Treasured Thoughts" Vol. #I, II, III, IV.; [pers.] My inspirations as swift as the waters. Nature is my education, the best teacher of man. I am a lover of birds, flowers, and all nature around. Now retired, look back on my childhood years and put lifetime thoughts into poems.; [a.] Morton, ON

LAMBRAKIS, AGIS
[b.] August 27, 1966; Cyprus; [p.] Nikos and Irene Lambraki; [ed.] Glyfada H.S., Athens University of Law; [occ.] Lawyer; [oth. writ.] Several poems ready to publish in collection, two scenarios to cinema almost finished, and a theatrical play now writing; [pers.] I have been greatly influenced by all the people that suffer every day with or without reason. I believe that we can make or create with God's help a better life and world.; [a.] Glyfada, Athens, Greece

LANGE, BRIAN ANTHONY
[p.] Mobios, Da True Player; [b.] October 24, 1987; Saratoga, NY; [p.] Brian and Paula Lange; [ed.] In progress at GGCA Budapest; [occ.] Student, Athlete, Musician; [memb.] SG Club, Silhouettes, Bible Speaks Church, GGCA Chess Club; [hon.] Various academic achievements, first place in art contest, Captain of Soccer Team, various trophies; [oth. writ.] "Death," "Time," "Justice," various short stories, lyrics for the band Free Perfect; [pers.] Poetry is just a hobby of mine. My poems are greatly influenced by my father, who is a pastor, and my personal belief in Jesus Christ, who is the only true meaning in life.; [a.] Burnt Hills, NY

LEE, LOIS YEONG
[b.] April 22, 1985; San Francisco, CA; [p.] Rubin K. Lee, Yeong J. Lee; [ed.] Attending middle school, seventh grade, at Seoul International School; [occ.] Student; [oth. writ.] Unite the World (poem), Death (poem), Spring Fever (poem); [pers.] I would like to thank my mother and my language arts teachers, Mr. Browne and Mr. Mitchell, for teaching the best they can for me. Also I would like to thank my family.; [a.] Seoul, Republic of Korea

LEPPER, JUDY
[b.] September 24, 1949, Tatamgouche, Nova Scotia; [p.] Lou and Olla Langille; [m.] John; September 20, 1969; [ch.] Jonathan Andrew, Justin Matthew, Jarvis Daniel, Julie-Ann Olla; [pers.] This poem was written with a very thankful heart. Landmark East School in Wolfville, NS has helped many children with learning difficulties, including my son, Jarvis.; [a.] Tatamagouche, NS

LEWIS, AIMEE ELIZABETH
[b.] 7/8/79, North Bay; [p.] James and Heannine Lewis; [ed.] Temiskaming District Secondary School; [occ.] Student; [pers.] "If you want to figure out the secrets of yourself, all you need to do is to write."; [a.] Temagami, ON

LEWIS, PATRICIA
[pen.] Pat Lewis; [b.] 17 March 1923; St. Louis, MO; [ch.] Ruth, Ken, and Sharon; [ed.] B.A. and M.Ed., McGill University; [memb.] Home and School Association, and too many more; [hon.] Valedictorian at each and every school level, award from Lakeshore Teachers' Association, Phi Beta Kappa, president of too many organizations to list; [oth. writ.] Articles about teaching. Still write column on social issues for Home and School News, Canada.; [pers.] We should all work to end war and hunger in our world.; [a.] Pointe Claire, QC

LIPSMAN, NIC
[b.] January 30, 1982; Tel Aviv, Israel; [p.] Izhak Lipsman, Sofia Lipsman; [ed.] Westmount Collegiate Institute; [occ.] Student; [hon.] Second Place, Provincial Essay Writing Contest—seven awards for academic excellence; [oth. writ.] Various poems, essays, and short stories published in school yearbook and school newsletter; [pers.] I firmly believe that the future will judge us not by our politics or conflicts, rather by the writings of the poets and authors who shaped our world and changed the way we see ourselves.; [a.] Vaughan, ON

LOPEZ, ROCHELLE GANAN
[b.] August 26, 1980, Atimonan, Quezon, Philippines; [p.] Romeo Lopez, Rachel Ganan; [ed.] Atimonan Central School, Leon Guinto Memorial College, Far Eastern University; [occ.] First year Mass Comm. Student; [hon.] Extemporaneous Speaking, Declaimer, Debater; [oth. writ.] Several poems published in high school paper—The Golden Mean; [pers.] Pens are mightier than the sword.; [a.] Manila, Atimonan Quezon, Philippines

LORENTZ, VICTOR JOSEPH
[ed.] Life; [occ.] Human Being; [memb.] Human Race; [pers.] I strive only to know myself.

LOVE, JONATHAN
[b.] September 19, 1974; Calgary, AB; [p.] James Love, Bernice Love; [ed.] B.A. English from University of Calgary LTCL (Licentrate degree from Trinity College, London); [occ.] Speech and Drama Teacher

at Mount Royal College, Calgary; [memb.] The Heebeejeebees, a cappella quartet; [hon.] 1993 Canadian National Speech and Drama Champion, the Dr. Leona Paterson award of recognition, the Outstanding Speech Perfumes Award by the RSTAA; [pers.] Luck, laughs, and fun to all! Thanks to Dr. Seuss and Dr. Pat.; [a.] Calgary, AB

LOVELUCK, ROYSTON
[pen.] Royston Loveluck; [b.] January 9, 1929; Bridgend; [p.] Edward Loveluck, Olive Loveluck; [m.] Meirion Hilda Loveluck; March 24, 1958; [ch.] Helen Margaret, Rosalina Catherine; [ed.] Technical College, Bridgend; University of Science and Technology, Cardiff; [memb.] Member Institution Electrical Engineers, National Trust membership; [oth. writ.] Several poems and articles published in local Church of England magazines; [pers.] Much of my writing reflects my Welsh background and culture. I admire the poets William Wordsworth and Dylan Thomas.; [a.] Chester, Cheshire

MACDOUGALL, BRUCE
[b.] May 29, 1925; Edmonton, AB; [p.] Ray and Phyllis MacDougall; [m.] Isabel MacDougall; September 5, 1953; [ch.] Bruce, Moira, Paul, Jane, Nancy; [ed.] B.A., L.L.B., M.D.W. D.D.; [occ.] Retired; [memb.] Writers Union Canada; [hon.] Doctor of Divinity Huntington, University Sudbury, ON; [oth. writ.] Hurrah for the Process (word), Rejoice in the Lord, (Abingdon), Time to Travel Light (United Church of Canada); [a.] Southampton, ON

MACKAY, BARBARA LYNN YOUNG
[pen.] "B", Bub, Barbie; [b.] April 16, 1960; Hamilton, ON; [p.] Shirley H. Seip, William J. Young; [m.] William Alexander Mackay; August 5, 1989; [ed.] Sherwood Secondary School, Mohawk and Sheridan College, Honours; [occ.] Sales Rep. Merch., Kimberly Clark, Inc.; [memb.] Glendale Golf and Curling Club, Christ Church Unity; [hon.] C.A.A.T. Scholarship Bursary College Bus. Admin., Provincial Curling Champion 1993 and 1997; [pers.] Don't quit before the miracle.; [a.] Grimsby Beach, ON

MADHOSINGH, ROBERT
[b.] September 23, 1941; Trinidad and Tobago; [p.] Deceased; [m.] Divorced; 1974; [ch.] Robert, Terrence, Anthony; [ed.] B.Sc. University of Winnipeg, B.Ed. University of Manitoba; [occ.] Physics Teacher; [memb.] Manitoba Association of Science Teachers, Manitoba Association of Physics Teachers, Manitoba Track and Field Association; [hon.] Editor's Choice Award 1997, 1996 International Poet of Merit 1997; [oth. writ.] Heartland Voice—Winnipeg Free Press 1995, Beneath the Harvest Moon 1996, A Treasured Token 1997, articles in Winnipeg Free Press, Toronto Star, Trinidad Guardian; [pers.] It is through denial of self and suffering with the poor and infirm that we are brought closer to the divine, and it is then that we are inspired to bring to light the plight of the oppressed on our spaceship Earth.; [a.] Winnipeg, MB

MAGILL, LIZA
[pen.] Liza Christopher, Velvet Kitten; [b.] November 8, 1970; [ch.] Ryan Matthew Magill; [pers.] If I had the opportunity to change one thing in my life, I would change nothing. I believe that everything that has happened in my life has brought me to this very point, which is right where I need to be.; [a.] Ontario

MAHARAJ, JENNIFER KAMINI
[b.] September 16, 1975; [p.] Arun Maharaj and Christina Maharaj; [oth. writ.] I wrote my first poem at the age of seven and ever since then it has become my favorite pastime. As I read through all of my poems, I've noticed that they have become more sophisticated; they have a lot more depth and every one has become special to me. Each poem describes a certain time in my life or an experience. I've always found it easier to express the way I feel through a poem rather then to talk to someone about it.; [pers.] I hope to pursue a professional career in creative writing and hope that my work would be enjoyable for others to read, and also that my experiences would show them that everyone is the same, it's just that sometimes we find ourselves in different situations. The key is turning your negatives into positives through something that you love to do and you will not stop on that road to success. One God, one love, one life!; [a.] Toronto, ON

MALLOV, IAN
[b.] 17 May 1984; Syracuse, NY; [p.] Jon Mallov and Ruth Faulkner; [ed.] Grade eight, Truro Junior High School; [occ.] Student; [memb.] Junior High School Band; [oth. writ.] Poem published in local paper, many unpublished poems and short stories, unpublished children's stories; [pers.] I have wanted to be a writer ever since 1993, when I was nine.; [a.] Truro, NS

MANGANO, MARISSA
[pen.] Marissa; [b.] August 2, 1981; Hamilton; [p.] Joe and Mirella Mangano; [ed.] Attending Cardinal Heights Middle School, grade seven; [hon.] Scholarship Award from Cardinal Heights School, soccer awards and trophies; [a.] Hamilton, ON

MARIJANAN, C.B.
[pen.] Christian Benjamin; [b.] February 16, 1955; Ommen, Overijssel, Netherlands; [p.] B. Marijanan, F.H. Marijanan; [ch.] Francina, Ismaël Joshua; [ed.] Primary school, Majo and Havo, two years teacher's school for History and Dutch language, most of all I have made self studies. Autodidact; [occ.] Singer, but at this moment unemployed. I have no contract.; [hon.] Several poetry performances and a publication in local magazine with Dutch poems; [oth. writ.] Songwriting—English, short stories in Dutch, poems in Dutch; [pers.] In my writing I hope to strive for a better world with love, honesty, respect, and understanding for everyone. Therefore we need a lot of imagination and our own free will to be good.; [a.] Assen, Drenthe

MARTIN, WILFRED J.
[b.] January 16, 1936; Kitchener, ON; [p.] Israel Martin and Carrie Martin; [m.] Sylvia Stockwood; November 15, 1962; [ch.] Wilfred, Carolyn, David, Daryl; [ed.] High school, self-taught beyond that; [occ.] Retired Airline Worker (telecommunications), currently amateur wood carver; [oth. writ.] Many unpublished poems, used for family occasions, etc. Most significant is 85-verse poem, "My Canada," depicting the land I love.; [pers.] I have a great love for the outdoors and the world around me, always attempting to see beauty where many people see only the ordinary and the mundane. Favorite poet is E.J. Pratt.; [a.] Port Coquitlam, BC

MASON, DAVID RICHARD
[pen.] Dai Mason; [b.] January 12, 1965; Porthcawl, South Wales; [p.] Richard S. Mason, Pearl, M. Ross; [ed.] B.A. (Hoas) Theatre degree (Majoring in writing stage plays, film, radio, and television), HNC in Management (a Scottism vocational qualification); [occ.] Caring for terminally ill person, working on redrafting, re-writing plays; after serving nine years in

the Royal Air Force as an Electronic Technician working on airborne fitted vocation . . . and so went to study at Rose Bruford College of Speech and Drama, working with actors, directors and technical people to develop my writing from the original idea to performance. Since leaving college, I have been working on my professional portfolio.; [oth. writ.] Listening for the Grasshopper (radio play), Yesterday's Child (epic style play), The Promise of a Rainbow (stage play), Divine Justice (musical comedy), Flowers in the Wind (film script), plus other plays for television and various poems; [pers.] Seek first the kingdom of God and all these things shall come to you. In the Christian faith, the way should be narrow, not the people. It is a faith of love and forgiveness, not judgement, and as a playwright I seek to help people see things from another perspective.; [a.] Beckenham, England

MASON, PAUL
[b.] May 27, 1944; Toronto, ON; [p.] Howard (Bud) and Margaret Mason; [m.] Carol; June 26, 1976; [ch.] Bonnie and Jason; [occ.] Self-employed; [pers.] Thanks to our two grandchildren, Ashley and Victoria, my wife and I have been blessed beyond words.; [a.] Midhurst, ON

MASSOUD, MARY M. F.
[b.] Cairo, Egypt; [p.] Dr. Farid Massoud, Mrs. Lily Massoud; [ed.] B.A. Honors in Eng. Lit., Cairo University, M.A. Eng. and Comparative Lit., Columbia University, NYC, USA, M.R.E. (emphasis on drama), Union Theological Seminary, NYC, USA, Ph.D. Lit. in English Lit., Air Shams U., Cairo, Egypt; [occ.] University Professor of English and Comparative Lit., Air Shams U., Cairo, Egypt; [memb.] On the Executive Committee of IASIL (International Association for the Study of Irish Literatures); Member of IBI (International Biographical Institute) Cambridge, UK; and member of ALTA (Association of Literary Translators of America); [hon.] Awarded the Dorothy Cadbury Fellowship to lecture of Selly Oak in Birmingham, England in 1977-78; Fulbright Scholar lecturing at the University of Utah, Salt Lake City, 1980-81; Visiting Prof. at the University of Indiana in PA, USA in 1983-84, and again in 1991-92; won the Air Shams Award for the best literature work of the year in 1997; [oth. writ.] Several poems published in local magazines, 80 plays (mostly in Arabic), one play, Our Father, translated into ten languages, author of the book Translate to Communicate (Chicago: David C. Cook); editor of Literary Inter-relations (Gerrards Cross: Colin Smythe, 1996); author of numerous critical works in the field of American, English, and Anglo-Irish literature; [pers.] The good that I can do, let me do it today, for tomorrow may be too late.; [a.] Cairo, Egypt

MASUDA, ALLAN
[b.] August 5, 1975; Manila, Philippines; [p.] Alfonso Masuda, Milagros Masuda; [ed.] B.S. Physical Therapy, University of Santo Tomas; [occ.] Physical Therapist; [memb.] Philippine Physical Therapy Association, University of St. Tomas Alumni Association, University of St. Tomas Physical Therapy Alumni Association; [hon.] Second Place—poetry (Filipino division), Ustetita Awards for Literature for the collection "Papi Lab"; [oth. writ.] Several collections of poems written in English and Filipino (I Love in Silence, Gay Blues, Sentiments, Papi Lab, Pira-pirasong Pagsuyo, Biyernes nang Minsang Tumilapon ang Aking Pag-iisip at iba pang tula); [a.] Kalookan City, Philippines

MATHEW, MUNDANKURIAN MATHUNNY
[pen.] Wordsmith, M. Mathew; [b.] August 12, 1936; Trichur, India; [p.] Mathunny and Kunjanamma Mathunny; [m.] Philo Mathew; May 3, 1965; [ch.] Six children: five daughters and one son; [ed.] National Diploma in Commerce, Co-op College Trichur; [ed.] Higher diploma in Commerce Co-operative Training, higher secondary: St. Thomas College; [occ.] No job (retired Bank Manager); [memb.] No memberships in Canada; [hon.] Not yet received in Canada; [oth. writ.] "Praise the Lord" is my first poem; [pers.] I am a retired bank manager from India. I retired on 31 August 1996 from The South Indian Bank Ltd., Trivandrum, Kerala, India. I have 38 and odd years service with this bank, out of which 26 years as an officer, 21 years as manager. My eldest four daughters are post-graduates and all of them married.; [a.] Surrey, BC

MATHEW, TAKWI
[b.] September 21, 1965; Nkwen-Bamenda; [ed.] Catholic school Bayelle-Nkwen, Government Bilingual Secondary School, Bamenda, Nacho High School, Bamenda, University of Yaounde; [occ.] Administrative Assistant, O' Level Technical G.CE, Cameroon G.C.E. Board; [oth. writ.] A plethora of unpublished poems; [pers.] The innate desire in making a positive difference in society through the pen, is the ultimate of he who succinctly dares; for man in man, not man on man, is man.; [a.] Bamenda, North-West

MAZURIK, DOROTHY
[pen.] Gran'ma Dorothy; [b.] February 28, 1928; Winnipeg; [p.] Oliver and Beatrice Lewis; [m.] Joseph Mazurik (deceased); May 4, 1946; [ch.] Gwendoline Ruth, Gregory Kenneth and Paul Joseph; [occ.] Retired School Secretary; [memb.] Member of the Parish of St. Timothy, St. Vital Legion #16; [hon.] Retirement celebration, and having some of my poems published in "The Path Not Taken" and "Best Poems of the '90s"; [oth. writ.] Mary and Me, The Eyes of a Child, The Many Faces of God, God's Love, Faith, and Spring; [pers.] To really come to appreciate nature, take a stroll with a small child and just see what you learn!; [a.] Winnipeg, MB

MCCARTNEY, DONALD M.
[b.] September 16, 1946; Nassau, Bahamas; [p.] Moreina Turner/William McCartney; [m.] Betty L. McCartney; August 21, 1968; [ch.] Donette and Dawn McCartney; [ed.] Teacher's Certificate—Bahamas, Dip. Ed. (equivalent)—Univ. of South Carolina Certificate (advanced), Management and M.Sc. Ed. University of Miami; [occ.] Former Educator, Deputy Chief Passport Officer, Ministry of Foreign Affairs; [memb.] Member of the Association for Supervision and Curriculum Development. Served as Chairman of National Advisory Committee to Government of the Commonwealth of the Bahamas on Industrial, Vocational, and Technical Education and Training; [hon.] Able Toastmaster awards and certificates for public speaking. Among the 10 Best Dressed male awards 1984 and 1985. Interviewed on UN Radio and featured as personality of the month March, 1990. Presented lead paper on "The Global Refugee Issue" at University of Nebraska's James E. Smith's Mid-West Conference on World Affairs. Nominated for Poet of the Year—1997. Awarded Poet of Merit Medallion—1997; [oth. writ.] Presently working on a manuscript of 17 poems to be published some time in the future. Also I am a columnist for the Community Journal, a local newspaper. Produce commentary for local radio

station 96.1 F.M.; [pers.] To those of us who have been given much of the bounties of the earth, a great deal is expected from us. We must give in the measure we hope to receive.; [a.] Freeport, Grand Bahama

MCGEE, DEBRA
[pen.] Debra McGee; [b.] April 29, 1956; Toronto, ON [p.] Aluster and Betty Keith; [m.] William McGee; [ch.] Tyler Keith McGee; [ed.] Ryerson Polytechnical University, Marketing Management Seneca College, Business; [occ.] Consultant/Writer for small business (entrepreneurs); [pers.] My poems reflect my belief that we can change our lives by changing our perceptions and reconnecting with our true spiritual essence.; [a.] Toronto, ON

MCGINN, RONNIE
[b.] February 7, 1943; Cork, Ireland; [p.] Jim and Pansy; [m.] Mary; September 8, 1966; [ch.] Juni, Diedre, Orla, Siobhian, Mavei; [ed.] New Bridge College, Kildare, Ireland; [occ.] Manger Dixies Showband; [oth. writ.] Song poem published in local papers, and also in The National Library of Poetry; [a.] Cork, Ireland

MCGOVERN, MIKE
[b.] May 8, 1979; Kingston, ON; [p.] Ed and Ann McGovern; [ed.] Grade 12; [occ.] Apprentice Electrician; [pers.] I like learning about dinosaurs in my spare time, and I often write poems that poke gentle fun at these Mesozoic "monsters." I am likewise captivated by time travel machines, and enjoy reading stories about them.; [a.] Cold Lake, AB

MCGUIGAN, KELLY
[b.] October 17, 1965, Montague, Canada; [p.] David and Joan McGuigan; [ed.] Montague Regional High, Holland College; [occ.] Casino Cashier; [oth. writ.] This is my first publication.; [pers.] I've just recently begun writing. I try to write from the heart and speak about issues which touch my own heart.; [a.] Montague, PEI

MCGUIRE, LOIS
[b.] April 13, 1933; Rob Roy, ON; [p.] Harry and Delle Bristow (deceased); [m.] Walter McGuire; September 15, 1956; [ch.] Michael and Leana; [ed.] Secondary diploma, Registered Nurse, Nursing Management; [oth. writ.] "My Twin" is the first poem I have published or submitted. I have written humorous anecdotal poems and short stories for retirement farewell parties for personnel in the medical field.; [pers.] Embrace all of life it's beauty, pulse, and song, and spirit will merge in muted harmony here, where we each belong.; [a.] Collingwood, ON

MCINTOSH, DAPHNE JOHNSON
[b.] August 6, 1966; Nassau, Bahamas; [p.] William Johnson, Sheila Johnson; [m.] Alcott McIntosh; February 27, 1988; [ch.] Ashley Simone, Jenay Tenille; [ed.] B.H.T.C, NAS. Bahamas, LA, Sorbonne University, Paris, France, The National University of Mexico, Mexico City, Mexico; [occ.] Restaurant Owner; [oth. writ.] "The Young Reader," a children's book; [pers.] I strive to provoke cultural awareness and to capture a realistic point of view, often with an idealistic edge.; [a.] Nassau, Bahamas

MCISAAC, KENNETH
[pen.] Ken; [b.] November 27, 1963; New Waterford, NS; [p.] Andrew and Florence McIsaac; [m.] Linda McIsaac; August 14, 1993; [ch.] One; [ed.] Graduated high school in Sydney, NS; [memb.] President of a Toronto-based Dart League; Queen Street Dart Rookies; [hon.] Dart Championships; [oth. writ.] I currently have an invention in writing but have no way of fulfilling because of funding.; [pers.] I have never been acknowledged for anything before. I am excited because this is the first.; [a.] Toronto, ON

MCNAMARA-COMEAU, JANETTE
[b.] March 31, 1962; Brandon, MB; [p.] Edith McNamara (June 22/21-February 4, 1996), Allan Charles McNamara; [m.] Michael P. Comeau; February 18, 1995; [ch.] Philip Alexander ('89), Jenna Noelle ('91); [ed.] OSSGD; [occ.] Domestic Engineer/ Pharmacy Technician; [memb.] I am a Beaver Leader (Sunshine) with Scout Canada; [oth. writ.] "You Will Be" published in Fields of Gold, "My Last Goodbye" published in The Glow Within. Poems published in Hudson Village Voice. I have made 3 poems into bookmarks (You Will Be, Your Garden, A Mother's Love) and they are being sold in the Village Bookshop with proceeds going to the Canadian Cancer Society in memory of Edith Joan McNamara, my mom whom I miss very much and who has been an inspiration to me my whole life. My family has also been source of inspiration.; [a.] St. Lazare, QC

MEANEY, LYNN L.
[b.] June 12, 1950; Oshawa, ON; [p.] Norm and Carrie Gammon; [m.] Glenn J. Meaney; August 14, 1990; [a.] Waterloo, ON

MEDERACKE, HRILINA TAGORE
[pen.] Hrilina Tagore-Mederacke; [b.] September 14, 1945; Calcutta, India; [p.] Sandaya Tagore, P.K. Tagore; [m.] Harald Kurt Medracke; January 20, 1993; [ch.] Alina, Rejoy, Ronnie; [ed.] Loreto House, Calcutta, India, Loreto College, Calcutta, India; [occ.] Managing Director, Firma Mederacke; [hon.] For music, dance, painting and other artwork, drama, etc.; [oth. writ.] Several poems; [pers.] Life is a dream.; [a.] Toronto, ON

MELLON, SALLY ALAINA
[pen.] Sally Alaina Mellon; [b.] February 29, 1984; Brockville, ON; [p.] Dana and Sharon Mellon; [ed.] Attending high school in Perth, ON, (Perth and District Collegiate Institute); [memb.] Perth Athletic Centre; [hon.] Received a scholarship after attending a mini-course in poetry at Carleton University, ON, Science, English, Best All-Around Student Awards at North Elmsley Public School, Public Speaking Award, 1997, Perth, ON; [oth. writ.] Other personal writings; [pers.] Through my poetry, I strive to express my innermost thoughts and feelings, from every facet of myself.; [a.] Smiths Falls, ON

MEREDITH, THOMAS MUIR
[b.] 19 July, 1947; Vancouver; [m.] Laurel; [ch.] Paul, Ashley, Jamie; [ed.] B.A., Certificate of Education, Pre-masters, at the University of Manitoba; [occ.] Director of Extension Studies at Collingwood School; [oth. writ.] "Saskatota" (a major simulation game based on Canadian separation) published by University of Manitoba, "Puck McMurphy" —short story contest winner; [pers.] Life is to be lived.; [a.] North Vancouver, BC

MICHALOSKI, MICHELLE
[b.] July 18, 1969, Citilliwack, BC; [p.] Mike and Donna Michaloski; [ed.] General Arts/Mount Royal College; [occ.] Sales Representative: Konica Canada/ Singer: TLO(Tong Louie Orchestra); [oth. writ.] Several poems published in local newspaper; "Let it

Rain" published in A Treasured Token; [pers.] I reflect mostly on relationships or lessons learned in life, for however painful they may be, they make us wiser and kinder people.; [a.] Chilliwack, BC

MILLER, JANINE
[b.] August 19, 1981; Bracebridge, ON; [p.] Douglas and Janice Miller; [ed.] Grade ten; [occ.] In high school; [memb.] Air Cadets, four years; [hon.] Corporal in Air Cadets for two years; [pers.] Oldest of three children, one sister and one brother, I write this way because it is my view of society today.; [a.] Parry Sound, ON

MILLER, SANDRA
[b.] January 13, 1981; Scarborough, ON; [ed.] Grade 11 student at Msgr. Paul Dwyer C.H.S; [hon.] Swimming awards; [oth. writ.] None published. I just write for fun.; [pers.] I believe that everyone has a guardian angel sitting on her shoulder. Mine's my good friend who helps me through the toughest times.; [a.] Oshawa, ON

MIZGALEWICZ, MAGDA
[b.] February 6, 1983; Krakow; Poland; [p.] Anna and Peter Mizgalewicz; [ed.] Primary school; [occ.] Student; [hon.] Student of Excellence 1995; [pers.] After coming to Canada in 1989, I realized that poetry is greatly underestimated. I wish to change that.; [a.] Oakville, ON

MOHANAN, P. K.
[b.] 19 November 1948; Kerala, India; [p.] P.U. Krishnan, Karthikeyani; [m.] Sukla Devi (43); [ed.] December 1977; [ch.] Dhritiman Kumar, 14; [ed.] Pre-university from Pandu College (Gauhati University), Assam, India; [occ.] Serving in Northeast Frontier Railway as Stenographer; [memb.] Life member of the Poetry Society (India), L-67/A Malviya Nagar, New Delhi—100 001, India; [hon.] Awarded first prize while in college for composing poems in college competition; [oth. writ.] "Love Lyrics" —a book of romantic poems accepted by state governments of Assam, Mizoram, and Kerala, and they have purchased 40, nine, and two copies respectively. Poem "Fluttering Wings" was composed on December 17, 1996 and poem "Desert" on February 15, 1996, both at Guwahati—781 012.; [pers.] Started composing poems from 1974. Born in a middle class family. Humble birth and bringing up. Father—landlord turned into pauper.; [a.] Guwahati, Assam, India

MONARENG, MARTIN P.
[pen.] Cornerstone; [b.] 30/6/47, Johannesburg; [p.] Monamere Simon; Queen Mary; [m.] Camelia Alzina; 8/5/90; [ch.] Maria, Lerato, Tumi, Jacob, Monare, Diane; [ed.] Matric; [occ.] Clerk, Poet, Author, Sangoma, Spiritualist Counselor with Crisis Centre; [memb.] National Library of Poetry, International Society of Poets, National Assoc. for Poetry Therapy, Pen International, Christian Apostolic Church in Zion, Musicians Union of South Africa; [hon.] Editor's Choice Award, International Poet of Merit Plaque, International Poet of Merit Medallion (ISP); [oth. writ.] "Breakthrough" —novel, short stories—That's Life, Don't Look Back, Hate the Love, Last Will and Testament, collection of poetry, some published in magazines and newspapers; [pers.] Life is similar to a snake, enticing, meandering and poisonous, dangerous if not treated delicately!; [a.] Johannesburg, Gauteng, South Africa

MOODIE, SHARON C.
[b.] November 8, 1967; Jamaica; [p.] Norma and Vernal Moodie; [ed.] Bathurst Heights S.S., Canada, Humbe College, Canada, Ardenne High School, Jamaica; [occ.] RPN (Support Care World); [pers.] "Words fitly spoken are like apples of gold in pitchers of silver," (taken from the Bible—I live by this biblical statement).; [a.] Malton, ON

MOORE, LENNIS
[pen.] Lenny Moore, Len Moore; [b.] August 7, 1942; Jamaica, West Indies; [ed.] Buff Bay Elem. School, Kingston Tech High School, Franklin Academy (USA), Devry Institute (Canada); [occ.] Private Peace Officer and Ind. Music Producer (part-time); [memb.] Songwriters Association of Canada—Society of Composers, Authors, and Music Publishers of Canada (Socan), Jamaican-Canadian Association; [oth. writ.] Freedom and Love (Author Music, 1973) Dream of a Lifetime, recent release on CD, Under the Moonlight (Ind) unpublished book in print—songs around Christmas (original songs—25) due in 1998; [pers.] I can always do better.; [a.] Toronto, ON

MOORE, MARY
[pen.] Mary "Em"; [b.] October 6, 1917; Harrow, England; [p.] Mr. and Mrs. A. Shervington; [m.] Ronald G. Moore (deceased); December 16, 1951 (second marriage); [ch.] Two—Roger and Philip; [ed.] High school senior, Oxford, diploma, and university—Trinity College Dublin, M.A. in Child Psychology; [occ.] Widow; [hon.] Nothing for writing M.A. in Child Psychology, lots of trophies for tennis but did not make Wimbledon, but I did officiate cousin of Donald Budge—great American tennis ace in the 1930s and 40s; [oth. writ.] Book poems titled "Some Verse" by Mary Moore and Friends. I am writing a biography called "One of Ten," being one of ten children, born during WWI.; [pers.] I live alone, quietly but fairly happily and content. I am a great-grandmother three times. I have played a lot of tennis and am still trying to play a little.; [a.] Scaborough, ON

MOORMAN, MYRA G.
[b.] August 31, 1922; Major Saskatchewan; [p.] Jim McCulloch, Mary O'keefe McCuloch; [m.] John Moorman (deceased); [ch.] Jim, Janet, Carol, Bob, Patricia; [oth. writ.] Many, including children's stories for personal use of eight grandchildren and seven, soon to be eight, great-grandchildren.; [pers.] God blesses and inspires me daily.; [a.] Abbotsford, BC

MORHART, DONNA
[pen.] Donacale; [b.] November 6, 1958; Regina, SK; [p.] Elvin, Lillian Cale; [m.] Randy Morhart; August 13, 1983; [ch.] Brianna, Heidi; [ed.] B.F.A. undergraduate, 1998, University of Regina, Maj. Ceramics, Multimedia; [occ.] Freelance Artist; [pers.] Some inhibitions become useful when deciding what to do with our inventions.; [a.] Regina, SK

MORRALL, BARRY
[b.] June 3, 1944; Auckland, New Zealand; [p.] John Morrall; [m.] Joyce Morrall; [ed.] Orewa District College; [occ.] Advertising Script Writer; [m.] NZ Poetry Society, Inc., NZ Japan Society; [oth. writ.] Wellington Hills, Wellington Skies, Haiku included in The Fist New Zealand Haiku Anthology, Haiku, Poems for a TV Age; [pers.] My celebration is my life: PS—your spring is our autumn.; [a.] Palmerston North, New Zealand

MOSER, JANICE
[b.] August 17, 1982; Sheet Harbour; [p.] Angus and Beth Moser; [ed.] Presently in grade ten; [occ.] Student at Duncan McMillan High School; [oth. writ.] Has

a collection of 68 poems to which I am adding on a regular basis.; [a.] Sheet Harbour, NS

MOTAZE, EMILIENNE
[b.] February 25, 1969; Yaounde; [p.] Dr. M. Motaze and Dra. Motaze; [occ.] Post-graduate Student; Writer, Customer Relations Officer; [oth. writ.] I have a collection of poems to my name, and have been represented on greeting cards, in anthologies, and in magazines.; [pers.] I believe that if we can all have the courage and humanity to allow God in our lives, our world can indeed be a better place.; [a.] Akwa Ibom State, Nigeria

MOYER, BARBARA
[b.] March 19, 1931; Thunder Bay, ON; [p.] Mr. and Mrs. C. Partington; [m.] William Moyer; [ch.] Gary, Rick, Jo-Anne, Jeff, Cathy; [ed.] Daniel McIntyre College, plus career in music field; [occ.] Retired with my poetry; [memb.] The Royal Canadian Legion; [hon.] An Editor's Choice Award in 1994 and 1997 with The National Library of Poetry. Also, third prize award in the North American Open Poetry Competition from The National Library of Poetry.; [oth. writ.] Published poetry in local magazines, as well as short stories; [pers.] Poetry is a rich, long-lasting bloom, graceful and delicate-like an orchid . . . it has distinction.; [a.] Winnipeg, MB

MYRE, SONIA
[b.] 05 April 1975; Hawkesbury, ON; [p.] Monique Lalonde, Francis Myre; [ed.] University of Ottawa, Department of Psychology (Honors); [occ.] Student; [oth. writ.] Several unpublished poems; [pers.] One should explore and embrace one's dark side.; [a.] Ottawa, ON

NEIL, JODY LYNN
[b.] April 6, 1984; Edmonton, AB; [p.] William Neil and Trudie Neil; [ed.] Attending Boyle School, currently in grade eight.

NETHERCOTT, ANNE
[pen.] Anne's Creations; [b.] March 29, 1921; Glenella, MB; [m.] George; November 29, 1952; [ed.] Grade 12; [memb.] Lioness Church Choir; [hon.] Implementation of social and public welfare, Bank of Montreal; [a.] West Lorne, ON

NEU, ELWIN
[b.] October 3, 1961; Kitchener; [p.] Herbert Neu, Erna Neu; [m.] Wendy Neu; September 18, 1993; [ed.] Eastwood Collegiate Institute (grade 12 diploma), George Brown College (Major Appliance Service program); [occ.] Major Appliance Technician; [hon.] Proficiency award in accounting for the highest overall average in Major Appliance Program; [a.] Campbellville, ON

NEUMANN, MELISSA
[b.] July 9, 1982; Calgary, AB; [p.] Helmut Neumann, Angie Neumann; [pers.] To succeed in life you have to succeed in yourself.; [a.] Calgary, AB

NICHOL, GLEN
[pen.] Glen Nichol; [b.] April 18, 1938; Winnipeg, MB; [p.] Sam and Frances Nichol; [m.] Lynn Nichol; August 22, 1970; [ch.] One daughter, Colleen 23, teaching in Taiwan; [ed.] Grade XI University Entrance Course, Diploma Course in Agriculture, University of Manitoba ('59); [occ.] Soils Technician, White Mud Conservation District, Neepawa, MB, ROJ ITO; [memb.] Member of a sweat lodge circle and honorary member of Sandy Bay Ojibway First Nation, Sandy Bay Res., MB; [hon.] Place three times in men's golden age 50 and over "grass-fancy" category Pow-Wow dancing, Connecticut; [oth. writ.] A dozen poems and the first chapter of a book about a young farmer and his brother on the prairie (fiction); [pers.] To create sufficient vision in other people's lives to cause them to believe in themselves and achieve the goals to which they aspire.; [a.] Riding Mountain, MB

NIELSEN, ELIZABETH BOGART
[pen.] Betty Bogart; [b.] USA; [p.] M. Westerbury; [m.] Jack Turgeon; March 28, 1968; [ch.] Niels L. Nielsen; [ed.] NYU, B.A. in English and History, Drama at New School, etc.; [occ.] Editor on newspapers; [memb.] Drama groups in NYC; [hon.] Nominal poetry prize, journalism 1980, swimming—gold and bronze medals, etc.; [oth. writ.] Many newspaper columns every week on local papers and poetry columns, Star TV scripts and stage plays, three produced in NYC and Chicago; [pers.] Having worked for US War Dept. in Italy for three years and also in hospitals full of war veterans where I became an anti-war advocate of peace, and thus am very interested in your fine anti-war efforts.; [a.] Portimao, Portugal

NOBLE, SARA
[b.] October 11, 1979; Windsor, ON; [p.] Ralph and Sarina Noble; [pers.] Believe in yourself, because no one else will tell you the truth.; [a.] Brampton, ON

NOORDYK, SUSANNE
[b.] May 1, 1942; London, ON; [p.] John and Edith Taylor; [m.] William Campbell; [ch.] Jacob, Anne, Irene, Billy, and Willy; [ed.] Grade 12 (OSSGD); [occ.] Housewife; [memb.] Hamilton Society of Model Engineers (O Scale Train Club); [hon.] Member of the Year, Skyway Bluegrass Club; [oth. writ.] Nonsense, verse, children's stories, other poetry, including haiku; [pers.] To live in this world, respecting all humankind, and to live in harmony with nature, Mother Earth.; [a.] Hamilton, ON

NORDRIK, TONI
[b.] December 4, 1978; Bergen, Norway; [p.] Anne-Lise and Helgo Nordrik; [ed.] High school; [occ.] Waitress in a cafe; [pers.] In some of my poems there's a reflection of me, and I think that poetry is a beautiful way of expressing your feelings. I want to say thank you for my family's support. Peace to all my friends.; [a.] Bergen, Norway

NORTON, KAREN
[pen.] Karen Norton; [b.] August 31, 1986; London, ON; [p.] Steven Norton and Jacinthe Norton; [ed.] Grade six primary school; [occ.] Student; [oth. writ.] Poems: Christmas is Coming, My House, It's the Dinosaurs' Time; [pers.] Always do your best at everything you do. Concentrate in things you enjoy.; [a.] London, ON

ODEDE, JOHN
[pen.] John; [b.] January 12, 1978; Bungoma, Kenya; [p.] C.A. Odede, Mary Odede; [ed.] KCSE—1996; [occ.] To proceed to the Local University 1998; [oth. writ.] Several poems published in the local newspaper; [pers.] Life gives hope to dreamless men who can't cope or attain success.; [a.] Nairobi, Kenya

OKEKE, IHEANYI
[b.] July 14, 1972, Unuahia, Abia St., Nigeria; [p.] Ebere Okeke and Cecilia Okeke; [ed.] Abia State University—Uturu, Abia State, Nigeria; [oth. writ.] Several unpublished poems—I am in the process of

compiling them.; [pers] I try to reflect the beauty of our environment in my writings, and also my writings reflect my particular mood. I've been greatly influenced by many African writers, but Wole Soyinka is someone I respect much. He is a genius who says so little but means so much, at times he's difficult to understand.; [a.] Owerri, Imo, Nigeria

PABALAN, OFELIA FRANCISCO
[b.] 7 November 1956; Kalookan City, Philippines; [p.] Moises Francisco, Avelina Francisco; [m.] Noel Pabalan; [ch.] Camille Pabalan; [ed.] M.Sc. Botany, University of Toronto; [pers.] This poem is for my late parents whose teachings will always guide me. My father's poetic talent had a great influence on my writing.

PAGE, EDWARD JOHN
[b.] September 12, 1936; Dartmouth, NS; [p.] Walter and Frances Page; [m.] Adele Florence; July 31, 1965; [ed.] Bachelor of Arts (Sociology) University of Western Ontario (UWO), University Extension Courses, several military professional development courses; [occ.] Retired Military Officer. Part-time Ready Reserve, private business ventures; [memb.] Chamber of Commerce, Royal Canadian Military Institute, Royal Canadian Military Association, Regiment, Poets Reading Circle, Army Cadet League of Canada; [hon.] Canadian Forces Decoration, The Queen's Silver Jubilee Medal, United Nations Medal, United Nations Supervisory Organization Middle East Medal; [oth. writ.] An autobiographic book (in draft), hundreds of unpublished poems, one poem published in Regimental History, entitled: A Tribute to a Fallen Comrade; [pers.] I have been influence by Shakespeare, Jonathan Swift, and so many others (Shelly, Tennyson, Whitman, Frost, Thoreau, etc.). Poetry comes from my heart and as the spirit moves me (for the most part).; [a.] Pickering, ON

PALMER, JEFFREY D.
[pen.] J.D. Palmer; [b.] June 10, 1970; Edmonton, AB; [p.] Don and Suzanne; [ed.] Graduate of San Diego Golf Academy 1991; [occ.] Golf Professional; [memb.] C.P.G.A., Golf Professionals Association; [oth. writ.] Personal journal, collection of poems and essays; [pers.] Strive to find understanding of my fellow man and myself through creative writing.; [a.] Victoria, BC

PALOMINO, DENISE
[pen.] Judy; [b.] December 1, 1969; Old Harbour; [p.] Delores Palomino; [ed.] Old Harbour Primary, Old Harbour Secondary; [occ.] Writer; [oth. writ.] Short stories, songs, articles in local newspaper, poems, etc.; [pers.] I'm a rastafarian for the last twelve years. My greatest desire is to excel as far as writing goes. Writing is my everything!; [a.] Jamaica, West Indies

PAPAGEORGIOU, ANASTASIA
[pen.] Anastasia Fardella; [b.] September 16, 1970; Montreal, QC; [p.] Frank Papageorgiou, Chryssa Fardella; [ed.] Lindsay Papageorgiou, Chryssa Fardella; [ed.] Lindsay Place High School, John Abbott College, graduated with a B.A. from Concordia University in Montreal; [memb.] Greek Orthodox Community of West Island, Distinguished Member of the International Society of Poets; [hon.] Has received several invitations to be published for her other writings.; [oth. writ.] Several poems have been published by The National Library of Poetry. "People, A Collection of Poetry" will soon be published. Currently working on a short story collection entitled "Eulogies."; [pers.] I hope my writing reflects honesty, or even maybe some form of truth. Perhaps it will expose my truth or reveal someone else's.; [a.] D.D.O., QC

PARUCHA, ALEJO G., JR.
[pen.] Galahad Parucha; [p.] Victoria and Alejo P. Parucha, Sr.; [m.] Juanita S. Supnet; [ch.] Joseph, Janette, Jonathan; [ed.] Bachelor of Science in Electrical Engineering, Mapua Institute of Technology, Manila, Philippines; [occ.] Postal Systems Technical Services, Canada Post Corp.; [oth. writ.] Nature As I Sense It, A Dream of Roses to Reminisce, Attitude Changed, and Are You Real?; [pers.] Nothing is worth doing unless it is for the love of God.; [a.] Scarborough, ON

PASSERO, SHARON MARIA
[b.] February 25, 1944; Buffalo, NY; [p.] Edward Stephenson and Helen Lahti; [m.] Frank A. Passero Jr; [m.] June 25, 1963; [ch.] Tony, Lisa, Gino, Dena; [ed.] Public School #56 (Buffalo, NY), Ridgeway High School (Canada), St. Mary's Business School (Buffalo, NY); [occ.] Horse Trainer, Housewife; [memb.] Campfire Girls (USA); [hon.] Golden Poet, Silver Poet x2, Channel 7 TV Poetry Contest (Buffalo, NY) '73; [oth. writ.] First poem published at age 11 (Buffalo Evening News); [pers.] I try to reflect upon the essence of the soul in all things.; [a.] Schomberg, ON

PATTERSON, JANE A.
[b.] August 11, 1936; Ramsey Isle of Han, UK; [pa.] Joan, William Leveson-Gower; [ed.] Ramsey Grammar School; [pers.] The poem, Memories, is dedicated to my grandfather, Captain Lawrence Richard Peel, the best person I have ever known.; [a.] Truro, NS

PAULOZZA, PETER
[b.] December 18, 1976; Toronto; [p.] Assunta and John Paulozza; [ed.] Humber College; [occ.] Student; [oth. writ.] Too many to list; [pers.] "Time has no meaning, nor does the soul, if by hate is feeding" by Peter Paulozza.; [a.] Mississauga, ON

PAULS, SHALYNN RENAE ALVENA
[b.] 25 June 1983; Abbotsford, BC; [p.] Ronald and Olvena Pauls; [ed.] Grade nine; [occ.] Student; [memb.] BLT (Bateman Leadership Team); [hon.] Public speaking award, citizenship award, Multiple Honor Roll Awards, Honor and Service pins, Gold Medallion for Reading and others, Honorable Mention for Grade Eight Leadership; [oth. writ.] Previously published in "Island Sunsets" of the Poetry Institute of Canada; [a.] Abbotsford, BC

PAYNE, PATSY
[b.] June 21, 1964; Oshawa, ON; [pers.] I dedicate my poems to my grandmother, Alice Vaillancourt, a much-loved English lady, and a lover of poetry.; [a.] Oshawa, ON

PEARS, PAUL JAMES
[b.] September 24, 1967; London, England; [m.] Fawna Marie Pears; July 25, 1996; [occ.] Finishing Technician; [pers.] Dreamers are the "Architects of the Future."; [a.] Whitby, ON

PEILIN, WEN
[pen.] Lydia; [b.] December 28, 1923; Beijing; [m.] Jiaxi Li; February 5, 1954; [ed.] B.A. (Sociology), 1949, Yenching University, Beijing; [hon.] A "Model University Teacher of Hunan Province," China; [pers.] Freedom through truth for service.; [a.] Hunan, China

PEREIRA, JENNIFER
[pen.] Lydwina Pears; [b.] April 15, 1984; Mississauga, ON; [p.] Carol Pereira and Christopher Pereira; [ed.] Grade eight at Blessed Edith Stein Elementary School.

I am hoping to go to Cawtrira: The School of Fine Music and Arts for Piano.; [occ.] Volunteer at Pet Vet, Telemarketer and Baby Sitter; [oth. writ.] I have written many other poems and books, but since this is my very first opportunity at getting my writing published, nothing else has been published. Hopefully in the near future that will change.; [pers.] Though only a teen, I see this sort of thing happen every day to loved ones. In my poetry, I try to help people understand that if we keep turning our backs on this type of thing, the madness will never end.; [a.] Mississauga, ON

PEREZ, JENNIFER
[pen.] Shirley Jane; [b.] June 7, 1997; Manila, Philippines; [p.] Narciso Perez Jr., Amelia Lacdao; [ed.] Fr. Michael McGivney, Catholic Academy; [hon.] Pearson Writes of Spring '96, Second Place, short story: A Note for Ricky; [pers.] From the demented and morbid imagination of a troubled woman springs forth the most beautiful collection of nightmares the world has ever known. Nightmares that could bring anyone down to their knees and make them weep gloriously.; [a.] Scarborough, ON

PERRY, GORDON L.
[b.] August 5, 1934; Quesnell, BC; [p.] Henry and Amy Perry; [m.] Marliss Shannon Perry; March 4, 1961; [ch.] Rae-llyn, Shannon, Scott, Mark; [ed.] Secondary, high school; [occ.] Professional Photographer; [memb.] Professional Photographers of Canada, Professional Photographers of British Columbia; [oth. writ.] Former Guest Columnist for local newspaper, The Cariboo Observer; [pers.] "Poetry is an expression of our inner self as it reacts to the world around us. Everyone should write a poem."; [a.] Quesnel, BC

POLEC, PATRYK
[b.] June 13, 1983; Poland; [p.] Elizabeth and Andrew Polec; [hon.] I received an award for the young talents, and I also received a thank you letter from Prime Minister Jean Cretien for writing a poem about Canada; [oth. writ.] I also play the piano at the Royal Conservatory of Music, and my piano teacher is professor Natalia Tyomkina. I began writing poems at the age of 11, and now, I am 14 years old.; [pers.] We can't forget about what inspires us to be better.; [a.] Toronto, ON

POPESCU, LILIANA
[b.] July 20, 1968, Turnu Magurele, Romania; [p.] Gheorghe Ioana, Tudora Ioana; [m.] Nicolae Popescu; [ch.] Mihai Gabriel, Dan Christian, Armin Nicolae; [ed.] Ph.D. in Mathematics, University of Bucharest; [occ.] Professor of Mathematics—University of Bucharest, Mathematics Department; [oth. writ.] "Tie" ("For You") 1994 and "Tarâmul Dintre Gânduri" ("The Realm beyond the Thoughts") (1997); [pers.] I believe the truth reveals itself to those prepared to receive it. (Sometimes it takes the shape of poetry, music, or mathematics, but always it is expressed through the sounds of silence that vibrate continuously in the universe, in all that is created.); [a.] Bucharest, Romania

PORRITT, DEREK
[b.] 14 August 1983; Three Hills, AB; [p.] Stan and Donna Porritt; [ed.] Prairie Elementary School, Rainbow Christian School, Nechako Valley Secondary School; [oth. writ.] Various articles about abortion, hard core, punk, all in underground magazines; also short stories and poems; [pers.] Dear Lord, remind us of our past and may it remind us to be humble. V-hoof Hardcore KIDS RIP. There is no excuse after death for your ignorance during life.; [a.] Vanderhoof, BC

PORRO, GEORGE PETER
[b.] May 19, 1958; Vancouver, BC; [p.] Dario Porro and Francesca Porro; [ed.] B.Ed., M.Ed., UBC (B.Ed.) U of Portland (M.Ed.), Technology Certification T.Q.S. (BC), Machinist Fitter (B.C.T.Q.S.) Millwright (B.C.I.T.); [occ.] Middle School Teacher and School Network Administrator, Mount Slesse Middle School, Chilliwack, BC; [pers.] Life, and all its glory and mystique, is an inspiration to be sad; however, it serves as a reminder of what is precious and important to mankind. I have been influenced by the likes of: Neruda, Frost, and T.S. Eliot, among others.; [a.] Chilliwack, BC

POTTEBAUM, RACHEL
[b.] November 10, 1981; Wisconsin; [p.] Nancy Alsbury; [ed.] Tenth grade at Saunders Secondary School in London, ON; [pers.] I may live in Canada, but I'm 100% American. Statement—Life is short, seize the moment.; [a.] London, ON

POWER, GORDON, JR.
[b.] August 8, 1947; Newfoundland; [p.] Gordon and Ann Power; [m.] Sheila Power; July 25, 1970; [ch.] Kelley Tracey, Matthew; [ed.] High school, vocational training school; [occ.[School Custodian; [hon.] Roman Catholic School Board, St. John's, NF Award of Excellence 1995; [oth. writ.] Various poems and one short story; [a.] Kelligrews, NF

QUAIT, PAMELA C.
[b.] September 13, 1973; Scarborough, ON; [p.] Glen H. Quait, Edith M. Quait; [ed.] B.A. (Hons) York University; [memb.] Canadian Federation of University Women, Aurora/Newmarket; [hon.] York University Sessional Academic Achievement List, York University Merit Award, Achievement in English Scholarship, Ontario Scholar; [pers.] For my first love—Rob McClelland. I have not been disappointed.; [a.] Aurora, ON

RATINEN, OSKARI
[b.] August 5, 1980; Siuntio; [p.] Pentti Ratinen and Irene Ratinen; [ed.] At the moment I'm in a high school (or "Luklo" in Finish) that is dedicated to self-expressional arts, Kallion Luklo in Helsinki; [occ.] Student; [hon.] None to be mentioned apart from making it into this anthology; [oth. writ.] Poems, lyrics, and short stories, most of them in Finish, are still in my desk drawer. I hope this success will help me on my way to a breakthrough.; [pers.] Don't try to make yourself the centre of the world, try to make the world the centre of yourself.; [a.] Siuntio, South Finland

RECSETAR, AMANDA
[b.] February 26, 1980; Saskatoon; [p.] Anita Richardson; [ed.] In grade 12, almost completed; [occ.] Simpson, Sask. SOG-four mo.; [memb.] Education right now. I am currently finishing grade 12. I am furthering my education later on (post-secondary education).; [hon.] Volunteering award in school, Math and English Bronze Award in school also.; [oth. writ.] "Rushing," "Life after Death," "The Pain He Didn't Share," "Before," "I Died for Beauty," and "The Running Mind"; [pers.] "It is not only necessary to love, it is necessary to say so." My English teacher has encouraged my writings throughout my whole life. I am very grateful to her.; [a.] Simpson, SK

REGIER, JENNIFER
[b.] 03 April 1982; Winnipeg, MB; [p.] Grant and Debbie Regier; [ed.] Presently enrolled in Kildonan East Collegiate; [occ.] Working Student; [hon.] Creative Arts Award Silver Medal—Water Polo, Bronze Cross and Bronze Medallion—Royal Life Saving; [pers.] One of my goals/dreams is to become a published writer. I believe dreams can come true if you follow your heart and I'm presently on the path fulfilling mine. Go for the gold!; [a.] Winnipeg, MB

REID, KATHERINE CHRISTINE
[b.] November 6, 1981; St. Catharines; [p.] Don and Edith Reid; [ed.] I am presently in grade 11 at Eden High School. In the future I plan on being a Financial Advisor and part-time writer.; [pers.] In my writing, my goal is to give people a sense of hope. I often use tragedy to express this. I believe strongly in two sides of looking at everything. In this poem, for example, you could see a lonely person or see how important life really is.; [a.] St. Catharines, ON

REIS, FRANCISCO
[b.] April 6, 1959; Santa Maria, Azores; [m.] Brenda Reis; October 25, 1986; [ch.] Skyler Reis; [ed.] Ongoing; [occ.] Colour Technician for PVC Plastics with the best company in the whole world, Vintex, Inc., Mt. Forest, ON; [oth. writ.] Songwriter, composer, arranger, percussionist; [pers.] "Equilibrium for the next millennium."; [a.] Brampton, ON

REYNO, MARY
[b.] December 8, 1936; Halifax, NS; [p.] John Coulson, Mary Coulson (both deceased); [ch.] David Kerby, Shelley Elizabeth, Kimberly Anne; [oth. writ.] First submission ever; [pers.] Love literature, spiritualism within, watching depth of achievement and support my three adult children (in memory of parents, sisters Helen, Helen's son Richard, together at rainbow's end, where another miracle begins.); [a.] Halifax, NS

REYNOLDS, ANTHONY
[b.] February 8, 1989; North York, ON; [p.] Apolonia and Ryan Reynolds; [ed.] Third grade at St. Jean Brebeuf School; [oth. writ.] My Dog Is Gone (first poem); [a.] Brampton, ON

RIBEIRO, INES
[b.] June 30, 1986; Toronto, ON; [p.] Luis Ribeiro, Ceu Ribeiro; [ed.] Richard W. Scott Elementary School, grade 6, grade 3 piano; [memb.] Etobicoke Youth Choir, school choir, York Figure Skating Club; [oth. writ.] Started Kidstreet magazine in my neighborhood; [pers.] I try to accentuate the positive in everyone's life, and to reveal pieces of myself.; [a.] Toronto, ON

RICHER, MELANIE
[b.] October 13, 1983; Ottawa, ON; [p.] Brian Richer, Muriel Richer; [a.] Maxville, ON

RICHMOND, ROBERT JAMES, JR.
[pen.] Robert James Richmond Jr.; [b.] February 15, 1973; Tilsonburg, ON; [p.;] Jim Richmond and Linda Richmond; [ed.] High school, soon to be attending college; [hon.] Hamilton Home Builders Association Award for small dwelling and design; [oth. writ.] Have filled several notebooks with my writing and waiting for an opportunity to share them.; [pers.] I have no set plan for writing. I just let my pen move, telling what I am feeling inside at that particular time.; [a.] Acton, ON

RILEY, RICK J.
[pen.] Rick J. Riley; [b.] January 30, 1968; Port Hope, ON; [p.] Richard W. Riley and Susan Orchard; [ch.] Daniel Riley, Sarah Riley; [ed.] Grade 12 OSSO, enrolled in Sault College, taking Liberal Studies program (GAS), then going to university after graduation; [occ.] Student in Sault College; [memb.] Members of The Canadians Foundations for the Study of Infant Deaths. (SIDS); [hon.] None at his time, but hopefully in the future; [oth. writ.] Have written many others poems but have not been published to date. Future, to write a fiction novel for publication.; [pers.] My poems are written from the heart and real life experiences. If my writing can help any other person have a different perspective in his life, then I will be satisfied. (Positive mind will conquer despair.) [a.] Sault Ste Marie, ON

RIVERA, MELISSA K.
[b.] July 22, 1982; Bronx, NY; [p.] John Rivera, Elena Gonzalez; [ed.] Academy of the Holy Spirit High School (tenth grade) [occ.] Student; [hon.] Math, English grammar, Spanish, Science, Social Studies, Miss Levittown Beauty Pageant First Runner-Up; [oth. writ.] Several poems not published, in both English and Spanish; [pers.] I am fully bilingual—Spanish and English.; [a.] Levittown, Toa Baja

ROBINS, ETHEL
[b.] 6 November 1915; Cherryfield, NB; [p.] Charles and Mabel Bulmer; [m.] George Robins (deceased); [ch.] Lois Goquen, Wayne Robins, Dawn Robins; [oth .writ.] Has written other stories and poems. This was the first attempt at having one published.; [a.] Summerside, PE

ROOTE, MARGARET
[pen.] Maggie Roote; [b.] October 31, 1957; Newfoundland; [p.] Stanley and Julia Young; [ch.] Bradley and Geoffrey; [ed.] Eastern H.S. of Commerce, Toronto, George Brown College, Toronto, Durham College, Oshawa, Centennial College, Toronto; [occ.] Clerk, Durham College, Oshawa, ON; [memb.] Hospice Durham; [pers.] I have never been afraid to die, only afraid of life.; [a.] Courtice, ON

ROUSSEAU, S. ELIZABETH
[b.] February 17, 1966, Sydney, NS; [m.] Divorced; [ch.] Ashley (3/15/90) and Lorgan (11/23/92); [occ.] Student at Camosun College, Victoria—Applied Communication program; [memb.] Victoria Women's Transition House; [hon.] Scholastic achievement; [oth. writ.] Unpublished collection of poetry, children's story, Magic Nation, short story, Imprisoned, published commentary in Esquimalt News; [pers.] If I can help you see the world through my eyes with my poetry, only then am I an accomplished poet. Through pain comes growth and from growth comes the ability to reshape the world in which we exist. The secret to happiness is freedom, the secret of freedom is courage. What is life if we choose not to live it?

ROWLEY, ROSEMARIE
[b.] July 10, 1942; Dublin; [ed.] Trinity College Dublin, B.A., M.A., M. Lit. Maynooth College; DIP Psych; [memb.] Poetry Ireland, The Byron Society, Gradhology Society; [hon.] First Prize Scottish International Open Poetry Competition 1996, represent Ireland The Ssalonini European Capital of Culture 1997; [oth. writ.] The Brother Pledge (1985), The Sea

of Affliction. Flight into Reality (book of 1989, tape 1996) essays; [a.] Dublin, Ireland

ROY, KAREN ANNE
[b.] February 13, 1953; Montreal, Canada; [p.] Alton B. and Marion A. Roy; [ed.] B.A. Psychology in 1977 from University of Guelph, Certificate in Drafting, 1978; [occ.] Retired from Drafting due to a heart attack in 1988; [memb.] Guelph Humane Society; [hon.] Honours degree in Drafting in 1979; [oth. writ.] Poem: If No More, No More Than This, published in The Glow Within; autobiography, Love Is Not Enough, unpublished as yet.

RUBIO, MARIA GERARDEE
[pen.] Din-Din; [b.] September 20, 1981; Manila Philippines; [p.] Dr. Francisco Rubio, Dra. Monica Rubio; [occ.] Student; [memb.] Journalism (Literary Editor), Children of Mary, Youth for Christ, dance troupe, science club, drama club, cadet officer; [hon.] School representative for declamation, oratorical, and writing contests. A 1 Filipino Child. First place On-the-Spot Acting, one of the three rep. of our school for the World Youth Day held in Paris, France last August, Ms. Science; [oth. writ.] Being Numb, Soul Mate, The Realm of Time, Back-off!, Figments of My Imagination, A Prayer, Sorrows, Abasement, Sorry I Lied, Discrimination, etc.; [pers.] Being an only child is not that hard when you have friends to count on. Never take your talents for granted, learn to use them and share them with others. Life is like a grain of sand that is easily blown by the wind. Love your family.; [a.] Lucena Quezon, Philippines

RUDDELL, VIVIAN
[pen.] Evelyn Bernadett Steele; [b.] 06 July 1958; Toronto, ON; [p.] Garfield Steele; [m.] Douglas Ruddell; 26 September 1987; [ed.] Grade II, St. Basils and correspondence course, certificate—Selena College, Upgrading—Arts and Technology; [occ.] Homemaker, volunteer work; [memb.] INFAW; [oth. writ.] Yes, many that don't rhyme.; [pers.] "He who has not sinned, cast the fist stone." I believe in fate and Jesus our God. I inspire people with my poems.; [a.] Toronto, ON

SAN MARTIN, JULIO GIANNI TORO
[b.] March 21, 1972; Santiago, Chile; [ed.] High school; [pers.] Influenced by the English Elizabethan dramatists and Romantic Poets.; [a.] ON

SANDERSON, AMY
[b.] August 13, 1977; North York, ON; [p.] Marjorie and David Sanderson; [ed.] Second year Honours Psychology at Brock University; [occ.] University Student; [pers.] Poetry is a reflection of the emotions of life that are tiny imprints that influence one's life.; [a.] Don Mills, ON

SANDIEGO, JOSELITO H.
[pen.] Joey Sandiego; [b.] May 28, 1970; Valenzuela, Metro Manila; [p.] Otilio C. Sandiego, Encarnacion H. Sandiego; [ed.] Sandiego Elementary School, Colegio de San Pascual Baylon, University of Santo Tomas, Colegio de San Juan de Letran; [occ.] Musician; [oth. writ.] Sweet Five Burning, The Birth of a New Day, Ethereal Lights, The Pleasure Pond; [a.] Valenzuela, Philippines

SCHECHTER, ODED
[b.] February 16, 1964; Jerusalem, Israel; [p.] Miriam and Yosef; [m.] Germick Hila Schechter; February 24, 1994; [ch.] 3-02 Rotem, Yehonatan; [occ.] Security Guard at the American Embassy, Tel Aviv, Israel; [memb.] Israeli Mountain Bike Union, Israeli Go-kart Union, Israeli Shotokan Karate and Black Belt Association; [hon.] Interview and article published in local newspaper in Jerusalem; [oth. writ.] Published poetry under my own auspices 12/91; [pers.] I quote a part of one love of my poems— "I try to be as good as bad can be. The clarity in my mind fighting living day after day decoding the inside of me. The vortex in me, I hold both edges of the extreme. My quest for mental balance—through radical means."; [a.] Tel Aviv, Israel

SCHELL, BOBBI JO
[b.] December 9, 1987; Wincham, ON; [p.] Bruce Schell and Bobbie Schell; [ed.] Grade four; [occ.] Student; [pers.] This poem was written for my aunt Marie to help her grieve the loss of her husband, uncle "Chick."; [a.] Wingham, ON

SCHOLES, SUSAN
[b.] September 30, 1960; Montreal; [p.] Joyce and Bill Scholes; [m.] Paul Guilbalt; November 2, 1985; [ch.] Maxwell, Fauve-Elise, and Tylee; [ed.] Regular high school system, then self-educated in different fields. B.H.S.A.I. in riding; [occ.] Housewife, Ostrich Farmer, and Writer; [oth. writ.] Just finished a children's book; [pers.] Searching for my grail has led me down many paths of different realities. Understand the journey will connect me to my grail.; [a.] QC

SCHROEDER, MARGARET
[b.] 10 March 1955; Flinflon, MB; [p.] John and Maureen Schroeder; [m.] Marcel Dubuc; 1991; [ed.] Bachelor of Science (1985), University of Manitoba; [occ.] Volunteer; [memb.] Independent Living Resource Centre (Wpg), writers' group for disabled writers; [oth. writ.] Several poems published in local newsletters and "Whisper of the Spirit" published in a chap book; [pers.] I suffer from a mental illness. I write the brutal truth as I see it from the depths of my being and from my own experience.; [a.] Winnipeg, MB

SCHUIL, MAUREEN
[b.] May 27, 1941; Johannesburg, South Africa; [occ.] Educator; [a.] Whitby, ON

SCOBIE, COREY
[pen.] Covey Scobie; [b.] January 4, 1981; Calgary, AB; [p.] David Scobie, Jennifer Scobie; [ed.] Enrolled in grade 12 at Lindsay Thurber C.H.S.; [occ.] Student; [pers.] Our time has come and gone. This is the end of the end, but only the beginning of forever—our last breath of smog, dirt, grime, and irony.; [a.] Red Deer, AB

SCOTT, LISA
[pen.] Lisa Martens; [b.] July 26, 1951; Winnipeg, MB; [p.] Abraham and Irene Martens; [ch.] Deborah Lee, Mark Anthony; [ed.] Nurse, Reflexologist, Alberta Vocational College, Canadian Armed Forces, Calgary College of Swedish Massage and Reflexology; [occ.] Nurse; [memb.] Royal Canadian Legion #154 Ogden Branch. I am also a member of the Massage Practitioners of Calgary, AB; [hon.] Certificate of Merit from Board of Education 1967 for essay written, various nursing awards; [oth. writ.] I have completed my first book of poetry and have started a book of short stories regarding my life experiences. The tranquility and peace I get from my writing truly is a gift from the father above.; [pers.] A minister once told me regarding my poetry, that I was a "modern day Psalmist" because I wrote from my heart.; [a.] Calgary, AB

SCOTT, THERESA
[pen.] Tee/Tereez; [b.] October 14, 1980; St. Croix, USVI; [p.] Germaine Scott, George Scott; [ed.] High school; [occ.] Student; [hon.] D.A.R.E. (Drug Abuse Resistance Education); [oth. writ.] I've been writing poems since elementary school, but this is my first poetry contest.; [pers.] My poems reflect on how I feel about things in my life, and my family as well.; [a.] St. Croix, USVI

SCRIBNER, MATTHEW
[b.] June 25, 1984; Montreal; [p.] Sherry Read and Ian Hale; [ed.] Kindergarten to grade seven; [occ.] Student; [pers.] I believe, above all, that all people are created equal and deserve the same freedom. This, however has nothing to do with my poetry.; [a.] Ottawa, ON

SEELEY, JASON C.
[b.] 14 September 1971; Ottawa, ON; [p.] Joan Seeley, Roy Seeley; [ed.] B.S. Math, University of Waterloo; [occ.] Consultant; [a.] Mississauga, ON

SEGUIN, JULIE
[pen.] August Jaysen; [b.] August 7, 1979; Richmond, BC; [p.] Ann and Denis Seguin; [ed.] Storefront School Broadmad; [occ.] Student; [hon.] English and creative writing; [oth. writ.] Wide variety of writings, this is my first publication.; [pers.] I urge you to be true to yourself, because in the end you are the only person you have to live with for the rest of your days. So, it's better if you are someone you like.; [a.] Victoria, BC

SEN, PRIYA
[b.] March 3, 1985; Ottawa, ON; [p.] Partha Sen, Nandita Sen; [ed.] Grade seven, Elmwood School, Ottawa; [occ.] Student grade seven at Elmwood School, Ottawa, ON; [memb.] International Tae Kwon Do Federation (Junior Black Belt), competitive swimming, King Fisher Swimming Club; [hon.] Winner First Prize, "Mother Mary" Essay Contest, Carleton Roman Catholic School Board, Ottawa—1993 (in grade three); [oth. writ.] Wrote several stories for fun, recently wrote my autobiography, won prizes at school for penmanship; [pers.] I have a deep interest in writing stories and poems. I enjoy writing!; [a.] Orleans, ON

SHAPIRO, DEBORAH E.
[pen.] Des; [b.] June 17, 1955; New Haven, CT; [p.] Theodore J. Shapiro, Ruth McGarkey; [ed.] LPN; B.A. (Education) in progress; [occ.] Technical Writer; [memb.] International Society for Technical Communication; Voices Israel—group of poets in English (former secretary); [oth. writ.] Poetry is Israel publications, short stories; edited several major scientific publications; [pers.] Seeking to be an overcomer, not just a survivor maranatha.; [a.] Haifa, Israel

SIKKA, PATRICK
[b.] March 7, 1979; Toronto, ON; [p.] Kathleen Lal Sikka; [ed.] Ascension of Our Lord Secondary High School; [occ.] Student; [hon.] English award, theology award, science award, Principal's award; [pers.] What you have is not as important as who you have with whom to share it.; [a.] Mississauga, ON

SOLINA, BEATRIZ LILIA
[b.] November 14, 1945; Rosario; [p.] Alfredo Solina (D), Renee Ricci; [ed.] HS: Normal #1—Rosario Tertiary: National Teacher Training College (INSP), Rosario; [occ.] Course Director A.R.I.C.A.N.A. (Rosario, BNC); [memb.] Tesol Artesol Aprir (Rosario Teachers of English Association), "El Circulo" cultural association; [oth. writ.] In English: articles on English grammar and poems in the Apair Journal. In Spanish: poems—Libro Annual XXXI (Assoc. Literaria "Nosotras"; [pers.] My writings are rooted in an inner urge for self-expression. I draw inspiration from Nature and from my own life experience.; [a.] Rosario, Argentina

SOUTER, JAMES B.
[b.] April 10, 1940; Nbicam; [p.] Alex and Ina Souter; [m.] Nellie I; November 30, 1963; [ch.] 12; [ed.] Part 12; [occ.] Disability; [memb.] House Humane Society, Prince Albert Ex Co., Ltd.; [oth. writ.] Have had several poems published; [pers.] Most of my poems are of the religion or native background.; [a.] Moosejaw, SK

SRIVASTAVA, RATIKA KIRAN
[b.] January 27, 1988; Halifax, NS; [p.] Rajiv and Rani Srivastava; [ed.] Faywood Public School, Toronto, ON; [memb.] Girl Guides of Canada; [pers.] Live in Toronto with my parents and younger brother, Roman. I like to write poetry, stories, and enjoy drama and drawing. I love art, especially works by Monet.; [a.] North York, ON

STANSFIELD, ESTHER RIVERA LIMSIACO
[b.] October 30, 1938; Talaban, Himamaylan, Negros Occidental, Philippines; [p.] Serapion Limsiaco and Rosario Grandea Rivera; [m.] Barry Lionel Pomfret Stansfield; June 10, 1967; [ch.] Richard Lionel, Valerie Elizabeth, Catherine Rosario; [ed.] Registered Nurse; [occ.] Portfolio Manager and Financial Manager for family; [memb.] Member of Chorale Ensemble, Philippine Folk Arts Society of Montreal; [hon.] Among the ten top scorers of the Philippine Nurses Board Exams 1958, Recipient Editor's Choice Award, present by The National Library of Poetry for Outstanding Achievement in Poetry 1997; [oth. writ.] Articles for Filipino newspaper; [pers.] Dream and hitch a ride with the stars, and all that's beautiful in heaven and on Earth and everything else would be less than significant.; [a.] Canada

STAUSS, RUSTI
[pen.] Rusti Stauss; [b.] January 28, 1941; Montreal, QC; [p.] William A. White and Mary Delaney White; [m.] Hans Stauss; September 22, 1982; [ed.] High school and home study courses; [occ.] Retired; [oth. writ.] Several small books of poetry—given to friends; [pers.] I enjoy writing about everything from fact to fantasy, sad, humorous, romantic, and happy. I grew up reading the works of Scott, Tennyson, and Moore.; [a.] Arucas, Las Palmas

STAVRAKOS, KONSTANTINE
[b.] January 29, 1976; Toronto, ON; [ed.] University of McGill, English Literature (major), Philosophy (minor); [occ.] Student, Poetry Editor for Scrivener (international arts journal); [pers.] My poetry primarily focusses upon urban environments, with special emphasis paid to cycles of repetition and stasis.; [a.] Richmond, ON

STEWART, SANDRA J.
[b.] February 19, 1965; Calgary, AB; [p.] Margaret and Joe Stewart; [m.] Marc Gaudet; September 15, 1990; [occ.] Self-employed "Cantina Express" mobile concession; [pers.] Success is the journey, not the destination.; [a.] Kelowna, BC

STIEGE, RUDI
[b.] September 7, 1943; [p.] Anton and Pauline; [m.] Patricia Ann; March 8, 1969; [ch.] Stacie, Judy, Elizabeth; [memb.] Royal Commander Region Branch

72, Pembroke, ON; [hon.] Worst Golfer of the Year 1987—Cobourg, ON (among others); [oth. writ.] Many and various unpublished works; [pers.] Purging the mind through poetry benefits many.; [a.] Pembroke, ON

STREILEIN, CARRIE
[b.] November 6, 1965; Victoria, BC; [p.] Andrea, Gary Letcher; [ch.] David Charles, Dustin Jonathan; [occ.] Dispatcher at Kelowna Cabs; [memb.] MADD Canada; [hon.] Peer Counseling, Communication, Parent Advisory Council (PAC), Pres. WRCS; [oth. writ.] Poems, parenting articles; [pers.] Learn to live and live to learn. When we stop learning we stop living. Every trial in life can be used as a learning experience,; [a.] Kelowna, BC

SUVEGES, CAPTAIN DENNIS
[pen.] Skipper; [b.] August 26, 1940; New Westminster, BC; [p.] George and Helen Suveges; [m.] Gail; [ch.] Mona, Clint, Lance, Scott, and Susie; [occ.] Tug Boat Captain; [memb.] Lions Club, Level and Curling; [oth. writ.] The Glow Within, Reflections, Tug's Wake; [pers.] Working on the water has influenced my writing. I enjoy like and all it offers.; [a.] Gibsons, BC

SVATEK, KURT FRANZ
[b.] January 26, 1949; Vienna, Austria; [p.] Franz Svatek, Trude Svatek; [m.] Herma Kurner, December 20, 1953; [ch.] Petra; [ed.] Goethe High School, Vienna Academy of Pedagogy, Vienna; [occ.] Teacher at a vocational school (Bookkeeping, Correspondence, Political Science); [memb.] Many literary organizations in Austria and Germany, Austrian Centre of International P.E.N; [hon.] P.E. Internal Haiku Association, Tokyo, Austrian National Library, Austrian Japanese Society, Vienna—Province of Vienna, Province of Lower Austria; [oth. writ.] Several poems, essays, short stories published in newspapers and anthologies; [pers.] I'll show the meaning and sense behind the words, I want show one's true colours, I'm also writing about the loneliness and homeless in our days.; [a.] Breitenau, Austria

SWAIN, PEARL DOROTHY
b.] February 10, 1916; Trenton, NS; [p.] Kenneth Cameron and Sarah Cameron; [m.] Charles Edward Swain; July 6, 1935; [ch.] Stephen Edward, Eleanor Ruth, James Joseph, and Richard Gordon; [ed.] I received a high school education—took many courses—nursed in mental hospital; [occ.] Writing, gardening, and painting, plus counseling children; [memb.] Rebecca Lodge; Gardening Club: teach Laubach—two or three people a year, also some church work. Each one teach one.; [hon.] Many copies of my first book, "Seen through a Window," have been sold and given away. His Holiness Pope John was sent one and I received his Apostolic Blessing.; [oth. writ.] Started writing when I was about 15. Sort of slowing down now. I am 81. You should read my "Teabery Hill." If you have ever eaten teaberries, it will take you way back.; [pers.] I love writing and have no problem to find the night words. But "A prophet is without honor in his own country." Ex: your wonderful Robert Frost, who has to go to England to gain recognition. My goal: To strive against racism and intolerance.; [a.] Westville, NS

SYMINGTON, KELLY
[b.] January 11, 1979; Edmonton, AB; [p.] David and Bernice Symington; [ed.] Kelly was in grade 12 at Hughender Public School at the time of her death. She had planned to go to Lakeland College after graduation.; [memb.] SADD—Students Against Drinking and Driving, Hughenden Community Choir, Hughenden United Church; [hon.] Kelly loved reading in general, and writing poetry. She had a beautiful voice and was an accomplished singer.; [pers.] Kelly's dream was to reach her graduation, because of this we used the theme "Grand Kelly's Graduation" at her funeral.; [a.] Hughenden, AB

TAYLOR, JOSEPHINE
[pen.] Josephine Bassi; [b.] July 19, 1949; Dublin, Ireland; [ch.] Two; [ed.] Sheridan College; [occ.] Social Service Worker; [pers.] Continually seeking balance of mind, body, and soul through journals, poetry, dream work, and unleashing the spirit within.; [a.] Burlington, ON

TAYLOR, MARY S.
[pen.] Molly Taylor; [b.] October 4, 1929; Eastlothian, Scotland; [m.] Michael W. Taylor; June 6, 1958; [ch.] Patricia A. Hughes; [ed.] College, Edinburgh, Scotland; [memb.] Lyford Cay Club, Bahamas National Trust; [hon.] Three Golden Poet Awards, Kiwanis Club, Bahamas Award for Service, 1988; [oth. writ.] Children's book— "Pepe from Flying Saucer Land"; [a.] Nassau, New Providence, Bahamas

TAYLOR-ARENAS, LE SAND DUANNE
[b.] November 27, 1977; Williamsburg, VA; [p.] Ralph D. Taylor and Nydia B. Arenas; [ed.] Antilles High School, Colegio Universitario Del Este; [memb.] Expose member 1996-1997, AHS Latter Day Saints; [hon.] Class poem and motto, PR Flag; [oth. writ.] 1,032 Poems; [pers.] If you have a voice, let it be heard, because only one's ideas and one's voice can change the course and events of time.; [a.] Rio Piedras, Puerto Rico

TAYS, MAUREN
[p.] Horace M. Tays, (deceased), Doris (Robinson) Tay; [m.] Jonathan Esterhazy; [ch.] Danishka; [ed.] High school, commercial college; [occ.] Administrative Receptionist, Computer Skills; [a.] Winnipeg, MB

TEIXEIRA, ANNA
[pen.] "Autumn"; [b.] May 20, 1963; Azores, Portugal; [p.] Arnaldo and Ema Teixeira; [ch.] Mark Andrew Adams; [ed.] George Brown College, Brockton High School, Toronto, ON; [occ.] Full-time Parent/Student; [oth. writ.] "Peace of mind" is my first publication. I've written and continue to write a lot of poetry.; [pers.] I wrote this poem at 19 years of age. I was 2 months pregnant. I reach my peace of mind through my faith, meditation, and life lessons!; [a.] Toronto, ON

THOMPSON, AUDREY
[b.] January 6, 1928; SK, Canada; [P.] Jim and Kit Johnston; [m.] Llyod W. Thompson; April 9, 1977; [ch.] Five; [ed.] High school plus 1 year business college; [occ.] Retired Bookkeeper; [memb.] I.S.P. ('95-96); [hon.] Five time E.C.A. The National Library of Poetry ('95-96—plus three for '97). As a child I won "Best of the Month" quite a few times!; [oth. writ.] As a youngster—always poetry and published then in weekly issues of the Western Producer out of Saskatoon, SK. Now am in five volumes by The National Library of Poetry (E.C.A.) for each, this will be sixth, published more recently in "100 Mile House Free Press."; [pers.] Life, love, memories, family, friends, and nature are my usual inspirations—I am usually trying to "Paint a picture of my feelings!"; [a.] Surrey, BC

THURSTON, FLORENCE
[b.] August 21, 1911; Petrolia, ON; [p.] George Alice, Kirk Patrick; [m.] James Thurston; August 27, 1932;

[ch.] Two sons and one daughter; [ed.] High school and business course, Gold Medal for Typing; [occ.] Senior Housewife; [memb.] People's Church in Wyoming, ON; [hon.] Sunday School Teacher for 30 years. Also taught handicapped students for a few years; [oth. writ.] Poem in 1967 to honour Canada's Centennial. Church history with poems and also for church monthly newsletter; [pers.] I believe poetry to be a gift from god to be used to inspire and comfort those in need of a spiritual touch.; [a.] Wyoming, ON

TIOSEN, NICANOR P.
[b.] January 10, 1953; La Paz, Leyte, Philippines; [p.] Nemesio Sr. and Corazon; [m.] Luviminda; March 24, 1981; [ch.] Feamor Vyn, Feliz Gemmavyn; [ed.] B.S. (Pre-Med.), Bachelor of Evangelical Ministry (B.E.M.), Master of Arts in College Teaching (MACT), currently taking Ph.D.—Major in Research and Evaluation; [occ.] Minister of the Gospel and Faculty Member at New Era University, Quezon City (College of Evangelical Ministry); [memb.] Religious-Iglesia ni Cristo; [hon.] Editor's Choice Award—1997 North American Open Poetry Contest; [oth. writ.] Even If It Takes a Lifetime (The Glow Within), I Beseech Thee (Pasugo—religious magazine), and other religious articles in Pasugo/God's Message published by the Iglesia ni Cristo; [pers.] Success does not come overnight, but I'm willing to wait even if it takes a lifetime.; [a.] Quezon City, Philippines

TRAGVAIR, SCOTT
[b.] January 6, 1977; Sarnia, ON; [oth. writ.] I have many other poems that have never been seen by anyone.; [pers.] I find writing poems a good way to release feelings and built-up pain.; [a.] Sarnia, ON

TZIMOULIS, MAE
[pen.] July; [b.] April 13, 1984; New Jersey; [p.] Aleka and Steve Tzimoulis; [ed.] Attending Bredon School at Gloucester, UK; [occ.] Student; [oth. writ.] Various short stories and poems; [a.] Thessaloniki, Greece

VALDEZ CRUZADA, MA. BONITA P.
[pen.] Bonette Valdez; [b.] April 9, 1965; Manila; [p.] Dominador Valdez, Maria Pailanan; [m.] Ernie R. Cruzada; March 19, 1996; [ed.] Bachelor of Science in Business Administration Accounting, University of the East, Computer Concepts and Programming, Systems Technology Inst., Secretarial, Ramon Magsaysay Vocational School, Book and Short Story Writing for Children and Teenagers, Institute of Children's Literature, West Reading, Connecticut, USA; [occ.] Executive Secretary, Conference Coordinator Faculty of Science, UAE University, Alain, UAE; [memb.] Literary Editor High School Organ "The Trailblazers," 1994 appointed Secretary and presently member, United Arab Emirates Filipino in the Emirates, Pro 1981 Maanuel Roxas High School Student Council, member local writers workshop; [hon.] Consistent honor student from elementary to high school, member of the honors class during college (University of the East), Subject Proficiency Awardee, Manuel Roxas High School, received certificates and medals for contests and symposiums attended; [oth. writ.] Literature and poems published in Gulf Weekly Magazine, Woman's Magazine and others, Deep Enchantments (in preparation) to be published by Watermark Press, short stories for children and teens (unpublished); [pers.] Along with my passion for thrill and excitement comes my intense quest for inner peace and contentment. I always go for whatever goal I pursue. I like positive changes and I know my limitations. As long as I have peace of mind and have enough means to survive, it's fine with me.; [a.] Al Ain, UAE

VALTONEN, HANNA
[b.] September 24, 1980; Jyvaskyla, Finland; [p.] Eija and Hannu Valtonen; [a.] Jyvaskyla, Finland

VASILEVSKI, CHRISTINA
[pen.] Christina Vasilevski; [b.] September 19, 1984; Scarborough, ON; [p.] Gorgi Vasilevski, Slavica Vasilevski; [ed.] Currently in grade eight. I plan on going to high school, then university.; [occ.] Student; [hon.] Grade seven Honours (both terms). Primary proficiency award in grade three. In grade five, one of my longer poems won me a spot in my areas speech art finals.; [oth. writ.] I have various small poems but this is the first time my work has been published.; [pers.] I have to become a world famous author one day and this is the first step to make my dream come true.; [a.] Scarborough, ON

VAUGHAN, HILDA
[pen.] Lola-Hilda; [b.] September 4, 1920; Swansea, ON; [p.] George and Winifred Vaughan; [ed.] Grade eight; [occ.] Retired; [memb.] Evangel Church of God; [oth. writ.] A poem, "God's New Day," published by The National Library of Poetry in the book called, "The Glow Within."; [pers.] God is the author, I am His voice and His hand to bring Glory to his own name through his very own works. For all of his words contain a message and in them are promise and purpose.; [a.] North York, ON

VORTMANN, BLONDINE
[b.] September 9, 1940, Bathurst, Canada; [m.] December 31, 1959; [ch.] Three; [oth. writ.] Completed my first novel in English: "In Search of the Farrezz." It's intriguing, full of suspense, fascinating discoveries, a positive outlook as we embark on a new century. Nearing completion: second novel in French: Biography on maternal grandparents.; [pers.] Recently retired. Now I have time to do things I always wanted to do.; [a.] Bathurst, NB

WAGNER, HARRIET ROCHLIN
[b.] June 8, 1922; New Haven, CT; [p.] Abraham and Elizabeth Rochlin; [m.] Benjamin Wagner; March 3, 1946; [ch.] Douglas Mark, Gary Alan, Kenneth David; [ed.] B.A. Journalism 143, Hunter College, NY, B.A. Early Childhood Ed: Concordia University, Montreal Institute of Children's Literature, two year correspondence course (US); [memb.] Great Books Leader, Writers Assoc. for Romance and Mainstream, (Warm) Co-Chairman Parkinson Foundation of Canada, Montreal Support Group; [hon.] Great Books "Y" Award, Film Arts Society Award, Parkinson Foundation Community Service Award; [oth. writ.] Worked for publishing houses in the US, moved to Montreal in 1946 to be married—worked in public relations for United Nations (ICAO). Then was a freelance writer for many years in MSE for the "Y" Beacon, MSE Gazette, Senior Times CDU Jewish News, Mining World (Saufraw). Have never written poetry before.; [pers.] My entire perspective on life changed when my husband of fifty years died quite suddenly in 1995. I find myself living in the past because I was hardly prepared to face the solitude of life without my dear partner. Through my children and grandchildren and friends, I am now trying very hard to find a satisfactory way to spend the rest of my life—a ranson raison d'etre, so to speak. Perhaps I'll turn to writing face again!; [a.] Westmount, QC

WALLACE, JESSICA
[b.] 15 October 1979; Winnipeg, MB; [p.] Doug and Cathy Wallace; [ed.] Carlton Comprehensive High School Graduate; [occ.] Working student; [pers.] Jessica has been writing poems and short stories since she could hold a pencil. Inspiration comes from personal life experiences. "The words come too fast for me to write them."; [a.] Prince Albert, SK

WARDROP, ANDREA ALLEGRA
[pen.] Allegra Wardrop; [b.] June 29, 1980; Vancouver; [p.] Nan and Norman Wardrop; [ed.] College student at Kwantlen University College (Richmond); [occ.] Student; [memb.] YMCA; [hon.] Distinguished Achievement Award for the YBC essay writing competition; [pers.] Our two most important tools in life are our ears and our mouths: our ears for listening, and our mouths for smiling.; [a.] Vancouver, BC

WATTERS, THERESA A.
[b.] March 1949; Toronto, ON; [p.] Arthur and Johanna Hume; [m.] Michael P. Watters; [ch.] Robert J. Beattie; [pers.] "One" should never take for granted, the beauty of this great land; it has a way of inspiring us all. This is why I write.; [a.] Orton, ON

WEBB, BRIAN
[b.] April 18, 1973; Winnipeg; [p.] Jack and Gwen Webb; [ed.] B.A. University of Regina; [occ.] Sasktel Representative; [hon.] Valedictorian of Dakota Collegiate Institute; [oth. writ.] Currently working on a larger work (novel) and I have a collection; [pers.] I enjoy testing the waters of poetic form. My poetry represents experiments in language and personal sentiment.

WHITE, TARA JANINE
[b.] January 31, 1985; Vancouver, BC; [p.] Cheryl White, Steve Rainforth; [ed.] I am currently attending grade eight; [hon.] Honorable Mention in poetry contest from Iliad Press; [oth. writ.] Lots of other poems. Fall Is on Its Way, and Whispers of the Wind are two poems currently in other contests.; [pers.] In my spare time I like to write poetry. This is one of my hobbies. Three other hobbies are drawing, horse riding, and playing my saxophone.; [a.] Nanaimo, BC

WHITTY M.D., ROBERT J.
[b.] August 16, 1928; Windsor, ON; [p.] Goldie T. and Adeline (Thompson) Whitty; [m.] Joanne (divorced 1976); 1956-1976; [ch.] James, Thomas, Diane, Melanie; [ed.] M.D. Degree, University of Western, ON, 1952—Internship, Residence, Harper Hospital, Detroit, Michigan 1992-1957, Surgical Specialty DAB 1957, CRCS 1957; [occ.] Retired; [memb.] Fellow American College of Surgeons; [hon.] Chief of Surgery, Grace Hospital, Windsor 1972-1975, Member Windsor Board of Education 1964-1970, Chairman two years; [oth. writ.] None other than article on treatment of prolapsing children's rectum—Harper Hospital Bulletin, 1955; [pers.] A great lover of outdoors, greatest joy was there in duck blind or fishing for speckled trout . . . places where God were near . . . close to mother nature . . . forced into only memories by multiple sclerosis.; [a.] Pickering, ON

WILLIAMS, B.V.
[pen.] B.V. Williams; [b.] September 17, 1937; London; [p.] Maude and Sydney Williams; [m.] Wanda Morey; January 1, 1994; [ch.] Rebecca and Shannon; [ed.] Dormers Wells Southall, Middlesea, Trinity College of Music, London; [occ.] Human Resources and Industrial Relations Consultant; [memb.] Member of Institute of Personnel Development; [oth. writ.] Poems published in anthologies and magazines; [pers.] I have been influenced by my experiences of life and strive to reflect them in my writing.; [a.] Burlington, ON

WILLIAMS, LYNDA
[b.] July 9, 1977; Mississauga, ON; [p.] Mary Anna Williams, Jim Williams; [ed.] Erindale Secondary School graduate; [memb.] Girl Guides of Canada; [hon.] Grade Ten Award English; [pers.] I make the best out of my life. My parents, teachers, and friends have been a great impact on my life.; [a.] Mississauga, ON

WLODARSKI, WANDA M.
[b.] June 19, 1923; Poland; [p.] Mary and Joseph Kopera; [m.] Stephen; [ed.] Secondary: business and Conservatory of Music; [memb.] MENSA, choirs: All Saints Choir, Etobicoke, Symphonic Choir; [hon.] Award for poetry in Hamilton, ON, various prizes for humorous poetry in clubs, organizations; [oth. writ.] Humorous poems to honor people: various anniversaries, welcoming poems to music, translated hymns to English hymnal, translated two books: (1) on religion and (2) on Numismatic, biography into English; [a.] Etobicoke, ON

WOLFF, MATTHEW ESPALDON
[pen.] Don Mateo; [b.] April 11, 1980; Guam, USA; [p.] Patrick M. Wolff and Vivian E. Wolff; [occ.] Student; [memb.] National Honor Society, SKIP Entertainment Company, Peer Mediation, "Peace Makers' Club" (pres.), Performing Arts Society (pres.), Boy's Varsity Volleyball Club (pres.); [hon.] First place choreographic competition at Jazz Dance World Congress at Kennedy Center, Washington, DC, 1996, Guam Rotary Club Youth of the Year, 1997; [oth. writ.] "Popcorn" poem published in Mc Donald's Foundation poetry book; [pers.] "You will find that what you are willing to settle for is exactly what you get."; [a.] Upper Tumon, Guam

WOLLINGER, PAMELA
[pen.] Hawkeye; [b.] November 4, 1962; Peterborough, ON; [p.] Floren and Helen Wollinger; [ed.] Behavioural Science Technologist diploma, Kingston, ON, Applied Multimedia Training Centre, AMTC, diploma, Calgary, AB; [occ.] Digital Graphics Advertiser; [oth. writ.] The Waiting, unpublished reality-based fiction of a 30-year-old man's struggle to find the truth about the self, his self. It's a harsh story of personal healing.; [pers.] I believe that in man's idyllic world, love is the key to happiness. To define it, cultivate it, and nurture it within ourselves is also key in regards to this. It's all in how we go about it.; [a.] Cornwall, ON

WONG, IRENE GRACE VALLEJO
[pen.] Irene, Dichi; [b.] August 24, 1973; Iloilo City, Philippines; [p.] Mrs. Sonia Vallejo Wong; [ed.] Elementary and secondary and Iloilo Chinese (Central) Commercial High School in Philippines, Bachelor of Science in Nursing and St. Paul College of Iloilo in Philippines; [occ.] Assistant Nurse in Gleneagles Hospital, Singapore; [hon.] Best in Handwriting Contest in high school, Cum Laude in Bachelor of Science in Nursing and St. Paul College of Iloilo, Philippines, CGFNS Board Passer, nominated as an Anesthetic Nurse (AU) in Gleneagles Hospital, Singapore Chairman in English Research Group (St. Pauls) in our senior years; [oth. writ.] De Javu, The Waiting, A Letter to My Sister, To My Best Friend, and several poems published in local magazines (Home Life Magazine), newspaper (Manila Bulletin); [pers.] I usually write

poems by mood and fascination. I am inspired by my loved ones and fascinated by what I see, hear, and feel about life. Poems are the expressions of my inner self, reflecting the reality of the outside world. I'm greatly fascinated by the image of Mama Mary and Baby Jesus and so came up with a poem: "Mother and Child" last 19th December 1996 in the Philippines.; [a.] Singapore

WREZOUNIK, IRMINA
[b.] December 12, 1942; Knihelfeld, Austria; [p.] Alois and Cecilia Windschek; [m.] Reinhard Wrezounik; October 7, 1967; [ch.] Sabine T. and Klaus Wrezounik; [ed.] Four years elementary school, four years secondary school, two years business school, one year private course photography, two years evening classes English and Italian languages, four years private course philosophy, psychology, and naturopathy; [occ.] Emergency First-aid Attendant and Housewife, retired; [memb.] Franz Nabl Institute, Graz, Austria (research of literature), Cunst and Culturworkstate, Yudenburg, Austria (literature and theater); [hon.] Honors by reading in the province. First prize in a mineral magazine with a short story, third prize in an advertising competition—all in German; [oth. writ.] Several publications in newspaper, journals in Austria and Germany, a poem book titled: "Aufdem Weg zur Schamanen Poesie!" An English translation is existent—title: "On the Way to Shamanpoetry!" The next book is in the works—present 1998.; [pers.] We are a part of nature; I respect and love her. She is my great mental teacher. I listen and look round about her and there are all the answers of our life-questions. Whenever I write, I attempt that the knowledge thought, changed in words, are going into the heart of humans.; [a.] Weisskirchen, Styria, Austria

YAGER, GILLIAN
[pen.] Gillian McMaster; [b.] October, 1977; Mississauga, ON; [p.] Sharon McMaster; [m.] Daniel Yager; November, 1997; [ed.] Queensway Christian College, received Ontario secondary school diploma, attended Humber College one semester; [occ.] Sales Associate, Au Coton; [memb.] Orchard Heights Tennis Association since 1991; [hon.] Received two character awards in grade eight for being humble and honest. I still readily pursue my interest in swimming, writing, and painting.; [oth. writ.] Many of my poems I have never submitted for publishing, but my friends encourage me to continue to do so and I also receive a lot of encouragement from my husband and family.; [pers.] I strive to reflect teenage issues such as "When You Need a Friend"; it was inspired by a good friend who was going through a rough time and needed comfort.; [a.] Mississauga, ON

ZANELLA, MARIA
[b.] January 10, 1958; Toronto, ON; [occ.] Office Manager; [oth. writ.] Several poems published in local magazine; [a.] Toronto, ON

ZAPANTA, MARY JANE
[pen.] Yours 4 Ever; [b.] June 9, 1982; Philippines; [p.] Lily and Eduardo Zapanta; [ed.] High school student; [hon.] English; [oth. writ.] Two other poems were semifinalists in another poetry contest. I have more poems that I have written but have not sent for publication.; [pers.] I write what I feel and what I encounter through my daily life. My dreams/daydreams influence what my poetry is revealing to the reader.; [a.] Guelph, ON

Index of Poets

Index

A

Abe, Teruo 133
Abel, Jennifer 17
Aceti, Andrea 84
Ackerman, Eileen 23
Adams, Kamerine 36
Agnew, Heather 101
Agostino, Andrew 59
Aguirrezabal, Pablo 82
Ahearn, Bonnie 115
Ahluwalia, Chatar 81
Aimal, Bushra 135
Al-Ajaji, Fajr 12
Albrecht, Christena 153
Aldaim, Dirar A. 9
Aldred, Laurie 56
Aliermo, Pacita Labayen 4
Aligaen, Giovani T. 224
Allingham, Melody Nicholls 23
Alsmo, Lola 40
Alsop, Cristin 128
Amin, Mornie 165
Amor, Julie Mahal 244
An, Yue 7
Anciro, Elena 197
Anderson, Mary Lou 182
Anderson, Ole 259
Andrada, Louella Marie E. 65
Andres, Glenda 49
Andrews, Doreen E. 198
Andrus, Barbara 121
Ang, Michelle 47
Ann, Tamara Eidsness 191
Ann, Veronica Lynn 184
Anthony-Hale, Scott 26
Argier, Michelle 51
Arkell, Jim 165
Arkilander, Adrianna 138
Armstrong, David 122
Ashtor, Gila 7
Aspland, Paul 37
Ategbole, Adepeju 33
Aubin, Melanie 200
Auron, Danny 73
Avery, Jodi 58
Ayre, Margaret 38

B

B., Robert 44
Babcock, Diane E. 5
Bacani, Anne Marie B. 135
Bagart, Betty 194
Bailey, Joyce Laura 129
Baiton, Dana 88
Baker, Charles E. 57
Baldwyn, Tamaara A. 147
Baraniuk, Charlotte 90
Barfoot, Dale 51
Baria, Rubella B. 205
Barkhouse, Angela 108
Barnes, William 182
Barnett, Rick 66
Barrett, Dayna Lynne 230
Barry, Mary C. 151
Basil, Michael Anthony 167
Basra, S. S. 37
Basson, Ian 250
Bastarache, Sophie 104
Battersby, Gloria 127
Batts, Miriam 170
Baumgart, Lakmini 94
Bayan, Rosalia A. 30
Bearns, Judy 91
Beaton, Ryan 132
Beaulieu, Nanette 130
Beckett, L. 23
Beckett, Teena 71
Bedford, Bernie 68
Beers, Jonathan 33
Beghin, Frank 41
Beilharz, Johannes 165
Beland, Bernard 49
Belanger, Jason Michael 15
Belisle, Sheena R. M. 117
Bergeron, Francine 183
Bernabe, Raissa 93
Berndl, Cornelia 159
Berry, Sharon 165
Bertschinger, Leonardo 107
Bickerton, Robert 200
Bignell, Brian 143
Billings, Carrie 111
Bilous, Donna 9
Bilusack, Beverly 202
Bird, Deanna 194
Birru, Ato Seyoum Dagne 160
Bishop-Scott, Megan 206
Blackstock, Erin 86
Boeur, Ronald J. 120
Bojarski, Christine 195
Bonnar, Kim 50
Bosomworth, David 4
Bossio, Anne 74
Boston, Lyndsey 39
Bouma, Beverly 184
Bouras, Konstantinos 210
Bowe, June L. 11
Boyd, Sarah 80
Boyes, Penny 207
Bracke, Rae E. 80
Bradley, Andre 29
Bradshaw, Jill 32
Branch, Stanley 59
Brandt, Angela 52
Brandt, Robyn 132
Brault, Cynthia 38
Breckon, Chris 163
Breen, Shelly 207
Bressi, Maria Carlino 34
Brewster, Eva E. 112
Brewster, Sylvia 8, 179
Brick, Kay 12
Brimblecombe, Pat 25
Brock, Jack 96
Brooks, Linda Grace 71
Brothers, Gary 20
Broughton, Vivien 243
Browatzke, Tyson 57
Brown, Allison 146
Brown, Courtnie 164
Brown, Darryl 214
Brown, Kimberly J. 15
Brown, Krista G. 17
Brown, Tanya 33
Browne, Emilie 256
Browne, Erin 147
Brownlow, Melanie 75
Brummet, Lillian 129
Brumwell, Carrie-ann 38
Brundritt, Carly Ann 81
Brunet, Louise 141
Bruni, Meghan 118
Bryan, Amanda 228
Buchanan, Gordon D. 199
Buck, Linda A. 12
Buitenwerf, Cynthia 118
Bunting, Mary T. 89
Burchall, Kia 182
Burchell, Joan Adams 3
Burgess, Leroy 140
Burke, Amber 206
Burke, Julie 35
Burlock, Paula 218
Burnett, Jim 92
Burns, Karen 99
Butcher, Gerald 123
Button, Kristy 256
Buzzell, Charlene 171
Byrne, Sybil 87
Byrnes, Cynthia 105

C

Cabotaje, Bernadette 151
Cadrain, Tara 217
Cameron, David 101
Cameron, Stan 188
Camerson, Joanne M. 115
Cammack, Constance 77
Campbell, Christine A. 159
Campbell, Jill 262
Campbell, Shirley 74

Campbell, William 242
Cardinal, Jayson 48
Carignan, Tracy 73
Carter, Anita 231
Cartwright, Michael D. 46
Castells, Mary Anne 29
Caulfield, Gerry 33
Caulien, Janice 41
Cayanan, Ester S. 69
Centritto, Luigino 111
Cesare, De Alessandro 19
Chai, Riyun 83
Chamberlain, J. M. 167
Chambers, Annette 27
Chander, Ravi 122
Chapman, Jeni 16
Chapman, Joan M. 215
Charbonneau, Johanne 63
Charron, Suzette 10
Chatten, Nancy 19
Chatten, Rosemary Armstrong 76
Chaudhuri, Dr. Anjana Rai 194
Cherry, Kailee Anne 24
Chevalier, Ken 261
Chijiiwa, Yoko 62
Chisholm, James Stanley 155
Chittick, Geraldine 200
Christensen, Andrew Campbell 30
Christensen, Angie Marie 229
Christopher, John 228
Chu, June 131
Chutko, Leah Jan 88
Citro, Mary Rosa Calvino 92
Clapp, Dominique 183
Clark, Candace 180
Clark, Evelyn Hunter 3, 21
Clark, Gina 93
Clark, Rosaline 14
Clark, Steven E. 23
Clark, Toni 246
Clarke, Maureen 78
Clarke, Melissa 119
Clearly, Angie 115
Cleet, R. H. 20
Clemente, Alexandre 5
Cliffe, Stephen 51
Clubine, Jonathan 46
Cochran, Edward 40
Coker, Lucinda 51
Collins, Maureen 11
Collis, Lyn 108
Cooke, T. K. 258
Coolen, Alana 11
Cooling, Sarah 173
Cooper, Tina 10
Copleston, Marjorie 26
Corbett, Patricia 169
Corpus, Eulogia Rojas 161
Corriveau, Janet A. M. 258
Costales, Melchor M. 170

Coughlan, Phil 89
Coumont, Alexandra 76
Counsell, Shirley Anne 218
Courtney, Gordon 208
Couvrette, Thaddeus Rogers 19
Covelli, Cleonice Biondi 148
Cowper, Robyn 39
Coxon, James R. 136
Crabs, Velma 257
Craig, Kathleen Loo 90
Craig, Shelley 204
Crain, Doris 241
Cross, Wanda 67
Croy, Shawna 104
Cruickshank, Angela 77
Cruz, Roanna T. 200
Cuell, Suzanne Y. 45
Cullia, Joseph 158
Culshaw, Kathleen 49
Cunningham, Jasmyne 24
Curé, Brigitte 132
Currie, Carl 116
Curtis, Adolf, Jr. 128
Cusack, Patricia 157
Cyr, Lisa 108

D

da Fonseca, Carla Marisa 107
Dabee, Vivi J. 138
Daculan, Michelle G. 106
Dafoe, W. L. 220
D'Agostino, Gina 11
Dalby, Ingeborg 158
Dale, Sonja 233
Dale, William 147
Damgaard, Sara 82
Danby, Christopher 201
Daniele, Stephanie 123
Dart, Kerrie 105
Davenport, Lisa A. 96
David, Ray Stasiulis 63
Davidson, Dolina 10
Davies, Lindsay J. 70
Davis, Christina 152
Davis, Teresa C. 229
Dawn, Pamela 31
Dawn, Shayne 16
Day, Stephen 249
Dayan, Shoshana 257
de Fiaño, Mirta R.B. 207
De Giorgio, Lorianna 68
de Oliveira, Ednilson Turozi S. 195
DeAbreu, Robert 217
Dean, Laura 160
Deegan, Debbie 59
Deforest, D. 156
DeMelo, Joseph 13
Demirdjian, Anoush 133
Demone, Candace 174

Denomy, Brenda E. 21
Desilets, Julie 186
Desmarais, Jennifer 244
Devine, Daniel Earl 24
Di Lello, Deanna 99
Dickens, Vera 64
Dilberovic, Vedran 106
Disanto, Lisa 110
Dobson, Russell 187
Dockrill, Reg 22
Doherty, Curits 150
Dominguez, Emilia 176
Domolewski, Betty 94
Donald, Doris Mae 122
Donalds, Pearline Ann 9
Doncaster, Viola 201
Donnelly, Richard M. 16
Dossor, Kristy 68
Doucette, Kandice 95
Doucette, Lorraine 170
Doucette, Mary 164
Doucette, Paul A. 32
Dougall, Jackie 205
Douma, Dawn A. 236
Downing, Robert 106
Doyle, Linda 70
Doyle, Lorraine 165
Draper, Joan D. 193
Drew, Mark 50
Druhar, Andrea 19
Drybrough, Gordon 99
D'Souza, Natasha 219
Dube, Dominique 113
Duda, Kamila 166
Duffy, Erin 99
Duffy-Bone, Debbie 125
Dugan, Stephen George 137
Dunston, Lola 170
Durack, Sheila A. 95
Dusterhoft, Katrina 56
Duval, Kevin 41
Dziedzic, Vernon B. 89

E

Edwards, Gerald B. 13
Egli, Christa K. 30
Ehman, Maureen 14
Emberly, Megan 254
Ender, Dieter 57
English, Shirley A. 88
Enopena, Severino 227
Enright, Gordon 3
Esak, Starla 135
Esannason, Jean H. 239
Esson, April 50

F

Fadl, Murtada F.M. 80

Fairman, Kay 42
Falkowski, Karen 18
Faminow, Peter S. 166
Fan, Connie 100
Feere, Aaron 171
Fehr, Rudy 253
Ferraiuoli, Veronica 159
Fetter, Corinna 130
Feusse, Lola 84
Fiala, Judy 153
Fiorini, Diane 103
Fiorini, Stephanie 190
Fish, Robert M. 135
Flanagan, Calvin 137
Fleming, Angelique 174
Fleming, Michael 125
Fleming, Paula 216
Fletcher, Claire 160
Fohring, Stephanie 100
Ford, Tracie 72
Francis-Browning, Paula 78
Franklin, Kim 170
Fraser, Gloria 235
Fraser, Peggy 60
Frick, Margot 199
Friend, Leila 16
Fuchs, Felipe 143
Fung, Derek 201
Fung, Victoria 97

G

Gagnier, Lisa M. 83
Gallinger, James 68
Garbarino, Carmen 13
Garland, Kenneth E. 187, 223
Garnatz, Jennifer M. 142
Garrett, Malcolm 42
Garrison, Diana Gwen 193
Gass, Carmen 114
Gautreau, Jennifer 37
Geier, Thomas, Jr. 113
Georgitsis, Tatiana 159
Gerena, Elba Yesi 92
Gerzanic-Hons, Hana 6
Ghumman, Dilraj Singh 79
Gianfelice, Rick 64
Gibbons, Clint 31
Gibbs, Diane J. 17
Gibson, Robert R. 234
Gilbert, Michelle 65
Giles, Margaret 118
Gillespie, Steve 6
Gilmore, Amanda E. G. 259
Gjesdal, Betty Loise 196
Glaster, Tracy L. 65
Glover, Damian 91
Gluckman, Brendan 98
Goddard, Tanya 52
Goguen, Susan 30

Gola, Slavomir 169
Golling, Carl James 261
Good, Brad 154
Gordon, Florida 142
Gordon, Gary L. 100
Gordon, Joan 193
Gordon, Leslie W. 181
Gorley, Terry 6
Gouzopoulos, Gloria 168
Graham, C. 131
Graham, Lloyd E. 47
Grandsoult, Michael 162
Grant, Mark 64
Graves, Maurice 259
Graves, Rachel Ivy 32
Graves, Sarah Jane 45
Gray, Erin 250
Greb, Robert 144
Grech, Vicki 44
Green, Amanda 174
Green, Paul 64
Greves, Ritchie 188
Grey, Joe 236
Grills, Debra 25
Grimes, Maxine 119
Grimsley, Donna F. 23
Grk, Marinko Croata 246
Grod, Natalya 234
Groening, Lori 113
Grondin, Stacy 171
Grosfield, David 240
Grozik, Tabitha 206
Guenther, Trojer 28
Gurevich, Alexander 263
Gustyn, Sylwia 227
Gutwillig, Eric 34

H

Haffner, Marilyn 72
Hahn, Melissa 255
Hall, Tammy 139
Halladay, Fran 238
Hamilton, Jason 154
Hamm, Agnes 53
Hamulka, Elizabeth 235
Hanak, Natalie 153
Hanson, Maureen 36
Hardjana, Astrid E. 17
Hardy, Tom 205
Hare, Amanda J. 183
Harker, Katelyn 149
Harrigan, Debra 183
Harris, Antonesha M. 255
Harris, Desmond D. 8
Harris, Marisa 240
Harris, Sheri 158
Harrison, Lauren Elysia 65
Hartal, Paul 140
Haughton, Harry S. 139

Hawkins, Linda 44
Haynes, Joanne Allong 182
Hayward, Christa 214
Headdon, Douglas C. 94
Heide, Rachel Lea 61
Heideman, Paul 203
Henderson, Christine 138
Henderson, Norma Sherk 254
Hendriksen, Joanne 238
Henrich, Cathy 11
Henry, Verona 229
Hernandez, Zeny 211
Herr, Claudia 243
Herrenkind, Petra 201
Herwig, Brooke 114
Hiebert, Keturah 205
Higgins, Kristi 218
Hill, H. Ross 119
Hill, Michelle 15
Hillyer, Erin R. 258
Hinrichs, Mallory 53
Hirschfeld, Linda L. Macumber 143
Hiseman, Heather 25
Hitchins, Dorothy I. 54
Ho, Stephanie 226
Hoch, Kimberley A. 126
Hodge, Winifred Jean 217
Hoey, Arlene 58
Hoffmann, Dorothy 70
Holdipp, Shinika S. 159
Hongisto, Helge 148
Hood, Florence Connolly 192
Horne, Sherri Ann 100
Hotson, K. 101
Hoyland, G. A. 160
Huang, Qing 136
Hughes, Natalie 185
Hughes, Tabitha Marie 158
Huguenin, Arlette 101
Hui, Winnie 129
Hundert, Michelle 58
Hurford, Melanie 7
Hussain, Aisha Magsad 237

I

Ibrahim, Ali 163
ImBeau, Jon 110
Inturralde, Martha C. 159
Ioannou, Mary 126
Iqbal, Sikander 200
Ivancic, Joseph 60
Izquierdo, Mariela 52

J

Jackman, Patricia 22
Jackson, Dani 125
Jackson, Rachelle 62
Jackson, William D. 85

Jacobson, Shirley 19
Jacquier, Kath 89
Jain, Neeraj 104
James, Bonnie 105
Janosevic, Milica 205
Janzen, Geneva 190
Jarosch, Rene Magnus 47
Jarvis, Stan 133
Jazz 55
Jean, Shirley Srigley 3
Jefferies, Kathy 32
Jeyaseelan, Nisha 181
John, Justina V. 204
Johnson, Lolita 156
Johnson, Noline A. V. 4
Jones, Christa 6
Jones, Darryl 28
Jones, E. 44
Jones, Eleanor 219
Jones, Kay 177
Joshua, Christine 28
Joudrey, Jackie 116
Joyce, Brian 206
Jurcovan, Ioana 116
Jury, Lisa 57

K

Kaiser, Glen 15
Kalekar, Vivek P. 182
Kallman, Suzanne 95
Kanda, Jagjit 208
Kandavanam, Vina 77
Kapadia, Sana R. 223
Karman, Doris I. 178
Karney, Bryan 215
Keith, Ryan 180
Kelley, Sis. Patricia 75
Kelly, Brian B. 94
Kelly, Catherine 194
Kelly, Dennis Joseph 9
Kelly, Erin 45
Kelly, Josie 113
Kendrick, Jennifer 165
Kennedy, Tia 110
Kernel, Virginia 201
Kerr, Megan 25
Ketchum, Clifford W. 3
Ketola, Irja 210
Khalaf, Bedoor 188
Khan, Rubaiyat 8
Khan, Tayyaba Jabbar 54
Khay, Sevendalino 111
Kianieff, Nevres 168
Kilander, Angelica 105
Killeen, Frances 35
Kilty, Tacia Lee 249
Kilvert, Stacey 79
Kiraly, Ilona 38
Kireef, Lisa 148

Kiriliuk, Aya 152
Kitney, Eva 155
Klassmann, Leda Suzana 149
Klimitz, Betty 4
Klosowski, Tom 142
Knot, Michaela 141
Kolman, Ari R. 257
Kowalchuk, Joyce 192
Kruschwitz, Monika F. 262
Kruse, Tatjana 143
Kunianthodath, Dr. Cherian 141
Kutney, Michelle 91
Kutowski, Karsten 142

L

Laborde, Patricia 199
LaCharite, Tanis 69
Laing, Allison 81
Lalonde, Serge 190
Lambert, William J. 153
Lambrakis, Agis 137
Lamothe, Amy 118
Lange, Brian 194
LaPlante, David 216
Larsen, Isabel E. 5
Latendresse, Gary 251
Laxdal, Jason 142
Lay, Steven 253
Leblanc, Andrea 44
Lee, Hor Ming 164
Lee, Lois Y. 114
Lee, Paul Anthony 122
Leffler, Paige 152
Leibner, Samara 111
Lemon, Mary B. 102
Leong, Simon 210
Lepper, Judy 247
LeRoy, Debra Lynn 157
Lévesque, Stéfan 199
Lewis, Adam 125
Lewis, Addana 94
Lewis, Aimee 237
Lewis, Amanda 182
Lewis, Patricia 80
Lilia, Beatriz Solina 178
Liliana, Popescu Elena 104
Linholm, Elsie Loke 7
Linton, Martin 46
Linyard, Shawna 31
Lipinski, Karen 70
Lipsman, Nir 147
Liscombe, Nicole 252
Lishchynski, Marc 245
Little, Danielle 211
Little, Stacy 68
Lloyd, Maxwell 58
Lockstein, Eileen 26
Lok, Ann 76
Loker, Chad 215

Lokke, Fini 4, 258
Long, Brian 103
Long, Michael Allan 9
Loo, Po Li 211
Lopez, Rochelle G. 196
Lorentz, Victor Joseph 118
Lorimer, Steven 60
Lotey, Prabhjot 39
Love, Jonathan 180
Loveluck, Royston 43
Low, Jaye 12, 224
Ludlow, Diana L. 221
Luimes, Brian H. 146
Lum, Ronnie 38
Lusk, Kristy 250
Lussier, Chantel 77
Lynch, Catherine 208

M

Macdonald, Yvonne A. 242
MacDonell, Tracy Lynn 141
MacDougall, Bruce 18
MacDougall, Chris 202
Mackay, Barbara Lynn Young 24
MacKenzie, Kyle 77
Mackney, Susan 46
Mackoy, Nelson James 18
MacLennan, Ian 8
Macneill, Sally 112
Madhosingh, Robert 248
Magill, Liza 258
Mahadeo, Mary 185
Maharaj, Jennifer 175
Maillet, Joanne 44
Majoros, James 66
Makeiff, D. Patricia 96
mallett, kim 129
Mallov, Ian 105
Mangano, Marissa 104
Mann, Sandy 169
Manning, Edythe 198
Manuel, Lisa 128
Marie, Cedric Jean 103
Marijanan, Benjamin 104
Marlow, Holly 252
Marshall, Melissa 128
Martin, Grace 46
Martin, Wilfred J. 130
Martinez, Providencia M. 69
Mason, Dai 172
Mason, Garry 147
Mason, Paul 92
Massoud, Mary 192
Mastromatteo, Patricia Anne 85
Masuda, Allan T. 194
Mathew, Takwi 170
Mathewson, Michelle 50
Mattapally, Sebastian 9
Matthias, Virginia 124

Matthie, Andrina 184
Maung, Su 33
Mavrow, Cecilia 22
Mayell, Sarah 14
Maypother, Shirley 105
Mazurik, Dorothy 161
McAdam, S. W. 206
McAndrews, G. 198
McCaffrey, John Paul 1
McCartney, Donald M. 230
Mccartney, Jessi 146
McDonald, Karen E. 198
McElligott, Sean E. 72
McEwan, Joan 145
McGee, Debra 175
McGinn, Ronnie 12
McGovern, Mike 127
McGuigan, Kelly 259
McGuire, Lois 109
McIntosh, Daphne J. 223
McIsaac, Ken 88
McIvor, Judy 69
Mckegney, Steven 131
McLaren, Ansel 172
McLeod, Gloria 137
McLeod, H. N. 5
McIlhinney, Tamara 57
McManamy, Marion R. 176
McMaster, Gillian 137
McMurray, K. 172, 173, 185, 236
McNabb, Hope 55, 245
Mcnamara-Comeau, Janette 210
McQuade, Kathleen 214
McRae, D. A. 152
Meaney, Lynn Lee 10
Mecl, Vera Marie 16
Medeiros, Eugenia 22
Mederacke, Hrilina Tagore 204
Mekhael, Amanda 166
Meldrum, Kirsty 247
Mellon, Alaina 40
Memon, Hinna 111
Menchenton, Cindy 51
Mendes, Lea 256
Mendoza, Davina 131
Meredith, Thomas 186
Messer, Angèle 185
Metcalfe, Vicki 191
Metzger, Lloyd H. 140
Michaloski, Michelle 63
Michaud, Shannon 242
Michelsen, Klaus 144
Miller, Janine 183
Miller, Robert L. 18
Miller, Sandra 117
Miller, Tara L. H. 15
Milner, Samantha 148
Minchan, Peggy Audrey 94
Mirc, Anton 260
Mitchell, Bruce 213

Mitchell, Eileen 232
Mitchell, James R. 245
Mizgalewicz, Magda 116
Mohammed, Patsy R. 178
Mohammed, Tariq 179
Mohanachandran, Dharsiga 164
Mohanan, P. K. 256
Monareng, Martin P. 176
Mondello, Sabrina 112
Moodie, Sharon 173
Mooney, Judy 6
Moore, A. G. 41
Moore, Len 198
Moore, Mary 10
Moorman, Myra G. McCulloch 161
Morgan, Gabriel 232
Morgan, Valerie 195
Morhart, Donna 98
Morin, Laura Diane Grona 111
Morrall, Barry 252
Morris, Rick 22
Morrison, J. Lindsay 182
Mortimer, Lane R. 251
Moser, Janice 187
Motaze, Emilienne 254
Moyer, Barbara 6
Mozak, Joelle 231
Mugambi, Michael 19
Muir, Cheryl 123
Muller, Susan 117
Mullings, Carl 254
Murphy, Noelle 189
Murray, Lena 168
Murray, Nancy 186
Murungu 149
Mushing, Marie 98
Myers, Lawrence 181
Myre, Sonia 244

N

Nagler, Frank 80
Nandkeolyar, Ritika 97
Neele, Arno 113
Neil, Jody 172
Neish, Barbara Ruth 173
Nelson, Brian 63
Nethercott, Anne 211
Neu, Elwin 117
Neumann, Melissa 45
Neverson, Nicole 125
Newton, Daniel 67
Nichol, Glen 203
Nichol, Terrance Keith 36
Nicholas, Rose 222
Nichols, Kristine 53
Nichols, Shirley 88
Nielsen, Rebecca 22
Niemi, Kristian 255
Nigro, Cristina 153

Nikolantonakis, Peter 123
Nikolic, Jackie 99
Noble, Phyllis 84
Noble, Sara 83
Noël, Maria 88
Noordyk, Susanne 29
Nordrik, Toni 201
Norman, David 136
Normandeau, Sherry 124
Norton, Karen 24
Nuttall, Jo Ann 212

O

Obinze, E. N. D. 8
O'Brien, Daniel T. 71
O'Brien, Elizabeth 167
Obuekwe, Nuala 167
O'Connell, Andrea 109
Odede, John 107
Ogilvie, Alda 130
O'Halloran, Shawn 212
Okeke, Iheanyi 56
Oliveira, Mariana 155
Oliver, Teresa 64
Ollson, Brenda J. 110
Olsson, Solveig 10
Ong, Ted 261
Oppel, Hanni 142
O'Toole, Michael 162
Ott, William 5
Owl, Rita M. 234

P

Pabalan, Ofelia Francisco 117
Page, Edward John 193
Palace, Paul 151
Palacios, Doris Elizabeth 134
Paletta, Anthony 145
Pallagi, Jodi 101
Palmer, Jeffrey D. 232
Palmer, Noelle 200
Palmer, Patricia 35
Palomino, Denise 53
Palumbo, Norma 39
Pani, Geeta 119
Papageorgiou, Anastasia 45
Paquette, Shirley 226
Parifsky, Eva 154
Parkinson, Amy 119
Parkinson, Beth 109
Parks, Angela 136
Partyka, Laura 131
Parucha, Alejo Galahad, Jr. 141
Passaro, Piera 29
Passero, Sharon 169
Pastuch, Nicole 251
Patel, Bharti 213
Patel, Rishad 145

Patrick, Vivien C. 262
Patry, Claudette 253
Patterson, Jane A. 56
Paulozza, Peter 95
Pauls, Beryl 92
Pauls, Shalynn 129
Paulsen, Noreen 31
Paulson, Kenneth 41
Payne, Patsy 65
Peacock, Sandi 82
Pears, Paul 135
Pearson, Brian 186
Pecnik, Sonja 149
Pederson, Tim 51
Peilin, Wen 172
Pentney, Cara 93
Perez, Jennifer 158
Perez, Raquel R. 71
Perry, Doreen 81
Perry, Gordon L. 100
Peters, Zachary 47
Peyton, Livia 159
Philip, Jeff 119
Philippe, Jane Collins 59
Pichota, Rose Marie 160
Pilkington, Charles 197
Pirroncello, Maria A. 163
Plata, Isabel A. 85
Pluss, Meaghan 231
Poet 256
Poggione, Tania 25
Polec, Patryk 50
Pommer, Stephen D. 177
Pompana, Michelle D. 177
Pope, Jc 206
Porritt, D. 237
Porro, George 140
Porter, Jean 16
Porter, Philip Edward 124
Porto, P. 52
Pottebaum, Rachel C. 45
Power, Gordon W., Jr. 211
Prebble, June Anne Malloy 64
Preston, Eva 11
Puyou, Lucia 254
Pyringer, Jessica 40

Q

Quait, Pamela C. 121
Quick, Brenda N. 122
Quigley, Eimear 52
Quintanilla, Joleen S. 195

R

Raco, Sandra 12
Radmore, Elizabeth 187
Ramballie, Melissa 125
Ramsden, Rowena J. 256

Ratcliff, Katherine 46
Rath, Kenneth 7
Rath, Kenneth R. 7
Ratinen, Oskari 137
Ray, Nyomie 117
Raycroft, Brett 68
Rea, Clive 171
Read, Patricia 116
Recsetar, Amanda 118
Rector, Andrea 143
Reddy, D. Veeru 173
Redford, Rachelle 186
Rees, Elizabeth 18
Reeves, Marian Heibloem 166
Regier, Jennifer 161
Reich, Jenni 107
Reid, Katherine 69
Reid, Laurie 13
Reiff, Daniel 128
Reis, Francisco D. 86
Renz, Tami 37
Revels, Sharon Lynn Fehr 233
Reyno, Mary 210
Reynolds, Anthony 27
Ribeiro, Inês 86
Rice, Hazel Harper 238
Richardson, Deanne 134
Richer, Melanie 80
Richmond, Robert J., Jr. 155
Riehl, Delphine 209
Riley, Rick J. 171
Rinaldi, Jennifer 40
Rivera, Melissa Karen 199
Rivest, Christine 192
Riviere, Bert 21
Robb, Sandra Cheong 28
Roberts, Garry 83
Robertson, Nicole 99
Robertson, Tish 198
Robins, Ethel 48
Robinson, Cathy 77
Rodier-Paris, Josianne 25
Rolley, Marguerite E. 220
Rolufs, H. 134
Romeo, Esther-Michelle 33
Romlewski, Melissa 146
Roote, Margaret 237
Rose, Brandy Lane 24
Rose, Sharon E. 156
Roth, Trudi M. 176
Rousseau, S. Elizabeth 258
Rovere, Lana 196
Rowley, Rosemarie 192
Roy, Karen Anne 27
Roy, Sebastien 107
Rubio, Maria Gerardee 209
Ruddell, Vivian 167
Rupnarain, Mala 32
Rutka, Karen 146
Ryan, Bonnie 179

S

Sabourin, Michael 67
Saeed, Mohsin 47
Sahagon, Gina 184
Salazar, Jocelyn Marybeth C. 66
Samant, Kalpana G. 42
Sampson, William J. 76
San Martin, Julio Gianni Toro 98
Sanderson, Amy 74
Sandiego, Joselito H. 18
Sapach, Carolyn 143
Saraogi, Vivek 230
Sarver, Dale 112
Saulnier, Kim 205
Saunders, Traci 164
Sawwan, Donia 124
Scala, Pasqualina 93
Schechter, Oded 155
Scheffler-Plath, Edeltraut 249
Schell, Bobbi-jo 111
Schmautz, Lindsay 204
Schneider, R. A. Bob 140
Schofield, Cheryl 243
Scholes, Susan 197
Schroeder, Margaret K. 59
Schuil, Maureen V. 154
Scobie, Corey 123
Scott, Anne 202
Scott, Lisa 207
Scott, Shawn 104
Scott, Theresa D. 81
Scourakis, Joanne 75
Scribner, Matthew 220
Searle, Morgan 257
Seeley, Jason 171
Seguin, Julie 55
Selby, Eleanor 3
Sellers, Delores S. 76
Selvaraj, Anita Luo 73
Sen, Priya 134
Sendao, Agostinho 17
Sestito, Ingrid Maria T. 86
Shantz, Angela 116
Shapiro, Deborah E. 58
Shariff, Farah 110
Shaw, Amanda-Beret 50
Sheldon, Kaye 57
Sheppard, Elizabeth 239
Shessel, Lindsay Fern 150
Shickluna, Christopher 149
Shinde, S. Nadini 259
Shiraishi, Tetsuya 71
Sidhu, Amanjote 28
Sieger, Robyn 120
Sikka, Patrick 221
Sikora, Horst Ulrich 59
Sillada, Danny C. 213
Silva, Jane 178
Simnett, Sarah 247

Simons, Marlene 70
Simpson, Deidre 20
Simpson, Lana 184
Simson, Shannon 257
Sinicropi, Melani 29
Sinn, M.C. Francisca 189
Siu, Stephanie 221
Slicer, Morag 100
Sly, Clarisse 228
Smail, Stacey 157
Smith, Angi 83
Smith, Lorelei E. 95
Smith, Margaret K. 74
Somasundram, Nakules 37
Somerville, Denise 97
Soto, Zut-ying 36
Souter, James 54
Spicer, Andrew James 53
Spray, Kellie 30
Srivastava, Ratika 130
Staal, Cory D. 112
Staats, Eleanor 176
Stansfield, Esther R. Limsiaco 195
Stapley, Sarah 246
States, Betti Ann 178
Stauss, Rusti 233
Stavrakos, Konstantine 87
Stead, Cheryl Ann 240
Stevens, Cory 102
Stevens, L. Monica 101
Stevens, Norm F. 87
Stewart, Sandra Joanne 75
Stiege, Rudi 62
Stoodley, Kathleen M. 61
Streilein, Carrie 31
Strohm, Elaine 62
Strub, Cassandra 185
Succhorab, Rudy 148
Suchet, Danielle 210
Suddard, Norma J. 17
Sultana, Nilofer 34
Summers, Jonathan 15
Surette, Alicia M. 65
Sutherland, Gloria 14
Suveges, Captain D. 164
Svatek, Kurt F. 89
Swain, Pearl 74
Swallow, Judy 124
Sych, Jennifer Elizabeth 36
Sylvain, Joan 58
Sylvester, Heather Giroux 48
Symington, Kelly 207
Szabo, Christian 106
Szalanski, Teodora 39

T

Tabert, Andreas 191
Tattam, Mona 150
Taylor, Josephine 155
Taylor, Marion U. 13
Taylor, Molly S. 106
Taylor, Naomi 41
Taylor, Olga 177
Taylor, Susan 37
Taylor-Arenas, Le Sand Duane 207
Tays, Maureen 87
Teed, Susan 63
Teixeira, Anna 158
Thilavanh, Bandasack 161
Thomas, Jennifer 235
Thomas, Nancy 179
Thompson, Audrey K. 5
Thompson, Marion 130
Thompson, Tim 74
Thompson, Vivian L. 241
Thornton, Michelle 38
Thurgood, Annie 226
Thurston, Florence 124
Tilson, Adrienne 61
Tiosen, Nicanor P. 14
Tottenham, Rebecca 47
Tragvair, Scott 98
Trahan, Chantale 144
Traill, Ted 255
Tratt, Greta M. T. 14
Traynor, John B. 101
Treybig, Kathy Lynn 222
Tribe, Margaret 225
Tripp, Janis 76
Tucker, Janet Renee 179
Tupper, Alexis H.D. 154
Turner, Gilese 146
Turner-Chambers, Melissa 113
Tzimoulis, Mae 176

U

Uppenborn, Jason 32
Ursell, John H. 30
Uys, Jasmine 53, 71

V

Valdez, Ma. Bonita P. 173
Vales, Jose R. 187
Valiquette, Robert J. 203
Valtonen, Hanna 204
Van Tine, Andrea 110
Van Walraven, Christine 251
Vander Loo, Andrea 175
Vander Zee, Karen 62
Vansickle, Willa E. 92
Vasilevski, Christina 75
Vaughan, Hilda 105
Vavaroutsos, Katherine 93
Vaz, M. 82
Veitch, John D. 222
Velis, Alfonso 154
Venantius, Andrea 86
Versteeg, Arlene 184
Vickerson, Ashley 75
Vijayaraghavan, D. 81
Von Keitz, Elizabeth 177
Von Muhlfeld, Bianca 79
Vortmann, Blondine 212
Vrdoljak, Diana 52
Vu, Quy N. 36

W

Wagner, Harriet R. 121
Waldo, Angie 82
Walinga, Shirley 78
Wallace, J. 122
Wallace, Jessica 123
Ward, Anna M. 13
Ward, Beth Ann 239
Ward, Kelly 39
Wardene, Delcia Abey 204
Wardrop, Andrea 225
Warnock, Peter 43
Warren, Jim 87
Warzecha, Katherine 95
Watters, Theresa 253
Webb, Brian 187
Webb, Michael G. 219
Webber, Jamie James A. 31
Webster, Elizabeth Seddon 211
Weekes, Edwin Ivan 56
Weymes, Jean 43
Whitby, David 249
White, Andrew 152
White, Tara J. 136
Whitecap, Cory 102
Whittaker, Paula 177
Whitty, Robert J. 155
Wickens, Elizabeth McLaren 82
Wiecek, Wesley 162
Wiffen, Alycia 152
Wiggins, Bruce 260
Wigley, Tasha S. 127
Wikstrom, Glynn 171
Wilkie, Kenna 258
Williams, B. K. 128
Williams, Elizabeth 211
Williams, Jennifer 139
Williams, Lynda 56
Williams, Norma Seymour 263
Willow, Jennifer 23
Wilson, Amanda 260
Wilson, Elizabeth 40
Wilson, Kent 90
Wimaleswaran, Siva 209
Winn, Ryan 117
Winnie, G. Kierstead 29
Winter, Lena 81
Wlodarski, Wanda 83
Wolff, Elana 86
Wolff, Matthew Espaldon 224

Wollinger, Pamela 227
Wong, Irene Grace 193
Wowk, Natalie 199
Wrezounik, Irmina 8
Wright, Samantha 147
Wydenes, Mike 241
Wysynski, Lorraine L. 89

Y

Yaqoob, Farzana 112
Yarde, Irwin Da Costa 248
Young, Ruth Ann 166
Yun, Sun Tze 225

Z

Zahran, Dina Mamdouh 216
Zammit, Anthony 126
Zanella, Maria 83
Zapanta, Mary Jane 248
Zasonski, Gloria 120
Zink, Evelyn C. 4
Zokol, Ken 36
Zorzi, Jeremy 129